EATING IN AMERICA

Waverley Root & Richard de Rochemont

EATING IN AMERICA

A History

William Morrow and Company, Inc. · *New York* · 1976

Brief portions of this book originally appeared in *Gourmet* magazine in different form, and have been adapted for use by permission. An article entitled "The Early American Larder" by Waverley Root is copyright 1975 by Gourmet, Inc. An article entitled "Early American Cookery" by Waverley Root is copyright 1976 by Gourmet, Inc.

Printed in the United States of America.

1 2 3 4 5 6 7 8 9 10

Library of Congress Cataloging in Publication Data

Root, Waverley Lewis (date)
Eating in America.

Bibliography: p.
Includes index.
1. Food—History. 2. Diet—United States—History.
3. Cookery, American—History. 4. Food industry and trade—United States—History. I. De Rochemont, Richard, joint author. II. Title.
TX353.R64 641′.0973 76-16145
ISBN 0-688-03096-3

Contents

EATING IN AMERICA

I

Independence Refused

IN 1776, "the Representatives of the UNITED STATES OF AMERICA, in General Congress, Assembled," adopted the Declaration of Independence, predated July 4, like an overdue check—it was, indeed, long overdue. It was actually signed, on the installment system, beginning on August 2, 1776, and ending only in 1781, when Thomas McKean, who had been in the Congress on July 4 but not on August 2, was authorized to add the last signature to the document.

The Declaration ended only one sort of link with England, and specifically said so: "We . . . solemnly publish and declare . . . that all political connection between [the United States] and the State of Great Britain, is and ought to be totally dissolved." America did not declare, did not desire, and did not attain independence in many other domains.

The fledgling nation did not declare independence of a legal philosophy which included such safeguards as trial by one's peers and the writ of habeas corpus. That newly created political entity, the American, had no desire either to dissolve his linguistic connection with England, a more lasting bond and a profounder one than that represented by any ephemeral political regime. Some Englishmen would certainly agree with H. L. Mencken that the American language has since acquired a degree of independence from the English language, but the Declaration was still saying "mankind are," a use of a plural verb with a singular collective noun which no American would write today, though an Englishman might. Such differences are minor; on the whole America, like England, remains heir to the mighty literary tradition of the English language.

English law and the English language are almost universally admired. There is another facet of English culture for which it would be difficult to say as much: the United States, in the exercise of its "inalienable Right . . . [to]

the pursuit of Happiness" might very well have seized the opportunity to declare its independence of the English cuisine. As a matter of fact, in 1776 it was already too late. The eastern coast of the United States had been occupied by English-speaking colonists for a century and a half, and they had made their choice. They had re-created in the New World the sort of cooking to which they had been accustomed in the Old. It must have taken a certain amount of obstinacy to do so. The foods they had been eating in England did not exist in America when they arrived there. The foods they found in America were unknown to England. A new and independent cuisine could have been built upon them. The colonists did not choose to do so. They turned their backs on most of the new foods, often refusing to eat them until after Europe had accepted them and reimported them to the land of their origin. The colonists brought over their former foods and overcame, with admirable persistence, the difficulties opposed to them by a hostile climate. American *native* cooking would remain thereafter a branch of English cooking. Americans might eat in French or Italian, Greek or Chinese restaurants, but at home, except at moments of deliberately exotic exercises with foreign cookbooks, the American housewife would maintain her cherished dependence on British traditions. Her cooking would remain, according to a well-worn saying, "as American as apple pie"—a dish imported from England.

Why did America miss the chance to achieve independence from one of the least admired institutions of the British Isles? It certainly never occurred to Thomas Jefferson, gourmet though he was, that he was answering that question, or even considering it, when he wrote in the Declaration of Independence:

> All experience hath shewn that mankind are more disposed to suffer, while evils are sufferable, than to right themselves by abolishing the forms to which they are accustomed.

The power of the forms to which one has been accustomed! This generalization has since been applied specifically to gastronomy by other writers: William James: "Few of us are adventurous in the matter of food; in fact, most of us think there is something disgusting in a bill of fare to which we are unused"; Peter Farb: "All cultures are much more likely to accept a change in a minor aspect of culture, such as a toy, than in something as major as a food crop"; Naomi Bliven: "Food preferences, like language, are obstinate cultural traits." Must we deduce that a change of governors, which America was willing to accept, was less important than a change of food, which it was not? Americans did not want independence from English cooking, however unappetizing it may have appeared to Frenchmen or to Italians. Thomas Jefferson and George Washington employed French cooks, but Washington in this respect was not the father of his country, or if he was, his offspring were unfilial. Probably he had no desire that his countrymen should follow this example. A French cook in the White House is simply a matter of prestige; at the moment of writing there is a French chef there who turns out, it appears, excellent milk shakes and double hamburgers. Americans admired French food, but for everyday use they preferred meals in "the forms to which they are accustomed." Their English fare could not even be described as a sufferable evil. They did not suffer from it, though some early French visitors to America did, just as they suffered from it when, instead of crossing the Atlantic, they crossed the Channel.

In resisting unfamiliar food, even unfamiliar food which most outsiders considered superior to that which was familiar, Americans were only perpetuating the example of their English ancestors, who, from time to time, had shown signs of a desire to profit by foreign example, only to revert quickly to comfortable conformity with the cooking to which they had been accustomed. "English cooking, after its first triumphant flourish in the early fifteenth century, became incurably domestic," Richard Barber wrote in *Cooking & Recipes from Rome to the Renaissance;* and when, after the Restoration, exiled aristocrats returning from France provoked imitation of the French cuisine, "there was a reaction . . . against the rule of the French in English kitchens . . . The first sign of it came from no less an authority than Patrick Lamb, chef to Queen Anne, in his volume of 1710, in which he extols the advantages of England as a food-producing country and the virtues of English food."

The American colonists, of the same steadfast, or, if you prefer, obstinate stock, held out against the blandishments of esoteric cooking. In the culinary domain they heeded the advice of George Washington "to steer clear of permanent alliances with any portion of the foreign world." England was not foreign, even in 1776.

II

The Seafarers

THE VERY EARLIEST written reference to the foods of America may well have been the observation in the Saga of Eric the Red that in Vinland the Vikings discovered "larger salmon than they had ever seen before." It was an accurate report. The Europeans who would arrive six hundred years later would be surprised also by the immodest dimensions of American salmon.

The Vikings were the first Europeans known to have reached America. They could have been preceded by others, but there is no record of it, unless you believe the legend that two early Viking explorers encountered an Irish colony which looked so threatening that the Scandinavians preferred not to approach them, though the Vikings were not noticeably timid.

The Norsemen left no culinary vestiges behind them, and very few traces of any kind, except perhaps a few blue-eyed Eskimos who today might still be taken for Scandinavians. Thorfinn Karlsefni brought cattle to the settlement he attempted to establish in Vinland, but when he gave up after two years he must have taken them back with him or else the natives killed them, for there were no cattle in America when durable colonization set in.

It is not surprising that the Vikings left no eating traditions in America. For one thing they had little to leave. For another, they did not stay long enough to impose any new eating habits on the natives. Apparently they only occupied Vinland sporadically between the first American landfall of Bjarni Herjolfsson in 985 or 986 and the last recorded visit of Bishop Erik Gnupsson in 1121.

Did the Vikings ever touch any territory now within the borders of the United States? Possibly they reconnoitered along the coast as far south as Cape Cod or even entered Long Island Sound; but there seems little reason to believe that they ever established any settlements there. Popular legend used to attribute the Old Stone Mill at Newport to the Vikings, but archeologists never took this seriously, and today historians believe they have tracked down its builder—Benedict Arnold, not *the* Benedict Arnold, but one of his ancestors.

The best-substantiated theory seems to be that the place (or one of the places) where the Norsemen established a colony was at L'Anse aux Meadows, facing Newfoundland's Strait of Belle Isle; ruins of what could have been Scandinavian structures have been found there, which carbon dating places confirmatively at about A.D. 1000.

Defenders of the thesis that the Norsemen colonized, ever so briefly, some section of New England, rely on indications in the sagas which they hold to be incompatible with a site so far north. Leif Eriksson said of Vinland that it "has no frost in winter, and bears vines." This does not sound like Newfoundland; but it does not sound like New England either. Elsewhere Vinland is described as *terra spaciosa et opulentissima,* spacious and extremely fertile. Wild grapes grew there so abundantly that the Vikings exported them to the homeland, proof, it is argued, that Vinland could have been no farther north than Nova Scotia. They also reported finding "wheat" there. It could not have been wheat, which did not exist in America until Europeans planted it; but it might have been corn, which can grow up to latitude 58 degrees north, in northern Labrador. As for grapes, they do not grow in Newfoundland now, but they probably did then.

It was not so very long ago that climatologists discovered that the world, until about the beginning of the last millennium, was warmer than it is now, warmer, indeed, than it has been at any time since, a fact possibly unknown to the proponents of the New England theory. When the Vikings discovered Greenland and Vinland, the most important food of Iceland was wheat, which at that time grew easily there, as it does no longer. Grapes could have grown quite as easily at latitude 50 degrees north, which is the level of L'Anse aux Meadows. We have, besides, other pertinent information in the sagas which can fix for us, more or less, the position of Vinland—observations on the length of the day. They place the country at about latitude 50 degrees north. One final indication: the Norsemen described Vinland as an island. Newfoundland is.

The Vikings may have explored some of the coast of what is today the United States. They might even have landed there; but so far we have no evidence of it. They may have been deterred from pushing farther south because time was running out. The cooling of the climate which would culminate in the Little Ice Age of the thirteenth century started not long after Vinland was reached, and was very probably one of the reasons why the Vikings failed to maintain their toehold in America. Ice began to obstruct the sea between Greenland and Vinland. The Norsemen went home, leaving no gastronomic contribution behind them.

The second discovery of America is seldom described by historians; but there *was* a second discovery, after Leif Eriksson and before Columbus. If the historians have all but ignored it, that is perhaps because historians are not comfortable when they cannot work from documents; and there are no documents about the second discovery. The discoverers were careful to provide none, for they wanted no one else to share what they had found.

They were Basque fishermen who, ever since the eleventh century, had been hunting whales off the coast of France, from St. Jean de Luz to Biarritz, which still carries a depiction of a whale hunt on its coat of arms. But by the fourteenth century, whales became scarce inshore. The lookouts who signaled the schools of whales which had once appeared promptly every year at the September equinox spotted them less and less often; the fishermen had been too efficient or the whales had become too smart. The Basques had to venture ever deeper into the Atlantic in pursuit of their quarry; and in the end the whales led them to the Grand Banks of Newfoundland, which, the Basques discovered, were swarming with cod. Cod fishing was less dangerous than whale fishing, and more profitable. The Basques changed professions. They must have known that there was an uncharted continent just beyond their fishing grounds; they may even have gone ashore on it, as they probably did later, for there is a locality in Newfoundland still called Port aux Basques. But they kept the news to themselves; they knew better than to show competitors the way to Golconda.

It seems likely that a handful of other fishermen did find the Grand Banks all the same; they may have shadowed the Basques—Bretons, Portuguese, perhaps a Spaniard or two. They will tell you on the Breton island of Bréhat that it was their fishermen who told Columbus of the continent in the western sea. Otherwise all those early fishermen kept their mouths shut. The secret of the cod fisheries was kept until 1497, when John Cabot discovered Newfoundland and told the world about it.

The Basques had been drawn to America by the lure of food—fish; but, like the Vikings, they left no food of their own behind to enrich the resources of the country.

The history of American food begins with the Indian.

III

The Not-So-Poor Indian

"LO, THE POOR INDIAN!" wrote Pope, who, it is true, had spiritual privation rather than material discomfort in mind; but from every point of view, the white man has always liked to believe that the Indian dwelt in a state of perpetual misery until Europeans arrived to improve his condition. In 1525, the Dominican Tomas Ortiz described the Indians as eating "fleas, spiders and worms raw." Apparently these tidbits never entered into any Indian diet, though the Indians of Arkansas and Missouri are believed to have eaten beetles, mites, ants, lice, grasshoppers, bees, wasps and termites in prehistoric times. It is difficult not to fall into the habit of referring indiscriminately to what "Indians" ate as though all Indians were the same; but there is as much difference between an Algonquin and a Hopi as between a Swede and an Italian. Swedes and Italians do not eat in the same fashion, and neither did Algonquins and Hopis. However, falling immediately ourselves into the error of generalization, we dare hazard the statement that at the time when Columbus discovered America, the great majority of Indians were probably eating better than the great majority of Europeans, if only because Indians shared the available food more equably—a fact noted by Roger Williams when he broke into verse in the midst of his normally sedate *Key to the Indian Language:*

> Sometimes God gives them fish or flesh,
> Yet they're content without.
> And what comes in, they part to friends
> And strangers round about.

They even parted to friends and strangers with a certain amount of ceremony, in a fashion hardly compatible with our view of the pre-Columbian Indian as an uncultivated savage. Many Indian tribes had well developed table manners. Grace before meat was a widespread custom. The Indians of the Northeast were accustomed to having a guest express formal thanks at the end of a meal, to which his host would answer, "It is well." The Plains Indians had a custom which modern housewives might well envy them; guests brought their own dishes with them and after the meal took them back home to wash them themselves. Politeness there demanded also that the husband wait on his guests, serving the men first, and assuring himself that everyone had been attended to before he sat down. In the Northwest, an Indian girl who wanted to find a husband was careful how she ate, for she was judged above all by her table manners—she was thought uncouth if she took too much food into her mouth at one time, or if she showed her teeth, or if she looked around the table while eating.

The complacent view of the American Indian as undernourished before benevolent Europeans undertook to improve his lot is based on comparison of Indian eating with that of non-analogous classes in Europe. Our conception of how Europeans ate a few centuries ago is warped to begin with, for until recently historians have had a tendency to restrict their observations to the comportment of kings and emperors, statesmen and their pampered mistresses, and the well-fed bourgeoisie; there has been only an occasional passing glance in the direction of the great masses which, in the centuries before 1492, were often subsisting on the fringe of starvation. At the same period, no Indian was feasting like the members of the privileged classes of Europe, but no Indian was faring as badly as the poorest Europeans either, unless everybody was starving together for reasons over which the tribe had no control and over which, when they were duplicated in Europe, governments had no control either.

Indian food was ill judged from the very beginning by colonists who were comparing it with what the well-fed were eating in their home countries, for they were members of the middle class; and their opinion was colored also by the circumstance that they did not like the kind of food Indians ate: it was unfamiliar. At least the Indian enjoyed a varied diet, except when the whims of Nature ruled otherwise, which was more than could be said for the pre-fifteenth-century poor of Europe, whose food was often deadly monotonous, in more than the figurative sense. Deficiency diseases do not seem to have afflicted most Indians. When scurvy appeared in North America, it was not among Indians, but among the sailors of Jacques Cartier, victims of their shipboard diet; the Indians of Canada cured them with a decoction made from spruce bark and needles, which supplied the vitamins they lacked. When some European regions adopted as their principal grain the one the Indians had been using all along—Indian corn, maize—pellagra broke out, first in northwestern Spain in 1730, and thereafter in Italy, in Bessarabia, in the Tyrol and in southern Russia—because the Europeans could afford nothing *but* grain. They ate maize and maize alone; and though it is a nourishing food, it is not a complete food. The Indians combined other aliments with it, fish, or pumpkin, or beans, or maple syrup, which supplied some of the elements corn lacked. Pellagra was unknown in America in Indian times. It appeared first among impoverished Negroes in the South, who, like the unfortunate European pioneers in maize eating, were trying to live on cornmeal alone.

When the white man arrived in America, he found Indians in several sections of the country cooking with considerable finesse. The fact is that the Indian had something to contribute to what was to become the cuisine of America. Despite the resistance of British eating prejudices, he managed to insinuate into our repertory more dishes than most of us realize.

At the time when Columbus discovered America, the Indians were using two thousand different foods derived from plants, a figure Europe could hardly have matched. Among their root vegetables, the white potato, and the sweet potato to a lesser degree, are familiar everywhere in the world nowadays; but they were unknown in Europe before Columbus. Completely strange to Europe also was the Jerusalem artichoke, which grew wild over much of the country and was eaten by the Indians, raw, baked or boiled. It is misnamed, being actually the root of a sort of sunflower; the Indians also ate the seeds of the sunflower proper, likewise a native American plant, now very popular in certain European countries, notably Russia, which never knew it until it had been imported from the New World.

Another underground plant which Indians ate avidly was the onion. Some writers have tried to deny them this plant, claiming that it was unknown in America until Europeans brought it there; however Bernal Díaz, who accompanied Cortés in Mexico, remarked about 1520 that wooden objects made by the Indians, for instance arrow shafts, smelled strongly of onion and garlic, and he seems to have been an alert observer. It is possible that this effect could have been produced by the native American onion-flavored ramps, but it is unnecessary to seek such an explanation. The fact is that native onions did grow wild in America—the nodding onion and the prairie onion among others—and the Indians were fond of them; wild onions saved Père Marquette from starvation in 1670. Wild leeks have always grown in the woods of the Northeast. The Indians also liked wild garlic (meadow garlic) and wild chives; they ate lily bulbs, too. One type of lily was so commonly consumed by them that its name today is the Indian cucumber.

The Plains Indians were great consumers of the starchy camas bulb (from the Chinook *kamass),* which they used to make bread. Other roots on their menu included those of the arrowhead (which they called the wapatoo, another Chinook word), a tuber which tasted something like salsify; and of the blue lupine, which tasted something like sweet potato. Indians also ate bitterroot (palatable when peeled); the biscuit root, also called Indian biscuit; the breadroot, or prairie apple; and the starchy corm of the familiar jack-in-the-pulpit, but you had better not try to emulate them unless you know how to rid it of its irritant raphides, as they did.

The hickory nut is Indian down to its very name, which comes from the Virginian Indian *pawcohiccora.* Southeast Indians made lavish use of pecan nuts, as Americans of the same areas do today. However the most important native American nut was the peanut, which has now spread all over the world and is one of the most profitable food crops for several African countries. The peanut was already an important item in the Indian diet two thousand years ago, if not on territory now in the United States, at least in Mexico, where it has been found in excavations dated that far back. Nuts were important for the Indians, for they could be kept in good eating condition almost indefinitely; so they made wide use of beechnuts, hazelnuts, chestnuts (Indians of the Yosemite area even succeeded in making horse chestnuts edible), chinquapins (Delaware Indian *chinqua mihn),* black walnuts and butternuts, from which the Narragansetts extracted oil. They were also ingenious enough to derive considerable nourishment from acorns, which they converted into nourishing foods all the way across the country from Virginia to California. The Hopi Indians often gathered them when more palatable foods became rare. Acorns were also pounded into a sort of flour and mixed with cornmeal, which thickened soups and, fried in fat, produced bread and cakes. Acorn oil was used for seasoning and as a spread for cornbread. The acorn has not disappeared from the menu even today. "Acorns," an American Indian wrote to one of the authors in 1972, "are the main ingredients of soup and bread made by many Californians. Even today, the pounding rocks can still be found where, over 40 years ago, my grandmother prepared her acorn-meal."

Pre-Columbian Europeans often lacked vitamins, but not pre-Columbian Indians. They were given to greens, great harborers of vitamins, which they ate raw, as salads, or popped into whatever happened to be cooking, soup or stew. Among the more recondite plants which the Indians treated as greens were the young shoots and stalks of the salmonberry; the sweet coltsfoot; the fiddlehead fern and the fern milkweed; and wild celery, which is not celery but tape grass, an underwater plant whose long ribbony leaves fit it for such treatment. It is hardly necessary to point to the dandelion, but there was another flower whose leaves and even blossoms provided a spicy salad for Plains Indians—the wild nasturtium, which served so regularly for this purpose that the first Europeans to cross the prairies named it Indian cress.

Bays and berries provided vitamins, too. The incoming Europeans recognized some of those the Indians were eating, or thought they did—for instance the strawberry, which did indeed exist in Europe as well as in America, but in a quite different species. Before the discovery of America,

Europe knew only the dwarf mountain strawberry; the larger fruit they found in America was christened by them the Virginia strawberry, through the accident that this was where they first came across it. Actually, it grows on both the Atlantic and Pacific coasts. The huckleberry and the blueberry, also found on both seaboards, looked familiar to newcomers, too, for they confused them with the English bilberry, and still do. With the raspberry they were on sounder ground; the American fruit which the Indians ate, though hardier and less damaging to the picker's hands, is essentially the same as its European counterpart.

Cherries were known to the Old World, but to the New World too, where many varieties grew wild—the black or chokecherry, whose scientific name today attributes it to Virginia; the pin or bird cherry, whose scientific name attributes it to Pennsylvania; and the sweet black cherry. Currants and gooseberries existed on both sides of the Atlantic, and so did plums; peculiarly American was the wild beach plum, from which the Indians made jam. The crab apple, known in Europe, existed in America too, but the apple proper was unknown to the Indians. There are some early references to melons—Hernando de Alvarado informed Coronado that a country which he had explored produced melons—but what could they have been? Types of squash unknown to the Old World? The melon proper came from Eurasia, and even the watermelon, now firmly associated with the American South, was a native of Africa, and was presumably one of the several foods which enslaved Negroes brought with them to America; neither could have existed there before Columbus, and consequently neither was known to the Indians.

A vegetable of which the pre-Columbian Indians enjoyed a monopoly was the squash, so American that its very name is Indian: it is a shortening of the Narragansett *askutasquash.* As this means literally something that is eaten raw, we are entitled to believe that this was the way the Indians ate it, at least at the time when it acquired its name, though they cooked it later. When Europeans first found it in America, they may not have realized that they were being confronted with something new, for Old World approximations of squashes also existed; but those of America were different and often superior. The Indians were alone in possessing the crookneck squash, several other delicate yellow summer squashes, the butternut squash and the sweet acorn squash.

When the white men came, they should have been surprised by American beans, but they were not. They were familiar with the broad bean of Europe and the haricot bean must have looked to them very much like the same thing, unless there were botanists among them. It would take some time for Europe to discover the exceptional qualities of the haricot bean; when it did, the American vegetable all but drove the European one off the market.

Europe had been more generous to its inhabitants than America in one important category of food—cereals. Europe had wheat, barley, millet, rice, rye and oats; the Indians had maize—an important grain, it is true. There was one major exception to this limitation, in the area extending a few hundred miles south from what is now the Canadian border between the Atlantic and the Mississippi, particularly near the Great Lakes. This was wild rice, which is not rice, but was so called because it does look something like its godparent, and, like the rice the Europeans who so named it already knew, grows in water. It was also called by whites Indian rice or water oats (by French Canadians "crazy oats"), and by the Indians themselves *manomin*—the good berry. It was sufficiently essential to the Winnebago and Chippewa Indians to prevent them from slipping into nomadism, though they were great hunters, for they dared not venture far from the region which provided their basic food. Around the Great Lakes, where wild rice grew with especial generosity, tribal wars were waged for control of the territories where it abounded. It is still largely an Indian product.

The products of the vegetable kingdom were of course the lighter part of the pre-Columbian Indian's diet; the heaviest was provided by game. American animals of the period seem, through some effect of climate or of feeding, to have been tastier than their European counterparts. Writing of American deer and elk, William Byrd of Virginia reported in 1737: "They are . . . not quite as large as the European ones, but on the other hand [of] much better flavor, and big and fat all the year long." There were also moose and bear, and in the Rocky Mountains the pronghorn antelope and the wild goat. Among smaller game, rabbits were available everywhere; the raccoon and the opossum were hunted particularly in the Southeast and still are; the squirrel might seem a trifle plebeian, but among the whites who later hunted and ate it was Thomas Jefferson. The porcupine is considered lowly meat by many, but it still has some fanciers in northern New England today, who maintain that porcupine liver is a great delicacy; and beaver is still eaten in the South and has been domesticated for the table even in France. Also considered edible by the Indians were the otter and the seal, the first eaten especially, the second exclusively, in the Pacific Northwest. Did they appreciate the groundhog? Why not? Georgia hillbillies do. The authors have come across no record of Indians eating skunk ("skunk" is an Algonquin word), but from whom else could William Byrd have discovered "the surprisingly sweet flavor of polecat meat?"

Among game birds, the turkey was of course king, but there was a wealth of others—partridges, quails, pigeons, plovers, larks, and ospreys. Waterfowl of all kinds abounded on the coasts—wild ducks, wild geese, and many others out of favor today, like the crane (the ancient Romans and Gauls ate it), the swan (also consumed by the Romans, and by Elizabethans as well), the coot (appreciated still in Italy's Polesine area) and the seagull (modern Italians eat the tern). Is the frog game? The Plains Indians liked frogs' legs, especially the fat meaty ones of the bullfrog. Indians also ate snails, and the Plains Indians gathered painted turtles, wood turtles, snapping turtles, and their eggs, which they considered a particular treat. And there were also, a rich feast, the giant turtles of the sea.

The sea turtle, or green turtle, nearing extinction off the coasts of the United States now, was then not only plentiful along the Gulf Coast, where a few still remain today, but also on the Atlantic as far north as Cape Cod. It was so important for Gulf Coast Indians that it has been called "the buffalo of the Caribbean." Was it because of the resemblance between the turtle's carapace and a shield that some Indians believed eating turtle meat before a battle would protect them from wounds? Turtle meat was held to have medical properties. Broth made from it was drunk to cure sore throats and was also fed to infants. Those rare and priceless delicacies of today, diamond-backed terrapins, were a commonplace for the Indians, who scooped them up in scores on the shores of Chesapeake Bay.

The sea was a rich source of food for the Indians. William Wood was stirred by the brazen plenty of the American seacoast to exclaim in 1639:

> The dainty Indian maise
> Was eat with clamp-shells out of wooden trays,
> The luscious lobster with the craw-fish raw,
> The brinnish oyster, mussel, periwigge,
> And tortoise sought by the Indian squaw,
> Which to the flats dance many a winter's jigge,
> To dive for cockles and to dig for clams,
> Whereby her lazy husband's guts she cramms.

When white men reached the Pacific coast they found it quite as bountiful. An early explorer reported that at spawning time the salmon choked the rivers so that "you could walk across on their backs."

Among the saltwater fish the Indians enjoyed were cod, lemon sole, flounder, herring, halibut, sturgeon, smelt, drum (on the East Coast) and olachen (on the West), though the last was less useful for eating than for lighting; it was so oily that it had only to be equipped with a wick to become a portable lamp, and accordingly was called the candlefish. West Coast Indians even hunted whales, which the Yurok Indians of California, who possessed an elaborate code of taboos, were prohibited from eating at the same meal with deer, not much of a hardship when they had deer. The Jesuit missionaries who traveled up the St. Lawrence and thence southward into New York's Finger Lakes country exclaimed at the presence of eels there and at the Indian skill in cooking them. Trout were of course present everywhere; but the fact that half the fishbones found in the 9,000-year-old Modoc Indian cave near St. Louis were those of the sluggish catfish induced archeologists to conclude that the Modocs were either too backward or too indolent to be efficient capturers of livelier fish. Perhaps there were simply more catfish.

Crustaceans were widely eaten: shrimp, crayfish, lobsters and especially crabs—giant ones in the Northwest, blue crabs in the East, especially the Southeast; only the meat of the claws and that which clung to the upper shell was eaten, along with the green liver on which the Indians doted. Shellfish came big on the West Coast too—the California abalone is big enough so that steaks can be cut from it; the geoduck is too big for its shell and cannot close it (the Indians gathered it ceremoniously twice a year at the extreme low spring and fall tides, provoked by what they called the "mad moon"); the bent-nose clam, of more reasonable dimensions, seems to have been an ancient favorite of the Indians, judging from the number of its shells in their kitchen middens. On Catalina Island alone, a single midden yielded twenty-two different species of shellfish. On the East Coast the clams which appealed most to the Indians were the surf clam, the largest on the Atlantic side; the hard-shell clam or quahog (from the Narragansett Indian *poquaûhock),* the one from whose shells they made wampum; and the soft-shell clam, alias the long-neck, alias the steamer. This last was their most popular shellfish, except for the oyster, on both Atlantic and Pacific coasts. On both coasts also the Indians ate mussels, but more sparingly and apparently with less enthusiasm. Oysters were also eaten on both the Atlantic and Pacific, and so were periwinkles, disdained in the United States today; but the French, the Italians and the Spaniards eat them.

What did the Indians drink with all this bounty? Water, mostly. But the tradition which blames the white man for first introducing them to alcohol is not quite unbreachable. The Indians had not learned to distill liquor, but this is not the only way to obtain alcohol. Fruit juice can ferment, and it would be curious if no Indian had ever happened to drink juice which had so turned; and as a matter of fact, a few of them did—the Cherokees, for instance, who made drinks from the fermented juice of wild fruits. There were also what for want of a better name we may call beers, of low alcoholic content, like those brewed from maple or corn syrup by the Indians of the Northeast, or stranger drinks concocted from such unpromising beginnings as the pumpkin. Some of the strongest pre-Columbian Indian drinks were those with which ritual intoxication was deliberately sought to provoke visions, which were invested with religious significance. Some western Indians drank mescal, the fermented juice of the maguey, for this purpose, while the Luiseño Indians of California achieved the same result with a drink made from the roots of the jimsonweed.

Did the Indians ever have wine? They had the makings for it and one account of the first Thanksgiving refers to wine made from wild grapes; but perhaps this was nothing but grape juice. The dour presence of the Pilgrims would not have encouraged roistering. It would be other, less abstemious, white men who would first introduce the Indians to hard liquor and, adding insult to injury, baptize it with a Chinook word—*hotchenoo,* hootch.

The first recorded instance of this corruption of the red man by the white man's liquor is the famous one of 1609, when Henry Hudson offered brandy to the Indians he found on an island in the bay of New York. Its effect on the unprepared Indians was powerful; their chief passed out. As a result, one version goes, the Indians baptized the place where this occurred with a Delaware word meaning "the island where we all got drunk"—Manahachtanienk. Most scholars prefer to believe, unpicturesquely, that what "Manhattan" really means is "high island." (So far as we know, nobody has tried to reconcile the two versions by rearranging this to mean "the island where we got high.")

What the Indians did drink in plenty was tea, brewed from sassafras or wild mint or the aromatic spicebush or, medicinal in taste and in purpose, the bitter leaves of the yaupon (from the Catawba *yopun);* the last, a powerful emetic, was known as "the black drink." They also had a cooling summer beverage, sumacade, made from the berries of the scarlet sumac. As they were particularly fond of this, they did not restrict its use to the hot months. They picked as many berries as they could find at their season of optimum ripeness, drying any surplus so that they could store them and enjoy this Indian lemonade all year round.

This thoughtfulness for the future does not accord very well with the popular image of the Indian as an improvident savage drifting rudderless and helpless across the seasons. If he was capable of looking ahead to assure a supply of an item as dispensable as a cooling drink, is it credible that he would have been heedless about more important foods? In fact, he was not. If he had been, the Pilgrims would not have survived their first winter in Plymouth. They lived on food they found in an Indian cache. The Indians knew, indeed, how to preserve food, not only to carry them through the winters, but to provide against unpredictable emergencies. They were aided by the fact that two of their most important foods were easy to dry, and would then keep almost indefinitely—beans and corn. In the Southeast the peanut was an equally good storehouse of nourishment. Meat could be smoked or air-cured, producing "jerky," which, later, the pioneers of the West would find so useful; the Indians were also the inventors of the long-keeping concentrated food called pemmican (Cree, *pimikân).* In the Northwest, salmon were dried, smoked and pressed into compact cakes which were stored in protective seal bladders; or they were simply smoked, producing what white settlers would dub "Siwash Cheese."

These careful, cautious Indians, hoarding food for the future and mindful of the fact that their climate could play unpleasant tricks upon them, are not as romantic as the Fenimore Cooper savages whose image springs to mind whenever Indians are mentioned. The Indian society was not composed solely of warriors, nor were all Indians nomads. Those who were had their own usually effective fashions of coping with nature. Meanwhile the more sedentary tribes did not sit back and wait for edible growth to offer itself for no more effort than the gathering. They farmed the land, and farmed it so well that they would surprise the first European witnesses of their labor.

IV

Indian Farming

"NEW WORLD AGRICULTURE was not only different from that practised in the Old World," Peter Farb wrote in *Man's Rise to Civilization,* "in many ways it was superior as well. Indians cultivated a wider variety of plants than did Europeans at the time of the discovery of North America, and they used horticultural techniques that were in many cases more advanced." According to Richard MacNeish, the natives encountered by the colonists of the sixteenth century "had made agricultural advances far beyond those of the Old World." In the dry Southwest, the Hohokam Indians ("those who have vanished," the name means in the Pima Indian language), were using irrigation two thousand years ago. In this part of the country the soil was fertilized with guano found on the floors of bat caves; in the Northeast the favorite fertilizer was fish; a fish was buried in each hill of corn, a trick some New England subsistence farmers use to this day. By their use of fertilizer the Indians replenished the soil with the nutrients their crops had drained from it and as a result they were able to remain on the same land for years; in contrast, the history of early white expansion in Virginia was a function of the exhaustion of unfertilized soil. Even after the white man began to profit by Indian know-how, he was a little slow on the uptake; for years after he became acquainted with maize he was still trying to sow it by scattering its kernels broadcast over the ground, because that was what he had been accustomed to doing with wheat. The Indians planted a few kernels in a hill, along with pumpkin seeds, whose vines spread over the space among the hills and finished ripening their fruit in the late fall on the same ground which by then the corn no longer needed—another trick white farmers have adopted.

Writers on Indian food have often referred to the "Indian triad," the three vegetables most common in Indian cooking—squash, beans and maize, the last fittingly named also "Indian corn." Of the three, the Indians probably did little to improve the squash: they took it as it came. The other two, however, seem to have improved under their care.

American Indians began cultivating the bean far back in their history, but probably not earlier than seven thousand years ago, the date ascribed to objects found in excavated Mexican caves which included beans. The beans were wild; cultivation had not yet started. But some time between 5000 B.C. and A.D. 1492, the Indians developed a bewildering variety of beans, whose diversity was in at least some cases deliberately achieved. The Pueblo Indians were slower in acquiring the bean from Mexico than was the case for several other foods which reached them from the same source—if it is true, as we are told, that it entered their diet only about 450 B.C.—but once they had it, they lost no time, especially the Papagos, who were nicknamed "the bean people," and the Hopis, who made it their object to produce beans of as many different hues as possible, starting from the large flat multicolored bean which is believed to have been the ancestor of all the Southwestern species. They developed at least twelve different kinds, ranging in color from black to white. The most prized were the yellow, blue, red, white, multicolored and black varieties because those colors symbolized the six cardinal directions (two more than the white man recognized) representing, in that order, north, west, south, east and, subtlely, up and down.

The Indians of the East probably developed their own beans independently. They were already widespread when the first explorers reached the Atlantic Coast; Cabeza de Vaca found them in Florida in 1528 and Jacques Cartier a few years later at the mouth of the St. Lawrence. String beans existed also; Cherokee women wound them into long chains and hung them up to dry in the sun, producing what were later dubbed "leather britches beans." Within a century after the discovery of America, several kinds of beans developed by the Indians were being exported to the Old World.

The bean was important to the Indian diet, but for almost all American Indians from British Columbia and Quebec to Chile and Argentina maize (an Indian word which the Spaniards had picked up in Cuba) was the basic crop and they were keenly aware of it. The Iroquois in the North accompanied its planting with prayer. The Creeks in the South, who believed in paying only on delivery, gave thanks ceremoniously when the crop had been harvested. In the West, corn dances were performed during the growing season to persuade good spirits to grant a bountiful crop or evil ones to withhold their malevolence. Corn was considered to have miraculous powers; later, the Zuñi would sprinkle it across their gateways to keep the conquistadores out. They must have skimped on the quantity.

Only a magical explanation could account for a magical food. The Navahos alone had two different legends to account for it. Some of their tribes remembered how a tremendous hen turkey had flown over their territory, dropping an ear of blue corn from under each wing; other tribes told a more complicated story. It recounted the appearance of a beautiful woman of non-Indian type, with long blond hair, who instructed an Indian hermit to set fire to the dried grass surrounding her and, when the sun had set, to drag her body by the hair over the scorched earth. He demurred at treating a woman in this fashion, but obeyed after she told him, "Wherever my body has passed, new grass will arise; when you glimpse my golden hair between the leaves, the grain will be good to eat." A similarly self-sacrificing spirit encountered a young Ojibway boy, challenged him to a wrestling match, and lost—purposely, one gathers—though the defeat was fatal to him. Following instructions his magnanimous adversary had given him before the bout, the boy buried him; corn rose from the grave. For the Iroquois, corn sprang from the footprints of a ghostly woman who strode across their fields; pumpkins as well as corn grew where she had trod.

Of all the pre-Columbian Indians of what would later become the United States, the Pueblo Indians of the Southwest were probably the most skillful farmers, if only because they were there first.

They were also encouraged to develop skill as farmers by another fact which at first thought might seem to have been more likely to discourage them: they lived in an arid and difficult region. They accepted this circumstance as a challenge, which spurred them on to solve the most difficult problems—for instance, that of irrigation. In our surprise at discovering that the Hohokam Indians in particular knew how to irrigate two thousand years ago, we have tended to exaggerate the extent to which the Pueblo Indians had recourse to this technique. It did exist, but it was exceptional and usually unnecessary, for the Indians were skillful at locating underground water and built their settlements near it. This tended to anchor them to fixed localities. The comparative permanence of Pueblo settlements meant that it was the same soil which had to be sown year after year; consequently the land had to be cared for so that it would retain its fruitfulness—hence the invention of fertilizer.

In the Northeast, the Iroquois, who have been called, possibly with excessive enthusiasm, "the Greeks of America," aroused the admiration of the Jesuits when they arrived, for their intensive cultivation of maize and vegetables and for their perspicacious choice of locations for their permanent settlements, established on the banks of rivers or lakes (for fish), where the terrain was flat (for cultivation) and whose surrounding woods lent themselves to clearing, promoting the growth of fresh underbrush to attract deer (for meat)—the closest approach any Eastern pre-Columbian Indians made to the domestication of large animals. Their vegetable gardens were laid out in orderly rows and were well tended. Among the Iroquois, it was the women who cultivated the soil, not in any subordinate capacity, as mere drudges for the magnificent males who hunted the game to go with their vegetables, but as the recognized owners of the land, and of its crops, too. The harvests belonged to them, and it was they who decided how the food should be shared, how much might be eaten at once and how much should be stored for a later day. They owned the lodges also. The importance of farming for the Iroquois was symbolized by the frequent festivals dedicated to various products of the soil. There were feasts in honor of strawberries, of beans, of corn, and of other crops.

The agricultural skill of the Indians of the Southeast impressed the Europeans when they arrived. John White, a member of one of Sir Walter Raleigh's North Carolina settlements in Pamlico Sound, marveled at the Croatan Indian villages "with houses made of bark and gardens where corn was planted in neat rows with beans climbing the stalks." Just inland from the Croatans, on territory which today straddles the states of Georgia, Tennessee and North Carolina, were the Cherokees, expert farmers too, who cultivated, among other plants unknown to Europe, the peanut and the sweet potato. The Cherokees belonged to "the five civilized tribes," which included also the Choctaws, the Chickasaws, the Creeks and the Seminoles, all good husbandmen.

A little to the southwest, in what are now Louisiana and Mississippi, the Natchez Indians based their whole existence on agriculture, and gave to their thirteen months the names of the foods appropriate to them. According to the Jesuit priest Maturin Le Petit, who visited them in 1699, their ideas of heaven and hell were largely gastronomic. The blessed would spend most of their time feasting, in a "region of pleasures, where all kinds of exquisite viands will be furnished them in abundance," while the damned would "be cast upon lands unfruitful and entirely covered with water, where they will not have any kind of corn [and] . . . will never eat meat and have no nourishment save the flesh of crocodiles and spoiled fish and shell-fish."

V

Indian Cooking

AMERICAN INDIANS—some of them—were not only sophisticated farmers, they were also—some of them—sophisticated cooks. The contribution American Indians made to the American cuisine is greater than most of us realize. We do not owe to the Indian the barbecue or mincemeat, as has been claimed, but we do owe to him the clambake, the idea of roasting peanuts, cranberry sauce, possibly codfish cakes, clam chowder, hominy, corn pone, pumpkin soup, Boston baked beans, Brunswick stew, and, of course, succotash. When the whites arrived, the Indians of the Northeast taught them to steam lobster, the Indians of the Southwest taught them how to deal with persimmons, the Indians of the Northwest taught them to plank salmon. After the Europeans imported the pig, the Cherokees invented Smithfield ham. The pioneers who opened up the Far West carried with them Indian jerky—strips of air-cured meat, often buffalo—and pemmican.

"Jerky" is a name that sounds English enough, a slangy version, one might think, of "jerked meat," whatever "jerked" might mean in this connotation. Actually the sequence was the other way around: "jerky" came first, and the evolution to "jerked meat" was a way to make the familiar, easygoing "jerky" sound a trifle more formal. "Jerky" was not English, but an Indian word, or more exactly a Spanish rendering of an Indian word. It comes from *charqui,* which, Reay Tannahill tells us in her meticulously researched *Food in History,*

> was made by cutting boned and defatted beef into quarter-inch slices and either dipping these in strong brine or rubbing them with salt. After the meat had been rolled up in the animal's hide for ten or twelve hours to absorb the salt and release some of the juices, it was hung in the sun to dry and finally tied up into convenient bundles. It looked, said one German traveler, like thick pasteboard, and was "just as easy to masticate."

Pemmican was bundled into packets of animal skin too, for keeping and carrying. Modern dieticians would be hard put to it to devise a better unspoilable and easily transportable food for men likely to be called upon to exert great physical effort. The iron ration of the Indians, it consisted of lean dried meat (proteins) pounded together with berries (vitamins) in melted fat (energy), sometimes with the addition of bone marrow. The inclusion of berries may have been prompted originally by a desire to give a little life to what otherwise would have been a somewhat insipid food, but whatever the original motive, the result was that pemmican was given life in a literal as well as a figurative sense. While Europeans were still allowing themselves to be afflicted with scurvy for neglect of foods containing the as yet undiscovered vitamins, the Indians had learned empirically which foods they required to remain healthy. It seems clear that they realized that the berries were not mere seasoning, but a necessary element in pemmican, for some kind of berry was included in pemmican in every part of the country where it existed. The Cree Indians used wild cherries, the Plains Indians used buffalo berries, the New England Indians used cranberries. Pemmican played an important role in the first crossing of the American continent: it was the basic food which in 1793 enabled Alexander Mackenzie, a fur trader, to travel from the Atlantic coast to the Pacific.

The development of Indian cooking, quite naturally, followed the development of the equipment at the Indians' disposal, as it did everywhere. We may reasonably suppose that the earliest method of cooking meat was to spit it on a stick suspended over an open fire; one development of this technique was to replace the stick by a grill, another to dig a trench in the ground in which to build the fire, whose heat would thus be confined more efficiently to the space in which it was meant to exercise its influence. In either case the kitchen was the great outdoors and the result was the barbecue. The American Indian cannot be credited with being the sole creator of the barbecue, a method of cooking so natural under primitive circumstances that it would practically invent itself everywhere, especially in societies accustomed to living outdoors most of the time.

But creator or not, the Indian was barbecuing his meat before Columbus, and when the whites arrived it seems indeed to have been the Indians who taught them, or recalled to them, this manner of cooking. The first settlers of Virginia, who came from a social environment unlikely to have been familiar with the barbecue, found the Indians utilizing it, and copied their example.

If the cooking of meat raised problems for a society without cooking utensils, the cooking of vegetables was even more complicated. Some vegetables (roots, for instance) could be roasted directly in the ashes or embers of a fire; but others called for boiling. In the period before they developed pottery capable of withstanding the heat of a fire, American Indians devised various ingenious methods for getting along without pots and pans. Several of them were variations of the technique which led anthropologists to nickname certain Indians of the pre-pottery period "the Stone Boilers." The principle was to find some container which, though it might be unable to resist flame, was nevertheless watertight. It would then be filled with water, and stones heated in a fire would be dropped into it until the water boiled, cooking incidentally whatever food, vegetable or meat, had been put in it also. The earliest watertight vessels were made of wood or bark (unless a rock with a sufficiently large hollow happened to be handy).

Plains Indians used another kind of cooking vessel, the stomach of a buffalo, or even the whole freshly killed animal, which was emptied of its internal organs and then suspended by its legs from pickets, back down, over a fire. Filled with water, the carcass provided a commodious receptacle, able to hold enough stew for a large company; but though either the buffalo or its stomach could be hung over a fire, it had to be a low one, and neither could be suspended too close to the flames. The heat of the fire was thus insufficient alone to cook the contents of this unusual pot, and had to be supplemented by heated stones submerged in the food. Permanent cooking vessels were also made from buffalo-hide leather, which must have given an interesting taste to the food.

It was probably the Pueblo Indians who first learned how to tress wicker baskets so tightly that they could hold water for stone-boiling; the Northwest Indians were soon achieving the same feat. The Southwestern Indians, always ahead of the others both in growing food and in cooking it, were also certainly the first to develop fireproof pottery which would enable them to dispense with the stone-boiling technique. By the time the white man arrived, the Southwest Indians had devised genuine ovens to which the Spaniards gave a name from their own language, *hornos.* Made of adobe and beehive shaped, they were used especially for baking corn bread, from meal made by spreading dried corn kernels on flat stone slabs called *metates* and crushing them with a stone rolling pin *(manos).*

Other parts of the country, instead of building ovens, dug them. Pit cooking, with heated stones or the embers of a fire providing heat at the bottom of a hole to steam the food which filled the rest of it, was no doubt invented before cooking pots existed; it remained in favor long after earthenware vessels which could resist fire were available because of the superior flavor produced by such slow even cooking; the white men would revive this technique some centuries later with the fireless cooker. If the hole were dug in the sand of a beach and the stones covered by seaweed, in whose steaming embrace fish, shellfish and even vegetables (sweet potatoes in their skins, corn in its husks) cooked fragrantly, the result was the still popular clambake; inland, and with other victuals than seafood, the pit became the beanhole, no longer utilized except by Boy Scouts. Thus Boston baked beans were born. The Indians pit-cooked their beans in maple sugar, and included a lump of bear fat. New Englanders replaced the maple sugar with molasses, the bear fat with salt pork, and retained the essential principle of long slow cooking. The Boston dish is basically the same as the Indian one. As for the brown bread which accompanies baked beans so perfectly, it is made today with a mixture of flours, but it still includes cornmeal, the only one the Indians possessed; and when properly made it is *steamed,* the way the Indians cooked it.

Plains Indians approximated the effect of pit cooking aboveground by burying roots in hot ashes, and Northwestern Indians by wrapping small pieces of game in fat, enveloping the packet in cedar bark, and setting it on hot stones so that the steam from the fat cooked the meat; or thin strips of meat were fried on hot stones. In the Northwest also tremendous roasts of large animals (bear, perhaps, or elk) would be suspended at an equal distance from three triangularly placed fires so that they would cook slowly all the way through.

Indians in several different regions discovered, apparently independently, the virtues of ashes in cooking. In the Southeast they learned that corn, soaked in ashes mixed with water, swelled, whitened, and changed flavor, and applied this knowledge to making hominy. Sometimes it was dried and pounded into the hominy grits still so popular in the South. Hominy is an Indian word, from the Algonquin *tackhummin,* meaning "corn without skin," and so is pone, from *appone* or *äpân* or *äbân,* depending on which dialect you prefer; corn pone and spoon bread are gifts of the Indian. In the West, the Navahos mixed a small amount of cedar ashes with the cornmeal from which they made their bread, and still do. They could not have known it, but cedar ashes are rich in the mineral salts which corn lacks and thus makes it a more nutritious food; the theory has been advanced that this use of ashes may possibly help account for the low incidence of cancer among Navahos. The American Indian quoted previously on acorn meal (who, it is almost unnecessary to explain, was serving at the time in the United States armed forces in Europe) wrote in the same letter that "cedar ashes . . . improve the flavor of boiled GI cornmeal weevils, at home and abroad."

The universal Indian bread was of course made from cornmeal, in innumerable varieties, beginning with the simplest, Northwest "buckskin bread," whose ingredients were meal, some form of yeast, and water. The many other Indian breads included sweet potato bread; chestnut bread; bean bread; hominy bread; wild potato bread; squaw bread in round flat loaves, made with potato yeast; Pueblo adobe bread, which shifted from cornmeal to wheat flour after the Spaniards introduced wheat; Indian bread, of mixed cornmeal and wheat flour, also, of course, after the latter arrived; carrot bread, when that vegetable was imported from Europe; molasses bread, which had to wait until the Spaniards brought in sugar cane; and bannocks, pancakes, ashcakes, corn pone and other floury foods. The Hopi had a special type of bread baked on ceremonial occasions, *chukuviki,* a little like a frankfurter bun, pointed at its two ends, which was wrapped in corn husks and steamed. The Hopi also made *piki,* a light flaky many-layered pastry like that which the Saracens invented and bestowed upon Europe; a Hopi girl who hoped to attract a husband was obliged to know how to make *piki.*

The fresh flavors of fruit highlighted many Indian dishes. The Seminole Indians of Florida cooked fish with wild grapes. The Iroquois stuffed ducks with grapes and, after the white man came, apples, and spit-roasted them. In New England, huckleberries and blackberries were added to stews, the wild beach plum was made into jam and the American wild cherry, too tart to eat fresh, was cooked into sweetness with the aid of maple sugar. Buffalo berries were also much too sour to eat, but, like persimmons, were tamed by the first frost. The Plains Indians gathered them then and mixed them in pemmican to give it zest, or mashed them into a cranberrylike sauce which was eaten with buffalo meat. The Hopi put squash blossoms into stews or deep-fried them by themselves.

The art of seasoning single foods, or carefully composed combinations of foods, was born at different times and utilized to different degrees in different parts of the country. The Pueblo Indians employed fiery chilies or hot peppers to spice their stews; they added coriander after they got it from the Mexicans, who got it from the Spaniards. Plains Indians, who had originally lined their cooking pits with hides, developed surprising subtlety when they had recourse instead to fragrant maple or sassafras leaves which imparted flavor to the food, used particularly in cooking ham after the white man had imported the pig. The Southeastern Choctaws ground sassafras leaves into a powder which was used to give flavor to various dishes and to thicken soups and stews. Wild mint was used in soups, stews and salads, and Indians also liked to season their dishes with the aromatic spicebush. The ingredient which gave special tastiness to Northwest Indian dishes was often the juniper berry, used with roast meat, stews or salmon. Pine sap was a seasoner of the Northeast, which also steamed large lobsters doused with sweet oil pressed from sunflower seeds.

The seasoning of a dish can also be affected by the liquid, or liquids, in which it is cooked; and in this field it seemed to the Europeans who first made contact with them that the Indians were handicapped by a grievous gap in their larder—the absence of milk. The Indians had no domestic animals and were not aware of this lack. They had learned how to derive from nuts liquids which could be used in cooking wherever Europeans employed milk—indeed, when the whites discovered them, they called them milks, the most important being hickory milk. The earliest account of the making of hickory milk seems to be the one published in 1588 by Thomas

Harriot in his *Briefe and True Report of the New Found Land of Virginia.* He wrote of the Powhatan Indians that

> they breake [the nuts] with stones and pound them in mortars with water to make a milk which they use to put into some sorts of their spoonmeat; also among their sodden wheat [maize], peaze [either a mistake or a post-Columbian addition to the Indian repertory, which would have been unlikely so early; the pea, like Thomas Harriot, was European], beanes and pompions [pumpkins] which maketh them have a farre more pleasant taste.

The most universal Indian dish, found almost everywhere, seems to have been succotash—naturally enough, since its two principal components, sometimes its *only* components, were also found almost everywhere. Succotash signified different things at different times in the same place, and different things in different places at the same time. When the authors were youngsters, and succotash was much commoner on American tables than it is now, it had settled down to a sober stability; it was invariably composed of corn kernels and lima beans, sweetened, thus combining the two principal and most widely spread vegetables of the Indian world. But before Columbus, and for that matter well into Colonial times, a guest of the Indians never knew what to expect when he was offered a bowl of succotash.

Succotash probably had no single place of origin, but appeared spontaneously everywhere that corn and the bean were found together, which meant in most of America. The exact meaning of the word, which appeared in different Indian languages in such varied forms as *sukquttahash, msakwitash* and *m'sick-quotash,* seems to have undergone a good deal of evolution, more, probably, than the dish it represented, which was simply the food being stewed in the cooking pot, whatever its contents might happen to be. The first signification of succotash, in some languages at least, seems to have been simply "husked corn," representing the bare minimum of what might be in the pot; one always had corn even when there was nothing else. Since even when there *was* something else corn was almost certain to be in the stew too, its name gradually became extended to cover everything that had gone into it. In the Narragansett language, the literal meaning of "succotash" at one period was "fragments," a pretty good description of the ingredients that composed the catch-all stew. The fragments were more or less certain to include both beans and corn, and, in hard times when game and fish made themselves scarce, nothing *except* beans and corn (sweetened in the North with maple syrup and in the South with bear fat), so "succotash" wound up meaning a dish combining only sweetened beans and corn.

Succotash must have gone back to a primitive era of Indian cooking when everything was normally boiled together in the same pot—or nearly everything, for William Byrd reported that superstitious Indians were afraid of provoking "the Guardian of the Forrest, by cooking the Beasts of the Field and the Birds of the Air together in one Vessell." There could not have been much concern for the taste of these improvised stews, into which anything might be tossed with little regard for its compatibility with the other ingredients; but as Indian cooking developed, it ceased to be tributary to the common pot and refined specialties were invented, especially in the almost urbanized Southwest, where Indians had been cooking longer. They had grown accustomed there to making fine distinctions. When a Zuñi squaw picked squash blossoms to serve as appetizers or to flavor her soup, she took care to gather only the large male flowers, which were considered the tastiest. The Hopis developed different strains of corn, each of which had its particular purpose. Yellow corn was the sweetest and was used for roasting ears; the kernels were eaten directly off the cob, as we eat them today. White corn was ground into meal, for cornmeal mush or bread. Red and blue varieties, which were less common, were also converted into meal, but for *piki* pastry, which was thus prettified, the red of the corn becoming a delicate pink in the pastry, and the dark blue a cerulean pastel shade. Pine nut soup was a favorite with all the Pueblo Indians, who were fond of these nuts and roasted them to munch, as we do peanuts. The prickly pear, the fruit of a kind of cactus, was converted into jelly; or its spines were painstakingly removed and it was dried in the sun, becoming a long-lived confection.

The Pueblo Indians stewed vegetables, green peppers or chilies, for instance, for their own sakes, or combined them with meat in stews; game and peppers was a favorite combination, with which they ate adobe bread, raised with natural yeast which they made themselves—at one period they were using potato yeast, but it is not certain that Southwestern Indians knew the potato in pre-Columbian times.

Since salmon was the principal food of the Northwest, there were many ways of cooking it, but the simplest was considered among the best: the fish, opened and cleaned, was pinched between two small branches cut from any handy tree, and pinioned between them too was a series of lateral twigs, like ribs, to hold the fish spread open before (not over) the fire. By turning or inclining the central branches, the amount of heat reaching various parts of the salmon could be regulated to insure even cooking. A delicate refinement, after the fish had been split open and cleaned, was to rub the interior with sweet ferns, imparting a delicate flavor to the flesh. The Northeastern Indians had two fashions of cooking what we would call planked salmon today. A king salmon was skewered to a piece of driftwood (which thus provided built-in seasoning) and held over a high flame to sear the fish and prevent its juices from escaping. The fire was then allowed to burn down, and the piece of driftwood with its attached fish placed on the embers to cook slowly and thoroughly. It would be charred on the outside, but succulently juicy inside, with a marked flavor of smoke. The other method consisted in making a sandwich of a salmon split open, flattened and enclosed between two thin slabs of alder wood, which was then laid over a bed of glowing embers. Too many salmon for immediate consumption were always taken during the spawning season, so the surplus was smoked for future use, much more heavily than we smoke salmon today; it was often left in the smokehouse for two weeks, emerging more brown than salmon-colored. Sometimes smoked salmon was also dried, seasoned and cut into thin strips, ready to be chewed between meals by anyone who felt hungry; this was "squaw candy." The red roe of the salmon was first spread out on the rocks to dry and then smeared on bread like butter.

Clams, mussels and barnacles were cooked, too—invariably, for they were never eaten raw; perhaps the Northwest Indians had experienced shellfish poisoning. The cooking method was to heat flat stones in the fire, and then place the shellfish on them to steam. There were often surplus shellfish, too, for the Pacific beaches were rich in them so, like salmon, they were smoked for future use.

The Northwest was the country of the potlatch, the most extravagant form of feasting on the continent. Not content with keeping up with the Joneses, the Northwest Indians, by means of the potlatch, strove to keep ahead of the Joneses. The potlatch was an occasion for conspicuous ostentation, which can reasonably be compared to the excessive largesse of Renaissance lords or Roman Emperors. Indeed, the proportion of his total wealth which the potlatch host squandered upon, or simply in the presence of, his guests, was certainly greater than that expended by the most profligate Oriental monarch.

The potlatch might mark an important event, like the marriage of a chief's daughter; or it might be designed to impress the host's peers or betters, to win preference for him, for instance when the case of succession to the chieftainship arose; or it might be given for no particular reason except to enhance the host's prestige, especially if he suspected that it was declining. It was not enough for the Indian notable who gave a potlatch to provide the best food obtainable, in quantities purposely much too great than was necessary (it would have been unbearably shameful if the guests had proved able to eat everything offered them), but he was also expected to give away a fortune in gifts—blankets, furs, edible oils, wood carvings: the possibilities were limited in those days. At a single Kwakiutl potlatch, the guests (who had previously eaten, among other delicacies, fifty seals) were gratified with eight canoes, six slaves, fifty-four elk skins, two thousand silver bracelets, seven thousand brass bracelets, and thirty-three thousand blankets. Indeed, the gifts were a more essential feature of the potlatch than the food; its very name came from the Nootka *patshatl,* to give. To convince those present, and everyone else who would hear about it, of his surpassing wealth, the host would often treat his guests to the spectacle of the simple destruction of riches, burning his reserves of oil, breaking up his canoes, or destroying the precious sheets of decorated copper which were the equivalent of money; some of them were almost three feet long and worth several thousand blankets. Certain exhibitionists went so far as to put their slaves to death and burn their houses; of course it was a simpler matter in those days to build another house than it would be now, and slaves could always be replaced from the next captives in an intertribal war.

Plains cooking was not particularly reputed among Indian cuisines, but George Catlin, who has left us perhaps our most remarkable collection of Indian portraits, was favorably impressed by a meal he was served by a Mandan tribe. This would have been in the eighteen thirties, but there was nothing on the menu that pre-Columbian Indians could not have provided; for that matter, the Indians of that region had probably not been much disturbed by white influence, for the land west of the Mississippi was still largely *terra incognita* at that period. We may assume that he was sampling the same sort of food the Indians had been eating before the discovery of America on the occasion he described thus:

> The simple feast which was spread before us consisted of three dishes only, two of which were served in wooden bowls, and the third in an earthen vessel . . . The last contained a quantity of *pem-i-can* and marrow-fat; and one of the former held a fine brace of buffalo ribs, delightfully roasted; and the other was filled with a kind of paste or pudding, made of the flour of the *"pomme blanche,"* as the French call it, a delicious turnip of the prairie, finely flavored with the buffalo berries which are collected in great quantities in this country, and used with divers dishes in cooking, as we in civilized countries use dried currants, which they very much resemble.

It was also apparently true in the Southeast that whites who sampled Indian food and reported on it were eating much as the Indians did before Columbus. When William Bartram praised the Seminole dish of red snapper steamed with oranges, it was one he could not have tasted before the Spaniards planted oranges in Florida, but the Seminoles had made the same dish before that revolutionizing event, using wild grapes for the fruit. Bartram did a good deal of eating with the Indians, and left us accounts of several of his meals. Of one Seminole feast he wrote:

> The ribs and choicest fat pieces of the bullocks [a dish the Indians could not have offered before the Spaniards imported cattle, but they could have used buffalo; in the meantime they had learned how to fatten beeves on corn], excellently well barbecued, were brought into the apartment of the public square, constructed and appointed for feasting; bowls and kettles of stewed fish and broth were brought in for the next course, and with it a very singular dish, the traders called it tripe soup.

Bartram then passed into what was then called West Florida, which, depending on exactly where he was, would have been on the coast of Florida,

Alabama, Mississippi, or Louisiana. There he made acquaintance with the Creeks, who, like the Seminoles, were one of the Five Civilized Tribes; more exactly, both were originally members of the same tribe, for the Seminoles had broken away from the Creeks, thus acquiring their present name: Seminole means "seceder" in the Creek language. The Creeks offered Bartram a meal, too:

> The repast is now brought in, consisting of venison stewed with bear's oil, fresh corn cakes, milk [necessarily post-Columbus too, unless it was hickory milk] and our drink, honey and water, very cool and agreeable.

Southeast Indian cooking was expert, and sometimes had to be—for instance in handling comfortroot, a relative of arrowroot indigenous to Florida, also called coontie, from whose stems and half-buried rhizomes the Seminoles made flour, *kunti.* There were several varieties of comfortroot, but all of them belonged to the genus *Zamia,* which requires careful handling and thorough washing to rid it of an undesirable alkaloid akin to curarine, a constituent of curare arrow poison. Comfortroot has disappeared from the menu nowadays, understandably, but a number of other Southeastern Indian dishes which we today consider typically American—and so they are, but not *white* American—have entered into the Southern cuisine. We have already mentioned hominy and corn pone, but for the latter we should perhaps specify that this was not a case of mere imitation by Europeans of a dish they had found among the Indians, but one of conscious education. Indian women deliberately taught the white settlers how to "bruse or pound [corn kernels] in a morter, and thereof make loaves or lumps of dowishe bread." Cornmeal is not too easy to handle at first for cooks formerly acquainted chiefly with wheat flour, so European women no doubt found it useful to be shown how the Indians moistened their cornmeal, flattened it into little cakes, and then baked it either on heated stones or on a paddle of green wood which would hold out long enough when held over a fire to allow the thin pone to bake; or the corn pone might simply be placed on the hot coals. The latter technique gave rise to the European name of "ashcakes," a literal description, and the former to "hoecakes," for the wooden paddle was replaced by the blade of a hoe when there was one handy (perhaps the whites also used the Indian hoe, whose blade was a large flat seashell).

Another food for which Indian women gave the Europeans their first lesson was the persimmon. The newcomers tried this mouth-puckering fruit and decided that it was inedible; the Indians told them that it was necessary to wait to pick persimmons until after the first frost, when they lost their astringency and could be used not only to make preserves, but also, dried and reduced to flour, to produce breads and puddings. Did they pass on also their fashion of studding cornmeal dough with blackberries or strawberries and thus producing the sort of dessert we call today a cobbler?

One dish credited to the Southeastern Indians is Brunswick stew, which, as it is made today, with only chicken and vegetables, is but a pale reflection of the Indian dish which preceded it—and might have been called, in some places and at some times, succotash, for it was composed of no fixed ingredients, but included anything and everything (except fish) which might be handy. It was contained in a pot which was left to bubble permanently over the fire. Its contents were periodically diminished as inroads were made upon them for a meal, and as constantly replenished whenever more food turned up. The corn and beans of succotash were almost always in it, but the favorite ingredients were game, both furry and feathered—squirrel, rabbit, turkey, or anything else that was handy. Why the whites called this dish Brunswick stew no one seems to know. Is it likely that Brunswick, Georgia, was trying to take credit for it? This would not jibe with the belief that the stew was so named in Jamestown, for Brunswick was first settled in 1772, and by then Jamestown had almost disappeared from the map. Another theory—but it is only a theory—is that the dish was named in honor of Caroline of Brunswick, wife of George IV, who became king in 1820; this would have been late for Jamestown too. The name remains a mystery.

The Southeastern Indians are often credited with having taught the whites to use gumbo, a suspicious assertion if you happen to know the origin of the word: it comes from Africa, *ngombo* or *kingombo.* Pre-Columbian Indians could not have cooked gumbo, or okra, for it did not then exist in the New World. It was Negro slaves who first brought it to America; what the Indians may have done, once okra had arrived, was to increase its palatability, and reduce its viscousness, by adding to it the gray-green powder which would then acquire the name of gumbo-filé. It is made from dried sassafras leaves. Sassafras is a native American plant, and the Southeastern Indians, notably the Choctaw, were experts in handling it; long before gumbo arrived they were already making the sassafras-leaf powder and using it to thicken soups and stews.

The Northeastern Indians made considerable use of fish, but the Pilgrims were slow to follow their example; they did not care much for fish, except eels. There were plenty of eels about. The Algonquin broiled them fresh, or smoked and dried them for future consumption. The Iroquois spitted them on twigs and broiled them (like those of the famous Italian eel-breeding city of Comacchio), or boiled them into a thick soup (like France's *matelote d'anguille),* or, as was the practice among the Algonquin, dried, smoked, and conserved them. Eels were included in an Iroquois feast which John Bartram (father of William Bartram) enjoyed in 1743 and described in his *Observations on the Inhabitants, Climate, Soil, Rivers, Production, Animals and other Matters worthy of Notice. Made . . . in his Travels from Pensilvania to Onandago, Oswego and Lake Ontario to Canada,* published in 1751:

> This repast consisted of three great kettles of Indian corn soup, or thin hominy, with dry'd eels and other fish boiled in it, and one kettle full of young squashes and their flowers boiled in water, and a little meal mixed . . . last of all was served a great bowl full of Indian dumplings, made of new soft corn, cut or scraped off the ear, then with the addition of some boiled beans, lapped well up in Indian corn leaves, this is good hearty provision.

Fish chowder was a popular dish among Northeastern Indians, but as this dish has been created spontaneously, in one form or another, along every coast in the world, we can hardly credit the Indians with having introduced it to Europeans. There was also a fish soup from which the fish had disappeared before the dish was served, like a French *soupe de poisson,* described summarily as "fish of any kind boiled in a quantity of water. It is then removed and coarse corn siftings stirred in to make a soup of suitable consistency." The Iroquois called it *u'nega'gei.*

Among vegetables, the Northeastern Indians made particularly lavish use of squash, even more than other American Indians, and especially of pumpkin. Both squash and pumpkin were baked, usually by being placed whole in the ashes or embers of a dying fire (in the case of squash, the acorn and butternut varieties were preferred) and they were moistened afterwards with some form of animal fat, or maple syrup, or honey; and both were also made into soup. When pumpkin was made into a soup, it often underwent some enriching which converted it into something more like a stew. A seventeenth-century Oneida recipe specified that pumpkin should be "boiled with meat to the consistency of potato soup."

The most important contribution of the Northeast Indians to American cooking is perhaps that which falls in the category of sweetening. For this purpose, Indians often used honey from wild bees, although the American insects were not of the same species as the European honey bees and could not vie with them as honey manufacturers. Maple syrup was the great sweetener, and more than that: it was also the all-purpose seasoner, which for the Northeast Indians took the place of salt. It impressed Europeans enormously, since the sugar maple did not exist in the Old World. Father Nouvel, a French Jesuit priest, wrote in 1671 of "a liquor that runs from the trees toward the end of winter and is known as maple-water." The Indians tapped the trees rather wastefully, slashing the bark with their tomahawks and letting the sap ooze out.

The colonists followed the Indian example in using maple sugar as their principal sweetener; two hundred years ago Americans were consuming four times as much as they do now. One reason for the popularity of maple sugar was that it was much cheaper than white sugar, made from the cane the Spaniards had planted in the West Indies, until at least 1860. True, the production of cane sugar involved the simultaneous production of the by-product of its refining, molasses, most of which went to the United States and was largely used there; but it was also in demand for rum, the product of a flourishing New England industry. Housewives were not always able to compete with the distillers. Hence maple sugar, at first the principal sweetener for the colonists, remained still a major sweetener until nearly the end of the nineteenth century.

It is conceivable that it is because maple sugar was their common seasoner that the American Indian exercised his most potent influence on the character of American cooking.

It might be argued that the sweetness maple sugar imparted to the dishes the Pilgrims cooked under the inspiration of the Indians helped to make sweetness a dominant feature of American cooking. The inhabitants of the British Isles who supplied the first colonists to Virginia and Massachusetts hardly required encouragement in this domain. They were already given to oversweetening (and overseasoning in general), and still are. "The English have a natural taste for highly seasoned food," Elizabeth David wrote in *Spices, Salt and Aromatics in the English Kitchen,* a judgment Latins would probably amend to read "too highly seasoned." The Englishman still eats treacle tart with heavily sugared tea, and piles salt on his plate before he tastes his chop; note that these two seasoners, each at one extreme of the gamut of seasoners, the sweet and the bitter, are the two which most completely overwhelm all other tastes and drown out delicate shadings of flavor; their overuse no doubt explains why both British and American food are so vulnerable to foreign criticism.

If the American cuisine is too sweet today—and any Frenchman or Italian will tell you that it is—the American Indian is not much to blame for it. It may be an intriguing intellectual exercise to wonder whether American cooking would have developed differently if the Northeastern Indians had been less devoted to maple sugar, but the answer is, probably, that it would have been much the same. The first American colonist brought his sweet tooth with him. Maple sugar, of course, did nothing to reeducate him.

The Indian contribution to the American menu was by no means negligible; but it has been absorbed, completely and utterly absorbed, into the culinary tradition the colonists imported with them. Despite the Indians, the cooking of America remained, and remains, the cooking inherited from the British Isles.

VI

Behold the White Man Cometh

BUT FOR THE GLUTTONY of wealthy Europeans, who needed spices to choke down food which was anywhere from slightly tainted to rotten (their principal diet was meat and fish), the official discovery of the New World might have waited for several decades. Columbus brought back many things, from corn to cacao beans, on his several voyages, but never that cargo of Spice Islands peppercorns he was seeking, which might well have paid for the whole enterprise. In the fifteenth century, spices in general were worth their weight in gold; in our time only genuine saffron can make that claim and it, now, is being replaced by a synthetic substitute in accordance with the Gresham's Law of gastronomy by which bad food drives out good.

Not that the European explorers, conquerors, adventurers, looters and slavers who colonized the West Indies and the southeastern shores of the future United States enjoyed much in the way of good food themselves. Their fare while at sea was too often salt meat and wormy bread, washed down with brackish water or a little wine. It was on his fourth voyage that Columbus fared worst, when his ships ran almost entirely out of supplies. "What with the heat and the dampness," his son wrote, "even the biscuit was so full of worms that, God help me, I saw many wait until nightfall to eat the porridge made of it so as not to see the worms." The ship's rat catcher made a tidy sum by selling his game to his shipmates at the price of beef. The first voyage was less trying, but nonetheless the Spaniards found shore food, strange though some of it was, a highly welcome relief. Once ashore they found conchs and oysters to eat raw, as well as various fishes. Columbus was welcomed with a feast of broiled fish fresh from the sea, bread the natives had made from pounded cassava root and corn, baked yams, custard apples and guavas; charmed by this fare, he described the natives as "no wild savages, but very gentle and courteous." They would get over this as they came to know the whites better.

In the Arawak villages of San Salvador, the Spaniards became accustomed to the cassava bread (after all they had little choice). Were they offered zamia bread also, by the Taino tribes of the Caribbean islands, with whom Columbus also established friendly relations? It was one of their staples. Zamia is sometimes called arrowroot, but it is not true arrowroot, nor is its "bread" derived from a rhizome, or root, but from the crushed stems of the plant, which it is advisable to wash with care. The Taino method of making zamia bread was to grate the stems and shape the resultant pulp into small spheres, which were then left in the sun for two or three days to rot, during which process they turned black and became wormy. Thus brought to the pink of perfection, the globes were flattened between the hands, like hamburgers, and cooked on a griddle. "If it is eaten before it becomes black and is not full . . . of worms, the eaters will die," the Tainos said, and they were quite right. The starch yielded by the stems contains, like comfortroot, an alkaloid called curarine, a constituent of curare arrow poison.

Zamia bread would not seem likely to have entranced the Spaniards, and they did not indulge either in an Arawak specialty, guinea pigs, which the Indians raised expressly for the table. However they did feast on *perros mudos,* the specially fattened barkless dogs the Arawaks roasted for great occasions. They came to like this dish, sometimes accompanied by roasted sweet potatoes, and on Columbus's second voyage they tasted pineapples, which they liked also. But they were appalled by the eating habits of the Caribs. Invading a village from which the inhabitants had fled, they found the prepared elements of a cannibal feast, choice cuts of human flesh, and tethered nearby two live young boys, *castrati,* who were being fattened for future use, and, as Samuel Eliot Morison reports, "twelve young girls, very beautiful and fat"; they were sent to Spain, where we lose track of them. As for the Caribs (whose name is etymologically linked to "cannibal" via the Spanish *caribal),* they survive today as a vestigial tribe on a reservation on the island of Dominica, and once in a while put on tribal costumes for photographing or filming. Their eating habits are conventional.

The Spaniards first encountered the foods of America in the West Indies, but they were to find many, perhaps most, of them in Florida a few years later, not only those we consider relatively humdrum today, like Indian corn in all its varieties and uses, beans from string to kidney, and squashes, all grown today in many parts of the United States, but also the exotic fruits peculiar to Florida—though some present there today may have been lacking then. There was a flow of foods from South and Central America via the West Indies toward Florida and the southern coast of the future United States, so some of Florida's present gastronomic treasures may have reached the state later than the first Europeans, transplanted either by the Spaniards themselves, or by subsequent white settlers, or by the Indians. The pineapple, for example, grows in Florida today, but it is not quite certain that it did then. The avocado was first described in 1519 in his *Suma de Geografia* by Martin Fernandez de Enciso, who saw it growing near Santa Marta, Colombia, but if it already existed in Florida at that date, the secret was well kept for almost four centuries. There are coconuts in Florida today, but there were none then, and even those we have now are the result of an accident: the schooner *Providence,* carrying coconuts from the West Indies, was wrecked off the coast of Florida in 1879; the nuts floated ashore and took root. Though the *Providence's* coconuts came from the West Indies, it is almost certain that Columbus never saw any there. The Spaniards reported fully on new foods encountered in the Caribbean area and in Mexico, but none of them ever mentioned the coconut. There *were* coconuts in America before Columbus, for they are pictured in pre-Columbian pottery, but they were on the wrong side of America to be found by Columbus, on the coasts of Chile and Peru, suggesting that the coconut, a great floater, had drifted across from the Pacific Islands.

One new food that impressed Columbus and his men probably did not then exist on what would later become the territory of the United States, though it does now, in Louisiana, Texas and California—the chili. The newcomers were quick to notice it, and no wonder, for the variety they encountered in the Caribbean was one of the most fiery of all, *agí,* and it was used as a universal seasoner. Pierre Martyr reported on it in 1493, only a few months after Columbus's arrival, and in the following year Columbus's doctor, Changa, called it *agí* and wrote that the natives used it to season meat and fish. Cassava also apparently did not grow in Florida and perhaps nobody thought it particularly necessary to introduce there a root which, if it did not receive the expert preparation the Caribbean and South Americans knew how to give it, could poison the eater. Bitter cassava especially contains so much poison (in the form of prussic acid) that Arawak Indians committed suicide by eating it, to escape Spanish torture. Some of the Caribbean yams which were served to the Spaniards also required skillful treatment to free them of toxins; it is not certain that they grew in Florida then, but they do now. Another new find which impressed the Spaniards in the Caribbean was the guava, also cultivated in Florida today, though probably not then.

Three of the most important vegetables discovered by Columbus in the Caribbean, however, were already thoroughly established on the North American continent. Columbus himself was probably one of the very first Europeans to see an American bean. He made the acquaintance of this food near what is now Nuevitas in Cuba, and no doubt he brought some back to Spain with him, since it was his habit to do so with all the new foods he found in America. If he did, the bean on its first appearance in Europe made little impression, if we may deduce this from the fact that the name eventually given it in Europe, "haricot," comes from the Aztec *ayacotl,* which suggests that it did not receive recognition until it arrived from Mexico, where the conquistadores who entered that country in 1519 discovered it.

Columbus also found sweet potatoes everywhere in the Caribbean, and likened them, curiously, to big radishes; he must have been thinking of their shape rather than of their taste. On the island of Santo Tomé the chief offered him a meal at which three or four different varieties of sweet potatoes were served. The sweet potato offered an alternative to cassava for making bread; Columbus called it *aje* bread, the native name for the sweet potato being *aje* or *axi.*

It was also in the Caribbean, of course, that Columbus discovered maize, alias Indian corn, alias sweet corn. The Spaniards ate it when they had no choice, but do not seem to have cared much for it. Columbus took corn aboard on the return trip from his first voyage to feed his sailors, who complained about it. The Spaniards do not seem to have been particularly broad-minded about what they ate (few peoples are), and in spite of their more or less forced acceptance of cassava bread and roast puppy thought the native aliments unwholesome and yearned for their accustomed victuals. Like the United States Army living on its Stateside food wherever it goes, the Spaniards ate as often as they could from the cargoes of supplies shipped to them from Spain, but the timing of ocean crossings was unpredictable in those days, and they were often obliged to depend on what was at hand, until they imported their accustomed foods to America for cultivation or raising.

In addition to vegetables, the Spaniards recorded the presence in the New World of various animal foods, some strange, some relatively familiar. The sea turtle was not new—it had been eaten by the ancient Romans—but Columbus's sailors were amazed by its profusion in the Caribbean. In 1503, during Columbus's fourth voyage, the discovery of two hitherto unknown islands was recorded in the journal kept by his son, Ferdinand, as follows:

> Upon Wednesday, the tenth of the same month of May, we were in sight of two very small and low islands, full of tortoises [sic], as was all the sea about, insomuch that they look'd like little rocks, for which reason those islands were called Tortugas [which, of course, means "turtles"].

The islands in question were not those which, for the same reason, bear that name today—the Dry Tortugas, which continue the arc traced by the Keys of Florida. They were Little Cayman and Cayman Brac, most appropriately, since it is precisely in the Cayman Islands that an effort is being made to replenish the turtle population of the Caribbean, where this reptile had almost become extinct.

The first European ever to lay eyes on an American bison was apparently Cortés, who saw one in Montezuma's zoo in 1521; the animal would not be reported again for twenty years, when the Spaniards encountered buffalos in great numbers in Texas and described them as "hunch-backed cows," later watered down to "wild cows," while the French, for once relatively unimaginative, put them down simply as "oxen" when they found them in Canada.

Nobody knows who sent the first turkey from America to Spain, where it quickly became a gastronomic success, but the first bird to have come from territory now included in the United States may very well have been dispatched by Miguel de Passomonte in 1511. Other accounts give the credit to Francisco de Córdoba, who saw turkeys in Yucatán in 1517, or Cortés, who met them in Mexico in 1519. Whoever discovered it, the turkey was quickly nicknamed for the members of that religious order who, more than the adventurers, interested themselves in New World eating, "cock of the Jesuits." The Indians' own name for the bird was *peru,* which, if it referred to the country now known by that name, was geographically erroneous, since the turkey's range did not extend as far as the South American continent; but it was not as wide of the mark as the names given the bird in various European countries. At a time when it was still believed that Columbus had reached India, the French, logically, called it the bird of India, *d'inde,* which has since lost its apostrophe to become today's *dinde.* The Germans and the Dutch, with admirable precision but deplorable inaccuracy, designated the bird as the Calcutta hen—*calecutische Hahn* and *kalkoen* respectively. The Germans have since retreated to *Truthahn,* but the Dutch remain committed to Calcutta. The English, in this period of geographical haziness, when any Oriental name could stand for any other, opted, as we know, for turkey.

Of the many European foods which, thanks to the Spaniards, found their way first to the West Indies and then to the mainland, one of the most important was the chicken. The first domesticated cattle seen in the New World were landed on San Domingo by Columbus in 1493, scrawny animals whose top weight, full grown, was a scant 100 pounds; the first to set hoof on territory which is now the United States were brought ashore in Florida no later than 1550. Texas would get cattle a little later, escaped from the herds of the conquistadores (along with horses), to become the ancestors of the Texas Longhorns, "all belly and no meat." Florida seems to have enjoyed priority over the Caribbean islands for the domestic pig (probably because the Mexican *javelina* or peccary was already obtainable in the islands), for the first hogs of North America were almost certainly the thirteen pigs introduced by Hernando de Soto in 1542 to supply a base near what is now Tampa.

Probably the single most important unique Spanish contribution to the foods of the United States (for imports like those of chickens, cattle and hogs would be duplicated later on English-speaking territory) was the orange.

The first oranges may have been planted in Florida by Ponce de Léon, which could have been as early as 1513, for the Spanish explorers were instructed always to carry citrus seeds with them and plant them wherever they went, so that citruses would be available as a cure for scurvy wherever the galleons might make a landfall after a long voyage; but the first date of which we are sure is 1539, when Hernando de Soto is known to have planted oranges in Florida. They were growing at St. Augustine in 1586 and vigorously too, for when Sir Francis Drake sacked the city in that year and had the trees cut down, the stumps put out new shoots which were soon producing oranges again. It is supposed that these were bitter oranges, otherwise known as bigarades, a theory which is borne out by the fact that most of the wild orange trees growing in the Florida wilderness are bitter oranges; for the most part they arose from seeds carried into the interior by Indians in the sixteenth century. The sweet orange would arrive later.

The adventurers who followed Columbus in the early years of the sixteenth century were interested in gold, not gastronomy; their eyes were fixed on the treasures which could be looted from the ancient Indian civilizations which crumbled at the approach of marauders on horseback and foot soldiers with firearms. They piled up a record of greed, brutality and daring; one would not expect such men to be particularly interested in agriculture. Most of the so-called colonists of the Spanish New World had no intention of settling down quietly and raising their own food.

The time inevitably came, nevertheless, when the conquistadores began to run out of civilizations to loot, and created extensive plantations for the cultivation of sugar cane, transplanted from Spain—the great money crop. A few of them had not waited to be forced out of freebooting into husbandry, but, being better businessmen or poorer soldiers, elected at once to settle for the relatively modest but surer profits of agriculture rather than for the more splendid but less dependable prospect of gold. There were even some among the 1,200 settlers landed from seventeen caravels by Columbus on his second voyage who concentrated on the acquiring of land as early as 1493. By 1512, sugar production was already flourishing on free land worked by free (meaning slave) labor. The Spanish government graciously rewarded its pioneers by granting them not only large tracts of land but also the populations which lived on them and had up to then been under the impression that the land was theirs. The owners supplied their slaves with imported food rather than locally grown produce; it seemed more reasonable to devote both land and labor to turning out molasses and sugar, eminently salable, than to use them for ordinary food production. The Spaniards quickly ran out of Indians, working to death those they had not massacred, and turned for fresh laborers to Africa. The American slave trade had begun.

The founders of plantations were in the minority. Most of the Spanish adventurers were like Cortés, who, when he was offered land by the viceroy, told him contemptuously, "I have come to gain gold, not to cultivate the fields like a peasant!" Cortés was to find it, but the Spaniards who moved into the two Floridas were less lucky, though they had gone there in the first place with appetites whetted by sailors who had landed on the Alabama coast in 1503 and reported that "the people wear hats of solid gold and life is gay and luxurious." When solid gold proved illusory in Florida, they showed less interest in colonizing the southeastern corner of what was to become the United States than they displayed in Mexico and Peru, where they had found what they were looking for. Perhaps they might have gone away and left Florida to its own devices if other explorers had not arrived on the scene ready to take over if the Spaniards permitted it, which was of course intolerable. Whether they wanted Florida or not, the Spaniards did not want anybody else to want it.

St. Augustine, founded in 1565, the oldest city in the United States, might never have been built at all if French Huguenots had not twice tried to colonize the Atlantic coast of Florida and claim it for France as "the fairest, fruitfulest and pleasantest [land] of all the world." They were driven out both times, but it appeared advisable to the Spaniards to fortify the region to keep them from coming back—hence St. Augustine. Later two more fortified posts were added on the coast of the Gulf of Mexico, also to keep the French, or anybody else, from encroaching on that sector—St. Marks and Pensacola.

Pensacola is an apt symbol of the vicissitudes of colonial life in the Southeast: it changed flags thirteen times between its founding in 1698 and its annexation by the United States. Mobile is another. The Spaniards made the first stab at settling on Mobile Bay, but didn't manage it. The French founded the city and named it for its Indians—Fort Louis de la Tribu Mauvilla; for eighteen years it was the capital of French Louisiana. The British removed it from the French, and the Spaniards removed it from the British. There was Dutch influence about, too.

It is the early history of this region which accounts for the cosmopolitan character of its food, which no other part of the country can equal, with the exception of New York City in this century after it had developed what is undoubtedly the world's most variegated display of food and the world's most disparate eating habits. The Europeans who at the tail end of the fifteenth century set out to conquer and plunder Peru and Mexico, and set up the islands of the Caribbean for their various way stations and outposts, were already surrounded by a varied food pattern of Indian origin. Some of the Indian comestibles were adopted *faute de mieux,* but remain to our day as part of the Creole cuisine. The slaves added new foods and new styles of cooking from Africa. The French dosage was measured out in installments, as political events dictated. It is no tribute to the Spaniards to point out that to this richness they were apparently able to contribute only two durable dishes—*jambalaya* and a sausage.

The Spaniards did not do much better in the Southwest, to which they were drawn by the same powerful magnet—gold. They never found any, but they were constantly hearing rumors of places rich in it, a little farther away (one may suspect that Indians who found them irksome guests told them tall stories to encourage them to go elsewhere); so they struggled on and on, most of the time into deserts, and their chroniclers record times of privation when they must often have been willing to trade the prospect of gold for the reality of food. One of the few Spanish reports of this period which carries any implication of plenty is the first description of the American buffalo, given, appropriately, by Alvar Nuñez Cabeza de Vaca (appropriately, because Cabeza de Vaca means "cow's head"):

> They also have cows, I saw them three times and I have eaten them. They seemed to me to be as large as those of Spain. Their horns are smaller than those of the Moors' cows, their hair is very long, like the wool of our sheep at the time when they change pasturage, it is of different colors, there are mottled ones and black ones. Their meat seemed to me better than that of ours and the animals fleshier. With the hides of the young ones, the Indians make mantles to cover themselves, they use those of the old ones to make shoes and shields. These animals come down from the North into the interior as far as the coast and spread out over more than four hundred leagues. During all this way, they follow the prairies, approaching the inhabitants to whom they supply meat to live on and a great quantity of hides.

Cabeza de Vaca also reported that the Indians got drunk on mescal made from the yucca, the first time that intoxication had been signaled among the Indians; all previous explorers had agreed that Indians did not drink alcohol.

The lure that drew the conquistadores into a thankless interior was the legend of the Seven Cities of Cibola, whose streets were paved with gold, while the doors of the houses were studded with emeralds. The mirage of Cibola drew the Spaniards on, none of them to gold and many of them to death. The most celebrated expedition was that of Francisco Vasquez de Coronado, whose men suffered incredible hardships and were reduced at times to living, like the miserable Digger Indians, on roots grubbed up from the ground, on insects, on lizards, and on snakes. At one time they attempted to imitate the Indians by eating the fruits of the cactus. "The men of the army ate a great deal of [cacti]," their chronicler related. "They all fell ill, with headaches or fever." Probably, lacking the Indians' knowledge of these plants, they ate the wrong kind of cacti.

When at last Coronado came in sight of what he thought might be one of the rich cities of Cibola, he decided to take it whether it was Cibola or not; he was in dire need of food. He attacked the following morning and occupied the settlement. It proved not to be a rich city with pavements of gold, only a Zuñi pueblo; but it gave him something which, for the moment, was more precious than any metal.

> We found there things we prized more than gold and silver [his chronicler related], namely maize, beans, and chickens larger than those of New Spain [they were turkeys], and salt better and whiter than I had ever seen during my whole life.

In the Southwest, as in the Southeast, it seems amazing that the newcomers, though they remained on the ground in person or in proxy for three hundred years, left almost no gastronomic traces behind them. What little Spanish flavor exists in the Southwest now does not, in all probability, go as far back as the Spaniards and not even as far back as the Mexicans who succeeded them.

For the failure of the Spaniards to leave a gastronomic mark on territories they held for so long there are a number of possible explanations. The most important, perhaps, is that they never really colonized the United States; they preferred to concentrate their attention on the territories where they had found what they were looking for, gold, which therefore constitute Latin America today. To the north they governed and converted but did not settle. Ruled, more or less loosely, by the Spanish viceroy in Mexico City, the Spaniards in the Southwest fell almost entirely into two narrowly restricted categories, the inhabitants of the missions and of the *presidios,* which offered strangely contrasting modes of existence. The colonial officials and their families lived in some style in houses furnished with European objects and ornaments; the Franciscans (who replaced the Jesuits and were replaced in their turn by the Dominicans) observed monastic simplicity and devoted themselves to the work of saving Indian souls. For both, the native peons did what work there was to do, indoors and out; there was virtually no European population. If the governing officials had any culinary competence, they could not have shared it with the natives, with whom they had no relations except those of oppressors. The missionaries were too ascetic to pass anything on, though they did initiate wine growing in California, chiefly to assure a supply of sacramental wine for the celebration of the mass. Only in the present century has the California wine industry become important.

In addition to the circumstance that Spain did not really colonize the Southwest (nor the Southeast either), there are two other possible explanations of their failure to leave any gastronomic legacy to the United States: first, the sort of men who came from Spain in pursuit of riches were not the sort of men who cared what they ate; secondly, even if they had cared, Spain had, in the gastronomic domain, very little to give.

In the history of American eating, the Spanish chapter remains almost blank. The Spaniards left a vacuum for the English-speaking colonists to fill.

VII

A Land of Plenty

IN 1607 colonists devoted to the English Establishment founded Jamestown, Virginia, and in 1620 colonists hostile to the English Establishment founded Plymouth, Massachusetts. Whether loyalists or dissenters in matters of politics and religion, both were conformists in matters of the table. They brought with them the gastronomic tastes, the culinary habits and the eating prejudices of the British Isles, and it had apparently not occurred to them that they might have to change them in an unknown country with a different climate and strange foods. In the end, they did succeed in holding to the familiar line; but not without difficulty.

They had come into a land of plenty. Everything was larger than in Europe: the salmon (Erik the Red had noticed it); the strawberries ("the wonder of all the Fruits growing naturally in these parts," wrote Sir Walter Raleigh. "The Indians bruise them in a Morter, and mixe them with meale and make strawberry bread"—the ancestor of strawberry shortcake); the lobster (their size impressed the Dutch of New Amsterdam, who claimed to have taken six-footers, but Adriaen van der Donck, the colony's first lawyer, was of the opinion that "those a foot long are better for serving at table"). When there was a storm at Plymouth, lobsters piled up in windrows two feet high on the beach; they were so plentiful and so easily gathered that they were considered fit only for the poor, who could afford nothing better; in 1622, when a group of new colonists arrived in Plymouth, Governor William Bradford was deeply humiliated because his colony was so short of food that the only "dish they could presente their friends with was a lobster . . . without bread or anything els but a cupp of fair water." The receding waves of storms also left behind them tidal pools brimming with crabs, offered for the taking. The Virginians could scoop up terrapin by the shovelful. Captain John Smith wrote that at Jamestown he found an "abundance of fish, lying so thicke with their heads above the water, as for want of nets . . . we attempted to catch them with a frying-pan . . . neither better fish, more plentie, nor more varitie for small fish, had any of us seene in any place so swimming in the water." He amused himself in the shallows by spearing skates with his sword: "We tooke more in owne hour than we could eate in a day."

The Hudson, whose waters were, in the words of its discoverer, "clear, blue and wonderful to taste," were full of shad, so plentiful as to be disdained; the Dutch ate them and enjoyed them, but pretended they didn't, lest they be thought common folk. All the same they made something of a cult of taking the first shad when they began to run in the spring; whatever date the shad had selected, the Dutch had decided that the proper time to begin fishing for them was March 11: hence shad was known as *elft,* the eleven fish.

The sturgeon was nobler; one could confess to eating sturgeon, though there were plenty of them in the Hudson, too, who swam far up the river; some of them weighed 200 pounds—they were referred to as "Albany beef." In Virginia William Byrd did not record their weight, but wrote that in summer they rose to the surface of the water in great schools, their backs protruding into the air "to warm themselves in the sun"—his interpretation of their motive, as we have no testimony from the sturgeon. "We had more Sturgeon, than could be devoured by Dog and Man," wrote John Smith.

More than thirty coastal rivers from the Connecticut to Canada were mounted each year by swarms of salmon returning from the sea to spawn; eels, sea trout and herring came, too, and of course there were brook trout everywhere, in such numbers that they seemed to be begging to be caught. Cod were the most common saltwater fish; it was for this reason that English navigator Bartholomew Gosnold gave its name to Cape Cod, eighteen years before the Pilgrims got there, in 1602. Francis Higginson wrote in 1630, in his *New-Englands Plantation,* "The aboundance of Sea-Fish are almost beyond beleeving, and sure I would scarce have beleeved it except I had scene it with mine owne Eyes"; he named as the principal fish of Massachusetts Bay, in addition to the cod, mackerel, sea bass, lobster, "Heering, Turbot [here he was mistaken: the turbot is not an American fish; he must have confused it with the flounder], Sturgion, Cuskes [related to cod], Haddocks, Mullets, Eeles, Crabs, Muskles and Oysters."

Much of this bounty was wasted, on the Pilgrims at least, narrow-minded in eating as in worshipping. A recent writer on the subject has asserted that the first New Englanders liked mussels and clams. That they ever liked mussels seems extremely unlikely; even today New Englanders as a rule do not eat them, and many pre-Columbian Indian tribes of the Northeast would not eat them either, though there were occasional exceptions to this rule. Clams became accepted in time, but it is on record that in the 1620s the Pilgrims fed clams and mussels to their hogs with the explanation that they were "the meanest of God's blessings." The oyster was more appreciated. The longest interstate conflict in American history is probably the "oyster war" between Virginia and Maryland, which started in 1632 and is not over yet (several fishermen were killed in one of its skirmishes as recently as 1959). This was a by-product of the favoritism of Charles I, who cut a slice off northern Virginia to make a domain for his friend, Lord Baltimore, and placed its Potomac boundary line, not along the thalweg, as is the usual practice almost everywhere in the world, but at the highwater mark on the Virginia side, thus making a present to Maryland, at Virginia's expense, of all the crabs and oysters of the region.

Besides fish, there was a plenitude of game. The same William Wood who had been so enthusiastic about fish gave his attention to this subject also in his *New England's Prospect,* published in 1634 (the authors do not guarantee the accuracy of his bestiary):

> The kingly Lyon, and the strong arm'd Beare,
> The large lim'd Mooses, with the tripping Deare,
> Quill-darting Porcupines and Rackcoones be,
> Castell'd in the hollow of an aged tree;
> The skipping Squerell, Rabbet, purblinde Hare,
> Immured in the selfe same Castle are,
> Lest red eyed Ferrets, wily Foxes should
> Them undermine, if rampird but with mould.
> The grim fac't Ounce, and ravenous howling Woolfe,
> Whose meagre paunch suckes like a swallowing gulfe.
> Blacke glistering Otters, and rich coated Bever,
> The Civet scented Musquash smelling ever.

Not all of these animals were eaten (except perhaps by the Indians) but most of them were, and William Wood did not even mention the birds—the passenger pigeon which was so incredibly numerous; the partridge, a ground feeder which an alert hunter can bowl over with a club; and first of all the turkey, which the Pilgrims are known to have eaten in 1621, at the first Thanksgiving dinner, and can hardly fail to have encountered earlier during their first full year in America, for whose successful termination (by successful they meant that many of them, to their own considerable surprise, were still alive) the feast was celebrated. It is perhaps not absolutely necessary to believe the legend that at the end of the meal one of the braves slipped silently into the woods and returned bearing, surprise, surprise, the first popcorn the Pilgrims had ever seen.

The first colonists thus found themselves in their new home surrounded by fish and game, and benefiting by the cultivated crops the Indians had taught them to grow—sweet corn, beans, squash, pumpkins, a few others. The forests were full of edible mushrooms, cherries and nuts; the fields were carpeted with strawberries, bushes offered lavishly their riches of blueberries, huckleberries, blackberries, raspberries, elderberries and currants; the shores were fringed with cranberry bogs and groves of the wild beach plum, and in Virginia sweet red and white grapevines spiraled up the trees. Virginia, according to one of its earliest settlers, writing in 1607, was "nature's nurse to all vegetables," to which a century later another added a description of that territory as having "so happy a Climate and so fertile a soil, that no Body's poor enough to beg, or Want Food, though they have an abundance of People that are lazy enough to deserve it."

It was a land of good cheer, or at least Captain John Smith found it so. He told of the "great heapes of corn" the Indians had stored away and of the "venison, turkies, wild fowle, bread and what else they had" which they furnished him. "The rivers become so covered with swans, geese, ducks and cranes," he noted during his first winter in Virginia, "that we daily feasted with good bread, Virginia pease [probably haricot beans], pumpions [pumpkins] and putchamins [persimmons], fish, fowle and diverse sorts of wild beasts, so fat as we could eate them." We may safely assume that John Smith had been accustomed to hearty Yuletide fare in Merrie England, but he was nevertheless deeply impressed when he was entertained by the Powhatan Indians at his first Christmas dinner in America. "We were never more merry nor fed on more plenty of good oysters, fish, flesh, wild fowle and good bread," he wrote, "nor ever had better fires in England."

The first settlers had come upon a land of plenty. They nearly starved in it.

The Pilgrims of Massachusetts and the Cavaliers of Virginia both actually would have starved during their very first winters in this well-stocked land and disappeared into oblivion like Sir Walter Raleigh's Lost Colony on Roanoke Island if it had not been for the Indians, who in Virginia knew they were supplying the white man with food but in Massachusetts did not. It was an Indian habit to stow away caches of long-lasting foods in various places where they might one day be needed; it was the Pilgrims' good luck to stumble on one of these caches, which kept them alive (some of them) over their first terrible winter. In the South, the Indians furnished the newcomers directly with enough food to assure survival (for some of them). Later the Indians would become less inclined to promote the survival of Europeans.

Assuring survival was not easy, whether in the North or the South. The epic of Virginia began in 1607 when three small ships, the *Susan Constant,* the *Godspeed* and the *Discovery,* commanded by the prophetically named Captain Christopher Newport, sailed into Chesapeake Bay four months out of London carrying 104 colonists who, after giving considerable thought to the matter, settled on the least favorable site in the area, half marsh, half peninsula (now, by edict of the James River, an island), and named their new home Jamestown in dubious compliment to James I of England, who had given them a charter but no cash. Jamestown was not fated to survive to see the birth of the Republic in 1776 (it succumbed to anemia about 1707) and its first colonists might have been justified in assuming that it was not going to survive at all. The *Discovery* returned to England after having put ashore enough food to last for four and a half months, and failed to return for more than six, by which time fifty-one of the original settlers had died from starvation or diseases abetted by malnutrition; yet this ship and another which followed it delivered 120 additional candidates for suicide. Jamestown burned down accidentally in 1608, but this hint from heaven was disregarded.

In 1609 the Indians, who had changed their minds about the sort of welcome appropriate for the white man, attacked the Virginians while they were planting the grain that was to have assured their food for the future, so the crop was lost before it was sown. The Indians also killed some of the cattle imported by the colonists, who themselves ate the rest, not being able to wait for the next generation to replenish the stock. When the flagship of a fleet bringing supplies was wrecked on the still-vexed Bermoothes, an event which came to the attention of William Shakespeare in time to get into *The Tempest,* it was the last straw; the colonists decided to give it up as a bad job. The entire population embarked on those ships which happened to be in the harbor, anchors were weighed, sails were hoisted—and lo and behold the battleship *Missouri* steamed anachronistically to the rescue in the guise of a rowboat bearing no less a personage than Lord de la Warr (hence Delaware), who had been appointed Governor of London's Plantation in the Southern Part of Virginia; his fleet, with three hundred more settlers and plenty of supplies, was becalmed down the bay. De la Warr, authoritatively, ordered the discouraged colonists ashore, and the colony was saved.

In Plymouth, where an even one hundred colonists would have landed if it had not occurred to two infants to be born during the nine weeks it took the *Mayflower* to struggle across the Atlantic, about half died in the three freezing months which followed their landing on December 11, from cold, privation, scurvy, starvation and, as in Virginia, diseases powerfully seconded by insufficient food. However the Pilgrims never entertained the idea of giving up and going home, which, indeed, no longer seemed entirely home to them, since they had been motivated in the first place by a desire to get away from England and its disinclination to respect their religious views.

The initial hardships of the colonists were to a considerable extent the result of their own shortcomings. A minor one was a characteristic unwillingness to accept any change in their eating habits; one suspects that the Pilgrims, dire as was their need, did not give as much attention as they should have to collecting foods which they did not like (fish, shellfish and lobsters, among others). The Virginians also could not or would not adapt themselves to the foods available locally, despite John Smith's enthusiasm for them, and elected instead to depend on supplies from England. They might have reflected that the *Discovery* had taken eighteen weeks to ferry them across the Atlantic to Virginia, a rather clear warning that it was not advisable to stake their lives on the speed of sailing ships; but they do not seem to have been very good at drawing conclusions from evidence.

A more important factor in exaggerating the hardships of life in a virgin America, which scarcely required exaggeration, was that the first English-speaking colonists of America were not quite the right persons to wring a living from a wilderness, even a well-stocked wilderness. What the situation called for was lumberjacks or peasants or laborers, men and women accustomed to working with their hands and with their backs. What it got, both in the North and the South, was refugees from the middle class. In England, the Puritans were largely merchants and industrialists; the *Mayflower*'s passengers included tradesmen, not immediately needed; artisans, many of whom would be valuable once the main problems of feeding and shelter had been solved; and "farmers," which usually meant small land-owners who had managed their properties while hired hands did the actual work. The indentured servants, who came to New England in a flow which started in earnest about 1630, were probably the most useful immigrants. This was true also in the South.

The Pilgrims landed on the shores of a sea teeming with fish, but they were indifferent fishermen. They were surrounded by forests full of game, but they were indifferent hunters. The land on which they settled was reasonably fertile, but they were indifferent farmers.

French and Portuguese fishermen had been operating on the Grand Banks since early in the sixteenth century, returning immediately to Europe with their catches, but the newcomers did not know how to take the cod, mackerel and flounder of the Banks and of their own coastal waters; indeed, they were not even very skillful inland, though a friendly Indian, Squanto, showed them how to scoop eels out of the streams in their hands. Perhaps it was because they did not like fish that the Pilgrims had brought with them no nets and little tackle; and what they did have was the wrong kind.

The Pilgrims had no experience in hunting either, for this was an activity which in England was restricted to the aristocracy and they were not aristocrats. Neither, for that matter, were the Virginians. Some members of the great English families had arrived in Virginia early, but quickly changed their minds and went home again. The word "Cavaliers" has deceived us about the Virginians. It did not mean that those so called were aristocrats; it meant only they they were royalists, of whatever class. With rare exceptions, the First Families of Virginia are not descended from the English aristocracy, but from men who first rose to distinction in the colonies. Like the Pilgrims, they came from the middle class.

As for tilling the land, the Pilgrims had been more accustomed to bending over the Bible than over the plowshare, while the Virginians, Samuel Eliot

Morison wrote caustically in *The Oxford History of the American People,* "seem to have been divided into those who could not and those who would not work." The quality of Southern colonists became even worse when, a third of the way into the next century, Georgia was founded, with charitable intent larded with self-interest, as a Utopia for the impoverished and a panacea for England's economic ills: "England will grow rich by sending her Poor Abroad." It did not take long for the Trustees charged with the settling of Georgia to reach the conclusion that persons "who had been useless in England, were inclined to be useless in Georgia likewise."

The Pilgrims had an excuse for their failure as farmers the first year, for they arrived in December, which, in the climate of New England (where, it is true, they landed by mistake, for they had been aiming farther south), was too late to store up food for the winter or even to prepare the soil for planting in the spring. The Jamestown colonists landed on May 14, and might have set to work at once to assure their own provisioning; unfortunately most of them, like the Spaniards, were more interested in hunting for gold than in breaking ground for crops.

The Pilgrims, paradoxically, were encouraged in the task of building up their own means of providing food by a situation which might very easily have discouraged them instead: they faced greater difficulties than the Virginians from a climate more rigorous than they had known in England. Virginians tried to counter the difference of climate by acting as if it did not exist. This was harder to do in New England, where winter spoke with a more resolute voice. The Pilgrims were obliged to find immediate solutions for the problems posed by the extremes of American weather. For instance, the cattle brought ashore in Virginia were turned out in the fields and woods to fend for themselves, in imitation of the practice in England, where it was possible to leave livestock on outdoor pasturage all year round. American weather, even in Virginia, did not lend itself to this method, but the Virginia climate was nevertheless sufficiently mild so that the colonists there could be excused for not immediately recognizing this fact. In New England there could be no such misunderstanding. The rigors of winter forced the Pilgrims to take immediate measures for providing shelter and winter forage for domestic animals, so when the first cattle arrived in 1624, three cows and a bull, they were cared for adequately. As a result, cattle of good quality had become plentiful in New England by 1640. The imported cows gave the Pilgrims their first taste of milk, for they had been less foresighted than the Virginians, who had brought goats along with them.

Psychologically, the Pilgrims were better prepared than the Virginians to meet the challenges of the new country. They are usually depicted as having quit England because of religious dissent, which is quite true; but it was not religious dissent alone, it was dissent all along the line. They wanted to have as little as possible to do with a government from which they were thoroughly alienated. They would have had to be reduced to dire straits indeed to swallow their pride sufficiently to beg for supplies or aid of any other kind from a monarchy whose every aspect they despised.

The Virginians, who accepted the church recognized by the state and were loyal to the monarchy which governed it, had no such inhibitions. They were entirely willing to accept support from the motherland, especially if that would reduce the necessity for applying themselves to manual labor, a sort of exercise properly reserved for the lower classes, to which they of course did not belong. But Pilgrims had no prejudice against manual labor. Indeed, they approved of it; it was good for the soul.

So the Pilgrims set to work, and within a single generation, New England became a farming community able to take care of itself. Its colonists adapted themselves when they had to, though grudgingly, to the fare of the Indians; at the same time they set to work to end this disagreeable necessity by importing and developing their cherished familiar foods—apples, for instance. Apple-tree slips were brought from England, and the Pilgrims had apples about ten years after their arrival; the trees flourished and bore plentifully in the New England climate. Many imported plants grew better on the virgin American soil than they had in Europe, peas, for example—after the first year, when the Pilgrims, unaccustomed to the heat of American summers, planted them too late, so they were practically burned up on the vines. Another Pilgrim import was the Italian honey bee, for "tree sweetenin' and bee sweetenin'."

The Pilgrims learned to hunt from the Indians and also how to fish, after a few disheartening experiences: in 1625 an attempt was made to establish a fishing industry at Gloucester, which had been founded two years earlier, but it failed and was temporarily abandoned. In 1628 the indomitable Puritans returned to the attack, this time with such success that in 1640 Massachusetts delivered 300,000 dried codfish to the market; before the end of the seventeenth century fishing was the main industry of Massachusetts Bay and New England was exporting dried fish to Old England.

Virginia was slower to achieve alimentary independence, and indeed did not try to do so; it achieved alimentary sufficiency all the same by continuing to depend on England for supplies, a tactic which had at first promised to be disastrous. But a new element had entered the picture—tobacco. Virginia, it used to be said, was built on smoke; it gave itself up to the almost exclusive cultivation of tobacco, which, despite occasional ups and downs, proved so profitable a crop that no planter wanted to tie up any of his land producing food; tobacco was able to finance its importation from England. The tobacco plantations were located, each in magnificent isolation, on the banks of rivers which the modestly sized ocean-going ships of those times could mount, to pick up the hogsheads of tobacco from the planter's private wharf; at the same time they unloaded the goods he had ordered from England: food, furniture, tableware, books, art objects, cloth for his ladies' dresses. Within a reasonable time, Virginians were eating high on the hog, a figure of speech very American and very appropriate also, since—exception made possibly for poultry—pork was America's first important meat from domestic animals, and would remain the country's most common meat for three centuries. Pigs and chickens were, of course, the easiest meat to carry to the New World by ship, and provided moreover the advantage that if unfavorable winds prolonged a voyage, they could be killed on the way to provide fresh meat for sailors and passengers.

The English colonies had to import these animals directly from Europe, though the Spaniards had brought them to Florida a century earlier. There was no dissemination of Spanish-imported foods, whether plants or animals, into English-speaking territory. The two communities co-existed but did not cooperate. This history of the European-imported gastronomy of the United States started only with the British colonists; what little the Spaniards had to contribute (and even the larger contribution of the French) would be tacked on later, after American eating habits had been irrevocably formed.

VIII

New World—New Foods

THE COLONISTS from Great Britain who marooned themselves early in the seventeenth century in an unknown world at the end of a slow and uncertain line of communications maintained by a minimum of sluggish ships were dismayed to discover that among the things from which they had cut themselves off were their familiar foods, the only ones they felt safe in eating. They do not seem to have given much thought before setting out to the circumstance that in the New World they would not find butchers, grocers and bakers ready to supply their needs, much less taverns to set ready meals before them. The Pilgrims, complained Governor William Bradford, a poor speller, "had no freinds to wellcome them nor inns to intertaine or refresh their weatherbeaten bodys."

Fish, at least, with a few exceptions, looked very much the same on the western shore of the Atlantic as on the eastern. Game animals might be different, but they did resemble, reassuringly, species already known in Europe. But the plants! They were all strange, except the wild cherry and a few berries, and thus potentially poisoners until they had been proven innocent. Some seemed less redoubtable than others because, though they were different, they recalled similar foods in Europe. But others were frighteningly foreign, including the most important food of all, and the most inescapable, since it was the only available cereal—maize, Indian corn.

The circumstances hardly permitted the newcomers to be choosy. During the grim early years of the 1600s, the problem was to survive. It was not a question of finding the foods one preferred, it was a question of getting *enough* food, no matter what its kind, on which to stay alive. Until they had had time to import known foods from Europe, which they did as soon as they could, the colonists ate desperately whatever they could lay their hands on. Indian corn was an alien grain they would almost certainly have scorned if there had been a choice, but there was none. The alternative was to eat corn or starve, and it was put urgently to the Puritans of Massachusetts and the Cavaliers of Virginia the very first winters each spent in the New World. Plymouth and Jamestown alike would have disappeared before they had taken root if their settlers had been unable to bring themselves to eat corn. They ate it. It was better than starving. Sir Walter Raleigh's men even reported courageously that it was "fair and well-tasted"; but they made acquaintance with it as it was prepared and served to them by Indians, who knew how to handle it.

Under ordinary circumstances, the colonists might have been expected to abandon corn as soon as grains they knew better became available, as they did soon, for rye, barley, oats and wheat were all planted in America in the seventeenth century. Adaptable as those grains are, they were slow to accustom themselves to a new climate and for a long time failed to give yields sufficiently important to drive out corn—particularly the grain the colonists would have preferred above all others, wheat. In New England wheat was attacked by a smut disease called "the blast"; in Virginia it did not do well either, for it was planted chiefly on land already exhausted by having grown one of the most soil-depleting of all plants, tobacco. As late as the end of the eighteenth century wheat was still so rare and so dear that it might as well not have been there at all, so far as the great mass of working people were concerned, though their chief food was bread. A laborer's average wage at this period was two shillings a day, which meant that it would take him four days at least to earn enough money to buy a bushel of wheat, whose lowest quality was priced at eight shillings and up. Sometimes he could afford rye, oat or barley bread, but as a rule he settled for corn (three shillings a bushel). Thus corn for two centuries remained almost unchallenged and had ample opportunity to ingratiate itself with the American palate. American cooks in the meantime had naturally set themselves to the task of developing dishes which brought out the maximum deliciousness of corn; by the time Americans were able to choose freely among different grains they discovered that they had been educated into liking cornbread. They took up the others, but did not abandon corn.

The second most important Indian vegetable, the American bean, was accepted without difficulty by the colonists. It looked, more or less, like the familiar European broad bean, and they did not know, and doubtless would not have cared, that it was of a different genus from its European cousin.

The third member of the Indian triad, squash, was immediately tolerable, too, for though there were no true squashes in Europe, there were other edible plants which resembled them. Even the most excessive among them, the pumpkin, was not exotic enough to frighten the colonists off.

Thus the three principal native foods were adopted by the newcomers, for reasons largely extraneous to their intrinsic merits, corn out of necessity, beans and squash because they could be compared to familiar foods. But it may seem odd today that the colonists failed to take advantage of two of the most important of New World vegetables, which are eaten universally today—the potato and the tomato. Yet two other American vegetables of lesser importance were accepted at once, finding their way quickly onto the tables of the Old World as well as of the New—the sweet potato and the Jerusalem artichoke. Then why not the white potato and the tomato, which were destined to be neglected for another century and a half after the other two had been accepted, and, indeed, were first tried out in Europe before they returned to the New World? The answer is simple: they were not there.

The sweet potato and the Jerusalem artichoke *were* there. The first settlers on the southern reach of the Atlantic shores found the Indians eating sweet potatoes and followed suit; the first settlers at its northern end encountered the Jerusalem artichoke and copied a similar example; but nowhere along the whole stretch of coast were Indians discovered using either the white potato or the tomato.

In the case of the sweet potato, it is probable that its honeyed taste helped it to achieve quick popularity in Europe and America. When it first reached Europe, imported at the beginning of the sixteenth century by the Spaniards, who named it *batata,* it was endowed, quite gratuitously, with the reputation of being aphrodisiac. For this or other reasons, it appealed to Henry VIII, who imported sweet potatoes from Spain and ate them in the form of pies, very sweet and heavily spiced; by the end of the sixteenth century many of his subjects were following suit.

There can be no doubt that for John Gerard, author of the famous sixteenth-seventeenth century *Herball,* "potato" meant the sweet potato, for in the 1633 edition of this work the chapter "Of Potato's" refers obviously to the sweet potato, and is followed immediately by "Of Potato's of Virginia," meaning the white potato. It was already so well installed by that time that Gerard apparently did not realize it was a native of America, despite his parenthetical remark that it "is called of some Skyrrets of Peru." Instead he tells us that

> The Potato's grow in India, Barbarie, Spaine, and other hot regions . . . *Clusius* calleth it *Batata, Camotes, Amotes, Ignames:* in English Potatoes, Potatus, and Potades. The Potato roots are among the Spaniards, Italians, Indians [he did not mean American Indians], and many other nations, ordinarie and common meat; which no doubt are of mighty and nourishing parts, and doe strengthen and comfort nature; whose nutriment is as if it were a mean between flesh and fruit, but somewhat windie; yet being roasted in the embers they lose much of their windinesse, especially being eaten sopped in wine.

The adoption of the sweet potato in Europe preceded the arrival of the first English colonists in Virginia, so that the strangeness of this vegetable had already been blunted for them before they arrived. The sweet potato also had the advantage, in those days when storage without spoilage was still a difficult problem, that it ripened late, and could therefore be installed in its winter quarters to be kept unscathed through the cold weather before it had time to wilt or develop mildew.

As for the Jerusalem artichoke, which is said to have first reached Europe in 1617, sent back from Canada, it too may have been aided by its sweetish taste, but probably even more by a fictitious familiarity resulting from the name given it by its discoverer, Samuel de Champlain, who came upon it in Indian gardens on Cape Cod about 1605, and called it an artichoke. It does not look in the least like an artichoke, but it does taste a little like one, and it may have been because Champlain hit upon this reassuringly familiar name that Europe took to the vegetable.

That the colonists were slow to accept it until Europe had set the example may be suspected by the name it had acquired by the time it was being generally eaten, *Jerusalem* artichoke. This was not a name which would have been likely to occur to the settlers of America (as a matter of fact, they first called it the Canadian potato, once again, probably, with the sweet potato in mind). We are no doubt on safe ground in assuming that the name, though not the vegetable, originated in Europe, both because it gained favor there more quickly and also simply because there were more people in Europe to influence language in the early seventeenth century than there were in America.

It seems probable that once again the name "Jerusalem artichoke" reflected the delusion that America was part of Asia, an error already illustrated by the name of the turkey, which was by no means the only case of the kind. Later, Europe, as soon as it had made up its mind to accept the white potato (which took a little time) dropped the Jerusalem artichoke, clearly outclassed.

Unlike the sweet potato, the white potato received little attention in North America until an adventurous farmer notorious for his temerity in experimenting with unusual plants started to grow it—Thomas Jefferson. He called it the *Irish* potato. This seemed curious, since we have long accepted the statement that the first potatoes sent to England came from Jefferson's own native Virginia, and were served in 1586, perhaps at the instigation of Sir Walter Raleigh, to Queen Elizabeth, who did not like them. It is true that her cook, confronted with an unknown plant, jumped to the wrong conclusion, throwing away the tubers and cooking the leaves.

But why had the potato disappeared from Virginia during two centuries? The fact is that, contrary to well established tradition, the potato had not disappeared from Virginia, for it had never been there. It was not a North American vegetable, it was a South American vegetable. The belief that it had reached England from Virginia was a simple error, which involved, not

Sir Walter Raleigh, but Sir Francis Drake. In 1586, Drake stopped at what is now Cartagena, Colombia, to take on supplies, including a tuber hitherto unknown to the English which was eaten by Indians. On his way back to England he made a detour to pick up some adventurous Englishmen who, starving to death, had decided to postpone the colonization of Virginia. It was natural enough to assume that the vegetable as well as the passengers had come from Sir Francis' last port of call. Among those who made this mistake was John Gerard, who published his authoritative *Herball* in 1597, and included in it the information that the potato was a native of Virginia. Once Gerard had said so, everyone accepted the pronouncement without question.

The potato was grown in Europe from the end of the sixteenth century, but as an ornamental plant; it occurred to nobody, after Queen Elizabeth's discouraging experience, to eat it (except perhaps to the kings of Spain, who seem to have been its first regular consumers). Most historians of food agree that the white potato met with long resistance before it was finally accepted in the Old World. In France, the parliament of Besançon even forbade its cultivation; it was believed to cause leprosy. Not until the end of the eighteenth century did France finally begin to eat potatoes in any quantity, in large part because there was a shortage of food after the Revolution. If the potato had become so thoroughly established in Ireland from the beginning of the eighteenth century that it acquired the name of that country, it was for the same reason—it was the bulwark against famine. The potato was very nearly the only crop that could draw sufficient nourishment from the poor soil of Ireland to feed its population. Even there it met resistance. Sir Walter Raleigh may have grown the first "Irish" potatoes on his estate at Youghal, not far from Cork, about 1588. They do not seem to have been taken up by others, for as late as 1633 the Royal Society had to urge that they be planted against famine, an admonition that does not seem to have been much heeded until the beginning of the following century. Ireland seems to have usurped the credit for this American vegetable definitely when tubers from that country were planted in 1719 in Londonderry, New Hampshire, whose name suggests that they might have come along with immigrants from Ulster.

In any case, the American potato had now become definitely the Irish potato. Americans showed no objection to ceding the title to the Irish, who had no other important vegetable to which they could attach their name, while Americans, who had many possibilities, could afford to ignore the potato. Indeed, they did more than ignore it; they stigmatized it as downright dangerous. Not until the eighteenth century had most Americans, though still not all Americans, resigned themselves to eating potatoes; but, abandoning with the utmost reluctance a prejudice of the century before, they were still insisting that potatoes were poisonous. Accordingly they were only eaten boiled, for it was held that boiling got rid of the toxins, which passed into the cooking water. As late as 1904 Célestine Eustis wrote in *Cooking in Old Créole Days:* "Waters in which vegetables have been boiled can be used in cooking, except potato water and cucumber water. They have been known to poison a dog."

It is perhaps less strange that the colonists were so slow about discovering the tomato that before it was grown in English-speaking America, the colonies were no longer colonies, but already the United States. The tomato also originated in South America, where the Indians seem to have displayed no great interest in developing it. Presumably it got to Europe first, carried there by the Spaniards in the sixteenth century; but Europeans were reluctant to indulge in it too. Planted in Spain, Portugal, Italy, France and England, it remained an ornamental plant for two centuries. Apparently it was the Italians who first dared eat it, and the French and Italians who induced the United States to follow their example. In the meantime the Europeans, particularly the Italians, had improved it. Thomas Jefferson was, as usual, the first to plant tomatoes, in 1781. An Italian painter introduced them to Salem, Massachusetts, in 1802, and they are first mentioned in New Orleans in 1812. The average nineteenth-century American remained chary about eating the "tomata," as it was usually spelled then. Not only was it considered poisonous, like the potato, but until nearly the beginning of the present century it was believed by many to cause cancer.

In the light of their reluctance to accept new foods, one wonders if the American colonists would even have welcomed the fruit of the wakwak tree if they had had the good luck to find it. It seems to have become suddenly extinct after 1729, when it was described as one of the new plants of the New World by a Turkish writer named Ibrahim Effendi, who failed unfortunately to state exactly where it grew—a pity, for it seems to have been a delightful plant. Its fruit, Ibrahim Effendi *dixit,* was "ripe and attractive women."

At the same time that the New World was sending new foods to the Old, the Old World was sending its old foods to the New. The colonists brought them in because they were used to them, liked them and wanted them; but the Indians were just as happy to have them as the Europeans. They adopted these unfamiliar products with greater open-mindedness than the Europeans had showed for the strange foods of America.

European fruits were not simply accepted by the Indians, they were pounced upon. For some reason, the Indians showed special avidity for the peach, which moved across the new territories faster than its introducers did. The Creeks and the Seminoles fell upon it when the Spaniards introduced it, and its cultivation spread so rapidly from one Indian tribe to another that by the time William Penn arrived a hundred years later to explore the Susquehanna region, he discovered that there was hardly an Indian plantation which was not growing peaches. Apricots were less widely favored, but the Cherokees grew enough of them so that by the eighteenth century they were running wild, dotting the countryside with what were called "field apricots." Pears and apples were well accepted by the Iroquois when Jesuit missionaries introduced them to their country. The Spaniards had, as we know, imported the orange into Florida early in the sixteenth century and it entered quickly into Indian cooking.

One of the most important of the new European foods, on its home ground, was wheat, but the Indians felt no great need for it, being already plentifully provided with corn; however it was grown to some extent by Indians, especially in the Southwest, where it had been introduced early by the Spaniards. Similarly rye, another crop the Jesuits gave the Iroquois, was not much cultivated by them. Vegetables played a more important role, increasing the variety of Indian foods, an element Indians seem always to have appreciated. Most of them were not too different from foods the Indians possessed already and knew how to deal with. They had always eaten a large number of greens, so they had no trouble assimilating purslane (also a gift of the Jesuits), lettuce, and, halfway between salad plants and more substantial vegetables, cabbage. Lentils, apparently first acclimatized among the Iroquois, were acceptable as another kind of bean. Among roots, the European onion was not too different from the American species, while the turnip and the beet could be referred to the roots the Indians already knew (the latter was treated like camas root, baked or roasted unpeeled). The carrot was perhaps the strangest of the root vegetables for the Indians; brought to the New World by the first colonists, it soon became so well naturalized that it escaped from vegetable gardens and reverted to the wild state in untended fields, where it is familiar to all of us as Queen Anne's lace.

The introduction of domestic animals by the Europeans caused a veritable gastronomic revolution among some Indians, notably the Cherokees, who had never known livestock before. The first cows were landed in Florida about 1550, the second at Jamestown in 1611; for the first time Indians had milk—and, of course, beef, though this impressed them less, since they already drew meat from the buffalo, which in those days existed not only on the central plains, but also in the East. English colonists saw them for the first time in 1612, near the present site of Washington, D.C., and they persisted in this part of the country until 1825, when the last bisons of the East, a female and her calf, were killed in West Virginia. The Cherokees, Creeks and other southern tribes fattened cattle on corn to produce tender beef. Pigs were fed on peanuts by the Creeks and the Seminoles, while the Powhatans, who also fattened them on peanuts, smoked their rear legs over hickory fires, thus presenting the white man with the technique which would later produce the famous Smithfield hams. Meanwhile the Jesuits had introduced cattle and hogs to the Iroquois in the North. Sheep were also adopted by the Indians; the Cherokees stuffed both suckling lambs and pigs with apples and nuts, and roasted them over the glowing embers of a dying fire. Sheep became even more important for Indians in the West, where the Navahos, still great sheepherders today, constituted their first flocks by stealing them from the Spaniards.

The most important gift the Indians received from the Europeans was not a new food, it was a new utensil: the iron kettle.

IX

Game

"GAME MADE THE SETTLEMENT of America possible," wrote Dale Brown in *American Cooking.* The statement, in this form, is perhaps a trifle sweeping, but the diet of the seventeenth century was indeed dominated by game, that of the eighteenth leaned heavily upon it, and it remained important in the nineteenth up to the Civil War. At the beginning game was the most abundant food and, with the possible exception of fish, the easiest to come by. The first colonists had no prejudices against it, for the game birds and animals of America were not alarmingly different from those of Europe. Even that strangest of American birds, the turkey, could be considered a cousin of the bustard or the capercaillie, both familiar to Europeans. Even after the importation and multiplication of hogs, the primary source of meat remained game, which renewed itself dependably even when hunted by the wasteful method learned from the Catawba and Tuscarora Indians of setting fire to the underbrush to drive animals out of cover toward waiting hunters.

For a considerable time after the arrival of the first settlers, game was not only the main *meat* of the colonists, it was often the main *food.* It may be that the American habit of heavy meat eating, which was to astonish many European travelers during the first two centuries of Anglo-Saxon presence in the New World, stemmed partly from habituation to a diet composed largely of game. The chief limitation to its use was that it would not keep. It was thus eaten chiefly during the cold seasons; when the weather was hot, there was no point in killing game unless it could be eaten immediately, or in killing more than the family could finish at the next meal. Preserving it, by smoking, drying, or pickling, was of course not impossible, but if meat were to be preserved, it was easier to deal with the pig.

One fact that impressed all observers was the great plenty of game in America; it was clearly inexhaustible. Both Jacques Cartier and Samuel de

Champlain marveled at the number of passenger pigeons which, on their migrations between Mexico and Canada, "darkened the sky." When we read that phrase nowadays we take it for a figure of speech, a picturesque exaggeration; but it is a simple statement of fact, literally accurate. Flights of passenger pigeons *did* darken the sky and a single flock might take several hours to pass. William Byrd described them as alighting on branches in such numbers that even stalwart oaks bent beneath their weight. Alexander Wilson, a Scot, and, what is more to the point, an ornithologist, so he may be presumed to be a competent witness, told of sighting a flock a mile wide and an estimated (by the time it took to pass) 240 miles long. He calculated that it contained 2,230,000 birds, which during their passage would eat 17 million bushels of acorns and beechnuts, which otherwise could be fed to hogs. They also ate other things, crops in the field, for instance, which explains why the Pilgrims did not give thanks for the blessing of the passenger pigeon. They did not see much advantage in having within reach of their blunderbusses several millions birds of which only a few score could usefully be killed for food, at the price of losing the grain which they expected to last them for a full year. The year 1648 was an exception: the crops failed without any assistance from the pigeons; the Pilgrims were glad enough to have the birds to eat in the absence of corn.

Peter Matthiessen, in his *Wild Life in America,* called the passenger pigeon "the most numerous bird ever to exist on earth," which it must have been if we accept his estimate that at its height there were nine billion passenger pigeons in North America, which would mean twice as many as all the land birds in that continent today put together. Considering their great numbers, it is stupefying to find John Josselyn writing as early as 1692 that "of late they are much diminished, the English taking them with nets." The implication was that the passenger pigeon was on its way out, a prophecy percipient but premature. A little less than half a century after it had been uttered, in 1736, pigeons were still six for a penny in Boston and farmers were feeding them to their pigs; a little less than a century later, in 1770, a hunter fired a single shot from his blunderbuss into a passing flock, and brought down 125 birds; a little less than two centuries later, in 1830, travelers reported passenger pigeons so abundant in New York that piles of them could be seen stacked up on market stalls wherever one looked; and as late as 1848 the Ohio state senate rejected a bill to protect the bird because "the passenger pigeon needs no protection." It was not an unreasonable position; at the beginning of the nineteenth century there were still five billion passenger pigeons in America; but they were only too easy to take. Audubon reported that in Pennsylvania he had once seen a man net more than five hundred dozen in a single day; that there were towns along the Ohio River which lived almost exclusively on pigeons for weeks at a time during their migrations; and that boats put in at New York loaded with pigeons that cost a penny apiece; 75,000 were sold in New York alone in a single day. Even after the Civil War, when hunters had been endowed with more efficient means of destruction, the birds were still plentiful enough so that their wholesale price varied between fifteen and twenty-five cents a dozen.

The opening of the twentieth century marked the end of the passenger pigeon: the last wild bird known to have been taken was killed in Ohio in 1900. The passenger pigeon population of America was reduced early in this century from the original nine billion to one—a bird in the Cincinnati zoo which died in 1914.

The turkey was so characteristically American that the country could have done worse than to accept Benjamin Franklin's suggestion that it be chosen as the national bird; wild turkeys, too, were abundant when the whites arrived. William Byrd described the sharp hissing of their wings when a large flock took off, and in Florida William Bartram complained of being awakened too early by "wild turkey-cocks saluting each other from the sun-brightened tops of the lofty cypresses and magnolias." In the spring, he wrote, the cocks "begin at early dawn and continue until sunrise from March . . . to April . . . the watch word being caught and repeated from one to another for hundreds of miles around; the whole country is for an hour or more in a universal shout."

In the seventeenth century, town dwellers unable to shoot their own turkeys paid a shilling for one. In 1820, wild turkeys were still so common and so cheap as to be disdained. They were a drug on the market; in Kentucky, farm chickens cost more. Europeans, who had had less opportunity to become blasé about the bird, were more appreciative. "The wild turkey is excellent," wrote Captain Frederick Marryat, who visited the United States in 1837. Turkeys were still plentiful as late as 1889, when Alessandro Filippini, chef of Delmonico's, asserted in *The Table* that "no game is more highly prized or more eagerly sought after in Europe than our American canvasback ducks, grouse and wild turkeys."

The canvasback duck! A gourmet's delight, as it always has been. It figures in the carefully preserved private recipe books of the great plantations which once bordered the Mississippi. "The great delicacies in America are the terrapin, and the canvasback ducks," Marryat wrote. He does not seem to have been much taken by the first, which he thought had to be an acquired taste, but "the canvasback duck is certainly worthy of its reputation." The ducks were still plentiful in the middle of the nineteenth century, for Charles Dickens reported in his *American Notes:*

> En route from Philadelphia to Washington, we crossed by wooden bridges, each a mile in length, two creeks, called respectively Great and Little Gunpowder. The water in both was blackened with flights of canvas-backed ducks, which are most delicious eating, and abound hereabouts at that season of the year.

Served at Delmonico's, the canvasback duck was rated a delicacy and a luxury; Filippini, who called it "the king of birds," insisted that it should not be overcooked, lest it lose the subtle flavor imparted to it by its diet of marsh plants, especially the tape grass also relished by the Indians, and that only the breast should be eaten. A slight dissenting note in the universal chorus of praise for the canvasback was sounded by Audubon, who wrote nostalgically in 1832:

> When a jug of sparkling Newark cider stands nigh, and you, without knife or fork, quarter a woodcock, ah reader!—But alas! I am not in the Jerseys just now . . . I am . . . without any expectation of Woodcocks for my dinner, either to-day or to-morrow, or indeed for some months to come. [He also appreciated the blue-winged teal:] so tender and savoury is its flesh that it would quickly put the merits of the widely celebrated Canvass-backed Duck in the shade . . . I myself saw a friend of mine kill eighty-four by pulling together the triggers of his double-barreled gun.

There was a wealth of other game birds besides the passenger pigeon, the turkey, the canvasback and the teal—among water birds, geese, mallards, pintails, and, for those with no objection to strong flavors (or with enough skill in the kitchen to subdue them), coot and rail (also called "mud hens"). Despite the reduction in their numbers as a result not only of hunting but of the draining of the marshes they frequented, some of these birds can still be hunted today, though no one should expect to come upon a sight like that reported toward the end of the last century by a boatman sailing off the coast of Florida, who disturbed a flock of floating ducks, which took wing, leaving on the water a blanket of down and feathers covering five hundred acres.

From the snipe, a bird fond of the marshes, the American hunter could move onto drier territory by shifting to the pursuit of its cousin, the woodcock. In Louisiana, the French hunted bobolinks, native to America, but of a calibre below that considered sporting by Anglo-Saxons, who usually abstained from shooting or trapping anything smaller than the mourning dove or the quail. The bobwhite quail is native to America, as its scientific name, *Colinus virginianus,* indicates, but it should have seemed familiar to Europeans all the same, since there are several varieties of quail in Europe. Plover were plentiful, too, so much so that during the single month of March, 1821, a professional hunter was able to deliver 48,000 golden plover to the market. The diligence of professional and amateur hunters, plus the urbanization which deprived them of living space, has eliminated from American fields and forests many birds which the early settlers found in large numbers. Common fare on American tables at one time were the prairie chicken (of which only a few still exist in the United States, in Texas) and the heath hen (the last one was killed on Martha's Vineyard in 1923). The Labrador duck, the Carolina parakeet and the Eskimo curlew are extinct.

The Eskimo curlew was an important food for our ancestors, but it seems to have been forgotten entirely, its fate obscured by the more publicized disappearance of the passenger pigeon. The curlew is related to the plover, the snipe and the woodcock, which gets it into tasty company, and Eskimo curlew seems to have been the tastiest of their kind. American hunters turned to them in the nineteenth century precisely because passenger pigeons were growing scarce, and the Eskimo curlew was considered next best. In preparation for its migrations it ate so heavily that its skin was stretched taut by its store of fat, so that when a shot bird hit the ground the skin frequently burst and the meat literally exploded from it, covering the ground with a sort of meat paste; New Englanders called it the "dough-bird."

In the day of the Eskimo curlew, game animals were as plentiful as game birds—big game and smaller game, of which some of the latter would be disdained today, though the South remains more broadminded than the North about what might be called marginal meats. Marryat reported that

> I have been in the game market at New York and seen at one time nearly three hundred head of deer, with quantities of bear, raccoons, wild turkeys, geese, ducks, and every variety of bird in countless profusion. Bear I abominate, raccoon is pretty good.

Marryat may have abominated bear, but this does not seem to have been the case for many of the earlycomers, and bear was plentiful. One reason for its acceptance may have been that its fat was useful in cooking, especially at the beginning, when there was no butter and no lard. Moreover, the early settlers may have been influenced by the Indians, who considered the black bear a primary food; in the South, the Choctaw knew at which season the meat was most desirable and when (at mating time, for instance) it was too strong. Young bear was naturally best for broiling, and a sort of shish-kebab was sometimes made by combining venison, turkey or duck meat with bear on a spit in such a way that in cooking the bear fat would flavor the other meats.

The bear seems to have been the largest animal which attracted the colonists. There is some mention of the elk in early writings, a little less of the moose (of which the prize morsel was the nose), and, what may seem more strange, almost nothing about the buffalo. The bison was probably too much of a good thing. Given the difficulty of conserving meat, what could a hunter do with an animal that weighed two thousand pounds, particularly if it were a male, which might carry as much as five hundred pounds more edible meat than the female? This consideration also accounted in lesser degree for the limited interest the colonial hunter showed for the elk and the moose; for that matter, even in the case of the smaller deer, he often took only the skin and a minimum amount of meat, leaving most of the carcass where it lay. If he wanted more meat than he could eat or carry, he could find it at his next stop; the white-tailed deer was present everywhere. It belonged to a genus native to America, and so did the black-tailed deer, as their scientific names indicate, *Odocoileus virginianus* and *Odocoileus columbianus* respectively. Venison was so plentiful in the seventeenth century that a quarter of a deer could be bought in New England for ninepence.

Among small game, the rabbit was of course common; Coney Island was thickly inhabited, not to say infested, by them, hence its name: "cony" is an earlier name for rabbit. Some American "rabbits" are really hares: the cottontail; the snowshoe rabbit *(Lepus americanus);* and the jackrabbit of the Southwest *(Lepus californicus).* Many of the other small animals eaten in the seventeenth and eighteenth centuries seem dubious provender to most of us today; but many colonists ate them then, and some Americans still do. The opossum feeds chiefly on wild berries, which gives it an agreeable flavor; young 'possum has been described as recalling suckling pig. Raccoon, of which there are two main varieties, the dark timberland animal and the saltwater yellow 'coon of the Southern coasts, are considered fine eating by many amateurs today, especially the former.

"Ate some beaver for dinner at the Governor's," William Byrd confided to his diary after an invitation to Williamsburg; and beaver is still eaten in the South today. The tail seems to have been the favorite part; an early description says that it tasted "like fat pork sandwiched between layers of finnan haddock." Squirrel was eaten by Indians and settlers alike, and in some country districts is still not disdained. The limit may have been reached with the muskrat, sometimes referred to, probably with sarcastic intent, as the marsh hare. But even this is still occasionally eaten in Louisiana, in a sauce so rich that the identity of the meat it smothers is hard to discern.

There was no lack of game in America when the first colonists arrived; but several counties in New York nevertheless thought it advisable to enact closed seasons on heath hens, grouse, quail and turkey in—1708!

X

The Food of the Colonies

FOR MUCH of the seventeenth century, American cooking might be described as a cuisine of survival: Americans ate what they could get, and were, not unreasonably, grateful for it—hence Thanksgiving. In the eighteenth, even before the presage of independence began to glow on the political horizon, American cooking started to pass from the level of artisanship (education by mothers of their daughters) to that of art, with the printing in Williamsburg, in 1742, of the first cookbook published in America—Eliza Smith's *The Compleat Housewife, or Accomplish't Gentlewoman's Companion*—which was successful enough to be reprinted in New York in 1764. This was simply a reprint of an English work, and so were all the other cookbooks brought out in America before the Revolution, like *The Frugal Housewife* of Susannah Carter, published in Boston. America would not have a really indigenous cookbook, born on its own soil and conscious of its own resources, until after the Declaration of Independence.

It is doubtful if the American housewife of the twentieth century, setting her automatic oven for the temperature she wants it to deliver and engaging the warning device which will remind her when it is time to take the roast out (or even shut off the oven itself in her absence), ever gives a thought to the conditions in which her seventeenth-century sister did her cooking. The woman colonist of the sixteen hundreds not only had no automatic devices to control her oven, she did not even have an oven. Cooking was done over an open fire on the hearth and the first fireplaces were pretty primitive affairs, made of stones cleared from the fields, patched irregularly together with mud. Thanks to incoming ships and improvements in local artisanry, these first crude structures were soon replaced by more workmanlike jobs of brick and mortar.

The first utensil the seventeenth-century cook enjoyed—often it was the only one—was a large iron kettle with three short legs which permitted standing it directly on the hearth over the flames or embers; or it might be hung over the fire, suspended by a hook from a lugpole made of green wood so that it would not easily catch fire; sometimes it did anyway, or was kept in use too long, so that, charred and weakened, it suddenly gave way and dumped the dinner into the flames. The tremendous kettle was heavy, too, even when empty; full, it might weigh as much as forty pounds. Manipulating it was an exhausting and even dangerous operation; burns were easily come by. The fireplace cook took minor difficulties in her stride—embers hopping into the soup, likely to happen if the wood of the fire were hemlock or chestnut, which have explosive tendencies; or, when meat was spitted over the fire, a common technique in those days, grease dripping into the flames, provoking sudden conflagrations. If the spit had to be kept turning, it was usually done by hand; but some ingenious families turned this task over to a dog on a treadmill.

The hazards of housewifery were decreased with the first great break-through in kitchen equipment, the replacement of the fixed lugpole by a hinged iron crane which could be swung out into the room to be loaded and then pushed back over the fire with a minimum of risk. "The crane did as much for the housewives of the seventeenth century as gas and electric ranges have done for those of the twentieth century," Jonathan Norton Leonard wrote in *American Cooking: New England.* The crane also had another major advantage. Before its advent, everything intended for a given meal often had to be cooked at the same temperature (it is true that in those days this was often an unimportant detail, since the whole meal consisted of the contents of the single big kettle, into which everything that was to be eaten had been thrown together as indiscriminately as for Indian succotash). The seventeenth-century cook was skillful at achieving the temperatures she wanted, though the process was more complicated than it would be three hundred years later. She began by choosing the correct wood for her purpose—usually oak or hickory, which burned more evenly and gave more heat than most of the others which were available. She then decided whether what she was going to cook should be placed over flames or embers; in the latter case she started her fire earlier so that it would burn down to coals by the time she was ready to start her cooking. Having no thermometer, she measured the heat by holding her hand over the fire. When the crane came in, it was garnished with hooks on chains of various lengths; by suspending her pots at different heights from the fire, she could boil the contents of one while simmering the contents of another—when she had another.

The seventeenth-century housewife not only had to make do without thermometers, she also had to make do without clocks, which were scarce and dear throughout the sixteen hundreds. She calculated cooking times by the progression of the sun; her cooking must have been more precise on clear days than on cloudy ones. Marks were sometimes painted on the floor, providing her with a rough sundial, but she still had to make allowance for the obstinacy of the sun in refusing to cast its light at the same angle as the seasons changed; but she was used to allowing for the vagaries of sun and weather. She also had a problem starting her fire in the morning; there were no matches. If she had allowed the hot coals smoldering under the ashes to go out, she had to borrow some from a neighbor, carrying them home with care, perhaps in a bed-warming pan.

As long as the sole cooking utensil was the kettle, it was often used for several purposes at the same time. If there were only one, its most important content was the catch-all stew. Hung above it, in its steam, brown bread might be cooking; or, a speedier process, lowered into the stew enclosed in a tin container, which prevented the liquid from reaching it, so that the bread was not boiled, but steamed. A sweet pudding wrapped in cloth might also be boiling in the stew at the same time. It has been maintained that stew and pudding did not exchange flavors. Perhaps not. Or could it have been that these mixed-food cooking habits had already begun to endow Americans with that inability to recognize fine shadings of taste of which they have been accused in our day?

After the kettle, the second utensil the seventeenth-century household was likely to acquire was a large frying pan. There were no smooth cooking-range surfaces on which to set it down, so, like the kettle, it had three legs. Its appearance caused it to be called a spider, which is why we call a frying pan, even legless, a spider today. Solitary tripods unattached to any specific cooking utensils began to appear also; set on the hearth, they provided support for vessels of different types, particularly round-bottomed pans which permitted quick warming up of dishes. Kettles themselves developed refinements. Some of them had covers with raised rims, so that live coals could be heaped on them, providing heat from above as well as from below. Straight-sided kettles appeared also, in which johnnycake or biscuits could be baked.

Baking was important in those days, when bread had to be made at home, so it was soon provided with more specialized apparatus. The first device was simply a sheet of tin, which could be fastened vertically outside the hearth to reflect the heat of the fire onto bread and biscuits, browning their top crusts while the heat of the hearthstone took care of their bottoms. It was not a very convenient device; the sheet of tin got in the way of other operations. It was supplanted by the Dutch oven, which at first was not the pot with a tightly fitting dome-shaped cover often given that name today, but a portable metal box set on the hearth with an open side turned towards the fire; it was often fitted with shelves so that several layers of bread, cakes or pies could be cooked at the same time. This was improved into the reflecting oven, about a foot square, made of tin, whose rear wall threw back into the oven the heat coming from the fire in front; it could develop higher temperatures when it was equipped with a curved canopy which radiated even more heat into the interior. This sort of oven was used especially for roasting game. A measure of the consumption of game in the seventeenth century is provided for us by some of these ovens which have been preserved, provided with six or eight hooks to permit cooking that many partridges or hares or cuts of venison at the same time.

Movable ovens were never as efficient as solid fixed ones, which began to appear in the seventeenth century as the art of masonry developed. The first permanent ovens were simply brick compartments built into the inside walls of fireplaces. A fire was lighted inside the oven itself until it had become sufficiently hot for baking; the embers were then scraped out and the doughy dishes which were to be baked replaced them. A tightly fitting wooden shield was forced into place over the oven's open side to keep the heat in, the temperature remaining hot enough for baking because the fire in the main fireplace prevented the oven in its wall from cooling. Baking was a chore performed perhaps once a week to provide enough bread to last until the next baking day. If the oven was big enough, everything was put in at the same time, the bread, which took the longest time to bake, in back, and cakes, pies and cookies in front, in the order of the time they required, so that each could be removed successively when done. If the oven was small, the different foods had to be baked one after the other, starting with those which took the least time and finishing with the bread, which was left in for as long as the oven remained warm. As living conditions improved and experience taught housebuilders how to design kitchens, the baking oven was moved outside of the main fireplace and given a flue of its own. The height of luxury was attained when it was dowered with a hinged iron door with a damper which could be opened or closed to alter the flow of air, thus controlling the intensity of fire and consequently the temperature for baking. The colonists could have done even better than this in the seventeenth century, but they failed to notice an innovation brought to America by Scandinavians—the cast-iron stove. Immigrants from Sweden, Norway, Denmark and Finland tended to settle in groups, setting up little ethnic enclaves in the New World, shut away from the surrounding country by an invisible barrier of different habits and customs. Within this psychological stockade, the Scandinavians enjoyed the convenience of the new stove; their Anglo-Saxon neighbors did not even realize that they possessed it.

A modern housewife transplanted by some interfering time machine into a sixteenth- or seventeenth-century kitchen would certainly be plagued by the total absence of glass. Before the Revolution, glass had to be imported; it was too expensive to be exposed to the dangers of the kitchen, and in any case it could not withstand the heat of a fire. Mixing bowls were made of wood, cooking utensils of iron, pewter, earthenware or stoneware. Today's housewife would miss also the convenience of stepping to the sink and opening a faucet when she wanted water. The lack of running water was not much of a hardship on farms, which had their own supply—a well, a spring, or even a running brook, though a brook could freeze solid during the winter—but townspeople were more seriously inconvenienced. Some city houses had wells in their backyards or courts, but as populations increased they were in grave danger of pollution. Those without access to a private well had to carry all their water from a public pump. No American city provided running water before the nineteenth century. Philadelphia, the cleanest city in North America, was the first to start work on a municipal water system, but that was only in 1801, and it was 1830 before it was really fully operative. By the standards of the time it must have been a splendid achievement, for it elicited a burst of enthusiasm from Charles Dickens when he made contact with it in 1842.

But Philadelphia was an exception. New York would not have running water until 1842, Boston not before 1848, and Chicago did not even achieve a drainage system until the Civil War.

During the seventeenth century, and for a large part of the eighteenth, cooking came pretty close to being a home monopoly; restaurants did not yet exist. Their birthplace was probably New York (then New Amsterdam), though New York was not America's largest city in the early part of the seventeenth century: Boston was, with Philadelphia second. If eating, or perhaps more importantly, drinking, outside of the home began in New York, it must be attributed to the somewhat stolid conviviality of the Dutch, who, however, started out at home, too, as Robert Shaplen pointed out in *The New Yorker* of November 10, 1956:

> The table around which the Dutch settlers practised their commensality was in the home and the food planked down on it had but one purpose: to satisfy hunger. Meals were as flat as they were functional—three of them a day, washed down with cold water. [Cold water? But hops had been introduced into the New Netherlands in 1629 (and into Virginia in 1648), so one suspects there was beer about.] As a rule, fish, fowl and roasts were thoroughly overdone [they still are, only too often, in the United States] and the idea of improving them with sauces seldom crossed a *huisvrouw's* mind; gravy was for fops. Fruit and vegetables were so little in demand that the local farmers scarcely bothered to grow them.

What seems to have been the first tavern in Manhattan was opened in 1642 on Coenties Slip by Willem the Testy, more formally known as William Kieft, Governor of New Amsterdam. At first taverns were frequented only by men, except on holidays, and were oriented more toward drink than food (the Dutch had imported Holland gin, too). However, excessive drinking was not encouraged; as soon as a man began to show his liquor, he was also shown the door; and when Peter Stuyvesant became governor, he imposed stringent regulations on gin stores. The British took over in 1664, but unsurprisingly did nothing to improve the quality of tavern food; however, public eating and drinking places did evolve under their influence toward the pattern of the coffeehouse, a substitute for the private clubs to which the English were accustomed. New York was pretty much alone in establishing taverns in the seventeenth century. The Puritans of New England were too tight-laced, the Quakers of Pennsylvania were homebodies and models of sobriety, and the colonists in the South were widely dispersed on isolated plantations, with no cities large enough to make the exploitation of restaurants profitable.

As the seventeenth century shaded into the eighteenth, Americans were still dependent largely upon game, to the detriment of agriculture. There was little incentive to stoop to the backbreaking labor of tilling the soil when the woods were full of meat and the sea of fish. Neglect of farming in the South was often laid to the lack of interest in exertion displayed by its settlers, but in the North, too, there were deterrents to the development of agriculture other than the competition of game. It was difficult to concentrate on exploiting farms when it was simultaneously necessary to defend them, against the Indians or the French or both. There was the Pequot War in 1637, the Indian War in 1644, King Philip's War in 1675 (a case of divine punishment visited upon Massachusetts because its young men were letting their hair grow long, the clergy explained), King William's War in 1680, Queen Anne's War in 1702, King George's War in 1744, the French and Indian War in 1755, Pontiac's rebellion in 1763, and a never-ending series of skirmishes which, if they did not gather themselves together into actions sufficiently coordinated to be officially designated as wars, nevertheless exposed farmers just as disconcertingly to constant guerrilla attacks, ambushes in the fields and massacres. Jared Eliot estimated that in 1758 alone at least five thousand men had been obliged to abandon their fields to fight the French or the Indians. "We are all military Men, as well as Farmers," he wrote, "our Circumstances being like that of the old Romans, from the Plow to the War, and from the War to the Plow again." In such circumstances it was not easy to plant seed, labor the land and harvest the crops (which were not infrequently destroyed by Indian raids before they could be gathered). It was with relief that the settlers welcomed the arrival of winter, when they might normally expect a respite from the incessant attacks, during which they could safely venture into the fields to prepare the soil for next spring's plantings; but they ran the risk of being caught outside their stockades, exposed in the open, if, after the first bite of frost, the weather turned temporarily mild again, as it so often did, and the Indians swooped down unexpectedly, out of their normal raiding season; it was for this reason that such weather was called Indian summer.

The Algonquins and Iroquois of the North were tougher characters than the Croatans or Cherokees of the South, which, however, had its Indian troubles, too—large-scale massacres in Virginia in 1622 and 1644, for instance, by Indians who resented encroachments upon their cornfields, not to mention the difficulties Powhatan imposed upon Captain John Smith himself, whose life was saved only because Pocahontas (who was twelve at the time) was in love with him, according to the famous legend—or more exactly according to John Smith himself, the sole recounter and only witness of the incident. The best evidence that Virginians were less hampered than Northerners in the pursuit of agriculture by the necessity of remaining constantly alert against the Indians lies in the fact that while the Pilgrims had to live in serried villages which could serve as fortresses if they were set upon, the Virginians were able with relative impunity to disperse themselves over the land in isolated plantations. Their failures at farming were therefore explained at the time, with, perhaps, less than entire understanding of their problems, as the result of their own fecklessness.

In 1687, Gilbert Chinard, in his *A Huguenot Exile in Virginia,* expressed himself as scandalized at the Virginians' neglect of their cattle, released in the fields and woods to fend for themselves, with no provision of food for the winter, and no use of their manure to fertilize pastures which might otherwise have provided them with better nourishment. He described "the poor beasts of a morning all covered with snow and trembling with the cold, but no forage was provided for them. They ate the bark of the trees because the grass was covered." Pigs were also turned loose to forage for themselves in the forest (some of them went completely wild, accounting for the razorbacks). "Hogs swarm like Vermine upon the Earth, and are often accounted such," Robert Beverly reported in 1705. He was not quite a dispassionate witness, but a man who chose to pose bumptiously, if not very convincingly, as a roughhewn, uncultivated backwoodsman, who displayed a chip on his shoulder to the English readers of his *Present State of Virginia,* which was published in London, announcing defiantly, "I am an Indian [which of course he was not] and don't pretend to be exact in my language." However, he was apparently right about the pigs, to which so little attention was paid that often they were not even entered on estate inventories of livestock. Virginia ate so much pork that William Byrd wrote they were becoming "extremely hoggish in their temper . . . and prone to grunt rather than speak." He also thought that cows were left to their own devices all winter in North Carolina not so much because this was an imitation of a habit permissible in the climate of England but because Carolinians were just too lazy to take the trouble of caring for their cattle. As a result, he reported, they lacked milk and had "custard complexions." This is not a symptom of shortage of milk, but it is of hookworm, which is not conducive to the expenditure of energy in caring for cattle or anything else. The South also had malaria to contend with. All the North had was Indians.

Observers continued to give bad marks to Southern agriculture throughout the eighteenth century. A Swedish botanist, Peter Kalm, wrote in 1748 that "the grain fields, the meadows, the forests, the cattle, etc., are treated with equal carelessness." In the same year, Jared Eliot expressed surprise that any progress in raising food had been made at all

> when we consider the small Number of the first Settlers, and coming from an old Cultivated Country, to thick Woods, rough unimproved Lands; where all their former Experience and Knowledge was now of very little Service to them: They were destitute of Beasts of Burthen or Carriage; Unskill'd in every Part of Service to be done: It may be said, That in a Sort, they began the World a New.

Less inclined to make excuses for his countrymen, the anonymous author of *American Husbandry* in 1775 called "the American planters and farmers . . . the greatest slovens in christendom." He criticized the planting of successive crops of corn to the exclusion of other plants which might have enabled the land to recuperate from the strain of producing this soil-exhausting crop (it is especially wasteful of nitrogen). "The land . . . after it is done with corn is of no more value than the sky to them," this author wrote. Virginians did not improve the situation by abandoning corn for a crop even more exhausting to the soil, tobacco, which drains it not only of nitrogen but also of potash.

The heavy hand of slavery was already imposing its deadening weight on Southern husbandry. Agriculture made more progress in the up-country of Virginia, and in the Carolinas, too, where individual farmers were able to exercise their own initiative away from the domination of the great plantations with their hordes of slaves. This region in the first half of the eighteenth century was already producing great herds of cattle, which were first rounded up in cowpens (hence the Battle of the Cowpens in 1781, fought at the site of one of these bovine rendezvous) and then driven to the ports to be shipped to England. In 1773 Josiah Quincy of Boston remarked on the coincidence between scarcity of slaves and flourishing agriculture:

> The number of Negroes and slaves is much less in North than in South Carolina. Husbandmen and agriculture increase in number and improvement. Industry is up in the woods, at tar, pitch, and turpentine; in the fields, ploughing, planting, clearing or fencing the land. Herds and flocks become numerous. Healthful countenances and numerous families become more common as you advance north.

British policy was partly to blame for the defects of American agriculture, especially in the South, where settlers in general agreement with the government were consequently more docile to its directives. Not only did England discourage or flatly prohibit trade with other countries than itself, thus damping American initiative, but it even dictated, with disastrous ignorance of the possibilities, the sort of crops it wanted America to grow. The British idea was to use the colonies to supply it with products that it was being obliged to import expensively because they could not be raised in the British Isles; the detail that the climate of America was even more unfavorable to them than that of England was not taken into consideration. Immeasurable ergs of energy were expended in Georgia in an unavailing attempt to coax silk out of the American mulberry tree, which was of a different species from the one to which Chinese silkworms were accustomed. The silkworms refused to cohabit with it. They preferred death.

There were other explanations for the slowness of the South to develop a self-feeding agriculture, one of which was supplied by no less eminent an authority than George Washington, who wrote to his friend Arthur Young:

> An English farmer must entertain a contemptible opinion of our husbandry, or a horrid idea of our lands, when he shall be informed that not more than eight or ten bushels of wheat is the yield of an acre; but the low produce may be ascribed, and principally, too, to a cause . . . that the aim of the farmers in this country, if they can be called farmers, is, not to make the most they can from the land, which is, or has been, cheap, but the most of the labour, which is dear; the consequence of which has been, much ground has been scratched over and none cultivated or improved as it ought to have been; whereas a farmer in England, where land is dear, and labour cheap, finds it his interest to improve and cultivate highly, that he may reap large crops from a small quantity of ground.

Both the South and North, however, had made considerable agricultural progress between the time of John Smith and William Bradford and that of George Washington. They had graduated rather quickly from the stage of being barely able to feed themselves, and had become able to ship foods to the homeland. Virginia had little to offer except tobacco (tobacco, most of the time, was enough), but she did ship pickled fish to England, and even apples (Albemarle Pippins) by 1759, if not earlier. New England had been even quicker in developing the apple. A document of 1649 suggests that apple growing must already have been a flourishing affair then, for in that year Governor John Endecott of Plymouth Colony bought two hundred acres of land from one William Trask, and paid for them with five hundred three-year-old apple trees. New England was exporting apples to the West Indies as early as 1741. South Carolina began exporting rice to the homeland shortly after 1680, the year when Captain John Thurber brought rice from Madagascar to that colony.

The North had a somewhat wider choice of products, but may not always have been quite judicious in deciding what to ship. In 1677, in the hope of charming Charles II into relaxing the crippling restrictions of the Acts of Trade and Navigation, Massachusetts sent him a handsome food package—ten barrels of cranberries, two barrels of samp (cornmeal mush) and three thousand codfish. This was an eminently representative sampling of the colony's resources, but its donors may have been a trifle out of touch with the tastes of the Merry Monarch, not to mention Nell Gwynn. "Wee humbly conceive," said the screed which accompanied these goodies, "that the laws of England are bounded within the four seas, and doe not reach America. The subjects of his majesty here being not represented in Parliament [could this have been the first formulation of the principle of no taxation without representation?], so we have not looked at ourselves to be impeded in trade by them." His Majesty conceived otherwise and the trade acts remained unaltered.

Massachusetts failed to send maple syrup or sugar to Charles II, or, apparently, to anyone else in England, though many farmers had learned how to make them. If maple sugar *had* been sent to England, it might very well have been rejected; it was a flavor too strange and too assertive to charm European palates; to this day it is virtually unknown in Europe. It "lacks the pleasing, delicate taste of cane sugar," according to a report dated about 1700, which perhaps meant that it was not in itself sufficiently neutral. When cane sugar began to reach the colonists from the West Indies, it was for a long time far too expensive for general use. Hence there was instead wide use of its cheaper by-product, molasses.

The abundance of cheap molasses created the profitable New England rum industry, which, according to Samuel Eliot Morison, played a beneficent role in early American history—beneficent, that is, for the white man. The Five Nations (Mohawk, Oneida, Onondaga, Cayuga and Seneca), he wrote, "whose fortified villages and extensive cornfields lay in central New York, were kept loyal to the English through the superior quality of English woolens and the high alcoholic content of West Indian rum." It may have been West Indian rum at the beginning, but it was soon New England rum, though made from West Indian molasses.

America also shipped to England another food the colonists had learned to appreciate, the green turtle, but in limited quantities, for in England it remained a delicacy, comparatively rare, never taken up by the mass of the population, which, indeed, never had a chance to find out if it liked turtle meat or not, since it existed only as an import and was consequently expensive. In America, where the turtle was abundant along the coasts from Texas to Cape Cod, turtle was a common and a favored meat; turtle barbecues were popular in New York in the eighteenth century and continued to be so well into the nineteenth. However, when turtle became rare as these singularly defenseless animals were gradually killed off,

Americans do not seem to have felt the disappearance keenly; turtle had always remained a little foreign to the spirit of Anglo-American cooking.

Simultaneously, the colonies were enlarging their own list of available foods. Some of the new aliments were undeserved gifts from the slaves, who carried seeds of African plants with them to the New World. The black-eyed pea, so popular in the South today, was introduced in this fashion in 1674; there were others—okra and the watermelon, for instance—but it is in the nature of things that we have no precise dates for their arrival. Meanwhile the colonists, for whom, in the beginning, a cow had been a cow and a sheep a sheep, whatever their quality, began to exercise more discrimination about the domestic animals they had imported. The Dutch had done so from the beginning; they had brought in Holstein-Friesian cattle in the early 1600s, if one may call them that at a period before the first herdbook had been opened; but, after all, the Holstein, registered or not, goes back two thousand years. After the British took over from the Dutch, they allowed Holsteins to die out, and it was not until the nineteenth century that they were reimported, to become the most important milch cows in the United States. Among sheep, the Leicester seems to have been brought into America shortly after the race had been stabilized in England, in 1755; one of the Americans who owned Leicesters was George Washington.

Husbandry developed more evenly in the North than in the South for a number of reasons. The South was discouraged from seeking diversity by the early development of one-crop economies, which provoked the phenomenon of the large plantation worked by slave labor. This initiated a vicious spiral, whose consequences for America would be all-important, for once the habit of using slaves had been institutionalized, the machinery was present which would lead inevitably to the development of other crops which demanded large-scale cultivation and would fix inescapably upon the South the "peculiar institution" which was to engender the most tragic episode in American history. After tobacco and, from 1680 onward, rice, the South would pass on to sugar cane and cotton, enrichers of the planters on the short term, impoverishers of the land (and of collective morality) on the long term. The Northerners were not tempted to ruin their soil by growing tobacco, which had initiated the big plantation system in Virginia, since this was a crop unsuited to the New England climate. (Only later would it be discovered that some types of tobacco can be grown successfully in the Connecticut Valley.) Corn did not deplete the soil in the North as it had sometimes done in the South, for the colonists had learned from the Northeastern Indians the trick of fertilizing with fish.

Fisheries developed rapidly in the North also, reaching in New England the highest point they would ever attain, relative to the economy as a whole, about ten years before the Revolution. It was in 1748 that a certain John Rowe moved in the Massachusetts House of Representatives that "leave might be given to hang up the representation of a Codfish in the room where the House sit [sic], as a memorial of the importance of the Cod-Fishery to the welfare of this Commonwealth." The motion met with general approval, if the skill of the anonymous artist who executed the memorial did not, for more than a hundred years later, in 1874, a visiting Latin-American revolutionist, Francisco de Miranda, noted that he had seen in the Massachusetts State House "the figure of a cod-fish of natural size made of wood and in bad taste."

Ever since the end of the seventeenth century, Massachusetts had been producing dried cod in greater quantities than Britain could absorb, either for her own consumption or for re-sale elsewhere—in the latter case, because she could not spare the shipping for its re-export. She was therefore obliged willy-nilly to open a breach in the Acts of Trade and Navigation to permit New England to export its cod directly in its own ships and to bring back cargoes from the ports where they landed it. This meant that Massachusetts sent its best fish to the Mediterranean (because that was the area among those where there was a demand for foreign cod which had been eating that fish longest and was consequently the most finicky), bringing back fruit. Second-run cod went to other overseas customers. The rest was delivered to the Caribbean (the best customer was Dutch Surinam) to feed the slaves of the plantations there; the ships brought back molasses for the rum distilleries. The New England cod fisheries were thus linked to the slave trade, and not in this fashion alone; the three principal currencies which in Africa were traded for slaves were Spanish money, rum, and salt cod, the last two from New England. The cod made many New Englanders rich, and the contemptuous term, "the codfish aristocracy," was coined to stigmatize them as parvenus. One of the most prestigious families of New England emerged from the codfish aristocracy, for it descended from George Cabot, who was captain of a codfish schooner in 1770 when he was only eighteen.

By the middle of the eighteenth century, America was eating quite well, quantitatively at least, and European visitors began to report that workers in the New World ate better than those of the Old, an impression based chiefly, it seems, on the heavy American consumption of meat—not always, it would seem, of prime quality. Thomas Cooper, in *Some Information Respecting America,* published in Dublin late in the eighteenth century, remarked that a great deal of meat was eaten in America but that much of it was "of a hard and oleaginous nature" (it was probably salt pork). An insight into the nature of American meat during this period may be afforded by the observation that Jonas Green, in his *Almanack for the Year 1760,* thought it useful to include a recipe "by which Meat, ever so stinking, may be made as sweet and wholesome, in a few Minutes, as any Meat at all."

Whatever its quality, the quantity of meat eaten in America must have influenced the Trustees of Georgia when they included large quantities of meat in the stores promised to those who would engage themselves to settle in that colony. The sort of persons they were trying to lure to Georgia (or, more exactly, to get rid of in England) were living on the edge of bare survival and were probably lucky if they tasted meat once a fortnight. The quantities of meat proposed to them, both for the voyage over and for their first year's stay in America, must have seemed fabulous to famished prospective emigrants. As set forth in their "Rules of the year 1735," the Trustees offered, in addition to certain items of clothing, arms, tools and cooking utensils, amounts of food which the beneficiaries certainly could not have afforded at home:

> Each working man will have for his maintenance in the colony for one year (to be delivered in such proportions, and at such times as the Trust shall think proper) 312 lbs. of beef or pork; 104 lbs. of rice; 104 lbs. of Indian corn [another indication that the Trustees were thinking in American terms] or peas; 104 lbs. of flour; 1 pint of strong beer a day to a man when he works and not otherwise; 52 quarts of molasses for brewing beer; 16 lbs. of cheese; 12 lbs. of butter; 8 oz. of spice; 12 lbs. of sugar; 4 gallons of vinegar; 24 lbs. salt; 12 quarts of lamp oil, and 1 lb. spun cotton; 12 lbs. of soap . . .
>
> The trustees pay their passage from England to Georgia; and in the voyage they will have in every week four beef days, two pork days, and one fish day.

Commercial catering existed in the American colonies even before the Revolution, especially in the North, which had a number of cities large enough to support restaurants. A celebrated example has persisted under the same name to this day, Fraunces' Tavern, opened in New York in 1770 by Sam Fraunces, popularly nicknamed "Black Sam" (he was a West Indian of swarthy complexion), who has been credited with "making our art of cookery more elegant." Legend credits George Washington with having been a customer of Fraunces, which is by no means improbable. Like the other Founding Fathers, Washington had been fortified for the task of creating a new nation by a background of solid eating.

(Sam Fraunces also ended the taboo against admitting women to bars, the first victory in a war which would not end until the last half of the twentieth century, when a New York court order forced the admission of women to McSorley's Old Ale House, then the oldest saloon in the city, which had held out since 1854. McSorley's had done its best (or worst) to keep the ladies out by offering its customers smelly Liederkranz cheese and Bermuda onions with their ale and porter, but they were persistent, and on August 10, 1970, the first woman entered; but the saloon's owner, faithful to tradition, continued to refuse to set foot in the place during business hours—for McSorley's, the last male refuge in New York, belonged to a woman, Dorothy O'Connell Kirwan, who died four years after the suppression of male privilege).

Fraunces' Tavern was not the first public oasis, though it was the most fashionable; as a matter of fact it was celebrated less for the excellence of its food than for the quality of its Madeira. It dated only from 1770, while in 1750 the tavern of Thomas Lepper, copying an English institution, had already introduced the "ordinary." This would be the *table d'hôte* today, reduced to its most literal meaning and its simplest dimensions. It offered no choice of dishes, but when the tavern keeper sat down early in the afternoon to his own warm dinner, anyone with a few shillings in his pocket to pay for it could sit down with him and eat the same meal.

The roadhouse did not appear until early in the nineteenth century. Neither the corner of Third Avenue and 125th Street in Manhattan nor Atlantic Avenue in Brooklyn are in the country now, but they were then. At the first address, the Widow Bradshaw specialized in chicken fricassee and at the second John Snedicker offered asparagus dinners—though according to most authorities, New Yorkers shunned vegetables until well into the nineteenth century. Nevertheless not everybody disdained vegetables in the pre-Revolutionary period; indeed, some which we consider modern discoveries may have been more common in the eighteenth century than in the twentieth. We are accustomed to think of broccoli as a twentieth-century revelation; but John Randolph, in *A Treatise on Gardening by a Citizen of Virginia,* written just before the Revolution, speaks of it as if it were well known in his time: "The stems will eat like Asparagus, and the heads like Cauliflower" (which also spots two other vegetables as familiar then). Vitamin-packed garnishes like watercress are not often mentioned as accompanying the all-protein diet which is usually ascribed to Americans of earlier centuries, but Randolph does not feel he needs to explain what it is when he refers to its "agreeable warm taste." Jefferson, a man of tremendous curiosity and a noser-out of new and better foods, ready to try anything, also grew a wide variety of vegetables. He raised European vegetables in Virginia and planted American sweet corn in his Paris garden when he was Minister to France.

It is possibly significant that a London traveler, who was so much impressed with the quantity of food thrust upon him at a Virginia plantation where he had been entertained that he wrote an article about it for the *London Magazine* of July, 1746, did not mention a single vegetable in the extensive list of foods he cited. "All over the colony," he wrote, "full Tables . . . speak somewhat like the old Roast-beef Ages of our Forefathers." Englishmen were accustomed to substantial breakfasts, but this one was overwhelmed at being served, fresh out of bed, with hashed and fricasseed meats and venison pie, and a choice of coffee, tea, chocolate, cider, beer and punch to drink. Dinner (in the middle of the day) did not include that American staple, pork, from which we may suspect that he was getting favored-visitor treatment, but no doubt he had enough to eat with beef, veal, mutton, venison, turkeys and geese ("wild and tame"), fowl ("boiled and roasted"), pies, puddings and assorted though unspecified desserts. Supper was quite as copious, "with some small Addition, and a good hearty Cup to precede a Bed of Down: And this is the constant life they lead, and to this Fare every Comer is welcome." Southern hospitality had gotten off to an early start, possibly because Virginians were lonesome. Virginia planters, each living on an estate without neighbors (though, it is true, with family, servants and slaves for company), demanded nothing better than to receive strangers who could bring to them a breath of fresh life and news from the outside world. George Washington himself is said to have kept slaves at a crossroads near Mount Vernon to invite any unknown who passed to come to dinner. The origin of Southern hospitality may well have been boredom.

XI

The American Revolution

FOODSTUFFS have to be counted among the causes of the American Revolution—or at least among the symptoms of its causes. Present in everyone's mind is the part played in the genesis of the rebellion by tea, but there were others as well: Madeira wine. Rum. Molasses. The turtle. Cod. Virginia called the Revolution the Tobacco War.

Tea was not the only foodstuff which the colonies were not permitted to import freely, nor were they allowed freedom of export for their own produce. The general principle was that the colonies were supposed to buy foreign goods, hence tea, from England, not directly from their producers; and to sell their own produce to England, not directly to the ultimate consumers. It was this second stipulation which caused the price of tobacco to drop ruinously in 1668. There was plenty of demand for tobacco on the Continent, but the English brokers wanted to supply it themselves, and pick up the middleman's profit. "Forty thousand people are impoverished," Governor Berkeley of Virginia wrote, "in order to enrich little more than forty merchants in England"—and also Charles II, who collected £100,000 in tobacco customs duties in 1675 alone.

One stipulation of the Trade and Navigation Acts was not particularly onerous—all colonial traffic had to be carried in "British ships"; but as this included colonial ships, it started on its way a New England shipbuilding and ship-operating industry which was to play an important part in American commerce, particularly in the handling of foods. And while tobacco and sugar, among other products, could be sent from America only to England, there were some exceptions to the general rules which were beneficial to American trade and American food production. New England could sell its cod anywhere, South Carolina could export rice directly to the southern Mediterranean, and the returning ships could bring back fruit, salt and wine without having to pass it through the mother country. Trade between North America and the West Indies was unrestricted, giving America a chance to show what it could do when allowed. Pickled beef and pork went to the Caribbean from New England, New York, and the Carolinas. The Connecticut Valley contributed potatoes and onions, Baltimore wheat and flour, Pennsylvania corn, and New England, of course, cod. On their return trips the ships brought back molasses from sugar refineries, and the American rum industry prospered. It was this which permitted molasses to replace maple sugar (in the North) as the most widely used sweetener. It was cheap. Sugar was expensive, but the refineries which made the sugar had as a residue great quantities of molasses which they were glad to sell for whatever might be offered. This situation was brought to an end by the rigid enforcement of the Sugar Act in 1760. A prohibitive tax (sixpence per gallon) was slapped on molasses, threatening death to the American rum industry. (It saved itself by fraud.) Then came the revenue act of 1764, which lowered the uncollectible tax on molasses, but created new onerous duties—on sugar and wine, for instance, especially Madeira, the colonists' favorite tipple, which they had hitherto been allowed to import free. The idea was to force the colonists to shift to port, supplied via England, at a duty of ten shillings per double hogshead as compared with the new impost on Madeira of an impossible seven pounds, fourteen times as much. The colonists retorted by declaring a boycott on "Punch and Madeira," declaring that they would "think themselves better entertained with a good Glass of Beer or Cider." There was of course no need to forego rum, manufactured chiefly in New England.

The tax on Madeira provided the British customs officials with an opportunity to run out of business a Boston merchant who had already been recognized as a trouble-monger, since he was known to be a generous contributor to the rebellious Sons of Liberty—John Hancock. An attempt to frame him was launched by accusing him of smuggling Madeira in his sloop, the *Liberty,* which the authorities attempted to seize, while Hancock risked arrest. A Boston mob roughed up the customs men and freed both Hancock and his vessel, in a parallel to the Boston Tea Party of 1773.

The act of 1764 was followed swiftly by the Stamp Act of 1765,

> the first direct, internal tax [Morison points out] ever to be laid on the colonies by Parliament; indeed, the first tax of any sort other than customs duties. It was a heavy tax, bearing on all classes and sections in America, the more so because the specified sums had to be paid in sterling. This meant that, in terms of colonial currencies, the tax was increased between 33 and 100 per cent.

One of its least appreciated provisions was that which imposed on liquor licenses a charge varying from one to four pounds on top of the local licensing fee already being paid. This increase in the cost of drinking was received with particular resentment because the colonists were already chafing under the obligation laid upon them to furnish free beer and rum to the British troops quartered in the colonies to keep them in order; the New York Assembly refused to grant credits for this purpose and was promptly dissolved by the Crown.

The Stamp Act proved unenforceable and had to be repealed, but was immediately replaced in 1767 by the Townshend Acts, named for the Chancellor of the Exchequer, who had forced his own hand by roaring in the House of Commons, while rather the worse for wear from an overdose of champagne, "*I* dare tax America!" Faced embarrassingly when he sobered up by the necessity of implementing his words or eating them, he tried to get out of the dilemma by a series of measures which looked tougher than they were, but retained the most detested impost, that on tea, as a symbol of Britain's right to tax the colonies. Unfortunately, tea had been selected as a symbol by the colonists also, as the Boston Tea Party was to demonstrate six years later. In the meantime many Americans began boycotting tea in principle, as they had Madeira; yet no less a patriot than John Hancock, hero of his own Madeira skirmish, offered tea to John Adams when he called in 1771. "I hope it's from Holland," Adams said, but he drank it all the same. Then the housewives of Falmouth announced that they were switching from tea to coffee, and Adams decided to do so too—along with so many others that America was well started on its way to becoming a nation of coffee drinkers.

One year after the Townshend Acts had been passed, in 1768, the Massachusetts Assembly drafted a letter to be sent to the other colonial assemblies protesting against them and suggesting "a humble, dutiful and loyal petition to our most gracious sovereign . . . to obtain redress." The sovereign was not at the moment in a gracious mood and instructed his government to order the Assembly to withdraw its letter. It refused to do so by a vote of 92 to 17, and was immediately dissolved. This provoked an almost burlesque episode in which the hapless green turtle, certainly unconscious of its symbolic importance, played a leading role.

At the time, one of the most stinging gadflies on the rump of the British government was an agitator named John Wilkes, a rather unsavory champion, who had organized obscene orgies and replied to Lord Sandwich, when the latter predicted that he would die either on the gallows or of venereal disease, "That depends, my Lord, on whether I embrace your principles or your mistress." However, Wilkes was handy as a symbol with which to attack the administration. He was then fighting to retain the seat in the House of Commons to which he had been elected but which many other Members were willing to deny him. He was hostile to the King. He was favorable to the American cause, in part, perhaps, because his elder brother had emigrated to America; and he may, indeed, have been in secret relations with the Sons of Liberty. He was also £20,000 in debt. The South Carolina assembly appropriated £1,500 to help pay his bills, and the Boston Sons of Liberty sent him two turtles. They had been carefully selected. One weighed 45 pounds: the anti-Wilkes fight had become particularly heated when the government suppressed No. 45 of his polemical newspaper, *The North Briton,* and Wilkes had adopted the number 45 as his symbol. The other turtle weighed 47 pounds: 45 + 47 = 92, "the Massachusetts patriotic number"—because it was the number of representatives who had defied the Crown in the Assembly vote. Paul Revere designed a silver punchbowl dedicated to the "Immortal 92," thickly engraved with slogans, including "No. 45" and "Wilkes and Liberty."

It may be assumed that this did nothing to improve His Majesty's Government's opinion of Massachusetts. In March 1775 the New England Restraining Act, intended to punish the recalcitrant colony for insubordination, was promulgated. It forbade the Yankees to continue fishing on the Grand Banks, which were the basis for its most important industry, that of dried cod. This might very well have been the *casus belli* capable of touching off the Revolution, but while the papers announcing this measure were still making their leisurely way across the high seas, another one was provided. New England still did not know of the deadly blow which was being delivered to its economy when British soldiers marched on Concord and were met by the Minutemen. A Cod War had become unnecessary.

If one subscribes to the thesis that the pursuit of agriculture, all things considered, serves the world better in the long run than the waging of wars, it must be considered regrettable that the imperious demands of the American Revolution diverted from their devotion to the soil two of America's ablest farmers, snatching them, like Cincinnatus from the plow, from the activity for which they felt a passionate vocation. George Washington at Mount Vernon (thirteen thousand acres, before, late in life, Congress granted him generous domains in the western lands) and Thomas Jefferson at Monticello (ten thousand acres) were both skillful practitioners of what since antiquity has been considered the noble art of agriculture. Both were unwilling to rest content with the passive role of mere ownership of land, but managed it personally, in detail, and intelligently; both were up to date in such matters as the theory of crop rotation, a new idea when Jethro Tull in England urged its practice in his *Horse-Hoeing Husbandry,* published in 1733, and thus gave a nickname to his first eminent convert, Lord "Turnip" Townshend, grandfather of the man who promulgated the disastrous Townshend Acts; both were experimenters seeking ways to improve animals and plants, Washington concentrating more on the former, Jefferson on the latter; and both, incidentally, were slaveholders opposed to slavery. "I am principled against this kind of traffic in the human species," Washington said, and Jefferson wanted to insert an anti-slavery clause into the Declaration of Independence; but to have tried to exploit a large Virginia estate without slave labor in the context of the times and the circumstances would not only have been impractical, it would have been quixotic, and would have exposed anyone who did so to the suspicion of being more peculiar than the "peculiar institution" itself.

Besides crop rotation, Washington interested himself especially in fertilization and stock management. He worked on experimental breeding with cattle, including buffalo at least once, but with what success is not on record. Wheat and tobacco were his principal money crops, but like Jefferson he believed that a plantation should be self-sufficient, producing everything it needed, especially food. Thus he ground his own corn in his own mill (so did Jefferson) and grew all the vegetables and fruit Mount Vernon needed, applying to the former three- and five-year rotation cycles. He had his private fishery arrangements to provide shad, bass and herring, largely for his slaves (Jefferson sent to the James River when the shad were running, had them brought back alive in barrels, and kept them in a pond until they were needed; he also had crabs collected in Chesapeake Bay).

Like Jefferson, Washington experimented with exotic plants, mostly trees, not exclusively for food (he planted palmettos, pepper trees and mahogany) and, like Jefferson, with slight success (the latter's chief failures were with olives and wine; he did establish a vineyard and produced wine of sorts, but he never dared offer it to discriminating guests). Washington did better with imported English grasses and grains, but his special pride in the vegetable realm was his peach and apple orchard. One may suppose that he grew cherries, but he seems to have made no particular reference to them, though this neglect would not justify us in concluding that it resulted from a life-long animosity towards the cherry which might confirm the veracity of the celebrated anecdote related by Parson Weems. Popular abridgement of that story has whittled it down to as acceptable a form as possible: "Father, I cannot tell a lie; I did it with my little hatchet." Probably few Americans today have read the original version; for the benefit of anyone curious enough to want to make acquaintance with it, here it is, in all its nauseating gooiness, as it was related in *The Life of George Washington: With Curious Anecdotes, Equally Honorable to Himself and Exemplary to His Young Countrymen:*

> "George," said his father, "do you know who killed that beautiful little cherry tree yonder in the garden? . . ." Looking at his father with the sweet face of youth brightened with the inexpressible charm of all-conquering truth, he bravely cried out, "I can't tell a lie. I did cut it with my hatchet."

Jefferson must have been cut out by nature for rural life, if we may judge from his definition of cities as "sores upon the body politic." Like Washington, he practiced crop rotation, but from that point on his special interests were a little different. He did not disdain the disciplines of animal breeding, for he imported special strains of hogs and sheep, but he gave more attention to vegetables. For eight years he recorded meticulously the first and last appearances of each of thirty-seven different vegetables on the Washington market, and correlated this information with his own carefully kept meteorological charts. He also made forays into fields related to farming and food, designing, for instance, a silver coffeepot which was inaugurated at a dinner in honor of Lafayette, and inventing an improved moldboard for plows which reduced resistance to their action, an exploit for which he received a number of awards, including membership in the official French agricultural society.

Jefferson assured himself a rich and varied food supply at Monticello by keeping his woods stocked with game (deer, hare, rabbit, turkey "and every other wilde animal" except of course predators); his ponds and streams with fish; his fields with cattle, sheep, goats and swine; his poultry runs with chickens, pigeons, guinea fowl and peacocks (the last, one supposes, for decoration); and his gardens and orchards with a great quantity of fruits and vegetables, some of which he obtained from abroad. Among the food plants we know he grew were apples, artichokes, asparagus, beans (of several kinds), broccoli, Brussels sprouts, cauliflower, celery, cucumbers, cymlings (a kind of summer squash), damson plums, eggplant, endive, Jerusalem artichokes, lettuce, peas (his favorite vegetable), peaches, peanuts, potatoes, raspberries, salad greens, salsify, Savoy cabbage, Spanish onions, spinach, strawberries, sugar beets (a real innovation, since sugar beets were practically unknown until Napoleon encouraged their cultivation to beat the Continental Blockade, and kept it secret as long as he could), succory (chicory), tomatoes and turnips. There were certainly others.

If Washington and Jefferson were more or less on an equal level as farmers, Jefferson was certainly the finer gourmet of the two. Washington did like to eat well, though he was not sufficiently interested in food to have left us many comments about it. He did once recall how, as a young surveyor, he had savored roast wild turkey eaten in primitive conditions, with a slab of wood for a plate. Food arrived on Washington's table lukewarm, because of the distance between kitchen and dining room, which did not seem to bother him. Jefferson took the trouble to avoid this disadvantage when he designed Monticello by incorporating into a wing of the main structure services relegated elsewhere to outbuildings, like the smokehouses and the kitchen. He explained one device he invented, a door pivoted top and bottom at its center, fitted with shelves which could be loaded with food on the pantry side and then swung around to transfer it to the dining room, as a means of securing privacy when matters of state were being discussed, so that indiscreet servants would not spread embarrassing rumors; but he was perhaps thinking also of reducing the time which would elapse between cooking and eating.

Jefferson called wine "a necessity of life," which certainly bespeaks the gourmet. He was only a gourmet, not a gourmand, for he was an appreciative but not a heavy eater. He told his physician, Dr. Vine Utley, that he had "lived temperately, eating little animal food, and that not as an aliment, so much as a condiment for vegetables, which constitute my principal diet." Vegetarians may see in this an explanation for the fact that when Jefferson died, at eighty-three, he still had all his teeth. However, Jefferson's confidence to Dr. Utley was made near the end of his life; he may have eaten more meat when he was younger. According to Captain Edmund Bacon, his overseer for twenty years,

> He was especially found of Guinea fowls; and for meat, he preferred good beef, mutton, and lambs. [His] broad-tailed sheep . . . made the finest mutton I ever saw. Meriwether Lewis' mother made very nice hams, and every year I used to get a few from her for his special use.

Washington and Jefferson, both well-fed, were moderate, reasonable men; one might well wonder if the events which led to American independence might not have evolved a little less painfully if all the colonists' ringleaders had, like them, been blessed with good digestions; the reactions of the comparatively extreme Samuel Adams may have been exacerbated by the stomach ulcers which held him to a diet of bread and milk.

Washington and Jefferson were of course exceptions, but good food was no rarity on the palatial Virginia plantations.

> Always in these great houses [wrote Eugene Walter in *American Cooking: Southern Style*], the tables were bountifully laid. When Philip Fithian came down from New Jersey in the 1770s to tutor the children of the Robert Carters at Nomini Hall with its 2,500 acres (part of Carter's holdings of 70,000), he was surprised to find Southern life pleasanter than he had expected. In a letter home he reported Carter's own estimate that the family and guests consumed annually "27,000 pounds of pork, 20 beeves, 550 bushels of wheat, besides corn, four hogshead of rum and 150 gallons of brandy." He also noted that one dinner included: "Beef and Greens; roast-Pig; fine boil'd Rock-Fish, Pudding, Cheese, etc. Drink: good Porter-Beer, Cyder, Rum and Brandy Toddy."
>
> Another visitor subsequently described the splendors of the table at Shirley Plantation, built by Edward Hill who married into the illustrious Carter family. "His service is all of silver and you drink your porter out of silver goblets . . . The finest Virginia hams, and saddle of mutton, Turkey, then canvas back duck, beef, oysters . . . Then comes the sparkling champagne—after that the dessert, plum pudding, tarts, ice cream, peaches preserved in Brandy . . . then the table is cleared and on comes the figs, almonds and raisins, and the richest Madeira, the best Port and the softest Malmsey wine I ever tasted."

George Bagby, author of *The Old Virginia Gentleman,* opened a window on more down-to-earth food when he set out to defend the thesis that Virginia bacon and greens were better than the same combination elsewhere, if only because Virginia pigs, like Westphalian pigs (Westphalian ham was highly esteemed in the colonies), were permitted to forage at large instead of being penned up, an observation which is hereby referred to the attention of today's meat raisers, who confine pigs and calves in narrow quarters and chickens in batteries to the detriment of their flavor.

Of course everybody in the South did not eat as the great planters did. Jefferson himself remarked that men and animals were "illy fed" on many Virginia tobacco farms, but it was not because they could not have done better, it was because "little food of any kind" was raised by planters unwilling to spare a few acres of land from tobacco to vary their diet.

In the North there was no equivalent of the sumptuous Southern manors; society was organized there in a different fashion. But food nevertheless was solid, plentiful and nourishing. In 1774, when the Continental Congress was meeting in Philadelphia, John Adams recorded that he had been entertained by Benjamin Rush, who put before his guests "the very best of Claret, Madeira and Burgundy. Melons, fine beyond description"; while at a four o'clock dinner given by Chief Justice Chew he had been offered "Turtle and every other thing—Flummery, jellies, sweetmeats of 20 sorts, Trifles, whip'd syllabubbs, floating islands, fools, &." One supposes that the meal included other items than turtle and desserts, but John Adams was a true American; he remembered the sweets.

In the North as in the South, Americans were eating well up to the very outbreak of the Revolution, with access to almost everything they wanted, including tea. By then the colonies were producing all the foods they really required; and as the country was predominantly rural, nobody lived far from the sources of supply.

Even *during* the Revolution Americans did not eat badly—including the armed forces, despite such harsh passages as the bitter winter at Valley Forge. The colonial soldier was better paid than his British counterpart, and was assured of regular rations of sugar, ginger, rum and molasses. (Both armies, of course, foraged for a good deal of their provender; Washington was obliged to "forage the country naked" at Valley Forge.) His soldiers were certainly not getting enough food there, but they may have suffered even more from want of warm winter clothing. Lafayette described them as "badly armed and worse clothed"; they were "barefoot and otherwise naked." But he had little to say about the difficulties of feeding the army at Valley Forge, though we know they were not lacking. Indeed, he did not say much about food at any time, except when it was a professional preoccupation, as when he had problems feeding the forces he commanded in the southern campaign which was to end in the victory of Yorktown.

Another period of famine for Colonial soldiers occurred in the Carolinas in the spring of 1780, when regiments from Maryland and Delaware moved to the relief of that area:

> On 22 June they reached Hillsboro, North Carolina [Samuel Eliot Morison wrote], after incredible hardships owing to the failure of the states through which they passed to furnish supplies. Soldiers went without food for days, then gorged on peaches, green corn and raw beef, with devastating results to their digestive tracts.

And then General Horatio Gates, taking over the command at Hillsboro,

> decided to advance on Camden; and, against everyone's advice, insisted on taking the direct route through the pine barrens where there wasn't enough food to support a hog, instead of following the longer wagon road along which there were many farms and well-affected people. This march, too, was attended by hunger and dysentery.

Such episodes were exceptional. Governor Jonathan Trumbull of Connecticut did a masterly job of supplying the troops with flour and beef throughout the war and a German baker of Philadelphia, Christopher Ludwig, shamed the merchants who had let the soldiers at Valley Forge starve rather than accept Continental paper for their goods, by furnishing the army with bread, pound for pound with the amount of flour issued him, although the government had offered him 135 pounds of flour for every one hundred pounds of bread, to allow him a profit.

In any examination of the role food has played in shaping history, it would certainly be exaggerated to maintain that it was because of food that France came to the aid of America during the Revolution. It was only a tangential fact that it was during a lunch that enthusiasm for the American cause was engendered in the Marquis de Lafayette.

Lafayette, who would not be eighteen for another month when this crucial lunch took place, was an officer of the garrison of Metz, a city given to good eating, a virtue which did not please Voltaire, who grumbled that Metz possessed twenty *rôtisseurs* (sellers of cooked meats) for every bookshop. The Duke of Gloucester, possibly more interested in eating than in reading, accepted an invitation to lunch with the army officers of Metz, whose culinary reputation may have been known to him.

During the meal the Duke gave vent to certain inflammatory opinions concerning his country's attitude toward the American colonies, though it may be suspected that he disapproved of that policy largely because he disapproved even more of his royal brother, to put it mildly. George III and the Duke of Gloucester couldn't stand each other.

*

> Do you realize [the Duke asked the French officers, including Lafayette, who was all ears] that England is engaged in losing its Colonies? . . . We didn't have the right to tax them without their consent. There is a sacred principle for the English: no taxation without consent . . . Why did we need, when we repealed the Stamp Act . . . to maintain the tea tax, hardly more than a symbolic duty . . . for no other reason than to humiliate them? We drove them to desperation. It's no longer a question of trade, a money matter, it's a question of honor. And made no mistake about it, gentlemen, the Bostonians are as good Englishmen as our people in London or Bristol. The English have always known how to resist when they have their backs to the wall. That's what they have just done at Bunker Hill; do you know that even farmers fired on our soldiers? They are holding a congress in Philadelphia. They have named a general-in-chief, a fine gentleman of Virginia, George Washington, who fought well against you over there in the service of my father.

Was this the first time that Lafayette heard the name of George Washington, whom he would come to idolize, and under whom he would later serve in what seemed almost like a father-son relationship? It is certain that this occasion remained deeply imbedded in his memory. It was fifty-three years later when he told the story of that lunch at Metz to Jared Sparks, the biographer of Washington; Sparks reported that he shook with emotion as he recounted it. His vocation for the American cause was born at that lunch. It is too bad that we haven't its menu.

When Lafayette achieved his ambition and joined Washington at his camp of Neshaminy in 1777, though the scanty clothing of the soldiers shocked him (and prepared him for the even worse shock he would experience later at Valley Forge), he found that they fared better so far as food was concerned. He discovered, indeed, that "at his headquarters, Washington had succeeded in establishing an almost Virginian atmosphere—copious meals, with plenty to drink, at fixed hours, and a semblance of etiquette." This did not mean that Washington took care of himself at the expense of his men; he was always ready to undergo personal hardship when the circumstances demanded it.

Officers from food-conscious France seldom recorded any lack of sufficient food, apart from those exceptional and inevitable shortages that occasionally arose through the exigencies of military campaigns. When the Comte de Rochambeau, commanding the forces France had sent to the aid of the Americans, accompanied by Lafayette, met George Washington for the first time in 1780, there was no dearth of good cheer. "There was an atmosphere of warmth before the great table of the inn, carved from a single trunk, covered profusely with cakes, bowls of punch and pitchers of cider which was nearly as intoxicating," wrote French historian Claude Manceron. And later, when Rochambeau dined with Washington:

> The meal was English in style, composed of eight or ten main dishes, some of butchers' meat, some of poultry, accompanied by several kinds of vegetables, followed by a second course of pastry, all of which fell under two headings, puddings or pies. After these two courses, the tablecloth was removed, and we were served apples and a great quantity of nuts, of which George Washington ate enormously for two hours, meanwhile proposing toasts and conversing. The nuts were small, dry and enclosed in shells so hard that they could only be broken with a hammer; they were served half opened and we seemed never to come to the end of extracting and eating them . . .

When on May 1, 1781, a discouraged George Washington confided to his diary the difficulties of his situation, he did not include a shortage of food among his troubles. The food was there, but getting it to the soldiers where it was needed was another matter. Less than a month earlier, in a letter written on April 9 to Colonel John Laurens, who had been dispatched to France to plead for financial aid, he underlined its necessity by explaining, "We cannot any longer even pay teamsters to transport our provisions, for they will no longer accept our scrip." Merchants were not the only Americans who put payment for their services first and patriotism second.

Meanwhile the British, or at least some of them, were having food difficulties too. Washington had not complained of lack of food in 1781, but Cornwallis did. He wrote wistfully from Wilmington to British headquarters in New York, "Let us quit the Carolinas . . . and stick to our salt pork in New York"; but he was ordered instead to Yorktown and defeat.

The campaign which ended in the British surrender at Yorktown was dominated for both sides by the problem of feeding the armies. We learn largely from Lafayette, who commanded in the South until Washington and his northern armies arrived to join him in the decisive action, how closely the operations were linked to the necessity of providing food for the rival armies, which had been milling back and forth within a restricted territory on whose meager resources both were trying to live. Shortly after Lafayette took command, his scouts told him that the British were advancing up the James River. "Their principal objective," he wrote to Washington, "is to seize Richmond, not so much because of its importance, but because of the quantities of provisions heaped up in the storehouses of the city." That he was correct in attributing preoccupation with food to Cornwallis was evident from a letter the British commander was writing to his superior in New York, General Clinton, at about the same time, in which he announced that to starve the Americans out, he was going "to destroy all the provisions in the neighborhood"—at a time when he expected that his own needs would be taken care of by the food of Richmond, which he thought he was about to capture. Lafayette disappointed Cornwallis by getting into Richmond himself twenty-four hours before the British appeared in the outskirts of the city. He was not able to hold it for more than two weeks, for Cornwallis greatly outnumbered him, but two weeks was enough. It gave him time to empty it of the stores which had made it so valuable a prize. "The public and private warehouses having been moved out of Richmond," he wrote to Washington, "this place becomes an objective of lesser importance."

At the same time, Lafayette was preoccupied with another facet of the food situation. He pushed his forces to heroic efforts, on the theory that it was important to occupy as many key points as possible before late summer or early fall, when he expected that a considerable part of his army would melt away as the soldiers went home to harvest the crops:

> Things are in such confusion here [he wrote to Washington in August] that we are having tremendous difficulty in amassing sufficient stores. Nevertheless I have been working hard to this end . . . We find in this state large quantities of steers, wheat and flour, but very little rum. We will have to appeal very soon to the State of Maryland. Water transport, I hope, will diminish our difficulties.

Meanwhile Lafayette received reinforcements—2,500 local militiamen and five hundred mountaineer riflemen. They appeared a motley lot to the French officers accustomed to the neatly uniformed highly disciplined armies of Europe, but they fought well on a minimum of food. According to the Chevalier d'Aucteville, captain of an engineering unit in France, detached for service in America,

> They constitute a corps of excellent riflemen, good shots, apt for guerrilla fighting in the woods, but not at all for combat in orderly ranks . . . They are all sober and patient, living on cornmeal, putting up with privation or delay without grumbling, capable of supporting fatigue and long marches, precious qualities which make them a real light infantry.

When Washington and his forces reached the combat area after painful footslogging through difficult country (and for some of them, a no less painful passage across Chesapeake Bay), the food situation was hardly improved, as French historian Claude Manceron pointed out in *Le Vent d'Amérique:*

> The rations of the soldiers were reduced to biscuits and cheese. It was necessary once more to beg flour of Shylock-De Grasse [the French admiral who lay with his apparently unriskable (and well-provisioned) ships prudently off the coast, not daring to enter Chesapeake Bay and join the battle; but he would redeem himself later]. The Americans consoled themselves by thinking of the English, short of everything, and without hope.

For Cornwallis had achieved a Pyrrhic victory when he took Yorktown and chose to concentrate his force there. Now he was shut up within the city, cut off from relief from outside by an encircling ring of French and American forces which tightened around him every day, though they were often fighting on empty stomachs—empty of food anyway. It was because most of the Americans were sleeping heavily, drugged by the rum they had swallowed in the absence of supper, that the British were able to attempt a sortie in the night of October 15, 1781. They were beaten back, not having even rum to sustain them. Since October 13, the besieged British had been living on nothing but biscuits. By the seventeenth Cornwallis was out of provisions, and had only a two-day supply of cartridges left. Starved out, he surrendered. The side that was least hungry had won the American Revolution.

America came out of the Revolution with its food resources intact, except for fish. A contemporary writer reported that the number of lobsters in the New York area had decreased because they had been frightened away by the cannonading of the Revolution, a statement which seems to overestimate either the importance of the artillery or the sensitivity of lobsters. Whatever the situation may have been for crustaceans, the catch of ordinary fish had declined, for the New England fishing fleet had been reduced to one-fourth or one-fifth of its pre-Revolutionary size; its fishing boats had been converted to privateers. The whaling industry was virtually wiped out, but recovered in time to receive the *coup de grâce* from the Civil War.

John Adams was not a Massachusetts man for nothing; he provided for the rebirth of the New England fishing industry by informing the British during the peace negotiations of 1783 that it was a case of "fisheries or no peace"; and he secured not only the right for Americans to fish in what remained of British America, but even to land fish taken on the Grand Banks on the coast of Newfoundland to dry and process them there before returning home. However, fishing never again regained the relative importance in the New England economy which it had reached before the Revolution.

A more temporary setback was experienced by the rice growers of the Carolinas. During the British occupation of Charleston and Savannah, the occupiers profited by the occasion to ship all Carolina's rice to British traders, including what should have been retained for seed. It was Thomas Jefferson, after he had been sent to Europe as the first ambassador of the United States to France, who smuggled rice out of Italy and supplied it to Carolina, whose rice industry was quickly on its feet again.

In the long run, New England profited by the changes which resulted from the Revolution. Freed of the restrictions imposed by the British trade acts, American ships could now go anywhere they liked to trade directly with foreign countries, which gave a tremendous fillip to New England shipbuilding and ship operating. For the next century or more the history of food and the history of the New England ships which carried so much of it throughout the world would be intricately entwined. In 1784 a veteran of Valley Forge named Samuel Shaw reached Canton in his ship, the *Empress of China,* carrying coals to Newcastle—that is, an important part of his cargo was composed of ginseng, which grew abundantly in Asia. But it grew even more abundantly in America, and there was a heavy demand for it in China, where it was considered a tonic and an aphrodisiac. The trade was profitable while it lasted, but it did not last long; the Chinese complained that American ginseng failed to produce the results desired. Other exports were found, and the ships returning from China carried the tea for which the United States was no longer dependent on England.

Ships from Boston delivered apples, cheese and—despite problems of conservation—even butter to India, while others ferried coffee northward from Brazil. George Cabot, the same who had outlived the epithet of the "codfish aristocracy" by progressing from cod fisherman to privateer captain to merchant trader, commissioned the first ship flying the American flag to arrive at St. Petersburg, in 1784, the beginning of the export of tobacco, rum and flour to Baltic ports. The first American ship to round Cape Horn was the *Thadeus* of Boston, carrying a cargo of missionaries whose object was to improve the happiness of the heathen by inducing the natives of Hawaii to renounce the terrestrial paradise they were already enjoying in favor of an austerity which would insure them a place in the celestial paradise forever. If you were asked today what city in all the world was, between the American Revolution and the War of 1812, the world's greatest pepper trading center, would it occur to you to name Salem? Yet this small port of a country which grows no pepper exported 7,500,000 pounds of it in 1805, most of which had been carried from Sumatra and from there was redistributed to the rest of the world.

Meanwhile American housewives were marking the victory of the Revolution and the political developments which followed it by creating dishes which they named Independence Cake, Federal Cake, Election Cake, Ratification Cake and Congressional Bean Soup—the ancestor of the bean soup which is a traditional item on the menu of the Senate dining room to this day.

It was while the Revolution was still on that a salutary foreign influence was first exercised on American cooking; the wartime alliance with France called attention to that country's gastronomic prowess, and encouraged emulation of it. The French themselves sought to underline the political alliance with a gastronomic alliance, and celebrated it by a touching gesture to demonstrate Gallic sympathy with the American cause: they took to eating turkey, scarcely a hardship, and even cornmeal mush sweetened with molasses, which should have been a little more difficult to take. It is true that they improved the mush with a dash of cognac or Calvados (applejack), and garnished it with whipped cream. Indeed they even used truffles to stuff the turkey. But despite these embellishments, their consumption of typically American foods demonstrated that their hearts were in the right place. On the American side, a similar gesture was a little less well documented. Americans were convinced that the French lived exclusively on salad and frogs. It was this belief, according to Samuel Breck, whose memoirs appeared a little belatedly in Philadelphia in 1877, which inspired Bostonians entertaining French naval officers, who arrived at Boston during the Revolution, to take the trouble of fishing frogs out of the swamps of Cambridge, with the best intentions in the world; but the French officers broke into a roar of laughter when one of them raised his spoon from the soup to discover a whole frog nestled in it.

French contributions to American gastronomy were happier, and were provided in two waves. The first came with the French alliance of 1778, during the reign of Louis XVI, and the second at the time of the French Revolution. The first made it fashionable to serve French cooking in America; the second sent exiles to the United States, who, lacking other means of livelihood, managed to make both ends meet by capitalizing on their knowledge of one of France's most salable assets, her cooking. "The *émigrés* who came following the French Revolution," Richard Osborn Cummings wrote in *The American and His Food,* "helped to educate the American palate. The celebrated Brillat-Savarin, author of the *Physiologie du Goût* [but not yet; it was first published, anonymously, in 1825], did not disdain to teach restaurateurs to make fondues, while his compatriot, Captain Collet, found it profitable to make ices in New York. Many lesser lights occupied themselves with spreading French tastes. They introduced bonbons and encouraged use of soups, salads, sweet oil, tomatoes, and fricassees."

XII

Between Two Wars

FRENCH INFLUENCE on American cooking, despite the alliance of the Revolution and the reciprocal sympathies it provoked, did not go very deep. It was limited to a few symbolic gestures. A civic feast held in Boston early in 1793 to celebrate the French Revolution was a sort of gastronomic counterweight to that of the French when they ate turkey and cornmeal mush as a way of demonstrating solidarity with the Americans during their Revolution. A whole ox, identified by a large sign as being a "Peace Offering to Liberty and Equality," was borne in triumph through the streets to a convenient open place which, in honor of the occasion, had been renamed Liberty Square, and there consumed with the aid of 1,600 loaves of bread and two hogsheads of punch; Revolution in France was saluted with considerable gaiety in Boston.

The value of French example lay more in providing standards against which to measure American culinary achievements than in contributing French dishes or French techniques to an American cuisine which was already set in its ways, ways antithetical to those of France, exception made for Louisiana, already an outpost of French gastronomy. This may have accounted for the *pot-au-feu* for which Dolley Madison was famous, for she was familiar with the cooking of Louisiana and fond of it. What purports to be her recipe was given by Célestine Eustis in *Cooking in Old Créole Days,* published in New York in 1904, considerably after Dolley's time. Miss Eustis reported that "the *pot-au-feu* is served daily in French families," which gave the French little credit for variety, and explained that the recipe "was given to me by an old colored cook who was brought up in James Madison's family, and she said [it was] served on Mr. Madison's table when he entertained the distinguished guests of the day"—but certainly not by this particular old colored cook, unless she was close to a hundred years old when she hobnobbed with Célestine Eustis.

There was also a German influence which could have contributed to the quality of American food, but apparently did not, exerted not on the cooking of food but on its production. The first Germans settled Germantown, Pennsylvania, in 1683, the vanguard of an immigration which increased considerably after 1727, until at the time of the Revolution more than half the population of Pennsylvania was represented by its 100,000 Germans. The Germantown settlers were mostly weavers from Crefeld and those who followed mostly indentured servants, none of them professional farmers, but hard workers; and they learned fast. Their quickly acquired know-how was not passed on to their Anglo-Saxon neighbors, in the opinion of Benjamin Rush, "the Hippocrates of Pennsylvania," for when he praised their achievements in *An Account of the Manners of the German Inhabitants of Pennsylvania,* it was in a fashion which by implication criticized the Americans:

> A German farm may be distinguished from the farm of the other citizens of the state, by the superior size of their barns; the plain, but compact form of their houses; the height of their inclosures; the extent of their orchards; the fertility of their fields; the luxuriance of their meadows, and a general appearance of plenty and neatness in everything that belongs to them.

But Americans at least were by now beginning to show consciousness of the importance of agricultural studies, for the country's first agricultural society was founded in 1785. Before this date, despite nearly two centuries in the New World, the colonists had paid little serious attention to agricultural science. True, the first agricultural book of America had been published in 1760 in Boston, Jared Eliot's *Essays upon Field Husbandry in New England, as it is or may be Ordered,* but it had not much influenced farming practices. As for the first serious systematic work on botany, the *Plantae Coldenhamiae,* in which Cadwallader Colden, Lieutenant-Governor of New York, described the flora in the neighborhood of his farm, nobody showed any great interest in publishing it (it is true that paper was hard to come by in those days and fonts of type rare), and it has indeed not yet been printed in full. It was only after the Revolution that a Connecticut minister, Manasseh Cutler, produced the first work on the flora of New England. The first agricultural fair ever held in the United States was organized in 1811 by Elkanah Watson, a businessman who bred Merino sheep. He was thus a beneficiary of an illegal act committed by the first United States Minister to Spain, who, if he felt a need for exoneration, could have referred to the example of the first United States Minister to France, Thomas Jefferson, who did not permit the law to stand in his way either when it was a question of bringing new food to America. The Merino, a highly superior sheep (its very name is derived, like "mayor" and "major," from the Latin word for "better"), had been developed in Spain since the twelfth century or earlier, and it was not Spain's intention to let anyone else profit from her labor. The law against exporting Merinos was severe and strictly enforced, but we may suppose that it was by use of that most extensible instrument, the diplomatic courier, that Colonel David Humphreys, first United States Minister to Spain, smuggled one hundred of these sheep, three-quarters of them ewes, out of Spain into Portugal at the end of his official mission. He shipped them to his Connecticut farm, and reportedly got from $1,000 to $1,500 for those he sold. This would no doubt have earned him a Senatorial investigation nowadays, but it was considered a meritorious action at the time; one acquirer of Merinos was Thomas Jefferson. To the Merinos, another American envoy (the United States possessed very efficient diplomats in its early days), Robert Livingston, Minister to France, added Rambouillets (descended from Merinos themselves), obtained, legally this time, from the famous flock established personally by Louis XVI. (Livingston published an *Essay on Sheep* in 1809.)

While American men were developing agriculture in a country which for the first time could market its produce for its own profit, an American woman had, in her fashion, published a Declaration of Independence from English culinary tutelage. Even after the Revolution, as before it, American women had remained tributary to the English for their cookbooks. The most ambitious to date, *The New Art of Cookery* by Richard Briggs, published in Philadelphia in 1792, was a reprint of an English book, and though American rivals would shortly start appearing, its 557 pages of recipes would not be equaled for another half-century. But in 1796 the first genuinely American cookbook appeared: *American Cookery, or the Art of Dressing Viands, Fish, Poultry, and Vegetables, and the Best Modes of Making Pastes, Puffs, Pies, Tarts, Puddings, Custards and Preserves, and All Kinds of Cakes, from the Imperial Plumb to Plain Cake. Adapted to this Country and All Grades of Life. By Amelia Simmons: An American Orphan.* The stop of orphanhood was pulled out to its fullest extent. "It must ever remain a check upon the poor solitary orphan," she wrote pathetically in her preface, "that while those females who have parents, or brothers, or riches, to defend their indiscretions, that the orphan must depend upon *character.*" Miss Simmons' character was quickly exhausted; it ran only to forty-six pages, vest-pocket size—the text was hardly longer than the title. But it was the first to contain such recipes as "cramberry sauce," "pompkin pie," pickled watermelon rind (then referred to indecisively as "American citron"), Indian pudding, slapjack and johnnycake, this last usually explained as a corruption of "journey cake," since this cornmeal concoction was supposed to be convenient for travelers to carry on trips through territories ill provided with feeding facilities. Perhaps so, though cornmeal breads are crumbly. But there is another less well-known explanation for this name, which gives credit to the Indians who taught the whites how to handle cornmeal: it is that the original name of johnnycake was "Shawnee cake."

Amelia Simmons' work quickly ran through four editions, picking up new recipes in the process, and was so successful that it was gratified by the sincerest form of flattery in 1808, when it was plagiarized by *The New-England Cookery* of Lucy Emerson of Montpelier, who, not content with pirating most of Amelia Simmons' recipes, also described herself as an "American Orphan," a status which must have been a guarantee of skill with the skillet, if not of gastronomic broadmindedness: "Gar-licks," wrote Miss Emerson, "though used by the French, are better adapted to medicine than cookery." So much for French influence.

It is possible that the American editors of still another English cookbook, Mrs. Rundell's *New System of Domestic Cookery,* reprinted in the United States in 1807, were unjustifiably severe when they wrote of American housewives, "There was a time when ladies knew nothing *beyond* their own family concerns; but in the present day there are many who know nothing *about* them." American women were at least sufficiently interested to buy this book and several others, including another autochthonous product, the *Universal Receipt Book or Complete Family Director,* published in 1814 by "a society of gentlemen of New York." This one followed a formula which would hold good throughout the century of combining food recipes with medical lore and useful (more or less) household information of all sorts: its first entry told how to make boloney, its second was a cure for jaundice, and its third gave directions for clarifying and preserving butter. Similarly far-ranging counsel was provided by a number of books which remained anonymous: "Home advice, with whispers to epicures," and another described as "By a Lady, with notes for dyspeptics." One nineteenth-century guide and cookbook was daring enough to explain how to tell male canaries from females (the males have larger feet), though presumably not for culinary purposes (however, a difference in flavor between birds of different sexes seemed to be indicated by one early recipe which called for "the brains of four cocke sparrows").

All of these cookbooks took it for granted that everyone was plentifully provided with food, and at this period perhaps everyone was. Grocery orders were made out in impressive quantities; Abigail Adams, the wife of John Adams, placed one in the summer of 1792, which was before her husband had become President, for brown sugar and oats—a barrel of the first, one hundred bushels of the second. City folk bought food in quantity partly because they stocked up on each item in its season for preserving and partly because roads were bad and trips into the surrounding countryside hazardous; whenever such a sortie had to be made, purchasers loaded up with all the food they could carry, to stave off for as long as possible the evil day when they would have to sally forth again. As for the farmers, they produced everything they needed themselves, buying almost nothing. A country store fifty miles from Boston, whose 1801 cashbook has survived for our information, reveals that the only foods its customers purchased were molasses, sugar, coffee, tea, chocolate, salt and biscuits: they spent more on tobacco, rum, brandy and other alcoholic drinks. Both food and drink were often paid for in farm produce—veal, butter, cheese. Every farm had its own cheese press, which often stood in a separate outbuilding, the buttery; but professional cheese making was getting under way, too, as Thomas Jefferson discovered when he was inaugurated as President in 1801. Supporters in Cheshire, Massachusetts, sent him a present of what was described as the largest cheese ever made, and probably it was: it weighed 1,600 pounds and was transported to Washington by sledge, taking three weeks to get there.

Another product—not to say another institution—got under way after, or indeed, in a way, because of, the American Revolution: moonshine whiskey. Up to the time of the Revolution, the colonies were not much given to whiskey drinking. The well-to-do preferred champagne, sherry and Madeira, the others drank rum, beer (even small children drank beer until about 1825 because the water was not trustworthy), or, above all, cider, which was cheap—three shillings a barrel in the late seventeenth and early eighteenth centuries—(including perry and peachy, made, of course, from pear or peach juice instead of apple), either sweet or hard. It would become hard very quickly if left to its own devices; when anyone took the trouble of distillation, the result was applejack, a heady brew; but it was hardly necessary to resort to it for a kick: hard cider all by itself was sufficiently authoritative and New Englanders who really wanted to go the limit mixed their rum with it, producing a beverage so redoubtable that it was called "stonewall."

Legally made whiskey, or at least legally made bourbon (that is, corn whiskey), has even boasted that it was a product of the Revolution, if you accept the claim made by James E. Pepper of Kentucky, emblazoned on the bottles he sent to market, that it was "Born with the Republic"; its brand name, accordingly, was "Old 1776." Actually his distillery, installed in a log cabin, did not begin operating until 1780, and he was far from being the first American maker of whiskey. Among those who preceded him were George Washington and Thomas Jefferson, both of whom had distilleries on their estates to make rye whiskey. They were not pioneers either. Colonists fortunate enough to own gristmills had been making whiskey for themselves or for sale to the neighbors since the seventeenth century. The first whiskey distillers in America were anonymous settlers from Ireland and Scotland who concentrated at first in western Pennsylvania and Maryland, and thereafter worked their way gradually down through Virginia into the southern mountains.

The first whiskey was rye; it was made from the grain the newcomers from the British Isles were used to handling. Then they tried mixing corn (since it was much cheaper) with the rye and approved of the result. The next step was to use corn alone, which produced a lighter and sweeter whiskey. Bourbon had been born. Ignoring James E. Pepper, annalists name Evan

Williams as the first to open a distillery in Kentucky, in 1783, and as the first to start making it in Bourbon County itself, the Reverend Elijah Craig, in 1789.

This was not moonshine, a creature of the law, for whiskey becomes moonshine only when it is made illegally and the tax levied on it has not been paid at this stage of its production; its very name indicates that it is liquor brewed surreptitiously at night, when smoke rising from stills cannot easily be spotted by the "revenooers."

The art of making corn whiskey was learned in America, to a considerable extent, by accident. Corn was made into whiskey in mountainous regions of Pennsylvania and the South in the first place not so much because of any overpowering desire for this particular type of strong drink, but because the terrain provided little flat land suitable for growing other grains. In the second place, corn was easier to keep and to transport out of the mountains in liquid form than in solid. As Albert Gallatin, the Swiss-born Secretary of the Treasury in Jefferson's cabinet, put it:

> We have neither means of bringing the produce of our lands to sale either in grain or meal. We are therefore distillers through necessity, not choice, that we may comprehend the greatest value in the smallest size and weight.

A second accident was the discovery of the value of aging. The whiskey makers barreled their product and carted it down to the tributaries of the Mississsippi to be shipped to the market of New Orleans. It had to wait for the spring rise of the rivers. It was discovered that the whiskey which waited longest tasted best at its destination.

There was no moonshine in the United States before 1791, for until that date whiskey making was not taxed; *all* whiskey was legal. But the young Republic was short of money. George Washington's Secretary of the Treasury, Alexander Hamilton, hit upon the idea of taxing, among others, distillers of whiskey.

The distiller reacted to the new tax with ferocity, and Congress quickly modified the law to eliminate some of its more obnoxious features, such as the snooping and the invasion of private premises that it had permitted. However, revolt still smoldered. Organized refusal to pay the impost led to what was the first instance in American history of invocation of the Constitutional provision which permitted the national government to call up state militias to enforce Federal laws. Thus, in 1794, the country was faced with the Whiskey Rebellion, a slightly comic episode which the government may be credited with having won, since the movement was put down and two of its ringleaders convicted—of treason! Washington sapiently pardoned them. Tempest in a two-ounce glass though it may have seemed, the Whiskey Rebellion caused the resignation of Alexander Hamilton.

Whiskey was also tangentially involved in other difficulties in 1808, when the Shawnee warrior chief Tecumseh and his twin brother, Tenskwatama, "The Prophet," a half-blind medicine man, led a revolt because the whites were encroaching on their territory. Some Indians had signed treaties alienating their lands, and also, generously, the lands of others, while under the influence of liquor provided by the buyers, so a boycott of rum and whiskey was proclaimed by the Indians. The Indians lost, of course, but their movement helped foster the bad blood between Britain and the United States which would eventually bring on the replay of the Revolution constituted by the War of 1812. Many Americans believed that the British had financed Tecumseh. This was almost certainly untrue, but the British Governor General of Canada was less than tactful when he provided refuge for Tecumseh and his warriors, causing Henry Clay to exclaim: "The militia of Kentucky are alone competent to place Montreal and Upper Canada at [our] feet." It would be exaggerating to attribute this agitation to the account of whiskey alone, but it did play its not inconsiderable part.

It was during Jefferson's presidency that an event occurred which was to have tremendous effects on American history in general and might have been expected to exercise a considerable effect also on shaping the American cuisine by adding a new element to its gastronomy. This was the Louisiana Purchase of 1803, which was slipped over on the country while nobody was looking by James Monroe, as envoy extraordinary to Paris, and Robert H. Livingston, United States Minister to France, to the vehemently expressed disapproval of many American politicians when they learned about it. (The Creoles did not like the idea either.) Fisher Ames, a prominent member of the ultra-Federalist "Essex junto" of New England, saw dire peril in diluting the pure principles of Anglo-Saxondom by taking in "the Gallo-Hispano-Indian *omnium gatherum* of savages and adventurers"; they might indeed have been able to impart a new and certainly not uninteresting direction to the American cuisine, but cooking had already become too firmly fixed in the Anglo-Saxon pattern to be budged, so the Creole gastronomy of Louisiana remains a local phenomenon.

In addition to the Louisiana Purchase, Jefferson's first term was marked by another momentous event, also part of the picture of the westward expansion of the United States and also destined to have more effect in other fields than in that of gastronomy. Jefferson, always curious himself about the local foods wherever he went, no doubt had in mind the possibility that some new aliments might be discovered when he gave his minutely detailed instructions to Captain Meriwether Lewis, an officer who had served in the militia which put an end to the Whiskey Rebellion, and a neighbor whom he had chosen (because of his mother's hams, perhaps?) to head what we know today as the Lewis and Clark Expedition. Among the many items on which Jefferson asked Lewis to report was the plant and animal life of the regions to which his party was presumed to be the first white visitors (but when Lewis found

Pacific Northwest Indians calling one another "son-of-a-pitch," he suspected that someone had been there before him); in preparation for the trip, Lewis went to Philadelphia for instruction in botany and zoology.

The expedition did not find much in the way of tempting new foods, though it did report on the amazing abundance of salmon in the Columbia River. The explorers reached it shortly after spawning season, and had to force their boats through thick swarms of floating salmon which had spawned and died. "The number of dead salmon on the Shores & floating in the river is incredible to say," Clark wrote in his journal, "and at this season [the Indians] have only to collect the fish Split them open and dry them on their Scaffolds." Otherwise the food lore collected by the party was less useful to the public than as a guide for future pioneers on what foods to take with them and what to leave behind, what to eat on the spot and what to avoid.

They started out in 1804 in a fifty-five-foot keel boat with sail and oars, plus two pirogues, loaded down with fifty kegs of pork (3,705 pounds), 3,400 pounds of flour, 2,000 pounds of "parchmeal" (corn), 750 pounds of salt, 600 pounds of "Grees" (lard?), and 560 pounds of hardtack—to nourish thirty-two soldiers, ten civilians, three interpreters, one slave (Lieutenant Clark's personal servant, York) and Lewis's dog Scannon; almost all were Virginians except Scannon, who was a Newfoundland. They were also all described as "good hunters, stout, healthy, unmarried young men, accustomed to the woods"; Clark, thirty-three when the group was organized for training the year before the actual departure, was the oldest; Lewis was twenty-nine. Their hardiness was proved by the fact that despite Indians, grizzly bears, rattlesnakes, miscellaneous hardships, and at times, even with their impressive stock of supplies, near-starvation, only one man died during their two and a half years in the wilderness, and he from a ruptured appendix. Lewis himself came close to being a second casualty, for one of his men, good hunter or not, was apparently afflicted both with bad eyesight and bad marksmanship. The first caused him, on a hunting foray, to mistake Lewis for an elk, and the second fortunately limited his error to shooting his captain only in the thigh. Lewis recovered. Hunting parties were frequent, for the main food of what had seemed at its departure a well-provisioned party turned out to be game. It was relieved from time to time by fish, and an occasional Indian dog. (Scannon was spared.)

There were times when the expedition was reduced to grubbing for roots, permitting the explorers to assess some vegetables until then eaten only by Indians. They were grateful to find the familiar Jerusalem artichoke and also wild sweet potatoes, from which they made "yellow loafbread." But the camas root, which the Indians ate with impunity, brought on violent attacks of dysentery. Perhaps they did not know how to prepare it. They did discover that another Indian food, the bitterroot, which at first trial seemed aptly named, ceased to be bitter when peeled. They had no difficulties with the cowas, or Indian biscuit root, which the local Indians ate as a vegetable, or converted into flour; the explorers compared its taste to that of celery. The breadroot, or prairie apple, a favorite food of the Sioux, also found favor with them. The most appreciated was the wapatoo, the chief locally obtainable food, which tided them over the winter of 1805–1806. "They are never out of season," Lewis reported. "They are nearly equal in flavor to the Irish potato and afford a very good substitute for bread."

The expedition dispelled one hardy mirage that had hung on for three hundred years. It disproved a theory that there might be a river mighty enough to connect the headwaters of the Missouri with the Pacific, despite the inconvenient presence of the Rocky Mountains. The dream of a Northwest Passage was over.

If the approval of all things French born of the Revolutionary alliance failed to convert the American public as a whole to adoption of one of France's most noted achievements, her cooking, it did have its effect at the highest level: the first four Presidents of the United States all appreciated the French cuisine and did their best to have it served on their own tables. Jefferson was even attacked for it, by Patrick Henry, who, hotheaded as always, lashed out at him for what Henry considered an effete taste for French cooking which had led him to "abjure his native victuals."

This was by no means the only demonstration in American history of the curious fact that in America it is politically disadvantageous to be known as a gourmet, as though there were something unmanly in being discriminating about, or even attentive to, what one eats. Gastronomic know-nothingism constitutes a special case of that anti-intellectualism which crops up so disconcertingly often in the United States, an extension of the yokel's distrust of anyone better educated, better mannered, or even merely cleaner than himself. This attitude was never more openly manifested than in the "log cabin and hard cider" presidential campaign of 1840, when the candidates were Democrat Martin Van Buren, up for reelection, and Whig William Henry Harrison, whose chief claim to fame was that it was he who had defeated Tecumseh and The Prophet on the Tippecanoe River. It seemed at times that the chief issue in the campaign was which candidate ate worse. In the battle for this honor, the tables were turned in bewildering fashion. It was Little Van, born in humble circumstances, one of the five children of a small farmer and tavern keeper, who was represented as the spoiled child of luxury, and Harrison, scion of the Virginia aristocracy, who was touted as the plain man of the people, proof against the demoralizing temptations of the table. As one of the poetic explosions of the campaign put it:

No ruffled shirt, no silken hose,
No airs does Tip display;

But like "the pith of worth" he goes
In homespun "hodden-grey."

Upon his board there ne'er appeared
The costly "sparkling wine,"
But plain hard cider such as cheered
In days of old lang syne.

One must admit that the Democrats did it to themselves. A no doubt badly inspired Democratic journalist of Baltimore started it all with a sneering article in which he expressed the opinion that if Harrison were offered a pension of $2,000 and a barrel of hard cider, he would prefer to retire to a log cabin with the cider than to enter the White House. The Whigs seized upon this opportunity with whoops of joy (a parallel close to us is the use Adlai Stevenson's supporters made of the photograph showing a hole in the sole of his shoe). As Samuel Eliot Morison reported:

> There were log-cabin badges and log-cabin songs, a *Log Cabin* newspaper and log-cabin clubs, big log cabins where the thirsty were regaled with hard cider that jealous Democrats alleged to be stiffened with whiskey; little log cabins borne on floats in procession, with latchstring out, cider barrel by the door, coonskin nailed up beside, and real smoke coming out of the chimney, while lusty voices bawled:
>
> Let Van from his coolers of silver drink wine,
> And lounge on his cushioned settee;
> Our man on his buckeye bench can recline,
> Content with hard cider is he.
> Then a shout from each freeman—a shout from each State,
> To the plain, honest husbandman true,
> And this be our motto—the motto of Fate—
> "Hurrah for Old Tippecanoe!"
>
> Maine lumberjacks, Buckeye farmers, and Cajuns in the Bayou country were shocked to learn that under Little Van the White House had become a palace "as splendid as that of the Caesars"; that the President doused his whiskers with French *eau de cologne* [and] slept in a Louis XV bedstead.

A he-man character was bestowed on Harrison by the assertion that he lived on "raw beef without salt," which may have startled him. Meanwhile Van Buren, in contrast, was attacked for reveling in the dangerously sybaritic luxuries of "strawberries, raspberries, celery and cauliflower." Even more devastatingly he was depicted as eating *pâté de foie gras* (French!) "from a silver plate," and *soupe à la reine* (French!) with, horror of horrors!, "a gold spoon." *Soupe à la reine* is not an extravagantly luxurious dish, basically chicken consommé, to which we have all grown accustomed, and even resigned, at its almost ineluctable appearance at the start of every institutional or charitable lunch or dinner; but Queen's Soup sounded dishonorably regal enough for political purposes.

The Whigs were betting that there were more hicks than sophisticates among the voters, and they seem to have been right. Van Buren lost the election; as it was very close—a few thousand votes could have reversed the result—we may be permitted to suggest that it was his shameless addiction to the reprehensible cauliflower that evicted him from the White House. Harrison was not to occupy it very long. He died a month after he assumed the Presidency. There is no reason for assuming that his demise was the result of imbibing unaccustomed quantities of electoral cider. But President Taylor did go to excessive limits in demonstrating the incompatibility of politics and gastronomy, or perhaps gluttony would be a better word, in America; he cut his term short by succumbing to a surfeit of cucumbers and cold milk after hardly more than a year in office, underlining subtlely the national overtones of this act by falling fatally ill at the ceremonies of July 4, 1850.

" 'Democratic' enthusiasm . . . made a virtue of crude and tasteless food," Daniel Boorstin commented, "and obsession with the delights of the palate was considered a symptom of Old World decadence." Politicians thereafter were careful to manifest disdain for the demoralizing subtleties of the table. The humblest and most down-to-earth foods alone were evoked in electoral periods. Political groups described themselves as "chowder and marching clubs," voters were invited to free feasts of only the most irreproachable nature, clambakes, barbecues and picnics at which the cheer was limited to that which could be held in the hand and eaten standing. (The modern $500-a-plate fund raising dinner is a phenomenon of financing, not of gastronomy.) In our own time, a Southern Senator was able to make political capital out of an attack on a State Department staffed by men accustomed to wearing striped pants and eating "fish aigs." What this defender of egalitarianism had in mind was caviar, which is, indisputably, fish eggs—like shad roe.

Jefferson may have acquired the eating habits for which Patrick Henry excoriated him during his stay in Europe as the first United States Minister to France; but he was in any case a pushover for the seductiveness of food. John Adams was less disposed to succumb to such seductions, but a mission to France modified his gastronomic attitude also. George Washington had never been exposed to French influence, unless Lafayette converted him, nor did gastronomy play in his life anything like as important a role as in Jefferson's. Nevertheless he employed a French steward, who was presumably responsible for the dinner Washington gave in New York in 1789, which Pennsylvania Senator William Maclay described as the finest he had ever attended; unfortunately his description of it is rather sketchy:

> First was the soup; fish roasted and boiled; meats, gammon, fowls, etc. This was the dinner. The middle of the table was garnished in the usual tasty way, with small images, flowers (artificial), etc.; then iced creams, jellies, etc.; then water-melons, musk-melons, apples, peaches, nuts.

However, the quality of Washington's food did not impress all visitors. A somewhat malicious woman guest of the Washingtons told how "she discovered that a fine-looking trifle was made with unusually rancid cream [how rancid was usual?] and whispered the news to the president, who immediately changed his plate. But . . . Mrs. Washington ate a whole heap of it."

The splendors of a presidential table should not have overwhelmed a Pennsylvania Senator; Philadelphia was accustomed to lavish eating. When John Adams, coming from a comparatively rural environment in Massachusetts (but he practiced law in Boston!), discovered the wealth of frivolities which ended the Philadelphian dinner already mentioned above ("jellies and trifles, fruits and nuts, syllabubbs and sweetmeats"), he found such feasts not only "elegant" (approvingly?), "mighty" (noncommittally?) but also "sinful" (reprehensibly, no doubt about it). However, after he had been sent to France in 1778 as a member of the American Commission he succumbed to sin and spoke testily of American criticism of French cooking as "a relic of colonial prejudice [which] belonged to the past." We may suppose that this attitude was reflected in the quality of the food served at the White House under the second American President, but it was apparently not remarkable enough one way or the other to have inspired much comment.

It was with the third President that gastronomy rolled over the White House like a wave. Thomas Jefferson's reputation as a gourmet had already been made long before he became President; and it may be that the most resented blow the British dealt him during the Revolution was the one which hit him, so to speak, in the breadbasket, when, finding themselves unable to deprive him of life or liberty, they did what they could to reduce his pursuit of happiness by destroying his cherished stores of food, including the precious contents of his wine cellar. This happened in February, 1781, when Jefferson was governor of Virginia.

It was during his period as governor that Jefferson was involved in an episode which does not show him in a particularly creditable light, but which is recounted in *Jefferson at Monticello,* edited by James A. Bear, Jr., on the authority of Jefferson's overseer, Edmund Bacon. Jefferson was a better farmer than businessman, nearly always hard up for money, partly as a result of his virtues—limitless hospitality, and a generosity of which practiced panhandlers often took advantage; Bacon told how, when frost had destroyed the corn crop at Monticello, he had to buy the grain at ruinous prices and cart it from a considerable distance to the estate:

> I could hardly get it hauled as fast as [Mr. Jefferson] would give it away [to poor neighbors also out of corn who came to him for help]. I went to Mr. Jefferson and told him that it would never do; we could not give ten dollars a barrel for corn, and haul it thirty miles, and give it away after that fashion. He said, "What can I do? These people tell me they have no corn, and it will not do to let them suffer."

It was during one of his hard-up periods that Jefferson sent agents to intercept all the droves of hogs on the way to Richmond and buy them all. Having cornered the market on pigs, he resold them to the capital's butchers at the price his monopoly enabled him to demand. They had to buy from him, but they expressed their opinion of the transaction by draping hog entrails over his fence all the way around his house; and for some time afterwards they never referred to him except as "the Hog Governor."

When Jefferson was sent to France as United States Minister in 1784, he took advantage of the opportunity to travel as widely as possible in Europe, and interested himself everywhere in food. He encountered waffles in Holland and brought back a waffle iron. He had a spaghetti-making machine delivered to him from Italy, superfluously perhaps, since one of his neighbors, Philip Mazzei, was an Italian grocer. Less superfluous was his deliberate violation of Italian law, when he smuggled two bags of rice out of the country in 1787, despite the fact that rice had already been brought to South Carolina and planted there in 1680. The rice Jefferson acquired was a highly superior strain developed in Piedmont, which was why the Italian government had enacted stringent measures against its export; it had hoped to maintain a monopoly.

After he returned from France, he bombarded American envoys abroad with requests for information on foods, or samples of them, first as Secretary of State in Washington's cabinet, and later as President. He had made a friend of the superintendent of the Jardin des Plantes, the botanical garden of Paris, while he was in France, and for twenty-three years after his return he received packets of seeds from him every year; besides planting them himself, he distributed them to private and public gardens throughout the United States, to assure the dissemination of possibly useful new food plants. He made himself a missionary for better food in the animal kingdom as well. Whenever he acquired good stock, he would advertise the fact, so that persons who wanted to improve their breeds could send him females to be covered by his males, on a basis of sharing the offspring. Thus his sheep (he had Merinos and broad-tailed Tripoline Barbary sheep, and no doubt others as well) and his hogs accounted for the establishment of many other fine flocks and herds besides his own.

The meticulous detail which characterized Jefferson's management of his estate was evident in the memoranda he prepared for Bacon when he left for Washington. They gave minute directions for finishing a watermill that was being built; for fencing; for planting ("a part of the field is to be planted in Quarantine corn, which will be found in a tin canister in my closet. This corn is to be in drills 5 feet apart, and the stalks 18 inches asunder in the drills. The rest of the ground is to be sown in oats, and red clover sowed on the oats. All the ploughing is to be done horizontally"); for wood cutting; for leveling the garden; for parceling out the various tasks among the workers, whom Jefferson named individually; for work in the nailery; for obtaining fish; for sharing out supplies to superintendents and laborers; for maintaining the hedges; for delivering produce to market; for filling in gullies; for handling the orchards ("the orchard below the garden must be entirely cultivated . . . a part in Davenport pea, which you will find in a canister in my closet; a part with Irish potatoes, and the rest with cow-pea, of which there is a patch at Mr. Freeman's, to save which, great attention must be paid, as they are the last in the neighborhood"); for building a house; and for assuring the year's supply of whiskey—thirty gallons. Even as President, when one might think Jefferson had too little time to pay attention to farming, he kept a steady stream of instructions flowing to Monticello: to build a dam, to make a wagon road, to weed, to fetch three mules he had bought, to cover the fig trees against approaching cold weather.

Jefferson's period as President was a merry one. The food served at the White House was impeccable, and it was of French inspiration. Jefferson was an unflagging host, who detested eating alone. "Man was destined for society," he maintained, and he demonstrated what he meant at Monticello, where it was a commonplace to make up beds for twenty guests or more; sometimes there were fifty. The culinary artistry of France had captivated him ever since the time when he had served as American Minister to the court of Louis XVI, and when he moved into the White House he installed there a French chef, Julien Lemaire, and a French *maître d'hôtel;* he also brought with him from Monticello two of his servants, Eda and Fanny, so that they could learn French cooking techniques in the kitchen of the White House; they became his cooks when he left office and returned to Monticello.

Jefferson's almost daily guests were rapturous about the quality of the food served at the presidential mansion, but there was a period when meals there lacked a certain decorum. Jefferson's concept of democracy was more militant than practical, and he was impatient with protocol. His invitations were sent out, not in the form his predecessors had used, in the name of "the President of the United States," but simply in that of "Mr. Jefferson." He boggled at seating in protocolary order the persons he had invited in this homespun fashion, and therefore no seating plans were provided for his dinners, no matter how many persons were present. The result was that every meal began with an unseemly scramble for what were considered to be the best places, especially by the women. If there had been a First Lady, she would undoubtedly have prevented these free-for-alls from the beginning, but Jefferson was a widower. It took a little time for him to surrender to the inevitable and allow protocol to move back in again. Order was thus restored, which was more in keeping with the sumptuousness which caused Jefferson to spend more than his salary on food, wine and service. He managed to run up a bill of $2,800 for wine alone in a single year, a difficult feat in those days; and after his retirement from political life he nearly ate himself out of house and home at Monticello, leaving when he died debts amounting to $40,000, a staggering sum in 1826.

James Madison seemed likely to prove a less promising President so far as feeding went; the only gastronomic item recorded concerning him before his presidency was a trifle ominous. He had neglected in 1777 to treat the voters to the customary rum and punch which rewarded their fidelity, and as a result had not been re-elected to the Virginia legislature. But there was his wife to reckon with, and because of her, Madison-sponsored French influence reigned at the White House even before Madison himself entered it. When the disorder of Jefferson's meals forced him to give thought to their management, he invited Dolley Madison, whose husband was then his Secretary of State, to act as hostess at the executive mansion. She introduced there, among other French dishes, that homely favorite of hers, *pot-au-feu.* She served it at the State Department, too, which caused the British Minister's wife to remark sniffishly of a dinner Dolley gave there that it was "more like a harvest home supper than the entertainment of the Secretary of State." Dolley put her in her place by retorting, "The profusion of my table . . . arises from the happy circumstances of abundance and prosperity in our country," a nasty dig at a time when the Bank of England had been obliged to suspend cash payments, when consols had fallen to their lowest ebb, when the sailors of His Majesty's Navy were mutinying for more pay and when England was having even more trouble than usual with Ireland.

But the British had the last word. Hardly had Dolley finished furnishing and decorating the White House than they burned it down, on August 24, 1814. About all she saved from the flames—personally, the story goes—was a Gilbert Stuart portrait of George Washington, the very one which, of all the many paintings Stuart did of his eminent subject, is the most reproduced today, for it alone has captured that expression of stern fixed devotion to duty which accords so perfectly with our idea of the inflexible integrity of the First President; it was the result of a new set of badly fitting false teeth which Washington put in while posing, causing him so much discomfort that he could not relax the muscles of his face.

XIII

As Others See Us

THE WAR OF 1812 confirmed what the American Revolution had asserted, "that these United Colonies are, and of Right ought to be, FREE AND INDEPENDENT STATES." There could no longer be any doubt about it; the United States existed and would continue to exist. Curiosity brought more and more European visitors to the infant Republic to gape at it in its cradle and among the things that interested them was how the fledgling ate. Most of them were more impressed by the quantity of American food than by its quality.

The man who should have been best qualified to assess American eating, Brillat-Savarin (who, a refugee from the Terror, preceded this wave, since he lived in the United States from 1794 to 1797), said little about it. He did record that he had been pleased by a dinner of mutton, vegetables and good cider at a Connecticut farmhouse—not exactly the sort of meal one would have expected to stick in the memory of the author of the *Physiologie du Goût*. But he was not inclined to criticize America and Americans; "I think everything they do is good," he once wrote. Besides, he was not yet a practicing gastronome. It may well be true that he taught Americans to make fondues, but this was not his way of supporting himself; he gave French lessons and played the violin in the orchestra of a New York theater in John Street.

In 1795, Constantin François de Chasseboeuf, Count of Volney, had also visited the United States, about which he was less enthusiastic than Brillat-Savarin, perhaps because he was accused in 1797 of being a French spy and had to beat a retreat to France the following year. In his *View of the Soil and Climate of the United States of America,* published in London in 1804, he expressed his astonishment at the unrefined solidity of American eating:

> In the morning at breakfast they deluge their stomach with a quart of hot water, impregnated with tea, or so slightly with coffee that it is more colored water; and they swallow, almost without chewing, hot bread, half baked, toast soaked in butter, cheese of the fattest kind, slices of salt or hung beef, ham, etc., all of which is nearly insoluble. At dinner they have boiled pastes under the name of puddings, and their sauces, even for roast beef, are melted butter; their turnips and potatoes swim in hog's lard, butter, or fat; under the name of pie or pumpkin, their pastry is nothing but a greasy paste, never sufficiently baked. To digest these viscous substances they take tea almost instantly after dinner, making it so strong that it is absolutely bitter to the taste, in which state it affects the nerves so powerfully that even the English find it brings on a more obstinate restlessness than coffee. Supper again introduces salt meats or oysters. As Chastellux [François Jean Marquis de Chastellux, in his *Travels in North America*] says, the whole day passes in heaping indigestions on one another; and to give tone to the poor, relaxed and wearied stomach, they drink Madeira, rum, French brandy, gin, or malt spirits, which complete the ruin of the nervous system.

A few years later it was the turn of Frances Trollope, mother of the novelist, who was perhaps not strictly objective in her feelings about America, since she had gone to Cincinnati with the intention of improving her depleted fortunes by operating a fancy-goods shop and had returned to England disappointed three years later, having failed to make a go of it. Her *Domestic Manners of the Americans,* published in London in 1832, was caustic and derogatory; food was among the things she had disliked. At one point she unbent to the extent of saying that a mixture of one part of cornmeal to two of wheat flour had made "by far the best bread" she had ever tasted, but otherwise she had nothing good to say about corn. It was eaten in many forms, she reported, "all bad," whether it was green, as in hominy, or in the many different cakes she had sampled.

From 1834 to 1836, the United States was exposed to the probing of Mrs. Harriet Martineau, a formidable figure who swept across the countryside catechizing the provincials with the aid of an enormous ear trumpet (she had been deaf since early childhood). She is stigmatized in American reference books for her "unfavorable critiques of America," yet she wrote of Americans that their "sweet temper diffused like sunshine over the land," and she praised "the practice of forbearance requisite in a republic"; nor was she always ungracious about the cooking, in her *Society in America* (1837) and *Retrospect of Western Travel* (1838). She breakfasted on "excellent bread, potatoes, hung beef, eggs and strong tea" at Stockbridge, Massachusetts. In Gloucester she tasted fish chowder for the first time and found it good. Sweet Springs, Tennessee, offered her stewed venison, ham, hominy and fruit pies. In Kentucky she found tender meat, fresh vegetables and champagne! Whatever it was she drank under that name, it could hardly have been worse than the New Jersey "champagne" of that period, made of turnip juice, brandy and honey, which Captain Marryat was to sample later and describe as not half bad. She was bowled over by what was considered a suitable breakfast menu at Montgomery, Alabama—cornbread, buckwheat cakes, broiled chicken, bacon and eggs, hominy, fresh and pickled fish, and beefsteak. In the South, she wrote, certainly with some exaggeration, that corn was more valuable than gold: "A man who has corn may have everything. He can sow his land with it; and, for the rest, everything eats corn, from slave to chick."

She found milk plentiful in the South only in Kentucky; in the Deep South it was "a great rarity." It was probably hard to keep. Sour food was not unusual and was apparently accepted as in the normal order of things. Mrs. Martineau told of being given a snack at a farmhouse in the interior of Virginia where all the food was sour—bread, coffee and butter. Her local driver stuffed himself with it and seemed to find it good enough. Mrs. Martineau asked him how he was able to down it with such good appetite and he answered somewhat beside the point that the road between this settlement and the coast had been opened only recently and its inhabitants were unaccustomed to food of good quality: "They have probably no idea that there is better food than they set before us."

Being English, Mrs. Martineau wanted mutton, but found it elusive. She was first told that Americans didn't like it, but in the South this statement was contradicted. "So far from mutton being despised, as we have been told," she noted, "it was much desired but not to be had." Her quest was not quite rewarded in Tennessee. "The dish from which I ate," she wrote of this occasion, "was, according to some, mutton; to others, pork. My own idea is that it was dog."

It was in 1837 that Captain Frederick Marryat visited the United States, to write two years later a "generally negative" account of the United States in *A Diary in America;* he was kinder to the country's food than to its institutions. "Miss Martineau does indeed say that she never ate good beef during the whole time she was in the country," he wrote, but disagreed: "The meat in America is equal to the best in England." He was less enthusiastic about the seafood:

> Oysters are very plentiful, very large, and, to an English palate, rather insipid. As the Americans assert that the English and French oysters taste of copper, and that therefore they cannot eat them, I presume they do, and that's the reason why we do not like American oysters, copper being better than no flavor at all . . .
>
> Fish is well supplied. They have the sheep's head shad and one or two others, which we have not. Their salmon is not equal to ours, and they have no turbot.

Marryat noted that in New York cooks who wanted fresh cream and butter could "send to the country" for them, which did not represent much of a journey since two-thirds of the island of Manhattan was still farmland. Participating in a Fourth of July celebration in New York Marryat marveled at the quantities of food in the stands set up along Broadway—oysters and clams, boiled hams, the exotic pineapple, pies and puddings, and of course all kinds of candy for America's already well developed sweet tooth. "What was most remarkable," he wrote, "Broadway being three miles long, and the booths lining each side of it, in every booth there was a roast pig, large or small, as the centre attraction. Six miles of roast pig! and that in New York city alone; and roast pig in every other city, town, hamlet, and village in the Union."

The Duke of Liancourt expressed his surprise that in the United States even the poor could afford salt meat for breakfast, salt meat or salt fish for dinner and more salt meat for supper. But salt meat three times a day was normal, as Henry Adams pointed out:

> Indian corn was the national crop, and Indian corn was eaten three times a day in another form as salt pork. The rich alone could afford fresh meat. Ice-chests were hardly known. In the country fresh meat could not regularly be got, except in the shape of poultry or game; but the hog cost nothing to keep, and very little to kill and preserve. Thus the ordinary rural American was brought up on salt pork and Indian corn, or rye; and the effect of this diet showed itself in dyspepsia.

Thomas Ashe, who had encountered in Kentucky the same phenomenon of three meals of salt meat a day, expressed the opinion in *Travels in America in 1806* that Americans even preferred it to fresh meat, believing the latter to be "unwholesome"—which may very well have been true, given the hygienic background of the times. Indeed, the aversion to fresh meat persisted even after it was readily obtainable, if an anecdote recounted in the July, 1887, number of *Century Magazine* is typical. It reported that a Maine timber operator supplied his lumberjacks with fresh meat in the belief that this would make them happy; instead they downed tools. "Your fresh meat, that's too fancy," their spokesman complained, "and hain't got strength into it." Salt meat was returned to the menu and the men went back to work.

The most illustrious foreign visitor to the United States before the Civil War—Charles Dickens, whose first trip to America occurred in 1842, when he was thirty—has been represented as anti-American, like Mrs. Martineau, and it has been suggested that he was prejudiced against the United States even before he landed because its copyright laws permitted publishers to pirate his books. Richard Osborn Cummings was apparently in agreement with the widespread opinion that *Martin Chuzzlewit* was in essence a libel on Americans when he wrote in *The American and His Food:*

> Dickens made Martin Chuzzlewit's journey from New York to the western development of "Eden" a travelogue of ill-health. Leaving a company of "spare men with lank and rigid cheeks," dyspeptic individuals who "bolted their food in wedges" and fed not themselves but "broods of nightmares," Martin had as train companions a "very lank" man and a "languid and listless gentleman with hollow cheeks." The hotel porch in the town where he changed to the river boat was filled with yawning, lounging men who kept their hands in their pockets, and the local land agent was a gaunt fellow with a twitching Adam's apple and wrinkled face. A reception was attended by men of a "ghostly kind," one of whom had "glazed and fishy eyes," and handshakes ranged from "the hot, the cold, the dry, the moist," to the flabby, "the shortlived and the lingering." The steamboat passengers were as "flat, as dull, and stagnant as the vegetation that oppressed their eyes." Among them was the "very straight, very tall, and not at all flexible in face or figure" Mrs. Hominey. Finally at his destination Martin was greeted by the sickly, "wan and forlorn" inhabitants of "Eden."

This was, indeed, hardly a flattering picture of the gastronomic situation in America, true or untrue; but the violent reaction to the observations of Dickens, of Mrs. Martineau, and of other foreign visitors who failed to praise American cooking to the skies, might justify the theory that Americans are abnormally sensitive to criticism, and that if any foreigner writes a book about the United States composed 95 percent of praise and 5 percent of dissent, he is sure to be set upon as anti-American. Dickens does not really sound like an implacable foe of Americans in what the *Reader's Encyclopedia* calls "his insulting *American Notes,"* a work of nonfiction written before *Martin Chuzzlewit.* When he was not embarked on a work of fiction, and consequently of exaggeration, he wrote of Americans that

> they are, by nature, frank, brave, cordial, hospitable, and affectionate. Cultivation and refinement seems but to enhance their warmth of heart and ardent enthusiasm; and it is the possession of these latter qualities in a most remarkable degree which renders an educated American one of the most endearing and generous of friends. I never was so won upon as by this class; never yielded up my full confidence and esteem so readily and pleasurably as to them; never can make again, in half a year, so many friends for whom I seem to entertain the regard of half a life.

Dickens did not devote very much space to food in his *American Notes.* Perhaps he did not spend enough time in the right places. He showed everywhere an almost morbid interest in visiting the local poorhouses, insane asylums and jails, none of which are noted for culinary finesse. When he does report on American cheer, he is hardly scarifying. He was entertained at private houses in Boston, where

> the usual dinner-hour is two o'clock. A dinner-party takes place at five; and at an evening-party they seldom sup later than eleven, so that it goes hard but one gets home, even from a rout, by midnight. I never could find out any difference between a party at Boston and a party in London, saving that at the former place all assemblies are held at more rational hours; that the conversation may possibly be a little louder and more cheerful; that a guest is usually expected to ascend to the very top of the house to take his cloak off; that he is certain to see at every dinner an unusual amount of poultry on the table, and at every supper at least two mighty bowls of hot stewed oysters, in any one of which a half-grown Duke of Clarence might be smothered easily.

And he also reported on a hotel experience in the same city:

> A public table is laid in a very handsome hall for breakfast, and for dinner, and for supper. The party sitting down together to these meals will vary in number from one to two hundred—sometimes more. The advent of each of these epochs in the day is proclaimed by an awful gong, which shakes the very windowframes as it reverberates through the house, and horribly disturbs nervous foreigners. There is an ordinary for ladies, and an ordinary for gentlemen.
>
> In our private room the cloth could not, for any earthly consideration, have been laid for dinner without a huge glass dish of cranberries in the middle of the tables; and breakfast would have been no breakfast unless the principal dish were a deformed beefsteak with a great flat bone in the centre [the T-bone steak was a cut unknown in Europe] swimming in hot butter, and sprinkled with the very blackest of all possible pepper.

Dickens seems to have done the greater part of his American traveling by boat; after all, canals and streams in those days were more dependable than the roads. It may well have been true that the food served on board to captive audiences was not the best the country afforded; here we do find echoes of the passages in *Martin Chuzzlewit* which so offended Mr. Cummings. There was, for instance, a canal boat in Pennsylvania:

> At about six o'clock all the small tables were put together to form one long table, and everybody sat down to tea, coffee, bread, butter, salmon, shad, liver, steak, potatoes, pickles, ham, chops, black-puddings and sausages. . . . the gentlemen thrust the broad-bladed knives and the two-pronged forks farther down their throats than I ever saw the same weapons go before except in the hands of a skilful juggler. [The next morning, at eight o'clock breakfast] everybody sat down to the tea, coffee, bread, butter, salmon, shad, liver, steak, potatoes, pickles, ham, chops, black-puddings, and sausages all over again. . . . Dinner was breakfast again without the tea and coffee; and supper and breakfast were identical.

On an Ohio River steamboat the atmosphere was not joyous:

> The company appeared to be oppressed . . . and had . . . little capacity of enjoyment or light-heartedness. I never in my life did see such listless, heavy dullness as brooded over these meals . . . I really dreaded the coming of the hour that summoned us to table; and was as glad to escape from it again as if it had been a penance or a punishment . . . sitting down with so many fellow-animals to ward off thirst and hunger as a business; to empty, each creature, his Yahoo's trough as quickly as he can, and then slink sullenly away; to have these social sacraments stripped of everything but the mere greedy satisfaction of the natural cravings, goes so against the grain with me, that I seriously believe the recollection of these funeral feasts will be a waking nightmare to me all my life . . . nothing could have made head against the depressing influence of the general body. There was a magnetism of dullness in them which would have beaten down the most facetious companion that the earth ever knew . . . Such deadly leaden people; such systematic, plodding, weary, insupportable heaviness; such a mass of animated indigestion in respect of all that was genial, jovial, frank, social, or hearty, never, sure, was brought together elsewhere since the world began.

Dickens' suspicion that the American diet was unhealthy echoed the opinion of the Count of Volney, who had written that Americans deserved first prize for a diet sure to destroy teeth, stomach, and health, and advised the government, for the good of the country, to undertake an educational program to teach Americans how to eat. But if many Europeans thought Americans ate the wrong foods, none of them reported that Americans did not get enough food. Its nature varied with time, place and ethnic background, but it was always plentiful. A frequent criticism was that Americans ate too much, especially too much meat, and specifically too much salt pork; and indeed, whereas in most countries "bread" serves as a synonym for "food," in America "salt pork" came very near to fulfilling that function; when an American wanted to say that he was coming to the end of his resources, he said that he was scraping the bottom of the barrel—it was the pork barrel which stood behind this metaphor. Listen to Fenimore Cooper's housewife in *The Chainbearer:*

> As for bread, I count that for nothin'. We always have bread and potatoes enough; but I hold a family to be in a desperate way when the mother can see the bottom of the pork barrel. Give me the children that's raised on good sound pork afore all the game in the country. Game's good as a relish and so's bread; but pork is the staff of life. . . . My children I calkerlate to bring up on pork with just as much bread and butter as they want.

But whether the food was salt pork or fresh woodcock, there was enough of it. Dale Brown, in *American Cooking,* of the *Time-Life Foods of the World* series, cites a letter an immigrant to the new country wrote home:

> Tell Thomas Arran to come to America; and tell him to leave his strap what he wears when he has nothing to eat in England, for some other half-starved slave. Tell Miriam there's no sending children to bed without supper, or husbands to work without dinners in their bags.

And of course the wealth of food was reflected in the waste which has so often shocked foreign observers in America. More peaches and apples "than would sink the British fleet" were left in Ohio orchards because no one wanted them, one stunned newcomer wrote home, while another said that the wheat lying ungleaned in an American farmer's field would "keep a whole parish for a week."

The evils of waste were not ignored by all Americans. In *The American Frugal Housewife* (1838), Mrs. Lydia Child wrote, "Nothing should be thrown away so long as it is possible to make use of it, however trifling that use may be." Her admonition seems to have fallen on deaf ears; for Elizabeth David was to remark, more than a century later: "In Chinese cooking everything that can be eaten is eaten, and in American cooking everything that can be thrown away is thrown away."

XIV

The Dangers of Eating

THE WAR OF 1812 reinforced the American tendency, initiated by the Revolution and the events which had led up to it, to turn from drinking tea to drinking coffee. Though the two wars for independence promoted this evolution, it would be exaggerated to attribute the change in American drinking habits entirely to war, or even largely to war, except to the degree that the two wars affected the real major factor in this development: Americans became coffee drinkers for the same reason that Britons became tea drinkers, not because of patiotism, but because of price. Even the first revolt against tea, the one which seemed most purely patriotic in its inspiration, began with a question of price—the increase in the cost of tea which ensued when England imposed upon it a tax of threepence per pound—though it was quickly transmuted into a question of principle, since the colonies contested England's right to enact such taxes.

American acceptance of coffee did not represent a turning away from an old favorite to embrace a new one. It was rather a reversion to the *status quo ante,* for until the middle of the eighteenth century England and America alike were devoted to the cult of coffee. If a change had occurred it was because Britain had tea to sell but did not have coffee to sell. Before Queen Elizabeth issued a charter to the "Governor and Company of Merchants of London trading with the East Indies," in 1600, Englishmen were not drinking much tea, and even after she did so it would take something like three-quarters of a century before they would really take it to their bosoms. Meanwhile the coffeehouses, representing a social phenomenon of considerable importance, were booming. In 1725 there were nearly two thousand of them in London, the city which accounted for the highest coffee consumption in the world. The atmosphere of the coffeehouses accorded perfectly with the cavalier style of life; the first Virginians, who came precisely from this group, arrived in America with an already well-developed taste for coffee. Indeed Lawrence Lawson wrote, in *A History of England and the British Commonwealth,* that the cavaliers of the eighteenth century were so thoroughly addicted to coffee that it might easily have become the leading beverage of England if it had not been so easy to smuggle untaxed tea into the country and sell it much more cheaply than coffee.

Coffeehouse society was less in the Pilgrim line, but all the same, following the example of the home country, Boston began serving coffee commercially twenty years before tea. The first license to open a coffeehouse was issued there in 1670, the first to open a tea room in 1690. New England was perhaps a bit confused about tea at first; in Salem there seems to have been some doubt as to whether it was a drink or a food: the leaves were cooked, salted, buttered and spread on bread, a habit which, understandably, did not last long. It is surprising that the colonies acquired a taste for tea at all when one considers how it was then made—boiled lengthily until it became strong and bitter, and then drunk without sweetening or milk. Yet, because tea was cheaper and easier to get, the colonies imported, as customs records attest, 1,866,615 pounds of tea between 1768 and 1772, paying duty on it, while nobody knows how much was smuggled in by the Dutch—possibly more.

It was in 1770 that George III's government rescinded most of the other Townshend taxes, but, with characteristic unintelligence, retained that on tea as a symbol, thus setting tea up as the target at which to shoot. In 1773 the Boston Tea Party occurred. "This Destruction of the Tea," wrote John Adams, "is so bold, so daring, so firm, intrepid and inflexible that I cannot but consider it as an Epoch in History."

Elsewhere the anti-tea campaign, though less theatrical, was quite as effective. In Philadelphia and New York, captains of ships carrying tea were dissuaded from entering the harbors, for fear, probably, that they would encounter reactions more violent than that of Boston. In Charleston the local officials, acting with commendable finesse, allowed the tea to be unloaded—and stored it in damp warehouses where it quickly succumbed to mold. In 1774 the Continental Congress voted a resolution against consuming tea, Madeira or port, all covered by British regulations. The merchants of the North and the planters of the South agreed not to import tea (unless smuggled), and heroic colonists started to drink raspberry-leaf and Labrador "tea," coffee not being available. The decline in tea drinking at this time was indeed inspired by political motives. But then the Revolution was fought, and at its end, Americans returned to drinking more tea than coffee; tea was cheaper.

When the War of 1812 again shut off easy access to tea, its price climbed to \$1.13 a pound when it could be had at all, and the country of necessity fell back upon coffee, by now obtainable from South America.

At the end of this war, tea started coming in again; but while the opening of Brazilian ports had now made excellent coffee readily available, the tea which was reaching the United States had become all too often execrable in quality. America was no longer buying from the experienced British East India Company, but was importing tea in its own bottoms; and the American ships were operated by companies which were carriers and nothing more. The American vessels simply picked up packages made ready for them by the sellers, and had little defense against such astute practices as including iron filings or tea-colored sand in the shipments to improve their weight.

The United States had become thoroughly accustomed to coffee and was not prepared to shift back to tea again, especially not when a cup of coffee was now cheaper. It was still considered elegant to serve tea in the afternoon at social gatherings but it was also smart to drink coffee, since the French preferred it. For Francophiles were rampant again, a result probably of the Anglophobia revived by England's second resort to open hostilities.

The War of 1812 had another direct effect on American food in the case of New England's all-important cod fishing industry. John Adams, politically embittered and alienated from his own party, had retired to private life, so the Treaty of Ghent was negotiated without the aid of that uncompromising New Englander, knowledgeable about cod, who had forced fishery concessions on England after the Revolution. The men who worked out the second peace treaty knew that fisheries were important, and their intentions were good, but they were diplomats, not fishermen, who did not know where the shoe pinched. Henry Clay was not even a diplomat, but fancied himself as a poker player; the British seem to have outbluffed him on this issue. They demanded that the United States abandon utterly all fishing rights off Newfoundland. This must almost certainly have been put forward solely for bargaining purposes, but in the face of the tough British position, the American negotiators no doubt felt that they had done quite well in securing for their countrymen the right to fish and cure their catches along certain stretches of the Newfoundland and Labrador coasts; unfortunately this represented a long step backward from the treaty of 1783, failing, for instance, to include any understanding about the purchase of bait, which any fisherman could have told them was essential. The disputes resulting from this failure were to continue for nearly a century, until the World Court in The Hague arbitrated the controversy in 1910. In the meantime it produced one beneficial result, the United States–Canadian reciprocity agreement of 1854, which was precipitated by the perennial debate over fishing rights for New England.

The observers of the twentieth century paint a grim picture of the food of the nineteenth century, "a monotonous round of badly cooked food," wrote Richard Osborn Cummings, restricted almost entirely to the few things that would keep—salt pork, dried beans, dried corn or cornmeal, and "barely a supply of turnips and potatoes in the winter months" (at least Americans had gotten over the belief that the potato was poisonous). "Vegetables, plentiful only in the growing season, were luxuries compared to salt meat and meal, prepared from corn which could be kept throughout the year. . . . City dwellers, like country people, suffered lacks of milk, fresh fruits and vegetables . . . lack of elements to be found in milk and fresh vegetables probably contributed to the decayed, spotted and missing teeth, common among both young and old."

At least there was a good reason for not eating fruit: it was dangerous:

> Fresh fruits, warned the *New York Mirror* in 1830, should be religiously forbidden to all classes, especially children. Two years later all fruit was held to be dangerous, and because of the cholera epidemic city councils prohibited its sale. Salads were to be particularly feared. [So there *were* salads!] . . . The *Chicago Journal* during the cholera of 1849 condemned the city council for not forbidding sales as had been done in other cities, since the "sad effects" of using such foods were "so apparent," and the *Democrat* carried a story about two boys who "partook freely" of oranges and coconuts and then went to the circus. "In a short time one was a corpse and the other was reduced to the last stage of the cholera."

Yet there were Americans who were not afraid of fruit, peaches in particular, and were even convinced that American fruit was especially excellent. James Fenimore Cooper thought so (of course he had the advantage of having lived in Europe):

> A French peach is juicy, and, when you first bring it in contact with your palate, sweet, but it leaves behind it a cold, watery, and almost sour taste. It is for this reason so often eaten with sugar. An American is exceedingly apt to laugh if he sees ripe fruit of any sort eaten with anything sweet. The peaches here leave behind a warm, rich and delicious taste, that I can only liken in its effects to that which you call the *bouquet* of a glass of Romanée.

But Cooper was not supported by the better-publicized members of the medical profession. Dr. Martyn Payne of New York argued that garden vegetables and almost every variety of fruit had been

> known to develop the deadly cholera; that the disease had developed and raged most fatally in the Delta of the Ganges, where the Hindus lived largely on rice and vegetables; and therefore those who would escape the disease in the United States should restrict themselves to lean meat, potatoes, milk, tea and coffee.

(It should perhaps be pointed out that Dr. Payne, medically trained though he was, committed here the same error as in popular usage of the word "cholera"—he confused Asiatic cholera with what was known in his time as "cholera morbus," otherwise gastroenteritis.)

Dr. Payne was perhaps not quite orthodox in recommending milk, for it too is often painted as dangerous, and, given the hygienic standards of the times, in many cases no doubt it was. Mr. Cummings noted that "most New Yorkers in 1840 had to drink swill milk which came from cows fed with distillery mash and stabled within the city limits."

Even if the milk were irreproachable to begin with, it might pick up bacteria on its way to market, because of unhygienic delivery systems. Said Cummings:

> Milk was brought in from the suburbs [of New York, but no doubt the same was true for other cities also] by boys or women who bore the milk in tin cans suspended from a yoke on their shoulders. . . . In the thirties, if really fresh milk was desired, one sent into the country by messenger to obtain it.

The rural regions did not seem to be much better off than the cities. It was especially in the country areas of the South and the Midwest that "the milksick," also called the slows or the trembles, was most common; it lasted well into the nineteenth century; Abraham Lincoln's mother succumbed to it. The popular explanation was that it resulted from drinking milk given by cows which had eaten white snakeroot. The explanation is not convincing. Snakeroot is not poisonous; it owes its name to the opposite quality, a popular belief that it is an antidote against snake bites, a theory in which it is perhaps advisable not to place too much confidence. It is more probable that "the milksick," whatever it was, resulted from the exposure of milk, a hospitable culture medium for germs, to unsanitary conditions.

Milk was not the only food which was treated with a casualness which would shock food inspectors today. Even in 1796, Amelia Simmons had complained about veal arriving at the market "flouncing on a sweaty horse." "At the opening of the nineteenth century," Cummings remarked, "methods of supplying perishables to the market were very primitive. Fresh meats were obtained from cattle driven through the streets to slaughter-houses located near the market stalls."

A frequent criticism of the American diet of the early nineteenth century is that Americans knew no other meat than salt pork. The pig *was* important, too important in the view of that famous educator, Horace Mann, who wrote in 1842, in his *Common School Journal,* that New England schoolchildren were less well housed than New England hogs. It is possible, however, that this observation on the monotony of one category of American foods has been a trifle overworked. It is true that Americans did eat a good deal of salt pork, another reason why the American sweet tooth developed to such inordinate proportions: "So much salt pork was eaten by so many Americans in the 19th Century," Dale Brown wrote in *American Cooking,* "that molasses, the most popular of sweeteners, was regularly used to subdue the briny taste." Pork was by far the most important meat in the opening Middle West and the South, where the prevailing diet was "hog and hominy"; but the Northeast ate a good deal of beef, and veal and lamb, too. Mr. Cummings presents the picture of a diet which so far as meat is concerned seems to rely almost entirely on the pig, but also gives a detail here and there which suggests an occasional modification of the monotony. He is understandably shocked that infants "were given meat before they had their teeth," but it may be significant that he says "meat," not pork.

The circumstance that gave America so much pork also operated for all other kinds of meat, accounting for the general European amazement at the quantity of flesh Americans consumed—the United States still possessed wide areas of cheap land. The same amount of soil which could produce one million calories of nourishment in the form of pork (or other meats) would produce roughly three million calories in the form of wheat (or other cereals). Europeans could not afford to use three times as much of their expensive land to supply their caloric needs through meat instead of grain, so their basic food was necessarily bread; Americans were able to eat their grain in the form of meat, any kind of meat; but pork was the easiest to produce since the pigs fended largely for themselves—"the hog cost nothing to keep."

Looking back to the first half of the last century, contemporary writers are even disposed to deny to the United States the merit which foreign observers had consistently, if grudgingly, consented to grant it—if the food wasn't good, it was at least abundant. It sounds less so in a description by Mr. Cummings of the situation about 1840:

> City wage-earners tasted but few perishable luxuries. They were probably better fed than laborers in Europe, but their diet was not comparable to that of those on the lowest income levels today. McMaster [John McMaster, in *A History of the United States from the Revolution to the Civil War*] observed that at the close of the eighteenth century unskilled workers, commonly paid two shillings a day at a time when corn was three and wheat more than eight shillings a bushel, rarely tasted fresh meat more than once a week. They ate bread, one of the cheapest sources of energy. Brayley [Arthur Brayley, in *Bakers and Baking in Massachusetts*] points out that in New England, where wheat was expensive, the poor used corn, rye, oat and barley meals for bread-making. As sugar was costly, molasses was a more common sweetening. . . .
>
> A common dish was blood pudding, which was a mixture of hog or sometimes beef blood together with chopped pork seasoned and stuffed in a casing. Hungry laborers would buy a pound of this for three or four cents and make a meal of it with butter crackers. Frequently the laborers raised their own supplies—that is, they notched the ears of scavenger pigs which fed on the offal of the streets. When New York City banished these scavengers by ordinance, the housewives fought with broom and nail the attendants of the hog carts sent about to collect them.

Certainly plenty is not indicated in a society where workers thought themselves obliged to eke out their rations by levying tribute on such ill-fed pigs, whose pork could hardly have been a gourmet's dream. Nor was it indicated either by the food budget of a Philadelphia family of three (mother and two children) for one week in 1833. The big item of their grocery bill was bread—sixty-two and a half cents' worth. Meat accounted for twenty cents, butter and potatoes for fifteen each, sugar (or molasses) for twelve, milk for seven, tea for ten, and salt, pepper and vinegar for seven: total outlay $1.48½. Let us not criticize this housewife for extravagance in buying bread instead of flour to make the bread herself; she had only a brick fireplace with which to cook, as was the case in most Philadelphia tenements of the period, and, having made the mistake of deciding to live in the city, she would have had to pay so much for fuel to bake bread on the inefficient hearth that the homemade article might well have proved dearer than "boughten" bread.

Possibly the presenter of this budget, one Mathew Carey, had gone to some pains to unearth an example which would appear as harrowing as possible; it may be suspected that he had a case to prove from the title of the work in which it appeared: *Appeal to the Wealthy of the Land, Ladies as Well as Gentlemen, on the Character, Conduct, Situation and Prospects of Those Whose Sole Dependence for Subsistence Is on the Labor of Their Hands.* The *New York Tribune,* presumably inspired only by a desire to ferret out the facts, presented a somewhat happier budget for a week for a family of five, also in Philadelphia, in 1851; but the passage of eighteen years may have accounted for an improvement in living standards. This time the chief item was for "butcher's meat," kind not specified, "2 lb. per day @ 10¢ per lb."—$1.40, nearly the total for the 1833 budget. This housewife made her own bread, so the sixty-two and a half cents she paid for a barrel of flour (coincidentally the same sum allotted for the week's supply of bread in the earlier budget) should really have been prorated over the eight weeks the barrel would last. Butter, two whole pounds of it, cost sixty-three cents; half a bushel of potatoes, fifty; four pounds of sugar, thirty-two; coffee and tea, twenty-five; milk, two cents a day (this would have allowed a fifth of a pint daily), and salt, pepper, vinegar, starch, soap (inedible), soda, yeast, cheese, and eggs all together added up to forty cents: total $4.26½. This was a considerable improvement, but it did not quite spell abundance.

According to Samuel Eliot Morison, in his *Oxford History of the American People:* "American cooking at this period was generally bad, and the diet worse."

XV

What Do the Cookbooks Say?

THE PEOPLE who wrote America's cookbooks in the first two-thirds of the nineteenth century seem not to have noticed that their food was monotonous and their culinary vocabulary limited; one of their striking features is precisely the variety of food with which they dealt. We may well wonder whether our pre-Civil War forebears were not more adventurous eaters than we are today, or at least than our fathers and mothers were yesterday. Twentieth-century Americans have been inclined to regard mussels as unfit for human consumption; recipes calling for them are found in early nineteenth-century cookbooks. The United States thought it had discovered broccoli in the 1920s; the 1820s knew it. Artichokes were considered a highfalutin European luxury not so many years ago; they turn up frequently in these books. Some foods which they take for granted—game, for instance, and turtle—have virtually disappeared since, for other than gastronomic reasons. Dishes could hardly have been drab, for aromatic herbs and spices were used freely; sharp spices no doubt played a particularly useful role in those days before refrigeration, preserving foods that were fresh and camouflaging foods that were not; and the frequency of their appearance, and of dishes like curries and mulligatawny soup, may also have reflected a romantic awareness of the role of Yankee ships returning from the Orient with cargoes of exotic seasoners.

Abundance is implied unconsciously in these early nineteenth-century cookbooks. Everything is on the grand scale. A single chicken does not exist. "Take a *pair* of large fat fowls," says the recipe for "rich white soup," in Eliza Leslie's *Directions for Cookery* (Philadelphia, 1828), naming the smallest conceivable unit of poultry; there were also two pounds of veal in this dish for good measure, along with a good many other things. Three pounds of beef, three pounds of veal and half a pound of ham went into "clear gravy soup," along with onions, turnips, carrots and celery; these ingredients were lightheartedly thrown away after their flavors had been boiled off into the water; only the consommé was kept. Meg Merrilies' soup called for four pounds of venison, a hare, a pair of partridges, a woodcock, "or any other game that you can most easily obtain," a dozen onions, two heads of celery and half a dozen potatoes. "This," Miss Leslie explains, "is the soup with which the gipsy Meg Merrilies, regaled Dominie Sampson" (in Sir Walter Scott's *Guy Mannering);* gypsies must have done well for themselves in those days.

In *Home Cookery* (Boston, 1853) Mrs. J. Chadwick offers a humble and, one would suppose, economical dish—bean soup; unsung in this name is its auxiliary seasoner, six pounds of beef (the really thrifty could fall back on pea soup, which required only four). To elevate her modest gumbo soup in the social scale, she suggested the optional adding to it of one hundred oysters; but oysters were prescribed as freely as salt in those times. Mrs. Leslie demanded two quarts of oysters for her oyster soup, minced oysters used fifty, pickled oysters one hundred and fifty, the recipe for "fine stewed oysters" called for two hundred and "spiced oysters" for four hundred. The country was in the throes of an oyster cult. Oyster express wagons heavily loaded with fresh oysters from Chesapeake Bay thundered across the Alleghenies, frequently shifting to fresh horses, delivering the shellfish so far inland that Abraham Lincoln, when he was living in Springfield, Illinois, was able to give oyster parties at which incredible quantities of this bivalve were devoured. Oysters were eaten raw, baked, fried, fricasseed, in soup, in pies, in stuffings, and riding triumphantly on top of grilled steaks. Every coastal city had its specialized oyster houses, and peddlers hawked oysters in the street. Oyster houses in Boston, New York, Philadelphia and Baltimore were plastered with signs reading: "All the oysters you can eat for six cents." Lobsters were no luxury either, so it was not extravagant for Mrs. Leslie to sacrifice three of them to make a pot of soup. Similarly her clam soup was made with fifty shellfish and her *plain* clam soup with one hundred—the thicker the clams, the plainer the soup.

Mrs. Chadwick gives a recipe for a cake one of whose ingredients is ninety eggs (plus the whites of nineteen more for the frosting). True, this was a wedding cake; an ordinary one asked only for the yolks of thirty-two. This carefree attitude toward the egg continued even into the Civil War period; Mrs. Horace Mann included in her *Christianity in the Kitchen* (1861) a cake recipe calling for twenty eggs as part of the batter which the cook was instructed to beat vigorously for three hours.

A corollary of this plenty was the assumption that everybody raised his own food. Early nineteenth-century cookbook authors seemed to take it for granted that everyone lived on a farm, and indeed in those days few persons lived far from one. The housewife, being the farm wife also, accordingly started from scratch. Miss Leslie's directions for roast pork note that "the pig should be newly killed" (in the morning, if possible, for dinner at two), which suggests that the cook, or her husband, was expected to do the butchering. Whether larger animals were supposed to be on hand, still alive, is not spelled out, but they were certainly not envisaged as far distant: for mutton soup "cut off the shoulder part of a fore quarter of mutton," so at least a substantial part of the animal had to be nearby, quick or dead; veal—"if you get a calf's head with the hair on, sprinkle it all over with pounded rosin and dip it into boiling water. This will make the hairs scrape off easily"; beef—"Take a leg of beef that has been freshly killed." Even sea turtles were still alive the day before they were expected for dinner, though a living sixty-pound turtle must have been a curious adornment for the New England farm of Mrs. Chadwick, who gave a recipe for "real turtle soup" which started from the very beginning with a vengeance—with cutting off the living turtle's head. There was a sea or green turtle cult in those days, too. Captain Marryat wrote that they were "to be had in plenty, all the year around," adding that he preferred them "decidedly" to what was nevertheless then considered (and still is, though it is now a rarity) the great delicacy in this category, terrapin—"rather an acquired taste," Marryat thought.

Eliza Leslie, though her book proves that she was no idler, balked at real turtle soup; but she provided directions for making mock turtle soup. "We omit a receipt for *real* turtle soup," she confesses, "as when that very expensive, complicated, and difficult dish is prepared in a private family, it is advisable to hire a first-rate cook for the express purpose. An easy way is to get it ready made, in any quantity you please, from a turtle-soup house."

O happy land of plenty, with turtle-soup houses on every corner and first-rate cooks available at the drop of a hat whenever a housewife needed one for an evening!

It is impossible to look through these old cookbooks without being struck by the quantity of dough which was crammed into the human system. Bread, rolls, biscuits, cakes and pastry are accorded the lion's share of their space. Mrs. Chadwick led her book with bread—beginning with instructions for making yeast (Eliza Leslie gave directions for making ordinary yeast, baker's yeast, bran yeast and pumpkin yeast). Mrs. Chadwick offered 134 recipes in this category, while Eliza Leslie, no doubt restraining herself because she had already covered the subject in her *Pastry, Cakes and Sweetmeats* (1828), confined herself to 124. Even E. Hutchinson's *New Family Book, or Ladies' Indispensable Companion and Housekeepers' Guide; Addressed to Sister, Mother and Wife* (New York, 1854), gives twenty recipes in this category (plus one for making yeast), though it prints only 155 in all: it was interested in many other fields of human endeavor besides cookery, as its title page indicates: *"The Very Best Directions for the Management of Children"* ("Never give medicine to a very young child. Many have thus lost darling children. It will, if not murdered, be permanently injured. . . . If medicine must be given at all, give it to the nurse"—if, one presumes, the nurse does not object); *"Instructions to Ladies under Different Circumstances"* ("Do not lace too tightly. . . . No woman who laces tight can have good shoulders, a straight spine, good lungs, sweet breath, or is fit to be a wife and mother"); *"Ladies' Toilette Table"* ("Better wear coarse clothes with a clean skin, than silk stockings drawn over dirty feet"); *"Rules of Etiquette"* ("The Teeth should be picked as little as possible, and never with fork or fingers"); *"Medicine, So that Each Person May Become His or Her Own Physician"* (for rattlesnake bite, "chew and swallow, or drink, dissolved in water alum, [the comma seems to have strayed a trifle here] the size of a hickory nut. Put thoroughwort leaves pounded on and keep wetting them with water. If the patient turns purple or black . . ." send for the doctor? No, have him drink some of the thoroughwort juice).

Astonishingly, this devotion to doughy dishes was manifested while cooking was still being done in open fireplaces. This was so normal in 1830 that it never occurred to Eliza Leslie to tell her readers that her techniques were adapted to working on the hearth. That could be taken for granted. Everyone understood it. Today we are jolted into realization of that fact from time to time when a detail in her recipes implies fireplace cooking. It is clear in her recipe for roasting a pig (the whole animal in one piece):

> Put the pig on the spit, and place it before a clear brisk fire, but not too near lest it scorch. The fire should be largest at the ends, that the middle of the pig may not be done before the extremities. If you find the heat too great in the centre, you may diminish it by placing a flat-iron before the fire.

When she took up the baking of bread, it is obvious that Miss Leslie had in mind one of those flueless ovens built into the side wall of the main fireplace:

> If it is a brick oven it should be heated by faggots or small light wood, allowed to remain in till burnt down into coals. When the bread is ready, clear out the coals, and sweep and wipe the floor of the oven clean. Introduce nothing wet into the oven, as it may crack the bricks when they are hot. Try the heat of the bottom by throwing in some flour; and if it scorches and burns black, do not venture to put in the bread till the oven has had time to become cooler.

She also recommended the Dutch oven for some kinds of baking, by which she apparently already understood the pot type which usually goes by that name today ("if you bake bread in a Dutch oven, take off the lid when the loaf is done, and let it remain in the oven uncovered for a quarter of an hour"); when she wanted to indicate the open-sided metal box which originally bore that name she called it the tin-kitchen.

Baking had to be done in those days not only without the aid of commercial yeast (introduced in 1868), but also without baking powder (introduced in 1856). Miss Leslie does not even mention baking soda, called saleratus in the nineteenth century, but Mrs. Chadwick, writing twenty-three years later, does.

> Until the end of the eighteenth century [James Trager writes], the only way to make baked goods light was to beat air into the dough, along with eggs, or to add yeast [but it had to be natural yeast, made by the cook] or spirits. Then, in the 1790s, pearlash was discovered in America; produced by burning wood, it was responsible for some of the wholesale destruction of American forests; but it revolutionized baking methods.
>
> Pearlash is potassium carbonate; it produces carbon dioxide in baking dough and makes it rise. The fledgling American republic exported some 8000 tons of pearlash to Europe in 1792. Four years later Amelia Simmons' *American Cookery* contained several recipes calling for pearlash.

A somewhat curious early form of yeast was a by-product of "apple beer," which sounds rather horrible, brewed from the leftover skins and cores of apples which had already served for other purposes. It was sometimes used to raise bread.

Good quality wheat flour was available at this period but expensive; durum wheat (imported from Russia) would not be planted in the United States until after the Civil War, but Oliver Evans had been producing bolted flour in his watermill since 1787, had patented his method in 1790, and the use of fine flour had become generalized by the 1830s. Miss Leslie suggested a little startlingly that you might like "a little Indian in your bread"; this turned out to be not an invitation to cannibalism, only recognition of the fact that cornmeal was so thoroughly associated with the Red Man that the single word "Indian" sufficed to designate it.

Another difficulty the early nineteenth-century cook had to face was the imprecision of her cookbooks. A criticism often made of them today is that they failed to specify exactly how much of each ingredient should go into a dish, either by weight or measure. Usually they did not do so because it would have been useless. Accurately standardized measuring cups and spoons were lacking and few kitchens were equipped with scales and weights. Eliza Leslie recommended that the housewife provide herself with whatever measuring equipment could be had, and Mrs. Chadwick offered a "Table of Weights and Measures, for those persons who have neither scales nor weights," but these two were among the most conscientious authors of their times, which no doubt accounted for the fact that their books enjoyed large sales over a long period. Most cookbooks did not bother with such details; the *New Family Cookbook,* for instance, ignored them entirely. Cooking times had to be approximate, too, even for those who owned clocks, if they had to put up with the uncontrollable vagaries of an open fire.

The number of recipes for game in these old cookbooks will surprise nobody; a symptom of its plenty is that Miss Leslie's book contains not only diagrams for cutting up a steer, a calf, a sheep and a pig, as might any modern cookbook, but also one for deer. She gives several recipes for deer meat (roast saddle of venison spitted before the open fire, venison steak, venison pasty, venison hams, cold venison hash, venison sausage, venison soup) and others for hare, wild duck, wild pigeon, pheasant, snipe, partridge, quail, grouse, woodcock, plover and reed-birds, alias bobolinks ("bury in ashes hot enough to cook them"): game birds, like chickens, are seldom encountered in the singular. There is no recipe in any cookbook known to the authors for a dish which has been described in the twentieth century as popular in the nineteenth—robin pie.

Modern writers who complain of the monotony they discern in the food served a century or a century and a half before they were around to sample it avoid mentioning fish, which does not support their thesis. Fish was plentiful all along the coast, which was where the great majority of the population lived at this period, and it was widely eaten. Miss Leslie gives four recipes for salmon (one with lobster sauce), plus directions for pickling and for smoking it. Sturgeon abounded in the same rivers; the Hudson was so full of them that children bounced their elastic muzzles like rubber balls on the streets of New York; Miss Leslie recommends lemon juice on sturgeon cutlets or steaks. The Hudson, and all the other Atlantic rivers, too, were likewise full of shad; Miss Leslie gives a mouth-watering recipe for this fish, stuffed and baked, and cooked in a port wine sauce seasoned with sweet marjoram, mace and cloves.

Directions for Cookery also treats halibut, mackerel ("immediately out of the water, it loses its flavor in a very few hours and spoils sooner than any other fish"), cod, salt and fresh (and cod roe), rock-fish, sea bass, blackfish, perch, trout, carp and catfish (the period would seem to have been not without finesse, judging from Miss Leslie's remark that "catfish that have been caught near the middle of the river are much nicer than those that are taken near the shore where they have access to impure food"). Other indications of delicacy of taste are lobster recipes making special use of the rich red coral which many Americans disdain today and the directions for employing the liquid of oysters and clams which modern American restaurants have a habit of washing away, along with most of the flavor.

A European impression that Americans were great meat eaters was exact. In the decade from 1830 to 1839, the per capita consumption was 178 pounds annually, or forty-five pounds more than would be eaten a century later, in 1930. Indeed, 1830's mark was not passed until 1970. The cookbooks do not bear out the assertion that pork was close to being America's only meat in the early nineteenth century, though it was indisputably very important. Miss Leslie gives recipes for whole roast pig, roast pork, roast loin of pork, stewed pork, boiled corn pork, pickled pork, pork and pease pudding, pork and beans, pork steaks (classically, with apple sauce), pork cutlets and pork pie. There are also boiled ham, broiled ham and ham pie. ("Ham should always be accompanied by green vegetables, such as asparagus, beans, spinach, cauliflower, broccoli, etc.," she wrote, which does not quite jibe either with the frequent statement that this period eschewed green vegetables.) Virginia ham already existed, but in her recipe for roast ham, Miss Leslie called snobbishly for Westphalian ham "if you can get it" (if you couldn't, she explained how to imitate it), and she marinated it in a bottle of Madeira or sherry.

There were recipes for roasting beef in the tin-kitchen; for baked beef if you had a real oven (this came with Yorkshire pudding); for boiling corned beef (served with French mustard, made by the housewife from "the very best mustard powder," tarragon vinegar and garlic, which could only be mixed properly with a wooden spoon); for broiling or grilling steaks; for beef à la mode; for beef stews; for beefsteak pudding or beefsteak pie; for boiled beef, enlivened with capers or "nasturtian" seeds; and for hashed beef and beef cakes, which it had not yet occurred to anybody to call hamburgers. There were ten recipes for veal, plus a dish little favored in America today, calf's head. There were nine recipes for mutton or lamb, and one for mutton ham; roast mutton was served with currant jelly, and a glass of port wine went into the gravy; mutton harico (sic) was cooked with carrots, turnips, onions and celery and seasoned with a bouquet garni, cloves and mace, which would have surprised Mr. Cummings, who believed there were no vegetables in those days. There was also a recipe for roast kid, a dish abandoned nowadays, unjustly; young kid is at least as interesting as young lamb. We can skip the many recipes for rabbit, pigeon, chicken, duck, goose and turkey ("Do not help anyone to the legs, or drum-sticks as they are called," reason not specified).

This would seem to offer a considerable variety of meats, and other cookbooks do so, too. *Home Cookery* has five recipes for pork, not counting pig's head and pig's trotters, outnumbered by thirteen for beef (including beefsteak and oyster pie), seven for veal (not counting two for calf's head), and ten for lamb or mutton (plus roast lamb's head). The *New Family Book* balances four pork recipes and two for ham with seven beef dishes and four of mutton, ignoring veal and lamb.

The daring of the nineteenth century shows up in the meat category, which included many items rarely or never eaten in America now—besides pig's or lamb's head and feet, these recipes offer beef tongue ("Beef's tongue is never cooked except for mince pies; but pickled and afterwards smoked is highly esteemed"), heart, kidneys (cooked with champagne!), or tripe; calf's sweetbreads or brains; pig's liver; and lamb tongue (not to mention the "lights" in turtle soup, otherwise the lungs).

The vegetables which the early nineteenth century did not eat, according to so many worthy authors, are nevertheless well represented. Miss Leslie, in addition to using vegetables as constituents of many other dishes, notably soups and stews, gives separate recipes for artichokes, asparagus, beans (dried, of course, but fresh limas and string beans, too), beets (in their fresh state), cabbage, carrots, cauliflower, celery, chestnuts, corn, cucumbers, eggplant, lettuce (in, of course, salads), mushrooms, ochras (sic), onions, parsnips, peas, potatoes (sweet and white), pumpkin, radishes, rice, rutabagas, salsify, spinach, squash (winter and summer), "tomatas" and turnips. There was also one which has since been abandoned, except in some remote country districts—poke, which has the disadvantage that its roots are poisonous, but the young leaves were eaten like spinach while the stalks offered the closest approach Nature has been able to achieve to the taste of asparagus (not very close, it must be admitted).

As for the tomato, represented as generally shunned because it was considered dangerous, it too fails, in the cookbooks, to live up to its reputation. It is undisputed that many persons believed until the twentieth century that eating tomatoes induced cancer, a fact too picturesque not to be noted, but the majority of Americans must have thought otherwise, or our cookbook authors would have felt themselves obliged to deal with this superstition. Miss Leslie gave recipes for tomatoes alone, included them in a dozen soups and stews, told how to make "tomata catchup," and provided instructions for preserving them. Mrs. Chadwick had four recipes for tomatoes alone, plus tomato soup and tomato catchup, and preserving directions. E. Hutchinson told how to make tomato sauce. None of the three seemed to harbor any doubts about the tomato, or even to be aware that anyone else did.

The early nineteenth century offered a full complement of vegetables for those who wanted them; that many Americans did not like vegetables (and in some parts of the country still do not) is another matter. Those who did ate them and had been eating them since colonial times. Jefferson served many vegetables on his table: the menu of one Jeffersonian meal which has been preserved for us comprises corn pudding, celery with almonds, scalloped potatoes with brown sugar, and puréed summer squash with bacon. He probably had company when he added to the same list of vegetables Virginia ham, *boeuf en daube,* and wild turkey—and also pickled Jerusalem artichokes and damson plum preserves to reinforce the representatives of the vegetable kingdom.

In February 1835, Hovey's *American Gardener's Magazine* wrote that expensive vegetables like broccoli, generally grown for the market in hotbeds, had fallen off in demand during the eighteen twenties, but had made a comeback in the eighteen thirties; and the tomato was being widely used in salads (which, in the United States, implied that lettuce was, too). It spoke also of the impressive and varied displays of fruit and vegetables on the markets of

New York, Philadelphia and Boston. Some of today's writers who missed this phenomenon may have been misled by considering the fresh vegetable and fruit situation at the wrong time of year, like a naïve foreign commentator who complained that Americans had no fresh vegetables out of season, completely forgetting that in the early nineteenth century vegetables were not available out of season anywhere in the world. It is probable that menus of the period which have been preserved and which make little reference to vegetables, whatever the season, fail to mention them because they came automatically with the main dish and were taken for granted. As Boorstin reported,

> In the 1830s, young ladies invited out to dinner who wanted to impress their escorts would request that their vegetables be served "in the French manner," which meant each vegetable in a separate dish. They could show their sophistication by saying that it somehow took their appetite away to see all their foods jumbled together on one plate, in the familiar American manner.

So the vegetables *were* there; and so were the fruits—not only home-grown ones like greengages, plums (often in the form of prunes), peaches, quinces, apples, raspberries, blackberries, strawberries, huckleberries, whortleberries, currants, gooseberries, cherries, grapes, cranberries, and watermelons, but also pineapples and coconuts from the West Indies, both popular at the period. Citrus fruits were less plentiful because they did not travel well, though lemons and limes stood up to voyaging better than oranges, which remained rare treats for the Christmas stocking until well into the twentieth century. The banana, even harder to transport successfully, is not mentioned in any of these early cookbooks.

Desserts were sumptuous. Miss Leslie lists ten kinds of pie (including molasses pie), twenty-four puddings (one based improbably on potatoes and another on green corn), sixty-four cakes, and twenty-six creamy desserts, plus various kinds of blanc-mange (and even *jaune*-mange!), junkets, and confections of gelatine. These last involved some problems which would appall a cook today, but were taken in the stride then. If the nineteenth-century housewife had no isinglass to make gelatine, she would render the gelling element from calves' feet; and for junket she would produce her own rennet either from chicken gizzards or (the heroic method) by removing the stomach from a calf, hanging it up in a cool place to dry for several days, and then turning it inside out, after which, according to *The Virginia Housewife* (1824), it was possible to slip off "all the curd nicely with the hand."

There were also sixteen kinds of ice cream (almond orange ice cream sounds perilously close to Howard Johnson) and an uncounted number of fritters, dumplings and unclassifiable sweets.

Mrs. Chadwick offered fourteen pies (including an apple pie with pork in it and what she called Persian apple pie, which turned out to be simply rhubarb), seventy-two cakes (including "upper shelf molasses gingerbread," which we may suspect means "top drawer"), eighty-eight puddings (including shaking Quaker and several types of "souffli"), nine kinds of fritters and fifty-five desserts in the quivery categories. Even the scant 155 recipes of the *New Family Book* included sixty-two desserts—nearly half the total.

The nineteenth-century housewife had a good many other chores to take care of in connection with her job as cook which nowadays are left to the supermarket. In addition to normal preserving, she made sausages—liverwurst, then called liver pudding; French bologna sausage, whose name reveals a certain amount of geographical confusion; head cheese, then called pork cheese; and a number of others. She not only churned butter, she also produced cheese. ("Place the cheeses in the hay-stack," Miss Leslie advised, "and keep them there among the hay for five or six weeks. This is said to greatly improve their consistence and flavor. Cheeses are sometimes ripened by putting them every day in fresh grass.") She concocted the variously flavored vinegars (cider, chili, horseradish, shallot, celery, tarragon, sweet basil, burnet, raspberry, sugar) and the versatile "catchups" ("tomata," lemon, mushroom, walnut, anchovy, oyster, lobster, and "sea catchup" because it was designed to keep at sea, a frequent preoccupation of these old cookbooks, which turns up in other recipes of very different kinds—for instance, "sea pudding," also meant for a ship's stores).

The early nineteenth-century housewife brewed the family drinks—beers (ginger, spruce, sassafras, molasses); wines (elderberry, elder flower, gooseberry, currant, raspberry and cider wine); cordials (cherry, strawberry, lemon, rose, aniseed); brandies (rose, lemon, noyau); punches (Roman, milk, Regent's)—and fox grape shrub, cherry bounce, ratafia, capillaire, orgeat, bishop, egg nogg (sic), sangaree, negus, Turkish sherbet, and, God help us, sassafras mead.

There seems to be no doubt about the abundance of food at this period; but the basic plenty was sometimes interrupted, temporarily or locally, by shortages which did not really represent failures of the food supply as much as failures of the money supply. The violent ups and downs of the economy and of financing during this period, sometimes the result of political inadequacies, often reduced the ability of certain individuals to acquire food; but the food was there. The high cost of flour caused food riots in New York in 1837, as the result of the sort of mishap which can still strike us today—the 1836 wheat crop had failed. But the following years saw a drop in food prices—rump steak was five cents a pound, calf's liver two, beef liver one—which lasted for something like a decade. The reaction to the drop did not indicate that Americans had been suffering too greatly from actual lack of food, for instead of increasing the amounts they bought of the low-priced essential foods when prices went down, they shifted instead, as most societies do in times of prosperity, from cheaper to more expensive foods—wheat bread instead of rye, a larger proportion of lean meats to pork, greater quantities of milk, more leafy vegetables and fruit. It was not more food, it was better food that they craved. It was significant also that farmers began to spend more money for food from outside sources, giving up as unnecessary the labor of producing foods which were onerous to raise. Whereas in the 1820s a farm family spent only about ten dollars yearly for food not produced at home, in 1833 it was estimated that one hundred dollars was being spent—for instance, for refined sugar, which replaced home-produced maple sugar or honey and the cheaper, though also purchased, molasses; or for flour, the most important single item in his diet, which the farmer had previously ground himself from home-raised grain but which he now preferred to buy from a miller.

So there was enough food: but how well was it cooked? It is a little late in the day to attempt to form now an opinion on the skill with which nineteenth century housewives executed their recipes—even at the time any such opinions would necessarily have been subjective—but the old cookbooks at least show that the women who used them were conscious of the fine points of cooking and were willing to take pains to achieve satisfactory results. A good sign would seem to be the considerable repertory of sauces—mint sauce, caper sauce, "nasturtian" sauce, celery sauce, white onion sauce, brown onion sauce, parsley sauce, mushroom sauce, egg sauce, bread sauce, wine sauce, anchovy sauce, oyster sauce and lobster sauce, among others.

Remarkable is the extent to which wine was used in nineteenth-century cooking, in a non-wine-drinking country—Madeira and sherry in such dishes as mock turtle soup and terrapin stew, claret in stews of hare and venison. The nineteenth-century housewife also went out of her way to produce such recherché dishes as "mangoes"—they were counterfeited from melons or peaches, though *Home Cookery* does give one formula for pickling mangoes and another in which they are included in "Achsjar pickles—East Indian recipe," for which the real thing seems to be meant. Mangoes may have been brought in by the Yankee clippers, which were certainly the providers of the pungent spices which were lavishly used, along with aromatic herbs, for the high seasoning of a cuisine which could hardly have been insipid. Mulligatawny soup, a favorite of the times, called for turmeric, cassia, coriander, black pepper and cayenne pepper; numbing doses of cloves flavored sausage meat; cinnamon and sweet and bitter almonds saved what otherwise would have been the blandest of milk soups; and cloves and mace, along with parsley, celery, sweet marjoram, basil, red wine, and currant jelly disguised the usually far from exhilarating flavor of domesticated rabbit.

The evidence of the abundance of food and of imagination in its cooking comes mainly from the cookbooks of the North; there were not many such publications in the South, perhaps not more than two of importance, Mrs. Mary Randolph's *The Virginia Housewife* (1824), sometimes described as America's first regional cookbook, and *The Carolina Housewife* (1847) by "A

Lady of Charleston." This is no more than a negative indication, probably discountable, for most of the best kitchen work in the South was being performed by cooks ill qualified to write about it—Negro slaves purposely kept illiterate. The "peculiar institution" accounted also for what is looked upon as evidence of backwardness in the production of food—the fact that the plow was little used in the South before the Civil War. A plow may have seemed an unnecessary investment when there were plenty of Negroes with hoes about, though a "prime field hand" between eighteen and twenty-five cost five hundred dollars in 1832; but after that his upkeep amounted only to $15 to $60 a year. It is difficult to assess the abundance or the quality of average Southern food in the absence of an average Southerner—that is, a member of the middle class, for there was not much middle class to occupy the wide gap between the plantation owner and the poor white, a group which already existed in those times and could hardly expect to rise to any comfortable standards of living in competition with the unpaid labor of slaves.

The famous "hog and hominy" diet was at least rendered a little less unhealthy by the prevalence on the Southern menu of greens, often ignored by food writers, perhaps as a food so lowly as to be unworthy of their attention, but providers of vitamins all the same. A significant passage in Frederick Law Olmsted's *Seaboard Slave States,* a product of his travels of the 1850s, suggests that slaves may have enjoyed a diet better balanced than that of many whites. Olmsted remarked that the more modest Southern planters lived on bacon (sometimes cooked with turnip greens), corn pone, coffee sweetened with molasses, and not much else, while their slaves had corn meal and salt pork, plus sweet potatoes of their own raising in winter. Some owners encouraged the Negroes to grow vegetables for themselves also, because they discovered that "negroes fed on three-quarters of a pound of bread and bacon are more prone to disease than if with less meat but with vegetables." It did not occur to the masters to draw any conclusions from this empirical observation for their own benefit.

If we may judge from the old cookbooks, the first three-fifths of the nineteenth century, far from being a period of monotony and of imited resources, was one of varied foods, prepared with ingenuity, unstinting pains and apparent skill, and of willingness to experiment with flavors, including exotic ones. The cooks, in the countryside at least, were very close to their raw materials, often growing or raising them themselves, and consequently conscious of their potentialities and eminently well equipped to deal with them. This seems to have been a time of solid honest grass-roots cooking, doomed to be choked off abruptly by the Civil War, and smothered thereafter by the urbanization and industrialization which followed it.

XVI

Refrigeration

THE CIVIL WAR would stimulate the change from home cooking and country cooking to professional cooking and city cooking; but the germs of three developments which would alter radically the pattern of American eating had already been planted. These were the improvement of refrigeration, the increased speed of transportation, and the industrialization of food processing. All of these helped to expand the variety of foods available to American families and to lengthen the seasons of those already present. To these may be added a fourth factor which was to change eating habits, a new preoccupation with the healthiness of the American diet; the birth of food reform movements began before the war, though they would develop momentum only after it.

The problem of keeping food from spoiling in warm weather was posed with particular acuity in the United States, whose extremes of climate astonished Europeans accustomed to more equable weather. An English visitor, Charles Janson, in his *The Stranger in America* (1807) described the contrast between winter and summer temperatures as so great that it imposed on "articles of life" seasons which were hardly perceptible in the British Isles. William A. Cobbett, another Englishman, who lived for a short time on Long Island, recounted in his *A Year's Residence in the United States* (1818) that, having slaughtered a lamb in August, he had tried to keep it from spoiling by hanging it in his well. Two days later he was obliged to confide to his diary: "Resolved to have no more fresh meat till cooler weather comes. Those who have a mind to swallow or be swallowed by flies may eat fresh meat for me." In her 1838 cookbook, Eliza Leslie advised that fish should be "put in ice until you are ready to cook them" and "even then do not attempt to keep a fresh fish until next day." Isaac Weld expressed his surprise in *Travels Through the United States* (1800) at the ravages of hot American summers, which caused meat to start rotting in a day, made it inadvisable to kill a chicken more than four hours before it was to be cooked, and turned milk an hour or two after it had been provided by the cow. Amelia Simmons, our "American orphan," had a solution for this problem: to keep milk fresh until you need it, leave it in the cow. One of her recipes, "To make a fine Syllabub from the Cow," reads:

> Sweeten a quart of cyder with double refined sugar, grate nutmeg into it, then milk your cow into your liquor, when you have thus added what quantity of milk you think proper, pour half a pint or more, in proportion to the quantity of syllabub you make, of the sweetest cream all over it.

She does not say where she kept the cream.

The earliest solution to the problem of keeping food fresh in hot weather was the farm pond flanked by the family icehouse, in which ice cut from the frozen pond in winter was preserved for as long as possible into the summer. George Washington, Thomas Jefferson and James Monroe all had such icehouses on their properties and all had difficulties in filling them and preserving the ice. It took a little time to learn how to manage ice, for instance to discover that if it were packed in sawdust it would be insulated from outside heat and would therefore keep longer. The efficiency of individual icehouses was gradually improved, and by 1846 *The Horticulturist* was telling its readers that an icehouse had to be considered as "a part of the comforts of every substantial farmer," to keep his meat, poultry and spoilable fruit in good condition. Before the Civil War the icehouse had become an indispensable element in a farm's equipment.

The problems of the harvesting and storing of ice on a larger scale were solved by two New Englanders, Frederick Tudor of Boston, an audacious and painstaking promoter who won the sobriquet of "the ice king," and Nathaniel Wyeth of Cambridge, whom he took into his business. Tudor solved the problems of preserving ice, even in warm climates (he began by shipping ice harvested from New England ponds to the West Indies and preserving it there long enough to sell it for the profitable production of ice cream and cold drinks) and Wyeth developed machinery to harvest blocks of ice of uniform size, essential for storing it aboard ships headed for warm climates so that the cargo would neither shift nor melt too rapidly during the voyage. Wyeth's horse-drawn cutting machine scored frozen ponds with parallel grooves in one direction, and then ran over them again at right angles to the first cuts, dividing the ice into a checkerboard pattern, from which the separate blocks when sawn apart could easily be pried up. He also devised a ramp running from the surface of the pond up to the top level of an ice house built on its shore, simplifying the storing of the ice. The cost of filling New England icehouses dropped from thirty cents to ten cents a ton and the summer loss from melting decreased from more than 10 percent to less than 8 percent, although the icehouse, originally built underground on the theory that ice would keep better there, had now moved aboveground.

After Tudor and Wyeth had transformed ice into an article of commerce, the United States entered the era of the iceman, the subject of much ribald joking and the central figure of a small facet of a vanished way of life, important enough nevertheless to affect the design of houses: they had to include a small porch built outside of their lockable doors so that the iceman could deposit his wares in the icebox even if there were no one at home. An order for ice was indicated by placing a square card in a window visible from the street along which the horse-drawn ice cart passed; each of its four sides carried a different number, so the amount wanted could be shown by placing the correct figure uppermost. Reading it, the iceman slid out a block of the stipulated size with his heavy ice tongs, hoisted it onto the thick rubber apron which covered his shoulder and back, and thumped the ice into the waiting icebox. By 1855, a Boston family buying ice in this fashion paid two dollars a month for fifteen pounds daily, or, alternatively, eight dollars for the whole time the warm weather lasted. The iceman became a folk figure of the times, seemingly so solidly established in American society that he would inhabit it forever; but he is nothing but a memory now.

The icebox, which bestowed upon the individual home the means of keeping its food unspoiled, may be dated in the United States from 1803, when Thomas Moore, a Maryland farmer, patented a chest insulated from outer temperatures combining a lower compartment for the storage of food with an upper one containing ice (a drip pan at the bottom caught the melted water, which it was the chore of the children to empty from time to time). Eliza Leslie wrote in one of her cookbooks, published in 1840, that an icebox was a convenience "no family should be without," and *Godey's Lady's Book* in 1850 called it a necessity of life, which situates for us the period at which the icebox had become a normal adjunct of the American pantry. As Daniel Boorstin wrote:

> The "Ice Age" of American diet—with its emphasis on sanitation, nutrition, and refreshment, on the health of the body rather than the pleasures of the palate—[but the pleasures of the palate were served, too] had begun. . . . By 1860 the household ice-box . . . was a commonplace in growing American cities; cookbooks took it for granted. . . . The rapid growth of cities put more and more people farther from the sources of fresh milk, meat, and vegetables, while the increasing number of household refrigerators enlarged the demand for ice. New Orleans, which in the late 1820s consumed less than 400 tons of ice a year, in one decade increased its consumption tenfold, in another decade twentyfold, and before the Civil War seventyfold. Within the same period ice consumption in such northern cities as New York and Boston increased almost as spectacularly. . . . By mid-20th century, the word "ice" in various combinations had provided more new compounds than perhaps any other word in the American language.

Hospitals were quick to make use of the now readily available ice, and taverns quite naturally followed. A wave of German immigrants arrived in the 1840s and established the lager beer industry, which required large quantities of ice too. From the providing of ice for individual use, refrigeration thus progressed to activities conceived on a larger scale. Some of the dates at which modern techniques of refrigeration began are surprisingly early, even if we neglect the example of Sir Francis Bacon, who in 1626 tried to preserve a chicken by stuffing it with snow; the experiment had no sequel except the death of Sir Francis, who came down with bronchitis from exposure. If new inventions were slow to come into general use, it may have been partly because the Civil War retarded the development of conveniences for civilians at the same time that it speeded up processes useful for providing food to the armies.

Cold storage began in 1858 when a schoolteacher named Benjamin Nyce patented the first cold storage warehouse, but though its benefits were so obvious that, once started, its use spread rapidly, it was slow starting because the war followed too closely upon its devising. Making artificial ice to end dependence on the natural product, and, consequently, on the vagaries of the weather (ice merchants suffered, though others rejoiced, from the mild winters of 1818 and 1890) came even earlier, in 1846, when John Dutton of Pennsylvania patented his compression process. This was followed by a number of analogous devices, but the production of artificial ice did not really get under way until after the Civil War, for up to then natural ice was usually cheaper. The most astonishing date of all is 1834, when Jacob Perkins, a New Englander whose specialty up to then had been improving the processes used to print banknotes, took out the first patent for mechanical refrigeration; it would be nearly a century before the mechanical refrigerator would become a taken-for-granted part of American kitchen equipment—not to mention the deep-freeze lockers which were its lineal descendants.

XVII

Transportation

REFRIGERATION had increased the availability of foods in terms of time; speedier transportation increased their availability in terms of space. In America's earliest days, fresh food was unlikely to reach markets more than a few miles from the place where it was produced, for it was not easy to get around. Roads were impassable in spring, when most of them became ribbons of quagmire, and rough going even in summer and autumn. Though it was easiest to move from one place to another in winter, when sleigh runners glided easily over snow covering frozen ground, winter was hardly a favorable season for delivering fresh fruit and vegetables to city markets. It was suitable enough for meat, which kept best then; but winter was not always a convenient season for slaughtering; fall was preferable.

It did not matter too much at first if food could travel only a few miles from its source, for nobody lived more than a few miles from a source. But the cities grew larger and the radius of action of the horse failed to increase correspondingly. Navigable streams provided one solution for the food transportation problem, at least for producing farms and consuming settlements lucky enough to be located on them. In the early nineteenth century, the effort to improve communications would be expended largely in developing boats to serve as carriers on docile waters and constructing canals where rivers were disinclined to cooperate.

The first ship to move by steam over American waters goes all the way back to 1787, when a vessel built by John Fitch performed that feat, but it would take another twenty years for a practical steamboat to begin to operate in the United States. This was Robert Fulton's *Clermont,* which, incidentally, did not start its career on American waters, but on the Seine in 1803, and might have stayed there if Napoleon had been impressed by the possibilities of the steamboat; but he was not, so the *Clermont* began its commercial operations on the Hudson in 1807, its 100 percent Americanism tainted for the second time by the circumstance that it had been fitted with an engine built in England. It covered the distance from New York to Albany in thirty-two hours, a convincing demonstration of the usefulness of steam for navigation. In another decade, the steamboat had reached America's greatest river. In 1817 one of them sailed up the Mississippi all the way to Cincinnati, and only two years later sixty stern-wheel paddle steamers were operating on the Father of Waters. They were a great improvement over the flatboats, which until then had been the chief cargo carriers on the river. The flatboat was not an ideal craft to which to confide perishable foodstuffs; the steamboat was not only safer, it was faster, an important detail when it came to moving fresh food. The speed was increased when an American inventor, Oliver Evans of Delaware, designed a high-pressure engine which took over from those of British manufacture. By the 1830s American steamboats were traveling faster than any in Europe.

The development of transportation, with special attention to getting farm products to market, was fostered by a nationalistic movement whose object was to bind the Union together and discourage sectionalism. Its chief proponents were Henry Clay and John Calhoun. "Let us," Calhoun said in 1817, "bind the Republic together with a perfect system of roads and canals." New York took him at his word that very same year and started the construction of the Erie Canal, an artery particularly well adapted to transport foodstuffs.

The benefit was immediately perceptible in the area the Canal served. Prices dropped. Flour, which in eastern coastal cities had often sold for as much as sixteen dollars a barrel before the opening of the Canal, now dropped to a figure sometimes as low as four dollars.

Not only did the Canal promote the exchange of goods, especially food, between its termini—Albany and Troy on the Hudson, Buffalo on Lake Erie—but it encouraged agriculture all along its course by giving Canalside farmers access to urban markets, and even to distant ones which could be reached from Buffalo across the Great Lakes in one direction, and in the other from Albany via the Hudson River to New York. The Canal was operating along its full length in 1825; by 1826 it was already running through the middle of a strip of land two miles wide which had been cleared and converted to agriculture. Philadelphia discovered that its cheapest route to Pittsburgh was via New York, Albany, Buffalo and Lake Erie; and the governor of Georgia complained that wheat from central New York was being sold more cheaply than wheat from central Georgia in Savannah—which, being a seaport, was receiving grain shipped cheaply by water via the Canal, the Hudson and coastwise steamships from New York. It was the

Canal which, by bringing merchandise from the hinterland to New York for transshipment by sea, made it America's most important port, leaving far behind its former rivals, Philadelphia, Baltimore and Boston.

Other states set feverishly to work to construct canals and develop water transport. Ohio connected the Mississippi, via the river for which the state was named, with the Great Lakes, in the process elevating Cincinnati into a great food center. Chicago sent its first cargo of grain to Buffalo to be loaded on Erie Canal boats in 1836. Until 1850 canal boats were carrying most of the country's bulky freight, including a large proportion of its food; but canals were then supplanted by a new and faster means of communication which had first appeared in 1826, only one year after the Erie Canal had entered into full operation—the railroad. No one dreamed at the time that it was destined to put the canals almost out of business within twenty-five years after they had been dug, and indeed the 1826 railroad was not impressive. It was three miles long and was called the Granite Line, for its purpose was to haul stone from Quincy, Massachusetts, to Bunker Hill, where a monument was being built. Its motive power was the horse.

But then the steam locomotive made its appearance. America's first railroad, the Baltimore & Ohio, was chartered in 1827 and began carrying goods for revenue in 1830; and railroads took over the task of increasing the diversification of food in the United States by making the products of one region available to others, and those of foreign countries available to all. Once again, cheaper transportation meant cheaper food. The Western Railroad was finished in 1841; in 1856 the *American Railway Times* called it the "regulator to the bread market of Boston." Norfolk, Virginia, became a truck gardening center for New York. The Carolinas and Georgia did not ship their fruit and vegetables all the way North by railroad, but it was railroads which carried their produce to the seaports from which they continued their voyage by coastal steamships. Inland railways brought green peas from New Orleans to Chicago in 1852; they sold for eight dollars a bushel.

The railroads not only enlarged the diet of the nation by increasing the range of foods once obtainable only in their own areas, they also improved the quality of foods already available almost everywhere; for instance, they gave the nation beef which was tenderer, tastier and cheaper than that to which it had been accustomed: tenderer, because cattle which rode to market instead of walking to it did not develop such tough muscles; tastier, because the same lines that carried cattle north and east also carried grain with which to fatten them south and west; cheaper because they lost less weight between pasture and slaughterhouse. The quality of pork improved, too, for before the advent of the railroad pigs had been bred partly for ability to walk to market, a factor which now ceased to be important; breeders could turn to the development of races which might be mediocre hikers, but could put on richer meat.

A parallel to the case of Cincinnati, made a great food center by canals, was that of Kansas City, made a great meat center by the location of a railroad bridge. The Great Plains, which Zebulon Pike, for whom Pike's Peak is named, had declared "incapable of cultivation," became the nation's granary because the railroads opened them up, and Florida the fruit and vegetable garden for the same reason; when the transcontinental railroad was completed, the orchards of the Northwest would reach a nationwide market, and California would be enabled to turn from gold to fruit. The ups and downs of the Georgia peach depended less on the quality of the crops than on the evolution of the railroads which carried the peaches to market. The invasion of the United States by the banana was a triumph of transportation in which both the railroads and ships played their part—saltwater ships now, for the Yankee clippers enriched immeasurably the food resources available to the United States.

Not all the Yankee clippers were Yankee; the title of the first clipper ship is often rewarded to the *Ann McKim,* which was built in Baltimore. She was launched in 1833, which is in accordance with the date generally given as that inaugurating the clipper ship era, represented as a development of the 1830s. It would seem that this date is too late; American craft had already achieved superiority on the oceans of the world at least a decade earlier. It was in 1824 that an Englishman commenting on the fact that the United States had captured the greater part of the trade between Liverpool and New York wrote:

> The reason will be evident to anyone who will walk through the docks of Liverpool. He will see the American ships, long, sharp built, beautifully painted and rigged, and remarkable for their fine appearance and white canvas. He will see the English vessels, short, round and dirty, resembling great black tubs.

It was a fact that the American Swallow Tail and Black Ball lines lorded it over the seas; and when Great Britain in 1849 repealed the Navigation Acts which had refused access to British ports to any non-British ships coming from Asia, the United States captured the lion's share of the China trade because of the greater speed of her ships. The *Nightingale* made Shanghai to London in ninety-one days, the *Sea Witch* linked Canton to New York in eighty-one, the *Challenge* raised San Francisco from Hongkong in thirty-three. The *Lightning* on its very first voyage set a record for the greatest distance ever logged in a single day, 436 miles, a mark which steam vessels would be unable to equal for many years. Financial crises checked shipbuilding after 1854, and when it was resumed after the Civil War, the emphasis for what were still sometimes called clipper ships had shifted from speed to economy. Besides, the steamships were getting faster.

The speed of the clipper ships was reflected in their high freight rates, which meant that they carried only luxury goods, high priced enough to be able to absorb the cost (from China, their great import was tea), and also destined them to transport perishable cargoes, mostly food—fruit from the Mediterranean, spices from Indonesia, wheat from Australia. A special use for these fast ships was opened up when gold was discovered in California, whereupon they carried passengers around Cape Horn, and food, too, to a land too busy digging for the precious metal to bother about digging for crops. The prices paid for food in San Francisco were fabulous. Eggs ferried all the way around the Cape could not have been remarkable for freshness, but they brought $10 a dozen, three months at least after leaving the East Coast, which was fast in those days.

In the East, as the speed of coastwise vessels increased, the danger of foods decaying en route diminished, and the North could call upon the produce of the South. New York enjoyed early vegetables and fruits shipped from Charleston; by the 1850s ships from Florida were delivering fruits and vegetables there twice a month; and by the middle of the century pineapples and coconuts were arriving from Cuba, from other West Indian islands, and even from Central America. The banana, a tenderer passenger, would have to wait until the 1870s to become common in Boston and New York, and until the middle of the present century to cross the continent, but there were occasional exceptions. The first recorded arrival of bananas in New York seems to date from 1804, when the *Reynard* delivered thirty stems of edible bananas from Cuba, thanks to favorable winds, moderate temperatures, and the circumstance that the fruit had been exceptionally green when picked. This may have been, like certain other sporadic cases of bananas reaching northern ports, Boston in particular, an accident, the by-product of the habit of taking this fruit aboard for the crew to eat during the voyage; sometimes there were leftovers which arrived in good enough condition to permit them to be sold, though oftener they did not. It was 1830 before a certainly deliberate importation of bananas to New York was risked, successfully, by the *Harriet Smith;* these may have been the ones that caught the eye of James Fenimore Cooper and caused him to report that "bannanas" could be found on the New York market; deliveries in his time—before 1851—must have been spotty. The story of the conquest of the United States by the banana is part of the story of the combined histories of the development of transportation and refrigeration, which converge about 1842, a year marked by at least four important advances in this field.

The first was not a realization, but it was at least a portent. The Boston & Albany railroad examined the idea of building icebox cars to ship fish from Boston to Michigan and bring game back; the idea died abornin', but would bear fruit later. Practical application of the transporting of perishables by rail was initiated, also in 1842, by the newly constructed Erie Railroad, which for

1842–1843 carried three million quarts of milk into New York, which swelled to six million for 1845–1846, and nine million in 1849–1850. Also in that year, oysters packed in ice were shipped by express to Buffalo, accompanied by an outburst of publicity, and in 1842 also Chicago received its first lobster; it got as far as Cleveland alive, but was there prudently boiled before continuing on its way to Chicago, where it arrived "as fresh as could be desired," according to the Chicago *Daily American.*

The publicity given these events seems not to have impressed the citizens of New York with the feasibility of transporting perishables by rail. They became alarmed at the amount of country milk flooding into the city, assuming that it must have been treated with chemicals, presumably noxious, to keep it drinkable, a theory which may just possibly have been implanted in suspicious minds by the dealers who were making handsome profits out of New York City's own "swill milk." A campaign of education had to be undertaken by the out-of-town dairymen, who explained that there were no additives in the milk (there are today, alas), but that it had been stirred with tin tubes filled with ice before being put on the train. This kept it cool until its arrival at New York, where it was immediately unloaded into a cooled warehouse maintained by the milk producers. The price of milk in New York dropped, consumption increased, and Lowell Mason, taxing his brains to produce *Little Songs for Little Singers,* created a ditty which proclaimed:

> Father 'tis thy kindness
> Gives us milk to drink,
> Milk, how pleasant tastes it,
> Very good, we think.

He continued in this strain for a number of stanzas which we hope we may be forgiven for not reproducing. It is not clear whether "Father" referred to the head of the family or to divinity, but in any case the thanks seem to have been misdirected. The credit should have been given to Frederic Tudor and James Watt.

XVIII

The Birth of Food Processing

AT THE BEGINNING of the nineteenth century, preserving food for the family was an important part of the housewife's labor; a century later, indeed, women would still be "putting up" fruit and vegetables in the fruitful months to eat during the long barren winter. This took care of the needs of persons living on the farms where the raw materials were produced; of relatives and friends of the farm families near enough to benefit by the industry of their rural acquaintances; and even of city dwellers whose markets were sufficiently well supplied and whose kitchens were sufficiently well equipped to permit them to plunge into the vapor-wreathed delights of home preserving.

It was the artisanal period of food processing. As each new vegetable or new fruit came into season, the housewife bought it in large quantities (in the city) or picked it (in the country), and threw herself into an orgy of canning (more exactly it was bottling). The preserve closet was an important room in the house, where shelves rising from floor to ceiling were crowded with long ranks of glass jars, displaying their colorful contents in mouth-watering profusion, each one identified by a little white handwritten label telling what was inside and in what year it had been put up; the provident housewife not only preserved enough stores to carry the family through the next barren winter, but through several barren winters if necessary (summers could be barren, too).

In the days before the technique of filling air-tight jars had been perfected, or before the necessary material was readily available, there were other methods of preserving, too. Peach leather and apple leather were made by drying the halved fruits in the sun until they reached a consistency which explains their name; cherries were dried in the sun, too. Quinces, boiled all day, solidified into what was called quince cheese. Limes and lemons were preserved with the aid of alum water. Jams and jellies kept well with only a protective headpiece of paper tied over the top of the jar, though when paraffin became available, a coating of melted paraffin poured on top of the jelly was better. In putting up fruits or vegetables the trick was to put in a great deal of sugar, particularly, of course, for fruits; it acted as a preservative. Mixing sugar with cream and boiling the two together preserved this extremely perishable food; poured into bottles and corked, with melted resin poured over the cork, "this cream," wrote Eliza Leslie, "if properly prepared, will keep perfectly good during a long sea voyage"—a recurring preoccupation in those days. Relishes lasted well, whether vegetable (piccalilli) or fruit (marmalade). Preserved watermelon rind, cut into decorative shapes, was popular, and so were pumpkin chips, in half-dollar size. Pickling was employed for a large number of foods—cucumbers and peppers, string beans and mushrooms, onions and tomatoes, cabbage and cauliflower, cherries and peaches, walnuts and butternuts, "mangoes" (actually muskmelon) and oysters.

Some other foods would not be likely to engage the attention of those few contemporary housewives who still do their own preserving. One of Miss Leslie's recipes tells how to preserve green ginger. Several ways are offered for conserving eggs; besides immersing them in a solution of lime slaked with boiling water (a gallon of water to a pound of lime), she recommended greasing them with melted mutton fat and then wedging them close together, small ends down, in a box of bran. This preserved them for two or three months, or they could be parboiled for one minute and buried in the same fashion in powdered charcoal; but there they were only good for a few days; it would hardly seem worth while to take the trouble.

But taking trouble was normal in those days. There were some methods of "preserving" which we would not be likely to call by that name today, since for us preserving presumes preparing food to keep for a considerable time. Miss Leslie tells how "to keep fresh shad": clean it, split it open, powder it carefully with a mixture of brown sugar, salt and cayenne pepper, and when it is wanted for cooking, wipe all the seasoning off and broil it: "this way of keeping shad is much better than to salt or corn it." How long would it keep? Two days. Preparing calves' foot jelly, starting from scratch with "a set of feet," which in the kitchen as on the calf seemed to mean four, was a long and painstaking process. How long would it keep? In winter, several days; in summer, "in ice, for two days; perhaps longer." Pickled oysters were packed into stone jars, where one might suppose they would have held out for some time, like other pickled foods. How long would they keep? "In cold weather . . . a week."

No matter how much trouble a housewife might be willing to take, she was originally limited to the produce of her own neighborhood; with the development of speedier transportation, her range was extended and more foods were made available to her. There were other restraining factors, such as the high price of sugar, often required weight for weight with the fruit being preserved. Only gradually did convenient equipment come to her aid. In the earliest days, stone or earthenware jars would be used to hold her preserves. Glass was at first not to be had at all; then it appeared, but not of a type into which a cook dared pour hot foods, much less boil container and all, in the common method of our mothers. It was not until 1858 that the Mason jar was patented, by which time industrial canning was already well launched; but many women would continue to prefer their own preserves to those of the factories, and so would their families.

Nevertheless the eating habits of the nation were gradually modified as commercial food processing developed, whether for better or for worse—probably a little of each. It has been maintained that the canning industry gave Americans a healthier diet, a debatable assertion. That it gave them a wider choice of foods is indisputable, but with the unfortunate corollary that regional differences, with all their rich culinary traditions, tended to disappear. Industrial canning certainly reduced the labor of the housewife, but sometimes also the pleasure of eating.

Modern food processing may be said to date from 1809, when a Frenchman named Nicholas Appert invented vacuum-packed hermetically sealed jars for food and was consequently gratified by a prize of twelve thousand francs bestowed on him by no less a donor than the Emperor Napoleon, who had been seeking some means of assuring a supply of unspoilable food for his armies. He saw to it that Appert's process remained a French monopoly for as many years as it could be kept from others, treating it as a military secret. It was inevitable that sooner or later others would hit upon the same principle, and when that occurred in the United States, the same preoccupation with feeding armies helped start commercial canning on its profitable way because of the demand for safe food in large quantities created by the needs of the Civil War.

Without waiting for the fillip of war, America had already begun to develop large-scale food preserving, using variants of Appert's system. The two pioneers in this effort were Englishmen, not Americans—William Underwood, who arrived in Boston probably in 1819, and Thomas Kensett, who landed at New York at about the same time. Both of them set up companies for preserving food according to Appert's technique, using glass containers. In 1825 Kensett took out the first patent for tin cans; and in 1839 the Kensett and Underwood companies both switched from glass to tin, with most other food processors following suit. When Henry Evans invented in 1849 a machine which reduced the hand labor involved in making tin cans, another impetus was given to the industry, which hardly needed one; it was doing very well already. The first foods canned commercially were lobster and salmon; by the end of the 1840s great quantities of other kinds of fish, of corn, of tomatoes, and of peas were also being sold in cans. The discovery of gold in California, all of whose food at first had to be imported, was a boon to enterprises capable of delivering foods unspoiled over great distances after considerable lapses of time. By 1850, Californians were complaining that the land was being buried under heaps of rusting cans and emptied bottles. Unperturbed by the peril to the environment, no pressing problem in those days, the Mills B. Espey company of Philadelphia alone canned ten tons of cherries, five tons of strawberries, ten thousand baskets of peaches, tomatoes and pears, more than four thousand bushels of plums, gooseberries and quinces, and uncounted thousands of bushels of assorted vegetables, all in the single year of 1855.

It was still before the Civil War when an ingenious and imaginative inventor named Gail Borden got his start on a career embodying all the elements of a story by his contemporary, Horatio Alger, whose heroes were invariably gifted with virtue and industry, and reaped accordingly the material success which such merits always command. Gail Borden, inspired, we are told, by the highest humanitarian principles, embarked on an enterprise in which he was appropriately rewarded by fame and riches. The story goes that Borden had been shocked into what later turned out to be a profitable activity by the fate of the Donner party, the hapless eighty-seven immigrants who, on their way to California, were trapped in 1846 in heavy snows which blocked the passes through the Sierra Nevadas; forty-seven of them survived by eating the others. Borden was moved by this horror, the legend continues, to vow that he would create concentrated foods which would save future adventurers from succumbing, in such dire circumstances, to starvation or cannibalism. "I mean to put a potato into a pillbox," he declared, "a pumpkin into a tablespoon, the biggest sort of a watermelon into a sauce. The Turks made acres of roses into attar of roses. . . . I intend to make attar of everything!"

That no crass commercial motives inspired him seems to be confirmed by the fact that his first attempt to produce attar was not a success. He spent six years, according to the official account, developing a meat biscuit. The Kent Kane Arctic expedition included the Borden biscuit among its provisions, but the number of persons heading for the Arctic or planning to become snowbound in the Rocky Mountains proved insufficient to provide a market for his streamlined pemmican; and stay-at-homes showed little interest in shrunken meat in a country which provided plenty of it in the untreated state. Possibly Borden, a man who held that eating was a waste of time and boasted of getting through his meals in fifteen minutes, had overlooked the element of taste.

He abandoned attar of meat and shifted to attar of milk; there he reaped his reward. Once again he had been inspired by the noblest of motives. The story this time is that during a rough crossing from London, his heart was wrung by the crying of immigrant babies, hungry because all the cows aboard ship were seasick and could not provide milk. The product of this harrowing experience was condensed milk, which he patented in 1856; it was an immediate success. It would probably have made him rich even if the Civil War had not broken out at the right time to provide him with a tremendous market for his product; but its usefulness for the armies was no small factor in helping Borden make a fortune.

XIX

Harbingers of Health

NOBODY COULD BE BLAMED for assuming that today's health food fanatics represent a very recent phenomenon, an alarmed reaction to the encroachments of a chemical industry which showers upon us a profusion of pesticides, weed killers and fertilizers, doses our natural foods with additives designed to preserve, color or falsify them, creates unnatural foods synthetically without benefit of any natural food at all, and adds to these direct interventions the indirect one of an all-pervading pollution of the earth we tread, the water we drink, and the air we breathe. Actually, however, food reformers appeared in the United States as early as the 1830s. They went overboard when they became enmeshed in their own ideologies, as they do today, but their crusades were sometimes well directed, no doubt by instinct, or perhaps empirically, for they could not have known why some of the dietary practices they advocated were beneficial. The Reverend Sylvester Graham had never heard of vitamins, but the foods he recommended provided them; Catherine Beecher did not suspect the existence of cholesterol, but the diet she preached was anti-cholesterol. The New Englander who in 1832 advocated the formation of a Society for the Suppression of Eating may seem to have been going a little far, but the name is not to be taken too literally; he was not in favor of ceasing to eat entirely, but only of restraining one's intake to the minimum amount of food which duly constituted medical authorities might decree to be necessary, and in any case going without dinner once a week. This was an example of an attitude not uncommon in the United States, where many persons (Gail Borden, for instance) regarded eating as a regrettable necessity—an attitude which may well be an offshoot of Puritanism.

It is probably true that many Americans over-ate at this period, though it should be taken into account that in those days more persons led an active outdoor life than do so today; that central heating had not yet reduced dependency on internal fuel for heating the human body; and that the climate was then in the chilly part of a cycle which later shifted to the opposite direction. The Yankee's day started, reported Sir William Howard Russell, correspondent for the London *Times* in the United States from 1861 to 1863, with a breakfast of "black tea and toast, scrambled eggs, fresh spring shad, wild pigeons, pigs' feet, two robins on toast, oysters," and continued unabashed in similarly lavish fashion for the more serious meals of the day. A reaction from heavy eating may have set in toward the middle of the nineteenth century because it was at about this time that the United States began to transform itself from an agricultural to an industrial society; there was also, as there so often is in America, a moralistic element.

It was probably no accident that the first, or one of the first, food reformers of the United States was a former Presbyterian preacher and agent of the Pennsylvania Temperance Society, the sort of man who might easily have been inspired by a Puritanical disapproval of self-indulgence and a feeling that there was something sinful about enjoying one's food. The Reverend Sylvester Graham may have started out from a basis of ascetic morality, but from whatever direction he arrived, he stumbled upon one principle with which we do not disagree today, the fact that different foods have different values. At the period when he became a food prophet, "it was widely believed," according to Daniel Boorstin, "that all foods had the same nutritive value. There was supposed to be one 'universal aliment' which helped the body grow, which kept it warm and working, and repaired the tissues." It did not much matter what you ate, as long as you ate enough of it.

Graham disapproved of dependence on any single major food, or even on a narrow range of foods, possibly because of disgust at gluttony and at addiction to the distrusted pleasures of the flesh, which he expressed by attacking the accepted heavy foods of his times. He advocated replacing them with natural food, which he defined as that which "the Creator has designed for man in such a condition as is best adapted to the anatomical structure and physiological powers of the human system," and simple food, not "compounded and complicated by culinary processes."

These principles led Graham to espouse the cause of fresh fruit and vegetables, clearly uncomplicated by culinary processes, at a time when the orthodox view was that fresh foods were dangerous. Highly respected doctors were blaming the cholera epidemic of 1832 on the eating of uncooked fruit, yet Graham was bold enough to tell Americans to eat it raw, and to eat more of it instead of meat, since meat made for hot tempers and sexual excess. He was especially critical of pork; he abhorred shellfish; and if he tolerated such animal foods as eggs, milk, and honey, it was just barely. Condiments which made for tastiness, a sensual pleasure, were anathema, even salt; as for pepper and mustard, and even such bland seasoners as catsup, they could cause insanity.

Since Graham disapproved of modifying foods from the fashion in which the Creator had presented them, it was natural that he should have adopted toward the food which is the symbol of all foods, bread (and the wheat from which it is made), the attitude which has embedded his name firmly in the English language. He opposed removing from wheat the bran with which nature had enriched it, for the purpose of arriving at fashionably white flour. This earned him the indignity of being mobbed by bakers in Boston. One wonders why, for what difference would it make to them if their customers ordered whole wheat bread instead of white bread? They could provide either. Perhaps they preferred refined flour because it keeps better in storage, but in this case they might have accommodated to Graham by keeping their flour in the form of bread, since he advocated eating one's bread slightly stale anyway—another means, perhaps, of curbing the indecent excesses of sensual pleasure.

Graham was aware that bran was somewhat laxative, making, in reasonable proportions, for digestibility; but its effect is achieved by irritating the stomach, so opinion remains divided about how much bran human beings ought to consume. What Graham could not have known was that bran has the merit of adding mineral salts and the still undiscovered vitamins to bread, elements which are to a large extent removed when wheat is milled into refined white flour. He was helped in his crusade for whole wheat bread by the circumstance, which to be consistent he should have regarded with suspicion, that whole wheat bread is excellent in taste; so today we are still eating graham bread, graham gems and graham crackers, all made from graham flour.

Graham's theories made a considerable impression in their time. Beginning in 1838 "Graham boarding houses" began to spring up all over the country, serving only meals in harmony with the food evangelist's teachings. Yet, dishearteningly, only a score of years after Graham had first enunciated his theories, depraved and unscrupulous millers were already sabotaging his efforts. The *Ladies' Indispensable Companion,* published in 1854, included a recipe for "Brown or Dyspepsia Bread," with this introduction:

> This bread is now best known as "Graham Bread,"—not that Doctor Graham invented or discovered the manner of its preparation, but that he has been unwearied and successful in recommending it to the public. It is an excellent article of diet for the dyspeptic and the costive; and for most persons of sedentary habits it would be beneficial. It agrees well with children; and, in short, I think it should be used in every family, though not to the exclusion of fine bread. The most difficult point in manufacturing this bread is to obtain good pure meal. It is said that much of the bread

> commonly sold as *dyspepsia* is made of the bran or middlings, from which the fine flour has been separated; and that *saw-dust* is sometimes mixed with the meal. To be certain that it is good, send good clean wheat to the mill, have it ground rather coarsely, and keep the meal in a dry cool place. Before using it, sift it through a common hair-seive [sic]; this will separate the very coarse and harsh particles.

It was in 1838 also that vegetarianism may be said to have had its beginning in the United States, since that was the year in which an American Health Convention endorsed vegetable diets; but America would have to wait until after the Civil War to achieve the formal organization of vegetarianism which had been consecrated in England as early as 1809; it was in 1813 that Percy Bysshe Shelley took time out from composing such sensual verse as the *Ode to the West Wind* in order to demonstrate, with a more commendable sense of duty, that the human body is designed to deal with vegetable foods and with vegetable foods only (he had perhaps neglected to examine the evidence to the contrary provided by human dentition).

Following in the footsteps of Graham, cookbook authors fired by his spirit provided the recipes for putting his theories into practical effect. Catherine Beecher, shocked at the large amounts of what she considered indigestible food which Americans were tucking away, called for more ascetic eating in *Miss Beecher's Domestic Recipe Book,* published in 1846. "The most injurious food of any in common use," she wrote, "is the *animal* oils, and articles cooked with them." Mrs. Horace Mann *(née* Peabody, one of the three famous Transcendentalist Peabody sisters of Massachusetts) ruled that "there is no more prolific cause of bad morals than abuses of diet." Like Graham, she exuded an evangelical odor of sanctity, and her cookbook, published in 1861, opened with a somewhat disconcerting Biblical tag: "There's death in the pot." Its title was *Christianity in the Kitchen.*

XX

Westward the Course of Empire

AS FARMERS, THE CHEROKEE were too efficient for their own good. Fifteen thousand strong when the whites arrived and hence one of the largest Indian tribes, they occupied territory which straddled parts of what are today the Carolinas, Georgia, Alabama, and Tennessee, where they quickly absorbed and applied such lessons in civilization as the newcomers were capable of expounding to them. They even paid the whites the compliment, in 1820, of organizing their own government on the basis of that of the United States.

The Cherokee lands were better suited for pasturage than for tilling, so after the domestic animals imported from Europe had multiplied sufficiently to leave a surplus for Indians to acquire, the Cherokee sapiently chose, from about 1790 on, to devote themselves primarily to raising livestock. They succeeded so well that in 1826 they were able to make the error of revealing to the white authorities that they possessed 22,000 head of cattle, 7,600 horses, 46,000 pigs and 2,500 sheep. Such competition was of course intolerable, so four years later they found themselves under orders to abandon their farms and move West; an aggravating factor may have been that gold had been discovered on Cherokee territory in 1828 (it quickly petered out). President Andrew Jackson's administration decided to take over the Indian lands in violation of a series of treaties granting Cherokee independence, with the somewhat irrelevant explanation that "God intended the South to be cultivated"—but apparently not by Cherokees.

The Indian Removal Act was passed in 1830, but Supreme Court Chief Justice Marshall ruled that American law had no jurisdiction over Cherokee territory. "John Marshall has made his decision," Jackson retorted. "Now let him enforce it." The Cherokee, showing more respect for the Supreme Court than had the President of the United States, refused to budge; so they were rounded up by troops under the command of General Winfield Scott and marched off to what is now Oklahoma in conditions so deplorable that an estimated four thousand of them died en route. It seemed that President Jackson in 1830 was no better disposed towards Indians than Lord Jeffrey Amherst in 1760, when he called them "an execrable race, more nearly allied to the Brute than to the Human Creation," and in a brilliant anticipation of biological warfare, suggested that they be issued infected blankets with the intention of killing them off by smallpox.

The Cherokee were of course not the only Indians pushed back beyond the Mississippi, into a territory then considered so distant, inhospitable and superfluous that the white man would never become interested in it. The Removal Act applied to eastern Indians in general; if the case of the Cherokee is cited oftenest, it is because they had become so particularly well adapted to the new situation created by European settlement and seemed so much more capable of cohabiting cooperatively with their white neighbors than any others, that their deportation seemed not only especially unjust but also particularly senseless, even inexplicable—except on the assumption that the whites were inspired by ruthless greed.

The Indians were relegated to territory which the whites then considered so indisputably a wilderness that they had no hesitation in granting it to them in perpetuity. The ritual wording of the new set of treaties drawn up to replace those which had just been broken guaranteed the Indians possession of their new lands "as long as grass grows and water runs." In the light of subsequent events in the areas covered by this sweeping promise, we can only conclude that they were visited shortly afterwards by an unparalleled drought which withered vegetation and dried up water courses—provoked, perhaps, by the feverish heat engendered when gold was discovered in California in 1848. The white man realized that he had not resettled the Indians far enough away, nor on sufficiently despicable territory; he followed the red man into the opening West.

The expansion of the United States westward was not destined to provoke much change in the eating patterns of the nation. The major new foods of America had all become known to the early settlers on the Atlantic coast. As they moved westward, they would come upon some slightly different fish or game animals or roots or berries, and meet on the Pacific coast some shellfish not quite like those of the Atlantic; but there would be nothing so startlingly new as to provoke any gastronomic revolutions.

Along the undefined and unofficial frontier which edged inexorably westward as adventurous, or simply feckless, settlers unable to make a go of it in a more organized society, moved forward, a pioneer society developed, whose circumstances were not such as to encourage culinary achievements. It is often maintained that the American attitude toward women, up to the middle of this century at least, was a product of the pioneer period, a psychological distortion which arose from the existence of an all-male society. A common American attitude toward gastronomy, contempt for the skills (or frills) of cooking, may go back to the pioneer period too. Men with no women in the kitchen to give loving attention to their food involved themselves in a relentless struggle for bare survival, and had neither time nor patience to concern themselves with the quality of what they ate. They gulped down whatever happened to be at hand—salt pork and beans mostly—without tasting it. Eating was necessary, but annoying; it was disposed of as quickly as possible. The mythology of those times might lead us to believe that the pioneer diet consisted chiefly of whiskey; it was not even good whiskey. If the pioneers passed down any eating habits to us, they were bad habits.

If the westward movement did not increase the variety of American foods, it did increase amply the quantity of food available. With very few exceptions, each step westward opened up territory capable of nourishing a population much larger than it was likely to acquire within any foreseeable future. American soil was, after all, everywhere virgin; the meager Indian population (estimated at under a million when the whites arrived, for the whole territory now covered by the United States) had not depleted the soil, nor had its hunting and fishing reduced to any appreciable extent the amount of animal food available.

The westward flow began, hesitantly at first, from the two extremities of the settled coastal regions, in the North through Ohio toward the Great Lakes, in the South through Kentucky and Tennessee toward the Mississippi (farther south the country was still Spanish, until 1821, or French, until 1803).

Kentucky received few good marks for its food from early visitors. Thomas Ashe, who visited the state in 1806, reported that Kentuckians ate salt meat three times a day, seldom or never had any vegetables, and drank "ardent spirits"—we may assume it was whiskey—from morning till night. On the first count, he added that Kentuckians actually preferred salt meat to fresh, which they thought was "unwholesome"—and in those times, before refrigeration was available to keep fresh meat from spoiling and before understanding had been acquired of the danger to human health constituted by the pig's parasitic worms, they may have been right. On the last count, Ashe was supported by the anonymous wit who in 1822 defined a Kentucky breakfast as "three cocktails and a chaw of terbacker." (Yes, cocktails *did* exist then.)

As for Tennessee, it did little to increase American food resources at that period since neither of its two principal crops, cotton and tobacco, were foods; yet foods would provide a good deal of the state's income by the opening of the nineteenth century—flour, bacon (and whiskey), which were floated downstream by flatboat, via the capricious Tennessee River, the Ohio, and the Mississippi, as far as New Orleans. Today Tennessee produces prize Jersey, Angus, and Hereford cattle, and picks up an appreciable amount of revenue from dairy products, hogs, corn and wheat. Its chief claim to gastronomic fame comes from the legendary generosity of its breakfasts, which customarily include, among a host of other edibles, thick slices of the state's luscious country ham.

In the North, when the United States inherited their western lands from the British, America was not quite sure what it had acquired. In 1787 Congress gave it a name anyway, as the first step toward identification, the Northwest Territory, defined as lying west of Pennsylvania, north of the Ohio River, east of the Mississippi and south of the Great Lakes.

Once again, new territory did not mean new foods, but it did mean more food. As soon as transportation facilities made it possible, Ohio shipped eastward substantial quantities of game, of which some species were already diminishing farther east. As the land was cleared, Ohio took on, little by little, the aspect we know today, that of a land of gently rolling fields, for the most part highly fertile, on which it now grows cereals, fruit, sugar beets, and that relatively recent discovery, soybeans, and raises cattle. But its most important contribution, from the historical point of view (for it is no longer of much agricultural or economic importance), was the creation of an eastern wine industry. One might indeed credit Ohio with being the very first wine-growing area in the United States, for California was still a foreign country when the first Ohio wine was produced.

The first winemaker was Nicholas Longworth of Cincinnati, who began experimenting with the Catawba grape in the 1820s; by 1830, wine was an important item in the economy of Ohio. It was from Ohio that the wine industry spread into New York State, where the child smothered the parent; today, with a little diligence, you can find New York wines, but it is hard work to locate a bottle from Ohio.

Indiana became a state in 1816. It has since, thanks to its undulating fertile terrain and a climate which, though invigorating, is not given to extremes, become one of the corn-hog regions of the United States. This couple, through whose happy symbiosis corn is marketed in the form of pork, provides one of the major bases of American eating. It is an expensive way to consume corn—it takes four pounds of corn to produce one pound of pork—but it follows an American tradition which from the beginning was based on a plenitude of meat resulting from a plenitude of fodder resulting from a plenitude of land. The land is a little more crowded now, but there is still enough room to permit the hog to be the leading citizen of Indiana, Illinois, and Iowa.

Americans met the prairies for the first time when they moved into Illinois, which still calls itself "the Prairie State." A land of fertile soil and hospitable topography, it allowed itself to be conquered easily. It is today a leading corn-hog state, and a producer of other grains also, and of soybeans.

The first Europeans to enter Michigan were French; in 1810, Michigan still had fewer than five thousand white inhabitants, most of them French. Its first contribution to the American larder was fish and game. Louis Armand de Lom d'Arce, Baron de La Hontan, who was fascinated by American Indians and praised the virtues of the primitive way of life, reported in 1687 that he had encountered there "trout as big as one's thigh." These were lake trout, which shared the waters with, notably, whitefish. As for game, there is still a good deal of it on the Upper Peninsula, including white-tailed deer. Michigan was the last stand in the United States of the woodland caribou; a few still lived on Isle Royale until 1927. Hunters in the Michigan woods make a catch-all stew from game which they call booyaw or boolyaw; it is an echo of the state's French past, for it represents an attempt to reproduce the French pronunciation of the word *bouillon.*

The state flower of Michigan is the apple blossom, the symbol of a category of food for which it is indeed important, fruit. Besides apples, Michigan produces great quantities of peaches, plums, canteloupes, strawberries and cherries, especially cherries, of which it grows more than any other state. Traverse City, Michigan, is the cherry capital of the United States, and rubs in that fact by devoting an entire week in July to a cherry festival. Michigan is also an important dairy state, the first in the Union to prohibit the sale of non-pasteurized milk.

Wisconsin became a state in 1848, the year when political upheavals in Europe drove a wave of immigrants to America, including the Germans who were to make Milwaukee famous for beer and Wisconsin for cheese. Not until 1860 did Wisconsin develop its first important commercial crop, wheat. Still a leading agricultural state, it is more important today for dairy products, and indeed describes itself on its automobile license plates as "America's dairyland." Few persons outside the state, and for that matter not very many within it, are conscious of another Wisconsin specialty—peppermint.

The first Americans to settle in Missouri were probably the seventy Virginians who in 1789 founded New Madrid (so called because the territory was then Spanish). "I come from a State that raises corn and cotton and cockleburs and Democrats," announced Missouri Congressman Willard Duncan Vandiver, in the speech that gave to America the immortal phrase, "I'm from Missouri; you've got to show me"; but he was seriously underestimating the area he represented. Missouri grows corn, wheat and soybeans, sells milk, poultry and eggs, and raises hogs, cattle, and the famous Missouri mule.

Arkansas became a state in 1836, but it made no particularly notable contribution to the nation's food supplies, although its eastern half is distinguished by fertile alluvial soil. It remains primarily an agricultural state, growing grapes, peaches, strawberries, watermelons, pecans, tomatoes, spinach, sorghum, and wheat; but some of the products from which it derives much of its revenue today were not developed until our own century—rice and soybeans in the 1920s, broilers (of which it quickly became the nation's second most important supplier) in the 1950s, and, even more recently, catfish: Little Rock is the headquarters of the Association of Catfish Farmers of America.

With Iowa, the United States gained one of its greatest food producing states. Iowa lies wholly within the area of the Great Plains. The first American settlers to enter the territory found it robed in high coarse grass, spangled with wild berries and gay with flowers. Except for a rare grove here and there, trees were confined to the river valleys. The topsoil went deep, and it was richly fertile. Iowa possesses more of what agronomists classify as Grade A land than any other state, and the highest percentage of cultivable land—85 to 90 percent of its total area. Nature had destined it to become the richest of the corn-hog states. Almost half of the cultivated land is devoted to corn, making it first in the nation for corn production; almost all of the corn is fed to animals, especially hogs, so that from the middle of the twentieth century the value of Iowa's livestock had outstripped that of all other states, even including beef-raising Texas, five times as big. Oats, barley, soybeans, eggs and milk are also significant to the state's economy.

The firstcomers to Minnesota found that its southern half was still in the prairies, open rolling land, but a region where the all-grass plains were beginning to give way to scattered woods of oak and other deciduous trees. The dark fertile loam of the south would prove excellent for cereals, while the northern part of the state, worked over by the glaciers of the ice ages, possessed fine deep rich soil also. Even the sandy east-central area was suitable for hay and root crops. Minnesota was clearly cut out for agriculture, and it became in time the United States' largest producer of butter, second largest producer of oats, third largest producer of corn, fourth largest producer of hay, and sometimes the fifth, sometimes the sixth, largest producer of livestock. It contributed also sizable quantities of soybeans, peas, barley, rye, sugar beets, potatoes and cheese. It does not grow much fruit, except apples.

When the United States established itself on the west bank of the Mississippi, it entered territory destined to become the great granary of the Republic—and failed to notice it. One might have thought that common sense alone would have suggested that an area capable of supporting sixty million head of buffalo could at least feed a few cows. But no: the first settlers accepted blindly the dicta of those who agreed with Zebulon Pike that the region was as "incapable of cultivation" as "the sandy deserts of Africa."

> I saw in my route in various places [he reported] tracts of many leagues where the wind had thrown up the sand in all the fanciful forms of the ocean's rolling waves and on which not a speck of vegetable matter existed.

Major Stephen R. Long, who in 1820 led a government expedition over the same territory, gave it the name of the "Great American Desert."

> In regard to this extensive section of country [he wrote], I do not hesitate in giving my opinion that it is almost wholly unfit for cultivation, and of course [of course!], uninhabitable by a people depending upon agriculture for their subsistence. Although tracts of fertile land considerably extensive are occasionally to be met with, yet the scarcity of wood and water, almost uniformly prevalent, will prove an insuperable obstacle in the way of settling the country.

It would be much later before settlers from the East would pour into Iowa to the strains of a song which proclaimed, "Ioway, Ioway, that's where the tall corn grows!" Until then it remained an article of faith that from Iowa and Nebraska to Arkansas and Oklahoma the land was fit for nothing but game. This probably accounted for the fact that the tier of states just west of those which bordered on the Mississippi did not become part of the Union until after the Civil War, except Kansas, which just made it—it became a state on January 29, 1861, seventy-five days before Fort Sumter surrendered and the war was on.

The first European to see Kansas was no doubt Coronado, seeking, in 1541, the mythical golden city of Quivira; when it proved nonexistent, the Spaniards left Kansas alone. They had been impressed there by the tremendous herds of buffalo (the state animal of Kansas) and so were the Americans when they arrived; the animal was already familiar to them, but not in such numbers. The slaughter of the buffalo was about to begin, but it would not end until well after the Civil War.

With Kansas, the United States had acquired another state capable of adding immensely to its food resources. Major Long had described it as "a sandy wasteland"; later, and better informed, commentators would call it the bread basket of the world. Major Long wandered rather far astray when he wrote off as infertile the state which would become the first for the production of wheat, mostly hard winter wheat, and would also rack up creditable scores in the raising of corn, oats, barley, sorghum, soybeans, potatoes, sugar beets, apples, and livestock.

XXI

Lands of Fable

NO SECTION of the United States has received more glowing, even fulsome, praise or more scathing abuse than the Lone Star State, for ten years a proudly independent Republic which on February 16, 1846, consented to become the twenty-eighth state of the Union, with the reservation that it might decide one day to split up its vast territory to become four more separate states. Up to now, this right has never been exercised, and the thought of eight more Texas Senators on Capitol Hill may have been a deterrent, even to Texans.

General William Tecumseh Sherman, no hero to the South on any count, is alleged to have said, "If I owned both Hell and Texas, I would rent out Texas and live in Hell." Were he alive today he would surely change his mind, but no Texan would ever forgive him. Nowhere in the whole broad land is there a population more aggressively defensive against criticism, or more avid of appreciation for its considerable achievements, its military prowess, its wealth, and its many-faceted patriotism. A secessionist state, despite Governor Sam Houston's desire to have it side with the Union, Texas weathered the Civil War with little battle action or war damage, but endured military rule and Reconstruction, the latter ending in 1874, with considerable resentment toward the damyankees. This feeling is latent today among most Texans, yet they are on the whole friendly and outgoing, especially in regard to foreigners, Europeans for instance.

Texas, or *Tejas* as the Spaniards spelled it, was an ill-fated area which can best be described as the northernmost Spanish province east of the Rockies. It was governed, theoretically, by the Spanish viceroy in Mexico City; but in nearly three centuries of colonial occupation, the Spaniards actually accomplished very little, and in 1821 their rule was succeeded by that of the newborn Republic of Mexico. Late in that very same year, Mexico authorized Stephen Austin, son of Moses Austin, a St. Louis banker, to bring into the province of *Tejas* three hundred colonist families, all Anglo-Americans. Their first settlement was on the Brazos River and was called San Filipe de Austin, not to be confused with Austin, the present capital of Texas. This was the beginning of a policy under which Mexico offered inducements to Americans to settle in Texas, rather shortsightedly it would seem, since the government could hardly have been unaware that there were Americans who coveted Texas. There were also Americans who didn't. When the question became acute, many of them were lukewarm, and some even heated, about adding to the United States what they probably considered as more desert; besides, the brashness of Texans had already become obvious.

In the light of a fairly widespread reluctance to receive the new territory with open arms, one might perhaps be tempted to discount any theory that the winning of independence by Texas was the result of wily machinations and general skulduggery motivated from the beginning by the intent to create a situation which would permit bringing Texas into the United States. "The story that the whole movement was the development of a deliberate and treacherous plot for the conquest of Texas," Frederick Law Olmsted opined, "appears a needless exaggeration of influences that really played a secondary part." He admitted nevertheless that "the land was fertile; that was the kernel of the matter. . . . We saw the land lying idle; we took it."

However it happened, and whether the United States annexed Texas or Texas annexed the United States, its entry into the Union was probably inevitable. In 1836 there were thirty thousand Americans living in Texas and only 7,500 Mexicans. It was not surprising that the English-speaking majority broke away from a not very effective foreign government with which it shared neither language, nor religion, nor culture. Texas became an American state, technically in 1845, effectively in 1846, when the Mexican War settled the matter.

It is with the arrival of the English-speaking settlers that we begin to know what and how Texans ate. Modern Texas (which, big as it is, is smaller than the original Republic of Texas, due to the loss of the territories which were ceded to the United States, along with California, for $15,000,000 and are now parts of New Mexico, Oklahoma, Kansas, Wyoming and Colorado) contains a variety of soils and climates, as well as areas of mountains, timberland, farmlands, range and pasture, and a rich coastal plain with a sub-tropical climate.

For the most part the colonists entered Texas from the northeast and spread out south and west. In these areas there were herds of wild horses and cattle, survivors of the animals the Spanish conquistadores brought with them, while to the north of the early colonized areas the plains were still the realm of the buffalo. The wild bulls of the cattle herds were dangerous; perhaps they had reverted to the wildness of the European aurochs, or ancestors even more remote. Today their descendant, the Texas Longhorn, picturesque rather than palatable, has been replaced by more stolid, beefy, hornless breeds: Angus, Hereford, or Brahma, and an attempt has been made to adapt the Charolais, France's prime beef animal, to Texas life.

Wherever the settlers landed, their first thought was to plant corn, the indispensable grain of the pioneer. Green ears could be eaten boiled or roasted, and the ripe kernels, grated, furnished a sweet sort of bread, or the makings of a porridge. Most valuable of all was the dried grain, which could be ground or pounded into meal. From the pith of the cornstalk something like molasses was sometimes made, and this could be used to sweeten cornmeal mush if no honey was available. From the cornmeal, various pioneer breads were made, if the settlers had a pan or two and a working fireplace, but milk and butter were scarce, despite the herds of cattle roaming just beyond the cabin door. A visiting Englishman wrote home that Texas corn bread was "a modification of sawdust." But, at least, there was no shortage of meat on Texas tables in the first half of the nineteenth century. Much of it was game: wild turkey, venison, bear, and buffalo, the latter prized for its tongue, which was tender, and tolerated for its steaks, which were tough. Wild geese, ducks, and prairie hens abounded, and in winter great flocks of pigeons sometimes came south. Hunters in 1838 traveled with a provision of venison, honey, and bear-oil as their iron ration, and William Ransom Hogan, in *The Texas Republic,* cites the report of one Nestor Clay, who took a party seven hundred miles up the Colorado River (of Texas) and down the Brazos in 1832, that they lived for two months "on different kinds of wild flesh: Buffalo, Mustang, horse, wild Cow, antelope, Panther, Bear, wildcat, mountain cat, Polecat, Leopard cat, together with a variety of fish, fowl, turtle, etc., making nineteen in all."

In the early days of Texas independence there were sharp contrasts in the way people ate. In Galveston, for instance, one could find restaurants with cakes and pies, shops that sold oysters raw and cooked, confectioners offering candies and ice creams. This reflected European influences, perhaps, seeping in from Louisiana and from the port. Then, too, the bottom lands of the coastal plain grew not only cotton but also tomatoes, melons, beans and pumpkins—and the inevitable corn and sweet potatoes. The government of the Republic of Texas needed revenues, and did not hesitate to put customs duties on essentials like bacon and wheat flour, which rose in price from ten dollars to seventy-five dollars a barrel. Also taxed were imported "apples, rice, molasses, raisins, beans, onions, sugar, coffee, tea, salt, mackerel and codfish. In 1838 Samuel Williams of Galveston . . . directed his wife to sell a town lot and buy several boxes of cherries."

But in the less favored areas, including the first capital of the Republic,

Washington-on-the-Brazos, the boardinghouses served a monotonous ordinary of fried beef, corn dodgers, sweet potatoes and black coffee, and only rarely had milk or butter. William W. Arnett arrived as a young man in Tyler County (possibly on his way to Houston or Galveston) and protested, "I can't see how a man can live as you folks do and be a Christian, for the ticks, the black mud, the sand flies, and musketoes—dry beef, black coffee, sweet potatoes and other hard features of your country would ruin me. . . . It is the most perfect purgatory of any place on the Earth." This was in 1845, and only about sixty miles from the fleshpots of Galveston. Down the Gulf Coast, at Corpus Christi, the same year, there were two hundred barrooms, selling mostly whiskey and brandy but also imported gin, champagne, claret and port. By 1842 cocktail mixing had been featured at the best hotels, where very fancy drinks, some still to be found in the classic Bartender's Guide, were offered at twenty-five cents each. Mexican dishes began to have some popularity, notably in the southern cities, and added a variety of format and flavors. Somehow *tamales* of cornmeal, chopped meat, and hot pepper, wrapped in a cornhusk and steamed, had more to offer than hoecake, johnny cake, or pone. *Chili con carne,* which Mexicans repudiate as not being part of their cuisine, and Texans vaunt as part of theirs, had not yet arrived on the scene in any of its "Tex-Mex" forms, but Texans adopted other Mexican ways of cooking eggs and meat, as has the whole Southwest in our times. On many tables there was quinine, offered beside the salt and pepper, while morning black coffee was also rated as a preventive of malaria. Texans to some degree adopted the habit of the siesta, which even today is referred to as "nooning" or "nooning it."

Before we leave the legends of the Lone Star Republic to contemplate those of the great trail-driving period, the War Between the States, and the days before the railroads came to Texas, let us remember that Easterner who died in Texas and was cured like a ham, smoked, packed in two barrels joined end to end, and shipped by boat to New York to his wife for burial. Nor is it fitting to discuss the Texas Republic without some reference to the Battle of the Alamo. Ours is from John Myers' absorbing recital *The Alamo:*

> For breakfast at the Alamo there was corn and beef, for lunch corn and beef, for supper beef and corn. The ninety or so bushels of corn and twenty to thirty head of cattle . . . was . . . almost their entire stock of food.

Myers also tells the story of Louis Rose, a former mercenary of Napoleon's army, who, when volunteers were called for, was the only man *not* to step forward across Colonel Travis's sword-drawn line. Knowing the jig was up, Rose cut out unhindered, leaving the defense only to dedicated men, each remembered while Rose is forgotten.

*

If old Texas was a fabulous land, especially as Texans tell it, old California was fabulous too, down to its very name. It was taken from a Spanish chivalric novel popular in the time of Columbus, in which "California" was an imaginary realm described, with a certain lack of precision, as being "near the terrestrial paradise." Many Californians would be willing to accept this description today as applicable to their part of the world, but the Spaniards who had discovered it showed no great haste to enter the terrestrial paradise. Perhaps the Spaniards had heard from the Indians reports which made California sound less like a terrestrial paradise than a terrestrial hell. A versatile state, it holds not only rich valleys, lush now with orange orchards, vegetable farms and vineyards, but also the desolate lowest point on the North American continent (280 feet below sea level, in Death Valley) and also the hottest (the Colorado desert, which shares with neighboring Arizona's lower Gila valley temperatures which sometimes reach 129 in the shade).

From the point of view of the acquisition of California by the United States, it was a stroke of luck that the discovery of gold was not made before a considerable number of Americans had already moved into the territory nor before the United States was capable of acting effectively in the area. But gold was discovered at Sutter's mill almost simultaneously with the American victory in the Mexican War—a war which many persons suspected was inspired less by the conflict over Texas than by the desire of President James Polk to lay hands on California, even before its mineral richness was known.

Americans were not unanimous about the desirability of enlarging the national territory. The legislature of the state of Massachusetts even called the Mexican War unconstitutional, an attitude explicable by the fear of anti-slavery circles that it might result in adding new slave territory to the Union.

There does not seem to be any exact information on when the first Americans entered California, but there was at least one there in 1824, for that was the year when Joseph Chapman planted a vineyard on land which is today in Los Angeles. In 1827 a French traveler remarked on the plentiful production of fruit and vegetables in California, and especially on the fine herds of cattle established by the missions. William Wolfskill, a Kentucky trapper whose name for that profession seems almost too good to be true, is caught on the scene in the 1830s, not trapping wolves, but making wine. Trade between California and the United States developed promisingly about 1840, attracting Americans to this part of Mexico. American settlers were cultivating the San Joaquin Valley in 1843, but in 1846 were still very few—five hundred according to one authority, seven hundred according to another, outnumbered but not submerged by ten thousand Mexicans and twenty thousand Indians.

With the discovery of gold, California, American now, abruptly changed character. The territory had launched itself upon an agricultural career, but with the gold strike California's farms were abandoned, and so were its towns. As ships from the East Coast reached California, their crews promptly deserted and went gold hunting too; by July, 1850, the harbor of San Francisco was clogged with five hundred vessels becalmed for want of crews. San Francisco was promoted from a small village named Yerba Buena, "good herb," from a local plant with a mint-like flavor, to a thriving, bustling metropolis of 25,000 citizens, mostly miners. In 1849, eighty thousand new gold seekers entered California, half coming overland, the other half on ships which had rounded Cape Horn. Three-quarters of the gold hunters were Americans, bringing with them Anglo-Saxon eating habits destined to overwhelm Spanish-Mexican ideas. The same phenomenon already encountered on a frontier inhabited by a society with no women in the kitchen was now repeated, strengthening the American tendency to neglect culinary niceties: women made up only eight percent of California's new population, and in the mining areas only two percent. The successful prospectors were heavy spenders; they had to be when it came to food, which was outrageously expensive. Since nobody in California wanted to raise it, everything had to be imported. Nevertheless, for unsuccessful, or not yet successful prospectors, San Francisco developed, in the 1850s, relatively modest hotels and boardinghouses, whose prices were reasonable in their context. Everybody sat down at a common table, and the food was hearty. Meanwhile, for epicureans among those who had struck it rich, a surprising number of French restaurants were opened. The first important one was named Le Poulet d'Or; there were not many linguists among the prospectors, who solved the problem of Gallic pronunciation by referring to it as the Poodle Dog. It was also at this time and place that the American Chinese restaurant got its start.

For the moment, the spectacular potentiality of California as a grower of food was neglected. Its new-found riches served chiefly, in this domain, to further the development of Oregon as a food-supplying state, catering to the Californian gold-rush population.

Oregon was still a wilderness in 1811 when John Jacob Astor's Pacific Fur Company opened there its first trading post, named, in subtle tribute to the boss, Astoria. Fur trappers heading for Astoria were probably the first, in 1811 and 1812, to start breaking what would become the famous Oregon Trail, at first a hardly discernible scarring of the soil by the hoofs of horses and oxen and the wheels of wagons wending their way west across the plains and through the mountains. One of the persons who became interested in Oregon was the same Nathaniel J. Wyeth who had been involved in the ice business in New England. He led an expedition to the territory in 1832, establishing on the way the trading station of Fort Hall, in the Rockies beyond South Pass, the bottleneck through which most westward traffic had to pass. The Northwest was not propitious. He failed lamentably and returned to Boston and ice.

Except for trappers and missionaries, travel to Oregon lagged. In 1840 the American population was only 150. The "Oregon fever" then seized upon the frontiersmen of the Mississippi Valley. New Englanders and Southerners, both of British descent, began to move westward in their covered wagons across the Oregon Trail, beating its faint track into the semblance of a road purposely planned and constructed. Their migration increased the population of the territory eightfold in 1843; but it was a little less than an invasion. The grand total was now 1,200 white inhabitants in all of Oregon.

Reluctance to undertake the harrowing journey to the Columbia River was understandable. There were two thousand miles of wilderness between Independence, Missouri, where the wagon trains started, and the Columbia. The passage took from four to six months, over plains often held by hostile Indians and then through the difficult passes of the Rocky Mountains; but here they were guided by the "mountainy men," trappers who knew every fold and bend of the tortuous terrain.

The covered wagons had to be loaded down with enough food to last the journey, though it was possible to count on taking game along the way and even on deriving some food from wild plants; but the arduous cross-country trek did nothing to develop a taste for luxurious eating. In *American Cooking: The Northwest,* of the *Time-Life Foods of the World* series, Dale Brown gave an excellent account of the culinary difficulties of the travelers:

> Nourishment was not the only criterion in selecting provisions: they had to be the kind that lasted, yet were compact and light to carry. Joel Palmer, who went from Indiana to Oregon in 1845 and wrote a widely read account of the journey, advised would-be followers in his footsteps that for each adult "there should be two hundred pounds of flour, thirty pounds of pilot bread, seventy-five pounds of bacon, twenty-five pounds of sugar, half a bushel of dried beans, one bushel of dried fruit, two pounds of saleratus [baking soda], ten pounds of salt, half a bushel of corn meal." He also urged the purchase of half a bushel of parched ground corn and a keg of vinegar. . . .
>
> Cooking equipment was restricted to essentials. Palmer's recommended list included a sheet-iron stove, a skillet, a Dutch oven, a tin coffeepot, tin plates, cups and saucers, two churns (one for sweet milk, the other for sour), and a large water keg. [So there must have been cows with the parties, unless they were prepared to milk buffalos.]
>
> It is to the everlasting credit of the pioneering women that they managed to feed their families three meals a day. Cooking conditions were, to say the

> least, primitive. Makeshift kitchens had the sky as a roof and the earth as a floor. The water was often brackish or alkaline. . . . Wood was scarce, and the women made their fires with hay, weeds, sagebrush and buffalo chips (dung). . . . Each fuel imparted its own special flavor to the food, and the wind often blew ashes into the skillet. . . . Because the heat from such fuels was unreliable, no woman could ever be certain whether the soda-rising bread she baked in her Dutch oven would come out scorched on the bottom or uncooked in the middle. . . .
>
> Breakfast usually consisted of bread with fried bacon or buffalo meat, washed down with hot coffee or tea [items omitted from Joel Palmer's list]. The midday meal was generally a meat sandwich and coffee, and supper was a repeat of breakfast. On occasion, the morning or evening meal might be varied a little with sour pickles, or beans baked in a pit of ashes and coals, or as a special treat, a dried-apple pie with a crust that had been rolled out on the leather seat of the wagon.

Some of the pioneer women developed special nomadic skills. They made butter by taking advantage of patches of rough going (most of the going was rough) to churn it by the heavings and tossings of the wagon. They timed the rising and kneading of their dough so that it would be at just the right point for baking when the evening halt was made, in an improvised oven manufactured by digging a hole in the side of any handy hillock. The less resourceful simply stocked up on preserved foods—sea biscuit, which could double as land biscuit when crossing the continent was like crossing the sea; dried beef or salt pork; jerky and pemmican, sometimes bought from Indians en route; dried corn; and "pocket soup," which was concentrated meat stock, boiled down and allowed to cool into a gluey jelly, which would keep for years and from which pieces could be cut off and dissolved in hot water as needed; and, of course, the ubiquitous dried apples.

Dried-apple pie was greeted with delight by some, but for others it turned up too frequently, inspiring protest from a poet of the times:

> I loathe, abhor, detest, despise
> Abominate dried apple pies.
> Tread on my corns and tell me lies
> But don't pass me dried apple pies.

Apples, undried, were to become one of the first crops by means of which Oregon would drain off some of the wealth of California, supplying them at fancy prices to the well-heeled gold miners to the south. Later the pear would become the particular pride and glory of Oregon, and the Rogue River valley the great pear producing region of the Northwest, but the apple got there earlier.

The first apple, a harbinger of the great fruit-growing region of the Pacific

Northwest, did not come from the trees which had been established long before in New England and Virginia, nor was it the gift of Johnny Appleseed, who never carried his favorite fruit farther west than Indiana. It was imported independently and directly from the same source which had supplied their original stock to the seventeenth-century colonists of the Atlantic coast—England. The story goes that at a farewell banquet given in London for one Captain Aemilius Simpson, who was about to set out for Oregon, a young lady impulsively handed him the seeds from an apple she had just eaten to plant "in the wilderness." Her act bore fruit near Fort Vancouver. However the real career of the Northwest apple began with American-grown fruit, when two professional nurserymen from Iowa, Henderson Luelling and William Meek, ferried apple seedlings across plains and mountains to the Willamette valley and began apple production there. Their market was California, where Luelling and Meek struck gold more surely than most prospectors. Their product was so valuable that they had to pack it in iron-bound thief-proof crates to ship it to San Francisco, where it sold for as much as five hundred dollars a bushel. Then California saw the light and in 1853 began to plant fruit on its own, sore news for Oregon.

But Oregon had other strings to its bow. Cattle could be raised there on almost no other food than the wild bunch grass, and sold most profitably to California, which in its obsession with gold had neglected its own herds of cattle. This made Oregon also a supplier of dairy products, highly profitable too. It turned out subsequently that Oregon was excellent wheat country as well. And then, of course, there were the salmon.

It was a little difficult to get fresh salmon to the California market quickly enough to be still palatable, but the fish lent itself readily to smoking, air-drying, salting or pickling. The Columbia is one of the greatest salmon rivers in the world, and in those days provided many times as much fish as could possibly be consumed within the area to which it could be delivered; it was well worth while to expend whatever effort might be necessary—the amount was not exorbitant—to preserve this easily taken fish for distant markets. Salmon, nevertheless, was one of the commodities which helped defeat Nathaniel Wyeth. Pickled salmon from the Columbia River was shipped all the way around Cape Horn to Boston, but there met with an unexpected mishap: the Treasury Department ruled that it was "foreign-caught fish," and imposed duty on it. This was not exactly consistent with the claim the United States would make to the Oregon territory a little later, but at that time (1831) most Americans thought Oregon too distant, too isolated—and perhaps too undesirable—to be made part of the Union. At best it might organize itself as an independent state, governed by Americans, which could become a sort of satellite of the United States, but not part of it. Thomas Jefferson himself, when Astoria was founded, envisioned Oregon as being organized by "free and independent Americans, unconnected with us but by the ties of blood and interest, and employing like us the rights of self-government." Even after the waves of immigrants began rolling over the Oregon Trail, a letter writer was quoted in the *Missouri Republican,* on June 11, 1844, as opining that "no man of information, in his right mind, would think of leaving such a country as this, to wander over a thousand miles of desert and five hundred of mountains to reach such as that."

But when California became part of the United States, it was difficult to allow the territory which was then providing much of its food to remain foreign; the salmon had to be naturalized.

XXII

War and Food

THE CIVIL WAR was fought by dyspeptic generals. This would not have surprised Sylvester Graham, if he had lived long enough to witness it; but according to Samuel Eliot Morison, the bad health of the warriors was not attributable to eating the sort of food Graham deplored, but was

> probably the result of constant exposure, lack of sleep, and bolted meals. George H. Thomas was the only general of either side who attempted to maintain a mess commensurate with his rank . . . General Grant suffered from splitting headaches [which may well have had their origin in an upset digestion, but public rumor did not lay that to food]; D. H. Hill from dyspepsia . . . Dick Swell, described at the age of 46 as an "old soldier with a bald head, a prominent nose and a haggard sickly face" . . . suffered from stomach ulcers . . . and lived largely on boiled rice and frumenty . . . Braxton Bragg's chronic dyspepsia, coupled with a mean disposition, made him the most unpopular general in either army . . . A. P. Hill "took sick" on the first day of Gettysburg; Lee became very ill at the most critical time on the North Anna River.

To this list we might add General Winfield Scott, "aged and infirm" when the Civil War broke out, and no wonder. He was seventy-five in 1861, though still commander of the United States armies, and should have been feeling some effects from his rugged record as a veteran of the War of 1812, of several Indian wars, and of the Mexican War. He may also have been suffering from delayed-action indigestion as a result of youthful indulgences in the pleasures of the table; the heinous charge of having a background of luxurious eating, always damaging for a Presidential candidate in the United States, was brought up against him when he was so ill-advised as to run for the Presidency, despite the disadvantage of being a dandy and a swashbuckler whose exhibitionism rubbed the public the wrong way. His unpopular airs were, according to the *Wheeling Argus,* the result of a boyhood diet of turtle and oyster soup, which had afflicted him with a fondness for plumes (the cause and effect relationship is a little hard to follow) and inspired in him a desire "to swim in the sea of society." He carried only four states, but he could pride himself on the fact that, as three of them were inland, he had been able to overcome their probable natural prejudice against oysters and turtles.

General Robert E. Lee's indisposition may have come from the stomach, for Lee ate badly most of the time during his campaigns. The Confederate commissary had difficulty getting food to its armies; Lee lived largely on commandeered cornbread and cabbage, tasting meat on the average only twice a week. Once when he invited some of his officers to dinner the best he could scrape up for them was a large platter of cabbage with a piece of pork buried in it, so small that everybody, out of politeness, refused it; in the end nobody got anything but cabbage. Lee may have become resigned to this somewhat monotonous vegetable; when he took Chambersburg, before the battle of Gettysburg, he called upon the community to provide twenty-five barrels of "Saur-Kraut" for his soldiers. He might have been seduced in this case by a specialty of the Pennsylvania Dutch, but it is more likely that he knew there was nothing else to be had. Just before Appomattox, Lee's surrounded army was half-starved; a train packed with provisions had been unable to reach the Confederate forces. They surrendered to General Grant and to hunger.

Food was an important factor in determining the outcome of the Civil War. The Southern states might have been expected to have an advantage when it came to food supplies, for they were still predominantly agricultural, while the North had become relatively much more thoroughly industrialized. But it was perhaps partly *because* it was industrialized and had therefore learned the techniques of organization that the North was able to mobilize more effectively the food resources it possessed. It was, besides, less fully engaged by the fighting than the South. The principal business, almost the only business, of the South was waging war, an effort which monopolized all its energies; its able-bodied men were almost without exception either in the army or in the government. The North had men to spare, able to busy themselves with other matters; outside the combat areas (which covered a greater proportion of Southern than of Northern territory) it was almost a case of business as usual.

The arable soil of the South was 100 percent mobilized for agriculture; the North controlled previously undeveloped land, which it was able to harness to the war effort. For forty years pioneers had been pressing the government to exploit its western lands, but the government had remained uninterested. Now that war had raised the urgent problem of feeding armies, the

Homestead Act was passed, with commendable dispatch, in 1862; it granted virtually free land to any settlers able and willing to make it productive. The new lands, broken now for the first time, had never been depleted by the growing of crops, and so furnished exceptional yields. The chief crops of the South, cotton and tobacco, were of a type which exhausted the soil on which they grew; when the plantations were converted to food crops, they produced disappointing harvests. In the industrial North, the intensified demand for food generalized the use of the mechanical harvester, which could deliver grain five times as fast as hand labor could handle it, along with other efficient machines which hitherto had been employed by no more than a handful of the biggest landholders. The South, since it possessed ample labor in its slaves, had neglected to manufacture agricultural machinery.

War, instead of reducing food production in the North, applied spurs to it; its farms produced more wheat and corn than it needed to feed its civilian population and nourish its armies. The amount of pork preserved for the market in the North was in 1865 twice as great as it had been in 1860; more than three times as much wool was produced as before the war. The element of luck was added to the element of effort: the war years were characterized by good growing weather. In Europe the conditions were bad. It was a time of crop shortages; the North therefore found in Europe a market for more than 400,000 bushels of surplus wheat and flour in 1862, more than four times the export of the whole nation in 1859. Not only did this put money into the coffers of war, it also exercised a direct influence on the policies of foreign countries tempted to throw their weight into the balance on one side or the other. England might have been inclined to give full support to the Confederacy to assure its supply of American cotton, for many British textile workers lost their jobs when the Union blockade cut off shipments from the South; but Britain was not ready, for the sake of cotton, to risk the loss of Northern grain, essential to save the British Isles from famine. "Old King Cotton's dead and buried," ran a popular song of the period, "brave young corn is King."

Another advantage the industrial North possessed was its ability to develop the infant industry of canning, which made it easier not only to preserve food but also to transport it. Transportation was the Achilles' heel of the South. Up to the end of the war the Confederacy probably had on its own territory enough food to supply all its needs, but it was in the wrong places; the difficulty was to deliver it where it was wanted. Shenandoah Valley farmers lacked storage space for their wheat, corn growers in southwestern Georgia were getting a dollar a bushel for corn, but in Richmond corn was so scarce that it was selling for fifteen dollars a bushel, while eggs cost a dollar apiece. Women staged a bread riot in Richmond in 1863 because of the high price of flour; yet there was plenty of it only 110 miles away—but, unfortunately, they were 110 uncrossable miles. Meanwhile Texas, far from the main battlefields, with a frontier open toward Mexico, was well fed throughout the war. Two months before Lee's surrender, General John Breckenridge, Confederate Secretary of War, announced that he had readied eight million rations; but they remained becalmed in the Deep South, and it was in Richmond and on the fighting fronts that they were needed. Even after the Confederate collapse, General Johnston's retreating army found plenty to eat in the Carolinas and Georgia, while President Jefferson Davis and his escort, retreating also, had no difficulty in getting food.

It was awareness of the South's vulnerability in the matter of food that accounted for Sherman's terrible march from Atlanta to the sea; its main objective may be described, a little summarily, as an attempt to starve the Confederate armies. Sherman's soldiers ate well, on commandeered turkey, chicken, and roast pork, before destroying everything they could not eat or carry away with them in the 2,500 six-mule wagons crammed with supplies for his 62,000 men. Moving through "the garden spot of the Confederacy," the Union columns found the Carolinas bursting with grain and beef cattle, and left them a desert. "We have devoured the land and our animals eat up the wheat and corn fields close," Sherman wrote in a report on June 26, 1864. "All the people retire before us and desolation is behind." Not only did Sherman destroy all standing crops, food stores, livestock and poultry, leaving a sixty-mile-wide stretch of barren ground behind him, but he also wrecked the railroads so thoroughly that they could not be repaired with the limited means at the South's disposal; it was thus impossible to move across the devastated strip the food which remained on its far side, in existence but unavailable. The Confederate commissary was forced to complete the work of Sherman by confiscating for the armies whatever food and animals Sherman had missed, with the result that Confederate soldiers, flooded with letters from their desperate twice-plundered families, deserted in droves to go to the rescue. "Two-thirds of our men . . . are absent without leave," Jefferson Davis put it euphemistically in September, 1864. General Johnston said he did not blame them.

Meanwhile the blockade of the Southern coast was depriving its hinterland of food from abroad—sometimes less because of the effectiveness of the Northern navy than because of the greed of the Southern speculators who were profiting from the situation. Bringing goods in through the blockade was an expensive business; the merchandise that got through had to pay for the merchandise that did not. The losses included the sinking of ships; the average life of a blockade runner was four and a half trips, and ship captains had to be paid as much as five thousand dollars—in gold—each time they took the risk of trying to break the blockade. This meant that only cargoes able to support a tremendous mark-up could be imported profitably—not staples, not the necessities of life which in some areas were so desperately needed, but luxuries—for example, coffee, which sold for five dollars a pound in Richmond. Moreover, since small craft were obviously better able to slip through the blockade than larger, more visible, ships, the cargo capacity of the blockade runners was limited, which ruled them out as carriers of bulky goods like grain. Some of the scanty space these small vessels afforded was preempted by the profiteers themselves, who saw no point in getting rich unless they could spend their gains for their own pleasures; so the blockade runners imported Paris dresses for the speculators' wives or fine French wines for themselves. The conspicuous spectacle of high living which they flaunted before the eyes of the citizens of Richmond, most of them living in penury, did not contribute to the maintenance of Southern morale.

Lack of food was far from being the chief cause of the Southern defeat, but the painfulness of its weight was recognized in one of Grant's first acts after Lee's surrender, when he rushed rations to the hungry Confederate soldiers. In the peace terms of Appomattox he stipulated, on his own initiative, "Let all the men who claim to own a horse or a mule take the animals home with them to work their little farms." "This will do much toward conciliating our people," said Lee, and no doubt it would have if it had not been for the insane assassination of Lincoln a few days later. Even so, private citizens in the North contributed, apart from what was officially provided by the government, an estimated four million dollars' worth of food for the relief of the South between 1865 and 1867, in striking contrast to the operations of the carpetbaggers.

If the South came out of the war with a crippled capacity for food production, the North was actually strengthened by it; war had promoted the growth of the food industry. The chief losers among Northern food producers were, once again, the fishermen, meaning chiefly New Englanders, the major shipbuilders and fishing-boat operators of the nation. New England had lost much of its fishing fleet during the Revolution and again during the War of 1812, and had not fully recovered from these blows when the Civil War arrived and decimated her shipping once more, a misfortune from which it never recovered fully either. During the war Confederate raiders destroyed 257 Northern vessels, of which the famous *Alabama* alone intercepted sixty-four; fifty-four of them were burned. The whaling industry based on New Bedford and Nantucket had also been hard hit by the Revolution; it had overcome this disaster and reached its highest point just before the Civil War, but virtually disappeared after it. This was not the result of the war alone, though the war may have delivered the *coup de grâce;* but whaling was vulnerable anyway, for oil had been discovered in Pennsylvania in 1859, and the reign of whale oil was ended.

For the infant food-processing industry, the demand created by the war was a stimulus which started it on the way to its present proportions, revolutionizing the eating habits of the nation.

Gail Borden, the father of condensed milk, found himself in what could have been a particularly favorable position when the Civil War broke out and he had a potential salesman on each side—one son in the Union Army, one son in the Confederate forces. He was spared the temptation of taking advantage of this situation, for the Federal government immediately freed him of any possible conflict of conscience by commandeering—with adequate remuneration, of course—the entire output of his large condensing plant, which he had foresightedly expanded almost immediately after the outbreak of the war. The Union soldiers liked condensed milk and after the war became propagandists for it, demanding it in civilian life and thus introducing it to their friends and families. Borden added another item to his line during the war, condensed blackberry juice, which he could produce with the same apparatus he used to condense milk; the government was a ready customer for this product also, which it used especially in its hospitals, for sick and wounded soldiers.

War demand was responsible too for the development of the processing industry for many other varieties of food, almost entirely in the North or in territories controlled by it. California had begun preserving fruit in bottles in 1860, but shifted largely to cans in 1862, partly because new canning methods had been developed the year before which cut canning time from five hours to thirty minutes; with a minimum of modernization, each cannery could then turn out ten times as much food. Canned fruit brought all the way from California was being eaten in the Union armies by 1862, mostly by officers, and was quickly followed by vegetables and other foods; the armies provided a ready market for anything that could be put into a can. In addition to the rations provided by the government, according to Francis A. Lord, in *Civil War Sutlers and their Wares,* the soldiers of the Union Army could buy canned meat, oysters, and vegetables, but showed an unmilitary preference for French sardines, salmon, and green peas. But Americans before the Civil War were already beginning to be spoiled by the variety of foods now being offered them by the development of canning. Even the Forty-Niners of the gold rush were singing of My Darling Clementine's slippers, made of "herring boxes without topses"; fish were put up in oval cans.

One result of all this was a geographical broadening of the food processing industry. The first canneries had been located on the Atlantic coast, for preserving had started, naturally enough, with the most perishable of aliments, seafood. The initial salmon and lobster were followed shortly afterwards by oysters. Seafood was canned especially during the colder months, and the slack was taken up in the summer by putting up small amounts of fruit and vegetables, more or less as by-products. When these became demanded items in their own right, canneries were established inland as well, notably in Cincinnati and Indianapolis. For these products also the soldiers who returned home after the war served as unpaid salesmen. Most of them had tasted canned food for the first time in the Army, and may have been more enthusiastic about it than they would have been under more normal circumstances; for preserved products compared well with such fresh foods as an army on the march could acquire; and they were equally palatable in all seasons.

Once again mechanical improvements gave added vigor to food processing. It was all very well to accelerate the manufacture of cans, but the advantages of greater speed remained limited as long as peas, for instance, had to be picked and shucked by hand. The availability of canned peas broadened towards the end of the nineteenth century when machines were invented to harvest them and divest them of their pods faster than hand labor could do it. This improved quality too, for greater speed in handling vegetables meant that they were fresher when they were sealed into the cans. Packing the salmon of the Northwest was hand work also, done mostly by cheap imported Chinese labor until 1882, when new immigration laws shut off the supply. This handicap was surmounted by devising a machine to clean and bone the fish. It was referred to, in an age prone to racism but unconscious of it, as "the iron Chink."

Meat packing was a little slower to profit by the war than fish, fruit, and vegetable preserving. The first great fortune made in this domain as a result of the Civil War was achieved after the war rather than during it, and was less the product of technical skill in preserving food than of financial acumen. Philip Danford Armour grew rich because he was a little quicker than others to foresee the Union victory, a little cleverer at drawing conclusions about what would happen in that event, and a little more daring in backing his foresight. As the war drew toward its end, with pork at forty dollars a barrel and going up all the time, Armour realized that a sharp drop in prices would occur when the North won. He sold pork futures with so accurate a sense of timing that when he had to deliver pork already paid for at the war-inflated price of forty dollars, he was able to pick it up at eighteen dollars. He made a profit of two million dollars, an unheard-of sum for the times. The great Armour meat packing business had been born.

XXIII

Beef and Buffalo

IN 1849, with characteristic effusiveness, Thomas Carlyle wrote to Ralph Waldo Emerson: "How beautiful to think of lean tough Yankee settlers, tough as gutta percha with most *occult* unsubduable fire in their belly, steering over the Western Mountains to annihilate the jungle, and bring bacon and corn out of it for the Posterity of Adam!" There was perhaps more enthusiasm than knowledge of American geography manifest in this passage; and the Forty-Niners might have been surprised at the idea that their objective was bacon and corn rather than gold; but in any case it was easier to write of annihilating American jungles before the Civil War than after it. The war constituted a sort of chronological barrier before which Americans might have been conscious of wildernesses to conquer but after which they were preoccupied mainly with industries waiting to be developed. Before the war, the United States was a society fundamentally agricultural and rural; after it, it became a society fundamentally industrial and urban. The war did not, of course, draw any sharp distinct impermeable line between the farm-oriented nation which preceded it and the business-oriented nation which was to follow it; the evolution from one way of life to the other had begun before the war, was inevitable, developed gradually, and would have happened whether the war had occurred or not. But the war did act as a catalyst which precipitated the process. As war so often does, this one induced the nation to spend more heavily and to apply more effort to bring about technical advances which served the cause of war than would have been mobilized to bring them about when all they served was the interests of peace. It was after the Civil War that the change of outlook became visible which moved the nation, for better or for worse, toward the industrialization and urbanization which changed its character.

In the domain of food, this meant a shift from raising one's own produce (or getting it directly from a neighborly farmer or fisherman) to buying it from a store—and in the kitchen, from the amateur to the professional, from the artisanal to the industrial. The *whole* process of readying food for the table was no longer carried out in the home; the first steps, often the easily abandoned ones of drudgery, were handled by some nameless enormous factory which delivered preserved, prepared or half-prepared foods to housewives who might have little more to do about them than to warm them up. The arts of cooking were communicated less and less from mother to daughter, but were learned from the directions on the label provided by the manufacturer, or, an intermediate step, from a cookbook.

The history of the processed food industry in the nineteenth century is very largely the history of the tin can. Early in that century, cans were made individually by tinsmiths. The long strips of metal from which the sides of the can were to be made were cut into pieces of the appropriate size by hand; the tops and bottoms of the cans were cut out one by one, also by hand; and sides, tops, and bottoms were soldered together, by hand. A skilled tinsmith could turn out fifty to sixty cans a day. But the individual tinsmith was already out of his depth in 1849, when Henry Evans invented his machine for pressing out mechanically the tops and bottoms of cans, the most time-consuming operation in their manufacture. Then some unsung benefactor devised "the joker," which replaced the hand-wielded soldering iron for closing cans. In 1840, two skilled tinsmiths had been able to turn out a maximum of 120 cans a day; in the early 1850s two unskilled men could produce 1,500 in the same time. In 1860, just before the Civil War, the annual output of the comparatively new processing industry had already reached five million cans of various foods, which seemed an impressive figure at the time. But then the men of the nation were called into military service, the army demanded more canned goods to feed them, and when they returned from the wars they insisted that their wives serve them, out of season as well as in, the unspoilable foods they had been eating in the service. By 1870, five years after the war, the nation was consuming thirty million cans of food annually. During the decade which followed, the product of the canneries increased, in terms of value, by 200 percent. Tomatoes, corn, and beans were the items most demanded.

Manufacturing techniques improved to keep pace with the galloping demand. Someone named Howe invented in 1876 a machine through which long lines of cans flowed unceasingly for automatic sealing. By the 1880s making cans had become an independent industry; the food handler no longer made his own, he bought them from a specialist. He was now too busy devising improvements in the methods of preparing foods to concern himself also with manufacturing their containers. In 1874 A. K. Shriver, a Baltimore canner, patented an autoclave in which food was treated with live steam, simultaneously reducing canning times and minimizing the risk of spoilage. Before the end of the century, the United States had become thoroughly committed to the eating of canned foods.

However one may feel about the salutary nature of fresh foods as compared to preserved ones, or about their comparative merits from the point of view of taste, one must admit that the flow of canned foods brought with it at least two indisputable benefits: it introduced millions of persons to foods which, at that period, they could never have eaten at all (inlanders enjoyed seafood, Northerners discovered pineapple and grapefruit) and, because canned foods were so easily transportable, they could be delivered, whether familiar or unfamiliar, to areas difficult of access, whose few inhabitants would otherwise have been reduced to local resources, often scarce or monotonous. The extent to which this privilege was appreciated is measurable by the amount customers were willing to pay for it. Colorado, for instance, which would not become a state until 1876 and was not easy to ship to because of an inhospitable terrain half mountain and half desert, was nevertheless already receiving in 1865, though its population was only about thirty-five thousand—not enough to encourage really difficult efforts on the part of suppliers—a wide variety of foods put up in cans. But Coloradans had to pay $1 to $1.25 per can for them, while Montanans were shelling out $2.25.

The manufacture of canned foods continued to rise dizzyingly. At the ten-yearly totting up of figures in 1970, Americans were buying twenty-six billion cans and jars of preserved food, with sweet corn, beans, tomatoes, and peas leading the vegetables, in that order, and peaches, applesauce, pineapple, and fruit cocktail first among the fruits. These are comparatively simple products, but a long list of more complicated foods was now available, at the end of an age of ingenuity during which canners, who had at first simply preserved fruit, vegetables, and seafood as nature had presented them, had progressed to more complicated confections. In 1897, for instance, it had occurred to a chemist named John T. Dorrance, whose family owned a small cannery in New Jersey, to apply himself to diversifying its products. He began experimenting with concentrated soups, and in 1898 his family was able to put on the market canned consommé, vegetable, tomato, oxtail, and chicken soups. This was the beginning of Campbell's. In Sharpsburg, Pennsylvania, a young man of twenty-five who was raising horseradish in his backyard began bottling it and peddling it to neighborhood grocers. They liked it, so he began putting up pickles too, followed by ketchup and then by relishes, until he discovered that his offerings had risen to the number of fifty-seven varieties. His name was Henry J. Heinz. In Chicago a grocery clerk accustomed to slicing off chunks from the enormous store cheese which stood on his counter, asked himself whether housewives would not appreciate the convenience of having reasonably sized portions of cheese provided for them under more measurable and less unsanitary conditions. He wrapped uniformly sized wedges of cheese in tinfoil and packed creamier versions in glass jars, acquired a horse and wagon, and drove through the streets selling cheese from door to door. *His* name was J. H. Kraft.

Armies fight on meat and especially, in this century at least, on beef. Yet the military demands of the Civil War which contributed so importantly to the rise of condensed milk and canned fruit and vegetables had little effect on the processing of meat. The Armour fortune, as we have seen, had its genesis not during the war, but at its end, and was based on pork, not beef, the American fighting man's ration. Gustavus Franklin Swift, whose brother was a butcher in Sandwich on Cape Cod, started the career which was to end in a meat packing empire as his brother's employee at the age of fourteen. He saved enough money to buy a heifer, butchered and dressed it, and began business on his own by driving a cart loaded with meat out of Clifton, Massachusetts, selling fresh cuts to housewives far enough away from the city's butcher shops to appreciate having fresh cuts brought to their doors. His profits enabled him to buy more animals and his meat route became a daily affair. But he did not graduate into operations of any size until well after the Civil War, when he moved backward along the route the cattle were taking, from Massachusetts to Albany, from Albany to Buffalo, and from Buffalo to Chicago, where he stopped in 1875 and set up his headquarters in the city which was destined to become the meat capital of America.

Americans have been great meat eaters from the beginning of their history and still are. No other country in the world eats more meat per capita, nor pays less for it in terms of proportion to total income. The United States contains less than one-fifteenth of the world's population, but it eats one-third of its meat. Americans have no doubt always preferred beef, but what they actually ate was necessarily that which was available, and for the first three centuries of white history in America, what was most readily available was pork. Nevertheless as early as 1854, *Harper's Weekly* reported that the commonest meal in America, from coast to coast, was steak; and at the beginning of the Civil War, Anthony Trollope, visiting the United States in 1861, reported that Americans ate twice as much beef as Englishmen. American suppers, he wrote, included "beefsteaks, and tea, and apple jam, and hot cakes, and light fixings, to all of which luxuries an American deems himself entitled"; and he recorded with amazement that four-year-old children not only demanded steak, they got it. In the present century beef consumption drew level with pork consumption and then passed it. From that time on it forged ahead steadily; during the last four decades, American consumption of red meat—almost entirely beef—has increased by a pound per capita every year, while pork consumption has remained stationary, despite the increase in population. Sheep, almost always described on menus as lamb, rate a bad fourth in American preferences (cattle get in twice, the order being beef, pork, veal, lamb), and are losing ground—there were 29 million in 1960, 18 million at most now. (This is not entirely a gastronomic phenomenon; the competition synthetic textiles give to wool is a consideration too.)

The average American eats about 180 pounds of meat a year (plus forty-six pounds of poultry and a little game); more than one hundred pounds of this is beef. Pork accounts for nearly seventy pounds, veal for a little more than four, lamb for a little less than four. These figures make it seem all the more astonishing that the Civil War did not speed up meat processing, and especially beef processing, at least to the extent that it speeded up fruit and vegetable processing, but a reason is not hard to find—fewer technical problems are involved in transferring tomatoes from the field to cans than in transferring steers from the ranges to cans: and indeed the consuming public did not particularly want steers put into cans, except in such secondary forms as corned beef and beef stew. The principal demand was not for canned beef, nor salted beef, nor smoked beef, nor dried beef, but for fresh beef, especially steak.

At the beginning supplying this demand presented no problem. Each settlement was capable of raising for itself as much beef as it needed, and no doubt felt it could go on indefinitely making meat rather than grain its basic food, at the cost of using three times as much land to achieve the same amount of nourishment, for the amount of land at the disposal of the colonists seemed unlimited. But the population of the East Coast increased rapidly; its inhabitants discovered they were not quite as rich in space as they had thought; and much of the land could be better employed for other purposes than grazing.

If Americans were to eat beef in the quantities to which they wanted to become accustomed, more spacious grazing lands had to be found. They *were* found, on a scale which once again seemed unlimited, in the Far West, then pretty much *terra incognita.*

There is a story which attributes the discovery that the West was ideal for cattle raising to the mishap of a heavily loaded governmental ox train which was blocked by blizzards in Wyoming toward the end of the Civil War. To save themselves, the drivers abandoned wagons and oxen. Returning in the spring to salvage anything that might be salvageable, they were amazed to find their oxen not only still alive, but well fed and healthy, having wintered successfully on whatever wild forage the land afforded. It may have taken Wyoming until the Civil War to discover that the West was good cattle country, but Texas had found it out a good deal earlier. Probably the Wyoming story impressed the public because it seemed so amazing that cattle which could not be left unsheltered from the mild weather of Virginia were able to fend for themselves in the open on territory exposed to Wyoming's harsh continental climate.

But it was not a question of climate, it was a question of grass. "There's gold from the grass roots down," California Joe, a celebrated post-Civil War guide, remarked sapiently, "but there's more gold from the grass roots up." Wyoming, and Texas too, produced spontaneously, without benefit of cultivation, what was known to botanists as grama grass, to incoming settlers as mesquite grass, and to hunters as buffalo grass: the last name is the most revealing. Grass that could nourish buffalo all year round could nourish domestic cattle all year round too. Well adapted to the arid climate of its region, buffalo grass would not wither away like Eastern grass (of which the best pasturage varieties needed to be sowed and tended) in periods of drought. It did not have to be harvested to provide hay for winter feeding either, it dried on its stalks and became standing hay, available and luscious, from a cow's point of view, throughout the winter. It actually grew better when grazed than when left to its own devices, for the cattle planted its seeds by trampling them into the ground and manured them with their droppings, assuring lush new growth in the spring. When deep snows buried the grass, the West provided other natural fodder in its low shrubs ("browze feed" the Texans called them), like white sage, referred to as "winter fat," which thrives on frost; it becomes more nutritious after the first freeze.

Texas not only had food for cattle, it had the cattle, waiting to be taken, whose ancestors had been imported by the Spaniards in the sixteenth century and abandoned in Tejas, where they had grown wild and become "more dangerous to footmen than the fiercest buffalo." The solution was, of course, not to remain a footman, but to get up on a horse: and behold, the cowboy! The pursuit of beef was about to open up an indigenous American life style so romantic, to outsiders at least, that it has been supporting the moving picture industry ever since.

The first Texas herds were thus composed of wild cattle, captured at considerable risk to life and limb, which in the next generation would become domesticated as the famous Texas Longhorns. They were very far from being the best beef critters in the world, which is why they are seen no longer, except in Wild West shows or at rodeos; but for their time and place they were exceptionally well cast. The original Spanish stock had come from dry parched country and their descendants had retained, in another dry parched country, the ability to stand up to hot Texas summers and to make do with a minimum of water. They had the wild animals' instinct for sniffing out water, so that in rainless summers cowboys would often let them choose their own direction and follow them to get water for themselves. They were good foragers for food too, and could survive on the poorest of rations; if grass were lacking, they could live on the shoots of the scraggly shrubs or trees, or on prickly pears, and if everything else was covered up by winter snows, a Longhorn would rear up, plant its forefeet against a cottonwood tree, and strip off the leaves and twigs. They tolerated winter cold as well as summer heat and were hardy resisters of disease; and they used their long horns to good effect in defending themselves from wolves.

Taken in hand by the Western cattlemen, the herds multiplied and prospered. Their self-appointed proprietors were burdened with none of the expenses which made beef dear in the East. In the beginning, he had not even been obliged to buy stock. There was neither sales price nor rent to be paid for the land. He did not have to buy fodder, fertilizer, or seed. He did not need to sow or to plow or to hay. He had no fencing to do, except for a corral or two, built from wood picked up on the range. He did not have to put up barns or stables or silos or any other large farm buildings, except quarters for his family and the help, which was not expensive either. A dozen cowboys, fed for the most part on the produce of the ranch, paid thirty to forty dollars a month each, could handle a few thousand cattle, and provide all the skills the ranch required, though there might be a few specialists among them—a blacksmith, a carpenter, a harness maker, and, of course, a cook. Cattlemen could make a good profit selling their beef animals for three or four dollars a head, in Texas; they were worth thirty-five to forty in Kansas or Missouri.

It seemed a perfect setup for a nation of beefeaters too. Vast expanses of open land were required to supply all the beef the nation needed; the West had them. A big market was needed to support a big meat-raising operation; the East could provide it. Industrial organization, capital and know-how was required to butcher, process, and deliver beef to the consumers; the Middle West was developing them and in time Chicago would become the center of the meat packing industry. Unfortunately, the rangers, the processors and the consumers were widely spaced; the only way to bridge the distances between them, before railroads, and to get fresh beef to the places where it was wanted, before refrigeration, was still to walk the steers to market; and the cattle were farther from the eaters than ever. In the circumstances the most important asset of the Longhorn was that he was a stout walker.

The legendary epoch of the cattle trails, the routes over which herds of Longhorns were driven north to the markets, dates back to before the Civil War. These movements occurred on a prodigious scale, hardly comparable to the placid processions of fifty or a hundred head which had earlier moved north from Georgia or east from Ohio. A Longhorn drive might consist of 2,500 animals with 1,200 to 1,500 miles to cover; instead of plodding along at the seven miles a day of more effete cattle, they would advance at least ten and perhaps twenty; that still meant anywhere from two to four months of steady slogging. The drives were possible only because there was unimpeded passage and free pasturage all the way from the Gulf of Mexico to Canada. The steers ate as they progressed; a common formula was a two-hour grazing period at the beginning of the day and another at its end. Even so, a 2,500-head drive might finish 375,000 pounds lighter than when it started out. The cattle might be sold as they arrived, scrawny animals which had eaten nothing but grass; or they might be finished on grain at their terminals, especially after the great Chicago stockyards developed, equipped as a matter of course with fattening pens. Or steers might be held over for fattening in the Midwest to build them up again before they were put on the road for a second trek to Eastern markets. The first herd of Longhorns thus to reach New York arrived in 1854; the citizenry flocked to gape at them.

Neither the cost of fattening cattle after the drives, nor the loss of weight suffered by those which were not fattened, added to the basic cost of the drive itself, was enough to account for the mark-up of 900 percent over Texas prices. That occurred because the cattle that got through had to pay for those that did not—and many did not. The nightmare of the cowboy on the drive was that the cattle might stampede; there were sometimes persons along the way who were willing to make them stampede—Indians, for instance. Three principal trails were followed by the drives, and all of them crossed Indian Territory. However there was less trouble from Indians than might have been expected, unless some of them happened to be short of food when a herd came by. As a rule Indians did not mind the whites passing through as long as they didn't stay; indeed the Cherokee, always adept at adopting the institutions of the Palefaces, legalized the passages by collecting grazing fees while the cattle were on their territory. Worse were white outlaws who, in an early version of the racket, stampeded the herds unless they were bought off. Even when no malevolence was involved, there was always the danger of spontaneous stampeding for no discernible reason when cattle were seized suddenly by panic in the night. The remedy the cowboys found for this added a new facet to American folklore: cowboy music. Before setting out on a drive, the wranglers riding herd at night would sing as they made their rounds, so that for their charges this *kleine Nacht-musik* became associated with the familiar setting of their home grounds, where they felt few fears. On the drive, the night guardians, ceaselessly circling the sleeping steers, kept up their serenading; the theory was that cattle startled at night in strange surroundings by unexpected noises or inexplicable movements, would be reassured by the strains to which they were accustomed, and would be lulled by them into a sense of security and a return to sleep; perhaps singing helped the cowboy morale, too. The night singing was at first often composed of nonsense syllables ("yippi yippi yay, yippi yay"), but it crystallized into the cowboy songs we know today, which developed a common style and became a distinct genre of folk music, authentically American.

When Texas joined the Confederacy, trail driving almost stopped; and when the war was over, in 1866, though the herds on Texas ranges had greatly multiplied, the Lone Star State was financially in bad shape. Fortunately the North was as anxious to buy beef as Texas was to sell it. The drives resumed, on a scale bigger than ever, but often over lessened distances. The business was becoming better organized; and the Civil War had at last begun to exert an influence on the development of the meat industry, indirectly, for it had stimulated the building of railroads, and the development of the railroads would soon revolutionize the fashion in which the flow of beef was canalized from the Texas plains to the Eastern markets.

The railroads, it must be admitted, did not want to revolutionize anything. Revolutionary ideas are rarely welcome to the established businessmen who are able to finance railroads, who tend to conservatism all along the line from the very fact that they have reached positions which give them something to conserve. The idea of Joseph G. McCoy seems today less revolutionary than simply logical. It was that the cattle drives should make a junction with the advancing railroads at some point as far west as possible, so that the steers could be moved the rest of the way by rail. Horrified, the Kansas Pacific said, "No"; the Missouri Pacific said, "No"; and not until McCoy had worked his way down to the modest Hannibal & St. Joseph, which was operating a line out of Kansas City with a prayer that it would eventually reach Chicago, did he find a line willing to accept bovine passengers. The next step was to select a city on the Hannibal & St. Joe for his cattle loading point. Obviously he could take his choice, for what community would not jump at a proposition which would create new jobs and bring money into town on a large scale? It turned out that the obvious was not obvious for everybody and that city fathers were as timorous as railroad presidents. Junction City said, "No"; Solomon City (misnamed) said, "No"; Salina said, "No"; and when Abilene said, "Well, all right," it was presumably because it had nothing to lose, being, in McCoy's not necessarily unexaggerated words (from his *Historic Sketches of the Cattle Trade of the West and Southwest)*,

> a very small dead place, consisting of about one dozen log huts, low, small, rude affairs, four-fifths of which were covered with dirt for roofing; indeed, but one shingle roof could be seen in the whole city. The business of the burg was conducted in two small rooms, mere log huts, and of course the inevitable saloon, also in a log hut, was to be found. . . . [But] the country was entirely unsettled, well watered, excellent grass, and nearly the entire area of the country was adapted to holding cattle. And it was the farthest point east at which a good depot for cattle business could have been made.

McCoy bought the whole town for $2,400.

A fast worker, he installed cattle yards, scales, a barn and other facilities for handling up to three thousand head at a time within two months, and then sent a rider down the trails to intercept drives already en route and induce them to shift destinations. A shorter trek, the saving of weight, and above all the chance to end their drives short of the territories in Arkansas and Missouri terrorized by the stampeders appealed to the cattle handlers, and they turned their animals towards Abilene. The first railroad-borne cattle, twenty carloads of them, left Abilene on September 5, 1867, in the same year in which McCoy had started to promote his project, and by the end of the year 35,000 steers had been routed through this city. Waking tardily, other railroad towns now began clamoring for cattle-loading facilities, and the future of one Midwestern community was assured when the Hannibal & St. Joseph decided to build a bridge across the Missouri at Kansas City, starting it on its way to its destiny as a great meat-packing center. By 1880 more than four million Longhorns had been put onto cattle cars at Abilene and other shipping points, and between the end of the Civil War and the time when cattle driving died a natural death, ten million steers had been walked to Kansas for shipment by rail—in conditions less than ideal, according to Richard Osborn Cummings:

> The cattle traveled hundreds of miles from the West on crowded cars tended by vicious drovers armed with steel-pointed rods and tail-twisters which were used to keep the exhausted beasts on their feet. They arrived emaciated, maimed and diseased. The blood of some was found on slaughtering to be as black as ink; the carcasses of others turned purple after a few hours' hanging.

What spelled the beginning of the end for the drives was the invention of barbed wire, introduced in 1875, or, if you prefer, the changing circumstances which made this new commodity a profitable item of merchandise. Farmers and cattlemen alike used it to fence their lands, the farmers to keep range cattle out, the cattlemen, after the bitter winter of 1886–1887, when steers died by the thousands on the open range, to keep them in. Open range was not so open any more; there was no longer free unobstructed passage in almost any direction the herds chose to take. Farms and even cities were getting in the way. The vast numbers of cattle moving over the shrinking trails began to overgraze the routes and it was not always certain that the animals would find along the way enough natural wild forage to keep them in good shape.

By the end of the nineteenth century it was all over.

The knell of trail driving sounded also the knell of the Longhorn. Whatever his shortcomings as a producer of quality beef, he had been tolerated for his toughness when he had to survive on unfenced range and above all for the stamina which enabled him to march to market. Cattlemen could now turn from breeding hikers to breeding beef.

In the East quality beef animals were already an old story, but there the original cows had been imported from the British Isles, then producing the best meat animals in the world. No less a person than Henry Clay had brought in the first English Herefords in 1817; the United States Shorthorn Herdbook was opened in the East in 1846; but it was only after Texas was ready to forsake the Longhorn that the first massive meaty black Aberdeen Angus reached the United States, in 1873. Texas breeders now began experimenting with hybridization of cattle in order to develop races which would be particularly well adapted to the climate and the pasturage of their region, using cattle from various parts of the world, English and Scottish breeds, of course, but also such less publicized animals as the Charolais, France's finest meat producer, and the Chianina, probably the best in Italy. They gave special attention to the Indian Brahman, seeking a hot-weather cow which would support the summer heat as well as the Longhorn but would be better eating. Crossed with the Aberdeen Angus, the Brahman produced the Brangus. The Beefmaster (a trademark) has Brahman, Hereford, and Shorthorn strains in its artificially confected ancestry. The greatest triumph of American breeding was the heaviest and hardiest of all these crosses, the Santa Gertrudis, described as the first authentic American beef animal, which is also possibly the one which gives the best beef. It was developed from Brahman bulls and Shorthorn cows on the King Ranch, under the aegis of its president, Robert J. Kleberg, Jr., who died in Houston, Texas, aged seventy-eight, in the fall of 1974. The Santa Gertrudis today is raised in forty-seven states and forty-five foreign countries.

By 1889, when Alessandro Filippini, chef at Delmonico, wrote a cookbook, he asserted in it that New York had the finest beef in the world, (it was finer beef than Texas was eating, at least, for New York bought the choicest Texas steers, leaving to the cattle raisers what the metropolis had rejected). But already, since 1880, the United States had been exporting beef to England, a first-rate example of selling coals to Newcastle.

The period of the great cattle drives not only opened an opportunity for the beef buyers of the North and East to change their eating habits, it also initiated new eating habits among the cattlehandlers themselves. According to J. Frank Dobie in *Up the Trail from Texas,* the chuck wagon, the traveling commissary from which the trail-driving cowboys and horse wranglers were fed, appeared a good many years after the first post-Civil War drives. Prior to its adoption, the men carried their provisions in sacks slung to their saddles, usually bread, bacon, salt, and coffee. Meat enough could be killed as they traveled along the trail. The chuck wagon itself evolved from the cart, sometimes driven by oxen, which carried the personal gear of the crew and the trail boss, and a few pots of beans cooked on the overnight stops. In its more or less final form the chuck wagon had a large chest for food supplies, fuel, water, pots and pans, and the tailgate served as a broad kitchen table for the cook.

On the drives, the cook hurried the chuck wagon forward past the slow-moving cattle to set up at the next planned stopping place and have food ready for the drivers when the herd arrived. He needed a good head start to give him time to bake the omnipresent red Mexican beans ("prairie strawberries," the cowboys called them). The staple was steak, of which a plentiful supply was always at hand; the slowest animals were naturally considered the most edible, and there was no nonsense about hanging beef—today's steak was yesterday's straggler. For tenderizing, pounding replaced hanging. The rest of the animal was taken care of by the occasional production of pot roast or beef stew.

It was on the trail that a famous cowboy dish was evolved: son-of-a-bitch stew. One of the cook's functions was to see to it that food was fairly distributed and that nothing was wasted; and though the cook ranked beneath the cowboy, the knight of the Plains, his authority was respected in such matters. Son-of-a-bitch stew came under the head of no waste, for it was composed largely of those supposedly lowly internal organs which even today many Americans disdain. The ingredients were variable, usually including the tongue, liver, heart, and sweetbreads, seasoned with a skunk egg (cowboy for "onion"), salt, pepper, and chili, plus one essential element—the marrow gut of a calf. Without a marrow gut there could be no son-of-a-bitch stew. It is the tube which connects two of the ruminant's four stomachs, filled in young animals with a substance which looks like marrow but is actually a digestive for cow's milk. It has a very special flavor, and it is as seasoning that it enters into this stew, to give it its distinctive taste. It is the son-of-a-bitch's soul.

Often the drive or range cooks were Negroes, sometimes they were Germans or Mexicans; their quality was good, mediocre or poor. Even when poor, they were at least always capable of turning out hot camp bread, made either with sourdough or baking powder and cooked over the coals of the campfire in a Dutch oven with other hot coals on its lid, at least for one meal of the day. If a cook were good, he might provide from time to time, as a special treat, dried-apple pies, fried or baked in the bread oven.

It was less than regal fare, but it stuck to the ribs and fueled the hard-riding, hard-driving, outdoor-living buckaroos who needed solid food more than finesse. The evocation of the chuck wagon today releases fumes of nostalgia, justified or not, and advertisers of canned beans plug their product by asserting that they exude "that good old chuck-wagon flavor." Since we don't know how chuck wagon beans tasted, who can say them nay?

*

Of the many aberrations of which man has been guilty, one of the most illogical might seem to be the massacre of the buffalo. At the same time and in the same place where one group of men was exerting valiant efforts to raise cattle and deliver them to market to satisfy a national demand for red meat, another group of men was working with equal diligence to eliminate the plentiful source of red meat that was already there. This makes for full employment.

The building up of Longhorn herds in the West began fifteen or twenty years before the Civil War and the destruction of the American bison began fifteen or twenty years before the Civil War. The War postponed the development of cattle driving as it postponed the pursuit of buffalo killing. When Charles Goodnight—one of those outsized characters the Old West so easily engendered (he married at ninety-one and sired a child before dying at ninety-three)—drove three thousand Longhorns across an uncharted trail to Wyoming in 1868 to feed the men who were building the Union Pacific and the soldiers who were protecting the railroad gangs from the Indians, he had to push through territory occupied by twelve million buffalo, many of them in Wyoming. The last southern buffalo was killed at Buffalo Springs, Texas, in 1879, four years after the invention of barbed wire presaged the end of the cattle drives, and the last of the northern buffaloes, save a few stragglers, were killed in 1883, by which time the cattle drives had dwindled to a trickle. The Longhorn and the buffalo were coeval. The buffalo probably provided tastier meat, but the Longhorn won. He represented human proliferation, which, inexorably, was gaining territory, while the buffalo represented primeval nature, which was, inevitably, giving ground.

When an eminent historian referred to Americans who "carelessly destroyed the buffalo," he implied an oversight of colossal dimensions; at a conservative estimate there were sixty million buffaloes roaming the plains when the first white men (Coronado's expedition in Texas) came upon their main body (some estimates go as high as a hundred million). Even at the lower figure, the bison population of America was the greatest any large animal had ever attained at any time and in any place in the history of the world. Early explorers, overlooking the plains from heights which permitted long views, reported again and again their amazement at the unbelievable spectacle of the thickly crowded black buffaloes grazing over the prairie as far as the eye could reach, millions of animals visible at the same time.

Getting rid of this many animals "carelessly" took some doing; "carefully" would probably have been a better word. The buffalo was, indeed, destroyed deliberately, except at the very beginning of the English-speaking population's acquaintance with the Western herds (the Spaniards made no inroads). Plains Indians had been living off the buffalo for as far back as there had been Indians and buffaloes, but had not made a dent in the herds even when they hunted by their most wasteful methods, setting fires in the high dry prairie grass or stampeding herds over a cliff. The chronicler of Coronado's expedition told how buffalo were driven in this fashion into a chasm: "so many animals fell in that they filled it up and the rest passed over their bodies."

When the Americans reached the big herds west of the Mississippi their first killings, though not yet aimed at exterminating the species, were, if you want, "careless," and in any case wasteful and wanton. Buffaloes were slaughtered not for their choice red meat, but, so to speak, for accessories. The reason for not tapping this rich source of food completely was the same which had prevented buffalo meat from becoming an important item in the diet of the early settlers of the East Coast: it came in too large a package. Imagine an 1820s Plains hunter who has felled a buffalo. At his feet lie 2,500 pounds of bison, some 1,250 pounds of utilizable meat: but utilizable by whom? The nearest potential market is perhaps a thousand miles away. Assuming the improbable—the wildly improbable—that he has a wagon capable of crossing a thousand miles of roadless country loaded with buffalo meat, it would spoil before he could deliver it.

As a source of food the buffalo was, at that time, useless—the whole buffalo, that is; there were connoisseurs for parts of it. The choicest morsels were considered to be the humps and the tongues. Even the humps were too bulky to be consumed far from the place of killing, but tongues were not, and they could be smoked on the spot to preserve them until they reached a market. Bison were killed by the thousands, their tongues were cut out to be shipped to luxury restaurants in the East or even in Europe, and the carcasses were left lying on the prairie for the coyotes and the buzzards. A vogue for buffalo carriage robes caused other thousands to be slaughtered for their pelts, while the rest of the animal, once more, was wasted.

About the only Americans who showed much interest in eating buffalo before the Civil War were the emigrants, for whom it offered a welcome supplement to the scanty and monotonous rations they had been able to carry with them on the long crossing of the Great Plains towards the Rocky Mountains. In pioneer times, the bison provided the most abundant source of fresh meat for wagon trains crossing the prairie—"humpbacked beef," the emigrants called it—and they seem to have thought it at least as good as domestic beef if not better.

The railroads, when they began to push westward, encouraged hunting for hides, which constituted a profitable item of freight. An efficient hunter might count on shipping one thousand hides East a year, and sometimes he sent the tongues along with them. Even before the days of the railroads, St. Louis alone received the pelts for 67,000 buffalo robes in 1840, and in 1848, when 250,000 buffaloes were killed, 25,000 tongues. The railroads were hostile to the buffalo, an animal not given to respecting the right of way. The Kansas Pacific ran special trains for hunters, who fired comfortably from car windows into the throngs of animals grazing along the tracks. They did not take the carcasses aboard to sell them for meat: the refrigerator car would not come into service until 1875. Railroads even hired professional hunters to kill off the bison; Buffalo Bill was working for the Union Pacific when he shot 4,280 buffaloes in twelve months.

Another enemy of the bison was the cattle raiser; buffalo competed with Longhorns for the available grass. One might ask why the Westerners from the beginning had not simply exploited the buffalo, already there, for meat; there would have been at least one advantage—buffaloes thrive on two-thirds the acreage required by the same number of Longhorns, and finish heavier. The buffalo was, of course, a wild animal, more difficult to handle than cattle; but for that matter the Longhorns were wild animals too when the Texans began to round them up. There was the difference that the Longhorns had centuries-old habits of domestication behind them and seemed ready to revert to them when they were taken in hand again; the buffalo might have been more obdurate. One can imagine the difficulties of trying to drive herds of buffalo to market instead of herds of Longhorns, not to mention those of inducing them to enter cattle cars, even if they had been domesticated in the meantime. In any case, whether the reasons for betting on the Longhorn rather than on the buffalo were good or bad, once the choice had been made the process was irreversible. Thus the men who had been sucked into the activity of promoting Longhorns continued to promote Longhorns whether it was reasonable to do so or not, and the men who had been sucked into the activity of destroying buffaloes continued to destroy buffaloes whether it was logical to do so or not. (Not all cattle breeders, parenthetically, disdained the buffalo. Charles Goodnight, when he abandoned cattle driving to go into cattle raising, kept a small herd of buffalo on his ranch, and crossed Polled Angus with them to produce an animal he called the cattalo.)

The most important motive of the whites in eliminating the buffalo was the desire to eliminate the Indian. The Plains Indians had developed a way of life which depended completely on the buffalo. If the buffalo disappeared, the reasoning went—and it was cogent—the Indian would have to disappear too.

The bison was first of all the Indians' principal source of food. His hide, scraped with the animal's shinbone and softened by rubbing in its brains, was cured and made into clothing, teepees, shields, saddles, harness, lassos, and bowstrings, which fired arrows whose points and guiding feathers were attached to the shaft with glue made from the hooves. Tendons and sinews were split and became thread. The hair was braided into rope. Stomachs were used for cooking pots and water buckets, bladders for raft floats. Horns were softened by steaming and shaped into spoons or ladles. Buffalo chips provided almost the only fuel in treeless country and were accordingly baptized "prairie coal." Even the children profited. The membrane which covered the bison's heart became a nursing bottle, the ribs became runners for sleds, and the dried scrotum, filled with pebbles, was baby's rattle.

The intent to get rid of the Indian by wiping out the animal on which he depended was expressed openly by General Philip Sheridan, when he said to the Texas legislature: "Let [the market hunters] kill, skin and sell until the buffalo is exterminated, as it is the only way to bring about lasting peace and allow civilization to advance." President Grant, whose record in respect to the conservation of resources is shaky at other points as well, saw eye to eye with Sheridan. In 1875, the United States Congress passed the first bill in its history on behalf of wild life, to protect the buffalo. Grant vetoed it, and the destruction of bison continued.

Deprived of their normal means of livelihood by the killing off of buffaloes, the Indians began raiding and looting white settlements for alternative foods. This convinced the whites, who were only too eager to be convinced, that the Indians were savages with whom it was impossible to live. The raided settlers called on the Army to protect them, and the Army organized punitive expeditions. Hostility augmented, for which the whites saw no solution except that of getting rid of the Indians, starving them out by killing *all* the buffaloes, the easiest way.

In spite of the lull in the campaign to kill off the buffalo which had been imposed by the Civil War, there remained in 1865 only about fifteen million buffalo. In that single year a million more were killed. Half of the remaining fourteen million had been eliminated by 1872. There was probably not a single bison left on the southern prairies by 1879, the year before the railroad penetrated the North, and permitted large-scale slaughter to take place there also. In 1883 the largest remaining northern herd, of ten thousand animals only (in earlier times single "families" of as many as four million animals had been reported) was wiped out in a few days by stationing sharpshooters at every waterhole within its reach—a joint operation by white hunters and Crees, who, not being Plains Indians, had no stake in the buffalo's preservation.

In 1886 a herd of six hundred bison took refuge in Yellowstone National Park, theoretically a general game refuge; but as the penalty for a hunter caught in the act of poaching was merely expulsion from the park (and who could stop him from coming right back in again?), only twenty bison remained by the spring of 1894. A nationwide census taken at about the same time counted 1,090 bison in the whole United States. Local inhabitants tried to protect a herd of bison in the Lost Park of the Colorado, which represented one-fourth of all the American bison left alive in the world, but poachers mowed them down one by one, and in 1897 the last four—two males, a female and a calf—were shot on behalf of a taxidermist who wanted specimens to stuff. The twentieth century opened with no wild bison left on the entire North American continent except twenty-one in Yellowstone Park and a small herd near Lake Athabasca in Canada, which had been placed under the protection of the Northwest Mounted Police in 1890. The buffalo, at least as a meat animal, was for all practical purposes extinct.

This is a story that has often been told, usually with indignation. It is true that it must evoke regret from all lovers of nature; but to how many of the indignant has it occurred to ask themselves what the result would have been if the deliberate slaughter of the buffalo had not been undertaken? It is difficult to put the question without falling immediately upon the answer: the result would have been the same, the buffalo would have disappeared. The thoughtlessness and the malice of man no doubt hastened the process; but in any case the existence of sixty million bison in the heart of the United States and the existence of Kansas City were incompatible. There may be some who would have preferred the bison to Kansas City, but this is irrelevant; the choice was not offered and could not be offered. Kansas City, like it or not, was bound to come, the bison was bound to go.

In 1905, the United States began to regret what it had lost. Theodore Roosevelt established a buffalo reservation near Wichita, stocked with twelve animals donated by the New York Zoological Society, an initiative which was followed by the creation of a national bison reservation in Montana. The process of resurrecting the American bison depended largely on captive animals in zoos or in private ownership, of which there were 969 in 1906. Canada bought the largest single herd in existence, which owed its survival to two Indians, a Pend Oreille named Walking Coyote, who had captured four young bison in 1873 and sold the thirteen animals to which they had increased in 1884 to a Flathead Indian, Michel Pablo, who brought their number up to 709. This left the United States 260 animals to start with, but under protection their numbers increased rapidly, for though a bison cow gives birth to only one calf a year, she remains fertile for forty years, and young bison are hardy. Today there are about eighteen thousand wild bison in Canada and twelve thousand in the United States, the limit for government-protected wild bison, since the government does not possess enough suitable grazing land to support a greater number. To keep the size of the herds down to this figure, they are thinned out yearly. The animals thus slaughtered provide one of the two sources for buffalo meat, now becoming again an appreciated Western specialty. The other, more important, is meat from domesticated bison, to whom private breeders are devoting grazing land because the operation is profitable. Buffalo meat today is worth about one-third more than beef.

How good is it? No less an authority than Alexandre Dumas, writing in the last century, said it has "a little sharp wild taste, recalling that of the stag"; but he was referring to salted jerky, not fresh meat. The pioneers did not note that it was particularly gamey, but they may have taken gaminess for granted, since game was commonplace in their day. Jonathan Norton Leonard, in *American Cooking: The Great West,* writes of buffalo tongue that it "was indeed splendid, its meat firmer, leaner, darker and smoother in texture than beef tongue and with a distinctive most agreeable 'wild' flavor"; but it is not specified whether this was from domesticated bison or from an animal of the free-roaming wild herds the government maintains. Most other buffalo tasters compare bison meat favorably with beef, describing it as rich, tender, and hardly distinguishable from beef except by a slightly sweeter taste. Gaminess is not mentioned, and it would seem that the domesticated buffalo has lost whatever wild flavor its ancestors may have possessed. "Buffalo meat resembles choice roast beef in flavor," Dale Brown wrote in *American Cooking: The Northwest,* and said of a buffalo steak (which was from a domesticated animal): "The meat was indeed tender, and just a bit sweet. It had none of the gamey flavor I had expected; it tasted like very good, very rich beef. There was hardly any fat and no gristle at all." Stewart Udall described buffalo meat as "more succulent by far than the steak of a Longhorn steer," not necessarily the height of praise, but Cleophus Griffin, chef for a New York Explorer's Club banquet, did better when he said, "Bison is better than beef. Best roast I ever cooked."

There are a number of buffalo-meat producers today in the West and Northwest, but not enough to supply the potential demand of the nation. The meat does not reach the East, for the total supply is snapped up on the spot by buffalo-meat enthusiasts in the West, and gets no farther. The best meat comes from young bulls, slaughtered at from two to three years of age. A three-year-old bull stands about six feet tall at the hump, weighs 1,500 pounds, and dresses out 750 pounds of meat. Unlike beef, which is considered best when marbled with fat (this is a criterion which is now changing), good bison meat contains little fat (instead of inserting itself between the muscles, it forms a three-inch-thick roll around the ribs, and is cut away) and no gristle.

The buffalo had been vanquished; the way was clear for beef—and for the development of Chicago as the greatest meat packing center in the world. Chicago had started early in that direction. In the days before cattle cars it was already receiving steers from the great drives, fattening them, and sending them off again, on foot, to the East; later they were transshipped by train. The arrival of the first cattle from the Southwest coincided with the importation of the restaurant from the East. The result was the steak house, as characteristic of Chicago now as the oyster house once was of New York; there are five hundred of them in Chicago.

Before Chicago found its vocation in meat processing, the most important meat-marketing center in the world, though it was not in the most important meat-producing center in the world, was Paris. Shortly after the Civil War, Chicago drew level with Paris, though it had then only one-tenth of the French capital's population, and then passed it. Obviously this meant that Chicago was supplying meat to a great many other cities besides itself; it was already on the way to its destiny as butcher to the nation, or even to the world.

The development of a national meat market began in circumstances not precisely ideal. Richard Osborn Cummings, who seemed to take positive pleasure in looking on the darkest side of things, described the early days thus:

> Before the development of the refrigerator car livestock came directly to the city on the hoof or by rail and, after purchase by butchers, were driven through the streets to slaughter-houses which were sometimes located in residential districts. These shambles, veritable pestholes surrounded by heaps of putrefying offal and pools of blood giving rise to horrible stenches, were tolerated until the close of the Civil War. But in 1865 Chicago, in 1866 New York, and then New Orleans and Boston banished the houses from certain districts or required the use of central abattoirs. The butchers objected to ordinances which deprived them of their time-honored rights and claimed that, because of the dangers of meat spoilage, it would be impossible for them to comply. Their cases were lost, however, the most important decision being rendered in 1873 by the United States Supreme Court in the case of the New Orleans slaughter-houses.
>
> Limitation of slaughter-houses was not only a step in the direction of improved public health through elimination of local nuisance; it also meant in the long run a more hygienic quality of meat, for the cattle car declined in importance and the refrigerator car became the chief source of the city's meat supply. . . . Under the new system the cattle were carried for relatively short distances in cattle cars from feeding grounds to the packing centers, where the great packers had plants equipped with machinery to expedite slaughter and efficiently cut up the carcasses. From their establishments the cut meats were sent by refrigerator car to be retailed in the butcher shops of the East.

Clearly, it was the refrigerator car which for Mr. Cummings marked the dividing line between the old era and the new. The refrigerator car was not an innovation of the railroads, resistant, as usual, to progress, but was imposed upon them, symbolically by the two men whose names more than any others marked the rise of the Chicago meat-packing industry, Gustavus Franklin Swift and Philip Danforth Armour—both of whom, incidentally, established themselves in Chicago in the same year, 1875, which ought to make this date a landmark in Chicago's history. When Gustavus Swift approached the railroads with the proposal that they operate refrigerator cars, he was, like Joseph McCoy when he called for cattle cars, turned down by several of them; their obtuseness was perhaps a little more understandable this time, for by now they had a considerable investment in cattle cars, loading docks and feeding facilities, and were not anxious to write it off in favor of something else. In the end it was the two meat-packing barons—only baronets then—who forced them into accepting refrigerator cars.

Gustavus Swift persevered in the face of a series of refusals by the major railroads, but at last found a single line, the Grand Trunk Railway, which would deign to move refrigerator cars (at rates cannily devised to make it just as expensive to carry dressed beef as live cattle)—if it didn't have to provide them. So Swift gambled most of his resources to build his own cars, ten of them to begin with. Armour built refrigerator cars, too. From that point on, their careers were destined to follow parallel courses and to employ comparable techniques.

When the railroads discovered, tardily, that there was money in refrigerator cars, as when they had discovered, tardily, that there was money in cattle cars, they began competing for the new business. This brought rates down to a more reasonable level, until it cost about the same amount to move a given weight of prepared carcasses as to move the same weight in live animals. Since 35 percent of the weight of a steer was cut away in the dressing, this meant an appreciable saving, which was increased by the fact that no allowance had to be made for the loss in weight suffered in transit by live animals nor for their occasional deaths in overcrowded cars. Beef prices came down, sales went up, and *Harper's Weekly* in 1882 referred to the period as "this era of cheap beef."

The operations of Swift and Armour constituted a triumph of organization. Every detail had to be worked out minutely in advance, against the obstacles resulting from the fact this was not yet an age of standardization: for instance, the railroads had not yet agreed upon a common gauge; each company spaced its rails at any distance which appealed to it, so Swift and Armour had to work out routes for their refrigerator cars which would send them over lines using the same gauge. Devices had to be perfected also for stopping the cars with a precision measurable in inches in front of the warehouses, refrigerated too, which received the meat in all important cities. Inside the cars, the carcasses were suspended from rails on movable hooks;

the warehouses were equipped with similar rails along which the hanging carcasses could ride. When a car arrived, both car and warehouse doors were opened, a hinged section of the warehouse rail was swung out and engaged with the end of the rail inside the car, making one continuous trolley for beef. The carcasses were rolled directly from one chilled atmosphere into another with no pause during which the meat might warm and spoil.

The skill in organization which was applied to getting the product to market was also utilized by the packers within what had become less slaughter-houses than meat factories. The killing, cleaning, grading and cutting up of the steers was reduced to an automatic process, so that there was a steady flow at a constant tempo from the point where the live animal entered the current to that at which its constituent parts left it, ready for shipment. The engineering genius involved in this operation was even more obvious when the Chicago packers began processing hogs, for though it was the particular problems of handling cattle that had started them on their way, it was inevitable that they would move on to all other meats eventually. Even at the beginning, when steers were leaving the packers only in the form of carcasses, pigs were being taken more completely to pieces in the Swift and Armour plants: at the very least, they were likely to lose their hams before the rest of the animal was sent on its way to the butchers. Very often they were cut up completely, the different parts turning up in a wide variety of prepared pork products. Pork was easier to preserve in various fashions—specifically, it was easier to can—and more of it could be salvaged with a minimum of effort by producing such items as sausage. The pig, like the steer, rode its even-paced way through the processing line, and underwent more manipulation during its odyssey.

Another field in which skill of organization was exerted was in that of the utilization of by-products: the principle was that everything was useful, nothing was to be wasted. The meat sellers did not content themselves with selling everything that was edible in a steer; they marketed all of its other components, too. While edible suet went into oleomargarine, salad oils and lard compounds, inedible fats were used for soap, glycerine, lubricants, and leather softening. While edible bones produced gelatine, inedible bones made glue. While intestines provided casings for sausage, lard, and cheese (edible) they were also used for goldbeaters' skin (inedible). Parts of the animal not considered fit for human food could still be cooked, dried, and ground. Bone meal enriched animal food, and so did dried blood, likewise employed for textile sizing, for waterproof glue, and for case-hardening steel. As for completely inedible by-products, the most important was the hide, which accounted for 7 percent of the animal's live weight. Body hair was used for felt, ear hair for brushes, tail hair for upholstery. As was the case for the steer, nothing of the pig was neglected. Hog bristles made brushes; hoofs were rendered into glue; internal organs which Americans refused to eat were sold to less finicky countries, or if they were of a sort that everybody refused to eat, became animal food; extracts and essences from the pigs' intimate chemistry contributed their active elements to medicines or found industrial uses, such as fertilizer.

There were still certain problems about putting meat into cans, especially beef. The trouble had been that no matter what beef was like when it went into a can, it came out stew. The cans were round, and in time the beef slipped and slithered inside and broke up into unappetizing messes. Two new inventions put an end to this: the first, a process for pre-cooking beef which shrank it to such an extent that no further shrinkage would occur in the can; the second, the designing by a Chicagoan named J. A. Wilson of a can shaped like a truncated pyramid. This held the can's contents solidly in place, and when it was opened at the large end, the meat inside would slip out intact, not only appetizing but even sliceable.

Most of the problems of the meat packers had now been solved. The public was being satisfactorily served, the industry was booming, and the name of Chicago had become synonymous with meat. But with the Spanish-American War, the industry suffered a jolt. Canned beef intoxicated American soldiers in Cuba, and some died from botulism, though Upton Sinclair was exaggerating when he wrote that " 'embalmed beef' . . . killed several times as many United States soldiers as all the bullets of the Spaniards." This gave canned beef a bad name for a while, though the fault actually did not lie with the meat packers. The bad beef came from Army stores which had been stocked years before in provision for an emergency, and it had not occurred to the commissary officers that beef, unlike bullets, cannot be conserved indefinitely. This end-of-the-century flurry about the dangers of canned meat quickly died down. "Neither customer nor butcher saw the cattle which furnished their meat," Richard Osborn Cummins noted, "but they were satisfied until they learned what was happening in the packing centers."

The person who told them what was happening, and possibly even more than was happening, in the packing centers was the same one who had coined the phrase "embalmed beef"—Upton Sinclair, whose *The Jungle* was published in 1906 and caused an immediate uproar. Sinclair pictured sausages as being made of spoiled meat treated with chemicals to disguise the fact that it had begun to rot, handled by tubercular workers (tuberculosis inspired then the same horror that cancer arouses now). There must have been *some* meat handlers who had escaped tuberculosis as well as the attention of Upton Sinclair, but it was a fact that packers were not overscrupulous about applying preservatives to meat already beyond preserving, plus additives of various kinds to mask its defects. The chief of the chemical division of the United States Department of Agriculture, Dr.

Harvey Wiley, well aware of this fact, had been decrying food adulteration and related abuses since 1883. The public reacted with alarm only when it read in *The Jungle* about

> cattle which had been fed on "whiskey malt," the refuse of the breweries [as a matter of fact distillers' grains are not bad cattle food, combined, of course, with other rations], and had become what the men called "steerly"—which means covered with boils. It was a nasty job killing these, for when you plunged your knife into them they would burst and splash foul-smelling stuff into your face.

There was government inspection of meat for sanitary reasons, but Sinclair did not describe the inspection as rigorous. He wrote of

> a government inspector who sat in the doorway and felt of the glands in the neck for tuberculosis. This government inspector did not have the manner of a man who was worked to death; he was apparently not haunted by a fear that the hog might get by him before he had finished his testing.

As a result of *The Jungle* and the campaign it inspired, meat sales dropped by more than one-half. The effect was long-lasting; packers were still trying to woo their customers back as late as 1928, when they launched an "eat-more-meat" campaign and did not do very well at it. They cleaned up their factories to an extent that made it possible for them to open them to the public; an excursion to the slaughterhouses became almost obligatory for tourists to Chicago. On the official plane, the scandal also produced results. The first Pure Food and Drug Law was passed in 1906 and was almost ironically named "Dr. Wiley's Law" rather than "Upton Sinclair's Law." It is true that Dr. Wiley actually had drafted its text, and he deserved all the credit the public might be willing to accord him, but without *The Jungle* it would probably have suffered the same fate as the bill Wiley had persuaded Congress to consider as early as 1889, which was voted down to the accompaniment of ridicule from the legislators and applause from the meat packers' lobby. This first Pure Food and Drug Law was not ideal, but it set a precedent, and would be improved by further legislation as time went on. Nevertheless, some of the additives which Dr. Wiley attacked as dangerous to health in the opening years of the century are still legally admissible in processed foods.

In the category of meat, specifically, the arousing of public consciousness had the effect of making inspection severer. All meats entering into interstate commerce (the Federal government had, of course, no jurisdiction over intrastate trade) were subject to examination and could not be sold unless they were stamped "inspected and passed." Beef was a special case; for this meat alone the inspectors certified not only its wholesomeness, but also graded it according to quality. That this applies only to beef is not generally understood by consumers; if you buy, for example, a ham stamped "Prime Quality," this is simply an assertion of the food processor, who is not likely to give his own work a low mark. The government does not grade hams.

The quality of beef varies with every carcass, so the inspectors assess each one separately. The categories, from the best downward, are prime, choice, good and standard. These are all the retail buyer ever sees, although there are three others, commercial, cutter and canner. These are grades which are not on sale in the butcher shops, but only to processors, who put them into such foods as sausage.

The faith the public accorded to governmental inspection and control of canned foods—not justifiably, let us hope—increased their acceptability, not only in the case of meat, but all along the line. Certain changes in living habits also tended to increase the use of commercially preserved foods. The shift from old-fashioned fuels, chiefly wood, which on farms and in country homes had made it possible to keep ranges permanently lighted, to gas and electricity, too expensive to use constantly, condemned many once popular and common dishes which demanded long cooking; but they could be warmed up quickly if bought ready cooked in a can. The cost of home preserving increased with the new fuels too, encouraging recourse to commercially canned goods whenever cost was an important factor; the homemade product was superior, but not enough so to justify much higher expense, or, perhaps more importantly, the amount of work the home preserver had to devote to her task, in comparison with the minute effort of opening a can. Increasing urbanization meant that more families were living in small apartments without attics or cellars, and with no space for a few hundred Mason jars; commercial preserves could be bought one or two cans at a time whenever they were wanted. Central heating became general, comfortable to humans but destructive to food. Some foods which would keep for a considerable time in old-fashioned houses spoiled in a few days where there was central heating; the solution of course was to keep them unspoilably, in cans. Everything seemed to be conspiring to bring about a shift from amateur individual home cooking to professional mass-produced commercial cooking.

The United States, for a variety of reasons, was first to undergo most of the changes which, for better or for worse, affected the character of modern living—and, incidentally and more or less accidentally, brought about the apotheosis of the can. By the nineteen twenties the United States was, qualitatively, processing more different kinds of food, and, quantitatively, "putting up" more food, than all the other countries of the world put together.

XXIV

Toward the Machine Age

THE HALF-CENTURY which elapsed between the Civil War and the First World War was a period of transition. From 1815 to 1860, the United States had been primarily bucolic. Everyday life was centered in the family, and when it reached out from the family into the society which contained it, it did so through group activities which constituted extensions of the family—the church social, the county fair (at which housewives competed for the prizes awarded to the richest cakes or the spiciest pickles), the lodge picnic, the Scout camp, or the summer seaside cottage. Most American families ate amateur cooking—by derivative meaning, cooking with love.

The march of progress from amateur to professional cooking had gotten under way, on a small scale, before the Civil War and vestigial remnants of the old school would persist after the holocausts of the two World Wars, but the greater part of the evolution from the old regime to the new occurred between 1865 and 1915. There was some resistance to it, much of which probably stemmed from simple dislike for changing established habits; it would have been rather difficult at that time to have looked deeply enough into the future to foresee, and dread, if dread were in one's nature, the horrendous developments in store for the nation in some sectors of its gastronomy. In addition to simple inertia, there was a certain opposition to the mechanization of food production which came from a quarter not primarily concerned with objecting to the industrialization of feeding, but to the industrialization of anything.

There was one special category of community which resisted change resolutely and affected American eating habits to an appreciable extent—the religious community. Since the factors which were altering so profoundly the nature of the foods being supplied to the citizens of the United States were almost without exception economic, it was only natural that the strongest resistance to them should come from utopian religious communities, impervious to the worldly and unworthy considerations of profit and, many of them, courageously successful in remaining deaf to the blandishments of Mammon.

Two religious communities in particular left their mark on American eating, the Pennsylvania Dutch and the Shakers.

> Of all the regional cooking styles in America today [wrote José Wilson, in *American Cooking: The Eastern Heartland*], perhaps the most enduring and distinctive can be claimed by the Pennsylvania Dutch, descendants of the German religious radicals who began emigrating to America at the end of the 17th century to join William Penn's thriving young colony for "schismatical, factious people," his "Holy Experiment" in religious tolerance. The cooking of this frugal, industrious and enterprising people—farmers then and farmers still—has changed little over the years.

The particular religious point of view of the Pennsylvania Dutch led to what would be described more accurately as simplicity than as austerity. They followed in particular those basic injunctions of the Bible, to till the soil and to multiply; the two are highly compatible, for there is nothing so useful on a good-sized family farm as a generous supply of robust sons, backed up by the equally sturdy daughters so plentiful in the Pennsylvania Dutch population. They constitute a community which limits its desires to the essentials—food, housing and clothing, of which the most important is food. Aside from a certain proportion of hard-working artisans, the population is made up almost exclusively of farmers, who concentrate on the quality of the food they produce, for they take pride in their business. Though they consider food God's gift to man, they do not look upon it as a free gift: it has to be earned, and they earn it. In the process, they work up good appetites: "Them that work hard, eat hearty," they observe. Hence the quality of their food and its nature. It is as tasty and as nutritive when it comes out of the soil, or off the tree or bush, or from the feeding pens, as good husbandry can make it; and it is put on the table in solidly appetizing rib-sticking dishes, not fancified or prettied up, but not without imagination either, and certainly not without loving care. To fail to do one's best with God-given food would be to disdain the bounty of the Creator. The God of the Pennsylvania Dutch, though an enemy of vanity, is no ascetic.

There is no incompatibility for the Pennsylvania Dutch between the enjoyment of food and the practice of religion even at the same time and in the same place. The Moravians, during sessions of hymn singings, pass around mugs of coffee and "love feast" buns; Amish half-moon pies are also called "preaching pies," because they are made in turnover shape to permit children to hold and munch them during religious services. Many Pennsylvania Dutch foods are inseparably associated with religious holidays. The Fastnacht dunking doughnut, for instance, is so called from the last day before Lent *(Fastnacht* in German), when it is traditionally eaten. The word "dunking" comes from the sect known as Dunkards, whose doughnuts are meant to be dipped in coffee or molasses before eating. Dandelion salad is a dish served especially on Maundy Thursday. Christmas is marked by special pastries, such as Lebkuchen (cookies) and "sand tarts." There are no religious inhibitions to deter wives and daughters from feeding husbands and brothers with all the skill and devotion they can muster (as long as they shun vain fripperies) and they do so. The Pennsylvania Dutch version of "the way to a man's heart is through his stomach" comes out: "Kissin' wears out, cookery don't."

The favorite meat of the Pennsylvania Dutch is pork, a preference inherited from their ancestral Germany. With characteristic disapproval of waste, they eat not only ham, roast pork, pork chops and pork sausage, but also find uses for parts of the pig which some finicky farmers might despise. The animal's stomach might not seem its most promising tidbit, but when it is stuffed with sausage meat and vegetables and baked in the oven it becomes the prized dish called hog maw. Pig's feet, treated with cider vinegar, are appreciated under the name of souse. Ears and muzzles go into head cheese, intestines make sausage casings. The ultimate economy comes when the scraps left over after butchering (but usually not the scraps alone, also such respectable portions as shoulder meat and the liver) supply the basis for a nationally known dish for which credit has been usurped shamelessly by the state's most famous city when it is called Philadelphia scrapple; the Pennsylvania Dutch maintain their copyright on this Pennsylvania Dutch dish by calling it pawnhass. ("Philadelphia" pepper pot is a steal from the Pennsylvania Dutch too.)

One might expect cooking low in key from the far from sybaritic Pennsylvania Dutch; on the contrary, they have developed a cuisine which reaches far for tastiness. They use a good deal of spice, favoring the shockers over the more subtle flavorers. One of the most used is saffron, which turns up in almost all chicken dishes, in many based on noodles, in soups and sauces, and even in sweet pastries. Since saffron is the most expensive seasoner in the world, this preference might seem to make hash of the Pennsylvania Dutch penchant for economy; but they are economical not in the sense of skimping on quality, but in that of abhorring waste: "Better a burst stomach than wasted food," they say.

The widespread use of saffron is rooted in history, or at least in history plus legend. Saffron is usually associated with the warm countries of the

Mediterranean basin, but the plant which produces it can put up with comparatively rigorous climates. From the fifteenth century on it was grown in Germany and used extensively in German cooking. According to Pennsylvania Dutch tradition, one of the families which migrated to the United States was in the saffron business, and brought a supply along, including, apparently, some plants. In the eighteenth century, as a result, the Pennsylvania Dutch, in accordance with their practice of producing for themselves everything they needed or wanted, grew their own saffron. Produced by their own labor on their own land for their own use, the market value of saffron was irrelevant; the Pennsylvania Dutch got into the habit of using it even more freely than had their ancestors. By the time they decided that on their soil and in their climate they would do better to concentrate on other crops, they had become so deeply devoted to the flavor of saffron that they never envisaged giving it up.

Many other strong spices and sharply flavored herbs play an important role in Pennsylvania Dutch cooking. The bite of coriander and of sage heightens the flavor of sausages. Ham is given pungency by being smoked over hickory or sassafras wood. Cloves add an exotic note to scrapple. The velvety Pennsylvania Dutch apple butter is more highly spiced than the now almost forgotten New England apple butter used to be. Cider vinegar is freely used for tartness, and what might be called its opposite among seasoners—sugar—is also much in evidence. Cakes and puddings are placed on the table at the beginning of a meal and left there until its end, an invitation to any eater to help himself to a sweet whenever he feels like it.

This simultaneous appreciation of the most assertive seasoners at opposite ends of the taste scale accounts for one of the most typical items on the Pennsylvania Dutch menu, the "seven sweets and seven sours," which bestow on it a riches of relishes. Among favorite Pennsylvania Dutch appetite teasers are bread-and-butter pickles, pickled green peppers stuffed with chopped cabbage, crisp pickled Jerusalem artichokes, pickled beets, watermelon rind pickle, several green tomato relishes, pickled walnuts, mustard-flavored green or yellow string beans, hard-boiled eggs marinated in beet juice, spiced cantaloupe, gooseberry catsup, and an endless assortment of jams and jellies.

The Pennsylvania Dutch sweet tooth, backed up by a redoubtable readiness to cope with starches, gives the Lancaster County housewife a rich repertory of cakes, cookies, and pies. One local specialty, known to all Americans at least as a picturesque name even if they have never encountered the dish, is shoo-fly pie, actually not so much a pie as a molasses cake, though it is baked in a pie-crust shell. Its name is usually explained as coming from the fact that flies are attracted by its sweet stickiness and must continually be shooed away, but there is another more recondite theory.

Crumbs are sprinkled on the top of shoo-fly pie, which it is alleged make it look to some observers like the head of a cauliflower; hence "shoo-fly" is supposed to be a corruption of the French word for cauliflower, *chou-fleur.* How a French word could have insinuated itself into this setting is not explained. Other typical Pennsylvania Dutch pies, some sweet, some not, are green tomato pie, vinegar pie, crumb pie and funeral pie (made of raisins). The most typical of all is no doubt *milich flitche,* a milk pie made from leftover pastry scraps primarily to provide between-meal snacks for hungry children, but not forbidden to others judging from some of its alternative names—grandmother's pie, poor-man's pie, promise pie, eat-me-quick pie, and schlopp.

The Pennsylvania Dutch were (and still are) natural enemies of the new values of the industrial age which were beginning to harden into their fore-ordained shape toward the end of the nineteenth century. Family centered, they could only be hostile to developments which would tend to break up the family. Forbidden by religious doctrine from having recourse to machines, they could not cooperate with an economy becoming increasingly dependent upon them. Accustomed to producing for themselves virtually all the food they ate, they looked with distrust on the patented aliments offered in cans, jars, or large economy packages in the supermarkets.

The Shakers presented a somewhat different case. They had no reason for bridling at an American society which was tending to break up families, for they had abolished families themselves: they practiced celibacy and maintained their numbers by adopting children, who became the wards of the whole community. Like the Pennsylvania Dutch, the Shakers believed in the inherent virtue of work, but they had no objection to augmenting their own physical strength by the adjunct of machinery. They were, indeed, exceptionally ingenious at contriving labor-saving devices, and have been credited with inventing a buzz saw, a threshing machine, a rotary harrow, a cheese press, a butter churn operated by water power, a pea sheller, a contraption which pared, cored, and quartered apples in a single operation, a round oven with rotating shelves to permit the simultaneous cooking of a number of dishes demanding different cooking times—and the clothespin. They seem also to have been among the first Americans to use the vacuum pan; it was in the Shaker colony of New Lebanon, New York, that Gail Borden discovered one in operation and was inspired by it to develop his process for condensing milk.

The Shakers, like the Pennsylvania Dutch, lived on their own produce; but while the Pennsylvania Dutch were content with raising quality food which would sell on its own merits without the intervention of high pressure salesmanship, the industry and ingenuity of the Shakers were devoted not only to improving the quality of their wares but also to marketing them. The Shakers, with the Pennsylvania Dutch, constituted an impediment to the development of mass marketing of food wherever an increase in scale meant a diminution in quality; but they were not basically and psychologically opposed to the type of society implied by the development of mass merchandising. They were tuned closer to the wave length of the evolving turn-of-the-century economy than the Pennsylvania Dutch were. One might put it that the mass food suppliers of the growing machine age had no objection to quality as long as it did not get in the way of profit and the Shakers had no objection to profit as long as it did not get in the way of quality; there was an overlapping area between the two approaches which left room for compromise. They were gifted with an ambivalence which permitted them to live with the old era and with the new; they constituted a sort of bridge between the age of amateurism and the age of professionalism. They were devoted to the ideals of the past, but they were prepared to translate them into the idiom of the future.

The Shakers, wrote Charles Dickens,

> are good farmers, and all their produce is eagerly purchased and highly esteemed. "Shaker seeds," "Shaker herbs," and "Shaker distilled waters" are commonly announced for sale in the shops of towns and cities. They are good breeders of cattle, and are kind and merciful to the brute creation. Consequently, Shaker beasts seldom fail to find a ready market.

Dickens, though no foe of exaggeration, had in this case exaggerated nothing. Shaker produce commanded premium prices because of the care devoted to assuring its superiority. The Shakers maintained plant nurseries and developed improved varieties of fruit. Shaker honey and Shaker maple syrup were more flavorful than the run-of-the-mill offerings of most of their neighbors. Shaker dairy products were richer (and their barns and stables were cleaner). The Shakers were, as Dickens implied, great herbalists; they reached a point at which they were able to supply 350 different kinds of herbs, roots, barks, seeds or flowers for culinary or medicinal purposes, and exported them to places as far distant as India and Australia. Their preoccupation with herbs inevitably had an effect on their own cooking, which made much use of chives, mint, chervil, rosemary, summer savory, borage and basil, great providers of vitamins, of which nobody had yet heard in the nineteenth century; but the Shakers, through instinct or empiricism, were dietarily well ahead of their times and were already eating green vegetables and fresh fruit at a period when many Americans thought they were dangerous.

> For 18th and 19th century America [José Wilson wrote in *American Cooking: The Eastern Heartland*], Shaker cooking showed a remarkably epicurean

> touch. Spinach was flavored with rosemary, apple pie with rose water. A delicate, fragrant herb soup combined chives, celery, sorrel, chervil, tarragon, nutmeg and chicken stock. There was even a recipe for *dolma,* which an enterprising Shaker sister of the community of North Union (now Shaker Heights) near Cleveland must have culled somehow from Middle Eastern cooking in order to make use of the leaves from the grape vines the Shakers cultivated on the shores of Lake Erie for medicinal wines and unfermented grape juice. In their early days the Shakers had nothing against the use of alcoholic drinks—hard cider and peach brandy from their orchards, fruit wines and cordials. But in 1828, in a sudden access of strictness, the mother community in New Lebanon banned the use of "beer, cider, wines and all ardent liquors . . . on all occasions; at house-raisings, husking bees, harvestings and all other gatherings."

This left the Shakers with the spring water they also bottled for sale, milk, and if not hard cider, at least sweet cider, for which a picturesque directive has survived in Shaker literature:

> Place the apples on the grass on the north or shady side of the barn to mellow. When at thirty feet distance you catch the fragrant apple aroma, they are ready for the press.

Shaker cooks are credited with having created oyster pie and corn oysters, with having first thought of baking ham in cider, with having developed a large variety of special breads, and with having conceived the idea of using the water in which vegetables had been cooked to enrich meat gravies, stews, soups, or sauces. They did not spoil vegetables by overcooking in order to produce a liquid to improve their gravies. "The long boiling of any vegetable in water extracts the salts that are so beneficial," a Shaker sister warned, a lesson not yet learned by many English and American housewives.

The Shaker women canned their fruits, vegetables, jams, jellies, relishes and preserves for the market before it was being done on a commercial scale, and the communities put them on sale with an astuteness which, again, was ahead of the times. Shaker seeds, similarly, were snapped up because of the convenient fashion in which they were offered. The general stores of the times kept their vegetable seeds in bins, from which they scooped up the loose seeds in approximately the quantity the buyer wanted; the Shakers seem to have been the first to come up with the idea of putting seeds in packets as they are so commonly sold today. They offered a wide choice. There were eight varieties of beans and the same of peas, six varieties of squash, and the same of carrots and beets, and different types of melons, asparagus, cabbage, collards, mustard greens, spinach, turnips, et cetera. Herbs were likewise put up in neat packages of convenient size. The Shakers also provided with their products what merchandisers today call a plus-value: they gave away recipes with them. It was a period when most cookbooks dodged the difficulties of giving exact proportions for the ingredients which went into their dishes, but the Shakers, ahead in this too, specified weights and volumes in terms of pounds, ounces, quarts, pints, cups, and tablespoons. True, many housewives did not then have the measures which would permit them to follow these directions; but the Shakers were prepared to provide them for any customers who wanted to order them.

Probably the most notable Shaker breakthrough was that they put on the market a basic compound whose formula included simply flour, baking soda, salt and shortening. Add water or milk, and you had pancakes. Put in sugar and flavoring and you could achieve, depending on your wishes, fancy breads, cookies, or cakes. It was the first ready-mix and it entitles the Shakers to be classed, for better or for worse, among the founders of food processing.

In the last third of the nineteenth century, despite the increasing temptations of processed foods, so easy to prepare and so effective in reducing the drudgery of the kitchen, the American housewife continued stubbornly to resist their assault on home cooking. She took pride in her own handiwork and it is hard to work up much self-satisfaction about opening a can. It had not yet occurred to women that cooking was a task unworthy of their attention, though some of them would begin to think so from the time when most of it was confined to persons held to be inferiors—the domestic servants who delayed the conquest of the kitchen by factory-produced products when they freed the mistress of the household from her more monotonous tasks.

> By the late 1870's [wrote Esther Aresty in *The Delectable Past*—she could have placed the date a little earlier], a new supply of household help became available in the waves of immigrants who arrived in America to share in its burgeoning prosperity. But if the mistress of a home expected the wheels to turn smoothly and meals to be cooked, she now had to be prepared to instruct the green newcomers.

The compensation for this burden was the delight that could be taken in exchanging anecdotes with one's friends about the comic errors of the "hired girl" over a hand of bezique or during the concoction of a crazy quilt. Unfortunately this relegation of the household tasks to Norah or Hilda convinced many women that it was beneath their dignity to enter the kitchen except to give orders, despite the adjurations of such ardent defenders of the dignity of the ancient and honorable pursuit of the culinary art as Catherine Beecher, certainly not one to accept a passive or secondary role in society for women; she was, on the contrary, a militant feminist who cried out indignantly in one of her cookbooks: "In what respects are women subordinate?" and added the parallel question: "Wherein are they superior and equal in influence?" She had an answer for this one: in the kitchen. Supremacy in this realm did not strike Miss Beecher as in any way demeaning, for she held that cooking was an art, and, one gathers, an art at which men were pretty poor sticks; woman's control of the kitchen gave her a weapon by means of which she could control everything else. She dedicated another of her books, this one written in collaboration with her sister, Harriet Beecher Stowe, to "the women of America, in whose hands rest the real destinies of the Republic, as moulded by the early training and preserved among the maturer influences of home." The hand that held the skillet ruled the world.

But though Miss Beecher felt that women should not relinquish the post of command provided for them by the kitchen, she saw no reason for accepting any servitudes connected with it if they could be eliminated. She advocated the rationalization and the simplification of the kitchen to free the cook from her more onerous chores, which would not only liberate her genius for its exclusive application to the esthetic aspects of cooking but would also give her time to concern herself with "the real destinies of the Republic." She found in the ship's galley the model for an improved home kitchen. The galley was indeed a first-rate example of the efficient organization of limited space to permit the preparation of food with a minimum of effort and the lessons to be learned from it became increasingly useful as the ratio of farmhouses to city apartments decreased, and it became less and less common for the kitchen to be the largest room in the home, and frequently its general living room. In the nineteen twenties modern kitchen designers would echo Miss Beecher's example, without knowing it, by looking for inspiration to an analogous example of the efficient utilization of space, the galley of the railroad dining car.

The growing industrial age was at this period working both sides of the street on the issue of whether women should get out of the kitchen or stay in it. One of its branches was devoted to improving prepared foods, whose ultimate effect would be to reduce almost to the vanishing point the amount of time that the housewife would be obliged to give to her kitchen. Another branch was offering her ever more ingenious equipment to aid her in her cooking, thus tempting her to give more attention to it. Not all the new inventions manufacturers put before housewives were unqualified advances, beginning with the most essential item of kitchen machinery, the stove.

Having failed to notice that Swedish immigrants had brought a simple iron stove to America as early as the seventeenth century, most American housewives were still cooking in fireplaces until after the Civil War, even in city apartments. Ranges had been available to them thirty years earlier, but they were formidable machines, cumbersome and complicated, and many of their first buyers, after herculean struggles with their many ventilators and flues, regretted that they had not left well enough alone and stayed with the fireplace. Not until the 1870s did an iron range appear which was easy for the untutored cook to handle; and even then some women were cool to it, including Catherine Beecher, who thought the brick oven in the wall of the fireplace was better for baking. The cooking stove also provided a continuous supply of hot water for the kitchen. Few cooking devices have been more flexible, more versatile, or more quickly responsive to the varying demands of the cook.

The chief disadvantages of the wood stove were the necessity of disposing of its ashes, the difficulty of keeping the kitchen clean, and the reserving of space for storing its fuel, the last a problem which became more acute as kitchens grew smaller with increasing urbanization. Urbanization also had the effect of increasing the distance between the tree and the stove, so that the housewife soon found herself paying several times more for transporting her wood than for the wood itself.

It was not until after the turn of the century that the kitchen range was redesigned to burn coal. A more compact fuel, coal was easier to transport, required less storage space (but still enough to create problems) and produced less ash; but it made it harder to keep the kitchen clean. The problems of cleanliness and of storage space were solved simultaneously in the nineteen twenties, when city kitchens were equipped almost universally with gas stoves. There followed flirtations with the fireless cooker and the vacuum kettle, but both gave way before the electric range of today, which operates undemandingly, requiring virtually no attention. It has contributed immensely to the liberation of women, permitting them to go out leaving the roast in the oven without being haunted with the nightmare of not getting back home in time to save the dinner from being burned to a crisp (or the house from being set on fire).

By the time cooking by gas and electricity had come in, the advertising man had come in too, so they were described as "economy fuels," to disguise the fact that this was precisely what they were not. The replacement of wood and coal by gas and electricity modified the cooking habits and the eating habits of the nation, and these modifications clearly resulted from the fact that the cost of fuel had now become a relatively more important element in the cost of food than it had been previously.

Wood or coal stoves were often kept burning continuously—especially on farms with woodlots, from which enough odd chunks of wood could usually be gleaned to keep the fire burning continuously with no cash outlay at all. This practice stopped abruptly with the advent of gas and electricity; nobody could afford to keep either of them burning all the time without ever shutting them off. The change banished one dish from the menu, in the city at least. In the days of the continuously burning stove, a catch-all kettle frequently simmered permanently on the back of the range, its contents changing constantly as they were drawn upon for one meal or replenished in view of another. The bubbling kettle could be fed with felicity by any good cook mindful of the dosage of the various vegetables or pieces of meat which she consigned to it whenever she had extra food. There was always an emergency repast on the stove, in the form of a usually rich stew, which often provided all anyone wanted for supper. It could almost be described as a free meal, since it was composed chiefly of leftovers which when gas and electricity came in would go only too often straight into the garbage can.

To the increased cost of the new fuels the household economy thus had to add also the cost of other dishes to replace this by-product of continuous heating. Another increment resulted from the fact that the advent of the quick-heating briefly burned fuels encouraged the replacing of dishes slow to cook, like pot roast, by quickly prepared ones, like steaks and chops; it happens that the latter are more expensive than the former. The permanently burning stove had served not only for cooking, it had also heated the kitchen, which now had to be kept warm by other means, and a separate installation was usually necessary to provide hot water, too. The Machine Age was the costly age.

The improvement of stoves during the late nineteenth and early twentieth centuries contributed enormously to easing the often exhausting work of the home cook; but it may be that easier cooking was achieved, to some extent, at the expense of quality. When the gas range came in, applying heat with an irreducible minimum of brutality to dishes some of which had responded better to the gentle glow obtainable from wood or coal ranges, a certain subtlety became unobtainable. But if the range of gas was more restricted, every gradation within that range could be obtained by turning the flame up or down through an infinite variety of shadings. Electricity reduced the flexibility provided by the gas flame to the number of arbitrarily chosen points built into the stove's rheostat; and when today's almost completely automated stove came in, the genius of the individual cook was almost annulled by it. In turning over part of her pains to machinery, the cook also lost her control over processes which were now performed unvaryingly by mechanical devices. The machine, unlike the born cook, cannot adapt its reactions to the myriad minute changes in the imponderables, whose skillful handling makes all the difference between competent cooking and divine cooking. Dare we suggest that the modern stove, superb though it is as a labor-saving device, makes it possible for almost anyone to cook acceptably but almost impossible for anyone to cook divinely?

If the perfecting of the stove tended to bring the mechanical age into the home and to undermine the practice of the cunning crafts of the kitchen by making the exercise of intelligence unnecessary, this was only a minor tangential contribution to the conspiracy of machines to reduce us all to the status of robots. The stove has not gotten out of hand nearly as badly as, for instance, the automobile, which has nearly completed its domestication of man. And smaller kitchen aids have, up to now, been held even more firmly than the stove to their roles as servants of the cook, not her masters. The ingenuity of the machine age was being applied to their development during the same period which saw the evolution of the stove, though in their case invention moved a little more slowly. Many basic kitchen utensils were about as efficient in their simplest forms as they ever could be: how, for instance, would one go about improving the rolling pin?

No objection could be made to the earliest of the minor kitchen labor-savers on the ground that their use decreased the intensity or the purity of natural tastes. What difference could it make to the flavor of an apple whether the knife which pared it were held in the hand of the cook or in the grip of a mechanical device? Apple parers must have been among the very first kitchen aids supplied to the American housewife. At least one had been invented as early as 1812; screwed to the kitchen table by a vise and cranked by a handle, it looked very much like the meat grinder which was standard equipment in all kitchens until its recent replacement by modern electric choppers, mixers, and blenders. The Shaker apple handler which came along later performed more operations on the fruit, but it had the disadvantage of being two feet long. In the late nineteenth and early twentieth centuries, uncountable thousands of kitchen helps were invented, some of them rather fearsome objects, like the one of which David Lack commented in the November 1969 issue of *Gourmet:*

> Surely it wasn't absolutely necessary to combine a cookie cutter, pie crimper, spice grinder, grater, apple quarterer, and cherry pitter into one masterpiece, yet such a model was actually patented. Just holding it posed a distinct problem of having the hand cut, crimped, ground, grated, quartered, and pitted simultaneously.

Most of the new devices were less dangerous and many of them were actually useful, though it must be suspected that in some cases women bought new examples of the ingenuity of inventors chiefly because of their novelty, abandoning them quickly to return to simpler implements, like the fruit knife. Though kitchen engineering produced a quantity of gadgets too ingenious to be practical, it is doubtful whether any of them actually denatured the taste of foods. It is not certain that one would dare say the same thing for our times, which have substituted the impersonal uncontrollable force of electricity for that of elbow grease, a primitive but infinitely variable form of energy. Famous chefs have been known to complain that electrically powered grinders, no matter how ingeniously equipped with accessories to permit a variety of gradations, frequently chop foods too fine and thus alter their textures, an element which has more effect on the perception of taste than most of us realize.

Since ancient times, the making of bread has been consistently the first culinary task which individual families have consented to turn over to outsiders. The first professional cooks to operate outside the home in both ancient Greece and ancient Rome were the bakers. Baking bread demanded more effort than any other common cooking task; the home cook was often relieved at being able to turn this hard work over to someone else.

Let it be recorded to the honor of the American housewife that the process of the degeneration of bread took a long time. She resisted this particular form of a quality-shattering invasion of the kitchen by the machine age for the entire nineteenth century. In ancient times breadmaking was even more onerous than it is now; it began with the grain, which had to be ground into flour at home. The American housewife at least did not have to grind her own flour; but she did have to knead the dough. This was hard work, but nineteenth-century cookbooks were generous of her time and effort. Some of the more considerate authors let her off with forty-five minutes of pummeling dough, but others prescribed twice as long and warned her sternly not to stop to catch her breath for "any pause in the process injured the bread." How much easier to go to the store and buy a loaf of ready-made bread! Why was the nineteenth-century housewife so reluctant to do so?

It must have been because she took pride in her bread.

"Americans traditionally have been excellent home bakers," Dale Brown pointed out in *American Cooking;* "indeed, many American women have been better bakers than cooks." "The true housewife," the Beecher sisters wrote, "makes bread the sovereign of her kitchen." During the nineteenth century, she received aid in keeping it so from the enemy—in other words, industrialism. The gadget makers helped her in her kneading by producing such devices as a tin bucket the size and shape of a milk pail which could be screwed to the kitchen table like a meat grinder; by turning a crank affixed to its rim, the housewife could rotate an S-shaped rod running from top to bottom of this contraption to knead the dough with which it was filled, exerting a minimum of effort.

A score of years before the Civil War, the American breadmaker received help in the form of a new leavening agent called saleratus, which changed its name later to baking soda. It was convenient to use, but required the help of an acid to perform its work; cream of tartar was the one usually chosen. In 1856, baking powder was devised; this provided the cream of tartar, or some equivalent acid, already mixed with the baking soda.

In 1868 commercial yeast became available in stores, and this took on its most convenient form in the familiar individual-sized foil-coated cakes of yeast. It was the last gift made by the food industry to the housewife to help her in her own baking; she would have to wait for nearly a century for another of comparable importance, and when it came it virtually shouldered her away from the mixing bowl and the creation of her own confections altogether. It was the ready-mix, for breads, pancakes and dessert cakes. The nature of what had been the home cook's pride was now determined outside of the home. She went to the store and bought her cake complete, in the form of a powder, all the ingredients present according to some manufacturer's formula, except the liquid. All she had to do was add the specified amount of milk or water and put the resulting paste in a mechanically controlled oven at the heat and for the time inscribed on the package. Anyone could do it—the most feckless and inexperienced male of the family or any child old enough to turn an electric switch. Frozen breads and frozen pastry completed the process of depriving the American woman of the pleasure of boasting of her baking.

While this evolution had been taking place for homemade bread, a parallel process was occurring for commercially made bread. As early as 1869 its progress, in terms of what today's jargon calls consumer acceptance, and its retrogression, in terms of the gourmet's criteria, had already reached a point alarming to the Beecher sisters. Defenders of mass-made bread were claiming that the home product lay heavy on the stomach and that commercial bread was lighter, and hence must be healthier and better than home-baked loaves. The Beechers treated women whose only standard for judging bread was its lightness as ignoramuses, unqualified to express any opinions about it. If bakers' bread was light, they intimated, that was its only merit; and for that matter lightness was in this case not a merit at all. "How else can they value and relish bakers' loaves?" the sisters asked scornfully, adding that commercial bread was "light indeed, so light that [its loaves] seem to have neither weight nor substance, but with no more sweetness or taste than so much cotton wool." The battle for bread became a Beecher family crusade when its most famous member, the Reverend Henry Ward Beecher, brother of the two cookbook-writing sisters, delivered in 1871 a blast of his own against professionally baked bread, though for a different reason: he attacked it not because it was losing its taste but because it was losing its nutritiousness. Aroused by the new practice of bleaching flour, he stigmatized it as killing "the live germ of the wheat" so that "what had been the staff of life for countless ages had become a weak crutch."

At the time when the Beechers spoke out, the women of America were still holding the fort for homemade bread. In 1900, 95 percent of all the flour sold in the United States was still being bought by individuals for use in home cooking. But then the surrender foreseen by the Beecher sisters came about. Changes in America's social pattern probably had as much to do with the victory of commercial bread as its convenience; for instance, a rapidly developing industrial and commercial economy was drawing ever more women out of their homes and into factories, stores and offices; and with the two World Wars, which increased immensely the business demand for women workers, few of them any longer had time for the lengthy process of baking bread. By 1970, the percentage of flour bought for American home use was no longer 95 percent, it was 15 percent.

Eating with regard to the healthiness of what one eats would seem to be justifiable in itself, and not to require appeals to morality, like those uttered by such cookbook writers as Mrs. Horace Mann or Catherine Beecher and her reverend brother, who believed that to eat badly was sinful. For them, eating in what they deemed to be an unhealthy fashion (for example, to excess) was synonymous with immorality. This attitude cannot be laid exclusively at the door of American puritanism; gluttony had been elected one of the seven deadly sins long before America was heard of. The example of the clergymen in stigmatizing unhealthy eating habits on the basis of morality rather than of hygiene infected scientists too, so that Wilbur O. Atwater, a professor of agricultural chemistry who published a considerable number of papers gravitating around the subject defined by the title of one of them, *Principles of Nutrition and Nutritive Value of Food* (1902), fell into the moral trap too. When he decided (on the basis of insufficient data) that American workmen were not eating enough energy-building foods for the efforts required of them, he was not content to rest his argument for changes in eating habits on the metabolic requirements of the human organism, but predicted that persistence in such evil ways would lead not to the improvement in morals for which everyone should be striving, but for a "fearful falling away."

Though the role of preachers and prophets as arbiters of everything was not seriously disputed, they were nevertheless amateurs, or at least not specialists, in this field, and the temper of the times was for professionalism. It was inevitable that the lead in a question that concerned health should be taken over eventually by professionals in health, that is, doctors. Even so, doctors ventured into this field not through the main portal of medicine but through the backdoor of theology, as though their right to intervene in a matter of health without ecclesiastical sanction was questionable. The lead in a direction which was to develop a whole new category of foods presented as being particularly beneficial to health was not taken by a doctor but by a religious leader, Mother Ellen Harmon White, spiritual head of the Adventist Church. However, she soon enlisted the professional skills of doctors, and her own theological input quickly became submerged in the activities of the doctors, especially of one doctor. In *American Cooking,* Dale Brown tells the story thus:

> God-given health and happiness are yours, [Mother White] promised, provided you eat two meatless meals a day, drink only water, avoid salt, spices and spirits, and do not smoke. High on her list of heavenly foods was Graham bread. In 1866 she founded the Western Health Reform Institute at Battle Creek, Michigan, and several years later hired Dr. John Harvey Kellogg . . . to manage it for her. Dr. Kellogg was not only to run the Institute: he was to take it over. He changed its name to the Battle Creek Sanitorium (it became known as the San) and he made it, as Ronald M. Deutsch has said in *The Nuts Among the Berries,* "a veritable fountainhead of faddism." Here the sick and the neurotic, the underweight and the overweight went for complete overhauling. "Bran does not irritate," said the good doctor. "It titillates!" And bran was on every tongue. In addition to being titillated, the patients were put on strange diets, suited, the doctor assured them, to their own special needs. The skinny were plied with 26 feedings a day, forced to remain motionless in bed with sandbags on their bellies to increase absorption of nourishment and not allowed even to brush their teeth, since any expenditure of energy might deprive them of a valuable calorie or two. Patients suffering from high blood pressure were served nothing but grapes; they were obliged to swallow 10 to 14 pounds of grapes a day.

An institution of this sort might have been expected to expire quietly, leaving no trace behind, once the absurdity of its methods had become apparent and the faddism or cultism which had supported it at the beginning had exhausted its momentum. What actually happened instead was that *Mother* White's *Reform* Institute (both of the italicized words sound overtones of religiosity) gave rise to a whole new category of foods, whose creation is represented as having been the result of an accident (Mother White might have called it the result of a miracle):

> One of Dr. Kellogg's pet theories [was] that people needed to chew dry, brittle food to keep their teeth in shape. . . . Part of the regular regimen of the San had been the endless munching of zwieback, but when a woman complained of breaking a tooth on it, the doctor vowed to provide a substitute, and he thereupon launched "experiments to produce toasted or destrinized cereals in a form which, while dry and crispy," could be offered to people with artificial teeth, sore teeth or diseased gums. Actually, the cereal his experiments yielded was suspiciously like another faddist's product, Granula; Kellogg dared to call his product Granola, but then thought twice about it when he was sued and quickly changed the name to Granose. In its very first year he managed to sell 100,000 pounds of Granose, and sales went on climbing ever afterward.

One of Dr. Kellogg's patients at the Battle Creek Sanitorium was named Charles Post. He had ulcers; after nine months of Dr. Kellogg's treatment he still had ulcers, but he had derived from observation of Dr. Kellogg a lesson more profitable than freedom from ulcers, the realization that there was money to be made from the combination of health and food. He began, in 1895, by inventing a coffee substitute which he called Postum. This was followed by a dry breakfast cereal of his own; since the religious inspiration behind the health food crusades was still powerful, he called it Elijah's Manna. Grocers, though not necessarily agnostic, did not react favorably to the name. Possibly they foresaw difficulties in persuading customers to pass through the streets with packages tucked under their arms blazing a phrase capable of misleading the neighbors into taking their carriers for evangelists of a new and dubious cult. Dr. Post therefore changed the name of his invention to Grape-Nuts, which proved more acceptable. He thus answered a question put long before by another creator, William Shakespeare. "What's in a name?" Shakespeare had asked. Dr. Post could have told him, "Everything." As all modern merchandisers know (but it was a new idea in Post's and Kellogg's time), a name easy to pronounce and easy to remember, especially if it implies, even vaguely, a promise of quality, will sell a product out of all proportion to its intrinsic merits or lack of them. Post cashed in on this principle with Post Toasties, a name almost singable. Kellogg also understood instinctively the importance of names. He came up with Kellogg's Toasted Corn Flakes, a name that scans and has endured. He had showed his awareness of the magic of names earlier, when he discarded the forbidding title of Western Health Reform Institute for that of Battle Creek Sanitorium. The sanitorium was not, as a matter of fact, actually at Battle Creek, but it was near enough to justify the name. Battle Creek was easy to remember. It had a historical ring to it, even if nobody knew what its history was, and Kellogg advertising publicized it to a point where it became synonymous with dry cereals. Rival food manufacturers hastened to annex the name to pick up any stray crumbs that might fall from Dr. Kellogg's opulent table, and at one time no less than forty competing breakfast food companies were all listing their addresses as Battle Creek.

Kellogg must have hit upon the best name: Kellogg's Toasted Corn Flakes is still the biggest seller of all American dry breakfast cereals, accounting alone for 10 percent of the business, despite the competition of sixty-five nationally advertised brands. Post's products have not done badly either; they formed the basis of today's mighty General Foods Corporation. Other classic breakfast cereals which achieved large sales included Shredded Wheat; Puffed Wheat and Puffed Rice, which were put over with the slogan, "The Food That's Shot from Guns"; Force and Quaker Oats, of which the latter differed from other patented dry breakfast cereals in that it was not a new form of food, but simply that old standby, oatmeal, offered in a trade-marked cardboard box instead of in bulk.

The American public, encouraged by skillful advertising and the will-o'-the-wisp promise of health, took breakfast cereals to its heart. Today they represent a $660-million-a-year business according to Dale Brown. It ain't peanuts—which would come in for some effective advertising promotion too, especially after 1890, which was when a St. Louis doctor invented peanut butter and vaunted its merits as a health food also; Americans eat nearly 250,000 tons of it yearly.

Cereal manufacturers have often devoted a large part of their publicity budgets to bearing down on the nutritive qualities (and thus the healthiness) of their products, but not everybody is in agreement. Sidney Margolius, in *Health Foods: Facts and Fakes,* quotes the opinion that breakfast cereals offer "no more nutrition than dirty fingernails." Today's food faddists say scornfully that "commercial cereals are garbage," and then urge us to switch to other brands of the same category of foods which must be garbage too, since the presently fashionable miracle-working substitutes fall roughly within the same area of nutritiousness. For that poet-champion of the lower-case letter, e. e. cummings, American breakfast cereals should be lumped together under a single pejorative heading: "battle creek seaweed."

In July, 1970, after nutritionist Robert M. Choate testified before a Senate subcommittee that most breakfast cereals had virtually no food value, some food manufacturers began to add nutrients to their products, but others, and not the least, stood pat and continued to produce breakfast foods that represented no gain for nutrition, no gain for gastronomy, but a triumph for the advertising industry. Nutritional or not, dry breakfast cereals have become so firmly established in American eating habits that they are hardly likely to be dislodged. They do have the advantage of coaxing their addicts into absorbing with them two other foods of unquestioned virtues—milk, one of the primary foods of the world, and sugar, a provider of energy. Americans did not really need to eat more sugar—they were eating too much of it already—but apparently they were not deriving from it as much energy as they should have. They were still too tired to sprinkle the sugar on their cereals without help. The food processors, always ready to oblige, accordingly offered cereals already sugared, in which Sidney Margolius found not only

> a nutritional inferiority in a package of sugar-coated flakes [but also] that the sugar had added 18 cents to the cost of the package. Analyzing the sugar content, he found that the consumers were paying for the frosting at the rate of 90 cents a pound, a somewhat high price to pay [it would be more now] to avoid sprinkling a little sugar over a bowl of corn flakes.

However the fact that eating cereals encouraged greater use of milk was beneficial, especially to children (some adults find it difficult to digest raw milk); and they appeared at a time when many children were not getting enough milk. It might be argued that the distribution system had not yet become competent enough to provide it for them: the hygienic conditions in which milk was being produced and handled in pre-cereal times were such that mothers might well have hesitated to give their children milk for fear that they might at the same time be giving them typhoid or tuberculosis. This was still the situation when Dr. Kellogg first got into the cereal business about 1870, but by a little more than a decade later milk would become safer.

In 1882 the first system of dairy inspection was set up, in New Jersey. By 1885, the Borden Company, which sold fresh as well as condensed milk, began delivering it in closed bottles, sounding the knell of the former system of ladling it out from open cans in grocery stores. In 1892 bacterial counts of milk offered for sale were inaugurated, and about a year later certified milk came in—meaning milk that was guaranteed to be free of dangerous amounts of bacteria when it left the dairy; there were still some risks after it got into circulation. These had been countered at first only by education, which became widespread about 1866, urging mothers to boil milk before giving it to children. For once education proved effective: an investigation in New York City in 1908 revealed that almost no babies were being fed there on raw milk. It is true that by this time pasteurization was becoming common; 25 percent of New York's milk and 33 percent of Boston's was pasteurized. Pasteurization was of immense value at the time, and it is doubtful if it could even be dispensed with safely today; but it does debase the flavor of milk, and even reduces its beneficial qualities by attacking its Vitamin C and calcium. One may well wonder whether we would be drinking pasteurized milk now if the tuberculin test for cattle had been perfected twenty years before pasteurization instead of the other way around.

Another food which underwent a change during this period was flour, and consequently bread, whether for better or for worse is still being debated. Sylvester Graham had fought against refined white flour before the Civil War; but there seemed to be an instinctive feeling that whiteness was a guarantee of purity, and against this Graham's reasoning, which in any case was not without flaw, failed to prevail. The shift to white flour which had begun in his time was intensified after the Civil War, largely because of mechanical developments. The milling of white flour had already been promoted by the invention in the eighteen forties in Hungary, a great wheat producing country, of a new type of flour mill which replaced the old rotary millstones with rollers. They squeezed the inner part of the wheat kernel out of its coating, depriving it in one operation of bran and germ alike. Wheat germ is highly nutritive, but it also contains oil which causes flour made with it to spoil in a few weeks, so bakers were glad to be rid of it. As the oil also darkens the flour, germless flour is whiter as well as easier to keep; it appealed to the eye of the guileless housewife, who was accordingly predisposed to believe the baker who told her that white flour was superior, especially as it did not occur to her that in the baker's vocabulary "superior" meant "more profitable." In 1870 the Hungarians hit upon another idea; they made flour mill rollers of porcelain, which produced an even finer, whiter (and longer keeping) flour. By 1881 all the mills in Minneapolis, which had become the great American milling center after the Great Lakes and Northwest regions took to growing wheat, were using porcelain rollers.

Whiteness became a symbol of quality in sugar too, helped along by an astute sugar industry. White sugar was easier to handle, less subject to spoilage, and permitted collecting a second profit for the service of refining it, so the merchants had every reason for extolling its superiority. Also it cost more, which helped to augment its snob value; no housewife with any pride dared put coarse cheap brown sugar on her table, thus earning the derision of her sisters. She might, however, use it in cooking, where its color wouldn't show, especially as it was both cheaper and sweeter. The refiner therefore set out to discourage the use of brown sugar in cooking also, by means of scare tactics. In 1898 it was "disclosed" that the discovery had been made in Dublin (at that period conveniently remote enough to make verification difficult) that a horrendous insect, which no doubt carried redoubtable diseases, infested brown sugar. The refiners sponsored an advertisement illustrated with highly magnified pictures of a frightful monster which described it as

> a formidably organized, exceedingly lively and decidedly ugly little animal . . . The number of these creatures found in raw sugar is exceedingly great and in no instance is raw sugar quite free from either the insects or their eggs. Brown sugar should never be used. . . . It is fortunate to note, however, that these terrible creatures do not occur in refined sugar of any quality.

The battle was won. White sugar ousted brown sugar. Here, however, time has wrought an ironic change. Snobbery, always a powerful factor in public eating, had accounted for the disappearance of brown sugar in the last century; it is accounting for its reappearance in this one. It is now smart to put brown sugar on the table; once lowly, it has become luxurious.

A less controversial evolution was now setting in, slowly, in a widening use of fresh vegetables and fruit. Although greater attention was paid to these foods after the Civil War than before it, it would still be incorrect to describe Americans as great eaters of either. Not until after the First World War would American mistrust of fresh fruit and vegetables be dissipated. It was a mistrust not without a certain reasonable basis. Fresh food spoiled, and the means for preventing spoilage were not yet perfected. Canned food did not spoil, or at least not often (it was not yet quite as dependable as it is now). It could be transported farther and kept longer; therefore many fruits and vegetables were being accepted canned, especially far from the places where they were grown, before they would be eaten fresh.

The earliest pioneer of fruit who has impressed historians was that picturesque American folk hero, Johnny Appleseed, who goes back to before the American Revolution. He was born in Leominster, Massachusetts, on September 26, 1774, and was christened John Chapman, a name few Americans would recognize. Artists like to depict him as a tall gaunt often wild-eyed figure, a bag slung across his shoulder from which he is scattering appleseeds like grain over a surprised soil. He might well have been wild-eyed, as befits a man with a mission. He was eccentric in manners, in dress and in religion (he was a Swedenborgian). But he was never so far off balance as to try to plant apple trees by sowing their seed broadcast; he knew too much about apples for that. He planted apple seedlings, expertly and rationally, in carefully established nurseries, beginning on the Atlantic coast and working his way inland. He was first noticed in this activity in western Pennsylvania in 1800, and by the end of the following year he had created a chain of apple nurseries from the Allegheny to central Ohio. At the time of his death, in March 1845, he had pushed his orchards as far west as Indiana, where he died at Fort Wayne.

Johnny Appleseed's contribution was to diffuse more widely a fruit already familiar. Four years after his death another outstanding figure in the world of fruit was born whose contribution would be that of giving his country unfamiliar plants. Luther Burbank was born before the Civil War but exerted his influence on American eating after it. He is credited with having created more than eight hundred new varieties of fruits and vegetables, but though he was the most prominent among them he was far from being the only horticulturist, botanist, or naturalist engaged in widening the number of flavors available to us. The names of many of them are perpetuated in the names of the fruits they gave us—the youngberry, the loganberry, the boysenberry. A seedless grapefruit appeared in California. Botanists solved the problem which had prevented the Incas, four or five centuries earlier, from developing the tomato—its tendency to dissolve into pulp unless handled with maternal care; tomatoes were now being grown which could be transported undamaged to market. New improved potatoes were developed and their area of distribution increased also. Irrigation came to California; the result was more and better canteloupes and watermelons, asparagus and lettuce.

It was an age of agricultural inventiveness, with scores of devoted naturalists laboring to lengthen for us the gamut of available tastes. Unhappily, it would turn out that the mighty merchants who determine what we shall be allowed to eat did not want it lengthened. The second half of the nineteenth century was characterized by the painstaking efforts of many men to put new edibles before the public; the second half of the twentieth century was characterized by the diligent efforts of many others to reduce the number of edibles that would be put before the public. A mass-market economy did not want to be bothered with a superfluity of products; it was more profitable to concentrate on handling a minimum number of foods than a maximum number. A great part of the work Burbank and his fellows had done was shoveled into the discard. What the food hucksters retained was varieties of greater transportability, longer shelf life and increased resistance to spoilage; what the favored fruits they selected to spread before us might taste like was a secondary consideration.

Nevertheless before the current was reversed, Americans had started to eat more fresh fruit and vegetables and a wider variety among them. By 1889 Alessandro Filippini dared write in his cookbook, *The Table,* "There is no place in the civilized world where the market for the supply of food is so well provided as in New York, both as to variety and excellence, and even as to luxuries." The chief influence in bringing this about had been the improvement of transportation.

The influence of convenient communications on expanding the food sources of any given region can hardly be illustrated better than by the case of the banana, whose introduction to the consumers of the United States was almost uniquely a function of transportation. Bananas were virtually unknown before the eighteen seventies, though there were plenty of them in the West Indies. It was from this source that an occasional bunch reached the country about the time of the Civil War. When bananas arrived in New Orleans, each fruit would be wrapped individually in tinfoil like a precious object and rushed to New York or New England, where, if it survived the journey, a single banana was worth a dollar. This trade was haphazard, unorganized and almost accidental, and because of the high perishability of the fruit, nobody considered exploiting bananas on a regular commercial basis until 1870, and even then it was more or less accidental too.

In that year a Jamaica planter gave two large bunches of bananas to Lorenzo Baker, the captain of a Cape Cod windjammer, who reached Boston with the fruit still in excellent condition; the weather must have been exceptionally favorable. He sold the bananas so profitably that he decided to make a business of ferrying them from the West Indies to the United States. His individual efforts were successful, inspiring him to increase the scale of the operation by organizing the Boston Fruit Company in 1885. Meanwhile another American, Minor C. Keith, had built a railroad in Costa Rica, good banana country. Baker and Keith joined forces: the United Fruit Company had been born.

Meanwhile refrigerator cars, already carrying chilled meat, had been adapted for the transportation of fruit and vegetables. The banana began spreading over the country wherever refrigerator cars could run, and as the rail network covered more and more territory, so did the banana. The banana boats were refrigerated too, insulated from outer heat by a layer of charcoal between a steel outer hull and a wooden inner one. Special speedy ships were constructed to carry nothing but bananas. One of the disadvantages of banana importing had turned out to be the hospitality of bananas to small snakes and large spiders, a plus-value unappreciated by housewives or even by grocers; the holds were made airtight and were pumped full of gases lethal to these undesirable stowaways. By the middle of the twentieth century the United Fruit Company owned more than 400,000 acres of Latin American banana plantations, operated over one thousand miles of railroads, and had an investment of $400 million in buildings and equipment in banana producing areas, not counting its extensive fleet of ships. The entire United States by now was feasting on bananas.

The technique of transporting tropical fruit had progressed a long way since the time in 1687 when Governor Dongan of New York had tried to mollify Governor Denonville of Canada by sending him a present of oranges at a time of dissension over the government of the Iroquois Indians, to receive from him a frigid acknowledgment of the gift of oranges with the observation that "it was a great pity that they should have been all rotten"; or, for that matter, even since 1859, when a ship started out from Puerto Rico with a cargo of 300,000 oranges consigned to New Haven—which, though the propitious month of January had been chosen for the voyage, received only ninety thousand of them, the other 210,000 having spoiled on the way.

Other tropical fruits too were now being shipped into the United States from the West Indies, pineapples and coconuts, for instance, increasing the variety of the menu; and coastwise shipping was transporting the produce of the Southern Atlantic states to the North, and vice versa. Ships brought in foreign fruits and vegetables not only for consumption, but also for planting and development in American fields and orchards—the navel orange from Brazil and the Valencia orange from Spain, the Eureka lemon from Sicily and the Lisbon lemon from, curiously, Australia. New types of cabbage were imported from Holland and Denmark. But it was the railroads which contributed most to the enrichment of the larders of all parts of the United States, in some cases literally creating new centers of food production, and then distributing their produce throughout the nation.

When the Civil War ended, the United States possessed 35,000 miles of steam railroads, of which only three thousand were west of the Mississippi. By 1890 there were 200,000 miles (more than existed in the entire continent of Europe), of which 72,500 had crossed the Mississippi. On May 10, 1869, the Union Pacific and the Central Pacific were nailed together with a symbolic golden spike, a poor metal for securing rails; but it was cautiously replaced by something sturdier, and less subject to theft, as soon as the official ceremony was over. Pacific Coast products could at last be delivered easily to the Atlantic markets, and vice versa. But it was expensive to run railroads 2,500 miles across the continent with no paying passengers or freights from the Rockies to the Mississippi, half of the total distance if you count from Salt Lake City, then an isolated outpost of the West, or three-fifths of it if you count from California. The two developed areas, East and West, had to pick up the tab of operating the trains over one thousand to fifteen hundred empty miles without lucrative passenger or freight traffic to share the cost, which meant that tariffs had to be set too high to attract the volume of traffic necessary to finance the exploitation of intercontinental railroads. They needed, and needed desperately, a population to fill the void. There was a nucleus for a population at hand in the thousands of workers who had been brought into the interior precisely to build the railroads which now needed customers. The railroad companies encouraged them not to return home, to the East or the West, once the job was finished, but to stay on the territory which they had opened. The government was willing to provide free land to homesteaders, and most of the railway workers had some savings; much of their living expenses on the job had been paid by the companies, and it had been difficult for them to spend their surplus money in a country virtually without stores. They were able, therefore, to buy seed, stock and tools, and, since foreigners were not eligible for homestead land, the railroads sold them farms or ranches on credit, out of the large holdings which they themselves had been granted to encourage their expansion. The new settlers discovered that what had been considered the "barren" central plains actually constituted a phenomenally rich granary; the railroads furnished the means for carrying the grain to market. They offered the economies of shipment by carload lots, they built or encouraged the building of elevators in the ports of the Great Lakes, and they delivered grain to seaports for transshipment onto ocean-going vessels, thus opening the way to foreign markets.

Grain had been grown in eastern Kansas and Nebraska before the expansion of the railroads, for the East, but now it could be delivered handily to the West as well; the farmers of these two states pushed into their western reaches, and their output increased vertiginously—868 million bushels of corn in 1866, over two billion bushels in 1891. Most of this reached the consumer in the form of meat, especially pork; the railroads carried the pigs to the Chicago packing plants and then carried the processed products away to what was now a nationwide market. Farther north, after the Great Northern Railway struck westward across the plains of Dakota, the grain was more likely to be wheat, which reached the consumer in the form of flour. The center of wheat growing shifted from Illinois and Iowa (which revenged itself by converting to corn and hogs) to Oregon, Montana, the Dakotas, and Minnesota, where the high-quality hard spring wheat this area produced was destined to make Minneapolis the capital of flour milling. Production skyrocketed in this area too—152 million bushels in 1866, 612 million bushels in 1891. It would not be too much of an exaggeration to say that it was the railroads which created the mighty American grain industry.

A reaction to this development was suffered by New England, which had been growing considerable quantities of wheat, barley, and rye. It had to abandon these crops when the railroads began delivering the produce of the giant farms of the flat central plains even to the Northeast at prices the tillers of the small hilly farms of this region could not meet, especially after the panic of 1873. New England had been raising fruit and vegetables too, but its orchards and truck gardens were doomed, except as small-scale furnishers of local markets, when the first freight-car load of fresh fruit reached the East Coast from California in 1869. A side effect of the conversion of the Plains to grain and of the Pacific Northwest and California to fruit and vegetables was the conversion of New England to dairy farming.

Many factors—climate, for instance—accounted for the quickly gained domination of the fruit and vegetable industries by the Pacific states, but the railroads must at least be given credit for hastening this evolution, by making it possible to deliver their produce fresh to any point in the country where there was a demand for it. They performed a similar service for many other areas where the scale was smaller. Thus by 1868 the Mobile & Ohio and the Illinois Central had reached into the Deep South, and were bringing the first fruit and the earliest spring vegetables of the Mississippi Valley to Chicago, following the ripening season northward. In South Carolina and Georgia a peach industry which had flourished between 1850 and 1870 had withered away almost to the point of extinction, since its fruit could not be delivered in good condition over a radius wide enough to permit an expansion of business which would keep pace with the expansion of the times: then the combined influences of the refrigerator car and the development of the hardy Elberta peach expanded the horizon, and once again everything was peaches down in Georgia.

A distance of a possible three thousand miles between producer and consumer was no longer an obstacle to the passage of fresh food from one to the other. By the opening of the twentieth century, a food available in any part of the country was available in every part of the country. With the exception of some exotic items which would have to wait for the airplane, the American repertory of foods was virtually complete, or as complete as its consumers wanted it to be.

The happy nineteenth century never heard the name of merchandising, yet in its second half the thing itself had already gotten under way. Before that the farmer or the horticulturist or the livestock breeder or the fisherman simply put the best food he could produce on the market and assumed that an appreciative public would reward him for his effort by paying for it in function of its quality. The merchandising philosophy of the day was expressed by Ralph Waldo Emerson or Elbert Hubbard as: "Make a better mousetrap and though you live in a forest the world will beat a path to your door." American ingenuity was soon to devise means for selling inferior mousetraps in the absence of better ones, or even in their presence, for a man who devoted all his attention to making better mousetraps was likely to be outdistanced by a man who concentrated on developing better methods of selling mousetraps, good or bad. The principle could be applied also to mousetrap cheese and other foodstuffs.

The moment at which skill in producing food began to be less relevant than skill in selling it might perhaps be located, if it has to be located at all, in 1859, when two citizens of Augusta, Maine, George Huntington Hartford and George F. Gilman, opened at 31 Vesey Street in New York a small store with large ambitions. It called itself, despite its modest dimensions, The Great American Tea Company, and at the time tea was indeed its sole preoccupation. It is a common assumption that the United States has always been a nation of coffee drinkers, but the fact is that more tea than coffee was sold during most of the nineteenth century. The Great American Tea Company may be awarded the credit, or saddled with the onus, for having first introduced modern merchandising methods and progressive publicity techniques to a naïve nation.

Under the first heading it initiated methods common enough now but revolutionary then, buying in enormous quantities to induce sellers to grant favorable prices, and as close as possible to the source to eliminate the profits of middlemen, achieving savings which, passed on to its own customers, enabled it to undersell competitors. At first Hartford and Gilman would go to the docks when a clipper ship came in and buy up its whole cargo; but soon they were importing their own tea from China and Japan direct. As a result they were able to offer tea at thirty cents a pound when other merchants were charging a dollar.

Under the second heading they dreamed up a publicity gimmick which was well ahead of the times: a red wagon pulled by eight dappled gray horses was driven through the streets of New York and a prize of twenty thousand dollars was offered to anyone who could guess the combined weight of horses and wagon; if anyone ever won it, no record of the feat is known to the authors. The color of the wagon matched that of the storefront, Chinese vermilion, with the name of the company lettered on it in gold, evoking the Orient from which the company's merchandise came. The same colors are still used in its stores today, though since 1869 the name has been different—The Great Atlantic & Pacific Tea Company. By the time of this rechristening, other lines had been added to tea, for instance spices, coffee, condensed milk, baking powder, and soap.

By 1876 there were sixty-seven A & Ps and by 1912 nearly five hundred, which, like the independent stores with which they were competing, carried charge accounts and delivered orders, a policy which was soon to be abandoned.

> Led by John Hartford, son of the founder [Daniel J. Boorstin wrote in *The Americans: A Democratic Experience*], the great expansion of the A & P chain came in 1912. Between 1912 and 1915, a new A & P store was opened every three days, to a national total of one thousand stores. Expansion was based on the cash-and-carry idea and on reduction of staff to make the one-man "economy" store. Meat, which soon became the largest single item, was not added till 1925. For the year 1929, total A & P sales exceeded $1 billion; in the following year, A & P stores numbered 15,709. [In the early 1930s the A & P was bowling over neighborhood groceries like ninepins, a phenomenon which would be repeated a score of years later by the supermarkets; by 1932 the A & P had bought up fifteen thousand small independent stores.] By 1933, A & P was doing over 11 percent of the nation's food business. After that year, there was a trend to larger stores, and the number of individual stores gradually decreased [the move toward the supermarket, keeping step with the increase in the number of automobiles, which made it feasible for buyers to shop farther from home]. But by 1971 the 4,358 A & P stores reached an unprecedented annual sales volume of nearly $5.5 billion.

It was thus in the nineteenth century that the movement toward mass merchandising began—an evolution possibly regrettable, socially and gastronomically, but ineluctable. It was a logical, and indeed inseparable, element in the movement of our society away from the family and from communal groupings—the small town in the country, the local neighborhood in the city. It is possible to be nostalgic about the days when food was retailed more intimately and more individually and on a smaller scale, but nostalgia is futile; the day of the neighborhood grocery is not going to return.

Packaging, a subdivision of marketing, is another word which was not in the vocabulary of the nineteenth century, though the phenomenon which it represented was taking on substance then. At the end of the Civil War—and for a great many foods even until the end of the First World War—a characteristic of retail food selling was that everything was presented in bulk. Great mounds of store cheese and golden butter rose from grocery counters; the clerk slashed away the amount demanded with a practiced hand. Milk was ladled out of an enormous tin milk can with a tin ladle and poured into the smaller tin can you had brought with you, while a tin scoop was plunged into the appropriate tin bin to bring out the sugar or flour or beans or raisins or nuts you wanted. Unwrapped candies were laid out in open cardboard boxes or on trays; the jellybeans were in a large glass jar into which a grimy juvenile fist might occasionally venture in exploration; other glass jars held spices which were doled out by guess and by golly. Onions, potatoes, turnips, carrots, cabbages and lettuce rested expectantly in their crates on the floor in front of a formidable barrier of barrels containing apples or pickles or cookies or crackers. It was no doubt an unhygienic system, but nobody worried much about that in the days before the extraordinary efficiency of the fly in distributing bacteria had been discovered, though if one of the kegs contained molasses it was considered good practice to keep it covered.

It took the twentieth century to work up shock about this state of things, and there were still examples extant to arouse it. As late as 1910 the Massachusetts Commission on the Cost of Living discovered an old-fashioned store on the outskirts of Boston, and described it, with deep disapproval, in these terms:

> The oatmeal or rolled oats, Indian meal, etc., are in open barrels just beneath shelves that serve as boulevards for countless rats and mice both day and night as they journey to their "ratskeller." Dried codfish may be found, as in ye olden days, whole and on the skin, lying exposed to all the dust for weeks and sometimes seasons. When one enters the door a bell rings, which calls the attendant from the barn, where he has been unharnessing or brushing the horses. Accordingly as one article or another is desired, he plunges his unwashed hands into the pork or pickle barrel, cuts cheese or butter, often drawing kerosene and molasses in the mean time [sic], and wiping the overflow on his coat sleeve or jumper. In summer no attempt is made to keep out flies, and much of the merchandise is open to them for food. The maple syrup bottles stand near by, and the keeper himself has been seen to take a swallow from them at different times, when his sweet tooth called.

One thing that could be said for the old-time store was that its smells were interesting—usually good, though perhaps not in the case of the example presented by ye Massachusetts Commission, but anyway interesting.

Many considerations were involved in the change from bulk to packaged foods, of which hygiene was one of the least; the profit motive counted more. Packaging saved money by preserving foods from damage and spoilage, by making them easier to transport, and by making them more compact for storage. There were even cases in which the package was largely responsible for preserving, ameliorating, or even altering its taste. For instance, the bonbons known as Lifesavers were originally offered in cardboard packaging; unfortunately the candies quickly took on a flavor compounded of the taste of the cardboard and of the paste which held it together. This disadvantage disappeared when some genius conceived the idea of putting them up in little tinfoil-covered tubes which not only preserved their taste until the tubes were opened, but even after they were opened and some removed, when the tinfoil could be folded back over the remaining candies to keep their flavor intact. Another example of the importance of the package to the food it contains can be found in salt, which used to be sold in little cotton bags. (The bag cost more than its contents, so that the price of salt varied with the price of cotton.) Unfortunately cotton could not prevent salt from caking in damp weather. When it was packed in waxed cardboard containers it was protected from humidity, permitting the Morton Salt Company to sell it with the slogan, "When it rains it pours."

Packaging is an almost mystical concept, which for the unimaginative may mean nothing more than enveloping food, or anything else, in some sort of covering; but for the philosophically inclined, what is essential about packaging is that it brings shape out of formlessness, for convenience of one kind or another. Thus the cracker in the general store's barrel was not packaged though it was in a container; but other foods, though still nude, were in this sense packaged—chocolate molded into a plaque or formed into a Tootsie Roll, even without wrapping, or an uncovered lollipop (its package was the stick).

The sausage, even uncovered, is packaged too, but it does have a wrapping, even though it is invisible: its ingredients are stuffed into a casing which in happier times was made from a pig's intestine, but now from a substance obtained from a chemical factory.

The materials which have been pressed into service for packaging are infinite, and the forms given to containers have borrowed from all the arts, and also from the sciences (the bottle shaped to fit the hand comes under the head of engineering). Packages exemplify architectural art (usually functional), sculptural art, the graphic arts, and, in a surprising apotheosis, the art of swindling. Tinfoil was one of the earliest preservative wrappings, which early in this century afforded schoolchildren a source of pocket money, for they saved the tinfoil from candy bars, rolled it into balls, and sold it to recuperators. Flexible metals have been shaped into squeezable metal tubes for mayonnaise and salad dressings (and toothpaste and shaving cream and artists' colors). The tea bag is a package. Wrapping your food at home in cellophane or using aluminum refrigerator or oven paper is packaging. So is putting ice cream into a cone (1904) or on a stick (1919). Food vending machines and automat restaurants are elaborate machine-age forms of packaging. So is the possibly villainous aerosol can, whose most noxious use is to propel frosting onto cakes or whipped cream onto desserts.

Packaging is ubiquitous today and we take it for granted; but it presents no exception to the rule that fixed habits, including bad habits, are obdurate to change. The open sugar barrel died in the end at the hands of packaged sugar, but it died hard. As late as 1928, 90 percent of all the sugar sold for household use was still being sold in bulk. Yet the American Sugar Refining Company had been pleading for years with its wholesalers to preach in their turn to retailers the advantages of the packaged sugar it was prepared to supply. Its arguments were cogent, as in one circular distributed in 1925:

> Do you know that it takes a man about an hour and three-quarters to weigh out a 350-pound barrel of granulated sugar in five-pound paper bags; that a man averages only about 69 five-pound bags when he weighs out a 350-pound barrel; that the five pounds lost by spillage and down-weight represent 1.4 per cent of the cost price of the sugar; that, in addition to sugar wasted, bags, twine and labor amount to about forty cents added to the cost per cwt. of the sugar; and—that 350 pounds of Domino Package Sugars means 350 pounds sold with a profit on every pound; that no time is lost and no material or sugar wasted; that, therefore, a retailer makes more money per pound when he sells Domino Package Sugars; and that he will appreciate your pointing out these facts to him, thereby enabling him to make more money on sugar?

The company was dead right, of course—in the context of our times, at least, which is that of large-scale operations. The neighborhood grocer who sold fifty pounds of sugar a day could ignore, in the interests of folksiness and the human scale, the subtleties of cost accounting, which added to the overhead such elements as wasted time, spillage and bits of string. Homespun methods of doing business might lose the neighborhood grocer ten cents a day, but he could afford that. The mighty supermarket could not afford to overlook the imponderables, for if its volume of business were ten thousand times that of the neighborhood grocer the daily loss would be one thousand dollars, if 100,000 times, ten thousand dollars. In other words, the bigger they are, the harder they fall.

The canned food industry was unable to supply the potential mass market represented by the United States until machines had been invented for fast inexpensive manufacture of cans. The processed meat industry was unable to supply that same market until machines had been invented which turned slaughterhouses into models of automation. Canning and meat processing constituted special branches of packaging which happened to develop early; their dependence on advances in machinery was echoed in other departments of packaging as well. Many kinds of foods were unable to supply the mass market until machines had been devised to provide them with the types of containers they required, even such simple ones as wrapping paper (first produced in rolls in London in 1807) and paper bags.

The paper bag, one of the earliest, usefulest and most versatile forms of packaging, became common in the United States after the Civil War, when every grocery had a supply in various sizes, in which the customer could carry away almost any purchase except liquids. Even as simple a container as the paper bag depended on machinery. The first American-made wrapping paper was produced about 1815 in Delaware, the first paper bags were made from it in Pennsylvania in 1852, but the first machine capable of producing the useful square-bottomed bags we know now did not appear until about 1870.

Cardboard containers had to wait for machines to develop them too. The first cardboard food containers were round or oval, the easiest shapes to make. They had the disadvantage that empty boxes waiting to be filled took up just as much room in the processor's plant as full ones. What was needed was a machine which would stamp out cardboard forms of the desired shapes and crease the resulting sheets so that they could be stored flat but folded quickly and easily around the merchandise at packing time. This does not strike us as much of a problem nowadays, but it was not solved until 1879, in New York, by one Robert Gair, who until then had been making paper bags. Gair's machines which produced the flat foldable cardboard cartons were quickly followed by others to do the folding; nowadays packing food for shipment is an operation entirely automatic.

Packing, it may finally be noted, somewhat tardily, is not quite the same thing as packaging, which adds a new and important element to the preparation of merchandise to be moved from one point to another, whether by the producer, the processor, the wholesaler, the retailer or the individual customer. "Packing," wrote Daniel J. Boorstin, "was designed to transport and to preserve, packaging was designed to *sell.*" It was normal that the science of packing should develop after the Civil War, a function of the expansion of the railroads, for it was becoming increasingly important to move large amounts of food by rail with minimum damage; and it was inevitable that the art of packaging should develop with it, for putting merchandise into more or less durable containers created automatically a need to identify it, if only by stenciling a carton with the shipper's name. A name alone was an embryonic sales message even if it was not so intended; a satisfied customer would naturally want to find the same product again, and now that it was identifiable he could ask for it by name. Adding a deliberate sales message to simple individualization was a development so natural that it may have begun before anyone was completely conscious that the package was becoming an advertisement. Even a trademark alone could serve this purpose. When the National Biscuit Company decided to stop selling soda crackers in bulk and put them into packages, probably because crackers are fragile, the biscuit makers consulted the Gair carton company for counsel on the ideal container. "You need a name," Robert Gair's son remarked. Thus Uneeda Biscuits were born, and the cracker barrel died.

One case in which packaging, in the sense of packing-plus-selling, was promoted by food processors with complete consciousness of what they were doing was that of dry breakfast cereals. Having very little to sell in the way of nourishment, the manufacturers had to invest heavily in persuasion. They benefited by an unexpected boon in 1907 when Dr. Harvey Wiley, in an unguarded moment, remarked that: "The cereal-eating nations of the world can endure more physical toil than the meat-eating nations." American dry breakfast cereals were not exactly what Dr. Wiley had in mind, but the cornflakes manufacturers were broadminded enough to overlook this and made maximum use of the observation all the same. (Several contemporary writers have lately asserted, on what authority we do not know, that it is meat-eating peoples who have always ruled the world. It is possible that neither opinion has ever been subjected to serious scrutiny.) The breakfast food industry perhaps deserves the credit for popularizing the personalization of products when it put Sunny Jim on packages of Force and a Quaker on boxes of Quaker Oats. The example was contagious. Uneeda Biscuits, though they already had a slogan in their name, dealt themselves a second trump by putting a little boy in a yellow nor'easter on their label; in more recent times we have been gratified with Popeye the Sailor Man spinach and Chiquita Banana. The package had become part of the product, and an advertising agency once announced candidly, "We couldn't improve the product, so we improved the package."

Packaging and mass marketing, once their techniques had been developed to excess, conspired to alter the objective of the grocer; he was no longer selling food, he was selling appearance. "You cannot sell a blemished apple in the supermarket," wrote Elspeth Huxley, "but you can sell a tasteless one." The philosophy of merchandising could no longer be summed up by, "Build a better mousetrap and the world will beat a path to your door." It had become, "Save the surface and you save all."

Is treating a tomato with ethylene gas to give it the bright red of ripeness, though it has been picked green and is destined to be sold green, except in color, a subtle form of packaging? It is at least a subtle form of adulteration. Adulteration is a practice too venerable to be laid at the door of mass marketing, nor can it be described as an invention of the Machine Age, though modern techniques have expanded its weaponry.

America's very first cookbook, that of the orphaned Amelia Simmons, took cognizance of the art of adulteration and warned housewives of the wiles of merchants no more honest than they had to be. Even in those innocent days, it appears, the gills of fish were peppered, or speckled with a little blood taken from fresher fish, or simply painted to cajole the buyer into believing that they were barely out of the water. Cheeses appetizing in color owed that asset not to their own normal ingredients but to the cosmetic action of "hemlock, cocumberries, or saffron, infused into the milk." As the nation grew more sophisticated, so did the adulterators:

> Overenthusiasm got quite out of hand [wrote James Trager]. Minced tripe dyed red was sold as deviled ham. Maine herring was labeled "imported French sardines" and put in fancy boxes with labels in French. North Dakota alone consumed ten times as much "Vermont" maple syrup as the state of Vermont produced.

Adulterants need not be harmful to health in order to be destructive to taste. There is the case of bread: unless they make it themselves, Americans have virtually no opportunity of ever tasting bread free from preservatives, anti-staling chemicals or dough conditioners. As a result when they visit France they become ecstatic about the quality of French bread. "How do the French do it?" they demand; but it is not what French bakers do that accounts for the tastiness of their bread, it is what they do not do. They do not put anything in it except the simple natural ingredients which have produced bread everywhere in the world for at least three thousand years. The big American baking companies have always maintained that the additives they put into bread, largely to make it keep, are not harmful. "Even assuming that these chemicals are harmless," retorted Dr. William Lijinsky of the Oak Ridge National Laboratory, "the advantage in selling bread that does not go stale for a week or more . . . seems to lie more with the baker and retailer than with the consumer." Both sides were using the words "harmful" and "harmless" in reference to health; there could have been little argument if they had been referring to taste.

When Dr. Harvey Wiley, chief of the bureau of chemistry in the United States Department of Agriculture, presumed to conduct experiments which demonstrated that some of the preservatives, colorants and other additives used in canned foods were dangerous to health, food processors denounced him wrathfully for "Socialist interference" and in 1911 they tried to get rid of him by charging that one of the experts in his department was discovered to be drawing a larger salary than that legally earmarked for his job. Wiley was exonerated, but resigned in disgust from governmental service the following year. Many food manufacturers were happy to see him go, but the structure he had left behind continued to make difficulties for them when they overstepped the line.

The exaggerations of food sellers had abetted the exaggerations of Upton Sinclair in helping Dr. Wiley to secure the passage, in 1906, of the Pure Food and Drugs Act, a long step in the right direction; but its effects were gradually vitiated by administrative and judicial decisions. A court action brought by the government against Kansas City millers in 1910 to prohibit the bleaching of flour was lost by the millers, but on appeal to the Supreme Court a retrial was ordered on a legal technicality. It never took place; the question of whether bleaching flour is or is not a violation of pure food regulations remains undecided. In the meantime we are eating bleached flour.

Whatever its occasional defects in application, we must nevertheless applaud the principles which inspired the Pure Food and Drugs Act. Its passage was one of the major events in the history of American food, chronologically a boundary marker between the 1865–1914 period of transition and the highly regimented present, and a product of a changing spirit—one of its happier manifestations.

XXV

The United States Fills Up

AT THE END of the Civil War, the American nation was organized into two discontinuous blocs of states, one starting on the Atlantic Coast, the other on the Pacific. The territory in between was a sort of No-Man's-Land, theoretically under American sovereignty, but the extent to which it was effectively organized was variable. Between these two parentheses, the interior was divided, rather than organized, into Territories, governed fitfully from Washington as its means permitted, with the exception of two holes in the political fabric, of undetermined status. One of them would eventually become the state of Wyoming, which it could be assumed was already subject to the authority of Washington, since it was completely surrounded by territory which was; the federal government maintained a few military posts within this vacuum to protect passing wagon trains from the Indians, but Washington had not yet gotten around to deciding what status should be given to the area. The other ambiguous region is now Oklahoma, but it was then called Indian Territory, or, better, Indian territory, with a small "t", for this was a popular designation, not a legal one. The government had not organized the area officially as a Territory like the others dignified by that name, and though the United States kept a watchful eye on it, it is difficult to define its relationship to a region which was *sui generis.* Several Indian tribal governments enforced their own laws there, but as far as Washington was concerned it could perhaps best be described as ungoverned—a situation which was not rectified until 1890, when it was made a Territory like the others.

Gastronomically, the United States gained little when it hurried Nevada into the Union in 1864, but its attractiveness did not consist in ability to provide food, but in ability to nourish the powers-that-be with two more

Republican votes in the Senate. The new state was so poor that it could not even support its Shoshone Indians, otherwise known as the Diggers, because they often had to grub for roots to find any food at all. Jedediah Smith, the first white man to cross the state from west to east, in 1827, called the Diggers "the most miserable objects in creation," and Mark Twain thirty-four years later described them as

> the wretchedest type of mankind I have ever seen . . . who produce nothing at all, and have no villages, and no gatherings together into strictly defined tribal communities—a people whose only shelter is a rag cast on a bush to keep off a portion of the snow.

Nevada pictures a plow and a sheaf of wheat among other assets on its state seal, but this is more of a boast than a report. The state's agriculture is minimal, and what little there is depends entirely on irrigation. The proportion of Nevada income derived from agriculture is so small that it is not even considered worth listing by the *New York Times Almanac,* which gives the sources of revenue as: services, 41 percent; government, 16 percent, wholesale and retail trade, 15 percent; transportation, communications, and public utilities, 8 percent; construction, 7 percent; finance, insurance and real estate, 4 percent; manufacturing 4 percent; and agriculture not even "also ran." One may assume that "services" covers the state's two most important crops, gambling and divorces. More orthodox ones are listed as barley, wheat, oats, corn, and, in the south, tomatoes, berries, apples, and other orchard fruits; but the state does not produce enough of them even for its own needs. Sixty-five percent of what little agricultural income Nevada does have comes from grazing, which accounts indirectly for the only gastronomic originality the state seems able to offer: for the past fifty years its sheep have been handled largely by Basque shepherds. Get into sheep country and you will come across Basque restaurants and hotels, but their fare is humdrum (true, "humdrum" may be above average in Nevada). Basques have lively eating traditions on their own territory, but it could be that the shepherds they send abroad are not the best culinary ambassadors to the infidels.

But Nevada does have deer and consequently venison.

The only new state created in the eighteen sixties was Nebraska.

The United States acquired it by the Louisiana Purchase, after which a few fur traders and explorers entered the region and reported sapiently that it was a near desert useless for agriculture, undeterred by the observation that its thick lush grass supported vast herds of buffalo.

With Nebraska, the United States gained a vast undulating plain of great fertility, confounding the dreary reports of those first pessimistic explorers. Its suitability for farming was almost implicit in its name: "Nebraska" is an Oto Indian word meaning "flat water," a term the Indians applied to the Platte.

Most of the state's rain falls usefully in the growing season, April through August. About a quarter of the population is employed in agriculture, Nebraska's single most important economic activity. Livestock and its by-products account for 70 percent of the state's agricultural income, for the large quantities of corn it grows reach the consumer chiefly in the form of meat—cattle are by far the most important, followed by swine, sheep, and poultry. Of commercial crops, corn comes first, wheat is second. Nebraska also supplies the country with appreciable quantities of oats, barley, rye, sorghum, sugar beets and potatoes.

Colorado became a Territory in its present borders in 1861. The first railroads penetrated it in 1870, a stimulus which multiplied the population nearly five hundred times; the 1880 census, taken four years after Colorado became a state, credited it with 194,827 inhabitants. Horace Greeley may have helped when he thundered, "Go West, young man!" He was thinking specifically of Colorado, where he was sponsoring a farming colony.

Colorado might not have seemed likely to contribute heavily to the food resources of the nation, for its specialty was mountains—more than a thousand higher than ten thousand feet, fifty-five higher than fourteen thousand and, though Colorado does not include America's highest mountains, it does rate as the state with the highest average altitude. Nevertheless, Colorado produces more food than its unpromising topography might lead you to expect. True, it is obliged, to do so, to rely to a large extent on irrigation; only California has more irrigated acreage, but all the same irrigated land accounts for only three million acres out of Colorado's 104,247 square miles; forty million acres are given over to dry farming and grazing, particularly the latter—two-thirds of the state's farm revenue is derived from animals and their by-products. Agriculture has been Colorado's leading industry since the middle of this century. Its position as a provider of various crops varies with the years, but it is usually the second state for the production of sugar beets, the fifth for potatoes and onions, the eighth for barley, and the ninth for spring wheat, cantaloupes and peaches. It also grows appreciable quantities of wheat, corn, beans, apples, and pears.

Game is still killed in quantity in the mountains of the western part of the state; but Colorado has a black stain on its record in this category. In 1897 it allowed the last small herd of buffalo on its territory to be exterminated for the sake of giving a taxidermist some specimens to stuff. Unabashed by this circumstance, the state has allotted its most impressive grave to a notorious slaughterer of the American bison: Buffalo Bill lies in a tomb blasted out of the living rock of Lookout Mountain, twenty miles from Denver.

The least appreciated contribution of Colorado to the agriculture of the nation is the potato bug. This destructive beetle is a native American, originally restricted to the high plains which lie east of the Rockies, whose favorite food used to be the buffalo bur, *Solanum rostratum.* When a close relative of this plant, *Solanum tuberosum,* alias the potato, was introduced into Colorado, the insect transferred its affections voraciously to the newcomer. It pursued the potato eastward, crossing the Mississippi into Illinois toward the end of the Civil War and reaching the Atlantic Coast by 1874. Since 1945, the damage it causes annually has been assessed at approximately $40 million.

The United States rested for more than a decade after Colorado became a state before adding others; then, in 1899, it splurged by taking in four more (and the year afterwards, two others).

With the entrance of the Dakotas, the nation gained two new states which were to be above all providers of food. North Dakota is the most rural of all the states, with 90 percent of its land in farms, 61 percent of its population rural, and 23 percent of its revenue derived from agriculture. South Dakota is the state which leads all others in the proportion of personal incomes derived from farming, over 28 percent. If North Dakota is second in this respect (23 percent) it is partly because in terms of money South Dakota's produce is of a kind more profitable per acre, and partly because some of North Dakota's income from food is disguised under the head of manufactures: the leading industry of the state is food processing. Foods, processed or unprocessed, are in both states the leading products.

North Dakota has had an agricultural economy ever since it became a state. Its leading item is livestock and animal by-products, cattle and calves accounting for more than half its revenue in this category, with dairy products second, and pigs and poultry tied for third place. Among crops the most important is spring wheat, which provides about 50 percent of the cash derived from all vegetables, followed by barley, durum wheat (North Dakota hard wheat is of particularly high quality), oats, potatoes, soybeans, sugar beets, and corn.

South Dakota leans even more heavily than North Dakota on livestock, the source of two-thirds of its cash farm income. In most years it is numbered among the first five states for the production of steers and calves, and among the first ten for hogs and sheep. Its leading crop is corn (it grows only hybrid varieties), of which normal production is a hundred million bushels on four million acres, which usually gives it ninth place among corn producing states. The state is usually tenth for the production of wheat and second for that of durum wheat.

Both Dakotas are propitious to those who want to wrest food directly from Nature. Wild fruit is abundant—wild plums, wild grapes, flowering currants, chokecherries, highbush cranberries, juneberries, buffalo berries, pinchberries, and serviceberries (pronounced sarvisberries). The fishing is good—trout in the western mountains, bass, pickerel, pike, carp and catfish elsewhere.

Most of the big game which once abounded here—elk, deer, antelope—has disappeared since the railroads came and the Indians went, but in the Black Hills of South Dakota you can still knock over an occasional mountain goat, the gamiest of game animals. There is still plenty of smaller game—Canada geese in South Dakota, pheasant in North Dakota, where the town of Mott, in its southeast corner, refers to itself as the pheasant capital of the country.

The last buffaloes in North Dakota were killed off in 1883. But South Dakota is making reparations now by raising domesticated buffalo.

Montana, since its very name comes from the Spanish word meaning "mountainous," might not seem a promising addition to the United States from the point of view of filling its larder, but it is fatter than it sounds. Its western two-fifths are indeed occupied by the Rocky Mountains, but this leaves a majority of the state to the Great Plains, high, gently rolling country which has proved apt for food production.

Nobody would have prophesied that Montana's future lay in farming in 1833, when the first few milch cattle were brought into the state. Missionaries imported some beef animals in the 1850s, for their own nourishment, along with several head of sheep. Stockmen began to show a feeble interest in the possibilities of grazing in the region in the early 1860s, but the real beginning of Montana's commercial livestock industry probably has to be situated in 1866, when a cattleman named Nelson Story drove a thousand Longhorns from Texas into Montana; only eight years later steers were no longer being driven into Montana, they were being driven out, for Eastern markets. The arrival of the Northern Pacific Railroad in 1883 stimulated the cattle industry by making it easier to deliver meat animals to their consumers. Meanwhile, sheep had become important in the territory also—from four thousand in 1870 they increased to 250,000 in 1880, and when they reached 6 million in 1900, Montana had the largest wool clip in the country. This inevitably made the state also a provider of lamb and mutton, but in those days before the advent of synthetic fibers, the first objective of the sheep raisers was wool. Today there are four times as many beef critters in Montana as people, and twice as many sheep. It is true that Montana counts only five inhabitants per square mile.

When agriculture supplanted mining as the main economic activity of Montana, a second shift occurred within the agricultural category from livestock as the principal source of farm income to crops—also a result of the arrival of the railroads, which provided transportation for the sort of produce which could be provided by dry farming. By the middle of this century, livestock was accounting for only 43 percent of the state's agricultural revenue, and crops were producing 57 percent of it. Agriculture today is the state's third most important source of income, 16 percent of it (government expenditures amount to 18 percent, wholesale and retail trade to 17 percent).

Wheat is the most valuable item, beef is second. Montana is the nation's third wheat-producing state, after North Dakota and Kansas. It also grows important quantities of barley. Other food products are sheep, dairy goods, poultry, pigs, sugar beets, corn, oats, and potatoes.

Montana's western areas are wild enough so that big game is still found there—deer, elk, moose and antelope. Geese, ducks, pheasant, and grouse are plentiful, and even sage hen is not to be disdained. As for fish, Montana's tourist advertising asserts that it is in particular the nation's Number One trout-fishing state and more generally its freshwater-fishing capital (it possesses between ten thousand and fifteen thousand lakes). Sportsmen there may take sockeye salmon, grayling trout, cutthroat trout, and rainbow trout, of which the last originated in the American West, though it has by now been stocked in distant waters all over the world.

The admission of the last of the four states which entered the Union in 1889, Washington, was less a new event than a re-play of an old one—the tardy adoption of northern Oregon, whose southern part, under its maiden name, had become a state thirty years earlier. Washington and Oregon had shared much the same history; they share also much the same food. The most conspicuous edible of the region is the salmon of the Columbia River, which is the boundary between Washington and Oregon. Seafood is important in this area too, where the fish, shellfish, and crustaceans, not having been informed that man was drawing a boundary there, peopled both sides of the line equitably with the same species. Oregon, once it acquired settlers, devoted itself to the cultivation of orchard fruits; so did Washington. Even so small but unusual a specialty as fireweed honey, gathered from a plant which springs up profusely after forest fires, appears in both states. One might also suspect Washington State University of having developed Cougar Gold cheese in order to provide a counterpart for Oregon's Tillamook Cheddar.

One advantage which Washington enjoys over Oregon is possession of Puget Sound. This arm of the Pacific Ocean, forty miles wide at some points, probes for two hundred miles into the interior, giving the area a milder climate than any other part of the United States equally far north. It is this natural feature which has also presented to Washington the credit for harboring one of the most prized crustaceans of the Pacific Coast, the Dungeness crab, which some connoisseurs consider the tastiest in America. It exists north and south of Washington also, but it took its name from the place where it seems first to have been noticed, Dungeness, which is on the strait leading into Puget Sound.

Crabs nevertheless rate last of the three principal money earners among Washington's seafoods. Salmon, of course, is first (850,000 pounds a year), and oysters second. Washington produces a particularly flavorful oyster, the Olympia, which is small for commercial exploitation, only an inch and a half across, but it is cultivated in Puget Sound all the same for an appreciative market. Easier to handle, though coarser in flavor, are the Pacific oysters transplanted from Japan in 1902, which are three times as big. Various types of clams reach the market too—several kinds of cockles, for instance—but the most distinctive and best liked ones are the kind the amateur clamdigger must hunt out himself and eat immediately, like the razor clam or the geoduck. Another prized product of the sea is a pink shrimp particularly abundant along this coast.

The fish of the Pacific provide a sizable amount of revenue for Washingtonians, among them rockfish (at least thirty-three species), cod, lingcod, sablefish, and smelt. Freshwater fish are plentiful too, but while those of the swiftly flowing streams are often native, those of the lakes are mostly imported, for many of Washington's lakes were barren before they were stocked by the government. There are native rainbow, steelhead, cutthroat, silver, and Dolly Varden trout, but the Loch Leven, Mackinaw, and eastern brook trout are imported. Also imported are the bass, perch, crappie, catfish, and sunfish which abound in the state now.

Washington is still game country, even big game country in its wilder regions—elk, deer, and bear. Smaller game includes ducks, geese, pheasants, grouse, and sage hens. The woods are rich in mushrooms—chanterelles, boletus, morels, milky caps, shaggy-manes and chicken-of-the-woods.

Livestock, dairy products, and poultry account for one-third of the state's farm income. Wheat and hops are important, but it is for fruit that the state is best known, especially apples. The Wenatchee Valley is the chief apple producing region, growing mostly the Delicious and Winesap varieties, which constitute 85 percent of the apple crop; the town of Wenatchee holds an Apple Blossom Festival each spring. The Yakima Valley grows not only apples, but also pears, melons, and grapes—and makes some wine, a fact almost totally unknown to the rest of the country.

The assimilation by the United States of what had originally been called "Oregon" was completed in 1890 with the admission of Idaho.

The food producing potentiality of the new region was harshly judged, not entirely without reason; after all, Idaho is mostly mountains. This does not quite excuse Washington Irving for referring to its "vast desert tracts that must ever defy cultivation," for he was speaking precisely of the only part of the state where this is flagrantly untrue—the plain through which flows the Snake River, the largest tributary of the Columbia, before passing through more violent scenery, including Hell's Canyon. It is true that Irving wrote before irrigation. This began in 1894, and by 1950 the state had fifteen thousand miles of irrigation canals and ditches, fed not only by the Snake, but also by 360 reservoirs capable of holding more than five million acre-feet of water. Adequate watering did wonders for the state's mainly volcanic soil, rich in lime and potash, though poor in nitrogen; but this deficiency was easily remedied by growing clover or alfalfa and then plowing it back into the ground to enrich it before shifting to other crops. After this treatment, Washington Irving's "vast desert tracts" turned into vast vegetable gardens.

It was not until the middle of the present century, however, that agriculture became Idaho's principal industry, employing one-third of the entire male working force and bringing in more revenue than any other activity ($500 million a year before the dollar depreciated). Manufacturing, the state's second industry, is creeping up on agriculture, but manufacturing includes canning the state's crops.

Agriculture in Idaho began with cattle raising in the 1870s when breeders began feeding their herds on land which the Nez Percé, Bannock, and Sheepeater Indians considered theirs, giving rise to sporadic fighting, a difference of opinion which was eventually settled in the usual fashion. Idaho still raises cattle and sheep, and derives some income from dairy products, but 95 percent of its farm revenue now comes from field crops. Everyone knows its most famous vegetable, the potato, superb for baking; Idaho's volcanic soil is perfect for growing big tasty potatoes. Few persons would dispute the assertion that no other state can produce better baking potatoes and only one—Maine—can equal them. Also important are sugar beets, beans for drying, peas for drying too but also for selling fresh and canning, onions, and peppermint. Idaho shares with the other two states once united with it in "Oregon" the specialty of growing hops for America's beer; and though it is not as important for fruit as Oregon or Washington, it does grow appreciable quantities of apples, peaches, pears, cherries, and plums for prunes. Its chief cereal crops are wheat, barley, oats, sweet corn for humans, and field corn for cattle.

As one might expect from the savage nature of much of its terrain, Idaho is good game country. Among big game animals are elk, moose, white-tailed and mule deer, pronghorn antelope, bighorn mountain sheep, black and grizzly bears (the black bear is edible; one may suppose the grizzly is too). Game birds include ducks, geese, pheasants, quails, doves, and sage hens.

Wyoming came into the Union in 1890, the same year as Idaho. It first became a food producing state with cattle. When Texas pasturage, which had once seemed inexhaustible, began to be overcrowded, many herds were moved to Wyoming—hence a couplet in a well-known cowboy song:

> Whoopee ti yi yo, git along little dogies,
> For you know Wyoming will be your new home.

Wyoming was especially attractive to cattlemen, for use of the public lands (which at the time meant pretty much *all* the land) was free until 1867; there was no pasturage fee. But the livestock raisers suffered a devastating setback in the winter of 1886–1887, which was so exceptionally cold that all water froze too solidly for the steers to be able to break drinking holes through it, while deep snow covered the grass. One-sixth of the cattle died, and the industry has never recovered from the disaster. There were two million steers in Wyoming before that winter, a peak never attained again; there were only half as many by the 1960s. It was after this holocaust that a picturesquely named territorial governor, Thomas Moonlight, decided that livestock raising was not Wyoming's forte, and tried to break up the open range into small farms. He was more or less right on the first point, but less right in thinking that Wyoming could do better with crops.

Despite Moonlight, animal breeders persevered, but the cattlemen ran into more trouble in the 1880s, when sheep began to come into the state. The famous battles between cattle raisers and sheep raisers were engaged, with Wyoming as their chief battleground. Sheep increased until there were six million in 1909, but at that point they reached a peak also, and by the 1960s were down to 2,250,000. Hogs, a specialty of corn country, have never been numerous in Wyoming. Poultry used to be fairly abundant, but chickens have now fallen off and turkeys, numerous in the 1930s, have practically disappeared from Wyoming farmyards. The fact is that Wyoming is not primarily an agricultural state. It is a mining state, whose destiny became consolidated with the development of oil (it also possesses 36 percent of the known uranium deposits of the United States).

Of what little agriculture is still found in the state, livestock remains the most important; 80 percent of the farms, and 80 percent of the farm lands, are devoted to raising beef or sheep (Wyoming is second only to Texas for its wool clip). The state's chief food products are, in that order, cattle, sheep, sugar beets, and wheat. There are lesser quantities of oats, barley, potatoes, rye, and corn.

One department of food in which Wyoming remains supreme is game. It may be considered symbolic that it was in Wyoming that a few bison in the Yellowstone Valley escaped the general slaughter of the nineteenth century; buffalo are now being raised as domestic animals in Wyoming. Still found wild in the mountains are many big game animals, estimated about a decade ago at 125,000 mule deer, 110,000 pronghorns, 35,000 elk, 10,000 black bears, 5,000 moose, 3,000 white-tailed deer, 3,000 mountain sheep, and 80 grizzlies. The cold swift mountain streams offer cutthroat, brook, rainbow, brown, Mackinaw, and golden trout, the warmer lakes, bass, crappie, and catfish. The most widely distributed game bird is the sage grouse, and there are also pheasants and, introduced from abroad, Hungarian partridge and Indian chukar. Also introduced into the state, but from other parts of America, were wild turkeys, after Wyoming hunters had killed off all their own birds.

Wyoming's Starr Valley has a rather unexpected specialty for a state which has never had many milch cows—a type of cheese akin to Swiss Emmenthal.

There are five thousand Holstein cattle in the valley, one-eighth of all the milk cows in the state, which provide four million pounds of cheese yearly. It is made by Mormon families who settled in Wyoming before the beginning of the century and are still there.

Utah was the last state to enter the Union before the beginning of the present century; it would no doubt have been admitted earlier if it had not been for the institution of polygamy: the Mormons did not want to give it up and Washington did not want to let polygamists in. The Mormons finally conceded the point in 1890, but only in 1896 did Utah achieve statehood.

The Mormons who settled Utah were an agriculturally minded lot, but the land on which they established themselves gave them singularly little help. The four thousand square miles of the Great Salt Lake Desert were less than responsive to farming, while the Great Salt Lake itself, seventy-five miles long by thirty wide, was so saline that almost nothing could live in it except brine shrimp. Nevertheless, Brigham Young dissuaded his followers from taking off after the will-o'-the-wisp of fortune in California. "Instead of hunting gold," he said, "let every man go to work at raising wheat, oats, barley, corn and vegetables and fruit in abundance that there may be plenty in the land." It was sound doctrine, but it meant hard work, given the uncooperative nature of climate and soil.

The first years were difficult; they left the Mormons with an obsession about food, or more exactly about a possible lack of food, which has left traces in their iconography. The honeybee which appears on the state seal is not a reference to the food it collects, at least not directly; the Mormons chose it as their emblem because it is a symbol of industry. But the bee is surrounded by sego lilies, which grow in the dry areas of the West, and the lilies *are* a reminder of the days of famine, when for want of more palatable food the Mormons ate the corms of this plant (they also ate thistle leaves and such unappetizing birds as hawks, owls, and crows). The Sea Gull Monument in Salt Lake City's Temple Square recalls another escape from starvation, the well-known story of the near loss of the first year's crops in 1848, when hordes of crickets fell upon the fields; the food was saved when great flocks of gulls, which must have followed their prey from afar, devoured the crickets before the crickets could devour the crops. The sego lily, understandably, is the state flower today and the sea gull is the state bird.

Utah is in little danger of famine now, but remembrance of those parlous days probably accounts for an admonition to the faithful to keep always on hand enough food to last each family for a year. The recommendation is widely followed, and accounts for the fact that while housewives in other states have often abandoned home preserving of foods in favor of letting commercial processors handle it, the art of home canning is still practiced diligently in Utah. Family supplies usually include unground wheat, with the result that home baking, also comparatively rare elsewhere, still gives the fortunate Mormons the kind of bread which many of us have not tasted since childhood. A common present for a Mormon bride is a small hand-operated flour mill; this is often symbolic, for she has also the option of taking her own wheat to a church-operated mill, which will grind it for her.

Utah's difficulty in feeding itself had always been due to scarcity of water. The first preoccupation of the original settlers was with problems of irrigation, and of necessity they developed great skill in solving them, but ambitious present plans for irrigation systems are running into a substantial snag common to most of the West, one which was not operative when the area was more sparsely settled. There is just not enough water to go around for all the demands now being made on it. State is in competition with state, community with community, and irrigation system with irrigation system everywhere in the West; the building of new dams and the creation of new reservoirs cannot keep up with increasing needs.

Less vulnerable to water shortages than crop farming is livestock raising; Utah's agricultural economy depends largely on grazing, and three-quarters of farm revenue is derived from livestock and its by-products. The state manages to make profitable use of 91 percent of its land, a feat of some magnitude on terrain so uneven that there are six climatic zones reflecting differences in altitude. Eighty-seven percent of the land is devoted to pasturage, yet from the scant four percent which remains Utah manages to wrest a considerable number of cash crops, attaining maximum yields for the difficult conditions under which many of them are raised. Her leading agricultural products are, in this order, cattle, dairy produce, turkeys, wheat, and barley, and the state also grows other grains, fruit (apples, peaches, apricots, cherries, berries, and melons), potatoes, sugar beets, beans for drying, and tomatoes, peas, and sweet corn for canning.

Like several other Western states, Utah is well endowed with game. Buffalo and elk became extinct long ago, but have recently been reintroduced, and once in a while a stray moose stumbles into the state from the north. Mule deer, the pronghorn antelope, and the brown bear have always been present, small game is represented by rabbits and squirrels, and there are ducks, geese, sage hens, pine hens, ruffed grouse, quail, and, an artificially introduced foreigner, the ring-necked pheasant. Trout, whitefish, suckers, and chub are native, and have been reinforced by additional species of trout, carp, catfish, bass, yellow perch, and grayling brought in from other states.

Yet Utah, despite its long-standing obsession with food (which emphasizes quantity more than quality) has never enjoyed a high gastronomic reputation. The reason is not hard to understand, but it is generally skirted cautiously, in a tactful attempt to avoid clashes with deep-seated taboos. Does one sense between the lines a reluctance to offend in, for instance, this passage from Jonathan Norton Leonard's *American Cooking: The Great West?*

> Today about three fourths of the population of Utah is still Mormon, so that everything that happens in the state is affected in some way by the rules and customs of their church. A stranger spending a few days in Salt Lake City may be surprised that the city, though obviously prosperous, has so few good restaurants. If he has much contact with the Mormons, he soon learns why: it is because Mormons eat at home. They also eat extremely well, and what they eat is strongly influenced by their religion.

In what direction is eating in Utah influenced by the dominant religion? In an anti-sybaritic, or if you prefer, an anti-gastronomic spirit, obviously. A limit is imposed to gastronomic finesse or sophistication whenever any foods are forbidden, in this case, most prominently, tea, coffee, and especially wine, a major factor in the development of any cuisine. These prohibitions were no doubt enacted in the service of high moral principles (so was Prohibition with a capital letter) and it can be argued that the gain is worth the loss; but it is clear that a loss exists. It exists not only in the outlawing of these items themselves, but also in some indirect results of their prohibition, results which usually go unnoticed.

It seems, for instance, that the human organism occasionally feels a need for mild stimulants. In the absence of such common stimulants as tea or coffee, one turns intuitively to some other provider of quick energy—sugar, for instance. It happens that Utah buys nearly twice as much candy per capita as the rest of the country, not counting the considerable quantities of homemade sweets which appear in the local social pattern. Dietitians often criticize American eating habits because an unhealthy proportion of sugar is included in them; Utah seems to be twice as excessive in this respect as the rest of us. Whatever the effect of higher sugar consumption on health may be, the effect on cooking is clear. A cuisine characterized by heavy sweetening cannot be a cuisine distinguished by subtlety: sugar is a bludgeon seasoner, which tends to stun all fine shadings of flavor. Whether in a good cause or not, the heavy use of sugar joins other factors stemming from the Mormon attitude toward food in setting limits on the extent to which their cooking can develop finesse and sophistication.

Oklahoma consists of a rolling plain sloping gently from northwest to southeast at an altitude of about 1,300 feet, which before the white man came was covered with vast herds of buffalo and populated by roving Indians, who established no fixed communities because they followed in their rovings the animals on which they were completely dependent for food, clothing and shelter. The land seemed designed expressly for agriculture, and Oklahoma is indeed considered primarily as an agricultural state, though the cash revenue derived from farming is exceeded by the value both of its mineral products (including oil and natural gas) and of its manufactures (but part of the latter consists of food processing). As 80 percent of the state's total acreage is in farm land, its classification as agricultural territory would seem quite justified.

At the beginning farming meant cattle raising, an important activity in the territory even before the beef producers had a legal right to be there. The nature of the terrain made Oklahoma also a natural host for those immense wheat farms which stretch across the prairie as far as the eye can reach. Wheat is by far Oklahoma's most important money crop; the state ranks third in the nation for wheat production. Unwise farming methods, such as plowing of grasslands, exposed the soil to erosion and provoked the appalling tragedy of the Dust Bowl of the 1930s. Thousands of Oklahomans were reduced to poverty, thus earning the contemptuous name of "Okies," in conformity with an American tendency to regard poverty as being a form of sin. The bitter lesson of this period was heeded. Oklahoma soil thereafter was managed with cautious efficiency, so that the state's problem in some later years actually became one of overproduction—as in 1970, when a bumper crop of 118 million bushels of wheat was not easily absorbed by the market.

Today beef cattle provide the leading source of agricultural income—there are more than three million Herefords, Aberdeen Angus, and Shorthorn steers in the state—followed by dairy products (including several million chickens) and hogs; there are also some sheep. Among crops, after wheat come sorghum, a poor second, oats, rye, corn, peanuts, pecans, and fruit. Walnuts, hickory nuts, plums, crab apples, grapes, cherries, blackberries, dewberries, strawberries, raspberries, huckleberries, gooseberries, currants, persimmons, and papaws are gathered wild.

An offbeat specialty which Oklahoma shares with Texas is mung beans, grown for Chinese restaurants, which convert them into sprouts.

Of the two Southwest Indian states, the last of the contiguous United States to enter the Union, Arizona is the poor cousin. Everybody who found it promptly forgot about it. It did not have the water of the Rio Grande nor the natural oases of New Mexico; so it was New Mexico which the Spaniards, and for that matter the Mexicans and the Americans after them, chose to develop first.

New Mexico's dry climate does not particularly fit it to be a food producing state, yet agriculture is fifth in the list of its revenue-producing activities. The chief form of farming is grazing, so cattle, dairy products and sheep head its exports, bringing in more than twice the revenue from crops, of which the two most important do not reach the dinner table, except indirectly—cotton perhaps in the form of tablecloths, hay, greatly modified, in the form of meat. Cotton is the chief crop in irrigated areas, winter wheat in dry farming country, which means about two-thirds of the crop-growing surface. Sorghum, corn, and beans for drying are the other chief crops, but some fruits and vegetables are grown in the Rio Grande and other river valleys.

Arizona was even less fitted to raise food than New Mexico. Manufacturing, largely for defense, is its leading industry, and mining second—with the reservation that since the last figures were compiled, tourism may have risen in rank. It is important in a state which possesses such spectacular attractions as the Grand Canyon (217 miles long, four to eight miles across at the top, a mile deep), the Painted Desert, and the Petrified Forest. (New Mexico has the Carlsbad Caverns.)

Agriculture ranks only eighth among the activities which provide income for Arizona's citizens; the state has had to fight hard for enough water to permit even this modest amount of farming. It is in perpetual conflict with Nevada and California over sharing the water of the Colorado, a difference which only the United States Supreme Court is able to arbitrate. Moreover the drilling of wells had to be restricted some years ago because the water table was dropping. The state nevertheless manages to produce cattle, dairy products, dates (which have to be pollinated by hand), barley, wheat and other grains, sorghum, potatoes, grapefruit, oranges, lettuce, and even wine (an overflow from California vineyards). There are also walnut and cherry trees.

Game is limited nowadays, with many animals protected. Hunters wiped out the native elk long ago, but Wyoming elk have been brought in to replace them. There are some pronghorns, several species of deer, black and brown bears, and the only native pig of North America, the Mexican javelina.

The expansion of the United States from its early territories of the Atlantic and Gulf coasts added more food, but no new foods, to the American larder. But when expansion continued beyond the bloc of the forty-eight contiguous states, the additions became more exotic, those of Alaska mildly so, those of Hawaii wildly so.

Alaska, the forty-ninth state, is enormous—2,200 miles long, 1,200 miles wide, one-fifth as large as all "the other forty-eight" (as Alaskans call the rest of the United States) put together, and twice as big as Texas, which, disgruntled at being displaced as the biggest state, says of Alaska, "Wait till it melts." Alaska harbors two glaciers, Malaspina and Bering, each as large as the state of Rhode Island, and the highest mountain in North America, Mount McKinley. It boasts of its size through its self-given nickname, "the great land" (or "the great country"), which it maintains is the significance of an Eskimo word which gives it its official name; but this is a mistranslation. The word which has been Anglicized into "Alaska" comes from the Alakshack language, from island-minded Aleuts; what it means is "the mainland." Another statistic about Alaska: it is two miles from the Soviet Union and five hundred from "the other forty-eight." You can see Russia's

Big Diomede Island from America's Little Diomede Island, when the fog lifts; but there are half a thousand miles of British Columbia between the southern extremity of Alaska's coastal spur and the state of Washington.

Apparently the fog did not lift in 1728 for Captain Vitus Bering, a Dane in the employ of Russia, who was looking specifically for the mainland, but managed to pass from the Pacific Ocean into the Arctic through the strait which bears his name today without sighting it. He may have glimpsed Alaska from his ship on the way back, in 1732, but this is not certain. However on his second voyage, in 1741, he went ashore, probably the first white man ever to set foot in Alaska. From that voyage he never returned. Weakened by scurvy, he ran his ship ashore on an island which also bears his name today, and died there. He would not have known that a common plant which grows along the Alaskan coast is scurvy grass; only later would Russian sailors discover its ascorbic properties and take great quantities of it aboard their ships as protection against the malady which had felled Bering.

Furs were thought to be the only asset of Alaska at first. It was on account of fur that Russia established Alaska's first permanent settlement on Kodiak Island in 1784 and consequently found itself, without much premeditation, in possession of Alaska. She developed the fur trade so briskly that by the 1850s the fur-bearing animals of the region had been seriously depleted and Russia began to show signs of willingness to sell out. Leaving Alaska had become all the more tempting since the Russians had tried to grow grain there and had failed. Consequently they had been obliged in 1811 to operate farms north of San Francisco, and to build forts to protect the farms, in order to supply food to a territory which couldn't supply it for itself. They moved out of California in 1841, considering that supporting Alaska was not worth the trouble. Nobody else showed any interest in acquiring a territory believed to consist mainly of ice until Secretary of State William H. Seward persuaded the United States to pay $7,200,000 for it in 1868—about two cents an acre. Consistent with its record of opposing every acquisition of new territory, the American public divided itself into two parties on the question of Alaska, one which derided Seward for his silliness in letting the Russians put one over on him, and the other which charged him with criminal profligacy in squandering the nation's money. Both called the purchase "Seward's Folly." Of course no one at the time, least of all the Russians, could have anticipated the discovery of gold toward the end of the nineteenth century, much less the still unappreciated richness of oil, which would be found in the twentieth.

It is not probable that even Seward expected Alaska to contribute food to the nation; it was an unpropitious symbol that its very first appearance in history had been stamped with scurvy. What could be expected of a country where winter temperatures could fall as low as seventy below zero; where only seventeen thousand of 350 million acres are cultivated; where the Federal Government owns 97 percent of the land because nobody else wants it, for it is either tilted up on edge, or covered with ice, or seething with volcanic activity (the Valley of Ten Thousand Smokes); and where the largest state has the smallest population, with only one inhabitant for every two square miles?

Yet the very name of Alaskans is a food name. They are called sourdoughs.

For many urbanized Americans nowadays the word "sourdough" carries little precise meaning, only a vaguely romantic association with pioneer he-men. Before Alaska became a familiar name for us, the mention of sourdough invoked the Far West and the chuck wagon; but a great many persons would be stumped if you asked them exactly what sourdough is. It is simply what used to be the first stage of foresighted breadmaking everywhere before it became possible to step out to the neighborhood grocery and buy commercial yeast or, later, baking powder. The East had almost forgotten what had preceded this labor-saving technique by the time the pioneers moved beyond the range of grocery stores and therefore had to revert to primitive do-it-yourself baking. The realm of sourdough narrowed where civilization moved in; but it continued to accompany pioneers to each succeeding frontier. The last frontier turned out to be Alaska, which therefore remained the ultimate possessor of the word, and of the thing which the word represented.

Sourdough is a starter for bread. Instead of making bread from scratch each time a few loaves were needed, and waiting, in the days before commercial yeast, for the natural yeast cells which are always floating in the air (unless the weather is too cold) to settle on the dough and multiply, releasing the gas which makes bread rise, the early housewife kept on hand a small amount of dough in which the concentration of yeast had already begun—a thick paste of flour and water which had accumulated the yeast which would be needed whenever bread was to be baked. In practice, there was usually some additional ingredient in the sourdough to generate yeast faster than by the *laissez-faire* method; some cooks put in hops, others used potato water. Each time a batch of bread was to be made, some of the sourdough went into the new dough made for the occasion as a sort of catalyzer, to start the yeast working and speed up the rising of the bread. Since yeast is a living organism, the sourdough had to be fed regularly; whenever some was taken out, it had to be replaced by new material. Many sourdough devotees hold that the starter should never be thrown out but kept in continuous production as long, no doubt, as its owner lived (it might even be handed down to an heir). The older it is, sourdough fanciers say, the better bread it makes; some Alaskan families have sourdough fifty years old. Purists frown on adding commercial yeast to the mixture, but it must be suspected that many cooks today cut corners on this precept. This is probably of minor importance; what counts is that the sentimental maintenance of the sourdough tradition means that Alaskans still eat that vanishing luxury, homemade bread; if you start out with sourdough, homemade bread is what you are going to have to produce. It is bread of dense texture and rich flavor, bread of a quality few of us "on the outside" get to taste nowadays, limited only by the shortcomings of today's over-refined flour.

However great our nostalgia for the old times may be, we can hardly avoid admitting that sourdough bread is better with today's butter (provided by a flourishing Alaskan dairy industry, based on the lush growth of vetch, peas, clover and various grasses) than with the "butter" of gold-rush days—the fat skimmed from the surface of water in which caribou horns had boiled for 36 hours.

No one, probably, makes caribou-horn butter nowadays, but some other ingenious old-time substitutes for foods difficult to find have hung on. Few persons could afford imported (and far from fresh) eggs in the 1890s, at two dollars a dozen. They ate seagull eggs instead and many Alaskans do still, for their distinctive flavor. Sweetening was another problem. Sugar was scarce, and there are no bees in Alaska to provide what has usually been the commonest sweetener wherever sugar has been lacking. Alaskans learned to stretch their short sugar supplies by becoming their own bees, extracting honey from blossoms without the aid of intermediary insects. What little sugar could be had to begin with was converted into syrup. Red and white clover and pink fireweed were then boiled in the syrup until all the sweetness of the flowers had been drained out and transferred to the liquid. This was called squaw honey, and some Alaskan housewives still make it. Other holdovers are relishes made from kelp and the use of moose (or even porcupine) fat in cooking.

The probability that Alaska would eventually do rather better than this might have been predicted early for at least two types of food, one for local consumption (game) and the other for potential export (fish). But how many prophets would have expected Alaska to produce crops? It seemed at first that the Alaskan climate ruled this out; but the original theories about the climate had to be revised in the light of experience.

Alaska has not one climate, but several; the mildest is that of its southern projection, which runs like a fringe tacked onto Canada down the coast, a lacework of islands off a narrow strip of mainland. Protected from Arctic winds by the mountains north of it, heated by the warm Japan Current, which also brings it plentiful rain, this strip enjoys a relatively temperate oceanic climate. Even the main body of Alaska, where it can become very cold on occasion (and even very hot in the summer, though it is short), is not, below the Arctic Circle at least, as frigid as you have probably imagined it. The January temperature of Fairbanks, in the interior, is about the same as that of Nebraska.

Alaska is thus not as hostile to growing things as most nineteenth-century Americans imagined. Nevertheless its most consistent source of food, and of revenue from food, has always been the one the prophets could have foreseen—its fisheries. The sea product we associate most readily with the state is the Alaska king crab, which thrives in the cold northern waters, where it has been known to reach a weight of twenty-five pounds, while its spidery legs spanned a distance of six feet. The king crab has long outsold its two rivals from these waters, the Dungeness crab and the snow crab, chiefly because it takes so well to freezing; but it has been over-fished and there is now a tendency to turn to the hitherto relatively neglected snow crab, which many connoisseurs prefer. Alaska is also the home of tiny tasty pink shrimp. They are delicious, but are not widely known outside of their area, for they do not keep well and have to be eaten quickly; however some of them are now canned, and so are several Alaskan bivalves. The state's deep-water scallops are larger than lifesize—eight to a pound, divested of their shells of course; they have become responsible for the development of a flourishing scallop-canning industry at Seward. Also canned are butter clams, razor clams, and geoducks, the last described as the world's largest intertidal clams. Razor clams and geoducks present the same problem as Alaska's pink shrimp, in more exaggerated form. Neither of them can close their shells completely, so their liquid runs off as soon as they are dug and they die before they can be delivered to market. They are thus restricted to consumption on the spot where they are taken, unless they can be gotten into cans very quickly, which some Alaskan canneries manage to do. Alaska has no oysters (except, possibly, along its southern strip); its waters are too cold.

In spite of the almost exclusive public awareness of the king crab as Alaska's contribution to seafood, it is not the state's most important export in this category. The most important is salmon (dried salmon has always been the staple food of Alaska's Tinneh Indians). The first salmon canneries were opened in 1878; salmon represents a yearly intake of approximately $100 million. Chinook and sockeye salmon are in particular demand; most of the roe goes to Japan, where it is esteemed as a great delicacy. Unfortunately a tendency has developed to set salmon nets too close to the river mouths and to leave them in place too long, so that few young salmon can escape to the sea, to mature there and return to spawn later. The survival of the salmon is thus threatened; the cod, similarly, has already practically disappeared from Alaskan waters (the so-called black cod still caught there is not a genuine cod, but a sablefish). However, halibut fishing is still important, and for the sportsman, the mountain country is a freshwater fisherman's paradise. Grayling and trout are so abundant in its almost inaccessible and consequently nearly virgin streams that one writer who managed to reach them has described fishing there as like stripping berries from a bush.

The native population (half Indians—Tlingit, Haida, and Tinneh—and half Eskimos and Aleuts) has been accustomed to procuring from the water other foods usually disdained by the whites—seal, walrus, sea lion, whale; the first three are less prized now, but some Eskimos still eat whale.

Most of the Eskimos have always depended, and often still depend, on a fish diet, supplemented in summer by berries and roots; but the minority who live inland owe their survival to the caribou (the same geography and the same sparseness of population which makes interior Alaska superb fishing country also makes it superb game country). Eskimos and caribou probably reached America together during the Ice Ages across the Bering Strait, when it could be crossed on foot. Wild caribou subsequently died out in Asia, leaving the North American animal the sole survivor, except for a few of a smaller species in Spitzbergen and Novaya Zemlya.

The inland Eskimos have been called "caribou Eskimos"; they were as dependent on these animals as the Plains Indians were on the buffalo, for food, clothing, fuel, sinews for sewing, bone for tools, and oil for lamps. The history of the buffalo is paralleled by that of the caribou. Great herds of millions of caribou covered the land in the eighteenth and nineteenth centuries; it is estimated as late as 1911 that there were still thirty million caribou in Alaska and Canada. But hunters mowed them down relentlessly for sport, cooking a steak or two over a bonfire on the spot of the kill and leaving the rest of the enormous carcass where it had fallen—just as buffalo were killed for tongues or hides alone. The slaughter of the caribou was less complete than that of the buffalo; there are still 600,000 caribou in Alaska, where only residents are now allowed to hunt them. Their meat tastes like heavier, gamier venison, provides good hams, and makes excellent sausage.

Some zoologists describe the caribou as a wild reindeer and think the only difference between the two is that the reindeer has been domesticated. An American missionary who must have had about the same idea, Sheldon Jackson, imported 1,280 Siberian reindeer into Alaska toward the end of the nineteenth century, and by 1920 Alaska was exporting reindeer meat to the United States. Alaskan reindeer reached a peak of 250,000 head and then, in 1939, Washington in its wisdom decided to award the monopoly of reindeer raising to the Eskimos. The Eskimos were good hunters but bad livestock handlers. One thing they did not do was to rotate their reindeer from one pasturage area to another, as the reindeer-raising Lapps of Finland do, with the result that the animals ate the lichen down to the bare ground—and lichen takes fifty to one hundred years to recuperate. Not only did the reindeer population drop, but so did that of the caribou, which fed on some of the same areas. Today the reindeer has nearly disappeared from Alaska, except for a herd belonging to the government.

No attempt has been made in Alaska to domesticate another large animal, the musk ox (more valuable for wool than for meat in any case). It is dying out, but, oddly enough, musk oxen transported to Vermont have been raised experimentally there since 1954.

The most important large game animal in Alaska aside from the caribou is the moose, of which there are believed to be 160,000—enough anyhow so that the Alaska railroad collides with and kills about five hundred of them a year, which has earned it the sobriquet of the Moose Gooser. If you can imagine what beef would taste like if the steer were a wild game animal, that is moose. A characteristic Alaskan specialty is moose meat, cut thin and air dried, like the famous Swiss *Bündnerfleisch.*

One very rare type of game is obtainable practically nowhere except in Alaska—the Dall sheep, named for William Healey Dall, who explored Alaska in 1865–1868 and wrote a book about it, *Alaska and Its Resources.* There are about forty thousand of them, but you have to get up into the high mountains to find them. The meat tastes like spiced young lamb. Mountain goat exist also in Alaska, but are not hunted for meat, though bears sometimes are.

Alaska is a berrypickers' Eden—raspberries, strawberries, blueberries, salmonberries, lingonberries, highbush and lowbush cranberries (neither of which are cranberries, but Alaskans make "cranberry wine" from them all the same), nagoonberries (alias wineberries), cloudberries, watermelonberries, sable crowberries, wild gooseberries, and, a trifle off center, rose hips; even the tundra produces anonymous edible though tart berries. Mushroom hunters are in luck too; there are a score of tasty species, among them the orange delicious, the chicken mushroom, the snail mushroom, inky caps, puffballs, boletus, and owl mushrooms.

So far we have been dealing with wild food, the sort it seems natural enough to find in wild country. Prepare now, if you happen to know little about Alaska, for a surprise: improbable though it may seem, Alaskan agriculture is by no means negligible. Alaska is not a leading farm state, but its produce nevertheless brings in several million dollars a year. The Russians did not succeed in raising grain there, but Americans in Alaska grow wheat, using, ironically enough, hardy varieties imported from Siberia. They also grow oats, rye, and barley.

More surprising still is that Alaska produces vegetables—vegetables which, in harmony with the scale of the land in which they grow, often reach dimensions unattained elsewhere. It is, indeed, an Alaskan phenomenon for those vegetables which will grow there at all to grow enormously. This can be witnessed especially in the fertile Matanuska valley, which runs inland from Anchorage, probably the state's single best farming area, which contains nearly one-half of the state's total cultivated acreage. Here seventy-pound cabbages have been raised. Rhubarb grows three to four feet high, oat stalks rise to seven feet. Wild strawberries are as big as some cultivated ones elsewhere.

The explanation for this gigantism is the length of the days this far north between the spring and autumn equinoxes (much of Alaska, indeed, lies north of the Arctic Circle, where the sun never sets at all in summer, though this area is not recommendable as farming country—but the best interior agricultural region is around Fairbanks, less than 150 miles south of the Circle). Alaskans claim that their produce is not only bigger but better, which is more than a mere boast too; once more it is explained by the climate. Alaskan plants receive sunlight in larger doses than in lower latitudes, which acts as an accelerator on *size* in growth; but they develop in average temperatures lower than those current elsewhere, which acts as a brake on *dispersiveness* in growth—that is, the rate of the plant's chemical exchanges with the atmosphere; its respiration is slowed down. Elements which farther south would escape into the air remain stored within the plant in Alaska, where they form sugar or other flavor-building compounds.

Alaskan farms are small and scattered; most of them are located on the deltas of streams. Many are dairy or poultry farms, so Alaska exports dairy products, poultry and eggs. Others produce lettuce, cauliflower, beets or carrots. Alaska is far from being ideal farming country, perhaps, but it is much more bountiful than we of the warmer "other forty-eight" are accustomed to realizing. How much more surprising from this aspect must the forty-ninth state look from the vantage point of the fiftieth! It is the Tropic of Cancer regarding the Arctic Circle.

Hawaii is probably the only state that ever entered the Union primarily because of food. Geographically, the inclusion in a basically continental power of a group of islands 2,100 nautical miles from its nearest important port (San Francisco) is something of an absurdity, a legal fiction like the legal fiction which extends the official limits of the city of Honolulu so far into its outlying islands that it is the only metropolis in the world which can boast that its population includes a considerable number of whales. Politically, its admission seemed so little necessary that the United States refused to accept it as a protectorate when that status was first solicited, in 1851, while later Congress refused twenty-two times to make it a state, until it became expedient to bring it in as a political counterweight to Alaska, for which statehood appeared more logical. Hawaii was acquired by an almost unique process, neither by conquest nor purchase nor annexation in the ordinary sense, but by its progressive approach to the United States through a series of ever tighter treaties deriving from what may be called economic drift—it was drawn little by little to the nation upon which it depended economically more and more, and this dependence was accounted for primarily by its two principal exports, sugar and pineapples.

It is something of a paradox that the state whose adherence to the Union was motivated partly by the question of food was in a sense the poorest, or at least one of the poorest, from the point of view of the variety and importance of the foods it knew originally. It is easy to think of Hawaii as a country of great alimentary richness because an impression of lush abundance is produced by the thickness of its tropical vegetation and the brilliance of its colors, which evoke an image of Oriental luxuriance. But the fact is that the Hawaiian Islands, like most Polynesian islands, were very poor in foodstuffs, and those which cater to their prosperity now were almost all imported, some of them quite recently—the sugar industry dates from 1835, the pineapple trade only from this century. The nature of the islands, volcanic masses heaved up ruggedly from the sea, gives them very little level ground suitable for the raising of the most important foods of man, cereals (only seven percent of the land is cultivatable) or for what is perhaps the second most important food once a society has become rich enough to eat its grain in its most expensive form, meat (only forty percent is fit even for grazing). Indeed the indigenous resources of the islands pretty much limited anyone who settled on them to a diet of seafood. For a long time no one did come to settle on them. The Polynesian islands were probably the last hospitable area of the world's surface to be inhabited by man, who reached them by a process of island-hopping, starting from Asia. The first arrivals in Hawaii probably dated from about A.D. 750.

The first European credited with having seen Hawaii was Captain James Cook, who landed there January 20, 1778, and named the archipelago the Sandwich Islands in honor of his sponsor, the Earl of Sandwich, the same one who gave his name to the article of food which he found the most convenient means for satisfying his appetite without obliging him to leave the gambling tables to which he was addicted. The islands first attracted the attention of Americans about 1820, when whaling developed there; anyone with a good pair of binoculars can still see humpback whales and their calves frolicking in their breeding grounds, the Alenuihaha Channel between the islands of Hawaii and Maui, from November to May. Missionaries, who were to play a considerable part in the development of Hawaii, started arriving at the same time. The first treaty with the United States was negotiated by a naval officer, Captain Thomas ap Catesby Jones. The rest was a succession of tiny steps, each one moving Hawaii a little closer to the day when it would become American territory in 1900 and an American state in 1959.

In that status, Hawaii is officially described as consisting of 122 islands, 114 of which total only three square miles in area put together. Besides this collection of mere islets and coral reefs, there are eight principal islands, one uninhabited, with Hawaii the largest, and Oahu, on which Honolulu and Pearl Harbor are located, the most heavily inhabited, with 80 percent of the total population.

What did these islands, then uninhabited, have to offer in the way of food to the first Polynesians when they arrived in their seagoing outrigger canoes? Fish, crabs, turtles, whales if they could catch them, and small birds—the ancient Hawaiians ate songbirds. Vegetable foods were necessarily scarce. The isolated islands of Hawaii, of comparatively recent origin, had had little opportunity to acquire edible plants, except those whose seeds could be carried by birds or which could float to new habitats. Some of the vegetable foods widespread in Hawaii now may have planted themselves thus before men were present to plant them, but nobody knows which ones. There was even less opportunity to acquire land animals. It is probable that the very first mammal in Hawaii was man.

Everywhere in the world, the most important staple food is bread, or, where cereals are lacking to make it, some starchy substitute. There were no cereals in Hawaii when the Polynesians arrived and it is almost certain that they brought none with them. The chief cereal there today, the only one really suited to the growing conditions, is rice; it does not seem to have existed in Hawaii before the nineteenth century. The Polynesians had two starchy substitutes for grain, breadfruit and taro. Most accounts say that the Polynesians brought both with them, implying that neither existed in Hawaii before them, and that both arrived at about the same time. What might have preceded the Polynesians was not exactly the genuine breadfruit, but its very close relative, the jack tree, or breadnut, much inferior in flavor. Birds could have sown the jack tree, for its fruits have seeds; the superior Malayan breadfruit has not.

The experts also credit the Polynesians with importing the coconut, which may not have been necessary; the coconut is a great floater which propagates itself by letting itself be washed up on suitable beaches. If it is true that it reached the west coast of South America by drifting from the Pacific islands, it could certainly have covered the shorter distance from one Polynesian island to another without help from man. However it reached Hawaii, it played an important role in shaping the patterns of Hawaiian eating, for coconut, which to Westerners of the temperate zones may seem a rather frivolous food, useful for confectioneries and desserts, but easily dispensable, is a vital basic aliment for one-third of the world's population; the very name of the coconut palm in Sanskrit means "tree of life." The coconut grows often in climates where milch animals are rare—in Hawaii they were non-existent for at least a thousand years—but all the uses in cooking of cow's milk can be supplied by coconut milk (which is not the liquid found inside the nut, but juice pressed from its meat). Coconut fat is chemically close to butter fat; in the regions where coconuts grow their milk is everywhere the basic cooking fat. The meat of the nut enters into a wide variety of Polynesian dishes; and coconut served as a sweetener before sugar cane moved into its territory. In addition, the coconut palm provides a vegetable which you would be unlikely to attribute to this source if you didn't happen to know what it was—what luxury restaurants call palm hearts, which are the terminal buds of the tree. The sap of the coconut palm can be processed into wine, spirits, or vinegar.

The first meat in Hawaii is supposed to have been provided by pigs brought to the islands by the first Polynesians—highly probable, for the pig had become strongly entrenched in southeastern Asia before the Polynesian islands were settled; long familiarity with the pig seems confirmed by the fact that pork is the favorite and festive meat of Hawaii. Captain Cook added European species of pigs and also goats to the islands' fauna in 1778, when he put ashore some of the animals he had aboard for food. They went wild in the Hawaiian woods, and in the unaccustomedly favorable climate of Hawaii multiplied so fast as to become a destructive nuisance to crops. Hawaiians, who like goat meat, hunt the wild animals, but do not bag enough of them to bring their numbers down. Goat is the only new meat for which they have shown any enthusiasm. The British explorer George Vancouver introduced cattle and sheep in 1793 (the first horse arrived in 1803), but Hawaiians do not care for lamb and while they will accept beef, prefer pork. Axis deer were brought into the islands in 1867.

Did the original fauna of the islands include a large edible bird, in addition to their small ones? There is a native Hawaiian wild goose called the nene (pronounced naynay), but how long it has been there is a mystery. It is believed to have evolved from the Canada goose, far enough back to have adopted terrestrial habits; it lives only in dry areas and has lost most of the webbing between its toes. Easy to hunt, the nene had been all but wiped out by the end of the 1940s. The Hawaiian conscience was then aroused, birds were bred outside of the islands and brought back to be released there, and the nene was named the state bird. Its numbers had passed one thousand by the beginning of the 1970s.

The authorities cautiously refrain from committing themselves about when the chicken arrived—"anciently," says one respected reference book, but refrains from including it in the list of the early Polynesian imports. It has been in the islands long enough so that those which escaped from domestication into the woods have had time to revert to the original form of the wild Indian jungle fowl, which is the ancestor of all the chickens in the world. On the other hand, a more recent origin has been argued from the fact that the chicken brought with it a form of avian malaria called bird pox or bumblefoot, which, infecting Hawaii's native wild birds, killed most of them off, which happened in the nineteenth century. However it is possible that diseased chickens had been in the islands for a long time, perhaps even for centuries, without transmitting their malady, for lack of a germ carrier. If we do not know when the chicken arrived, we do know when the disease carrier arrived—1826. It was in that year that a ship named the *Wellington,* which had last filled its water casks in Mexico, took on fresh water in Hawaii, first dumping out what was left of their Mexican water; it contained mosquito larvae. These were the first mosquitoes in Hawaii; they set to work at once to transfer bird pox from the chickens to Hawaii's defenseless birds.

Other edible birds which have been brought into Hawaii successfully since include, among domestic birds, the turkey, and among game birds, the pheasant.

When the reference books credit the first Polynesian settlers with having given Hawaii the ohia, or Malay apple, they are probably right; when they put sugar cane into those first incoming canoes, the assertion is dubious; and when they tell us that the first imported plants included the sweet potato and the arrowroot, they are necessarily wrong: both are natives of tropical America, unknown anywhere else until seven and a half centuries after the Polynesians reached Hawaii. It may be admitted that in the case of arrowroot, they may be only half wrong, having simply repeated uncritically an imprecision of the English language. True arrowroot belongs to the genus *Maranta,* and, being American, could not have been imported by ancient Polynesians. But they could have brought along *Curcuma angustifolia,* a member of the ginger family, called in English today East Indian arrowroot, or, what the reference book writers may have had in mind, *Tacca pinnatifida,* a palm which the Hawaiians had already naturalized before the arrival of the first white men, who baptized it the Otaheite arrowroot. Both of these plants grow in Hawaii today, and so does genuine arrowroot, transplanted there from the West Indies.

Much of the ancient Hawaiian vegetation, whether indigenous or attributable to the Polynesian settlers, has disappeared since whites first became acquainted with the islands. Captain Cook saw, and was impressed by, a gourd called *ipu nui* which he said could hold from ten to twelve gallons of liquid; it is extinct now. Some imported plants reacted to a changed environment as had the European pigs and goats, flourishing so lavishly that they drove out native species less fitted to survive. The guava and the blackberry, for instance, dispossessed original vegetation which competed for the same types of soil and location. "On the island of Oahu," Robert Wallace tells us, "about 85 per cent of all the native vegetation has been wiped out and replaced by plants brought in by man." The gastronomic pattern of the islands was considerably altered by the disappearance of old food plants and the development of new ones, brought in by the successive waves of immigrants from one country after another.

> In the early 19th century [Rafael Steinberg wrote], New England missionaries and whalers and traders introduced corned beef, salt fish, stews, chowders and corn bread. Chinese plantation workers brought in rice, the stir-fry method of cooking, and Asian vegetables like soybeans, Chinese cabbage and lotus roots. With the Japanese sugar-cane workers came charcoal braziers, new kinds of noodles, a taste for seaweed, and the sugar and soy sauce teriyaki marinade—which remains the most popular way of preparing meat in Hawaii today. Koreans arrived with their *kimchi* (pickled cabbage) and hooked the islanders on the taste of garlic and chili, and the Filipinos introduced jack fruit [ah?], mung beans, bitter melons, and the powerful *bagoong* fish sauce. From Europe came the Portuguese, who left their mark too. The bright red-and-white vans that peddle their

> fluffy, sugary *malasada* doughnuts roam everywhere in Honolulu, especially at sporting events and festivals. A Portuguese bean soup, thick, spicy, with an insistent taste of sausage and garlic, has also become a favorite among Hawaiians of every ethnic background. Even the Scots, who arrived in smaller numbers as sugar technicians [shades of Robert Burns! sugar in the Highlands?] and plantation overseers, added their special touch to Hawaii's menus: scones and shortbread. . . .
>
> The whalers' jerked beef now turns up as *pipikaula,* a tasty dried meat tidbit essential to every well-planned luau, or Hawaiian feast. And the salt fish dear to the missionaries has been transmuted into the excellent *lomi lomi* salmon. *Lomi* means massage in Hawaiian, and *lomi lomi* salmon in its basic form consists of thin salted salmon fillets that have been squished in water by hand to remove some of the salt and break down the fibers.

And then came the American arrival in force, with a result reported by the *Encyclopaedia Britannica:* "Most people eat foods similar to those consumed in the mainland United States." Hawaiian supermarkets offer today all the familiar trademarked brands dear to Denver, Dallas, and Kansas City, plus Hawaiian foods which have been naturalized American along with Hawaiian citizens. Names like poi, luau, laulau, limu and hau pia shout lustily from cellophane bags, tin cans, glass bottles and cardboard cartons: sterilized exoticism.

Some native foods have resisted assimilation, especially those of the sea. There are more than 650 species of fish in the waters around the islands, aboriginal of course (but the present freshwater fish—trout, black bass, carp and catfish—were imported). Ocean fisheries bring in several million dollars annually, the most important fish commercially including *aku* and *ansahi,* in English, ocean bonito and yellow-fish albacore (until they get into cans, when both become tuna). Hawaiians enjoy one privilege which most of the world has lost—the right to eat genuine turtle. One of the last places left where the green sea turtle comes ashore to lay its eggs is in the Hawaiian Islands National Wildlife Refuge; the great animals, some of which weigh as much as three hundred pounds, are protected while they are there, but once outside of the Refuge they are free game and may be taken without limit as to size or number. Of the other products of the sea, one of the most prized is the Kona crab, of particularly delicate flavor. The superior Hawaiian coffee (a late immigrant, of course) is also called Kona; it is the name of an area on the west of the island of Hawaii where coffee is raised and crabs are plentiful.

The other survivors from the earliest days are mostly fruits. The bright red huckleberry-shaped ohelo berry played a part in the Christianization of the islands. It was sacred to Pele, the goddess of volcanoes; the berries, appropriately, grew thickly around the active Mount Kilauea, considered to be her abode. According to popular belief, anyone who ate ohelo berries there without throwing a few into the crater for Pele would be swallowed up instanter in a burst of lava—excessive punishment for petty larceny, it would seem, but of course it was aggravated by *lèse majesté,* a crime to which constituted authority, whether temporal or spiritual, has always been sensitive. A particularly exhibitionist convert to Christianity chose to defy Pele by munching ohelo berries on the rim of her particular volcano, not only withholding the goddess's share, but at the same time pelting the crater with stones. Nothing happened. The populace drew the natural conclusion that Pele had been outranked in the celestial hierarchy.

Some other fruits considered native to Hawaii are actually foreigners which have acquired new habits in a new habitat, for instance the white strawberry, which remains that color even when ripe; it developed this peculiarity after having been imported from Europe and America.

Native Hawaiian cooking has tended to become lost in the influx of foreign foods, except as a folkloric spectacle staged for tourists, a development which, in most of the countries where it has occurred, has resulted in adulteration of the individuality of characteristic local cuisines, since their most salient features are almost automatically those least acceptable to visitors from other cultures, and accordingly are watered down to appeal to outsiders. There seems no reason why this should not happen in Hawaii also, especially as so few old Hawaiians are left to maintain tradition. There were 300,000 natives in the islands when the whites and their diseases arrived, but by the second half of this century there were only twelve thousand full-blooded Hawaiians left (two percent of the population), plus eighty thousand part Hawaiian and part Asiatic. As a normal day-after-day diet, the pre-white cuisine of the island (sometimes not quite literally a cuisine, a word which implies cooking, for many foods, including fish, were eaten raw) has pretty much disappeared. It surfaces when a luau is staged, whether for visitors or for islanders playing with the old customs rather than perpetuating them, as the Old Far West is played at on dude ranches. "Luau" is a feast now, but originally the word meant only "taro," a plant which plays an important role in Hawaiian feasts—its chopped leaves go into *laulau,* leaf-wrapped packages of steamed food, like fish and pork or fish and chicken (Hawaiians like to combine meat and fish), while the pounded roots make poi, the starchy paste which was the closest approach to bread the old Hawaiians knew. A universal food for natives, poi has not often won the affection of passing visitors, many of whom have hit independently on the same description of its taste, that it is like stale library paste (library paste, it may be remarked, could serve as food in a pinch, when it is made, like bread, from flour and water). Derogatory estimates of poi from outsiders are usually received with indignation by permanent white residents, but when no outsiders are in hearing, they refer to it among themselves as "mashed elephant." Poi is used to make baby food, for consumers too young to resist.

The *pièce de résistance* of a genuine luau should be that idolized aliment, the pig. It is cooked in a pit dug in the ground *(imu)* with the aid of heated stones; the animal is stuffed with hot stones too, cooked simultaneously from the inside out and from the outside in, so thoroughly that its roasted flesh falls apart when hoisted out of its underground oven, which is the way the natives like it; nowadays it is often cooked less lengthily to meet the demand of foreign customers. Other foods are steamed at the same time, wrapped in leaves—*ti* leaves for fish, to which they impart a musky flavor not appreciated in, for instance, cooked fruit, which is accordingly wrapped in banana leaves instead. Only men are allowed to cook in the *imu,* in obedience to an ancient taboo. The most exotic food likely to come out of the *imu* is *limu,* edible seaweed, which may not hold out much longer except for the Japanese, the world's greatest seaweed eaters.

The *ti* which furnishes leaves for oven paper, and *kava,* both very old plants, probably brought in by the Polynesians, but possibly native, provide alcoholic drinks obtained from the liquid pressed out of their roots. In the old days it was simply allowed to ferment, resulting in a mildly titillating brew no stronger than beer. About 1800 the whites introduced the Hawaiians to the ministrations of the still, enabling them to promote *ti*-root juice into a vicious counterfeit of rum productive of super-hangovers, called *okolehao.* Considerably tamed, this beverage can now be purchased by the incautious in liquor stores, along with bourbon and gin. Tamed also is the original native cooking, in a compromise cuisine known as *hapa haole,* half white men's. It is distinguished largely by a habit of wrapping foods for cooking in *ti* leaves instead of aluminum paper. Most of the American population prefers whole white men's food, imported chiefly from the continental United States, which is one of the reasons why the cost of living in Hawaii is higher than in any of the other forty-nine states.

The islands could, if they wanted to, grow almost any needed food instead of importing it, but producers prefer to concentrate on the most profitable crops, which no doubt makes sense since they have so little arable land to work with. Hawaiian agriculture today is a large-scale operation, very different from that of the old days, which fastened upon the islands a peculiar system of land division admirably designed as a function of the mountainous terrain. Each land-holding family group was assigned a parcel of land called an *ahupuaa.* Triangular in shape, its apex was located at the highest level, and the holding descended, widening as it went, to the sea and even into it, for property rights extended for some distance into the water. Thus each property included all of the necessities of existence, which were found at varying levels—wood from the top of the *ahupuaa,* taro from the flooded terraces a little farther down, yams and bananas still lower, domestic pigs and cultivated vegetable plots where the ground flattened, coconuts from the palms on the beach, and seafood, the most substantial part of the diet, from the water, where fish were often trapped in pools created by building semicircular stone walls out from the beach; some of them, more than a thousand years old, are still there.

Hawaii's most important agricultural product today is sugar. It supplies one-seventh of all the sugar consumed in the United States (the first cargo to pass through the Panama Canal after it opened was Hawaiian sugar). Three-quarters of the cultivatable land is used for sugar cane, which means only 221,300 acres, about the area of New York City. Sugar cane growing in Hawaii is highly technical and completely mechanized; the result is the highest yield achieved for this crop anywhere in the world. The second most important crop is pineapples, also highly mechanized. The fruit has been regimented into growing to dimensions which will fit the machines which are to process it. If nature asserts her prerogative of unpredictability to the extent of permitting pineapples to reach an inconvenient size, the rebellious fruit are simply abandoned in the field. Rice used to be the third, and relatively important, Hawaiian crop, but of recent years there has been a tendency to import rice, or equivalent cereals, in favor of converting the land on which it used to grow to sugar cane.

Agriculture is the leading industry of Hawaii, a development which it would have been wildly irrational to predict two centuries ago, given the penury of Hawaiian foods and a terrain which seemed to destine the islands to almost anything except agriculture. Its present vocation represents a triumph of mind over matter. Hawaii, lacking food of its own, has demonstrated a remarkable ability to exploit the foods of others, more successfully even than their original possessors. If you asked people anywhere in the world where they thought the pineapple originated, it is probable that the poll would give a majority vote for Hawaii—not unreasonably, since Hawaii now produces 75 percent of all the pineapples sold in the world; but, as we know, the pineapple is a native of tropical and subtropical America. The macadamia nut originated in Australia and was first planted in Hawaii less than a century ago; but the islands now enjoy a virtual world monopoly on the commercial production of macadamia nuts.

Even the ukelele originated in Portugal.

XXVI

The Tepid Melting Pot

THE ENTRY OF HAWAII into the United States provided a test case of the instinctive American rejection of any foods incorrigibly foreign to the eating habits imported from the British Isles. It brought within the political borders of the United States a completely exotic gastronomic tradition, that of Polynesia, but it proved to be so basically incompatible that it failed to exercise the slightest influence on the cooking of the United States. For good or for ill, the United States was perhaps a political melting pot, perhaps a cultural melting pot, perhaps an ethnical melting pot, but it is not a culinary melting pot. Its capacity for digesting esoteric gastronomic contributions is narrowly limited.

The cuisines which were most successful in infiltrating American kitchens were those which resembled the cooking of England—Dutch and German, for instance. Even Scandinavian cooking proved a little too foreign, and is confined chiefly to Scandinavian ethnic enclaves in the United States. More exotic cuisines, even those which originated in the United States itself, but in response to foreign inspiration, are not felt to be native, but alien. They do not lose themselves in the main current, but remain regional phenomena, like the Creole cooking of Louisiana. American Chinese cooking, as distinct a variation as Szechwan or Pekin cooking, though it did develop on a base of Cantonese cuisine brought to the Pacific coast by immigrants from Canton, has not entered into the main stream of American cooking either, despite the travesties of a few of its dishes available throughout the country in cans. The Spanish were on American territory long before the Anglo-Saxons, but the Spanish gastronomic vocabulary has added little to the American vernacular.

There even seems to be a tendency, when for some reason a dash of extra-American inspiration seems desirable, instead of risking the addition of a genuine foreign dish to the American repertory, to invent instead an American dish with a foreign name and a vague resemblance to a foreign creation, but which is actually, and reassuringly, a native-born citizen of the

American kitchen, consequently acceptable to American tastes; dishes of this kind too are often restricted to the areas which created them.

Swiss steak and Russian dressing are not worth considering in this category. They are concoctions entirely American and the reasons for which somebody decided to tack a foreign label upon them are not readily discernible. There are other American dishes, however, whose foreign names are explicable by their own nature. There is, for instance, chop suey, which has gotten around the country, in restaurants or in cans, though the many Americans who eat it certainly do not think of it as part of their native fare; yet it was invented in the United States and was unknown in China until very recently, when it began to be imported into that country for the delectation of the American visitors beginning to arrive there. Tokyo is full of restaurants offering Chinese cooking, but the only one which makes chop suey is a big establishment specializing in American food for its American clientele. One of the stories told to explain the birth of chop suey is that it was devised to feed the Chinese coolies brought in to give the American land transcontinental railroads; in the process, they gave the American language the word "chow"—as in "chow mein." Their idea of satisfactory chow was rice plus vegetables and, if possible, a little meat. The Chinese laborers were hard workers and their employers were willing to give them the food they wanted to encourage their continued efforts, but the railroad gang cooks knew little about Chinese cooking except the vague ideas they had been able to gain from the Chinese food of San Francisco. They did their best, and what they came up with was chop suey, simple but acceptable.

Cioppino sounds authentically Italian, but both the dish and the name were invented in San Francisco, with the freest of fantasy in both cases. Cioppino is a seafood stew which admits of infinite variations, oftenest built around crab, and the Italian-looking word is explained as a reduction of the English word "chop" to its Italian phonetic equivalent.

Vichyssoise sounds authentically French, but it was invented in New York in 1910, and is unknown in France except in hotels frequented by Americans, who ask for it on the assumption that they can enjoy a taste treat by eating the real thing on what they assume is its native heath. The first request of this sort seems to have occurred in 1946 or 1947, and the obliging restaurateur who was asked if he could make a Vichyssoise soup responded by producing one based on carrots, to the surprise of his transatlantic customers who were familiar with it as being made with leeks and potatoes. It was a natural error, for the distinctive characteristic of Vichy dishes for the French is that they contain carrots. French chefs have now learned from their American clients, and if asked to produce Vichyssoise will come up with a French imitation of this American invention.

Chili con carne sounds authentically Spanish, which it could hardly be, for the Spaniards had never seen a chili before they reached America; it was an element of Indian, not of Spanish, cooking. The Spanish name could have been explained by a Mexican origin, but the only persons who deny that provenance more vehemently than the Texans, who claim credit for it, are the Mexicans, who deny paternity with something like indignation. One Mexican dictionary even goes so far as to define chili con carne as "a detestable food with a false Mexican title which is sold in the United States from Texas to New York." Texas to New York covers a lot of ground, but chili con carne does make it, in cans, whose contents Texans often refuse to recognize as representing the dish fairly. Canners often put beans, lots of them, in what they sell as chili con carne, since beans are cheaper than meat; beans in chili make Texans see red. This dish is believed to have been invented in the city of San Antonio some time after the Civil War; it grew in favor after the development of chili powder in New Braunfels in 1902 (by a German, incidentally, a spicy ingredient in the melting pot). (One also hears with apprehension that cuteness has crept in; at least one chili con carne maker puts out his product labeled One-Alarm, Two-Alarm and Three-Alarm, depending on the intensity of its chili-generated heat, and even one version called False Alarm, which has no chili in it at all.)

Although Texas has annexed the credit for the particular type of cooking found along the Mexican frontier, Arizona may get closer to the Mexican formula than Texas. The cooking of Arizona, indeed, is so closely linked to that of Mexico that its Tex-Mex food not only leans heavily on the Mex component in general, but even on a specific type of Mexican regional cooking—that of the state of Sonora, which is just across the border. Sonora is wheat-growing country, so Arizona tends to make *tortillas de harina,* wheat tortillas, instead of using Indian corn, more common in the rest of Mexico. Sonoran food is less violently spiced than that of most of the other Mexican states; Arizona goes in for comparatively mild chilies, which it grows itself along the border. One dish that Arizona borrowed from Sonora deserves special mention, a soup containing tripe, green chilies, onions, and mint called *munodo:* it is good for hangovers.

If Tex-Mex food is more specialized in Arizona, it is more widespread in New Mexico, largely because Arizona today has few descendants of the old families of the Mexican era, but New Mexico has many of them. They call themselves Spanish-Americans and maintain the culinary traditions of the past, including many dishes more Spanish than Mexican; they reached the United States via Mexico, but were introduced to Mexico by the Spaniards, who seem to have been particularly prone to importing desserts. There are anise-flavored cookies which appear especially during the Christmas season; of the two kinds of anise in the world, one is a native of Egypt and the Near East, the other of China: the Aztecs did not have anise and they did not have Christmas either. The little hot breads called *sopapillas* are served with a sauce containing cinnamon, a favorite spice of Spain. Cinnamon is used too in *capirotada,* Spanish bread pudding, which is sometimes enlivened with a shot of brandy or, less authentically, of whiskey; it then becomes *capirotada borracha,* drunken bread pudding. The baked pudding called *panocha,* however, is a genuinely Indian dessert, although it gets a dash of cinnamon today, an innovation after the Spaniards arrived. That it is basically Aztec is marked by the fact that it is made from sprouted wheat. Sprouting wheat makes it sweeter; the Indians used this means of sweetening their desserts because, until the Spaniards came, they had no sugar.

Despite the competition of Arizona and New Mexico, Texas remains the state where the most Tex-Mex food is found, if only because it is so much bigger. Texans are given to boasting about how hot they like their chilies, an addiction to explosively spiced food being apparently a test of he-manship. Indeed Texans go so far as to seek out a spice even hotter than chili, which its original users, the Indians, seem to have abandoned with a sigh of relief when it ceased to be necessary. In pre-Columbian times, the Indians made a fiery powder from a red berry called the *chiletepín,* with which they coated buffalo jerky to preserve it; they were careful to wash off as much of it as they could before venturing to eat the jerky. Texans today deliberately gather these berries wild and use them in a sauce guaranteed to make the hair curl.

In their pursuit of stronger flavors, Texans also eat a dish which many Americans regard with the utmost distrust—kid. Actually kid is tastier and has more character than lamb, which Texans disdain, though whether primarily as trenchermen or as cattlemen it is difficult to say (they refer to lamb chops contemptuously as "wool on a stick"). Kid is one of the meats which can be cooked by a technique to which Texans seem to have decided they hold the copyright, though it has been highly developed in places as diverse as Greece and Mongolia, Sardinia and India. In the United States, its existence has sometimes been attributed to the example of the American Indian, and it may indeed have been from the Indians that the Virginians, during the first century of white settlement in their area, picked up the idea of barbecuing pigs or large fish—sturgeons, for instance. Turtle barbecues were popular in eighteenth-century New York. Acadians go in for barbecues too, which may account for the picturesque theory that the word comes from the French *barbe à queue,* "from whiskers to tail," evoking the image of an animal roasted whole. As a matter of fact Acadians, nowadays at least, though they barbecue meat in great chunks, do not go in for animals entire. ("Dudes!" one might imagine Texans snorting scornfully, but you would not be likely to find a whole steer roasting at a Texas barbecue either in these effete times—nor be put to the virile ordeal of spooning the brains directly out of a barbecued calf's head, as you might have been invited to do fifty years ago. Calves' or steers' heads are still prized dishes at Texas barbecues, but they are not usually set entire on the table.) A more probable derivation of "barbecue" is from *barbacoa,* usually presented as a Spanish word, though the

Spaniards probably picked it up from the Arawak Indians. It meant, in any case, the green-wood grills which the Indians set up over holes dug in the ground in which smoked heated stones or the embers of a fire which had been allowed to burn down to its glowing coals, over which they cooked game or fish. Whether the word was originally Indian or Spanish, it passed into English via Spanish, thus partly justifying the proprietary attitude adopted toward the barbecue by once-Spanish Texas.

"Barbecue" is a noun, a verb, an adjective, and in Texas it can be a major social event, as it was whenever the late President Lyndon B. Johnson called in Walter Jetton to prepare one of his barbecues at the LBJ Ranch on the Pedernales River. Chef Jetton presided over the wood fires in the roasting pits, the charcoal fires in the shallower broiling pits, and the Dutch ovens where the beans were simmering, with the East Texas hot-guts (a spicy sausage) ready near by. Accessory foods like steamed ears of corn, potato salad, spicy cole slaw, pickles, sliced onions, and sourdough biscuits were at hand for loading the big tin plates after the basic meats were served by the cooks who sliced them hot and doused them with barbecue sauce. No Texas barbecue is authentic unless *two* sauces figure in its presentation. The first is the "sop" or "mop" which is essentially a marinade, applied to the meat before and during cooking, often with a small string kitchen mop, hence the name. A typical sop might contain beef-bone stock, salt, mustard, garlic, chili powder, paprika, bay leaf, hot pepper sauce, Worcestershire, vinegar oil, and (alas!) monosodium glutamate; this sauce is lavishly used in basting the meat, and may be saved from one barbecue to another (and from one kind of meat to another), growing stronger and more flavorful as it matures. The second sauce, called "barbecue sauce," is served apart, for splashing over the meat (in this case called "the barbecue," whether it be beef, veal, pork, lamb, goat, or poultry), and is never used in cooking. Jetton's formula contains tomato ketchup, cider vinegar, sugar, chili powder, salt, water, chopped celery, bay leaves, garlic, chopped onion, butter, Worcestershire, paprika, and black pepper, all brought to a boil and simmered briefly, then cooled and served.

San Antonio can supply greater choice for the restaurant diner than most American cities. In 1840, thanks to an influx of German immigrants, there were beer gardens on the banks of the San Antonio River; as the former capital city of the Mexican province of *Tejas* it was flamboyantly Spanish in architecture and manners, and today there is nearly a third of the city's population which is of Spanish or Mexican descent and loyal to their ancestral eating habits. Restaurants catering to this clientele go far beyond the usual Tex-Mex cuisine and offer authentic Mexican dishes not found elsewhere north of the Rio Grande. In the markets of San Antonio, which is a truck-gardening center shipping produce to Dallas and Fort Worth, Mexican stores sell the *metates* and *manos,* mortars and pestles made of stone for grinding corn for tortillas and such; *molcajetes* for milling spices and *molinillos* for preparing foamy chocolate are on display, while candy men, their trays on their heads, peddle sweets made of cactus, sweet potatoes, pecans, and sugar. At sidewalk stands, women offer warm *tortillas, tamales* and *tacos.* Perhaps a pair of guitarists wander busking among the shoppers. From the nearby military establishments, young airmen ask the way to Matamoros Street, notorious in the days when San Antonio was a wide-open town.

Residents of San Antonio often entertain guests from the north by giving them a cocktail party on one of the launches which ply the San Antonio River; a *mariachi* group of Mexican musicians provides entertainment for the boating party. In San Antonio the two cultures, Spanish-Mexican and Anglo-American, seem to have merged more happily than in other cities of the Southwest, despite the massacre of three hundred citizens by Don Joaquin Arredondo on August 20, 1813, and the bloody siege of the Alamo in February and March of 1836, both events ever in the memory of Texans.

Tex-Mex food might be described as native foreign food, contradictory though that term may seem. It is native, for it does not exist elsewhere; it was born on this soil. But it is foreign in that its inspiration came from an alien cuisine; that it has never merged into the mainstream of American cooking and remains alive almost solely in the region where it originated; and that, above all, when an American from any other part of the country enters its territory and makes acquaintance with it, it *feels* foreign to him.

Edge eastward from the realm of Tex-Mex cooking and you will find yourself confronted at once by another example of native foreign food—Creole cooking.

Creole cooking is that of a melting pot, but not the general American melting pot. It is a mixture of French, African, Indian, and Spanish cuisines, cheerfully unconscious of the very existence of Anglo-Saxon cooking. It was put together partly on the mainland and partly in the West Indies, whose populations are also made up chiefly of the descendants of Frenchmen, Africans, Indians, and Spaniards; its islands transmitted their own particular amalgams to America's Gulf Coast.

No regional cuisine in America has received so much attention, practically all of it complimentary, as the Creole cuisine found at its best in New Orleans and in the neighboring Teche country of Louisiana, and in modified form the length of the coast.

In trying to put together the culinary jigsaw puzzle and to trace its origins we should not overlook the presence of Chinese and East Indians, imported as free labor after the British, French, and Dutch abolished slavery, decades earlier than the United States, nor forget that the French and Spanish refugees who fled the islands during the slave uprisings brought some of their household mulattoes, with their many skills, to add to the already French tradition of New Orleans, where finally the whole complex skein was to come together in what was certainly North America's first gastronomic statement.

Of the varied ethnic groups which cooperated in creating Creole cooking, the French, the last to arrive, are generally accorded the major share of the credit, which they probably deserve (but perhaps not quite as exclusively as many persons think). The first contributors to Creole cooking were of course the Indians. The Spanish arrived second, and the Negroes probably third, for slavery had already become well established before the Acadians, driven out of Canada and Nova Scotia, reached what with their aid was to become Creole territory in the second half of the eighteenth century. The greater visibility of the Acadians accounts for the remark, in a generally knowledgeable book about Creole cooking: "Among the finest, and certainly the most famous [of Acadian dishes] is jambalaya," which is rather unkind, for while the Acadians have endowed this territory with any number of dishes for which they can be given credit, jambalaya is almost the only one which can be claimed by the Spaniards. It is easily recognizable by anyone familiar with Spanish cooking as a form of *paella.*

Another dish often credited solely to the Acadians, or Cajuns as they are now called, might be described more exactly as an excellent example of the way in which the various separate cuisines of the Caribbean region have merged to create Creole cooking, a new gastronomic style. This is the fish chowder still called in Louisiana by the French name of *bouillabaisse.*

Every country with a shoreline has some sort of fish or shellfish stew, call it *bouillabaisse,* call it *zuppa di pesce,* call it *chowder,* but only Louisiana has discovered and perfected the gumbos, fish dishes thickened either with okra, an import from Africa brought in by slaves, or with *filé,* made by pounding sassafras leaves with a pestle of black gum wood and drying them in the oven, or in the sun, as the Choctaw Indians did. (The powder is added to the gumbo only after all boiling has stopped, it should be noted.) Neither okra nor *filé* is an impressive ingredient taken on its own; okra pods must be young and tender if they are to be eaten as a vegetable; if too old or badly cooked they are either slimy or stringy, and at best need some accompanying flavor, while *filé* has only a secondary use as a medicinal tea of dubious efficacity. In gumbos, any sort of fish, shellfish, frogs' legs, or even poultry or turtle meat, may be used, though *gumbo z'herbes* has only greens or tender herbs, no flesh or fish, and is traditionally served on Maundy Thursday. A bowl of any gumbo, with its accompanying rice, is a unique treat in taste and texture, and there are as many variations as Louisiana has parishes or as New Orleans has restaurants.

New Orleans *bouillabaisse,* though French in name and largely French in inspiration, is nevertheless a hybrid creation, for it contains both *filé* powder and gumbo, alias okra. *Bouillabaisse* is thus an apt symbol of the synthesis of diverse elements which have fused so harmoniously in many other dishes so well that Cajuns are loath to admit that their originals came from elsewhere. Many of them are convinced that such creations as *pompano en papillotte* (the fish cooked in a paper envelope also containing a *velouté* sauce of crabmeat, shrimp, mushrooms, white wine and cream or bechamel) were actually first invented in their city, not in Paris. They will concede that Marseilles has priority for *bouillabaisse,* but may honestly claim that the New Orleans version, based on a variety of fresh fish lightly cooked and a mixture of spices, represents a new incarnation of this famous dish, whose merits are such that Louisiana may justly claim it as its own. One of the persons it impressed was William Makepeace Thackeray, who wrote of it:

> This Bouillabaisse a noble dish is—
> A sort of soup, or broth, or stew,
> Of hotch-potch of all sort of fishes,
> That Greenwich never could outdo;
> Green herbs, red peppers, mussels, saffron,
> Soles, onions, garlic, roach, and dace:
> All these you eat at Terre's Tavern
> In that one dish of Bouillabaisse.

Creole *bouillabaisse,* remarkably, does not give the impression of a hodgepodge, of a mosaic put together from the rags and tatters of more or less unrelated cuisines. It is thus a perfect representative of the Creole cuisine, which has become more than the sum of all its parts. Somehow the magic of the bayou country has cast a spell over the disparate components contributed by the distinct ethnic groups which lived there, blending them into a cuisine of distinctive character. Creole cooking is no longer a borrowing, it is a cuisine with a soul all its own, harmonious and consistent. This triumph must have been achieved little by little, accretion after accretion, as each successive wave of conquerors or refugees reached the propitious territory of the Mississippi delta.

The French settlers arrived in two main waves, the Acadians driven out of the north by English Protestants in the 1750s and 1760s and the aristocrats fleeing the Terror twenty or thirty years later. Many of the richer emigrés, coming from France after the Revolution of 1789, seeking refuge where they knew they would find countrymen speaking their own language and descended from their own culture, even though they were of a class considerably more humble, or fleeing the West Indies as a result of slave revolts, were able to bring with them some of their favorite domestic servants and a taste for the best in food and drink. The Acadians were on the whole a poorer, sterner lot, having come from Normandy and Brittany to the piney barrens of Nova Scotia, where they barely managed to survive prior to their eviction, recounted by Longfellow in *Evangeline.* To them the rich Louisiana bottom lands of LaFourche and Teche (from an Indian word *tenche,* snake), with its bayous teeming with fish and crustaceans, its woods and swamps full of game from bear to squirrels, was the eighteenth-century equivalent of striking oil; it changed the Cajun character almost completely. Though they remained as devoutly Catholic as they had ever been, they became gayer, more boisterous, fond of sports, and fond of drinking.

When the Acadians settled into their new homes in Louisiana's Embayment, as the ever-varying maze of slow-flowing tributaries and brackish inlets is sometimes called, they found that the Indians of the Choctaw and Chickasaw tribes had much to teach them in simple gastronomy. For one thing, the Indians considered the black bear a primary food source, and the Cajuns accordingly ate bear too, and still do when they can get it. Today the Louisiana black bear is close to becoming an endangered species, though from time to time bear meat turns up on the New Orleans market, and Creole cookbooks provide explicit instructions for hanging and marinating bear meat, which is then usually braised slowly in stock or in the marinade itself.

By the time the Acadians arrived, there was another variety of big game in fair supply, the wild boar. This was no native of the Mississippi delta, but a European pig brought to America by the Spanish explorer Hernando de Soto. De Soto landed near what is now Tampa in 1542 with thirteen porkers in his supply train, and although other explorers and settlers of the American South brought pigs which eventually ran wild, Louisianians like to think of their wild boar as having a true Creole ancestry, that is to say, in this case, Spanish, with no native intermixture. There would be a native intermixture later, when pigs of a more domestic nature escaped from the plantations of the English-speaking Atlantic coast and mated with the Spanish stock, which no doubt possessed the seductiveness of Latinity and savagery.

Still plentiful throughout Louisiana is the white-tailed deer, and the principal New Orleans restaurants prepare it well in a number of ways, but one cannot say that it is an essentially Creole food, though the idea of braising it in bear's grease, Choctaw fashion, is purely local.

Louisiana claims to have nearly seventeen million acres of forest land, some of it marshy, and there is an abundant population of muskrats, squirrels, and rabbits, plus two kinds of raccoon, the dark timberland animal and the salt-water yellow 'coon of the wetlands, which is now a protected animal in most of the State. Any or all of these are eligible for inclusion in that famous Southern stew, *burgoo,* popular at barbecues and picnics. The Acadians were familiar with rabbit, which they had eaten in France and in Nova Scotia, but the muskrat, or marsh hare, may well have given them pause. Nowadays the preferred recipes for muskrat involve boiling the meat until it separates from the bones, which are removed, and presenting it in a thick sauce savorous with mustard, egg yolks, and sherry.

Opossum and raccoon are prepared for the most part as they are throughout the South, parboiled and roasted with yams, or marinated and baked, but the Louisiana touch is the addition of garlic and available herbs. These are back-country dishes, not likely to turn up in any restaurant in the cities. Nor are any of the squirrel stews to be found on town menus, though the Cajuns look forward to sampling them at country picnics, fairs, and camp meetings. Perhaps an exception should be made for "squirrel ravioli," prepared in the usual Italian way with minced squrrel meat, sautéed with garlic and bacon fat and lightened with spinach or watercress, as the stuffing.

When it comes to feathered game, Louisiana has perhaps the most favored situation of any state in the Union. Although its wild non-migrant fowl are few, they are varied in nature. The wild turkey is hunted enthusiastically by Cajuns and visiting sportsmen, as is the bobwhite quail the French-speaking hunters call *perdreau.* Bayou people have traditionally hunted the mourning dove, which in most of the nation enjoys protection under state game laws, but owes its survival in Louisiana, perhaps, to a superstition that it is bad luck to shoot one when it is on the ground. The Cajuns have not been handicapped by any other British traditions of shooting, and since the earliest days have hunted down the tasty bobolink, known to gourmets the world over as the *ortolan,* which when cooked is usually crunched head, bones and all. In the Delta region the prize bird to shoot is the snipe *(bécassine),* which frequents the marshes and is famed for its evasive flight pattern when flushed. In the somewhat drier pine woods a lucky shooter may find the snipe's cousin, the woodcock *(bécasse),* a bird with nocturnal habits of feeding.

Hardier, or hungrier, back-country Louisianians occasionally seek coot and rail (generally known as "mud hens") and cook them with special precautions to rid them of their strong taste, soaking them in lemon juice and necessarily skinning them since the skin contains an evil smelling oil which protects the bird from the damp, but does nothing for gourmets. They are hardly worth the effort, particularly since the same regions of tidewater and marsh are annually visited by thousands of migrant geese and ducks which find their way down the Mississippi Flyway each year, some to stay and winter in the Delta, others to continue on to South America after days of feeding and rest. Mallard, teal, and pintail are featured in many recipes attributed to the kitchens of the great plantations which once bordered the Mississippi and its estuaries, vast houses built in the Greek Revival style of the first half of the nineteenth century, when sugarcane production made the fortunes of Creoles and settlers from the North alike. Every relation of the origins of Creole cuisine stresses the importance of the *roux,* the mixture of fat and flour so basic to all French cooking, the addition of liquor from the stock-pot (which might have its foundation of meat, fish, shellfish, or poultry, or some combination of these) and then the all-important herbs and spices. Rice, of course, is the preferred starch of the southern parishes, while corn bread in various forms is favored in the North.

French is the language of cooking in Louisiana. In other states, French names appear on the menus seemingly to intimidate, but in Louisiana they are part of the normal language. Terms like *daube glacée, bisque d'écrevisses, gâteau aux fraises, sauce piquante, étouffée, beignets,* and *pain perdu* (lost bread, otherwise French toast) are household words in Creole country. Delicatessens (or *charcuteries)* offer *fromage de tête de cochon* (head cheese) and sausages with names like *ponce* (stuffed pig's stomach), *boudin, chaudin* and *andouille,* of which the last proclaims its French origin by nature as well as by name—the sausage stuffing is not ground, American style, but made of cubed meat as in France; as in France too, *andouille* is hot with spices, but the Creole version reduces its pepperiness by basting it with sugarcane syrup during the smoking process. A sausage called *chaurisse* sounds French, but it is probably a corruption of *chorizo,* the small-caliber dark red hotly spiced Spanish sausage which may therefore constitute, with jambalaya, the total overt Spanish contribution to Creole cooking.

A large proportion of the Acadians came originally from Normandy, where it is the habit, in the middle of a heavy meal, to toss down a slug of Calvados, the renowned Norman *eau-de-vie* made from apples, on the theory that it will burn a hole in the stomach's contents and make room for more. The Cajuns do the same thing with applejack, but there it is no longer the *trou normand,* the Norman hole, as in France, but the *coup de milieu,* the mid-time swallow. The end of the meal brings *café brûlot.* If you drink milk punch, you are gratified with a Cajun joke—it is called *la suissesse,* the Swiss woman. All this is pure French, but it can sometimes happen that this language comes into collision with English, with slightly comic effect—for instance, if a Cajun housewife is confronted with unexpected guests and has hastily to improvise something out of nothing to feed them, what does she call her improvisation? Why, *le make-do,* of course.

In New Orleans, native gourmets will tell a visitor that if he wants the ideal Creole dishes he must go to the bayou country, where at some legendary inn on the water's edge, perhaps in Terrebonne parish, or LaFourche or Plaquemines, gumbo will have surpassing freshness, crabs will have been cooked in a magical broth of fresh herbs, and the jambalaya will be made with oysters gathered that very morning. This verges on sheer fantasy for the average visitor, for unless some native Louisianian is there to guide him to such an establishment he will never find it, and if he does, he may be disappointed in that his *aubergiste* was not sufficiently forewarned, or that the crawfish are not in season, and so he may have to make do with the *plat du jour.* This will probably be a good, spicy dish, perhaps a pompano, snapper, or even a flounder plainly cooked, with rice, beans, or a vegetable combined with herbs as the *garniture,* but it will not be what he had hoped for.

Such an excursion will at least get you into crawfish country.

Louisiana catches more crawfish (alias crayfish, crawdads, bay crabs, freshwater crabs, freshwater lobsters, creekcrabs, yabbies, or mudbugs) than any other area of equal size in the world—eighteen million to twenty million pounds a year—and consumes four-fifths of them itself. The town of Breaux Bridge (population five thousand) has been dubbed Crawfish Capital of the World, which will surprise Nantua, France, if it ever hears about it. Breaux Bridge is in the Atchafalaya basin, which crawls with crawfish; the town holds a crawfish festival every other year, including a crawfish eating contest and a crawfish race, in which the penchant of the crawfish for setting off in unpredictable directions has been outwitted by designing the race course in the form of a circular target, with starting gate at the bull's-eye and the finish line at no matter what point on the circumference. Between festivals, Louisianans fall back on crawfish picnics in season, preferably under a full moon, hold gay and messy indoor "crawfish boils," or enjoy cornucopias of boiled crawfish bought from street vendors to eat *al fresco.*

A kindred specialty of Louisiana, though not an exclusive one, for it is shared all along the coast to Florida and then northward up the coast into Chesapeake Bay, is that great American delicacy, the soft-shell crab—usually the blue crab, though the term applies to no particular species but only to a crab at the molting period, when, having split and crawled out of its old hard shell, it is for a few days or hours sheathed only in a yielding skinlike covering, so that it can be eaten *in toto,* softened "shell" and all. Lake Pontchartrain is good crab territory, but the bayou country is even better. Crabs are caught near molting season and caged in submerged boxes along the shore, where they are kept under stern surveillance. The boxes are checked daily to spot any crabs which show signs of being about to shed their shells. When they do, they are nicknamed "peelers" and transferred into another box, visited oftener. When the crucial moment seems imminent, those crabs which are in the most interesting condition are moved once more, into the box of "busters," which is inspected four times a day; as soon as the crabs emerge from their shells they are fished out of the water and whisked away to market.

A Louisianan author has described his state as divided into the North, land of Anglo-Saxons, Germans, and similar non-Latin types; the South, where the French and Spanish descendants of the immigrants from Europe and the West Indies are, with the transported Acadian French, the dominant stock, and the City, by which he means New Orleans. These divisions prevail today. The North, by contrast with the other two, has a more austere, less rollicking approach to life—and to cookery—but it does not divorce itself from Creole cuisine. It just doesn't practice it the way the South does, not for any lack of good ingredients, for there are fine fish and river shrimp to take the place of seafood from the Delta; but there is more restraint in the use of herbs and spices, and less improvisation. We might put it: less of the Latin spirit.

Alabama, or more exactly the region around Mobile Bay, is in a way more French even than Louisiana, for the Spaniards were less successful in hanging on there than the French were. It was in 1702 that the French founded the settlement of Fort Louis de la Tribu Mauville, which by attrition became Mobile, and two years after that it was the site of an event which had an appreciable effect on eating in that area. This was the arrival of twenty-three young women described as *filles du roi,* daughters of the King, a designation not to be taken too literally. All it meant was that Louis XIV had sponsored their trip from France to provide wives for his distant but loyal subjects. The ship on which they arrived was named for a legendary symbol of maternal devotion, the Pelican; and the sort of conduct the King expected from his wards may be deduced from the fact that the box of useful objects he provided for each contained a rosary and a set of needles. The records do not tell us how skillful the girls were at needlework, but they were keenly interested in another feminine domain, the kitchen. They protested against a diet composed exclusively of game, fish and whatever could be gathered wild in the forests. Their husbands obediently set to work to clear the ground and till the soil. Under the inspiration of these handmaidens of Venus and of Ceres, agriculture was born on the shores of Mobile Bay and the gastronomic resources of the region improved.

Two years after the arrival of the brides-to-be at Mobile, the experiment was repeated in Louisiana when a group of young Frenchwomen was shipped to New Orleans, then a mere outpost (Biloxi was the first capital), by the Normandy-based Bishop of Quebec at the request of the Sieur de Bienville, who felt his soldier-colonists would be more contented if they had wives. The girls protested at the monotonous local diet of corn, the mainstay of their ordinary, and demanded wheaten bread such as they were used to in Paris, whence most of them had come. Their protest to the Governor was not wholly in vain, though no wheat was available, for he turned them over to his own housekeeper, one Madame Langlois. This worthy woman, an Acadian, had learned a number of ways of preparing the native foods from squaws of the friendly Choctaw tribe. She is said to have taught the brides how to grind corn into meal, and to make corn bread, as well as the art of bleaching corn into hominy or grits. Today Madame Langlois is credited with having brought *filé,* the sassafras powder, into the Creole culinary vocabulary, having borrowed it from the Indians.

In the neighborhood of Mobile Bay traces of French still remain in the culinary vocabulary, for instance High Holy Mayonnaise. Nothing could sound more irreverently American, but this actually represents an attempt by Anglo-Saxons to pronounce *ailloli,* the French word for garlic-flavored mayonnaise, still a specialty of this part of Alabama. Though it has nothing to do with foreign contributions to American cooking, may we be permitted, while we are on the shores of Mobile Bay, to shed a tear for one of America's great shellfish, the Bon Secour oyster (again a French name, albeit misspelled), which once supported scores of oyster bars ringing the Bay? Few oyster beds have survived the discharge of industrial wastes into the water.

In today's Florida also, foreign strains persist. The Spanish contribution, as in Louisiana, was minimal, and so was that of the next outlanders, who arrived in 1767. There were 1,500 of them, who were settled at New Smyrna to produce indigo and were referred to as "the Minorcans." Some of them actually did come from the Spanish Balearic island of Minorca, but there were also Greeks and Italians among them. Their descendants are still there and they are still called Minorcans by other Floridians, but they do not seem to have contributed to the regional cuisine. This was not the case for another influx of immigrants, who did import a native cuisine to which they remained faithful on the alien soil of Florida. These foreigners were Greek sponge fishermen who made their home at Tarpon Springs, near Tampa. They still support a Greek Orthodox church and call their favorite foods by their Hellenic names. Here you will find that semi-liquid appetizer, half dip, half spread, known to everyone familiar with the Near East, compounded from olive oil and eggplant, here called *melanzane.* The Greeks regale themselves on the characteristic goat cheese of their country, *feta,* and sip the pale but powerful anise-flavored apéritif, *ouzo.* Their example did not seep into the surrounding territory to modify or enrich Florida cooking.

It is the latest wave of immigrants which has had the most impact on Florida's food and oddly enough what they have added to it is an element it should have had from the beginning, but missed the first time around—the Spanish touch. This is now being provided, on the rebound, by the thousands of political exiles who have poured in from Cuba, bringing with them a thirst for *café Cubano,* a hunger for black beans and rice, and a disinclination to abandon Cuban culinary traditions. Cuban food is basically Spanish, more so than Tex-Mex cooking, though it has inevitably picked up some Indian and Negro overtones during its evolution on its island. It seems probable that this school of cooking will become a permanent addition to non-American American cuisines, if only because of the large number of Cuban immigrants now established with every appearance of permanence in Florida. They may be expected to preserve their native cuisine in their new home because, like the Tarpon Springs Greeks, they stay together.

Today there are two kinds of "Spanish" restaurants in Florida—those which pile on a spurious Old Spanish atmosphere in the dining room (to make up, one suspects, for an absence of color in the kitchen) and offer a menu dripping with Spanish names representing dishes which are usually spurious too; and Cuban restaurants, which have multiplied in the last few years to serve the newcomers.

What Tampa calls "Cuban sandwiches" are made of Cuban-type bread, sliced open and filled overpoweringly with ham, pork, sausage, cheese, and dill pickles. Street vendors offer deviled crab, hotly spiced, the way Cubans like it. *Verzada* is a thick vegetable (beans, potatoes, onions, greens) and pork (ham, bacon, blood pudding) soup. Favorite appetizers are *bollitos,* little deep-fried balls of black-eyed peas and garlic creamed together. The classic Spanish chicken with rice *(arroz con pollo)* is necessarily a fixture in Cuban restaurants. *Alcaporado* is beef stew highlighted by raisins and olives, and *bolichi,* a specialty of Key West, is beef wrapped around hard-boiled eggs.

French influence did not seep over into Florida from Louisiana and Alabama. Florida did attract a few illustrious early French citizens, but they arrived as individuals and exerted no influence on the local cooking. Indeed the most illustrious among them did not arrive at all, but entered Florida history only as an absentee landlord. This was no less a personage than the Marquis de Lafayette, to whom a grateful if tardy Congress voted in 1824 the sum of $200,000 and a township—a unit of land roughly six miles square—to be chosen from part of the unsold public domain; he picked Florida. In 1831 he arranged for about fifty Norman peasants to settle on his property, which was near Tallahassee, where they were supposed to cultivate vineyards, plant olive trees, and start a silkworm industry based on mulberry trees. Not surprisingly the colony failed, since none of these projects was suited to northern Florida, and Normans are no great shakes at tending grapevines anyway; but the Marquis, who never actually saw his property, sold the land for $103,000 and thus came out of the deal more advantageously than a good many later acquirers of Florida real estate.

Another highly placed French immigrant actually took up residence in Florida personally—Achille Murat, nephew of Napoleon Bonaparte, son of Joachim Murat, and bearer of the title of Crown Prince of the Kingdom of Naples, of which his father was King until an unfortunate sequence of events led him to face a firing squad on the very day his brother-in-law, the Emperor, debarked at St. Helena.

Having heard of the charms of Florida, Prince Murat rented a small house with a garden, bought himself a slave, hired another free servant, and found that he could live nicely and entertain at dinner once a week for about one hundred dollars a month. A couple of months later he found a plantation that pleased him where the Matanzas River and Moses Creek met. There were 1,200 acres, for which he paid under two thousand dollars, and with it acquired eight field slaves, a female cook and two Negro children. At Parthenope, as the place was called, the principal crop was sugar cane, but it also grew tobacco, cotton, oranges, and other fruits. Murat had the aid of a good neighbor, Joseph Hernandez, who shared his considerable knowledge of agriculture with him; a Minorcan, Hernandez, who must have sprung from that 1767 colony of indigo cultivators, later became the first Florida territorial delegate to the United States. We may hope for the sake of his reputation that the influence he exercised on Prince Murat was solely agricultural, not gastronomic, for Murat set a somewhat original table, serving alligator steaks, roast crows and boiled owls. He was not an admirer of his Floridian neighbors, whom he described as "not very industrious." He observed also that the white traders cheated the Indians, corrupted them by selling them guns and liquor, infiltrated their culture by imposing on them such modern folderols as blankets, and in many cases swindled them out of their lands—not the last time that land swindling would be heard of in Florida.

One wave of outlanders which washed into Florida, or at least into Florida's farthest extremity, Key West, cannot be set down as bringing with it a foreign influence, for it was made up of persons committed to the same culinary tradition as other Americans, that of England. The first Key Westers were Britishers, fiercely individualistic inhabitants of the Bahamas who slipped across to the Keys before Florida became part of the United States, swearing that before they would pay what they considered unjust and excessive British taxes they would "eat conch." This does not seem to have been meant as a compliment to the conch, but eat conch they did, and discovered that they liked it. They are still eating it, and take no offense at their nickname, "the conchas."

The conch (pronounced "conk") is a spiral-shelled marine gastropod which tastes like an exotic type of clam, sweet, and reminiscent of the sea. With rare exceptions, it is eaten only in Florida, and even there chiefly in the gastronomic enclave of Key West. The southernmost city of the United States, Key West is the terminal point of an archipelago of twenty-five islands and their satellite islets which swings in a flat curve southwest from the tip of the peninsula. The Keys are the only truly tropical area of the United States, with a climate which might have given them a unique fauna and flora, and consequently one more special cuisine, if they had covered more area and had been blessed with more water. The defect of the area in this latter is underlined by the name of some of the islands which prolong the Keys, the Dry Tortugas. "Tortugas" of course means "turtles," once plentiful off Florida, and an occasional specimen is still sighted off the Keys; but as a rule a Floridian who wants to taste turtle must settle for the artificially raised animals of which the Cayman Islands are now making a specialty. Imported alive, these turtles are kept until wanted in stockades constructed in the water along the shore, known to the untutored as "crawls" and to the more sophisticated as "kraals." The word and the idea were borrowed three centuries ago from the Dutch of Curaçao and Surinam.

Turtle is tough, and so is conch; the usual way of dealing with either of them is to pound it into submission, as California does with abalone. However Nature, which often manages such things well, has provided a natural tenderizer on the spot where it is needed. Conch becomes more malleable if marinated in the juice of the Key lime, a fruit which grows here alone—especially if it has been allowed to ferment, in which case it is usually converted wickedly into a lethal liquid known as Old Sour. The ordinary lime grows in southern Florida too, where it is called the Persian lime. It is, as a lime ought to be, bright green outside with yellow flesh inside. The Key lime perversely reverses this color scheme; being yellow, it is often taken for a lemon, but when cut open its pulp shows a distinctly greenish tinge. It is smaller than ordinary limes, juicier, and has a flavor sharper and more assertive.

The conch is only eaten in Florida though it is found elsewhere; but the bivalve known as the amber pen shell is not found elsewhere in the United States. It is the only true pen shell in American waters; what are called, in Florida, and in their case also as far north as the Carolinas, the stiff pen shell and the saw-toothed pen shell are imposters. If, wading over a mixed sand and mud bottom, a habitat dear to pen shells true or false, you cut your foot, the chances are good that you have found a pen shell; a nastily disposed bivalve, it has a habit of lying just under the surface, sharp edges up. Pen shells have a single strong muscle, like scallops, so they are often sold as scallops. It is not a particularly reprehensible substitution, for the pen shell is sweet and tasty.

Every visitor to Florida encounters the coquina, though not necessarily in a culinary context. Its small shells, adorned with such a variety of gay colors and diverse patterns that it is difficult to find two that are alike, are pounced upon by owners of souvenir shops. Coquinas, also called pompano clams, calico clams, butterfly shells, or variable wedges, are better decorators for broth, soup or chowder; coquina broth is such a favorite regional dish that you may run across it in restaurants, as well as in private homes, in spite of the fact that you are hardly likely to find this clam on the market, for it is too small—three-fourths of an inch long—to be commercially interesting. Even smaller is the wedge shell, another Florida shellfish which is excellent eating if you are willing to take the trouble of handling a half-inch bivalve.

The coon oyster is a little less Lilliputian, two inches long. This is still too small to interest the market and means that a good deal of labor is required to reap a relatively small quantity of meat, but it is worth the trouble. These little oysters are superb deep-fried in little clusters in a batter of beaten egg and breadcrumbs, and they are also good for soups and stews. A taste for them is shared by the raccoon; this accounts for the name of the shellfish. Coon oysters attach themselves to the roots of mangroves growing at the water's edge; at low tide, when the roots, and the oysters, are exposed, the coons scamper out to feast on them.

The Florida crustacean par excellence is the stone crab, which exists all the way from North Carolina to Texas; but Florida makes a cult of it. Possibly timid crab hunters in other states are afraid of it. Its heavy—and dangerous—claws, peach colored and black tipped, are so prominent and so impressive that they have stamped their image deeply into the Floridian consciousness; as a result those great paired horseshoe-shaped staircases which sweep majestically upward in old Southern plantation manors are called in Florida "crab claws." The body meat of the stone crab is excellent, but it is not eaten—not in Florida, at least. There, gastronomically as well as morphologically, the crab is all claw: it is the only part eaten. Indeed, only *one* of the two claws is eaten. The crab population is maintained by throwing the crab back into the water after one claw has been broken off; he needs the other to defend himself if he is to remain alive and propagate crablets. After two years he has two claws again, having grown a new one to replace the missing member.

Another glory of Florida seafood is the spiny lobster, again not exclusive to the state, but Florida makes more ado about it. The spiny lobster is not a true lobster, like that of New England, but a crustacean of a different character; it prefers warm water, while the genuine lobster likes it cold. In Europe, the lobster appears on the Atlantic Coast, the spiny lobster in the Mediterranean; in America, the lobster revels in the gelid waters of the Labrador Current, the spiny lobster starts in North Carolina, appears all along the Gulf Coast, and turns up again off California. (A favorite way of cooking spiny lobsters in the Florida Keys is to stuff them with chopped fish and heighten their flavor with Key lime juice, but the authors have even more reservations about this treatment than they have about spiny lobsters with garlic. It is hard to improve on the flesh of this crustacean as Nature presents it, particularly by stuffing it with fish of inferior taste; but lime juice is not a bad idea.)

Gulf shrimp, which have risen inordinately in price and in popularity, are the great cash crop for Florida fishermen, who share this wealth with their neighbors from Key West to Mexico. Long gone are the days when humanitarians beseeched Louisiana slave owners not to oblige their field hands to eat shrimp more than a few days a week; in our times a shrimp cocktail (four to six medium shrimp of prawn size, hung on the edge of a glass of hot ketchup or chili sauce) costs the American diner, from coast to coast, what he paid for his whole dinner a decade ago, and has become the standard appetizer to precede the frozen steak, tenderized and micro-wave broiled, with foil-wrapped baked potato and mixed green salad, to which he is profoundly and enthusiastically addicted.

Foreign and exotic certainly is a food otherwise associated especially with Polynesia, considerably downgraded in Florida by being given the not very appetizing name of swamp cabbage. A more appropriate description, the one you are likeliest to see on menus, is palm hearts. It also appears in some luxury restaurants which serve it as "millionaire's salad," for it is necessarily an expensive food; to get at the heart (which is actually the terminal bud), you have to cut down the whole tree which bears it—the sabal palmetto. This tree, one of the smallest of the numerous family of palms, is native not only to the east coast of Florida, but also to the entire Atlantic Coast as far north as North Carolina; but Florida (a palm-conscious state which has chosen the palmetto palm as its official tree) seems to be the only place which sacrifices its sabal palmettos for food.

Although it is in the southern third of Florida that we should find our most markedly foreign foods, the citrus fruits of the center, though no longer confined to Florida, were of course originally foreign too, and indeed the orange remained so for the greater part of the country until the present century. Nevertheless at least one orange grower, probably the first Florida citrus magnate, was already doing well at the end of the eighteenth century with oranges shipped to distant buyers—Jesse Fish, who in 1776 sold 65,000 oranges and two casks of juice to London. The English liked Jesse Fish oranges because they were exceptionally juicy, as Florida oranges still are, which made them ideal for use in mixed drinks. Two years later Fish followed up his oranges with sixteen hogsheads of juice, so he should perhaps be considered as the founder of the Florida orange juice industry. Despite this example, orange production stagnated until the United States acquired Florida in 1821, which gave a fillip to the industry. Orange production increased, but at a leisurely rate, although fast sailing ships were now carrying the fruit up the Atlantic coast to the North; but New York, Philadelphia, and Boston were getting more citrus fruits from the Mediterranean than from Florida, transported by clippers which passed through cooler waters, so that their fruit traveled better; however, losses were still important enough so that oranges remained a luxury, available only to the well-to-do.

Freezing weather is the nightmare of orange growers, but the danger has been slightly attentuated by the development of new varieties of oranges in the United States which are a trifle better attuned to the climate. One of the American oranges born in Florida is the Parson Brown, a popular early-fruiting orange widely grown by many persons who perhaps have no idea why it is so quaintly named. It perpetuates the memory of Nathan L. Brown of Webster, a nineteenth-century preacher whose pulpit income proved less than sufficient; he supplemented it by growing oranges. A mutant appeared in his grove about a hundred years ago, and it was from that tree that all the Parson Brown oranges of today are descended. A more celebrated Florida-developed orange is the Indian River variety, which all by itself rescued the orange-growing industry at least twice. Its first opportunity came on February 8, 1835, when the thermometer dropped to twenty-one degrees below freezing and stayed there for fifty-six hours. All the orange groves of Florida were wiped out except one, the property of a certain Douglas Dummett, whose orchard was strategically placed on the Indian River in a unique mini-climate which proved immune to the freeze. Buds from his trees replenished the Florida orange groves. In the winter of 1894–1895 the cold struck again, twice; the Dummett grove was again almost the sole survivor and became once more the savior of the Florida orange. No doubt the notoriety the Indian Rivers gained from their extraordinary resistance helped make them famous throughout the world, but it was true too that the special climate and soil which saved them had also the effect of making them the sweetest oranges of Florida, and hence the most sought after. Ships were dispatched from Russia especially to carry Indian River oranges to the Czar, and *Blackwood's Edinburgh Magazine* wrote, "The Indian River orange is not to be mentioned in the same breath with ordinary oranges. It is a delicacy by itself, hitherto unknown in the world, and which Spain need never attempt to rival." Oranges from this region still reach the market stamped "Indian River"; special legislation protects the name from being usurped by oranges grown outside the charmed area.

In addition to perishability in transport and vulnerability to frost, another factor retarded the acceptance of the orange—prejudice against a fruit frequently looked upon as a carrier of cholera. On February 18, 1854, the Chicago *Daily Democratic Press* printed an article by a reporter who had been assigned to cover a display of sub-tropical fruits in a local market, and inquired wittily: "Lives there one with taste so dead, who never to 'hisself' hath said, I can't bear to suck an orange?" and answered, "Guess not!"

Orange production increased slightly after the Civil War, when Northerners attracted to Florida by the climate went in for orange growing; one of them was Harriet Beecher Stowe. However, the Mediterranean continued to remain the first furnisher of oranges for the North until the 1880s, when two new developments changed the picture: insulated ships were built, veritable floating ice-boxes, to deliver oranges by sea, and at the same time the railroads began to reach deep into Florida, providing fast land transport for the fruit. The orange industry was flourishing by the 1890s, and in 1894 more than a billion oranges were exported from Florida, before the momentary setback caused by the 1894–1895 freeze. But in spite of this increasing production, it was not until after the First World War, when specially adapted refrigerator cars were devised to carry them, that oranges finally became easily available to every part of the United States. The per capita consumption of oranges, which had been only 6.69 pounds in 1899, doubled to 13.81 in 1919, nearly doubled again to 25.4 pounds in 1931, and in 1939, when food rationing was imposed, oranges were so plentiful that they could be purchased with the free blue stamps issued to the needy. By this time, Florida was growing every member of the orange family, mandarins, tangerines, clementines, sweet oranges, bitter oranges, blood oranges and double blood oranges. "Blood oranges grow well in Florida," wrote John McPhee, "but they frighten American women," possibly the only thing that does.

After the Second World War, the trend was reversed. Until then, the United States rate of consumption of fresh oranges per capita was the highest in the world; in twenty years it dropped 75 percent. What had happened was that Americans abandoned the orange itself for standardized orange juice concentrate, now so thoroughly accepted even in Florida that, with orange trees all around you, you will find it difficult to get fresh orange juice unless you squeeze the fruit yourself. Ask for orange juice in a Florida restaurant and you will get concentrate, as orange juice drinkers do everywhere else in the country.

Florida is orange juice country par excellence, for the Florida orange, generally speaking, is a juice orange, while the California orange is a table orange. According to John McPhee in *The New Yorker* of May 7, 1966, in one of a pair of articles later expanded into a book which covered the subject of oranges so thoroughly that it has become virtually impossible for anyone else to write about them without plagiarizing him:

> An orange grown in Florida usually has a thin and tightly fitting skin, and it is also heavy with juice. Californians say that if you want to eat a Florida orange you have to get into a bathtub first. . . . In Florida, it is said that you can run over a California orange with a ten-ton truck and not even wet the pavement. The differences from which these hyperboles arise will prevail in the two states even if the type of orange is the same. In arid climates, like California's, oranges develop a thick albedo, which is the white part of the skin. Florida is one of the two or three most rained-upon states in the United States. . . . The annual difference in rainfall between the Florida and California orange-growing areas is one million one hundred and forty thousand gallons per acre. For years, California was the leading orange state, but Florida surpassed California in 1942, and grows three times as many oranges now. California oranges, for their part, can safely be called three times as beautiful.

But the appearance of Florida oranges also, when they are designed to reach the ultimate consumer intact, as Indian River oranges do, for instance, is not neglected by their sellers. "Citrus packing houses," Mr. McPhee observed, with Florida in mind, "are more like beauty parlors than processing plants."

Relatively few Florida oranges have escaped the juice plants ("Fresh oranges have become . . . old-fashioned," McPhee has remarked) since the technicians learned to take the constituents of the orange apart and put them back together again in proportions less variable than those of Nature. This preserves, more or less, the nutritive qualities of the fruit when the product is honest, but there are watered juices on the market which advertise, for instance, that they contain "more Vitamin C than orange juice," a deceptive statement, for the joker is that the mixture doesn't contain much orange juice—10 percent perhaps, the rest being sugar and water. Its touted Vitamin C is likely to be synthetic and the Vitamin A found in normal oranges almost completely missing. Floridian producers of orange juice actually made from oranges are presently worried also by the appearance on the market of completely synthetic "orange juice," which has never been nearer to an orange grove than the inside of a chemical factory.

Florida grows every kind of citrus fruit which it is commercially advantageous to grow. Altogether it produces two-thirds of the total United States citrus crop, which accounts for more than one-third of the state's agricultural revenue. Over one-half of the citrus crop is frozen, mostly as juice. Despite this versatility, the orange remains king. Florida's fifteen million orange trees produce over 80 percent of all the oranges grown in the United States (Florida also provides a majority of the tangerines), a yield greater than that of the second, third, and fourth orange producing countries of the world (Spain, Italy, and Mexico) added together. A grateful state has selected the orange blossom as its official flower. For the lemon the situation is the exact opposite. California produces 80 percent of all United States lemons. Florida grows them too, but they do not loom large in her economy.

Almost exclusively Floridian, however, is the lime; the southern part of the state grows almost all the limes eaten in the United States; but Texas has recently begun to produce a few.

However grapefruit production may be divided among the four states which are its chief growers—Florida, California, Texas, and Arizona—Florida must be granted the credit for developing its modern version, whose popularity as an appetizer or a breakfast food is relatively recent. Its ancestor, "the mother of grapefruit," was the pomelo, also called the shaddock because, it seems, a British sea captain named Shaddock first brought its seed from the East Indies to Barbados in 1698. The pomelo was slow to catch on, for it was not particularly admired and was even referred to sarcastically as "the forbidden fruit"—forbidden not by divine fiat but by its own inhospitable nature. Disconcertingly large, pear-shaped, and with a thick loose rind, it was far from juicy and its pulp was coarse; yet from this unpromising beginning the modern grapefruit was developed, almost exclusively in Florida, possibly with the aid of a natural mutation or two. The success of the improved fruit was statistically consecrated when its per capita consumption in the United States rose from 3.86 pounds in 1919 to 8.32 in 1931. Pink grapefruit was created in Bradenton, a little south of Tampa; one wonders why. Experimenters in Florida have now gone back to the source and are seeking to improve the pomelo itself, retaining its pristine form.

After the orange and its fellows, the fruit most persons would be likeliest to associate with Florida is the avocado, or alligator pear. The first person known to have taken it seriously was a horticulturist named George B. Cellon, who, circa 1900, learned by experimentation that grafted trees could be induced to perpetuate superior strains of this fruit in Florida, and to deliver avocados of commercially desirable uniformity in size, appearance and quality. The tree grew well on the light sandy soils of Florida, and an avocado industry was launched in that state, an example followed shortly afterwards by California.

Of the three main varieties of avocado (there are countless sub-varieties) the most determinedly tropical is the West Indian, which can be grown nowhere in the United States except in southern Florida. Taking advantage of this natural monopoly, Florida has concentrated on the West Indian fruit, while California cultivates the hardiest, the Mexican variety. (The third, the Guatemalan, stands midway between the other two.) The Florida tree is quixotic, but never niggardly; year in, year out, an adult tree will yield between forty and eighty pounds of fruit, but every once in a while especially favorable weather produces a bonanza year, multiplying the crop by five or even ten times.

Americans were slow about taking avocados to their hearts, and in its early prudish days their growers dared not advertise the merit which, privately, they considered likely to prove its strongest selling point. A resourceful publicity man found the solution: he had a representative of the avocado raisers' association deny with indignation the false and malicious rumors that the avocado was aphrodisiac. Sales rose.

The list of fruits grown in Florida which no other state can produce is long. Most of them are handled on a small scale, but they are luxury foods which bring high prices because of their rarity. The mango was first planted in Florida in 1889, when only a single variety was available, the Indian *mulgoba;* today Florida grows more than fifty different mangos, some originally imported, some developed on the peninsula itself—among them the red mango, which is red; the green mango, which is green; and the mango, no adjective, which is colorless, or as nearly colorless as a fruit can be: it is an abashed low-keyed gray-violet which seems to be striving for invisibility.

One commercial success is the papaya, a popular breakfast fruit in southern Florida, whose deep-yellow to salmon-colored pulp, slightly sweet with an agreeably musky undertone, reminds many persons of the musk-melon. It is best known outside of the state in the form of juice. The papaya contains papain, the active principle of meat tenderizers. Floridians wrap tough poultry or meat in papaya leaves overnight before serving them.

The food of Florida today might be described, unkindly, as characterized by an overwhelming abundance of raw materials and a rather spectacular absence of good cooking. Even without taking into account the very special types of food available in the state, if we compare what Florida makes of the less unusual fish and vegetables it possesses with what the nations of the Mediterranean littoral have done with the same ingredients, it appears that here is a case of abundance wasted. Nature has always been lavish with Florida, but good Florida cooks have always been rare.

What happened to Florida? What prevented its foods from shaping its cuisine, as foods usually do—which in this case should have created something exotic and, in that sense, foreign? Perhaps it was because Florida was invaded early by that enemy of exoticism, that all-too-American destroyer of anything foreign, strange or imaginative, whose presence has always been disastrous for gastronomy—the booster.

Toward the end of the nineteenth century, a New Jersey horticulturist named John S. Collins, who had been lured south by the enticing prospect of getting rich from Florida's soil and climate, opened up a new source of wealth for the state as a result of failure as a farmer. He missed making his fortune raising coconuts in the 1890s, missed again with avocados at the turn of the century, and finally decided that the real money crop of Florida was not fruit but vacationists. He turned out to be right, but, a sort of Midas in reverse, did not profit personally from his perspicaciousness, for though the small hotel he built on a bare sandpit inhabited by a few out-of-elbow beachcombers prospered, he overexpanded and had to sell out; so it was others who cashed in on Miami Beach. The beachcombers of Palm Beach were somewhat better dressed, for Palm Beach was strategically located where the annual hurricanes drove valuable cargoes ashore from ships which broke up along the coast, but the Florida tourist boom drove the beachcombers away from Palm Beach too, or perhaps it would be more accurate to say that they were replaced by a different type of beachcomber, even better dressed, if not overdressed or underdressed as circumstances might dictate. The change was not appreciated by everybody. Henry James described Palm Beach culture as "a hotel civilization" and Alva Johnston said it was "high life in a boarding-house."

Palm Beach was promoted, or demoted, to this level by some fairly curious characters, for exotic men as well as exotic fruits flourished on the Florida soil. There was, for instance, Colonel E. R. Bradley, who supplied an indispensable element for success by opening a gambling casino, the Beach Club. There was the dynamic self-taught architect Addison Mizner, who, without benefit of diplomas or construction licenses, built some rather sensational homes in a style vaguely Spanish for the millionaires who had begun to wend their way to Florida (the best publicized example was the two-story villa which he forgot to supply with any means of reaching the second story from the first; he tacked a flight of stairs onto the outside of the house, converting an oversight into an innovation). There was General T. Coleman duPont, a leading pacer in the stable Mizner got together to boost the lavishly planned development called Boca Raton (he also acquired the services as a spellbinder of William Jennings Bryan). There was Paris Singer, of the sewing machine Singers, who built what he intended to be a hospital for wounded officers of the First World War; peace disconcertingly broke out, so he turned the hospital into the exclusive Everglades Club. There was Clarence H. Geist, who in 1928 opened in the Boca Raton complex another club so luxurious that despite the stock market crash he was able to charge its members five thousand dollars a year for the privilege of spending as much more as they wanted in the club's facilities.

None of the promoters of touristic Florida seemed likely to turn it in the direction of gastronomic distinction. Paris Singer was a chronically sick man, hardly disposed to the pleasures of the table. General duPont, a somewhat primitive practical joker, thought it made for the success of a meal to serve the guests rubber frankfurters or flannel griddlecakes. Clarence Geist hired famous chefs to turn out for his high-priced club elaborate dishes with which he could not cope himself, because of his chronic dyspepsia. Addison Mizner had stomach ulcers, which he treated by wolfing down huge portions of ice cream slathered with preserved Canton ginger. Many of their more prominent customers symbolized a civilization which could not get along with its food. There was Snider of Snider's Catsup, one of the world's most efficient condiments for smothering all tastes but its own; Adams, the tycoon of chewing gum, a product whose popularity is greatest among people suffering from nutritional deficiencies; Emerson of Bromo Seltzer, who had reaped a fortune from the indigestion of others; and at least two patent-medicine millionaires, Dr. Kilmer the Swamp-Root King, and Dr. Fletcher of Castoria ("Babies cry for it.")

These harbingers of bad eating blazed a trail which has since become a super-highway over which thousands of successors have poured into the state, bringing with them gastronomic habits which often do little credit to the places they come from, and in any case bear no relation to the food of Florida as it is known to natives, who by now must be greatly outnumbered by invaders. The newcomers have imported various life styles, of which two are readily apparent on the East Coast alone, at least to those sufficiently familiar with Florida to realize that this playground of the well-to-do is not the homogeneous slab of luxury which it may seem to be from a distance. Actually there is a sharp contrast between the two chief ways of life which have been established there, that of the super-rich luxury of Palm Beach and its satellite communities, where elegance has been carefully nurtured and opulence restrained, and that of the staggering flamboyance of Miami Beach, where conspicuous extravagance is the rule rather than the exception. Even more representative of the American way of life is the colonization of Florida by the middle class, particularly by the retired and the elderly, and by the upwardly mobile working-class families who intend to share the generally agreeable climate with the rich and retired and at the same time find employment under sunny skies. Each group has brought with it its own style of eating and has made only slight concessions to local conditions.

The (relatively) poor Floridians of our day buy their food supplies in supermarkets and consume huge amounts of processed, canned, packaged, or frozen food like their fellow-citizens elsewhere. Their restaurants are mostly of the fast-food type, ranging from the hamburger, cheeseburger and fish-

and-chips stand to those of the fried-chicken-and-french-fried-potatoes specialists, and, in the retirement centers such as St. Petersburg, elaborate self-service cafeterias that offer a balanced variety of low-priced foods appealing to elderly folks from all parts of the country.

The huge and flashy Miami Beach hotels set out luncheon on buffets which groan with a seemingly unending variety of *hors d'oeuvre* including smoked and pickled fish, *pâtés* of game or poultry, shellfish, crab, shrimp in mayonnaise, fried prawns, pickles, cheeses, green and cooked salads, cold boiled spiny lobsters. For the main course there is a choice of cold meats, and a number of hot casserole dishes, with suitable garnishes. Then comes the display of desserts, the moment of temptation for those who are torn between their resolve to diet and lose weight and their feeling that they might as well get their money's worth on the "modified American plan," which includes breakfast, and, as a rule, one meal. There are fresh fruits and compotes, ices and *bavaroises,* frosted cakes of alluring shapes and colors, pastries, tarts, *schnecken* and *strudel,* with whipped cream *ad libitum.* This super-smörgåsbord is not Florida food; its almost exact duplicate is offered at the famous Catskill resort hotels north of New York whose clientele is not unlike that of the great Miami Beach caravansaries.

Meanwhile the once exclusive domain of Palm Beach has suffered degradation too, which might be dated from 1942, when the United States Army took over the Boca Raton Club; after the war it became part of the hotel empire of J. Meyer Schine. The Schine management introduced a gastronomic ritual which met with high favor among the affluent guests who have always favored Boca Raton with their patronage. It was called the "Steak Roast Dance" and was held outdoors, near the pool and beach. A string of charcoal grills, each made from a fifty-gallon oil drum split lengthwise and propped up on legs, was presided over by a double rank of chefs and *sous-chefs,* under the supreme command of a *rôtisseur.* Fires in the grills were maintained at hot, medium, and slow. Prime loins of beef, aged three weeks in the hotel's meat room, were cut into fourteen-ounce steaks, which could be grilled rare, medium rare, medium, medium well-done and well-done. With the steak came corn on the cob and baked potato. Once the order was received, the steak was first seared on the hot fire, then transferred to the "medium" grill, or, if need be, to the slow fire while the diners finished a whirl on the dance floor. It was a pageant of flames and white-hatted *rôtisseurs,* which satisfied, apparently, as many as six hundred putative steak lovers in an evening. The Schine system has since been widely imitated at Southern resorts and even in the Caribbean tourist islands; it has become perhaps the most typically traditional tourist meal for the whole area. One glimpses dimly, through the smoke of charring steaks, the buccaneers of the sixteenth and seventeenth centuries seated around a fire waiting for their *boucan* to be served.

*

Of all the immigrants who came to America from other territories than the British Isles, those whose cooking most resembled the English cuisine which the Anglo-Saxons and their accompanying Celts brought with them were the Dutch. Their contributions were plentiful but, because of their kinship with English cooking, they were absorbed into the American cuisine almost without trace.

The Dutch settlers of New York were cut out to be transmitters of good cheer. They were mostly well-to-do, brought to the new land by the Dutch West Indies Company, the sister of the Dutch East Indies Company, which had made Holland rich from the spice trade. They occupied large fertile estates along the Hudson, producers of plenty, and they had behind them a tradition of hearty eating which they honored in doing well by themselves in the new country. An essential item in the equipment of the Dutch-American *huisvrouw* was a copy of *The Wise Cook and Housekeeper,* a Dutch cookbook published in 1683, replete with rich recipes. Washington Irving's *The Legend of Sleepy Hollow* is of course a work of fiction, but his documentation seems to have been accurate when he drew for us a picture of a Dutch tea:

> Such heaped-up platters of cakes of various and almost indescribable kinds, known only to experienced Dutch housewives! There was the doughty doughnut, the tender "olykoek" and the crisp and crumbling cruller; sweet cakes and short cakes, gingercakes and honeycakes and the whole family of cakes. And then there were apple pies and peach pies and pumpkin pies; besides slices of ham and smoked beef; and, moreover, delectable dishes of preserved plums, and peaches, and pears, and quinces, not to mention broiled shad and roasted chickens, together with bowls of milk and cream, all mingled higgledy-piggledy, with the motherly teapot sending up its clouds of vapor from the midst.

This was tea, remember; one wonders what they ate when they really set their minds to it.

Irving was right in using the world *olykoek* (literally "oil-cake") in its Dutch form; the word was employed by English-speaking housewives for about a century before it was replaced by English equivalents (the diminutive *koekje* became cookie). *Oliebollen* did not last long in the vocabulary but it did in the kitchen—it means "dumplings." Waffles were Dutch too and so were pancakes (*pannekoeken*). One word which held out well through the nineteenth century was water souchy, good kitchen English for the soup known as *waterzooie* in Dutch and Flemish. Some other words are with us still. Crullers are the kind of doughnuts which are twisted into a tress, for *krullen* means to curl (hair, for instance). *Cool sla,* cabbage salad, has of course become cole slaw; in the nineteenth century housewives who had forgotten, or never known, that *cool* is Dutch for "cabbage," were already miscalling the dish "cold slaw," which gave illegitimate birth to "warm slaw."

German cooking, like Dutch cooking, was compatible with American fare; but instead of dissolving in the national cuisine and becoming lost in it, it merged with it without losing its own identity. German dishes, virtually unmodified, were simply added to the existing American repertory, usually under their own names, which were so thoroughly adopted that it seldom occurs to their users that they are not English—names like sauerkraut, pretzel, pumpernickel, bock beer and (misspelled) zwieback—zwieback probably seems to most Americans less strange than its English equivalent, rusk.

The German contribution to the melting pot was more important, and began earlier, than most Americans realize today. The Germans of whom Americans are most conscious as constituting a separate group are not even called Germans—the Pennsylvania Dutch. It was they who settled Germantown, now part of Philadelphia, in 1683, attracting by their presence other Germans who did not share their religious practices.

As the country grew inward from the coasts, new German immigrants gave up the habit of stopping in the ports where they landed and moved into the interior, concentrating in certain regions which for one reason or another took their fancy. Political refugees from the revolutions of 1830 and 1848 were numerous. In the 1830s, 30 percent of all the immigrants who entered the United States were German.

Moving outside of the cities, many Germans bought land, notably in Wisconsin and Missouri, and exploited their farms with the same skill and industry which had so impressed Benjamin Rush in eighteenth-century Pennsylvania. Anyone who has perused nineteenth-century American cookbooks must have been surprised at the frequency with which Westphalian ham is called for; was it really necessary for the United States to import hams from Germany? We may suspect that they did not: these were Westphalian hams made in the U.S.A. In Iowa, German descendants make "Westphalian" hams today, soaking them in brine for four weeks, smoking them slowly over hickory fires, dusting them thickly with finely ground black pepper, and hanging them in a dry place for several months to ripen.

German-Americans have contributed most generously to the American larder in the fields of cheese and sausage (beer falls under a separate heading). Limburger is sometimes described as the only German cheese reproduced in America in significant quantity (even so it is in limited demand in the United States, being too strong for most American tastes), but as a matter of fact it is not German, but Belgian. The role of German-Americans has been less that of introducers of the German cheeses with which they were familiar in the old country than that of skillful manufacturers of cheeses from any country. The United States imitates many of the widely eaten cheeses of the world, and it is often German-Americans who preside over the imitating. This is partly the result of the geographic accident that the greatest proportion of Germans has been concentrated in the most important dairy state, Wisconsin; 72 percent of the population of Milwaukee was of German origin in 1900, and the Germanic character of the state is marked by towns bearing such names as New Berlin and New Holstein.

Many persons assume unconsciously that two fairly well known cheeses made in America are of German parentage because of their Teutonic names, but in both cases they are wrong. One is Munster, which has the peculiar property of inducing a country which ordinarily plays hob with foreign accents to become suddenly meticulous about its name, and to apply conscientiously to its first vowel the German umlaut; unfortunately the name of this cheese is not Münster, as it usually appears in the United States, but Munster; it does not take an umlaut. The cheese is not German, it is Alsatian, and since Alsace is in France, where the letter U is normally pronounced in the fashion which has to be indicated in German by placing an umlaut over the letter, it requires no diacritical embellishment. However spelled, it is a luscious soft cheese, rather unassertive in flavor, for which reason it is often enlivened by being sprinkled with caraway seeds.

Liederkranz certainly sounds German enough, but actually it is one of the only two cheeses which authorities in the matter are willing to admit as genuine native creations, all other American cheeses being held to be derived from European ancestors. One might be tempted to call Liederkranz derivative too, since it was born accidentally in an attempt to reproduce in the United States the German cheese known as Bismarck Schlosskäse; something went awry and the result was Liederkranz. Since this happened on the national territory, it has been ruled that Liederkranz is a native-born American; but its name, and the names of its promoters, are in that case even more potently symbolic of the role played by citizens of German extraction in providing America with cheese. Liederkranz was, for once, a cheese not originated in Wisconsin, but in Monroe, New York. It was first produced there in 1892 by Emil Frey, a German-American cheesemaker. Frey sent a sample of it to one of his customers, Adolph Tode, a German-American delicatessen owner. Tode was a member of the German-American Liederkranz ("wreath of song") choral society. He distributed it among his fellow German-American singers, who found it good. So it was put on the market under the name of Liederkranz.

The other indisputable American cheese is Brick, mild when young, but considerably stronger in taste as it grows older, which is the way connoisseurs like it. Whether it is a German-American creation or not is uncertain, though it seems reasonable to believe so, since it was first made, in 1877, in predominantly German Wisconsin (and has remained a cheese of the Midwest, little known to Americans on either coast). The inventor of Brick was John Jossi, a name of baffling origin, perhaps Swiss.

Since the two cheeses authoritatively described as the only ones which are really American nevertheless owe their inspiration at least to German forebears, one hardly dares attempt to claim originality for any others, such as Cougar Gold, developed at Washington State University; or California's semi-soft Monterey or really soft Monterey Jack; or Oregon's Tillamook, which indeed gives itself away when it is put on the market under the name of Oregon Cheddar. The United States is rich in Cheddars, sold candidly under that name—Wisconsin Cheddar, of course, plus New York Cheddar, Vermont Cheddar, Favorite Style Cheddar, Caraway Cheddar, American Cheddar, and just Cheddar. Colby, Coon, Cornhusker and the spiced Sage are also variants of Cheddar. American Blue covers a good deal of ground, including cheeses inspired by Danish Blue or Roquefort or Gorgonzola or Stilton. Other American-made cheeses which look back to one or another European ancestor are the Chantelle of Illinois; Cold Pack, which sometimes has herbs in it; Connecticut's Pineapple, named for its shape; and New York's Poona, reminiscent of Limburger.

Originator of cheeses or not, the United States is the world's largest cheese-manufacturing country, making twice as much as the world's second producer of cheese, France; but of course the population of the United States is more than four times that of France. Americans eat nine pounds of cheese per person per year (eleven, if you count the process spreads for bread called cheese by their manufacturers, though they are not quite real cheeses; some of them are more palatable than most cheese *aficionados* are inclined to admit—for instance, Clifton Fadiman, who described them as "solidified floor wax"). Frenchmen consume twenty and one-fourth pounds, Norwegians nearly twenty, Danes nearly nineteen, Swiss seventeen and a half, Swedes seventeen and one-third, Dutch over seventeen, and Germans a little less than sixteen.

The German influence on American food is exercised even more vigorously in the case of sausage than in that of cheese. There are more than two hundred different kinds of sausage on the American market; it is a safe guess that German-Americans make a majority of them. The German-settled city of Milwaukee boasts more than fifty sausage manufacturers, many of them with obviously German names. In this category of food, Germans are not simply the makers of sausages which may have appeared originally in other countries, they are also, in many cases, their originators. Germany, after all, is perhaps the world's leading concocter of sausage; many of the types found there have been transferred almost unaltered to the United States.

A sausage is likely to be called, in the United States, with no feeling that a German word is being invoked, a wiener or a wienie; the diphthong in "wiener" is even spelled and pronounced correctly, which is rare for words adopted from other languages. It is true that "wiener" is often used to mean "frankfurter," necessarily a contradiction, since both words are place names, and they refer to different places. "Wiener" is of course short for *"wiener-wurst,"* Vienna sausage. We use the same word currently in "Wiener Schnitzel" (veal cutlet, Vienna style), while "frankfurter," also of course, means "Frankfort sausage."

In the frankfurter, Germany gave the United States its most popular—one is tempted to write, its most American—sausage; 15,100,000,000 of them (1,500,000,000 pounds) were eaten by Americans in 1974. Yet it first appeared honestly under its genuinely foreign aspect, if it is true that its original appearance in the United States was at the Chicago World's Fair, or Columbian Exposition, as a German exhibit. Another account, however, credits a Bavarian named Antoine Feuchtwanger with having sold frankfurters in St. Louis well before that date, while a third says that a certain Charles Feltman introduced the frankfurter into this country at Coney Island; it was in any case often referred to slangily as "Coney Island chicken." The frankfurter became a favorite food at baseball games, easy to hold in the hand when nestled in its specially tailored bun, and eminently fitted for outdoor munching. It is supposed to have been at a ball park that the frankfurter impressed itself upon the man who, more than any other single person, divested it of its alien character and made it thoroughly American—the cartoonist Tad (T. A. Dorgan), who drew a cartoon in which he endowed a frankfurter with a tail, legs and a head, so that it looked like a dachshund. The frankfurter has been called a "hot dog" ever since, even in snack bars in France and Italy, where it is sold to American tourists under that name in the belief that the frankfurter is a Yankee invention.

The frankfurter is in principle a pure beef sausage, and that is what it was indeed in the youth of the authors, when it was as luscious as a food of this sort is capable of being. It was usually bought from a street vendor, clasped in its frankfurter bun, daubed with an excessively yellow mustard, and no nonsense about such extraneous frills as piccalilli, cole slaw, or sauerkraut. It has since deteriorated sadly. Today's frankfurter contains on the average 28 percent fat, crowding the legal limit of 30 percent, which is far too much: but it is an improvement over the 51 percent of fat which some frankfurters had reached before this abuse forced the imposition of a maximum fat content in 1969. Before 1969 frankfurters had also begun to substitute for expensive beef such cheaper meats as mutton, pork and even goat, a practice horrifying to devotees of the genuine sausage. The 1969 law restored beef to the frankfurter, but leniently permitted its replacement up to a limit of 15 percent (by volume) with poultry meat. It is also permissible, though reprehensible, to pump water into frankfurters in a proportion no greater than 10 percent, making the total water content more than 55 percent, for the meat itself is 49 percent water. The result might have been sad to the sight if the frankfurter makers had not discovered that their product could be given the reassuring pinkish glow of health by dosing it with nitrates and nitrites, whose potential effects upon the human system many dietitians regard with alarm.

Other place-named German sausages reproduced in the United States include Braunschweiger (Brunswick sausage), made of liver and such bits of pork as are left over after the animal has been cut up; Berliner processed sausage; and Thuringer, also called summer sausage, of the cervelat type. Also popular in the United States are the domestic imitations of the fat Bratwurst (Thuringian too, a pork sausage there, a pork and veal sausage in America); the red garlic-scented Knackwurst; Brockwurst; Mettwurst, Weisswurst (white sausage); and, of course, Blutwurst, blood pudding. This last, found in all hog-slaughtering countries, has penetrated the United States from other sources as well. We have already met the French *boudin* in Creole country, where, as in France, it is an essential accessory to the feasts of the Christmas-New Year's season, and so it is in Sweden, where it is the custom to serve it at breakfast on Christmas Day. Swedish housewives in Minnesota go to considerable trouble to produce blood pudding for that occasion, which is difficult because, for some mysterious reason, a state law forbids slaughter-houses to sell pork blood, the essential ingredient for this sausage.

Germany gets a good deal of help from other countries in providing America with its rich variety of sausages. Italy probably ranks second in this respect. After the frankfurter the next most popular sausage in the United States is boloney, spelled by purists Bologna, after the city of its origin; but even in this form the name has become so thoroughly Americanized that the Pennsylvania Dutch see no anomaly in naming one of their sausages Lebanon Bologna (referring, of course, to Lebanon, Pennsylvania). Boloney appears to be an American attempt to reproduce Bologna's mortadella, but it is a much muted version of that famous sausage, without the peppercorns which in Italy make it spicy. (There is also an American mortadella on the market, sold under that name.) Italian too, of course, is the widely eaten sharp hard salami; there is a moister Jewish salami. Liverwurst may have reached the American larder through Jewish sources rather than German; it is not always easy to distinguish between Jewish and German contributions to the food of the United States. It is Swiss-Americans who have given us the veal Kalberwurst and Landjaeger.

The Spanish sausage which has already made a disguised appearance under the name of *chaurice* in Creole cooking exists also under its Spanish name, *chorizo,* both in Tex-Mex cooking and in the diet of the Basques whom this country imported to exercise here their unparalleled competence in herding sheep; *chorizo* is made expressly for them in Fayette, Idaho. In Chicago *kielbasa,* a pork sausage flavored with caraway and garlic, is manufactured for the many Poles of the region. There is also a Swedish potato sausage, made, like Swedish blood sausage, especially in Minnesota, and, again like Swedish blood sausage, a feature of the Christmas holidays;

despite its name, it is not devoid of meat—ten parts of potato to three of beef and one of pork, plus seasoning.

But are there no *American* sausages? It would not be surprising if there were none, for sausages, like cheese, date from antiquity, and all the possibilities might well have been exhausted before America was discovered. However, the plain ground-pork breakfast or country sausage, usually flavored with herbs—thyme, or sage, or rosemary (in Pennsylvania Dutch country coriander is added)—is apparently native; a version which combines two parts of lean beef with one of pork is also included in nineteenth-century American cookbooks. Indiana "whole-hog" sausage, which avoids the inferior parts of the pig in favor of lean loin and shoulder meat alone, appears to be indigenous too. Finally there are the special sausages which were more or less improvised where unusual meats turned up—reindeer and caribou salami in Alaska, buffalo "Braunschweiger" in South Dakota (made of the liver, tongue and heart of the animal), and venison sausage in the Upper Peninsula of Michigan, where Italians and Swedes make their own varieties of venison sausage as well, the first with plenty of garlic, the second with potatoes and onion.

The German element in American cooking is not confined to cheese and sausage; at only a slight remove from the latter is what is considered today a food as thoroughly American as the frankfurter, the hamburger, which, of course, takes its name from the city of Hamburg, where it is known as American steak; no country has a monopoly on ground beef. (The fact that "hamburger" has given rise to senseless words like "cheeseburger" is one of the many signs which betray the increasing degeneration of the American language.)

The German penchant for doughy foods, added to our Dutch inheritance, has helped to make dumplings a normal element in American cooking. Jelly doughnuts were well known in Germany before they reached the United States. Rye bread has been accepted as not too alien, but pumpernickel continues to seem a trifle foreign to many.

Sauerkraut has become nationally accepted, perhaps not as a full-fledged American dish, but sufficiently so to prevent anti-German feeling from driving it off the menu during World War I; it was simply rechristened Liberty Cabbage. Examples of the German habit of contrasting sweet and sour elements in the same concoction are familiar especially in those parts of the country where German-Americans are numerous. Sauerbraten is a thoroughly accepted food in many localities; Hasenpfeffer, with its vinegar-and-spice sauce applied to rabbit (ideally, it would be hare), is somewhat less widespread; and dishes like spareribs stuffed with apples and prunes are usually only to be found in Wisconsin or other centers of German settlement. Was *gefüllte Fisch,* if we spell it in German, or *gefillte fisch,* if we put it into Yiddish, a German or a Jewish gift to the United States? Jewish cooking turns up especially in the large cities of the East, in New York first of all, where Second Avenue and tributaries like Essex Street provide mosaics of Central and Eastern European cuisines, strained through Jewish cooking; is potato pirogen with sour cream, for instance, a Jewish dish in itself or simply a dish transported by Jewish immigrants from some European country, perhaps Roumania? That rich hors d'oeuvre, chopped chicken livers moist with the chicken's fat, is certainly Jewish. If poppyseed appears on a roll or on the glazed egg bread called *challah,* we are no doubt justified in considering these breads Jewish, but was it Germans or Jews who decided to embed caraway seeds in rye bread? It seems safe to credit the rich pastrami to Jewish cooking; the variety of smoked salmon called lox also seems to be authentically Jewish; and there are, of course, those Jewish foods about which cults have been built up, like that cousin of the doughnut, the bagel, which it is perhaps necessary to be Jewish to appreciate.

If Dutch food lost itself almost completely in American cooking, and German food did so partially, most other foreign cuisines established beachheads in America, but never got much farther. One minor exception might be cited, if we dare class as foreign a contribution from the British Isles; it is peculiar in that it represents a survival in America of an entity which has all but disappeared in its land of origin. The Cornish language has died out in Cornwall; and to the outsider, at least, it appears that the population of this southwesternmost prolongation of England has become indistinguishable from that of the rest of the country; but the mark of Cornwall still remains in Michigan and Minnesota, which still make Cornish pasties. Thus America maintains a Cornish tradition, for Cornish pasties in the United States serve the same purpose for which they were created in Cornwall—to give miners a complete lunch in one piece. A doughy envelope of the right shape and size to fit into a miner's lunch pail was filled with meat at one end, vegetables in the middle, and fruit at the end; baked in the morning and wrapped so that it would stay warm until noon, it provided a full meal for the miner, who began eating it at the meat end and worked his way through to dessert at the other. The tin mines of Cornwall, which were already being worked in prehistoric times, are practically played out now, but in 1830 miners from Cornwall emigrated to Wisconsin to work the lead mines there, bringing with them Cornish pasties and saffron cakes. Today it is the iron-ore miners of Minnesota and the copper miners of Michigan who carry in their lunch pails the same food which centuries ago served the tin miners of Cornwall. Another apparition of unusual foods from the British Isles turns up in Idaho, where a number of Welsh immigrants settled in the nineteenth century, and such specialties of the old country as *bara brith,* raisin-and-currant bread, are still eaten.

Scandinavian immigration into the United States was early and considerable, as in Delaware's New Sweden, where the Swedes were eliminated in a few decades by the Dutch, and the Dutch in a few decades more by the English, but it has had no appreciable effect on the national cooking. This is largely the result of the tendency of Scandinavians to build up their own homogeneous settlements, within which they perpetuate the traditions of their former countries, with a minimum of cultural interchanges with the surrounding population. Scandinavian enclaves thus sprang up here and there in the United States, more or less at random, composed of persons who had known one another in Europe and tended to remain tightly linked in America and to develop their own miniature societies, sufficient unto themselves.

Most of the Scandinavian enclaves today are not in the East, but in the northern Middle West or the Northwest. There are Swedish colonies in Washington, Nebraska, Iowa, Illinois and Minnesota, which offer visitors lingonberries with Swedish coffee bread, or Swedish cakes and cookies—spritz rings, cherry twists, *sandbakkels, fattigmannbakels* (poor man's pastry), and *pepparkakor* (pepper cookies, which have become favorites in Utah since Swedish converts to Mormonism introduced them there). There are Norwegians in Washington, the Dakotas, Iowa and Wisconsin, who bake for special occasions the lofty pyramidal *kranskake,* along with such pastries as *goro, berlinerkranser* and *krumkaken,* and even abandon themselves to the lye-cured cod called *lutefisk,* whose failure to enter into the general American cuisine is easily understandable. Also apart from it are such Norwegian-American dishes as barley soup, *tykmelk* (clabbered milk with bread crumbs and sugar), *rømmegrot* (sour-cream porridge), potato lefse, Norwegian flat bread, *torsk* (fresh cod), *rullepølse* (cold rolled spiced beef), *spekejøtt* (smoked dried lamb), and *søtsuppe* (sweet fruit soup). Danes helped to found the dairy industry in Wisconsin; Racine numbers a considerable proportion of Danes in its population. Like Danes everywhere, they enjoy specialties such as *leverpostej* (liver paste), *frikadeller* (meat balls), *rødgrod med fløde* (a currant and raspberry pudding with cream), *aebleskiver* (small puff-ball shaped doughnuts served with jelly), and a large ring-shaped, sugar-sprinkled sweet bread called *kringle.* Everybody, of course, believes himself to be familiar with Danish pastry, but in America, unless you find a Danish housewife who makes it, it is unlikely that you have ever tasted the real thing. In New York there are Danish pastry shops in Brooklyn, and large cities in the rest of the country harbor similar oases, but otherwise what is foisted off on the unsuspecting consumer as Danish pastry would be consigned to the garbage can in Scandinavia. There are Icelanders in North Dakota (but more of them across the border in Canada) who maintain a very ancient tradition by making *skyr* (milk, egg, sour cream and sugar), an ancient Viking dish, eaten with berries in season, and, a more recent creation, *vinarterta,* a seven-layer cake with fillings of puréed prunes and apricots, flavored with vanilla and cardamom. Finns have settled in Washington, Idaho, and anywhere else where Swedes are found, particularly around Lake Superior, where they spoil themselves with their native *piirakka* (rice-filled pasties), *lohimuhennos* (salmon chowder), and black bread.

Polish immigration did not really get under way until 1834, after an unsuccessful revolution; one notable arrival, in 1848, was that of Big Mike Goldwasser, grandfather of Senator Barry Goldwater. There are many Poles in both Milwaukee and Chicago, where, in addition to their own special kinds of cheese and sausage, they find in their neighborhood groceries such foods as their cheese-flavored *pierogi* and the fat round *pacski* buns, which do not figure in the American larder. Neither do the foods of the Czechs of Iowa and Nebraska—roast pork with dumplings; the round Bohemian *kolaches,* their pastry enriched with fruit and nuts, sold in American stores in Cedar Rapids; Slovak poppyseed cakes; and Moravian coffee cakes, sugar cakes, and half-moon cakes.

It is in the larger cities of the East, notably in New York, that a spate of Japanese restaurants has come into being in the last decade. More stylized in service than the Chinese, but with a smaller repertory of dishes, these places have enjoyed a certain success with Americans who have lived in Japan and with visiting Japanese businessmen. Most successful is a chain of neo-Japanese steak houses, founded by a Nisei (American-born), where eight diners sit at a counter surrounding a metal hot plate on which the steaks, prawns, and vegetables are cooked, sliced, and shared out by a Japanese "chef" who simultaneously performs a sort of sword dance of flashing knife and fork, while chanting appropriate gutturals, which, according to the founder of the chain, have been carefully rehearsed.

The Latins remain. There are many French-Canadians in the Northeast, but their gastronomic influence is nil. French Huguenots left only the faintest memories in Baltimore and Charleston. As for the French restaurants scattered throughout the United States, the few which are genuine remain extra-territorial and transmit none of their spirit to American gastronomy. The others pay tribute on their menus to the French language, but little to the French cuisine. Besides the Spanish influence in Tex-Mex cooking, in Louisiana, and, via Cuba, in Florida, there are Puerto Rican restaurants in New York, but they have contributed nothing to American cooking. The sole gift of the Portuguese seems to have been Portuguese sweet bread, still findable on Cape Cod.

Italian food provides a special case. The Italian restaurant has always been an article of export, but while it has retained its foreign, and even often its picturesque aspect, some of its foods have nevertheless worked their way into the American kitchen. Macaroni with cheese does not impress one as an exotic dish nor does spaghetti with tomato sauce; noodles in one form or another are universal wherever wheat is grown. Perhaps various forms of pasta may take on a more esoteric air when we deck them with clam sauce or

Bologna *ragù,* but even so they have become more or less naturalized and so have such dishes as Italian meat balls or veal scallopine. Perhaps the Italian cuisine comes nearer to being compatible with the American because it is basically amateur cooking and rustic cooking, and so is American. French cooking, prestigious though it is, is professional and sophisticated, and thus accommodates itself with difficulty to an American cuisine which has never turned in this direction.

New York is, in a sense, the greatest gastronomic melting pot in the world, but it is a melting pot in which nothing melts. You can find there restaurants offering virtually all the cuisines of the world, but the city is weak on American cooking. Each of the foreign cuisines available in New York remains isolated in its own context. They do not borrow from one another, they do not merge their separate styles into a common amalgam. The gastronomic melting pot of New York is an accurate reflection of the gastronomic melting pot of America: a vast catch-all stew into which the most varied elements have been thrown, but within which each element remains undissolved, refusing to release its juices into a homogeneous medley. This result would have surprised Harriet Martineau, who had predicted a different denouement:

> America was meant to be everything [she wrote]. . . . There are many soils and many climates included within the boundary line of the United States; many *countries;* and one rule cannot be laid down for all.

But one rule *has* been laid down for all. Despite all the foreign contributions which have been offered to it, American cooking remains as uncompromisingly Anglo-Saxon as it has been from the beginning, at least in spirit.

XXVII

American Restaurants

AN INCIDENTAL RESULT of the influx of immigrants into the United States was that it provided somebody to run America's restaurants. For some mysterious reason Americans whose ancestors came from the British Isles have never been very good at this. They distrusted alien foods and, because they were on the spot first, succeeded in maintaining a cuisine more or less immune from them; yet they trusted alien cooks to prepare their meals. American housewives of Anglo-Saxon background, at least in the days before pre-cooked frozen TV dinners, did very well in the home kitchen, feeding their families bountifully; and in the early days a family might include as many persons as a small restaurant could serve. Talent in this direction did not seem to be transferable from the amateur to the professional plane. When it came to restaurant cooking, Americans of the old stock abdicated in favor of foreigners; but as the once-foreigners moved into their second and third generations and became Americans too, they often acquired, as though it were a necessary condition of citizenship, the American lack of interest in restaurant cooking which produced the strange phenomenon of a country where, in the luckier regions, at least, one ate well at home and badly in restaurants. In the unlucky regions, one ate badly in both.

American ineptitude in the restaurant field goes far back. In 1848, Captain Frederick Marryat wrote that

> the cookery in the United States is exactly what it must be everywhere else—in a ratio with the degree of refinement in the population [which he cautiously forbore from trying to assess]. In the principal cities you will meet with as good cookery in private houses as you will see in London, or even Paris.

In private houses, note. Marryat did not commit himself about restaurant cooking, and though other Europeans had an occasional good word to say for food they had eaten in American homes, it is difficult to find a recommendation for restaurants. Some of them did make uncomplimentary remarks about the quality of professionally produced food, but what seemed to annoy Europeans even more was the conditions in which it was served. They objected to the promiscuity, with everyone sitting down together; to the lack of individual choice (the food was plunked down on the table, and that was that, take it or leave it—true, there was usually a considerable variety from which you could choose what you wanted, but it was all put on the table at the same time, encouraging free-for-all battles as the customers competed for the choicest meats); and the inexorability of eating hours fixed rigidly for the convenience of the management, not for that of the guests. It was a case of "come and get it," and if you didn't come right away, you wouldn't get it. There could be no disobedience to the peremptory summons sounded by the startling dinner gong which had aroused the wrath of Charles Dickens and would affect Anthony Trollope in the same fashion, as Daniel J. Boorstin tells us in *The Americans: The National Experience:*

> A traveler who found himself sharing his dinner table, and called upon to chat familiarly, with a miscellaneous company of common soldiers, farmers, laborers, teamsters, lawyers, doctors, ministers, bankers, judges, or generals, soon discovered that Americans considered the desire for privacy a vice akin to pride ... Captain Basil Hall, traveling the country in 1827–28, complained that ... to have a meal alone was a rare luxury, never secured without an extra fee, and usually not available at any price. Anthony Trollope, thirty-five years later, wistfully recalled the wonderfully private luxury of an English inn—one's tea, one's fire, and one's book. "One is in a free country ... and yet in an American inn one can never do as one likes. A terrific gong sounds early in the morning, breaking one's sweet slumbers, and then a second gong sounding some thirty minutes later, makes you understand that you must proceed to breakfast, whether you be dressed or no. You certainly can go on with your toilet and obtain your meal after half an hour's delay. Nobody actually scolds you for so doing, but the breakfast is, as they say in this country, 'through.' ... They begrudge you no amount that you can eat or drink, but they begrudge you a single moment that you sit there neither eating nor drinking. This is your fate if you're too late, and therefore as a rule you are not late. In that case you form one of a long row of eaters who proceed through their work with a solid energy that is past all praise."

Another detail which annoyed some British visitors was what was called the American Plan, which had become the standard arrangement in the United States from about 1830 on. "It is the invariable custom in the United States," Thomas Hamilton wrote in 1833, "to charge by the day or week; and travelers are thus obliged to pay for meals whether they eat them or not." This was less irksome for Continental Europeans, who were accustomed to the *pension,* which also quoted its prices for rooms and meals together; one was not obliged to eat the meals, only to pay for them. For practical purposes the American Plan did not make much difference outside of a few of the larger cities, for there were no restaurants. The hotel dining rooms were all there was, and sometimes there was only one hotel. Even in New York, wrote Samuel Eliot Morison, there was only one restaurant in 1845, but we may suspect him of being severe in defining "restaurant," for he added that there were nevertheless "plenty of 'eating-houses.' " It would seem that only hotels in cities with restaurants capable of offering competition would have needed to bind their clients to their own tables by means of the American Plan, yet it prevailed in restaurantless cities and, perversely, it was precisely in a big city with enough good restaurants to provide formidable competition that a first-class hotel, for the first time since the American Plan had become standard, announced that it would operate on what it was decided to call the "European Plan" to differentiate it from the other: you were charged for your room, paying only for such meals as you actually ate in the hotel. This bold step was taken by the Parker House of Boston, opened to considerable fanfare in 1855, which did not have to worry too much about competition. Its own dining room was one of the best eating places in Boston, capable of wooing customers away from the restaurants; a large proportion of its diners was made up of persons who were not staying at the hotel.

The American public eating habits which early British visitors to the United States found so disconcerting betrayed a good deal about the spirit with which Americans approach the table; and though most of us have acquired manners somewhat more elegant than those of the nineteenth century we have perhaps, basically, not changed a great deal. The American attitude today is still, often, that of persons who do not really like to eat. Eating is unfortunately a necessity, however distasteful it may be, and there is no getting around it. It has to be done. So it is dispatched as quickly as possible, without time-consuming ceremony.

Is this a by-product of the Puritan spirit? Dawdling at the table is time wasted; enjoying one's food is self-indulgence. When we sit down to eat we are in danger of succumbing to one or the other, or both, of two of the seven deadly sins—sloth and gluttony. We escape by bolting our food with scant attention to its quality. American restaurant operators are probably Puritans too, who strive to lead us not into temptation by serving us food which is, indeed, not tempting.

Does Puritanism explain also the curious dichotomy of American cooking, always considered "good" when executed at home by amateurs, potentially "bad" (or should one say "evil") when executed in restaurants by professionals? Good cooking results from a labor of love, and love, as we all know, is admirable when unpaid for, but despicable when offered for sale. The restaurant chef who so far forgets himself as to give loving care to his cooking, thus catering for pelf to the sensual appetites of his customers, is, to the

Puritans, dangerously close to pandering. For the salvation of his soul, he will be best advised to consider his function as purely therapeutic and banish affection for food from his kitchen.

The home cook is in a different position. She can let herself go, being the handmaid of one of those rare situations in which the Puritan ethic permits a cautious unbridling of the emotions. She prepares her food for occasions in which the stigma of self-indulgence is avoided, since the food itself plays only a secondary role in the service of some primary purpose of undisputed virtue—at home, the unification of the family and the demonstration of maternal and conjugal devotion. If she bakes her most elaborate cake for friends invited to tea or for bridge, or, in the country, simply for "a nice visit," her motive is the promotion of friendliness and neighborliness (but let her beware lest she fall into another deadly sin—that of pride).

Even on the professional side of the picture, attention to quality is forgivable if it is put at the service of some noble principle. There exist in many large American cities businessmen's luncheon clubs where a conscious effort is made to enlist the skills of gastronomy; but this does not constitute a soul-destroying surrender to the selfish demands of sybaritic stomachs and taste buds, but a harnessing of the seductive art of cookery to the worthy purpose of promoting trade and industry, whose smooth functioning is necessary to keep us all prosperous, happy and consequently grateful. In a similar spirit, fine, and consequently expensive, cooking is also a specialty of those restaurants whose real vocation is to serve as informal chambers of commerce, evident in the nickname given them of "expense-account restaurants"—frequented, that is, chiefly for business reasons by persons whose thoughts allegedly are far from the unavowable motive of self-pampering.

Gourmet eating, then, is justifiable when its necessity is presented, almost as a burden, as a part of the tasks imposed upon toilers by duty. Yet how much more admirable are those who, despite having justification for fine eating in the pursuit of a worthy cause, choose instead to shun the fleshpots all the same. They are the martyrs of our time, who can only approach in a mood of self-sacrifice the sort of food put before them at dinners to raise funds for charity or for political campaigns. It says much for the virtue of our Congressmen that, though they eat there as a matter of duty, they tolerate in the dining rooms of the Senate and the House of Representatives what *The New Yorker* once described as a "cuisine . . . at its zenith, mediocre."

It is possibly a combination of the Puritan conviction that good eating is bad eating, and the he-man ideology inherited from our pioneers, who felt that it was effete to be choosy about one's food, which accounts for the fact that American restaurants succeed best with the simplest types of food presented in the humblest fashion. Richard Osborn Cummings was right in recognizing, as a significant trend in American restaurant eating,

> the growth of chain restaurants and cafeterias which in the late nineteenth century had begun to supplant the old-fashioned corner restaurant with its greasy, seldom-changed menu. The first to employ the system of keeping down the cost of food by letting patrons wait on themselves were quick-lunch establishments for businessmen. The Exchange Buffet, opened in the commercial district of New York in 1885, where patrons helped themselves and ate standing, was for men only. But the Automat, a German idea, where nickels dropped into slots released desired food, was open to both sexes. With increased employment of women in business, smaller families, and apartment living, eating out became more customary, and restaurants and cafeterias increased greatly in numbers.
>
> Cafeterias became particularly popular in the twentieth century. Several social and philanthropic organizations run by women had established cafeterias in Chicago during the early nineties. [And in New York too, where they were joined later by consumer cooperatives, which remained non-profit organizations by dividing their surpluses periodically among the customers in proportion to their expenditures.] A manager of one of these early experiments recognized the commercial possibilities of the idea and set up her own establishment. Another woman was inspired to adopt the plan for a public restaurant opened in Los Angeles in 1905. The principle of "see and select one's food" drew the crowds, and a branch was opened in San Francisco. In Washington cafeterias appeared about 1915 and increased rapidly in numbers during the crowded days of the war. One of the larger chains, Childs, during the war period and the early twenties tried to capitalize on the new knowledge of nutrition by including in parentheses after each item its caloric value.

Be snobbish about it if you will, but these establishments, devoid of fuss and feathers, frequently offered better food, even from a gastronomic point of view, than many more pretentious establishments.

The foods which accorded with the psychology that produced this type of restaurant—the Puritan-plus-pioneer psychology, if we may be permitted to simplify—the foods which seem most typically American, the foods Americans make best, bear an obvious family relationship to one another, but it is a little difficult to put the finger on their unifying characteristic. What is the common denominator which binds them together, the essential element which accounts for their unmistakable likeness? Is it that they are rustic? Is it because they are well fitted to be eaten in the open air (as at barbecues, clambakes, and shore dinners)? Is it because many of them can be held in the hand for eating (hamburgers and hot dogs in their buns, Western sandwiches, corn on the cob)? Is it because they are adapted to being eaten standing up? Perhaps the best answer is that which was dredged out of the collective consciousness only a few years ago, when people began to talk about "fast foods," a description which covers a considerable variety of our most

American edibles. This would have been considered a valid characterization of American provender by those early foreign visitors who were impressed, and frequently depressed, by the speed with which Americans got through their meals. Speed in eating was in the American tradition, and it was intensified when feeding became fast in the most literal sense because it was carried out in motion, or at best during pauses in motion so brief that there was no time to realize that there had been an interruption in the state of movement. Acceleration in the speed of eating resulted from the coincidence that the development of restaurants and the development of railroads occurred during the same period; the latter had more effect upon the former than we usually realize today. Improvement of railroad freight services widened the variety of foods available to consumers; the growth of railroad passenger services was largely determinant in fixing the fashion in which those foods would be prepared and served in American restaurants—first of all, in a hurry.

It was Captain Marryat who provided one of the first reports about the incidence of railroad travel on eating habits. It dates from 1839, which means in the first decade of American railroading. At that time the trains stopped to let passengers eat—but not long. Meals had to be choked down in a headlong rush.

> The cars stop [Marryat wrote], all the doors are thrown open and out rush all, the passengers like boys out of school, and crowd round the tables to solace themselves with pies, patties, cakes, hard-boiled eggs, hams, custards and a variety of railroad luxuries too numerous to mention. The bell rings for departure, in they all hurry with their hands and mouths full, and off they go again until the next stopping-place induces them to relieve the monotony of the journey by masticating without being hungry.

Forty years later, in 1878, conditions seem not to have improved, for another critical Briton wrote in that year of a breakfast break on the Union Pacific Railroad:

> We stopped half an hour to hurry out and get breakfast [this was a generous allowance; fifteen minutes was often considered long enough for breakfast, and indeed was so in this case, for the account continues]: All ate as if for their very lives and the result was that we were all through together a quarter of an hour before it was time to start.

It must have been the wrong place, or perhaps too early in the morning, for this disgruntled passenger to have been soothed by the charms of the Harvey Girls (possibly the first manifestations of the spirit which later would give us hostesses, carhops and eventually "topless" waitresses), who graced the chain of railroad-station restaurants established in 1876 by Fred Harvey. They needed gracing, if one may judge from a *New York Times* editorial sparked by indignation at their misnaming as "refreshment saloons."

> There could not be a more inappropriate designation for such abominations of desolation. Directors of railroads appear to have an idea that travelers are destitute of stomach; that eating and drinking are not at all necessary to human beings bound on long journeys, and that nothing more is required than to put them through their misery in as brief a time as possible. It is expected that three or four hundred men, women and children . . . shall rush out helter-skelter into a dismal, long room and dispatch a supper, breakfast or dinner in fifteen minutes.

A more appropriate name for similarly primitive purveyors of food, whose establishments were indeed modeled upon the railroad-station "refreshment saloons," appeared in the language within a decade of the Civil War, Daniel J. Boorstin tells us in a brilliant, vivid—and revolting—description of early railroad travel in the United States, set forth in the chapter called "The Democracy of Haste," in *The Americans: The National Experience.* It was, he writes, " 'lunch-counter,' offering both rapid service and enough discomfort to discourage the customer from lingering over his meal . . . an American invention of the era, a by-product of railroad travel." Later its name would become even more brief: quick lunch.

Another new word would now be added to the American language thanks to the railroads and their catering—diner. It seems a logical and an obvious idea now; it was revolutionary in the mid-nineteenth century. The first dining cars added a certain degree of comfort and convenience to the business of eating while traveling, but not much. They were not, in fact, really dining cars, designed for that express purpose, but ordinary baggage cars requisitioned for a new function and equipped for it simply by fixing down its center a long table about which the customers could cluster. It was nothing more than the lunch counter mounted on wheels.

At this point there appeared on the scene, providentially, a man whose object was to convert railroad travel from a hardship to a luxury.

George M. Pullman gave his attention to the problem of sleeping on trains before he turned to that of eating on them. He produced his first sleeping cars in 1858, and in 1863 created a much improved model whose first example he named the Pioneer. The success of the sleeping car encouraged Pullman to devote himself to the dining car. He designed a coach especially planned for eating, with rows of tables arranged against the two walls of the car, leaving a center aisle through which waiters could pass to serve passengers no longer condemned to battle for their food. Each car included a kitchen cleverly designed to provide the cook with all the equipment essential for preparing hot meals, compactly and efficiently fitted into a small space—the chuck wagon of the Machine Age. The Detroit *Commercial Advertiser* waxed enthusiastic about what it called "the crowning glory of Mr. Pullman's invention"—the "cuisine department containing a range where every variety of meats, vegetables and pastry may be cooked in the car, according to the best style of culinary art." Apparently the press had been granted preview privileges, for this article appeared in 1867, but it was only in 1868 that the first luxury Pullman dining car actually entered into commercial operation, on the Chicago and Alton Railroad. Mr. Pullman must have agreed with the *Commercial Advertiser* that the cooking in his diner represented the best style of culinary art, for he challenged comparisons with almost reckless boldness by baptizing his first dining car the Delmonico. This may not have been entirely an empty boast, for the railroads seized upon this new asset as a means of promoting railroad travel (as airlines later would advertise their food as well as their speed), by seeming to lavish loving care on the food.

> Dining car menus in 1870 offered seventy-five cent meals of oysters on the half-shell, porterhouse steak, quail, antelope, plover, fresh trout and terrapin, with second helpings on the house [James Trager informs us]. There was champagne at every meal, including breakfast, and passengers ate in the splendor of Turkish carpets, French mirrors, fringed portières and rare inlaid woods. The Denver and Rio Grande made a specialty of mountain trout, the Union Pacific was famous for its antelope steaks, the Northern Pacific for its grouse and salmon.

The last-named also advertised itself as "The Line of the Great Baked Potato"—it crossed Idaho. We may also add to Mr. Trager's list the scrapple of the Reading Railroad and the terrapin stew of the Baltimore and Ohio. The railroads were, obviously, living on the fat of the lands through which they passed; and if they could find no local specialty to publicize, they fell back upon simple opulence—the Chicago and Northwestern Line offered thirty-five main courses and twenty-five desserts in 1877, but this was, of course, expensive—one dollar.

The quality of railroad food did indeed remain high (allowance made for the conditions under which it had to be cooked and served), until the Second World War; one could eat better in motion than in the restaurants of many of the cities at which the trains stopped. It was only when the railroads surrendered ignobly before the competition of the airlines and allowed their passenger services to degenerate shamefully that their food became as abject as all the rest.

Pullman's innovations brought in their wake changes which he could hardly have anticipated when he set out to provide better sleeping and eating accommodations for railroad travel. The changes his luxury diners produced had their effect in the general domain as well, altering, for example, the design of home kitchens. The lessons learned through improvement of dining-car cooking compartments were applied for the benefit of the housewife, as apartments became progressively smaller and roomy kitchens were supplanted by kitchenettes. The most visible effect of the dining car was demonstrated in the domain of public restaurants, however, where tribute was paid to it by direct and deliberate imitation. Small eating places were built in the shape of dining cars—lunch wagons, which were often called diners. Unfortunately they dispensed with the smooth suave service of the Pullman cars and reverted from their separate tables to the long counter running along one side of the room, behind which a short-order cook plied his limited skills. The railroad-station lunch counter had returned from its sophisticated sojourn between the rails to the primitive *status quo ante.* Puritanism had triumphed.

When George M. Pullman named his first luxury dining car the Delmonico he was drawing a parallel with an institution which was promoting gastronomic elegance on stable foundations during the same period when Pullman was promoting it on wheels. The single restaurant which Samuel Eliot Morison had been willing to concede to the New York of 1845 was Delmonico, or Delmonico's, as it was alternatively called; several other writers have awarded it the same monopolistic position. "In 1825" (the year when the first Delmonico reached the United States), wrote José Wilson, in *American Cooking: The Eastern Heartland,* "there were no restaurants, as we know them today, in New York or anywhere else in the country." This observer was writing from the strict constructionist position, refusing to accept as restaurants establishments which indulged in other businesses at the same time that they provided food. This ruled out inns, taverns and hotels (though the City Hotel, established in 1794, was still constituting serious competition for Delmonico half a century or so later; for that matter, one of the eleven incarnations of Delmonico which appeared in New York before the line petered out was itself part of a hotel).

No matter. Whether or not Delmonico's was all by itself at the beginning (it would certainly not be at the end), it was destined to become the symbol of a new age of restaurant eating which took possession of New York like a tidal wave (and sent out side eddies into other cities as well), the result of the fresh fortunes which were being made in railroads, in shipping, in mining, in building, in manufacturing, in speculation—and in food. In the heady atmosphere of mounting millions—fewer than twenty millionaires in the entire United States in 1840, over one hundred in 1880 (one of whom was Lorenzo Delmonico), over four thousand in 1890, and forty thousand in 1916, when the rhythm of lavish spending began nevertheless to slow down—some of the plentiful money was bound to be spent for luxuries of the table. Eventually luxury would swell into extravagance, and extravagance into conspicuous waste, until the high jinks of what it was agreed to call the idle rich would become both grotesque and contemptible, even to themselves, and the Era of Wonderful Nonsense in eating would collapse in shame and of its own weight. Expansion could not last forever, but while it lasted somebody had to take the lead in satisfying the Gargantuan appetites of the parvenus and the refined appetities of the aristocrats and the intellectuals. It happened that this somebody was, collectively, the Swiss family of Delmonico.

The Delmonicos got into the restaurant business more or less by accident. None of them had ever been trained in the *haute cuisine* which they nevertheless introduced to New York, and the first of them to reach the United States, John Delmonico, was neither a restaurant manager nor a chef, but the captain of a three-masted schooner which plied between New York and the West Indies. He decided at thirty-seven that he had had enough seafaring, a profession into which he may have stumbled in the same directionless fashion in which he was to stumble into running restaurants, for nothing seemed to destine to the sea a man brought up in Switzerland, rich in Alps but short on oceans. No alternative activity beckoned him from land; he just wanted to get away from sailoring. Perhaps it was the fact that his native Ticino was wine country which gave him the idea of opening a wine store on the Battery, where he was still in touch with the sea and perhaps with old friends from the windjammers, whose ships could deliver the French and Spanish wines which he sold directly from the barrel for home consumption. Business proved good, so a year later he added his older brother Peter to the enterprise. Peter was neither a chef nor a restaurateur either, but he had managed a pastry shop in Berne, so he added that experience to John's newly acquired talent as a vintner and the pair opened Delmonico Brothers at 21–23 William Street, offering sit-down facilities to sippers of wine, spirits, coffee and chocolate and nibblers of pastry, candy, and ice cream. For the sake of keeping the record straight, suppose we call this establishment Delmonico I. This was a success too, so in 1831 the Delmonicos hired a French chef and converted the place into a full-fledged restaurant. Its European food was different from anything to which New Yorkers were accustomed. It quickly became fashionable to frequent the place. One novelty which attracted customers was such foods as eggplant and endive, which the Delmonico brothers dared put before the hitherto carnivorous New Yorkers. Thus from its beginning Delmonico's assumed the role of converting Americans to more balanced as well as to more refined and more luxurious eating.

> Delmonico . . . helped Americans to discover delicacies in their own backyards [Daniel J. Boorstin wrote]. . . . One of his achivements was to help Americans discover salads; and he showed how salads could be made from common New World plants. He popularized ices and green vegetables [ices had already appeared on the tables of George Washington and Thomas Jefferson, but perhaps they were less easily available to persons without presidential kitchens]. . . . Delmonico's restaurants . . . set a standard for New York gourmets which . . . made that city, next to Paris, the restaurant capital of the world.

The particular Delmonico to whom Mr. Boorstin was referring was the third to arrive, Lorenzo Delmonico, only nineteen at the time; but he was destined to prove himself the genius who would achieve that feat of making New York the runner-up of Paris. A nephew of John and Peter, he was imported in 1832 when his uncles needed help, for, finding themselves turning away more persons than they could serve at Delmonico I, they had opened Delmonico II on Broad Street. This prospered also—success had become a Delmonico family trait—so three of Lorenzo's brothers (Siro, François and Constant) were sent for too, to lend a hand.

At the end of 1835 the Delmonicos suffered their first bad luck: a fire got out of control in lower Manhattan, and destroyed a good many of its buildings, including Delmonico I. The indomitable family bought land on South William Street and built Delmonico III, larger and (was this already Lorenzo's influence?), embodying a surer taste in its interior decoration—though, if this was intended as an oblique reference to the fire, there may have been a touch of exaggeration in flanking the entrance with two marble pillars brought from Pompeii. Delmonico III was described in the New York press as having been conceived "upon a scale of splendor, comfort and convenience far surpassing anything of the kind in this country." Meanwhile competition in the field of fine catering appeared, between the fire and the opening of Delmonico III, in the establishment on lower Broadway in 1836 of the Astor House, which hoped, no doubt, to sweep up some of the crumbs which were falling from Delmonico's table. Together with the ancient City Hotel, the Astor House would indeed, in succeeding years, attract many large banquets, though it never achieved the reputation of Delmonico, while the City Hotel appeared in comparison with either of them as stiff and stuffy. Neither of them could match Delmonico's in serving small parties or individual diners. It was Delmonico's which attracted the most notable visitors from France, arbiter of fine eating, like the visitor for whom a reception was given at Delmonico III in the first year of its existence—Charles Louis Napoleon, who fifteen years later would become Emperor Napoleon III.

> Not long after the South William place opened [Robert Shaplen wrote], Lorenzo was able to draw up a seven-page *Carte du Restaurant Français* of stunning splendor and variety. Printed in English and French in parallel columns, and still adhering to the custom of listing prices in both dollars and shillings, it offered meats, fish, and game prepared in ways that few New Yorkers had even heard of, and presented vegetables and salads as if they were something to be prized. All à la carte, the menu began with nine soups, or, as alternative starters, eight side dishes, such as lobster salad and *saucisson de Lyon.* Next came fifteen varieties of fish, including such newcomers to Manhattan tables as stewed eels, and codfish with oyster sauce or capers, and these were followed by eleven beef dishes—boiled, à la

> mode, broiled, or roasted with truffles, mushrooms, or olives, and so on. Then, there were twenty kinds of veal, ranging from a conservative veal with white sauce to a daring fricasseed calf's head and stuffed calf's ear; seven kinds of mutton (a meat never popular with New Yorkers); twenty-nine kinds of poultry, including "chicken pie, financier fashion," "a leg of chicken, in paper," and pigeon "stewed or broiled, with peas;" and eighteen kinds of roast game, among them woodcock, snipe, plover, and grouse. Of the eighteen vegetables available, several—endive, watercress, artichokes, sorrel and eggplant among them—were utter strangers to most Delmonico customers. The menu wound up with sixteen varieties of pastry or cake and thirteen stewed or fresh fruits and preserves, and on its back was a list of sixty-two imported wines, champagnes, sherries, and Madeiras. A bottle of 1825 Château Lafitte sold for three dollars, and so did a bottle of Château Margaux of the same year. A bottle of Heidsieck champagne cost two dollars and the best Madeira eight dollars. A bottle of sauterne or red Bordeaux could be had for as little as fifty cents.

Not everybody admired Delmonico II and III, though it may be suspected that some of its detractors were incapable of recognizing its achievements because their previous eating experiences had not educated them sufficiently to permit them to appreciate Delmonico food. Mayor Philip Hone, after his first visit to Delmonico's, confided to his diary that he had eaten in Delmonico II, where "we satisfied our curiosity, but not our appetites." However Mayor Hone soon became a Delmonico habitué and in the 1840s and 1850s, the Philip Hone Eating Club held many of its gastronomic gatherings there.

Similarly banker Samuel Ward was on his first visit critical of the wine, though one may suspect that it was because his taste had been perverted by the sugary vintages which Americans had been drinking since Colonial times.

> I remember entering the café [Ward wrote forty years after the event] with something of awe, accompanied by a fellow student from Columbia. The dim, religious light soothed the eye, its tranquil atmosphere the ear. . . . I was struck by the prompt and deferential attendance, unlike the democratic nonchalance of the service at Holt's Ordinary, in Fulton Street, at Clark & Brown's, in Maiden Lane, and at George W. Brown's, in Water Street. . . . I reveled in its coffee, the chocolate, the *bavaroises,* the orgeats. . . . The Burgundy disappointed me and did not prove comparable to the March & Benson Madeira of those days. But we rose from the table with a sigh of regret that our next visit would have to be postponed until our next pocket-money day. We dined perfectly for half a dollar apiece, if not less. The cost of a dinner at George Brown's, or Clark & Brown's, was a shilling downstairs, upstairs, a quarter of a dollar.

Exception made for the reservation about Burgundy, this hardly constituted an indictment, and an older and richer Ward later became so favored a client of Delmonico's (which was no longer serving half-dollar meals) that he was allowed, when he gave a dinner there, to go into the kitchen and make the sauces himself. This worked out better in his case than in that of another person who was accorded the same privilege, a shipping magnate named Ben Wenberg, who produced in Delmonico's kitchen a sauce for lobster from a recipe which he said he had discovered in South America. The house approved of the sauce to such an extent that it adopted it, and listed the dish it accompanied as Lobster à la Wenberg. Wenberg wore out his welcome quicker than the sauce did, by precipitating a brawl in the restaurant which caused him to be barred from Delmonico's. The sauce stayed, renamed Lobster à la Newburg. Another attempt to honor a valued customer was frustrated by the incomprehension of the public: the creamed chicken dish listed as Chicken à la Keene, for Foxhall Keene, the free-spending son of a successful Wall Street speculator, is still with us, but we call it Chicken à la King.

The most voluble detractor of Delmonico's was probably William Makepeace Thackeray, but he seems to have been preoccupied more by what the food cost than with how it tasted. On his first visit to the United States he was entertained at Delmonico's by a group of admirers, headed by Washington Irving, and was delighted; he, of course, ate free. When he invited a few of his hosts for a return meal, also at Delmonico's, he was thrown into a state of shock on discovering that the bill came to four pounds per person. This no doubt warped his judgment of the fare, which he then decided was "so-so and the wines . . . were quite ordinary." He wrote to the poet Bayard Taylor, "Don't, don't give a dinner at Delmonico's. I did it yesterday and it is a sin [the author of *Vanity Fair* may well have been a Puritan] to spend so much money on the belly."

The first Delmonico, John, died while deer hunting in 1842. Peter, the survivor of the two original brothers, who was getting on, left the leadership in managing the business to Lorenzo, who thus became in fact, if not yet in title, the boss of Delmonico's. His first ordeal was the second disastrous fire in the family's history, again a disaster also for lower Manhattan, in which Delmonico II was burned down. One year later Delmonico IV was opened, close to Bowling Green; it was both restaurant and hotel. Two years later, Peter, now sixty-two, decided that he wanted to retire completely. Lorenzo became the sole head of Delmonico's, of which he was already the real manager. He was thirty-five. He would direct Delmonico's mounting destinies for three decades more.

The times were propitious for bringing prosperity to restaurants, particularly pretentious restaurants. Hitherto most American eating and most American entertaining had taken place at home; now the rich were seeking a broader playground; and a restaurant like Delmonico was prepared to provide it. Delmonico's did not simply profit idly and undeservedly from this change in social habits, it had been largely instrumental in provoking it. It had raised dining out to the status of an event by providing the sort of background and the kind of food which made it an adventure. Its success in remaining the one New York restaurant above all others where it was smart to be seen, where presence was often rewarded by finding one's name in the eagerly scanned society columns of the newspapers, was not a gratuitous gift of the circumstances, but a result achieved by unflagging effort and the exercise of a certain psychological flair, particularly on the part of Lorenzo, though one might wonder if some of the tactics adopted by Delmonico's, which turned out to pay off, were not arrived at partly by accident. It was, for instance, a shrewd stroke to present menus in French, thus annexing the prestige of French cooking and tapping the exploitable element of snobbery, as Delmonico's had done since the time of John the Founder—or was it? Could it have started simply because John and Peter were more at home in French than in English? The relaxed, agreeable atmosphere of their first restaurants, and the increasingly luxurious settings which succeeding Delmonico establishments displayed may have sprung from a motivation no more complicated nor calculating than the natural pleasure a home owner feels in making his dwelling as attractive as possible, transferred to business premises. Another detail for which Delmonico's became noted was the emphasis it put on appetizing, carefully prepared vegetable dishes; it may have been inspired by the fact that the Delmonicos liked vegetables themselves.

Later Lorenzo certainly used psychological tactics with astute awareness of what their effects were likely to be. He no doubt realized that there is nothing likelier to make the public fight to get into a restaurant than an apparent attempt to keep them out, though when he established a blacklist of persons Delmonico's did not care to serve, it may also have stemmed from a desire to keep out the boisterous, who were by no means in short supply in New York. Lorenzo raised prices at a certain stage in Delmonico's evolution, which was not unjustified, given the quality of the food and service, but he probably had in mind also the advantages of creating another element of exclusivity.

Lorenzo's perspicacity extended also to the choice of locations for his restaurants. He sensed early that the center of gravity in New York was moving steadily northward, and he moved uptown with it. Another element of his success was that he paid his help well; Delmonico's was therefore able to acquire and to hold the services of the most skillful chefs and the suavest *maîtres d'hôtel.* When, in 1861, the Maison Dorée on Union Square (another exploiter of the prestige of French) was on the way to becoming a dangerous rival of Delmonico's because of the brilliance of its chef, Lorenzo simply outbid the Maison Dorée for him. His name was Charles Ranhofer, French despite his apparently German name; he was Alsatian. Though only twenty when Lorenzo hired him, he had already served in the kitchens of a princely house in Europe and had come to New York as chef for the Russian Consulate. He presided over Delmonico's cooking for thirty-four years and eventually became a sort of gastronomic dictator who refused flatly to prepare, even for the most valued clients, any dish at a season when he felt, in his own phrase, that it would not "cook well"; the customers meekly assented.

But for all his astuteness, the most important element in Lorenzo's success was the banal Horatio Alger principle of hard work, coupled with unrelenting attention to detail. He never forgot, as too many restaurants operators do once their establishments have attained a certain reputation, that the basic element in the industry of feeding the public is food; if it is not of the first quality to begin with, no amount of skill in the kitchen can improve it. The foundation of fine cooking is know-how in buying its raw materials. The public seldom realizes how many of the world's most famous chefs refuse to delegate the choosing of the raw materials to anyone else. Lorenzo was not the chef, but he knew food. It was his habit to rise every morning at four and do the day's buying in Washington Market and the Fulton Fish Market, garbed inappropriately in cutaway and top hat. He finished the day's shopping at 8 A.M. and then went back to bed to refresh himself for a reappearance, a few hours later, in the restaurant. At first Delmonico's often had difficulty finding on the market the unaccustomed fruits and vegetables it wanted for its tables, so the family bought 220 acres of land in Brooklyn and raised its own, tailor-grown to Delmonico specifications. Similar care was devoted to ordering exotic products from abroad and scouting distant sources for unusual foods—for instance, Delmonico's is believed to have been the first restaurant in New York to serve avocados.

These principles were already in full application when Delmonico IV was opened and confided to the management of brother Siro. It developed a special character of its own, that of a place of rendezvous for the sort of celebrities who get regularly into the newspapers for other reasons than the possession of wealth. Jenny Lind developed a habit of eating her after-theatre suppers there, following the concerts she gave in 1850 and 1851 at Castle Garden. Louis Kossuth, the Hungarian revolutionary, enthusiastically received when he arrived in the United States as an exile, lived during the same years in the Delmonico hotel and ate in its restaurant. Leading politicians and other persons influential in the councils of the municipal and national governments conferred across Delmonico's well-spread tables—Horace Greeley; Chester A. Arthur, before he went to the White House; and, somehow not on Lorenzo's blacklist, Boss Bill Tweed of Tammany Hall, before he went to jail. But the new restaurant soon found itself too far downtown, left behind by the rapidly growing population of New York (it nearly tripled in the two decades before the Civil War), which continued to flow uptown. Lorenzo sold out in 1853 and opened Delmonico V at the corner of Broadway and Chambers Street. Meanwhile the competition was growing too; in 1858 the Fifth Avenue Hotel opened on Madison Square and for a score of years was rated the best hotel in New York by the same class of persons who considered Delmonico's its best restaurant. It served excellent food.

Fashions in elaborate eating were changing again. The newly rich, and even some of the older rich, were going in for spacious, well-equipped mansions on Fifth Avenue where they could give lavish dinner parties at home, while balls and banquets bringing together hundreds of people at a time were held in public halls or hotels with room enough to accommodate them. This was beyond the scale of Delmonico's, which in any case preferred a sedate subdued atmosphere to the crush of crowds, considered more appropriate to the circus than to the dining room. It undertook, however, to cater for such functions, not only in New York, but as far away as Newport, where some of its richest patrons maintained chateaux overlooking the sea. The largest affair over which it presided, winning overwhelming esteem despite unruly attendant circumstances, was a ball given in honor of the Prince of Wales, later Edward VII, in 1860. There were four thousand guests, too many for any New York restaurant to handle, or for that matter, for any hotel ballroom of the period, so the Academy of Music was requisitioned. Even so, four thousand represented an exclusive gathering, since there were 300,000 persons outside to see the Prince of Wales arrive, of whom at least 100,000 no doubt wanted to be inside. The Prince was young and gay (a word unambiguous at that time); an attempt was made to entertain him in a fashion which it was hoped he would find amusing. Unfortunately the only persons sufficiently august to be charged with receiving the heir to the title of King by the Grace of God of Great Britain, Ireland and the Dominions beyond the Seas, Emperor of India, had left their days of gaiety far behind them. The ball was "managed by sexagenarians," according to the *New York Herald,* which added:

> Such a splendid study of antiques of both sexes has never before been enjoyed in this city. It seemed like going back to the Pyramids. . . . To see the old fellows hobbling about, interfering with everybody, elaborately disarranging other people's plans and having none whatever of their own, was exceedingly ludicrous.

The ball was something of a shambles, but Delmonico's, in charge of the supper room, so far as anyone could be said to be in charge of premises overrun by a milling mob, salvaged whatever could be salvaged for the honor of New York by the superb quality of its food. The menu, printed in gold on white satin for the royal guests and in bronze for the riffraff, was what the gay blades who were running the affair would probably have described as *nec plus ultra.* This is what the four thousand, or as many of them as could fight their way to the tables, were offered to stay their hunger:

Consommé de Volaille
Huitres à la Poulette

Saumon
au Beurre de Montpellier
Truites

Filets de Boeuf à la Bellevue
Pâtés de Gibiers à la Moderne
Pains de Lièvres Anglais Historiés

Galantines de Dinde à la Royale
Cochons de Lait à la Parisienne
Terrines de Nérac aux Truffes

Jambons de Westphalie à la Gendarme
Langues de Boeuf à l'Escarlate

Mayonnaises de Volailles
Salades de Homards à la Russe

Grouses
Bécassines
Bécasses
Faisans

Gelées au Madère
Crèmes Françaises
Petits Fours

Macédoines de Fruits
Glaces à la Vanille et Citron
Charlotte Russes

Pêches, Poires, Raisins de Serre, etc.

PIECES MONTEES

La Reine Victoria et le Prince Albert
Le Great Eastern
La Vase de Flora
Silver Fountain, etc. etc.

Reading the menu was as close as many of the guests got to the food, but *The New York Times,* always conscious of its grave responsibilities, chose to ignore this fact and concentrate only on the merits of the caterers.

> In the details of decoration and equipment [it wrote], there was scarcely anything with which the most fastidious taste could quarrel. The crest of the Prince of Wales blazed out in plumes of diamond-like light over the floating folds of a vast tent of pink and white drapery, lined along one side with buffet tables, singularly neat and brilliant in service, and really attended to by a regiment of most faithful and active waiters, marshaled under the orders of Lorenzo Delmonico, and perpetually supplying a regulated and orderly stream of admiring, but more or less appetized, guests with all the delicacies which the house of Delmonico so justly prides itself on "creating" with the true artistic power. We may frankly say that we have never seen a public supper served in a more inapproachable [literally *le mot juste,* but this was probably not what the reporter meant] fashion, with greater discretion, or upon a more tactfully luxurious scale.

Readers who consulted no other paper than the *Times* would have missed the real record-breaking aspect of the occasion: never since Balthazar's Feast had so much food of such high quality been spilled on so many persons, or, alternatively, on the floor. The irreverent *Herald* reported that since no one could move in the jam-packed supper room, food had to be passed over the heads of those present so that "wine [of the finest vintage], cream, and jellies

. . . were liberally sprinkled upon elegant dresses." But the food and drink, whether used for sprinkling or for consuming, was unanimously admitted to have been beyond criticism.

The Academy of Music where this shindig was held was on Fourteenth Street, and with the tide of fashion still flowing uptown, Washington Square had ceased to be the northernmost permissible limit of social activity. Lorenzo decided to locate on Fourteenth Street too, adding to Delmonico III (managed by Siro Delmonico) and Delmonico V (managed by Constant Delmonico), Delmonico VI, on the corner of Fifth Avenue and Fourteenth Street.

Delmonico VI opened just in time to play host to the first of the exclusive dinner dances, which he called cotillions, dreamed up by Ward McAllister, the terror of social climbers, who had decreed that high society was limited to The Four Hundred (because that was the maximum number of guests who could be accommodated in Mrs. William Astor's ballroom). The "Ward" came from his uncle, Samuel Ward, the same who had been allowed to make his own sauces in Delmonico's kitchen; he was thus a pampered Delmonico client by inheritance. Always in favor of being plentifully supplied with money provided he did not have to work for it, McAllister first tried feathering his nest by inheritance, unsuccessfully, so he married money instead. He retired for life at the age of twenty-four, and set himself up as the *arbiter elegantiarum* of society, powerfully aided by its real queen, Mrs. Astor, exerting a despotic sway over candidates for admission to the *Social Register,* not to mention those already in it who wanted to stay there. His dictatorship extended to the gastronomic domain as well, though he may have cheated a bit in establishing competence in this field. He had a farm, which permitted him to pose as a knowing producer of food, and liked to invite friends to picnics there (it was perhaps largely for this reason that he popularized picnicking among a social class which up to then had not much appreciated this simple pleasure of the poor); when his guests came, he borrowed cows and sheep from neighboring farmers and scattered them about his property to give it the appearance of an operational food factory. However, whether his reputation as a gourmet was earned or spurious is beside the point: he had it, and consequently his approval was as valuable to Delmonico's as Delmonico's deference was useful to him. A good many of the restaurant's most profitable dinners were given at his instigation, and no doubt others were due to him indirectly, when it became known that his advice to party givers was, "Tell Ranhofer [Delmonico's chef] the number of your guests and nothing more, and you will have perfection." He did not bother to add, "if you can afford it," for if you could not afford it you did not belong to Ward McAllister's world.

McAllister does not seem to have been directly responsible for the most expensive dinner held at Delmonico's before ostentatious feeding began to get completely out of hand (prior to 1875, say), after which the sky was the limit. As a matter of fact there were *two* most expensive dinners, depending on whether you go by the total bill or the price per plate. 1865 was the year of the dinner for which the total cost was highest—$20,000, which we will not attempt to turn into today's equivalent, but it would certainly multiply this figure several times. The host was Sir Samuel Morton Peto, an English businessman, and the guests were one hundred New York tea and coffee merchants, so the occasion falls into the category of expense-account eating. It is not certain that Sir Samuel had time to recoup his outlay through deals made with his guests before he was unfortunately prosecuted for fraud two years later in his native England, which must have saddened Lorenzo, who never liked to hear of his customers going to jail, though several of them did.

The most expensive dinner per person was served in Delmonico's at the beginning of the 1870s; paradoxically it proved, in a way, Chef Charles Ranhofer's contention that Delmonico's was not excessively expensive. He even made the observation, heretical for a man in his position, that "the most expensive dishes are not always the most palatable," and presented a sample menu composed of Delmonico dishes of the first quality which, accompanied by a recommendable table wine, cost only twelve dollars for three persons. This was a somewhat lower estimate than that of journalist Richard Harding Davis, who had described Delmonico as a "place where you can get a good square meal, well cooked and fitly served, for about seventeen dollars," at a time when this would have been an outrageous price. Delmonico's prices of that period do not sound outrageous to us today, they sound philanthropic.

> Somebody just dropping in to take pot luck on the evening of Monday, September 12, 1898, for example [Robert Shaplen wrote], would have found roast larded partridge, at two dollars and fifty cents, the most expensive item on the menu. Venison cutlets with purée of chestnuts were a dollar, roast lamb with mint sauce was sixty cents, as was an artichoke with Hollandaise sauce, and Niagara or Delaware grapes were forty cents. Use of the chafing dish was a quarter.

Actually it was not the cost of the food which was making Delmonico's a rich man's preserve but the extras: special service in private rooms, flowers, decoration, music, fine wines and spirits, and above all favors for the guests (at one Delmonico dinner each lady present was gratified by a souvenir in the form of a solid gold bracelet, which certainly set the host back more than the dinner did). The most expensive per-person dinner proved Ranhofer's point in that while it came to four hundred dollars a plate, an unheard-of sum for the times, the larger part of this amount was accounted for by the expensiveness of the gift offered to each of the ten guests—a scale model of the luxurious boat owned by the host, a fervid yachtsman.

Ward McAllister seems to have been the inspirer of a unique gastronomic contest in 1867—at least he reported it in his book, *Society As I Have Found It*—the result of bets exchanged among three of Delmonico's best heeled patrons, Leonard Jerome (whose daughter subsequently became the mother of Winston Churchill); William Travers, whose reputation as a wit may possibly have been won partly by wealth sufficient to induce acquaintances to overlook his stutter and explode into laughter at his palest sallies; and the august August Belmont, Prussian-born, at that time New York's leading banker. Each of them undertook to offer for a score of guests a dinner which would outdo those of the other two, and in accordance with McAllister's well-known penchant for Delmonico's, all three, naturally, commissioned that restaurant to produce the winning dinner, and hang the expense. The contest turned out as it had to—it was judged a three-way tie. Its chief contribution to gastronomy was ice cream with truffles on it, "strange to say, very good," McAllister wrote.

In 1868 a Delmonico dinner which attracted wide attention was the one offered by a group of publishers to Charles Dickens on his second visit to America. The first had left a certain bitterness behind it; Americans, no doubt oversensitive, had resented Dickens' observations about the United States in his *American Notes* and in *Martin Chuzzlewit,* which had not given good marks to American food—and disapproval on this score from an Englishman was disapproval indeed, given the difficulty of producing food worse than that of England. Delmonico's put itself out to make him eat his words, along with its cooking, employing among other blandishments the kittenish device dear to restaurateurs of giving nonce names to some of the dishes served, which had no real meaning since they had never been used before and would never be used again—*crème d'asperges à la Dumas, petites timbales à la Dickens, truites à la Victoria, agneau farci à la Walter Scott, côtelettes de grouse à la Fenimore Cooper.* Despite the speciousness of these non-descriptions, the quality of the food was so genuine that Dickens, in a mood of euphory, rose to his feet, possibly with a certain difficulty,

> to record that wherever I have been, in the smallest places equally with the largest, I have been received with unsurpassable politeness, delicacy, sweet temper, hospitality, and consideration, and with unsurpassable respect for the privacy daily enforced upon me by the nature of my avocation here and the state of my health. . . This testimony, so long as I live, and so long as my descendants have any legal right in my books, I shall cause to be republished, as an appendix to every copy of those two books of mine in which I have referred to America. And this I will do and cause to be done, not in mere love and thankfulness, but because I regard it as an act of plain justice and honor.

What was probably the most famous dinner ever served at Delmonico's occurred in 1873 and has gone down in restaurant history under the name of the Swan Banquet. Edward Luckmeyer, an importer and shipowner, had received an unexpected windfall, in the form of a government check for ten thousand dollars, sent him on the flimsy pretext that he had overpaid his taxes. Stunned by this unaccustomed munificence, Luckmeyer decided to spend it all on one Gargantuan breakfast; and to whom could he turn for realizing this project if not to Delmonico? The meal for seventy-two guests which resulted was described by the restaurant's head waiter, Leopold Rimmer, as

> the greatest affair that ever could be got up in any land . . . The table was eighteeen feet wide and as long as the hall; it had a big lake in the middle with a big cage over it; there were swans swimming around in it; there were large trees with rustic bird cages, and singing canary birds, and two fountains, stones and sand just like a natural park. Tiffany built the big golden cage; it was a sight.

Rimmer did not point out that the flowers had a utilitarian as well as a decorative aspect but Ward McAllister, who was present, did:

> The table covered the whole length and breadth of the room, only leaving a passageway for the waiters to pass around it. It was a long extended oval table, and every inch of it was covered with flowers, excepting a place in the centre, left for a lake, and a border around the table for the plates. The lake was indeed a work of art; it was an oval pond, thirty feet in length by nearly the width of the table, inclosed by a delicate golden wire network, reaching from table to ceiling, making the whole one grand cage; four superb swans, brought from Prospect Park, swam in it, surrounded by high banks of flowers of every species and variety, which prevented them from splashing water on the table. There were hills and dales; the modest little violet carpeting the valleys, and other bolder sorts climbing up and covering the tops of those miniature mountains. Then, all around the inclosure, and in fact above the entire table, hung little golden cages, with fine songsters, who filled the room with their melody, occasionally interrupted by the splashing of the waters of the lake by the swans, and the cooing of those noble birds . . . these stately, graceful, gliding white creatures.

Noble, stately and graceful, no doubt, but the swans proved less well attuned to the decorum of Delmonico's than the diners, who behaved, though the swans did not. Perhaps they were accustomed, when they dined out, to less formal settings, more like the Brooklyn park from which they had been brought—Niblo's Garden, say, which from 1829 until the Civil War was the most famous of the "winter gardens" frequented by New Yorkers in their thousands (of German inspiration, though William Niblo was Irish), where eating ranked lower than drinking, dancing, listening to the band, or watching vaudeville acts or plays. It is probable also that the Prospect Park swan handlers, when they rented their birds to Delmonico's, neglected to mention that it was mating season, when swans turn ugly. In the middle of the meal, two of the males staged a battle royal; fortunately Tiffany's gold wire held.

> McAllister was not ruffled in the least, which is understandable [Dale Brown wrote]—he had been moistening his throat with floods of Blue Seal Johannisberg, "incomparable '48 claret, superb Burgundies, and amber-colored Madeira." And then, just at the very moment when he could hardly bear the exquisite pleasure of it all any longer, "soft music stole over one's senses." So ravished was McAllister by the $10,000 dinner that he neglected to tell what he had to eat at it.

This oversight was rectified by Chef Ranhofer in his 1,200-page cookbook with four thousand recipes, *The Epicurean,* as we are reminded by José Wilson:

> Ranhofer's book records the menu for this grand occasion. . . The eight courses ranged from *consomme imperiale* and shrimp bisque through hors d'oeuvre, a fish course of red snapper and *paupiettes* of smelt, fillet of beef, chicken cutlets, canvasback duck and cold asparagus vinaigrette. After a pause for a palate-refreshing sherbet, the 75 [sic] diners forged on with saddle of mutton, truffled capon and various vegetables, winding up with a galaxy of desserts, glazed fruits and bonbons. Seldom can a tax refund have given so much digestion-taxing pleasure to so many.

Enriched by truffle ice cream and battling swans, Lorenzo Delmonico, still following the flow of society northward, moved farther uptown in 1876 to open Delmonico VII on Madison Square, which was becoming the fashionable area for dining out. Not only was the Fifth Avenue Hotel, a serious competitor, located there, but so was the new Hotel Brunswick, which had developed a cuisine second only to that of Delmonico's itself. Several exclusive clubs which prided themselves on their food were nearby too. John Jacob Astor and his brother William inhabited twin houses a few blocks to the north on Fifth Avenue, on a site destined to harbor later the old Waldorf-Astoria Hotel, another famous caravansery, since supplanted in its turn by the Empire State Building. From the moment that Delmonico's moved to Madison Square, where Lorenzo entrusted its management to still another recruit from the family, his nephew Charles Delmonico, it dominated the neighborhood, maintaining its position as New York's top restaurant, though competition was tougher now. In a city where fifty years earlier Delmonico's had been described as the sole restaurant, there were now between five and six thousand, born partly of Delmonico's example, but more importantly of the changing times. The Madison Avenue restaurant was, of course, the best yet. The *Tribune* called it "the pride of the nation," and continued:

> Yesterday morning at seven o'clock precisely the three members of the Delmonico family of restaurateurs—Lorenzo, Siro and Charles—were found at their new rendezvous of gastronomes on Fifth Avenue, the house having

been opened to the public at that hour. The three Delmonicos did not begin to receive their guests in any great numbers until late in the day, when a steady stream of celebrities—social, plutocratic, artistic, journalistic, legal and every other shade of professional gentlemen, including a sprinkling of the clerical—poured through the door of the café, a salon of almost Saracenic splendor, and sauntered in and out, hat in hand, all over the beautiful building. The soft, yielding carpets, the costly gildings, the rich paper on the walls, the sumptuous silver service, the solid rosewoods and oak panelings on the café, were all admired in their turn. . . . The recent great increase of American travel in Europe, and familiarity with the most famous restaurants of the old civilization, have taught our citizens to appreciate their debt to the Delmonico family. . . . There is now no restaurant in Paris or London or Vienna which can compete with our Delmonico's in the excellence and variety of its fare. . . .

The Madison Square restaurant was indeed to prove the best, or at least the most profitable, of any restaurant the Delmonicos operated before or after it. As the Madison Square establishment, being the farthest uptown, automatically replaced as the most *chic* the Fourteenth Street Delmonico VI, Lorenzo sold the latter, and at the same time moved Delmonico V *southward,* thus transforming it into Delmonico VIII, at Broadway and Pine. A move in this direction might seem contradictory, but it took into account the growing importance of the financial district. He also opened Delmonico IX at Broadway and Worth, but soon abandoned this one, which left him with four restaurants, Delmonicos III, V, VII and VIII. Delmonico VIII, the flagship of the fleet, became even more brilliant than its predecessors; not only was it frequented by the rich, but also by successful, and publicity provoking, literary lions—Mark Twain, William Dean Howells, Bret Harte, Oscar Wilde when he visited the United States, before his disgrace of course, and even so unplayboylike a foreign customer as the philosopher Herbert Spencer. This injection of intellectualism into Delmonico's world may have helped to preserve it from the extravagances which were now beginning to run wild in the conspicuous revels of "high society" and of the unco rich, which were not encouraged at Delmonico's, for which the Swan Banquet had represented just about the limit.

Lorenzo was mercifully spared the degrading spectacle of the antics of an upper crust which was rapidly progressing from the tasteless to the odious as the century toiled onward toward its end. Having fed every nineteenth-century President of the United States beginning with James Monroe, though some after and others before they occupied the White House, he died in 1881, leaving an estate of two million dollars. Almost symbolically, the death of the greatest of the Delmonicos, the man who had created more than any other single person the cult of gastronomically substantial eating in New York, occurred in the same year as the opening of an establishment destined to become Delmonico's most formidable rival, partly because it would be willing and ready to open its doors to the sort of tomfoolery in high-altitude eating which Delmonico's was never able to bring itself to tolerate.

This was Louis Sherry's, but its rivalry did not develop immediately. Another restaurant important in the gastronomic history of New York opened a year later, in 1882—Lüchow's, which may not have constituted quite direct competition for Delmonico's, since its specialty was German cuisine rather than French; but it appealed to serious *Feinschmecker,* as did Delmonico's, for in its field it gave equally careful attention to the quality of its own type of European cuisines, and like Delmonico's it imported fine vintage wines, especially, of course, Rhine wines. It was reputed for its game, prepared in a fashion antithetical to that of Delmonico. For some reason it proved particularly attractive to musicians, of no matter what school—Victor Herbert, Enrico Caruso, Ignace Paderewski, and Richard Strauss were all among its customers. Lüchow's would outlast Delmonico, and continues to feed New Yorkers more or less in its traditional fashion at its original Fourteenth Street address, despite changes of management.

It was early in the 1880s also that still another harbinger of future competition for Delmonico's first appeared, in 1883, when a certain Oscar Tschirky, a Swiss like the Delmonicos, came to the United States and found a job as a busboy at the Hoffman House, also on Madison Square, from which he could watch the entrances and exits of the elegant customers of New York's Number One restaurant. According to his memoirs, he was engaged in his favorite distraction of observing Delmonico's from the vantage point of the Hoffman House one evening in 1887 when he heard its doorman call for Lillian Russell's carriage. "At that moment," his version of the incident continues, "Miss Russell came out with a party of friends. I was captivated by this fleeting glimpse. She was the loveliest woman I had ever seen." The next day, burning, we may suppose, with desire, he applied to Delmonico's head waiter for a place on his staff. He got the job. The enemy was within the gates—for Tschirky, of course, though still in the bud, was to become Oscar of the Waldorf.

The preliminary mustering of counter-Delmonico forces began at a time when the Delmonico army itself was weakening. Siro had died a few months after Lorenzo, and Charles thus found himself the last male survivor of the Delmonico line, the others having disappeared through death, disability or disinclination. François, deciding that the restaurant business was not for him, had bowed out many years earlier. Constant had committed suicide in 1873 in grief over the death of his wife. Sole responsibility seems to have been too much for Charles; and his cares were aggravated by unfortunate ventures on the stock market. In 1883 he suffered what was politely described as a nervous breakdown, and in January of the following year he eluded the apparently not quite intensive vigilance of the male nurse charged with keeping him out of trouble, wandered off alone into a snowstorm, and was found several days later frozen to death.

There was still a Delmonico in Delmonico's however, for though the male line was extinct, the female line was not. Of Charles's two sisters, one, Giovannina, had married and thereby become Mrs. Theodore Christ; but the other, Rosa, who had remained single, was still in possession of her maiden name. Mr. and Mrs. Christ had already disappeared from the family roster even earlier than the male Delmonicos, in 1874, when they made a business trip to Paris and died there in an epidemic of the black plague. They left three children, Lorenzo, Charles and Josephine, who were brought up by Aunt Rosa, head of the business since Charles's death. Charles had bequeathed a one-fifth interest in Delmonico's to each of the children, while Rosa held the remaining two-fifths. It seemed that when Rosa died, there would be no Delmonicos left to carry on the family traditions. Lorenzo, though he had been given the name of the most talented of the Delmonicos, probably in the hope that he would emulate him, had no taste for the business; but Charles and Josephine had, so they proceeded to rectify the shortage of Delmonicos by changing their names legally, giving a slight twist to their patronymic in the process. This made them respectively, Charles Crist Delmonico and Josephine Crist Delmonico. Rosa quickly realized that in Charles the family genius had found a new avatar, and she retired to the wings to leave Charles in control. He turned out to have inherited the genius of his granduncle and followed faithfully in his footsteps, applying the principles which had enabled Lorenzo to keep Delmonico New York's best restaurant. It remained the best.

With a fine feeling for continuity, Charles Crist Delmonico in 1890 bestowed new life upon the oldest of the surviving properties and the first to have escaped destruction by fire, Delmonico III. He built a new eight-story building on its site, converting Delmonico III into Delmonico X. A pair of hand-me-downs were retained from the previous building—the Pompeiian pillars.

The year 1890 was marked also by another stirring in the restaurant world, a development potentially ominous, from Delmonico's point of view. Louis Sherry's confectionery shop had given birth to a catering service, which had been mightily aided by its location. Only a block away from the Metropolitan Opera House, Sherry had succeeded in winning the between-acts catering concession, lucrative in itself, but, even more important, a strategic position from which to impress wealthy potential private employers of caterers with his competence. He had worked up a flourishing home catering business among the same sort of persons who ate at Delmonico's (and frequented the opera), and he now delivered what amounted to a challenge to the older establishment. He closed his Sixth Avenue place and opened a luxury restaurant, equipped, like Delmonico's, with a general dining room and private dining rooms of varying sizes—and also with large ballrooms. It was clear that he was going after Delmonico's clientele; the better to woo it away, he had set up shop in a more fashionable location, north of Delmonico VII, at Thirty-seventh Street and Fifth Avenue.

This frontal assault from without was paralleled by a bit of boring from within. Oscar Tschirky had been steadily working his way upward in Delmonico's. When he was put in charge of the private dining rooms, he had the satisfaction of assigning himself to wait on Lillian Russell and her nearly inseparable companion, Diamond Jim Brady, the first time they appeared at Delmonico's after he achieved his new position, or so he wrote in *Oscar of the Waldorf.* When he heard that a great new hotel was about to be opened, he prepared, on the Delmonico letterhead, a recommendation praising his own merits and asked the most wealthy, distinguished and desirable customers he served, one after the other, to sign it. He accumulated eight large pages of signatures, which he then took to the manager of the still unopened hotel as an earnest of the kind of custom he could attract to it. The Waldorf-Astoria began business in 1893, with Oscar as its head waiter. He installed there an innovation which, as a standard fixture of exclusive restaurants, has plagued diners-out ever since—the plush rope behind which customers praying admittance can be lined up to wait, patiently or impatiently, for the staff to pass on their worthiness.

In the Waldorf's formal Palm Garden or its adventurous Roof Garden, open to the sky, Oscar again had occasion to serve his idolized Lillian Russell and Diamond Jim Brady. They also remained customers of Delmonico, but as a matter of fact the archetype of a new sort of restaurant which was now springing up, Rector's, in the hail-fellow-well-met vein, was more in accord with their life-style. Also, though neither of the pair were hard up for money, and though Rector's was not exactly cheap, it was still cheaper than Delmonico, no negligible detail when one ate as much as they did. "Jim Brady is the best twenty-five customers we have," George Rector said, and he considered his custom so valuable that when Brady remarked regretfully that Sole Marguéry could only be had in the Paris restaurant which had created it and had given it its name, Rector took his son out of college and sent him to Paris to take a job in the Marguéry's kitchen and burglarize the recipe—or at least that is the story which was told at the time. It goes on to report that after several months of espionage, the Rector scion succeeded, and when the first American-made Sole Marguéry was plunked down before Diamond Jim, he devoured nine orders of it one after the other before going on to the next course.

This represented no record for Brady. A normal dinner for him, according to Rector, began with two or three dozen Lynnhaven oysters, six-inch giants rushed up from Maryland expressly for him. Then came half a dozen crabs, two bowls of green turtle soup, and, in Rector's words, "a deluge of lobsters," a term which he redefined more precisely, on request, as meaning six or seven. This whetted the appetite for a double portion of terrapin, two canvasback ducks, a large sirloin steak with appropriate vegetables, and, when a tray of French pastry was presented for dessert, its entire contents. That Brady was only a glutton, not a gourmet, seems evident from the fact that he did not drink wine, the almost irreplaceable accompaniment for this sort of food, nor, for that matter, even beer. He accompanied each enormous repast with several large glasses of his favorite drink, freshly squeezed orange juice or, alternatively, lemon soda pop. After such a meal, lingering at the table for after-dinner talk, he would dip from time to time into a box of chocolates placed handily near his plate by the knowing waiters who served him. The correct amount to tamp down such a meal was about two pounds.

For most persons, a dinner of these dimensions would have required the next twenty-four hours for its absorption; Brady ate six meals a day. Breakfast consisted of pancakes, hominy, eggs, cornbread, muffins, steak, chops and fried potatoes, washed down with a gallon of orange juice. At half-past eleven he ate two or three dozen shellfish to stave off the pangs of hunger until lunch, an hour later—oysters and clams again (he was a great guzzler of seafood), deviled crabs, a couple of lobsters, roast beef, salad, and two or three wedges of different kinds of pie. With orange juice. Tea was slight: shellfish again, accompanied, for a change, by lemon sole. Dinner has already been described. If he could rise from the table afterwards he might go to the theatre, an appetite-provoking exercise, which had to be followed by supper—the traditional hot bird and cold bottle, except that in Brady's case this meant *several* game birds, and the bottles held orange juice or lemon soda. Though Brady himself drank so badly, as a host he treated his guests better. More than five hundred bottles of champagne were consumed at a dinner for fifty which he gave at the Hoffman House, Oscar Tschirky's first place of employment, in honor of his racehorse, Gold Heels, which had just proved itself to be aptly named by winning a large purse. On this occasion, Brady's guests tied on the feedbags at four P.M., and did not finish eating until nine the next morning—seventeen hours of stalwart stuffing, and stalwart drinking too, if his guests drank ten bottles of champagne apiece (could the management have padded the bill?) The dinner cost $100,000, but as at Delmonico's, it was the extras which counted—the favors were diamond brooches for the ladies and diamond-studded watches for the men. Brady had to live up to his nickname, which came from the $87,000 set of diamond studs and cufflinks he wore in the evening, part of a jewelry wardrobe estimated at $2,000,000. He had evidently profited from his profession of selling heavy equipment to railroads at a period when railroads were proliferating like weeds, but more rewardingly. His heavy eating may have begun in the days when, in his business capacity, he had an unlimited expense account with which to entertain railroad presidents and purchasing agents or it may have started earlier, at the training table provided by the free lunch counter of his father's saloon. Free lunch counters in those days were as lavish at their end of the social scale as were Delmonico's, Louis Sherry's, and Rector's menus at the other. Richly supplied buffets stretched temptingly halfway down the long bars, making it unnecessary for the patrons to interrupt their drinking to eat. The free lunch counters may have been weighted a little heavily toward salted or spicy aliments, great provokers of thirst, but this was hardly unreasonable when saloonkeepers had to get their money back in an era of five-cent beer.

It is easier to understand Brady's gluttony than that of his most constant dinner companion, Lillian Russell (real name, Helen Louise Leonard), the popular music hall and operetta singer, who shattered all conceptions of feminine delicacy by eating dish for dish with him; she remained nevertheless for thirty-five years the idol of American males, including Oscar of the Waldorf, running through five husbands and nobody knows how many lovers. She shared with Diamond Jim a passion for corn on the cob lashed with great gobs of melting fresh farm butter, a dish never included in thinning diets; and indeed neither of them was thin. America's dream girl weighed more than two hundred pounds; but the nineteenth century liked its women ample. As for Brady, when he died in 1917 at the age of fifty-six (from digestive troubles), his stomach was found to be six times normal size.

From the point of view of Delmonico, Diamond Jim Brady's preferred hangout, Rector's, was flashy and vulgar. It belonged to a new, brash type of restaurant which had been nicknamed "lobster palaces" (Churchill's, Charley's, Bustanoby's, and the Knickerbocker were other celebrated examples of the species). They were the appropriate places to dine with chorus girls, who in the popular imagination lived exclusively on champagne and lobster. At Delmonico's one did not dine with chorus girls, one dined with heiresses, and even with heiresses one dined with all the world as chaperons. No one was allowed to eat behind closed doors in Delmonico's; and even with the doors wide open, one couple could not occupy a private room, even a married couple. Delmonico's believed that there was safety in numbers, and the more-than-two rule for use of the private rooms was inflexible. When so important and long-standing a client as August Belmont ordered dinner for four in a private dining room, and through some misunderstanding the Belmonts' guests did not show up, the headwaiter refused to let Belmont and his wife enter their reserved room. Purpling at the jowls, Belmont bellowed for the boss. Charles Delmonico was immediately produced, and informed Belmont politely but firmly that Delmonico's did not serve couples in private rooms. The Belmonts ate in the common dining room with the populace.

Delmonico's prudishness left one field wide open for Louis Sherry's, that of the stag dinner. Without Sherry's, where could "the awful Seeley dinner" have taken place? The host, Herbert Barnum Seeley, had no claim to fame except that he was a nephew of Phineas T. Barnum. Seeley had tried to stage his party, for twenty persons, at Delmonico's behind closed doors, but Delmonico's would have none of it. The feature of the evening was a dance performed on the table by Little Egypt, who had won notoriety and wild success at the Chicago Columbian Exposition in 1893 by the liveliness of her dancing and the brevity of her costume. To forestall any criticism on this second count, she left it off, ingenuously or ingeniously, at the Seeley dinner, except for its black lace stockings and high-heeled shoes. Some envious person must have tipped off the authorities as to the nature of the program, for after waiting politely for Little Egypt to finish her number, the police, who must have been waiting just the other side of the keyhole, burst in, accompanied by headline-hungry reporters who had been tipped off too. Unfortunately for the history of journalism and the edification of posterity, snapshot photography had not yet become practical; the photographer who wanted a clear image in those days had to request his subject to remain relatively still for a few seconds, and remaining still was not one of Little Egypt's gifts; besides she had an urgent appointment with the paddy wagon.

Delmonico's closed its eyes resolutely to this sort of thing and pursued its virtuous course unperturbed. Virtue did not have to be its own reward in this case; it was not lack of prosperity which caused Charles Delmonico in the middle of the decade to close two of his four restaurants, Delmonicos V and VIII. He may have felt that he was spreading himself too thin, but the chief reason was that the location of these two no longer corresponded to the distribution of Manhattan's population. He retained the oldest establishment, Delmonico X (né III); the South William Street site served the still growing financial quarter, whose bigwigs might lunch at Delmonico's downtown and dine the same day at Delmonico's uptown. In 1897, Delmonico's uptown became even farther uptown. Charles built Delmonico XI, destined to be the last of the line, at the corner of Fifth Avenue and Forty-fourth Street. It was, as usual, bigger and better than its predecessors. The main restaurant, with Louis XVI furniture and wall coverings of green and yellow satin, was on the ground floor, as were the Palm Room and the café. The second and third floors contained private dining rooms of various sizes and diverse decoration, while the fourth floor was a roof garden—in name only, for it was indoors, not open to the elements like that of the Waldorf-Astoria; perhaps that was why it never became popular.

Louis Sherry did not propose to allow himself to be upstaged by his rival. He promptly followed Delmonico's north, commissioning fashionable architect Stanford White to build a *twelve*-story building diagonally across Fifth Avenue from Delmonico; it opened in 1898. Despite Sherry's edge in size and the inclusion among its regular customers of such prized persons as banker Pierpont Morgan and newspaper publisher Frank Munsey, the weekly *Illustrated American,* in an article entitled, "The Fight between Delmonico's and Sherry's," bet on the aging David against the youthful Goliath. "It will be a fight to the death," it predicted, "with the odds in favor of Delmonico's. This hostelry has such a loyal following that a dozen eating establishments would not hurt it."

Delmonico's left to Louis Sherry, without regrets, the honor of staging the Horse Dinner given by C. K. G. Billings for thirty members of the New York Riding Club, whose steeds were brought up by freight elevator to the restaurant's main ballroom on the fourth floor, which may have caused some alarm among diners on the third floor, although the horses' hoofs had been muffled by cushioned bags. This precaution seems to have been taken less to spare the feelings of the third-floor customers than to spare the flooring; with a further thought for its well being, a covering of turf had been laid down. The horses were eased up to the central table and mounted with the aid of small flights of steps placed beside every second horse for the convenience of cavaliers who, Riding Club members though they were, had not reached the point where they could afford to eat at Louis Sherry's without acquiring an age and a girth incompatible with rodeo performances. They did manage to stay in their saddles throughout the dinner without anyone's being thrown, while waiters dressed as grooms fed oats to the horses and waiters dressed as waiters fed a fourteen-course dinner to the hussars. The problem of how to get to the provender was solved by harnessing a small table across the withers of each animal, from which the rider, with some effort, could eat, and that of drinking by making it an all-champagne dinner. With only one wine, it was possible for each guest to carry his own supply in his saddlebags, and suck up the champagne as desired through a rubber tube—*brut,* one hopes. The cost of this feast was given as $50,000. It must have been conceived, remarked Ralph Pulitzer, publisher of the *New York World,* "in the spirit of desperate and dogged travail."

In 1901 Charles Delmonico died suddenly of a heart attack; but the indomitable Aunt Rosa was still alive, and she returned grimly to the active direction of the business from which she had hoped to free herself fifteen years earlier. She died in her turn in 1904, handing over the reins to Charles's sister Josephine—the last of the Delmonicos.

American habits in high-level eating were changing again. Antics like the Horse Dinner had been badly digested by public opinion. Newspaper readers who had once turned avidly to the society columns to participate vicariously in the glittering and fascinating revels of the rich, looked sourly upon them now as the reprehensible divertissements of wastrels.

Newsworthy banquets were still being held, but the spirit behind them was different. In 1905, for instance, a dinner at Delmonico's celebrated the seventieth birthday of Mark Twain; 172 other writers were present to pay tribute to him. Twain, always a remarkable speaker, moved his hearers alternately to tears and laughter. William Dean Howells described the food as "the best Delmonico could do," which sounds ambiguous, but he meant it as a compliment.

In 1919 the Waldorf-Astoria staged a memorable meal in honor of a personage from abroad whose functions guaranteed restraint—Cardinal Mercier of Belgium. It was, besides, Ember Day, when meat could not be offered to Roman Catholics. The Waldorf did itself proud all the same, with fish and vegetable hors d'oeuvre, canteloupe filled with fruit salad, potato soup, lobster Thermidor, salmon steaks with mousseline sauce, potato balls, hearts-of-lettuce salad, Port Salut cheese (a delicate reference to the sacerdotal vocation?—*salut,* of course, means "salvation"), peach Melba, and *petits fours.* This was a sumptuous meal for Oscar of the Waldorf, whose influence on New York restaurant eating had taken the direction of simplifying menus and cutting down on their abundance, in principle a healthy tendency, but one wonders whether the inspiration came from gastronomy or from economy. Oscar, after all, was not a man of the kitchen, he was a man of the dining room. The only dish he ever invented was Waldorf Salad, a questionable combination of lettuce, diced apple, celery and mayonnaise (today's chopped walnuts were added later, by another hand). Oscar was less expert in cookery than in snobbery. He may be credited with having promoted the attitude which cowed customers into accepting the standards of *maîtres d'hôtel* and headwaiters as the ultimate criterion of social behavior, especially in matters of dress. Greater sobriety was nevertheless desirable enough, and it accorded with the new temper of the times; Oscar's success may be ascribed partly to the circumstance that the public was weary of waste and in a mood to prefer less extravagant eating. To measure the extent of this evolution, one has only to put side by side the menus of the 1860 Delmonico supper for the Prince of Wales (later Edward VII) and the 1919 Waldorf-Astoria dinner for the Prince of Wales (later Edward VIII):

Tortue verte à la Waldorf
Celéris   Amandes salées   Olives
Crabes d'huitres à la Newburgh [sic]
Poitrine de pintade farcie, sauce diablée
Pommes douces à la Dixie   Coeurs de laitue à la française
Pudding au riz à l'américaine
Café

And with what wines was this feast washed down? Alas, Prohibition had set in. The only beverage to which the menu owned up was White Rock mineral water. Could refreshments unlisted on the menu have been available also? When reporters asked the Prince what he thought of Prohibition, he answered, "Great! When does it begin?"

"The best restaurants in the world are, of course [of course!] in Kansas City," reads the first line of Calvin Trillin's *American Fried,* a conversation stopper if ever there was one. This recalls an observation of Alexandre Dumas in his *Le Grand Dictionnaire de Cuisine:* "The best *andouillettes* [tripe sausage] I have eaten . . . are the *andouillettes* of Villers-Cotterets," a place of which few other Frenchmen had ever heard, in connection with *andouillettes* or anything else. Dumas was born in Villers-Cotterets and Calvin Trillin was born in Kansas City. It is unlikely that anyone else would nominate as a leading harborer of good restaurants a city whose most famous palace of gastronomy was one which, at about the period when Herbert Seeley was serving Little Egypt for dessert, was far enough ahead of the times to gratify the wealthy cattlemen who made up the bulk of its clients by having their appetites attended to by waitresses who were not only topless, but bottomless also.

If Kansas City is not a great restaurant town, then what place in the United States is? One name presents itself immediately: New Orleans. New Orleans not only possessed restaurants of historic importance at the same time as New York, in the heyday of dining out, but it still possesses them. New Orleans has not been content to fall into the broad American pattern of our times, in which the nation's hosts from coast to coast serve a slightly embalmed shrimp cocktail in a ketchup sauce, a tenderized steak burned outside, still frozen inside, a tinfoil-wrapped baked potato, a salad with premixed dressing, and a gelatine pie or dessert topped with synthetic whipped cream, and call it cuisine. On the contrary, the better New Orleans restaurants stress the native Creole specialties which are little known outside of Louisiana, the neighboring Gulf Coast of Mississippi, and a bit of Florida. There is considerable variation, of course, among restaurants, but any city which can lay claim to a full score of *maisons sérieuses,* establishments which make a definite attempt to provide superior food cooked in a careful way, certainly deserves to be counted high in our hardly overcrowded hierarchy of gastronomic centers.

And such restaurants! From the very best, which are very good indeed, to the most ordinary, which can be very poor, the New Orleans establishments have escaped the dread uniformity which marks the general run of eating places in most American cities. So well publicized has been the food and music of the French Quarter that every tourist seems to know what he came for, and the city fathers see to it that he gets it. Even though there has been a falling-off, in recent years, in the quality of New Orleans restaurant food (a fact to which even loyal *Orléanais* subscribe) it has not been more severe than in such other gastronomic centers as New York and San Francisco, and has been palliated, if not compensated for, by the maintenance of a congenial atmosphere and friendly, unhurried service.

Antoine's heads every list, having served New Orleans and the world for more than a century and a quarter, since 1840. It is in the heart of the French Quarter, the menu is French, and except for the renowned Oysters Rockefeller and the elaborate crawfish bisque, the cuisine is basically French of the nineteenth century. The *pompano en papillote,* cooked in parchment, has a rich sauce of shrimp, crabmeat and mushrooms worthy of a Normandy *auberge,* though there are those who believe fresh Channel sole is a fish superior to the vaunted pompano.

Breakfast at Brennan's is an institution in New Orleans, though by local standards Brennan's is a Johnny-come-lately, founded only yesterday—1946, but it is already into its second generation—the son of founder Owen Brennan has taken over a good deal of the active management, along with his aunt, so Brennan's, like Delmonico's, may be developing one of those family dynasties which in the history of restaurants produce restaurants of history. As for Antoine's, it is into its third generation.

The sort of breakfast Brennan's provides would have pleased Diamond Jim Brady, except for its alcoholic content; the tradition of the house is that breakfast begins with an eye-opener—milk punch with a brandy and tangerine base, or better yet a Ramos gin fizz. Brady would have replaced this with orange juice, but afterward he would no doubt have gone along with Brennan's celebrated Eggs *Hussarde,* of which the name, in an attempt to straddle two languages, has gotten both its gender and its number twisted (ham and poached eggs on toast, with Hollandaise and *marchand de vin* sauce, plus a grilled tomato). A dessert of flaming pancakes can follow. Diamond Jim would have passed up the *café brûlot,* because of its brandy, but might have accepted New Orleans chicory-flavored coffee with milk instead.

Galatoire's on Bourbon Street completes the trio of classic New Orleans restaurants; it goes farther back than Brennan's, to 1905, and thus within the period of great restaurants marked in New York by the life span of Delmonico's—1825 to 1923. Once more it is a case of what seems to be something like a *sine qua non* for the development of a restaurant of historical importance, its direction within a single family for more than one generation; Galatoire's parallels Delmonico's in another fashion: there has been a descent from uncle to nephew, as happened twice in the Delmonico line; but founder Justin Galatoire's nephew is flanked by the founder's daughter, and a grandson is in reserve. Galatoire's, known for its rigorous impartiality in allotting tables—first come, first served—offers Creole and French dishes only a trifle less elaborate than Antoine's. Its followers rate its shrimp remoulade the best anywhere, and maintain that its gumbos are better than any served in New Orleans' famous French Quarter. Here too are many dishes straight from the classic French cuisine, such as trout *amandine* and dessert *crêpes.*

Visiting these three establishments, one acquires the credentials to talk about New Orleans cuisine with casual strangers, but it is not the whole story by any means. Recently Henri Gault and Christian Millau, the well-known French gastronomic writers, experienced in rating the hotels and restaurants of their own country, spent more than a fortnight in New Orleans and came up with the verdict that the best food in the entire city was to be found in the

Hotel Pontchartrain, outside the French Quarter, which is frequented by the city's aristocracy. The hotel itself is of medium size and thoroughly modernized; its restaurant is called the Caribbean Room for no discernible reason. Though no heavy emphasis is given to Creole dishes, the important ones are usually available, according to the supply of ingredients to be found in the local markets. Quality is uppermost in the minds of the proprietors (two generations of Aschaffenburgs) rather than mere picturesqueness.

Every resident of New Orleans has his favorite place, which he will hesitantly recommend if pressed. One which has perhaps attained historic status is the Bon Ton Café on Magazine Street, just outside the Quarter. "Greatest Creole and Cajun dishes in town," said an informant, which could be accounted for by the fact that its owner is a native of bayou country. This is the place where New Orleaners go to eat crawfish in season, from November to July.

After New Orleans what city still has restaurants worth remembering? Boston?

A unique quality of the historic restaurants of Boston is that almost all of them were dedicated to the New England cuisine, in contrast to New York's famous eating places, which kowtowed to the prestige of French cooking. Valid gastronomic traditions are almost invariably built around foods locally available, and this was the case for Boston, whose seafood has always been important on its restaurant menus. The city's most famous dish, Boston baked beans, however, did not appear on them, except in establishments of such low quality that they were called, in disdain, "beaneries," for the Bostonian's opinion of the sort of beans that were served in restaurants (or put up in cans) has always been low. In Boston, baked beans were the product of the home, where they could be cooked slowly and lovingly; less care was given to canning them for the barbarians west of the Connecticut River or south of Plymouth, who could not be expected to appreciate the real thing anyway. Nowadays Boston does not supply them at all. Friends Brothers, the last canners of baked beans in Boston, who had been using since 1928 the same recipe, which they claimed had been handed down since Pilgrim days, moved Down East to Portland, Maine, in 1974. Beantown isn't Beantown any more.

The Boston eating place best known outside of its own area is probably the Parker House, because of Parker House rolls,

> as much of a tradition in the United States as any bread [wrote James Beard]. They were created . . . by the Parker House in Boston, which was one of the great nineteenth-century hostelries. They have been copied by every cookbook author and every baker in the country. . . . Parker House rolls should be delicate, soft, and rather sweet, typical of American rolls in the nineteenth century, and they consume butter by the tons.

In the early days of the Parker House the filet mignon could literally be cut with a spoon, and its cooking was the pride of New England. Founded in 1855, and thus in the same period of rampant restaurantism that saw the rise of Delmonico, the Parker House is still an important name in Boston, but it has lost a little of its finesse, perhaps because its clientele has.

The Parker House was owned by the J. R. Whipple chain, which also operated Young's Hotel, well worthy of being listed in the gastronomic history of Boston. It was expensive, but worth it; the classic meal there early in the twentieth century was oysters on the half-shell followed by the establishment's renowned planked sirloin steak, which might run, depending on its accompaniments, to ten or fifteen dollars for four, plus a dollar to headwaiter Hoxter. This was a lot of money in those days, but when one was in a more economical mood there was always the United States Hotel on Atlantic Avenue, which served a smashing Sunday dinner for a dollar a head, composed of eight or nine courses, including tidbits like lobster, of excellent quality. The cooks were probably Negroes; the waiters were, which was true of Young's also. Both have disappeared now, but two other hotels of the same period are still flourishing mightily.

One is the Ritz-Carlton, born during the Delmonico-dominated period too. Associated loosely with the original Ritz of Paris, it was for collegians of the day the place to which one repaired for dinner in the stratosphere, suitably attired in tails (Boston considered the Tuxedo vulgar). A hostelry which was pretty close to being a national monument in those times, the Rizt-Carlton in our days has descended closer to the normal level for hotel dining, with a smaller and hardly adventurous menu, though its food continues to be excellently cooked and its range is reasonably wide: it can give you such a supposedly humble dish as Boston clam chowder (not so humble when it is well made) or a fine bottle of French wine.

The other Boston hotel of the great restaurant period has maintained its high position to this day, and perhaps even improved on it—the Winter Place Hotel. It dates from the great period too, the 1880s; it was the finest restaurant in Boston then and it still is. When the French gastronomic writers Gault and Millau toured the United States to compile their restaurant guide to America they described it as "the most seductive, the most prestigious of Boston and, without doubt, of the whole East Coast." It was a favorite of the late socialite and gastronome, Lucius Beebe. The Winter Place Hotel? you may be asking yourself in bewilderment. In the 1880s, yes; its present name is Locke-Ober.

The Winter Place Hotel was operated by Louis Ober, whose name suggests French origin; he was in any case enamored of French. Locke-Ober is the exception among major Boston restaurants in that it originally specialized, not in New England cooking, but in French. Its founder even ordered wood paneling and mirrors from that country to decorate his dining room, though whether it was from France or elsewhere that he procured Mademoiselle Yvonne, surname unknown, does not seem to be on record. Mademoiselle Yvonne is the name of a lush painting of a young woman, approximately life size, whose costume consists of a wine glass held lightly in the hand. It shocked the lights out of a city where "they dress the bacchantes / In bicycle panties," as a rhymester of the period put it when right-thinking organizations prevailed upon the Boston Fine Arts Museum to apply a bit of artfully disposed drapery to Frederick William MacMonnies' statue, the Bacchante, when it was acquired by the Museum. (It is still there, but minus the veils now.) The dining room of the Winter Place Hotel was frequented by men only; as Boston is a place of tradition, Yvonne is still there too, in the ground-floor restaurant which serves men only. The painting is hung against the wood-paneled casing of the stairway by which parties containing ladies mount to the second-story dining room, the only spot from which Yvonne cannot be seen.

In 1891 a retired merchant-marine captain, Frank Locke, opened a de luxe cafe next to the hotel, stocked with a rich selection of domestic and exotic beverages; it became a Bostonian habit to stop at Locke's for a drink before moving on next door to dine at Ober's. Union was clearly indicated, but it had to be a shotgun marriage: a liquor company bought them both, and Locke-Ober was born. The next step came in 1901 when a Frenchman named Emile Camus succeeded to the management, closed the hotel, and astutely added Bostonian cooking to the French cuisine; today you can order either, and either will be superb. The restaurant is still on Winter Place.

A classic Boston restaurant of a quite different type is Durgin Park, opposite Faneuil Hall Market, aggressively humble—sawdust on the floor, dishes and coffee mugs of unbreakable thickness. It is inelegant, but it is not trying to be anything else. It gives all its attention to the food, and the steaks, seafood, and blueberry pie served there stick in the memory.

Jacob Wirth's served German food—sauerbraten, sauerkraut, pig's trotters—and still does; nothing has been changed there for a hundred years, except that it occurred to somebody to install electricity. Another old classic is the Union Oyster House, whose building is three hundred years old; but the restaurant is younger—it dates from 1826, so it is now a century and a half that it has been serving some of the best oysters, clams, and lobsters in Boston.

Most Frenchmen who visit the United States and cover ground there pronounce San Francisco (not, surprisingly, New Orleans) their favorite city; given French fussiness about food, this should imply a high gastronomic rating. San Franciscan food has deteriorated of late years, but it remains true that you can do better there than in almost any other important American city, except New York, New Orleans, or Boston, and in its enthusiasm for dining out it surpasses Boston, where one goes to restaurants for the sake of their food, not, as in New York, New Orleans, and San Francisco, in the same spirit in which one goes to the theatre.

The restaurant history of San Francisco parallels that of New York. It started at about the same period and under the same impetus—the acquisition of sudden riches; in New York this newfound wealth came from industry and business, in San Francisco from mining. The boom in San Francisco was more sudden than in New York. The gold rush occurred in 1848, and in 1850 the Tadisch Grill, specialty seafood, the oldest restaurant still open in San Francisco, was already functioning. San Francisco's Delmonico period, so to speak, might be fixed as beginning in 1875, when the Palace, "the world's greatest hotel" in the estimate of San Franciscans, opened its doors with, precisely, a chef from Delmonico directing its kitchens—Jules Harder. One year later the Palace was host to a dinner which recalls some of Delmonico's banquets, slightly self-seeking, one might suggest, since it was given in honor of Nevada Senator William Sharon, who happened to be the owner of the Palace. He had made much of his money from his share in the precious metals of the Comstock Lode, which is why each guest found beside his plate a menu (in French, chic in San Francisco as in New York) engraved on a plaque of silver from the Comstock Lode which, if he chose to melt it down, would have been worth forty dollars, no negligible sum in 1875; it was perhaps to discourage such disrespectful treatment that each menu bore, incised on its back, the name of the guest to whom it belonged.

In San Francisco as in New York, the Nineties were Gay; then, in San Francisco as in New York, the atmosphere changed as the newly rich, who had a tendency, in the joy of its unexpected possession, to throw their easily won money about ostentatiously were replaced by their children, brought up in more sophisticated fashion and less tempted to brandish wealth since they were used to it. At the same time San Francisco, like New York, was so deeply submerged by a wave of foreign restaurants that the American element in its restaurant cooking became more or less lost in the flood of cosmopolitanism. San Francisco can give you good French, Italian, German, Danish, Middle Eastern, Moroccan, Greek, Balkan, Yugoslav, Russian, Spanish, Caribbean, Mexican, Peruvian, Indian, Indonesian, Filipino, Korean, Vietnamese, Thai, and every local variation of Japanese and Chinese food, in its impressive Chinatown or out of it, plus the inextricably mixed and the utterly unidentifiable; but it is short of American food. In Arthur Bloomfield's 1975 *Guide to San Francisco Restaurants,* of the eight to which he gives three stars, his highest award, three are Italian, two are Chinese, one is Japanese, one is French, and one is, more or less, Polynesian—Trader Vic's, which exists in several copies in a number of cities and, whether it is a restaurant or a circus, seems always to be successful.

There *are* American restaurants in San Francisco, especially restaurants devoted to Southern cooking, but they do not rank very high on the culinary scale. Restaurants of historical longevity, except Tadisch (founded, though, by a Yugoslav sixty-eight years before there was a Yugoslavia), turn their backs on American cooking. Jack's, which dates from 1864, offers French cuisine, and is so conscious of the unassailability of its ancient position that it sometimes seems to be not merely resting on its laurels, but leaning on them. Schroeder's, founded in 1893, which could not bring itself to let women in for forty-two years, is devoted to German cuisine.

Visitors can always explore along Fisherman's Wharf in search of seafood, whose purveyors like to refer to their places as "grottos," with about even chances of making a find or falling into a tourist trap. One of the surest ways to avoid the latter is to keep out of restaurants which go in heavily for atmosphere. A bad sign, though not necessarily a damning one, is waiters who go about their work with tasseled Sicilian fishermen's caps on their heads, which not so long ago might have been seen in the same neighborhood actually adorning genuine fishermen. Though the tasseled cap is no longer fashionable for San Francisco fishermen (discouraged from wearing it, perhaps, because of its usurpation by waiters), it should not be thought that Fisherman's Wharf itself has degenerated into picturesque uselessness. Fishing boats still tie up there and provide the restaurants with the rich variety of seafood the coast affords—Dungeness crab, for instance, or the fifty-two different varieties of rockfish found there. There are also numberless varieties of tasty clams, so it is a little disconcerting to learn that the Old Clam House imports its raw materials from Chesapeake Bay.

Chicago has not developed restaurants which have left their mark on history, unless you count the collective mark of its steak houses. The old and modest Whitehall Hotel has more or less cut itself off from recognition by excessive reticence, for the public is not admitted to the more interesting of its two restaurants, which is organized as a private club; it admits women at dinner, grudgingly perhaps, but they are barred at lunch. The private dining room offers French cuisine, but the public restaurant could hardly be more determinedly American; it is a temple of sturdy breakfasts (corned beef hash on the popular side, sweetbreads on toast for the effete) and of husky drinks (brandy eggnog and Bourbon milk punch). If Chicago's much touted Pump Room is considered by posterity to have made history, the question will arise whether it forms part of gastronomic or theatrical history. From a French point of view it belongs rather to the latter.

> This highly celebrated establishment (though abandoned little by little by its millionaires) [wrote Gault and Millau in their American guide] is inhabited by firebugs. The custom, widely spread in Anglo-Saxon countries and in some spurious large Italian (or even French) restaurants, of pouring

brandy on the dishes and setting fire to it has made the glory of this house. In our opinion, except in a few precise cases, this practice of "flaming" is highly reprehensible, falsifies taste, and makes the dining room look like a city bombed with napalm.

Philadelphia, where the lavish nature of a dinner he attended once shocked John Adams, possesses one of the oldest gastronomic traditions in America—normal enough, since this "great and noble" city, as the visiting Lord Adam Gordon called it in astonishment, was for a considerable time the metropolis of the Colonies. As befits the senior gastronomic city, it is Philadelphia which preserves the cookbook George Washington's mother gave to his wife so that she could feed her son in the fashion to which he had been accustomed. It told how to make a "frykecy of chicken" (George Washington's spelling was erratic too; perhaps he learned his letters at his mother's knee), "dress a dish of mushrumps, make a lettics tart or a hartichoak pie," or "make Red Deer of Beef"—Washington could not tell a lie, but apparently his mother could. There is a legend that Philadelphia's famous pepper pot soup was created by a Pennsylvania Dutch cook for Washington and his soldiers at Valley Forge, which seems unlikely.

Despite the antiquity of its gastronomic traditions, Philadelphia is less of a dining-out city than New York, New Orleans, or San Francisco. Philadelphians seem to prefer eating at home to eating at restaurants, and one of the city's most characteristic forms of feeding outside of the family circle is often kept as private as possible by that Philadelphian institution, the eating club, of which there are more than a hundred in the city. Indeed the dean of them all is virtually a secret society, which maintains its privacy deliberately and jealously.

Far and away the most venerable of all Philadelphia's eating clubs [José Wilson reported in *American Cooking: The Eastern Heartland*], and even today surrounded by a veil of secrecy the CIA might envy (members say they are "not authorized" to discuss any of its activities), is the State of Schuylkill, or the Fish House as it is better known. Here originated the famous and lethal Fish House punch and also, reputedly, the technique of planking shad, a claim the Indians might contest. By a neat piece of semantics, the Fish House calls itself the oldest formally organized men's social club in the English-speaking world (London clubs of an earlier date were not, apparently, formally organized).

When the club was formed in 1732 it was with the intent that a small group of Quaker gentlemen, among them Penn's secretary, might spend an idyllic day every now and then dawdling on the banks of the Schuylkill River . . . shooting game birds and fishing and cooking their catch for dinner, with no wives or servants present. It was this choice of locale that led to the club's original name, the Colony in Schuylkill (the name was changed to the State in Schuylkill after the Revolution). Since 1732 the club has moved its location and its ancient clubhouse (known as the Castle) four times, losing in the process not one smidgeon of its elaborate rituals.

Apprentices, who may be in their fifties or sixties, have to wait for a member to die or resign before they may be elected, after passing a test that calls for tossing a mess of perch in a huge iron frying pan. Meanwhile they come in for most of the work and not much of the fun. Although an apprentice helps with the cooking and passes the punch with which the opening toast is drunk, he may not take a drink or sit down to eat until invited, and it is his job to set the table in a most particular and exacting way. According to the number of members and guests present, a certain distance, precisely marked on a numbered stick, must be maintained between the nose of George Washington's head on one plate and the nose on the next; and the Madeira glasses, butter plates and flatware all have just as rigidly prescribed positions . . .

A city with such gastronomic traditions could hardly fail to have preserved some honored restaurants from its culinary past, and Philadelphia is indeed not without them. Bookbinder's was founded in 1865 (again the great American restaurant period) and has been in the same family for four generations. It now calls itself Old Original Bookbinder's to distinguish it from the newer Bookbinder's Seafood House (the specialty of the Old Original is seafood too); the Seafood House is run by a member of the Bookbinder family also. The first Bookbinder's is associated with a dish little known nowadays, snapping turtle soup, but even there it has lost its old-time favor. Today's eaters seem to be afraid of it; it is too far off the beaten track for contemporary American tastes, increasingly standardized and unadventurous. It is probable that the quality of the dish today is not what it was when the complicated recipe which is still used unchanged was devised more than a century ago, for there are very few snapping turtles wandering the streets of Philadelphia nowadays; when the restaurant makes snapper soup it has to send to Oklahoma and Missouri for frozen turtle meat.

Another historic house in Philadelphia is the Bellevue Stratford Hotel. Under that title it dates only from 1902, but it was created from a merger of the Hotel Stratford with the old Bellevue, which reaches well back into the nineteenth century. Three years after the merger it was the site of the Philadelphia Assembly, an annual social event which combined dancing (one of the dancers in 1790 was George Washington, then fifty-eight) with rich eating, and the Bellevue Stratford did its duty nobly on this occasion, with oysters in cream sauce, Virginia ham, fillet of beef in aspic, roast capon, roast pheasant, and terrapin, among other dainties. Terrapin, a rare dish nowadays, is still one of the specialties of the Bellevue Stratford.

Terrapin used to be a trademark of Baltimore, a good restaurant city in its time, whose standards were defended with vigor by that hearty eater, H. L. Mencken; but one hears little about its food today. It was, and is, a fine place to eat soft-shell crabs too, and so is its neighbor, Washington, D.C.; but the political capital of the country is far from being its gastronomic capital. Aside from one or two seafood restaurants and such political sideshows as the Occidental, where pictures of politicians plaster the walls, there is little to report about Washington. One suspects that it may have been a better eating center in its early days, when Major Pierre l'Enfant, the Frenchman who laid out the city, endowed it with two markets, one of which, the Eastern Market, has recently been restored. It seems to have been a colorful spot in the days when Thomas Jefferson enjoyed visiting it, and wrote after one of his explorations there: "If heaven had given me a choice of my position and calling, it should have been a rich spot of earth, well-watered, and near a good market for the production of the garden."

What has happened to Charleston, the capital of she-crab soup? Is gastronomic history being made in San Antonio, where you can even dine on canal boats? To what other American cities can we look for notable restaurants? Cincinnati, perhaps, for Grammer's, founded in 1872, which is still serving the hearty German cooking with which it began more than a hundred years ago?

And Kansas City?

Is it possible that the authors were too hasty in appearing skeptical about Calvin Trillin's claim for the restaurants of his native city? They feel, uneasily, that he may be closer to the American eater than they are, when they describe its restaurant history in terms of Delmonico and Louis Sherry; and Mr. Trillin writes so well that he almost convinces them that such eloquence cannot be mistaken. Unfortunately the fame of Kansas City eating places has not reached them, so all they can do is pass on his recommendations: Jess & Jim's, "the best steak restaurant in the world"; Bryant's, "the single best restaurant in the world," redoubtable for its spare ribs with barbecue sauce, accompanied by "the best French-fried potatoes in the world"; Mary-Mac's for pot likker; Zarda's Dairy for banana splits; LaMar's Do-Nuts for (need we say?) doughnuts; the Toddle House for hashed brown potatoes; Kresge's for hot dogs with chili; and Winstead's for hamburgers. The specialties of these gastronomic emporia are a far cry from the sort of victuals Delmonico put before the Prince of Wales, but it is possible that they are closer to the heart, and stomach, of grass-roots America.

Mr. Trillin's *American Fried* gives a good deal of attention to hamburgers, as they are presented in one place or another, an interest which would no doubt have been deplored by such foreigners as Gault and Millau, who referred scornfully to "hamburgers, cheeseburgers and other foods for toothless old men." This comes very close to being an insult to the flag, for hamburger is very much an American national dish, and one might have wished that Mr. Trillin, while he was extolling it, had told us where and when it entered the American larder. This was certainly an event worthy of being recorded in

American gastronomic history, but it is probable that Mr. Trillin does not know where it began, and, for that matter, that nobody knows.

However in January, 1974, Kenneth Lassen, owner of Louis' Lunch in New Haven, Connecticut, threatened with eviction to make room for a projected medical center, told the press that if he were put out, "a piece of American history will be sitting on the sidewalk." *What* piece of American history? The invention of the hamburger. It was his grandfather, Louis Lassen, he said, who had been the first man in the United States to put a chopped beef patty between two slices of bread, thus creating the American hamburger; and he, Kenneth Lassen, was still serving them as their inventor had done—between slices of toast, without ketchup, pickles, or other modern folderol which would have falsified their natural flavor. The authors have no idea whether this claim is valid or not; but they know of no other.

If the great period of American home cooking fell between the War of 1812 and the Civil War, and if the great period of restaurant cooking fell between the Civil War and the First World War, the second did not quite wait for the actual arrival of war to lay it low. The excessive luxury of restaurant eating had already begun to wane well before the war, partly because the war was casting its shadow before, but more importantly because social patterns were changing. In 1916 the oldest Delmonico restaurant, Delmonico III on South William Street in the financial district, was closed for lack of custom, after ninety-three years of honorable service. For years it had been almost deserted at night, when the offices which had displaced homes were empty; it had lived on long business lunches, which had now become few, short, and frugal. All that remained of the Delmonico empire was Delmonico XI, at Forty-fourth Street and Fifth Avenue, which was dying too—"half show place, half mausoleum," Robert Shaplen wrote of it. Three years later Josephine Delmonico sold Number XI too. Delmonico's subsisted, as a name and a building, but there were no Delmonicos connected with it any more; and where this great restaurant family could no longer succeed, how could anyone else expect to do better? It lasted only four years more. On May 21, 1923, thirty invited guests sat down with the ghosts of Ward McAllister, Diamond Jim Brady, Lillian Russell, and August Belmont, for the last dinner ever served at Delmonico's. The most famous of all American restaurants had lasted just four years less than a century.

Its runner-up, Louis Sherry, had already given up. It closed as a restaurant in 1919, reverting to its original status as a confectionery and catering business. Sherry's did make another stab at restaurant operation in 1921, but it did not last.

No New York restaurants since have had anything like the influence of Louis Sherry's or Delmonico's or the Waldorf-Astoria or even Rector's on the evolution of restaurant eating; but a few others which made their mark—and are now, most of them, gone—contributed enough to the history of dining out to deserve mention before we abandon this subject. For instance:

(1) Le Pavillon, a spin-off of the French Pavilion at the World's Fair of 1939. Its proprietor, Henri Soulé, spawned through the former members of his staff, from chefs to busboys, nearly as many French restaurants as the face of Helen launched ships. At his death his relict inherited La Côte Basque, still operative, which Soulé had substituted after moving Le Pavillon elsewhere in a moment of pique with his landlord, who had been refused a choice table and as reprisal had bought the building to annoy Soulé.

(2) Lupovitz and Moscowitz, with the Café Royal, and the old Ratner's, vanished from Second Avenue as the lower East Side Jews who appreciated their fine mid-European cuisine and *gemütlich* atmosphere left the old neighborhood for uptown, and for suburbs more in keeping with their improved economic situation. Today, though Greater New York has hundreds of delicatessen restaurants offering the traditional "appetizing" food favored by Jews, only a handful announce themselves as "kosher," while the majority describe themselves as "Continental," and do not observe Jewish dietary laws. In the great resort hotels of the Catskills, north of the big city, kosher cuisine is generally available, lavishly served and often well-prepared. Some of these hotels have a history contemporaneous with, though far less glamorous than, Delmonico's and Sherry's. Grossinger's and the Concord have become legendary for their luxury and the diversity of their recreational facilities, and in the profusion of eatables offered their guests they recall the latter days of the previous century.

(3) A whole category of restaurants, those devoted to seafood, once numerous and of wondrous quality in New York, might be considered the direct descendants of the oysterhouses which once impressed Charles Dickens. Alas, most of them now have become standardized reminders of their old selves. In those palmier days, before the techniques of congelation reached their present point of perfection, and when the offshore waters were less worked over by foreign trawlers and the inshore grounds less polluted, there were more available ocean-fresh fish and shellfish for New Yorkers. Lobsters, too, were plentiful and reasonably priced, and in summer there were excellent "shore dinners" to be had from Hoboken to Cape May, New Jersey, and from Coney Island to Montauk. After the Second World War the picture changed. Few of the old New York fish restaurants have been able to maintain their quality; but among the best are Gage and Tollner, founded in 1879, in the heart of Brooklyn, serving the finest soft-clam belly roast in America and doing it with great gaslight era style, and Sweet's, a clamorous place which claims to be even older, across from the old Fulton Fish Market, a landmark which is gradually being moved to the Bronx, as Les Halles of Paris was displaced to Rungis.

XXVIII

Drinking in America

THROUGHOUT THEIR HISTORY, Americans have never been content with the taste, or lack of taste, of water. All Europeans who could afford it were drinking large quantities of alcoholic beverages at the time when America was discovered because the quality of the drinking water was not dependable. Either they avoided it altogether or mixed it with wine or spirits to improve its taste; and if Americans were heavy drinkers from the beginning of their history it was largely for this reason too; their settlements could not provide adequate supplies of pure water. Since the English were themselves heavy drinkers, it is all the more remarkable that Americans were able to astonish them by their intake; yet almost all of the numerous British visitors to the Colonies and then to the young United States were struck by the amount of liquor Americans drank. This was perhaps the result of the climate, more bracing than that of the British Isles, which permitted absorbing greater quantities of alcohol with relative impunity.

The earliest colonizers of America came from wine-drinking territory. When they landed, they tried hard to make wine grapes grow in northern Florida and elsewhere along their colonizing routes, but the vines, transplanted from Europe as cuttings and as rooted plants, failed to flourish for various reasons. Later, Spanish authorities who feared competition with their own flourishing wine industry at home ordered the vineyards to be destroyed, but of course not all of them were ripped up; the futile Prohibition gesture of the 1660s failed as the later ones would do also.

The Spanish action, of course, was not Prohibition as we understand it today, a policy undertaken for moral motives; it was simply crass commercialism. Prohibition in America—where it began very early—was part of a very American philosophy: Puritanism. The habit of heavy drinking which it fought stemmed from a tradition very American too, the result of nearly three centuries of pioneering, when the man of muscle and of daring was the man of romance—whose he-man philosophy held that one proof of virility was ability to hold one's liquor. The history of American drinking can be seen as a never-ending battle between these two tendencies.

The first manifestations of the Puritan-Prohibitionist spirit in America appeared in the seventeenth century, directed against the "inferior" races, and against whites only in the eighteenth. The inferior races were of course, the Indians and the Negro slaves, who appeared in English-speaking America almost as soon as the British colonists did, in 1619. There were differences of opinion about whether to let the Indians drink, but there was none about the slaves. In their case the verdict was unanimous: no matter how you looked at it, alcohol was not for them. If the Negro were viewed as a worker, he should not drink, for that would lessen his efficiency. If he were viewed as a servant, from whom deference was demanded, he should not drink, for that might tempt him to become that abomination of the Lord, an "uppity nigger." If he were viewed as a prisoner, he should not drink, for that might tempt him to rebellion. If he were viewed as a human being—but to whom would it occur to regard him as a human being?

In the case of the slave, there was always the underlying fact that he was a piece of property and should not be exposed to the possibly deteriorating effects of liquor, lest the property be damaged; nobody minded damaging the Indian. He could indeed be damaged by the white man's alcohol. In addition to the few mild brews some Indians had developed to drink with their food—near beers, one might call them—many of them had long known various fermented tipples which served for social and ritual purposes, varying with the tribes and the availabilities of plants or fruits, which seemed to do them little or no harm. Their response to the white man's hard liquor, however, was disastrous. Seemingly they acquired an addiction, or at least a craving, for alcohol which led them to become easy prey for unscrupulous traders who got them drunk and swindled them outrageously.

Not only were unscrupulous traders in favor of selling strong drink to Indians; so, often, were Colonial governors, either to keep them in a bemused, ineffective and consequently manageable state, or even, more simply, to kill them off through alcoholism. "If your Excellency still intends to punish the Indians farther for their barbarities," wrote Henry Gladwin, commanding the British forces at Detroit, to Lord Jeffrey Amherst, who had just defeated Pontiac, "it may easily be done without expense to the crown by permitting a free sale of rum which will destroy them more effectually than fire and sword."

The Indians themselves were aware of this danger, including Pontiac, the Ottawa Indian leader, who said, "Our people love liquor and if we dwelt near your old village of Detroit, our warriors would always be drunk." He called eloquently for the suppression of the liquor trade, but the rum sellers knew how to deal with this sort of opposition; they plied an Indian of a rival Illinois tribe with enough strong drink to induce him to murder Pontiac with a tomahawk at Cahokia, near St. Louis, in 1769. This slaying of the chief who is described by the *Encyclopedia Britannica* as "one of the most remarkable men of the Indian race in American history, possessing a commanding energy and force of mind, combined with subtlety and craft, and a power of organization," caused the Ottawa to make war on the Illinois, who were almost completely wiped out, a result which Henry Gladwin would have regarded with equanimity.

Forbidding Negroes and, on occasion, Indians to drink alcohol was not quite a pure example of the Puritan spirit, for its motivation was more practical than moral, though it did contain that element of Puritanism which holds that inferior classes (meaning those which are not making the rules) cannot be trusted to cope, as, of course, their superiors always could, with insidious temptations like that of liquor. Probably the first experiment in what we might call pure Prohibitionism in America was the attempt in 1733 by General James Edward Oglethorpe and the Trustees of the newly founded colony of Georgia to ban alcoholic drinks there completely. This was justified on the not wholly unreasonable grounds that drinking would not help the immigrants to cope with the rigors of colonial existence; but it is to be suspected that another strong motive was a feeling that the colonists belonged to that category of inferiors who had better be guarded from contact with intoxicating liquors because they would be incapable of exercising self-control in their seductive presence. The first settlers of Georgia were misfits in England, who were being shipped to America precisely because the mother country wanted to be rid of them. They had been considered in England as unruly individuals, but, once herded together into a controlled population constrained to social conduct from the beginning by pre-established rules, it was presumed that they could be converted into usefulness.

> The paternal interest of the London Trustees led them beyond land and labor to morals [wrote Daniel J. Boorstin]. To preserve the colonists against luxury and indolence, they sought to protect them against strong drink. Soldier-settlers had to be sober to defend the border. The problem of drunkenness, which was still far from solved in London, seemed easily soluble in a new colony. The Trustees aimed to dispose of it by their Act of 1735, which declared that "no Rum, Brandies, Spirits or Strong Water" could be brought into Georgia, that kegs of such liquors found in the colony should be publicly destroyed, and that sale of liquor should be punished as a crime.

(Beer, of course, did not count as liquor; it would have been quixotic for Englishmen to refuse beer to other Englishmen, however disreputable and however distant, at a period when everyone in England drank beer in preference to water, the beer being safer.)

However, there was also a commercial element in the problem, which, as usual, triumphed over impractical moral considerations. Georgia was not the richest of colonies; about the only thing it had to export was lumber. There was an eager market for it in the British West Indies, whose trees were not of the right kind to supply the construction needs of the sugar planters; but the planters had only one export of consequence too, the products of their cane. The sugar went to England; there remained rum, or molasses which could be converted into rum, the only currency in which the West Indies could pay for Georgia pine. Georgia perhaps did not need the rum as badly as the West Indies needed the timber, but it did need money; and rum was, ultimately, money. Trade was mighty and did prevail. The West Indies got its wood and Georgia took the once forbidden rum in exchange. It was by then no novelty in the colony. Bootleggers from the Carolinas had long been doing a booming business in Georgia; the chief effect of admitting rum legally was to make it cheaper.

The only Americans practicing genuine sobriety, not always faultlessly, in the seventeenth and eighteenth centuries—sobriety, that is to say, which was chosen by their own free will, not imposed upon them by law—were the Quakers. In the early eighteenth century many of them were indeed living in rather more luxury than we are accustomed to associate with them today, especially in Philadelphia, but always with decorum. After all, it was they who had settled Philadelphia, governed it, and made it America's largest and most prosperous city; they conducted themselves accordingly as the successful men they were. They dressed elegantly, in the best English taste, powdered wigs and all, and they did themselves well at the table, but as gourmets, not gluttons. William Penn himself set the style for good living; he had the reputation of being a first-class host. Quakers did not get drunk, but they drank; and when they drank, they drank the best—fine French burgundies and bordeaux and, of course, that early American favorite, Madeira.

The English Quaker community began to wonder whether its American offspring were not losing sight of the austerity proper to their sect. Some visiting Quaker dignitaries expressed this opinion; eventually it began to spread among American Quakers themselves, inspiring a movement for plainer living. At the Yearly Meeting in 1777, the consensus of the Friends present was in favor of a reformation—especially "a Reformation in Respect to the Distiling [sic] and Use of Spirituous Liquors amongst Friends and the Polluting Practice of keeping Taverns, Beerhouses, etc." Quaker luxury was toned down a little. Meanwhile the Quaker spirit remained that of control of one's self, not control by law; of temperance, not of Prohibition. The Quakers did not try to keep their neighbors' houses in order, after their own concepts of orderliness; when they ruled in Philadelphia, they did not impose their ideas of proper conduct upon others, as most of the New England settlements did. In regard to drink, they avoided both forms of excess—the positive excess of drunkenness, the negative excess of total abstinence.

The only alcoholic drinks available to the original colonists were those they brought with them—if they lasted out the voyage, which was not always the case: cargo space was limited and thirst great. The *Mayflower* passengers put beer aboard, but not enough. It was probably not shortage of beer alone that decided the Pilgrims to land at Plymouth in the unpromising month of December instead of pushing farther southward, as they had originally planned, but beer is specifically mentioned as contributing to their decision. A diary kept by one of the passengers explains, in an entry dated December 19, 1620, why Plymouth was chosen, or imposed, as the point at which to land: "We could not now take time for further search or consideration; our victuals being much spent, especially our beere."

The newcomers thus had to develop their own manufactures if they wanted to drink—and they wanted to drink. Probably their very first alcoholic beverages were made from the fermented juices of the fruits and flowers they found in the New World when they arrived, like elderberry wine or dandelion wine. If such drinks were not the first made by English-speaking colonists (the Dutch were already on the spot, drinking their own brews), they came very early. William Penn's wife, for one, made gooseberry wine; her recipe has been preserved in a book of Penn family recipes dating from 1702:

Too make gosbery wine or of any other fruit

Take to every galan of gosberys
A gallan of watter,
bruse the gosberys and pore the water one them,
Lett it stand a weeke straining it often.
[add] as many pounds of sugar as gallans of [gosberys]
then Lett it Run through a gelly bagg:
tunn it up
you may boyle it in a furnis.
in a fortnight or 3 weeks you may drinke it—

Theoretically, the Pilgrims might have been able to acquire beer immediately in their new country, for the first private brewery in America had been established by two Dutch colonists in a blockhouse on the southern tip of Manhattan Island in 1612; and in 1622 a public brewery was opened in New Amsterdam at the order of Peter Minuit, its first governor. It may be suspected, however, that trade between the Plymouth Bay Colony and the New Netherlands was not brisk in the 1620s; besides, did the Dutch have a surplus to sell? They must have been using imported raw materials at the beginning, for the first hops were not introduced into Dutch territory from Europe until 1629. (They were planted in Virginia in 1648, and presumably before that in New England, where beer from the beginning was made with hops.)

Beer can of course be made without hops, but not without suitable grains, preferably barley, except by stretching the definition of beer to the breaking point; grain was lacking in the New World too. When cereals were planted in New England they did not do well at first, as we have already seen; for that matter, neither did the hops. Until European grains had become acclimated, beer was made from corn, which does not sound particularly entrancing. Corn beer disappeared, unregretted, as soon as more suitable cereals became available to the brewers. In the meantime, some expedients even more desperate had been tried—"beers" made from persimmons in the South, and in the North from maple syrup, pumpkins, Jerusalem artichokes, or spruce bark.

The Dutch maintained their head start as brewers, a vocation for which destiny had clearly marked them when it decreed that the first Dutch-American child should be born in the blockhouse where the first Dutch-American beer had been brewed. Its name was Jean Vigne, again the unmistakable stamp of fate, since Vigne means "vine." He could have no other lot than that of providing drinkables for his fellowmen, and he did indeed become a brewer. By the time he was old enough to open his own establishment it was in a place where there were already so many breweries that its name was Brouwer Street. Its beer makers supplied the four ale houses which Manhattan boasted in 1676, as well as customers farther afield. New Amsterdam also had at that time six wine taverns, offering imported vintages and of course Dutch gin, *jenever,* also known as blue ruin or strip-and-go-naked.

In New England the Massachusetts Bay Colony took official notice of the existence of beer for the first time in 1634 by fixing its price at "one penny a quart at the most"; but five years later inflation obliged it to double the ceiling. At the time when the first price fixing occurred, there was not even a licensing law in Massachusetts. When the first one was enacted, in 1637, just one license to brew beer was awarded, an exclusive privilege granted to a certain Captain Sedgwich for having jumped the gun, obviously, since the order granting the license described him as the man who "hath before this time set up a brewhouse at his great charge, and very commodious for this part of the country." In Pennsylvania, the first brewery began business in 1683; it was opened by William Penn himself, on his own property.

Pennsylvania was in a good position to go into brewing. For some reason the grains which were so reluctant to grow in New England did much better in Pennsylvania—barley for beer, and rye, which therefore went into much of the first American whiskey, whose history began in this state. This was a later development, however; not much whiskey was drunk in America before the Revolution.

Drinking possibilities were enlarged when the colonies acquired apples—early in their history, for the Pilgrims brought both seeds and cuttings with them. Allowing six to eight years for the trees to come into full production, we may assume that they were drinking cider by 1630. New Jersey first planted seeds from England in 1632 and apparently outdid the mother country, for the visiting Swedish botanist Peter Kalm wrote that he had never tasted better cider anywhere.

Cider was a favorite drink among the colonists. Sweet cider is refreshing and healthful, but it has the disadvantage for those who want to avoid alcohol of fermenting on its own initiative, thus becoming hard cider, about which an old saying went: "Cider smiles in your face and then cuts your throat." The reputation of hard cider is probably exaggerated. Naturally fermented cider contains not much more than eight percent of alcohol (16 proof). It may be its comparative mildness which accounts for the fact that nobody in the United States today makes it on purpose, for sale, obliging anyone who wants it to buy imported hard cider, usually the French produce of Normandy. Cider was much used in cooking in Colonial times, not only for its own sake, but because there was a shortage of other cooking liquids.

Hard or not, cider was not considered as really strong drink before the Revolution; it was consumed by those who maintained that they did not drink, like John Adams, who put down a pitcher of hard cider at breakfast every morning—which did not prevent him from reaching a robust ninety-one years. He took a rather Puritan view toward food and drink in general, but was capable of backsliding. He noted of one dinner that "I drank Madeira at a great rate and found no inconvenience in it." This was before he went to France in 1778, after which he seemed no longer to feel that there was any inconvenience in drinking wine.

Thomas Jefferson, a gourmet of temperate habits, drank no alcoholic beverages except wine and cider, though he provided stronger brews for his guests, for whom his table was always furnished, according to his slave Isaac, with "plenty of wine, best old Antigua rum and cider." He took great pains about the last, producing his own at Monticello.

The juice of the apple became more powerful when it was distilled. The result was called applejack, otherwise known as "Jersey lightning." New Jersey does indeed seem to have been the place where it was first made, in 1698, by a Scot, William Laird, seeking, no doubt, a substitute for his native whisky. Laird & Company of New Jersey still has a virtual monopoly of the manufacture of applejack in the United States, though its production has not been quite continuous since the time of its creator; but it has stayed in the same family, for it was a descendant of William Laird who founded the present company in 1780.

The apple gave rise to another early beverage, apple beer, made, according to an old recipe, as follows:

> Peel your apples and dry the peelings in the sun or by the stove [it would have been "by the hearth" at the beginning]. Put them in a crock and add enough boiling water to cover them. Cover the crock and let it sit for one or two days, until all the flavor comes out of the peelings. You may add some sugar if you want.

There the recipe stops, abruptly. The sentence might have ended, "if you want more alcohol." It sounds like an ignoble beverage, and it does not seem to have lasted long.

Historically and economically, the most important alcoholic drink made in the Colonies was rum. It played a large part in building up the economy of New England; it helped develop the slave trade; and from time to time it embroiled the relations between England and America: if the Revolution had not been sparked by tea, it might have been by rum (or Madeira, drinkables all three).

A number of factors combined to make New England important for rum, and rum important for New England. One was the inefficiency of the methods used to extract sucrose from the juice of the cane, which produced a richer molasses and consequently a richer rum. It was not profitable to ship molasses, a bulky cargo, to the mother countries in Europe, and it was not even profitable to convert it into rum in the islands. The best system was to ship the molasses to the spot where there was a market for rum, and make the rum there. The cheapest place to which to ship rum from the West Indies was somewhere else in the New World, and that somewhere else turned out to be New England, for New England had the ships to carry it and something to exchange for it—cod. Ship building became important in the economy of New England, and rum was in large part responsible for it, because of the existence of molasses as a cargo. As the rum trade developed, more and more molasses was demanded to make more and more rum which obliged the building of more and more ships to carry more and more molasses. The shipbuilding industry of New England was built on cod and rum.

Rum played a particularly unsavory role in New England commerce, the development of the slave trade. Slaves could be bought in Africa with New England dried cod and also with New England rum. An unscrupulous activity, it was not unnaturally carried on by unscrupulous methods. "Worter your Rum as much as possible," Captain Simeon Potter of Rhode Island instructed one of his shipmasters, "and sell as much by the short mesuer [sic] as you can."

The combination of rum and slavery produced one of the most astonishing letters in early American history, written in 1682 to "ye Aged and Beloved Mr. John Higginson" by Cotton Mather, a man little given to Beloving any of his fellowmen, however Aged:

> There is now at sea a ship called the Welcome, which has on board an hundred or more of the heretics and malignants called Quakers, with W. Penn, who is the chief scamp, at the head of them.
>
> The general court has accordingly given secret orders to Master Malachi Muscott, of the brig Porpoise, to waylay the said Welcome, slyly, as near the Cape of Cod as may be, and make captive the said Penn, and his ungodly crew, so that the Lord may be glorified, and not mocked on the soil of this new country with the heathen worship of these people. Much spoil can be made by selling the whole lot to Barbadoes [the original spelling], where slaves fetch good prices in rum and sugar, and we shall not only do the Lord great service by punishing the wicked, but we shall make great good for his ministers and people.
>
> Master Muscott feels hopeful and I will set down the news when the ship comes back.
>
> Yours in ye bowels of Christ,
> COTTON MATHER.

Master Muscott was unsuccessful, thus sparing to history the tolerant William Penn, but leaving behind for our edification a letter which is a perfect example of the Puritan-Prohibitionist mentality.

Rum became one of the main pillars of the New England economy, particularly that of Massachusetts, where Medford in particular became famous for its rum.

> The West Indies trade [according to Samuel Eliot Morison] was the main factor in New England prosperity until the American Revolution; without it the settlements on the northern coast would have remained stationary or declined. . . . Rum . . . replaced hard cider and home-brewed beer as the drink of the country.

Rum, beer and cider were the drinks of the average pre-Revolutionary American, along with tea when it was available. The quality, however, were drinking imported wines and spirits from the earliest Colonial days, and the Founding Fathers were no exception. George Washington's favorite tipple seems to have been Madeira, which in the latter half of the eighteenth century was customarily fortified by the addition of a bucket of brandy to a hogshead of wine, a procedure which made it more efficiently exportable. In pre-Revolutionary days, when the colonists deeply resented British laws requiring that all European goods going to America should be shipped in British bottoms, the island of Madeira (whose wine was not European merchandise, since Madeira lay off the coast of Africa) was exempt from this restriction. Thus a bottle of Madeira became a symbol of defiance of the King's oppressive interference with the Colonies' right to trade; but when England clapped a prohibitive tax on it in 1764, the colonies immediately boycotted it, as we have seen, and the measure had to be rescinded.

The boycott had been something of a sacrifice, for Americans preferred Madeira to all other wines. Heavy sweet drinks accorded with the tastes of the times, and Madeira filled that bill. If so temperate a man as John Adams could find "no inconvenience in it," it need not surprise us that the more jovial Benjamin Franklin indulged in it unblushingly; he once excused himself to a friend for writing him a rambling letter by explaining that he was in the middle of the evening's second bottle of Madeira.

George Washington does not seem to have been bothered by a sense of sin about drinking. It is true that he was educated in the pragmatic school of Virginia local politics.

> When George Washington ran for the [colonial] legislature in 1758 [Reay Tannahill wrote], his agent doled out almost . . . 3¾ . . . gallons of beer, wine, cider or rum to every voter. The great man himself was concerned over the extent of this hospitality; he feared that his agent might have been too niggardly.

Thomas Jefferson, perhaps America's nearest thing to a Renaissance man, was so expert in the matter of wines that he could select three red château-bottled Bordeaux wines which even today are tops in their class, and refer to a white Bordeaux which can only be the fabled Château d'Yquem, undoubtedly the world's finest natural sweet wine. It may have been when he was totting up his heavy wine bills that he acquired the conviction that duties on wine ("a necessity of life," he said) should be kept as low as possible, though the reason he gave was that "no nation is drunken where wine is cheap." He was economical, though, in at least one aspect of his drinking; he was careful to have all the bottles saved so that they could be used again; glass bottles were costly in those days.

Though Jefferson held that "good talk and good wine" were among the best things in life, he meant, literally, wine, not including spirits. He did not use strong drink himself and did not approve of those who did. "The habit of using ardent spirits by men in public office," he wrote after leaving it, "has often produced more injury to the public service, and more trouble to me, than any other circumstance that has occurred in the internal concerns of the country during my administration."

Benjamin Franklin liked to eat and drink well, a quality which endeared him to the French when he arrived in Paris to represent America. His tastes were like theirs—he preferred French wine to English beer. Could this have been in part because beer was associated with one of the most painful experiences of his life? When, on January 29, 1774, he appeared before the

Privy Council of His Majesty George III at a room in Whitehall Palace, called "The Cockpit" from its use in the days of Henry VIII, the atmosphere should have been relaxed by the mugs of stout on the table, but it was not. Facing thirty-five of the King's most influential advisers, Franklin heard Attorney-General Alexander Wedderburn call him a spy, a traitor, a thief, a potential assassin, and, worst of all, a rebel. He was not allowed to answer; that would have been unseemly. The Privy Council's report to the King caused Franklin to be stripped of his functions as Postmaster General of the Colonies. At least one writer has suggested that this may have helped to contribute to his distaste for the beverage served on that ill-fated day, beer "as black as bull's blood and as thick as mustard."

Wine was another matter. Franklin lost no time after taking up residence in Paris in building up a well-stocked cellar.

His wine and his table quickly became celebrated in Paris; his cheer remained unaffected even by amorous disappointment, when, at the age of seventy-four, Poor Richard failed to win the hand of the widow of the philosopher Helvetius despite an ardent courtship. Franklin "always knew how to suffer in Epicurean fashion," French historian Claude Manceron remarked, describing the fare offered by Franklin to his cronies at a time when he should decently have been plunged into despondency by the rejection of his suit:

> Red Bordeaux and white, including some very old vintages, champagne and *"white mousseux,"* red Burgundy and sherry to wash down the two principal dishes of meat and poultry (or game), followed by "two kinds of *entremets,* two dishes of vegetables and a platter of pastry, with hors d'oeuvre of butter, pickles, radishes, etc. Two bowls of fruit in winter (four in summer), two sorts of stewed fruit, a platter of cheese, one of cookies, one of candies,"

served, let us hope, not quite in that order. At one of these dinners, the company sang, to a familiar air, verses composed by Franklin's friend, the Abbé Morellet, several of whose innumerable stanzas paid tribute to Franklin's devotion to Bacchus:

In very free translation, which it must be admitted sacrifices some meaning to rhyme and rhythm, they go as follows:

He's a great man, and politic,
And yet at table no dull stick.
Though busy forming a new state
He takes time out to celebrate.
First serious, and playful then,
Versatile thus is our Ben.

Never has a nation fought
For aims with greater import fraught:

Their independence they design
Because they want to drink French wine;
That is the aim of all the men
Who back the plan of our Ben.

. . . The English, reaching 'cross the sea,
Tried to reduce our friends to tea,
Inhumanely, causing great pain
To Brother Ben.

If now our heroes plow the sea
To bend Britain in victory
It is because, among their ends,
They want to give fine wine to friends,
Subtle, silken,
The kind that pleases Ben.

I do not see why we should land
On England's God-forsaken strand.
What would we do on soil so drear
It knows no other drink than beer?
A sad omen,
Thinks our Ben.

By the time the Revolution was won, American drinking habits were pretty firmly established; the gentry drank their hard liquor with a certain style or protocol, inherited from the English for the most part, while the mass of the people drank to get drunk, or to produce an eye-opening jolt which later in the day would be followed by a nip here and there as an analgesic against the aches or frustrations of long hours of work. Beer and cider, though inebriating, were considered much as present-day soft drinks are, as thirst quenchers and an accompaniment to food. In those days the food most people were eating was not necessarily very palatable, and something with which to wash it down was welcome. A laborer might receive part of his pay in rum (or, later, whiskey), doled out to him for daily consumption, giving him the strength, it was believed, to carry on.

Ceremonial drinking was firmly entrenched, as it is today, part and parcel of all the milestones of life, baptisms, weddings, anniversaries of all sorts, and funerals as well. In celebration of a consummated business deal, drink was obligatory. Spirits were both medicine and anesthetic for the physicians and surgeons of the early days, and for the military the surest way of maintaining morale among the troops. "Dutch courage," or *jenever,* came to New Amsterdam with the first settlers, and the *Mayflower* on its various voyages brought hard liquor from England, enough to tide the Puritans over until they could start their own distilling industry, producing mostly rum.

Europeans visiting the young United States were astonished at two things—the American consumption of meat and the American consumption of strong drink.

> Americans ate and drank so much [Dale Brown wrote in *American Cooking*] that dyspepsia was almost a national disease, and they were an easy prey for medicine quacks peddling nostrums and elixirs. Whiskey was the American wine (although to be sure, good wine, especially Madeira, continued to be imported . . .). Diluted with water, hard liquor was drunk at mealtimes, and in between meals as well. Even ministers and children drank it; boys 12 years of age or less were known to enter stores where whiskey could be had, saunter up to the clerks, "and tip off their drams."

The meals at which hard liquor was taken included breakfast.

> For most early Americans, young or old, male or female [John Kobler explained], the day began with a tumbler full of rum or whiskey taken upon arising as an "eye-opener." They then sat down to a breakfast accompanied by a copious flow of spirits. In the South it might be mint-flavored whiskey or a fruit cordial. In New York the breakfast beverages were likely to include . . . Dutch gin. . . . In New England hard cider and rum were favored. At 11 A.M. everywhere offices, shops and factories closed while the employees repaired to tavern or pothouse for their "'leven o'clock bitters," a liquory interlude that was repeated daily at 4 P.M. So faithfully did the inhabitants of Portland, Maine, honor the observance that on the dot of 11 and again at 4 a bell in the town hall tolled. The term "bitters" covered a multitude of potent concoctions, among them toddies, a mixture of rum, sugar and the pulp of roasted apples, drunk hot or cold according to the season; slings or long sups (half spirits, half water, sweetened and spiced); flips, also called tiffs (rum, beer and sugar, to which a burned bitter flavor was imparted by stirring with a red-hot "flip iron"); meridians (brandy and tea); manathan (beer, rum and sugar); hotchpotch (the same, warmed); sillabub (warm milk, wine and sugar). . . . Rum, whiskey and brandy sluiced down lunch and dinner, and before bedtime prayers a nightcap or two was deemed an indispensable precaution against night chills.
>
> Besides these more or less fixed drinking periods, numerous opportunities for a nip arose in the course of an average day. Shopkeepers would stand a barrel of rum by the entrance and, when customers dropped in to pay a bill or place a large order, urge them to help themselves. Social calls almost always began with a welcoming dram and ended with a stirrup cup.
>
> Though rum and whiskey remained the liquid staples of both rich and poor, the rich householders stocked imported liquor as well, a favorite being arrack, a fiery Far Eastern brandy distilled from palms, and heavy sweet wines like port, malaga, canary and madeira. New Yorkers doted on sangaree—red wine, water, lemon juice and nutmeg—while their New England peers were partial to mead and metheglin, distillations of honey and yeast.

Mr. Kobler's list of tipples is by no means exhaustive. His sillabub was England's syllabub, which dated from at least the sixteenth century; the last syllable of its name may have come from "bubble," for originally the drink was made by milking a cow into a bucket of wine, causing it to froth up. Recipes for it varied from place to place; in the South it was more of a dessert than a drink: brandy, sherry, sugar, lemon juice and heavy cream were whipped together and the result was eaten with a spoon. In the same category of combinations of cream and spirits were milk punch (brandy or rum, sugar, unskimmed milk, nutmeg, with lemon juice optional) and, of course, eggnogs, also copied from England. These were of varied ingredients; rum or whiskey alone might be combined with cream, or both of them together (the whiskey would be Bourbon in the South), while there were any number of other combinations. A recipe frightening in its prodigality toward the egg is given in Célestine Eustis's *Cooking in Old Créole Days:*

> Yolks of thirty-two eggs and thirty-two heaping tablespoonfuls of powder sugar, beaten to a froth. Add to this one and a half pints of brandy and one-half pint of Madeira or sherry wine. To this add two and a half quarts of whipped cream; then beat the whites of the thirty-two eggs to a stiff froth, and stir all thoroughly together, the whites of the eggs being added last of all.

Mr. Kobler's sangaree was a transatlantic re-edition of Spain's *sangria,* which in its mother country usually includes slices of lemon and orange, plus pieces of whatever other fruits happen to be in season, all immersed in the wine, itself sometimes fortified with liqueurs. In early America, it could be made even with beer; Eliza Leslie's *Directions for Cookery in Its Various Branches* permits it:

> Mix in a pitcher or in tumblers one-third of wine, ale, or porter, with two-thirds of water either warm or cold. Stir in sufficient loaf-sugar to sweeten it, and grate some nutmeg into it. By adding to it lemon juice, you may make what is called negus. [From its inventor English Colonel Francis Negus, deceased in 1732, who would never have dreamed of putting ale in it.]

Flip was far from being the only alcoholic drink which was served heated; the period had a penchant for hot drinks, perhaps because of the climate. They were so common that the flip iron gave an expression to the language; it was also called a loggerhead, and in barroom fights red-hot loggerheads were often pressed into service as weapons: hence the phrase, "to be at loggerheads."

Caudle was an invention of the Hudson Valley Dutch, a hot punch based on Madeira. Mulled wine was thinned with water, flavored with nutmeg, cinnamon and cloves, brought to a boil, and then taken immediately off the fire, sweetened and served. It was also called Gluhwein, which did not mean

Glue Wine, but Glowing Wine. Mulled cider was made by boiling clove-flavored cider and pouring it over hot beaten sweetened egg, the whole sprinkled with fresh nutmeg. The most durable of these ancient heated drinks (excluding grog, which is international) is still occasionally produced triumphantly in New England, by a host or hostess mindful of tradition—hot buttered rum. The rum is heated, but not boiled; thinned with water (optionally, not obligatorily); sweetened and flavored with cinnamon; and poured hot into pewter tankards (preferably). Thin slices of hard butter are placed on the table, permitting each drinker to dissolve as much of it in his brew as pleases him, where it spreads over the surface with all the appetizingness of an oil slick on harbor water. The reasons for which this drink has been so lovingly exalted, and which have kept it in the repertory, escape the authors, who find that its chief quality is greasiness. Call it Glue Rum, if you like.

Punches were various and popular; the name implied the presence of rum, but sometimes the rum tended to get lost in a labyrinth of other ingredients, as in Célestine Eustis's Buckner Punch:

> For each quart bottle of champagne mix and add one wineglassful of good brandy, one wineglassful of good rum, one wineglassful of good arrack, one wineglassful of good kirsch, one wineglassful of good anisette, one wineglassful of good Maraschino, one wineglassful of good Curaçao, two slices of ripe pineapple, two slices sweet orange, one toddy glassful of pulverized sugar. At first put in a small quantity of ice, and later fill the bowl with large lumps of ice. It should stand three hours before using [or, preferably, indefinitely?].

Champagne appeared in this recipe and often enough in others when it was desired to put on the dog, but it would not seem that it had yet become a familiar drink for Americans, if we may judge by the conduct of a selected group of proper Bostonians. Shortly after the Revolution, the French consul at Boston, in a praiseworthy attempt to promote the products of his country, gave a champagne party for some of the city's important, and importing, citizens. The taste suggested to them a mild and innocuous beverage, a sort of sparkling cider, say—*sweet* cider—and while they showed great appreciation of it at the moment, they went home in such a state (and no doubt woke the morning after in such a state) that they were not inclined to switch from their accustomed sherry and Madeira to champagne.

Those who were not in the champagne or sherry or Madeira brackets had a large choice among less sophisticated, but not necessarily less potent, beverages. Shrub was made of brandy, wine, water, sugar, and lemons, allowed to mature together in a stone jug and then bottled; or the name might indicate the boiled skimmed sweetened juice of some small fruit given authority by an admixture of brandy—fox grape shrub, gooseberry shrub, currant shrub, or cherry shrub. In the case of the last, substituting whiskey for brandy and leaving the cracked pits of the fruit in the liquid for three months' mellowing, made it cherry bounce. Cordials were simply crushed or cut-up fruits allowed to stand in spirits until their flavors had been transferred to them—strawberry cordial, quince cordial, peach cordial; there was even rose cordial, made not from rose petals, but from rose leaves. Add crushed fruit pits (preferably almond shells) to a cordial and the result was ratafia (one recipe included a grain of ambergris, an expensive ingredient). Use crushed almonds alone (plus lemon rind, clarified honey and, after the rest had ripened together, rose water) and that was noyau (the French word, precisely, for the pit of a fruit). Bishop was essentially claret or port and roasted oranges.

Besides these drinks, every housewife knew how to make "weed wines," which meant a homemade fermented beverage derived from any product of field or garden—and almost anything could be turned into "wine": flowers (dandelion wine, elder-blossom wine, locust-blossom wine), grain (barley wine), roots (beet wine, carrot wine), vegetables (spinach wine, tomato wine), herbs (mint wine, geranium leaf wine), fruit (apricot wine, cherry wine, cider wine), and of course berries (blackberry wine, raspberry wine, strawberry wine). Some of these beverages seem quite capable of creating sentiment in favor of prohibition, but it did not work out that way: the drinkers, despite the sort of brews they were being invited to drink, remained in the ascendant.

> In 1792 [John Kobler informs us], there were 2,579 registered distilleries in the United States, which then had a population slightly above 4,000,000. Production, as reported to tax assessors, totalled 5,200,000 gallons, and consumption, counting imported spirits, came to 11,008,447, or an average of about 2½ gallons for every man, woman and child in the country. Within the next eighteen years the number of distilleries increased to 14,191, and consumption, again taking into account both domestic and foreign spirits, tripled. Yet the population had not even doubled. This brought the per capita consumption to almost 4 1/2 gallons. If, moreover, the probable nondrinkers were omitted and the number of illicit stills estimated, the average annual intake of the actual drinkers appeared vastly greater—at least 12 gallons.

In the opening years of the nineteenth century, the American tradition of lusty drinking was in full flower, manifest—a little too manifest—in the prestigious groves of academe and accepted even by the ultrarespectable hard-headed handlers of actuarial statistics. Harvard University itself operated a private brewery and its Commencement exercises were growing so alcoholically merry that stern measures had to be taken against "the Excesses, Immoralities and Disorders" which were accompanying the bestowing of degrees. Excess in this direction was human and comprehensible; but in the other, abstention from bacchanalian lightness of heart was suspect and abnormal, for instance in the estimation of one insurance company which imposed a 10 percent surcharge on life insurance premiums for non-drinkers, who obviously lacked virility. The abstainer was described as "thin and watery, and as mentally cranked, in that he repudiated the good creatures of God as found in alcoholic drinks." The man of sobriety was not a good risk.

Every history of Prohibition in America pays tribute to the Quaker Anthony Benezet, a truly inspired reformer. He sought changes in educational methods, was an abolitionist, and pleaded for humane treatment of the Indians too. In 1774 a pamphlet he had written earlier, *The Mighty Destroyer Displayed, in Some Account of the Dreadful Havock made by the mistaken Use as well as Abuse of Distilled Spirituous Liquors by a Lover of Mankind,* was published in Philadelphia, the first American broadside in the long and still unfinished war of the Drys against the Demon Rum. For Benezet, drinking was

> an evil so amazingly great that, did not useful experience too fully prove it, it seems incredible, that any whom it concerns could possibly be so negligent as not to use the utmost endeavors to suppress the destructive MAN-BANE.

Like Thomas Jefferson, Benezet thought to reach temperance by taxation, but their approaches were slightly different. Jefferson favored turning drinkers away from strong liquor and toward the moderation of wine by reducing duties on the latter to the minimum. Benezet argued in favor of

> laying such high taxes upon distilled spirituous liquors . . . as will make the drinking of it sufficiently expensive to put it out of the reach of so great a number of insatiable drinkers.

Another great name of the period, and one which lent a certain scientific luster to the temperance cause, was that of Dr. Benjamin Rush, surgeon, Philadelphia Medical College professor, Physician General of the Army, and, assuring his prestige, a member of the Continental Congress and a signer of the Declaration of Independence. As a practicing Quaker he responded to the ideas of Benezet on slavery and on drink, and in 1785 brought out his seminal *Inquiry into the Effect of Ardent Spirits,* a study which depicted in detail the effects of liquor on the human organism, some of them more lurid than demonstrable. For instance, Dr. Rush cited the case of a rum-soaked individual who, belching heavily in the neighborhood of a candle flame, became a victim of alcohol combustion and was thus destroyed. Although Dr. Rush possessed an impressive array of medico-scientific credentials, his descriptions of the effects of drink are closer to the lurid rhetoric employed by the series of reformed drunkards who were to lecture to entranced audiences in churches and temperance halls across the United States for decades later than to the language of clinical research.

The temperance gospel of Dr. Rush spread to New York State as a result of the conversion of Dr. Billy James Clark, a young doctor at Moreau, in the Hudson Valley, who had his practice among the rough, hard-drinking rivermen and farmers of the region. Though he is reported to have spent some time carousing in a local tavern with the Congregationalist pastor, it was when a close friend of both of them came near to death from an overdose of rum that Billy James felt the full impact of the older physician's grim admonitions. With the similarly converted pastor, Reverend Lebbeus Armstrong, Dr. Clark founded the Union Temperate Society of Moreau and Northumberland, whose history was written by Armstrong in *The Temperance Revolution.* The Temperate Society was not the biggest, nor yet the best, for many of its hundred-odd members were backsliders, but in 1808 it was the first of many such, preaching temperance by moral suasion.

In 1836 the convention of the American Temperance Society, claiming to represent five thousand local groups and a million and a quarter members, brought wine, cider, and beer under the same tent as ardent spirits, and asked that its members refrain from any and all of them. They were skeptical about the existence of moderate drinkers, over any extended period of time at least, holding that one drink led to another, and that great alcoholics from little tipplers grew. For this theory they could have found support in the experience of an eminent personage of the eighteenth century, Dr. Johnson, of whom Boswell wrote, "He has great virtue in not drinking wine or any fermented liquor, because he could not do it in moderation." An unfortunate result of including hard cider in the list of proscribed drinks was that some zealots felled whole orchards of apple trees, "the Devil's kindling wood."

Another result of the Temperance Society's bold call for total abstinence was the birth of the word "teetotaler." There were now two kinds of pledges, one of abstention from strong drink, the other of abstention from everything; when the Society signed up new members who promised not to drink at all, they marked the letter T against their names, for "total." T, total, teetotaler! (This seems a trifle likelier than the story which attributed this word to a stutter. According to this version a stammering English advocate of temperance proposed at a meeting, "Mr. Chairman, I finds as how the lads get drunk on ale and cider, and we can't keep 'em sober unless we pledge 'em tee-tee-total.")

Meanwhile the Dry divines were making converts everywhere. By 1833 there were temperance societies in twenty-three states, subdivided into five thousand local societies. They were not just preaching abstinence, they were getting results: four thousand distillers had been shamed into shutting down their establishments, six thousand liquor sellers had gone out of business, and the operators of one thousand merchant ships had stopped loading liquor for their crews to drink aboard ship.

In Baltimore, the Reverend Matthew Hale Smith inspired six roisterers to found the Washington Temperance Society in 1840. With no evidence that the Father of His Country had any interest in teetotalism, nor for that matter in militant temperance of any kind, the name nevertheless assured success for the movement which, with seven hundred members in Baltimore, spread to Springfield, Illinois, and in 1842 signed up a thirty-three-year-old local politician, Abraham Lincoln. Queried on his personal stand on the issue of abstinence, Lincoln, who was for moderation, not prohibition, replied, "I am not a temperance man, but I am temperate to this extent—I don't drink." His reply reflects the distortion the Drys had already inflicted on the word "temperance." A few years later the Washingtonians disbanded, since they refused to fall in line with the hellfire preachments of the churchmen, thus incurring the wrath of that aggressive clergy which was later to make national Prohibition possible.

Among the mullahs of abstinence, none was more popular on the lecture circuit than John Bartholomew Gough (1817–1886), whose qualifications as a spellbinder were almost perfect. Apprenticed to an upstate New York farmer, he managed to get himself released from indenture, after which he found work in a New York bookbindery, and eventually as an itinerant actor in the popular theater of the day, which consisted largely of broad farce and vaudeville numbers. J. C. Furnas, in his *The Life and Times of the Late Demon Rum,* recounts with sympathy the career of Gough, who had been a drunkard for most of his young manhood, losing job after job in the theater and out of it, practicing ventriloquism and monologues, singing in squalid dives, losing his wife and child in poverty, getting himself arrested as drunk and disorderly, and chronically suffering from the DT's. Rescued by Joel Stratton, a Worcester, Massachusetts, Dry who persuaded him to attend a Washingtonian meeting, he signed the pledge after confessing his downfall to the assembled members. As one who had been through the worst agonies of alcoholism, his hold on his audience was more real than any he had ever known as an actor, and by the time he was pretty well dried out and recovered from his withdrawal symptoms he was able to earn small fees speaking to other temperance groups. Perfecting his "routine," Gough found himself much in demand, and was able to earn a living which exceeded anything he would have previously dared to hope for, and with it the acclaim of which every actor dreams. In Boston in 1845 his lecture sponsors sent a four-horse open carriage to meet his train, and treated him as a genuine hero. Furnas quoted Gough's second wife as relating that when Gough came off the platform after one of his lectures, "he dripped with perspiration; his clothes were wringing wet . . . he was in a state of collapse. Hours of attention were necessary to soothe him . . . with bath and food; nor did sleep come till long past midnight." Sincere persuader, genuinely concerned for his fellow man? Or inspired Thespian, intoxicated with his own eloquence and emotion? Perhaps both. Even at the top of his career he backslid at least once, and was found after several days' absence in New York, semi-unconscious in a whorehouse, and confused as to how he got there. His reply to critics of his behavior was straightforward, and foreshadowed what present-day Alcoholics Anonymous preaches. Gough said, "Very well . . . if I am so weak-minded that I cannot drink in moderation, thank God I am strong enough to let it alone altogether. . . . You cannot make a moderate drinker out of a drunkard. . . . It has been tried over and over again. Total abstinence is absolutely necessary to save a man who has once been a drunkard."

Until the Civil War came along to distract attention from the hard-driving prohibition movement which was fueled by the Protestant clergy, the impassioned lecturers, and by the various ritualistic orders such as the Rechabites and the Sons of Temperance, the young nation had swung temporarily at least into a phase where temperance was to be a matter of enforcement, rather than persuasion. Whatever caused thirteen states, New York included, to vote for prohibition on a statewide basis has long been studied by historians. None of them discounts the influence of the Order of Good Templars, which was social, fraternal, and militant. Its members, some of whom had very elaborate titles, were for total abstinence, against any local licensing of drinking places, and, contrary to previous practice among such orders, admitted women to full membership. The Templars had lodges everywhere, and undoubtedly exerted social pressure upon any candidate for local or state office for adherence, even grudging, to the dry cause.

The Catholics of the prewar period had never shown much enthusiasm for the drive for prohibition. In the early nineteenth century many of those in the United States were newly arrived Irish, and sensed that shutting down the drinking places was aimed against workingmen in general and the immigrant from Erin in particular. Then, too, the ritualism of the Templars and similar groups smacked of Freemasonry, disapproved by the Church. Yet one of the most successful missionaries for temperance (as opposed to prohibition) was an elderly Capuchin friar who had come to America to bring the thanks of the Irish people for the aid sent from the United States during the potato famine of 1846–1847. Father Theobold Mathew had already been preaching total abstinence in Ireland, and continued to sign up Catholics wherever he went on a two-year lecture tour of the Northeast, the Middle West and parts of the South. Yet in 1849 and 1850 this modest but effective lecturer did much to impress the need for temperance upon a traditionally hard-drinking sector of the American public. The authors, both New Englanders, do not forget that in the first quarter of the present century no parade of Irish-American societies in Boston was complete without a marching delegation of "F.M.T.A.'s," the loyal members of the Father Mathew Total Abstinence Society. The good priest left America for home in 1851, and died in Ireland in 1856, one of the uncanonized saints of the temperance cause.

The need of the Union (Federal) Government to raise funds for the prosecution of the Civil War set the Dry movement back, since liquor, with beer, provided a tempting target for the Internal Revenue people, who were able to collect a dollar a barrel for beer and up to two dollars a gallon for spirits. The eminent taxability of booze has always been an argument against its abolition.

Even before the Civil War ended, public attention began once more to focus on the issue of temperance. John Kobler blamed the beer barons. Their annual production at the time exceeded two hundred million gallons, Kobler reports, and the brewers soon managed to have their tax cut down to sixty cents a barrel. Later the tax on spirits was reduced to fifty cents a gallon. It was such goings-on that soon stirred the Dry forces to riposte with militant action.

They found a truly formidable ally in the emerging American womanhood which during the Civil War included Clara Barton, Dorothea Dix, and Dr. Emily Blackwell, pioneers in organizing nursing care for the wounded, and, in hundreds of cities, other women who had organized the branches of the United States Sanitary Commission and made them work efficiently throughout the war. These were the same women, by and large, who had supported the temperance activities on the grounds that their sex and the children for whom they were responsible were the first victims of male drunkenness, and the poverty and neglect it could cause. The saloon, where no respectable woman would ever be found, was to become their field of battle, and the scene of some of their most picturesque victories. For years they had made up the bulk of the audiences listening to the temperance lecturers, but despite the fact that the campaign for women's rights, spearheaded by women like Susan B. Anthony, had been gaining strength, its leaders were not admitted to the high and all-male councils of the temperance movement. The action taken in 1853 by Mrs. Margaret Freeland of Syracuse, New York, should have forewarned them. When a saloon keeper, whose place had furnished her husband the firewater which led him to beat her up to a point where police intervention was required, refused to cut off her mate's supply, Mrs. Freeland took a stout club to the door of his bar, entered, and smashed every bottle and glass within range. Counsel retained by the local temperance people got her acquitted. The tactical war of women against the saloon had begun. It was to be pursued by groups of women who camped in front of saloons and knelt in prayer, groups that sang hymns, others who noted down the names of recognizable topers. Ingenious harassment was provided by one woman who, tired by rival saloons' boasting of their free lunches, rounded up a troop of hungry moppets and sent them charging in to eat their fill, on the pretext that their fathers had squandered the family food budget over the bar.

Alcohol is an auto-disintoxicant; so is excess. Excess generates reaction to its own abuses. The drinking habits of the early nineteenth century were excessive. They aroused the reaction of the women who bore the brunt of the excesses of their men, whose protests were all the more effective because they were so clearly justified. The embattled women contributed largely to the successes scored by the Puritan-Prohibitionists, whose motives were perhaps slightly different—ideological and moralist, with touches of killjoy-ism and holier-than-thou-ism. The Prohibitionists gained ground because the virile drinkers had gone too far. But though they were losing ground, relatively, the party of the drinkers had not disarmed; it was precisely during the period when temperance and abstinence movements were growing that the drinkers were leaving their mark on an American language which was endowing itself with a vocabulary different from that of England, richly endowed with homely or humorous or wry or picturesque or extravagant words and images.

> One common activity which left a rich legacy to our spoken language [Daniel J. Boorstin wrote in *The Americans: The National Experience*] was the drinking of alcoholic beverages. Wentworth and Flexner [Harold Wentworth and Stuart Borg Flexner, in their *Dictionary of American Slang*] observe that *drunk* is the concept with the greatest number of slang synonyms in the American language. This is due, in part, to the enrichment of our vocabulary by words from immigrant tongues; also, perhaps, to the immigrants' special need for the solace of drink. Whatever the explanation, Americans, more than others, seem to have enjoyed talking about their drinking. The basic American vocabulary of alcoholic conviviality dates from what Mencken called "the Gothic Age of American drinking as of American word-making"—the years between the Revolution and the Civil War.
>
> In that age we already find the essentials of an American drinking vocabulary. *Bar-room* (1807) and *saloon* (1841) were Americanisms for which there appeared countless euphemisms. Ask the *bar-tender* (1855) *to set 'em up* (1851)! Do you want only a *snifter* (1848), or do you prefer a drink precisely measured by a *jigger* (1836), a *pony* (1849), or a *finger* (1856)? Ask for a *long drink* (1828) unless you prefer your whiskey *straight* (1862; the English word was *neat)*. Would you like an *eggnog* (1755), a *mint-julep* (1809), or some kind of *cobbler* (1840), for example a *sherry cobbler* (1841)? The more unfamiliar inventions of the Gothic Age include: a *horse's neck, stone-fence* (or *stone-wall), brandy-crusta, brandy-champarelle, blue-blazer, locomotive,* or *stinkibus.* The world-famous *cocktail*—destined to become one of the most prolific American inventions, linguistic or otherwise—came not from a later era, but from that same Gothic Age. Its first recorded use, in the Hudson, New York, *Balance* (and *Columbian Repository)* on May 13, 1806, explained: "*Cock tail,* then, is a stimulating liquor, composed of spirits of any kind, *sugar, water,* and *bitters*—it is vulgarly called *bittered sling*. . . . It is said, also, to be of great use to a democratic candidate; because, a person having swallowed a glass of it, is ready to swallow any thing else."

This list could undoubtedly be extended indefinitely. There are the words the moonshiners gave us—*busthead* and *popskull* for badly made whiskey; and even for the better products *ruckus juice* (pronounced "rookus"), *conversation fluid, corn squeezin's* or just *corn, white lightnin'* or just *white, cove juice, thump whiskey, headache whiskey* and *blockade whiskey* (because moonshiners were called "blockaders," by analogy with blockade runners). There are countless other names *(whaler's toddy* in New England) and nicknames (*essence of lockjaw* for applejack) for various drinks. *Tom and Jerry* (a hot drink containing rum, brandy, milk, butter, beaten eggs, and spices) sounds American, but is not; it is named for the two heroes of *Life in London* written in 1821 by the English sports writer, Pierce Egan. There are also those courteous barroom toasts, *mud in your eye* (or *spit in your eye), down the hatch,* et cetera, common in American usage, though their American origin cannot be guaranteed.

There were other now forgotten words in the drinkers' vocabulary, for instance "barrelhouse," meaning a place which kept beer, wine, and spirits in a row of barrels on the counter to serve customers who arrived with their own bottles, for the wine or spirits, or buckets, if it was for beer. The beer buckets were called "growlers" and carrying your brew home in them was "rushing the growler."

The drinkers, and the suppliers of the drinkers, did not limit their effort to enriching the language. They were also enriching the drinkables, with valiant disregard of the attacks being launched against them. It was the period of development of American whiskies, legal (rye, bourbon) and illegal (moonshine).

The reason why whiskey was little drunk in America before the Revolution may have been its harsh quality; it was also expensive. Rum was cheaper because of the constant availability of molasses from the West Indies, while grains like wheat or barley remained dear; the former still cost nearly three times as much as corn at the end of the nineteenth century. Rum was easier to make successfully than drinks distilled from grains and, being coarser in its essence, could be tolerated even if the degree of success achieved was not elevated. The average American, when he wanted hard liquor, settled for rum, while the well-heeled chose brandy.

What changed American drinking habits in the nineteenth century and made whiskey a national drink was an improvement in techniques. About 1800 a process was developed for the rectification of spirits; continuous-operation stills were invented in 1826 by Robert Stein and in 1832 by Aeneas Coffey; the so-called Liebig condenser appeared at mid-century. It now became possible to make in the United States whiskey of a quality which could compete, on a price basis at least, with the expensive brews imported from Ireland and Scotland, countries which had learned to make good whiskey in pot stills without benefit of sophisticated equipment (they still do).

It was in the nineteenth century therefore that the United States developed the two types of whiskey which are particularly American, rye and corn, whose beginnings we have already chronicled. In both cases a considerable element of accident was responsible for their evolution. The Scotch and Irish settlers who made the first American whiskey, mostly in western Pennsylvania and Maryland, did not choose rye deliberately as its basic grain because that was what they had been used to in the old country; they used rye because rye was what they had. Scotland and Ireland did indeed occasionally put rye into whisky (Scots and English spelling) or whiskey (Irish and American spelling), but they preferred barley. However, barley, like wheat, was slow in acclimating itself to the American climate; rye accepted citizenship more promptly, and thus became the grain of the first American whiskey. By the time barley had become more plentiful, the makers of rye had become used to it and had decided that they liked it. Rye whiskey was established.

Rye whiskey is aged in new charred oak barrels; the discovery that charred barrels add flavor and tannin in whiskies was an accident . One account alleges that a fire in a West Indian rum distillery scorched barrels without destroying them; they were consequently used all the same to hold rum, when it was found that the flavor of the liquor stored in them was improved; thereafter barrels were charred purposely, and the same process was later applied to whiskey with success. A different story is that during the process of barrel making in Kentucky, staves which were being heated so that they could be bent into the required shape were charred by accident, with such good results that this thereafter became standard procedure. A third tale attributes this innovation to the economical character of a cooper who burned out the interior of barrels which had held fish so that whiskey could be put in them without tasting of the sea. The most fanciful story tells of a farmer who buried several barrels of whiskey beneath his barn to age; lightning struck the barn, it burned down, and the barrels beneath it were charred; but their contents were improved. The law does not require that rye whiskey must be struck by lightning, but it does now stipulate that it must be aged in new charred barrels, usually made of white oak. A mixture of grains may be used, but at least 51 percent of the mash must be rye for the product to have the right to be sold under the name of rye whiskey.

The favorite whiskey of the United States is bourbon, American par excellence, since it was not only created on American territory, but also is made, in majority at least, of America's own grain, corn. The birth of bourbon was aided by a number of accidents too. The first was the Whiskey Rebellion of 1791, which caused some whiskey makers to move to Kentucky in the hope of avoiding taxation; Kentucky at that time had not yet been incorporated into the United States. The government quickly caught up with the distillers, for Kentucky was made a state in June of the following year; but it took a little time to organize Federal tax collecting there, which gave the distillers breathing time; even after tax collecting *was* organized, on paper, it was still only spottily effective on the ground, rendered difficult by the geography of the States. Whiskey makers opposed to the idea of taxation simply took to the hills and a not inconsiderable number of them are still there, unreconciled to this day with fiscality.

The second accident which contributed to the development of bourbon was perhaps not an accident; it was the finding in Kentucky too of the pure mineral-free limestone spring water which had made the fortune of the Pennsylvania brewers. It is possible that the whiskey makers had prospected before they moved, and knew what to expect of Kentucky.

Accidental certainly, however, was the circumstance which created bourbon. The displaced distillers had been manufacturing in Kentucky what they had been producing previously in Pennslyvania—rye whiskey. But then the rye crop failed; when the supply became sparse, the distillers, in desperation, eked it out with corn—and discovered to their surprise that the mixture produced a beverage lighter in body and sweeter in taste than rye. They stayed with corn, and the result was called bourbon from the county where it was first made.

Bourbon and corn whiskey, however, are not synonymous. Compared with bourbon, corn is a crude beverage, consumed oftenest in rural settings (a certain rusticity is indicated by the popular name for it, corn likker) or among the poorer persons in urban populations. It is held in official disdain; legislation which required that bourbon and rye must be aged in charred barrels and in new ones makes no stipulation for corn; any old barrel will do. The only specification this brew has to meet to be labeled "corn" is that its mash must be made at least 80 percent from corn. While both rye and bourbon are limited to 160 proof at distillation, corn can come out of the still as strong as anyone can take it, and it is not necessarily reduced to less potency afterward before it is offered to the unwary customer. Corn can be a very raw drink, for whose appreciation a certain amount of fortitude is required.

Bourbon, on the contrary, is a drink for connoisseurs; the adjective they use oftenest to describe it is probably "noble." The present legal specifications for bourbon are that it should not test at distillation more than 160 proof; that it should be aged in new charred barrels for at least four years; and that at least 51 percent of the mash should come from corn. These are minimums; many bourbon makers do better. Some of them age their whiskey for six years; some use up to 80 percent corn; the rest of the grain is usually rye (but some distillers prefer wheat) and barley. And as whiskey distilled to a lower alcoholic content is fuller bodied and richer in taste, it is sometimes distilled at no more than 125 proof. Before being offered for sale, whatever its strength at distillation, it is diluted to somewhere between 80 and 100 proof, strong enough for anybody.

No true Kentuckian would think of using any other liquid than bourbon in that most romanticized drink of the South, the mint julep.

> The Honey of Hymettus [said the nineteenth-century Judge Soule Smith of the mint julep] brought no such solace to the soul. The Nectar of the Gods is tame beside it. . . . Bourbon and mint are lovers . . . in the same land they live, on the same food are fostered. . . . Like a woman's heart, mint gives its sweetest aroma when bruised.

Kentuckians agree about the bruising (of mint, that is); they crush it in the sweetened syrup added to the bourbon in the classic juleps served at the Kentucky Derby; but not all Southerners do. Some of them insist that the mint should be left uncrushed. Opinions on the proper way to make mint juleps are defended in the South as fiercely as the honor of women; mayhem lurks in the mind when a Kentuckian meets a Southerner so benighted as to prefer rye, rum, or brandy in his julep. Even when there is agreement on bourbon, there is no harmony on the amount of bourbon which is proper; the ideal dose for julep fancier A is an ounce, for julep fancier B two ounces, for julep fancier C three ounces; there are no doubt champions for fractional amounts as well. Those persons who put carefully chosen spring water into their juleps are scandalized at the blasphemy of heretics who draw their water simply from the faucet. You are blessed or damned depending on whether you serve your juleps in a glass or in a mug of silver or aluminum. Whatever the container, the reverent will not touch it with their bare hands when placing it in, or removing it from, the refrigerator in which it is put to cool before consumption; this might prevent the outside of the glass or mug from frosting evenly; women have been known to put on gloves while preparing juleps.

Bourbon falls in the category of straight whiskeys, which are unmixed beverages, offered in the fashion in which they leave the hands of their makers. United States law adds that they must have been distilled at no more than 160 proof and must have been aged in the wood at least two years. Blended straight whiskeys are mixtures of two or more, all of them straights. But blended whiskey, without other qualification, is something else again; it is a mixture of a straight whiskey with neutral spirits; the result is lighter and less expensive; 25 percent of all the whiskey sold in the United States is blended whiskey.

Starting at scratch about the beginning of the nineteenth century, the United States has become today the world's largest producer—and largest consumer—of whiskey.

As the making of legal whiskey became more and more a matter of technique, it became less and less romantic; but glamor continued to surround the makers of illegal whiskey—the moonshiners, so called because they sometimes worked at night by moonlight when smoke rising from their hidden stills could not be spotted from afar by vigilant tax collectors.

Moonshine was (and is) made chiefly in the southern Appalachians of West Virginia, Kentucky, and Tennessee, and the Ozarks south of them. Moonshining became solidly established there, not simply because the rugged hills furnished cover against tax collecting agents, but also because the very nature of the land imposed this activity upon them as almost the only way in which they could make a living. In the up-and-down terrain of this unfertile country, where only small patches of fairly level and slightly better land capable of growing corn interrupted the pine woods, this grain, almost the only possible crop, could not be produced on a profitable scale; and what little was produced could not be transported readily through the rough country to city markets in the form of grain. Both problems could be solved by converting corn into whiskey, easier to deliver and salable at a profitable price—provided its makers enjoyed the differential resulting from non-payment of the excise tax to offset the surer quality of the tax-paying commercial product.

The avoidance of taxes did not weigh heavily on the consciences of the operators of illegal stills. A former moonshiner told an interviewer for *The Foxfire Book:* "I felt like I was making an honest dollar, and if it hadn't a been for that stuff, we'd a had an empty table around here."

The temptation to take to moonshining (or to stay at it) was strong from the beginning when, in 1782, before bourbon had even been invented or the territory had become a state, the price of whiskey was officially fixed in Kentucky at $15 a half pint or $240 a gallon, which must have surprised the refugees from the Whiskey Rebellion. This was a thumping price for the times, with the government as the greatest gainer; it guaranteed that moonshiners could make money even if they were obliged to chalk up to profit and loss from time to time the cost of a seized still. The high impost also made the moonshiner all the more romantic; he was succeeding in evading a considerable tax, and was admired for it by all those who would have liked to be able to do the same (virtually everybody) but were unfortunately not in a position to get away with it. This was no doubt an anti-social attitude, but the hard fact is that the tax collector has no friends—a sentiment pushed so far in moonshine country that the revenue agent, a century ago, risked being shot at on sight.

To prevent the confiscation of their stills, which frequently represented a considerable investment, the moonshiners over the years developed various ingenious methods of camouflage, most of them based on the theory that they were likeliest to be spotted from above, by lookouts on the crests (nowadays the big danger is still from above—the airplane). Log sheds were built over stills and covered with branches: or live saplings were bent over them; or stills were placed under trees which had fallen across ravines; or holes for stills were dug in the bottoms of gullies and branches placed over them; or the still was placed in a cave with vegetation veiling its entrance; or a space just large enough for the still would be hollowed out in the middle of a thicket; or a large spruce would be bent down sufficiently to hide a still beneath it; or a room in which to work might even be built underground. One master psychologist placed his still on the main road, screened only by a few trees. He reasoned that the revenooers would never look for a still in a spot so exposed; they never did.

Smoke was a giveaway. Various means were devised to get rid of it. A moonshiner might start his fire before dawn, giving it time to settle down to producing heat, not smoke, before daylight; or he would rig up a pipe to return it to the firebox; or he might even pipe it to a stream, where it would emerge under water. These devices are unnecessary now. In *American Cooking: Southern Style,* Eugene Walter quotes an Ozark mountaineer on the reason why:

> We pretty nigh got them fellers [the revenooers] foxed now. We burn butane in our stills, and it don't make no smoke. They used to jes' set in their cars on some ridge [about the time of Prohibition, probably] and wait to see the smoke curlin' up from outa the pines in the valley, then come chargin.' Now they can't see doodley-squat.

Because stills had to be located well up in the hills near a source of water, government agents frequently walked up a stream, with a reasonable chance of finding a still if they went high enough; moonshiners countered this by locating their stills in "dry hollows," through which no water ran; then they would tap, higher up the slope, a stream descending through a different valley, diverting what they needed by means of a wooden trough which could be dismantled and hidden after each run, or perhaps through a buried pipe.

"Revenooers," of course, developed their skills too. They looked for "signs" even at considerable distances from stills, where moonshiners might be more careless—sugar or meal spilled on a road, a brick in the woods where no brick had any reason to be, cut branches, presumably used for camouflage. They listened in the woods for sounds of hammering or stills thumping as they went into action. Or they simply sniffed the air; there is little a moonshiner can do to suppress the odor of his product. But, as is true of many types of police operation, their most helpful aid was the informer—usually motivated by spite. "Th' lowest man I know," one moonshiner exploded, "is one who wins your confidence, buys your liquor, and then turns you in. I believe there's a special place for people like that after they die."

In the nature of things, there can be no reliable statistics on the extent of moonshining; but from time to time there have been more or less informed guesses. In 1878, the Commissioner of Internal Revenue reported that in the Southern Appalachian states "there are known to exist 5,000 copper stills."

How many other unknown stills may there have been? In 1952, twenty thousand illicit stills were reported to have been seized, and it was estimated that an equal number were still in operation. In May, 1968, the Atlanta *Constitution* alleged that there were 750 stills in Georgia alone, with a mash capacity of more than 750,000 gallons. In 1974 the Distilled Spirits Council of the United States complained to the authorities about the intense competition from moonshine whiskey. It ventured no figures, but if the illicit output was enough to bother the representatives of the lawful industry, which for the first eight months of that year had handled 230,491,739 gallons of distilled spirits, the amount of moonshine must have been impressive.

There is one sign that the moonshiner's day is about over; he is losing the support of his neighbors. Why? Because, say the old-time moonshiners, now too old to make it themselves, we have emerged from "the good old days when the whiskey that was made was *really* whiskey." Quality has been forgotten in the pursuit of quantity. Moonshining has been taken over, says *The Foxfire Book*,

> by a brand of men bent on making money—and lots of it. Loss of pride in the product, and loss of time taken with the product increased in direct proportion to the desire for production. . . . People used to take great pride in their work, but the pride has left and the dollar's come in," [said one mountaineer, while another even approved openly of the increasing success of the revenooers, an attitude which would have been all but unthinkable a few years ago, because] "the operations are so much bigger now, and sloppier. If the Feds can't get 'em, the Pure Food and Drugs ought to try. That stuff they're making now'll kill a man."

"Moonshining as a fine art," concluded *The Foxfire Book* regretfully, "effectively disappeared some time ago."

The activities of the Prohibitionists were retarded by the approach and then the outbreak of the Civil War. Abolition had become a more urgent cause than Prohibition; and after the War began the government needed all the money it could get to wage it, including the far from negligible revenue derived from liquor taxes. Even the militant women whose prewar activities had been so effective were for a time distracted from the war against rum by the war against secession. But after a breathing spell for reconstruction, they were back in the lists—with a vengeance.

Of all the direct-action advocates, none surpassed Carry Amelia Moore Gloyd Nation, who had founded a white ribbon chapter of the Women's Christian Temperance Union in Medicine Lodge, Kansas. In 1880 Kansas had adopted statewide prohibition, but Carry, daughter of a Fundamentalist Kentucky planter and his clearly psychotic wife, became unsettled by the existence of seven illicit dram shops and a bootlegging drugstore in Medicine

Lodge, and heckled the town fathers until all but the drugstore were shuttered. With the help of a Baptist minister's wife, Carry raided the drugstore, sledgehammer in hand, and smashed the ten-gallon keg holding its supply of bootleg whiskey. The druggist decided to leave town, and Carry, exhilarated by her success, prepared for a career as the catalyst for hundreds of women reformers, churchwomen mostly, who by direct action lent force and color to the war on drink. By her own account, it was on June 6, 1900, when she opened her Bible at random for guidance (a practice not unknown to religious reformers) and cast her eyes on a text from Isaiah bidding her "Arise, shine: for thy light is come, and the glory of the Lord is risen upon thee." Further urging came from an inner voice directing her to go to Kiowa, a few miles away, and wreak her wrath upon the illegal saloons that flourished there.

Three saloons were vandalized by Carry, who burst in with bricks or stones in hand and hurled them at whatever seemed smashable, such as bar mirrors and rows of bottles. When the local catchpolls apprehended her, she pointed out that the joints themselves were operating outside the law, and she was let go. John Kobler lists the Midwestern towns Carry raided as Wichita (where in addition to glassware she ruined a barroom nude entitled *Cleopatra at Her Bath),* Enterprise, Topeka, Des Moines, and Chicago. From there she moved east and south to Cincinnati, St. Louis, Atlantic City, Philadelphia, and New York, where former heavyweight champion John L. Sullivan refused to confront her when she went to his saloon, presumably on mayhem bent. Behind Carry, who had adopted a hatchet as her symbol, was a stream of women who espoused her tactics, along with those of what was later to be called the "pray-in." As the years went by, Carry, through her own exaggeration of her threat and her exploits and by that of the popular press, became one of the synthetic notables found regularly in United States history, more acclaimed for her eccentricities than for her single-minded devotion to her cause. By the time of her death, in her sixties, she had become worn out and somewhat demented. But, as no other single person ever did, she called attention to the negative aspects of the old-time saloon, and started a war on drinking places which goes on to this day, though the wave of American prohibition has receded, seemingly never to return.

Hundreds of women who lacked the brass and showmanship of Carry Nation indulged in sporadic if less spectacular forays against illicit saloons in Illinois and Ohio after having heard the inspirational lectures of Dr. Diocletian (Dio) Lewis, a dropout from Harvard Medical School who practiced nevertheless as an unlicensed healer until the day the Homeopathic Hospital College of Cleveland, Ohio, honored him with a degree.

A particularly successful Lewis appearance at a Presbyterian church in Hillsboro, Ohio, in 1873, appears to have triggered what came to be known as "The Crusade." (The title was later to be pre-empted by a successful group which *opposed* Prohibition.) Soon the ladies of the Middle West, upstate New York, and even parts of the South were parading, picketing, praying, and smashing, in an evangelical fervor which as it cooled down became manifest in another form, the Women's Christian Temperance Union—"We See to You" as the irreverent were to call it. Its first president was a heroine, one of the Army nurses of the Civil War, Mrs. Annie Wittenmyer of Keokuk, Iowa. Though there was no lack of talent or energy among the dauntless women who had cared for the Union soldiers in hospitals and on the battlefields, and who had crusaded so valiantly against the Demon, it was not until the WCTU came under the leadership of Miss Frances Willard that it realized its full potential. Rising from a local office to become Secretary of the national WCTU under Mrs. Wittenmyer, Miss Willard familiarized herself with the levers of command much as Stalin did in Lenin's lifetime, and five years later took over the presidency, which she held to her death on February 17, 1898. Under her reign the organization mixed into many reformist causes, though the main theme was the accomplishment of total national and constitutional Prohibition. Other targets, for each of which she usually created a special department in the WCTU, were tobacco, the double standard of morality, bad language, obscenity in any form, prostitution and its concomitant "white slavery," provocative fashions in women's dress, polygamy, desecration of the Sabbath, gambling, and intercollegiate sports. There were more easily recognizable good causes, too: the enfranchisement of women, prison reform, child welfare laws, adult education to stamp out illiteracy, and world peace.

The extraordinary woman who headed all this was born in 1839, to a theological student and his schoolteacher wife in Oberlin, Ohio. Frances and her younger sister were brought up in an atmosphere of Spartan fundamentalism, with strict Sunday observance and an eagle-eyed chaperonage that kept them far from any contact with boys. In this climate, Frances developed into a traditional tomboy, wearing trousers, playing and working as a boy might. In her autobiography she relates her furious crushes on girls, and her coolness toward boys. Her tendency to romantic attachments with females developed during her student years, and later when she became a teacher at her alma mater, Northwestern Female College at Evanston, Illinois. A most successful teacher, she became president of the college in 1871, and was appointed dean of women when it was merged with Northwestern University. At this point "Frank" (as her intimates called her) decided to devote herself wholeheartedly to the Temperance (read "Prohibition") cause.

It was natural that Frances Willard and Anthony Comstock, founder of the New York Society for the Suppression of Vice, should have seen eye to eye, and she saw to it that the blessing of the WCTU was put on the super-snooper's campaign against nude statues and art-school life classes. It was natural and reasonable that in an era of Victorian repression and hypocrisy no recorded inquiry into the emotional and psychological state of this extraordinary woman, blessed with aggressive energy beyond that of almost any man, seems to exist. Her own accounts of her relationship with her women friends in the United States and in later years with Lady Isabella Caroline Somerset, president of the British Women's Temperance Association, are warm and loving, but fail to answer the question of whether or not the affection was consummated. At the end of the last century we had not yet entered into the age of instant Freudian interpretations. Miss Willard stands today in the Statuary Hall in Washington (the old House of Representatives), in purest white marble, paid for by the state of Illinois and accepted by Congress in 1905, representing not only an eminent personage of the state, but the first woman to take her place in that monumental collection.

Oberlin College was to continue to write its name large in the history of Temperance through the career of one of its male graduates, Reverend Howard Hyde Russell. At a meeting held at his alma mater on May 24, 1893, Russell persuaded the executive body of the Temperance Alliance of Ohio to set up an overall state organization to work with any church or lay body which was devoted to the Dry cause. Unlike the WCTU, which was concerning itself with multiple causes, the new group was to stick to its knitting, the defeat of booze; unlike the perhaps equally single-minded Prohibition Party, it was to present no candidates, but would support any candidate of either party who would subscribe to the Dry program. The idea caught on, not only in Ohio, which had proved to be one of the focal points, with Kansas and upper New York State, of all anti-liquor programs, but as far north as Minnesota and as far east as the District of Columbia, where in 1895 a national convention of local groups announced the formation of the Anti-Saloon League of America. It was destined to become one of the most successful pressure groups in our history.

Also from Oberlin came Wayne Bidwell Wheeler, whom Russell picked as his assistant after learning of the young man's campus career as a Dry lecturer. Russell and Wheeler gathered around them a dynamic group of clergymen and began to solicit funds for the League. Founder Russell himself became a specialist in extracting funds from the very rich, including the John D. Rockefellers, father and son, Andrew Carnegie, Henry Ford, and Samuel Kresge. Pierre S. DuPont contributed at first, though later he was to defect and become an advocate of repeal, once Prohibition was established nationally. Not much support came from Catholics and Jews, nor from the Episcopal and Lutheran churches, but Methodists, Baptists, Presbyterians, and the fundamentalist sects of the so-called Bible Belt provided a reported two million dollar yearly war chest, enough to fuel a propaganda machine which included a newspaper, *The National Daily,* two weeklies, and two monthly magazines, plus pseudo-scientific pamphlets on the evils of drink and the saloon, and a variety of colorful promotional materials. With Wheeler and Russell were such notable figures as William Eugene Johnson, renowned as "Pussyfoot" for his foxy exposures of fraud and corruption on the part of state officials who were, like most of their kind, only half-heartedly enforcing dry laws, or not enforcing them at all. A master of covert operation and entrapment, he extracted from Theodore Roosevelt a commission to enforce Prohibition in the Oklahoma Indian Territory. With a fine disregard for legality Johnson and his deputies smashed and raided in all the Indian reservations of the West. Monumentally brazen, and physically fearless, Johnson rounded up some five thousand offenders and got most of them convicted during the five years he held his commission.

As cold a personality as "Pussyfoot" Johnson was hot, the Southern Methodist divine (eventually Bishop) James Cannon, Jr., dominated the Dry forces in Virginia, and from a secure position as head of a women's college and publisher of a Richmond daily newspaper, gained a national reputation as lobbyist for the Anti-Saloon League in Washington. His career included a high point in pressure application when he got the personally Wet Senator Warren G. Harding to endorse the Eighteenth Amendment.

But the hero, or the villain, as the case may be, of the pre-World War One drive for Prohibition was Wheeler himself. Having proved himself as a lecturer and organizer in Ohio, he studied law in such time as he could spare from League activities, and when Western Reserve University gave him his degree in 1898 he became the Ohio group's attorney. By 1916 Wheeler was in Washington as general counsel for the League, head of a nation-wide organization of churchmen, lecturers, lobbyists, and volunteer reformers who were prepared to do whatever was needed to swing the dry minority behind any candidate who was promising to vote their way.

The declaration of war by President Wilson on April 16, 1917, delayed action on Prohibition legislation, but probably made its passage more certain. New slogans and anxieties were developed by the war hysteria: grain should be conserved for food, not distilled into liquor; brewers were mostly of German origin, hence suspect; we should sacrifice everything to the war effort, including drink; and so on. When the proper moment seemed to have arrived, Anti-Saloon League pressure developed on Senators and Congressmen to let the resolution for the Prohibition amendment come up for a vote. In the hopes that a limiting clause requiring that the states ratify the amendment within six years might mean that it would never be ratified, the hesitant Senators agreed to clear the resolution. Wayne Wheeler, who knew better than the Congress how many votes could be mobilized for the Dry cause across the country, accepted the proviso with good grace.

The rest is history. The joint resolution passed the House and Senate in December, 1917, and by January 16, 1919, the Eighteenth Amendment was ratified by the required thirty-six legislatures, to become effective one year later. Many times it has been said that Prohibition was something "sneaked over in wartime" against the will of the American people. The record seems to indicate that it had been sneaked over in the elections of 1916, the year of Wayne B. Wheeler's triumph. Just what did this Dry victory represent?

(1) It was (perhaps) the last victory of the rural nativist Puritan mentality, exemplified by the fundamentalist Protestantism of the backwoods churches, over the urban "foreigner-corrupted" elements.

(2) It was expressive of the American concept of reform by law, valued as much for its moral statement as for its chances of success. And it was backed by glaring evidence of almost total disregard of human values by the makers of booze and the keepers of saloons. The problem was real enough; the solution offered was impossible and ludicrous, seen in retrospect; and those who tried to enforce it matched the liquor dealers in disregard of human values—and even, in the name of law enforcement, of disregard for the law.

(3) In the South it reflected the intention of the whites to control the former slaves, alleged to be potentially violent when they had access to liquor. In the North there were industrialists who felt that liquor impaired workers' efficiency (true enough) and that with the saloons closed, agitation for unions, et cetera, would be discouraged (which proved palpably false).

"The California wine grower who killed himself [at the beginning of Prohibition], believing he faced ruin," John Kobler wrote in *Ardent Spirits,* "could scarcely have imagined that during the next five years in his state alone, grape acreage would expand sevenfold from 97,000 to 681,000." There are only about half a million acres of vineyards in California today, but Mr. Kobler's figure is not improbable; the expansion of cities has decreased the amount of land available for vineyards.

The statement as it stands seems to imply that Prohibition was a boon, not a blow, to California wine growing; but it represents a simplification of an evolution rather more complex. Most authorities would probably agree that Prohibition, in the long run, harmed the adolescent American wine industry, qualitatively if not quantitatively; and it had even harmed it quantitatively before it was enacted. California had achieved some wines of excellent quality before the present century opened, and the influx of immigrants from the wine-drinking countries of southern Europe—six million in the first fifteen years of the twentieth century—was steadily increasing the number of its potential customers. By 1912, the annual production of California wines had reached fifty million gallons; but at this point the success of the Dry forces in arousing public opinion against drinking, which caused many municipalities and several entire states to enact local Prohibition statutes, reversed the tendency. Although wine-drinking immigrants continued to pour into the country between 1912 and 1915, production in the latter year had fallen to not much more than a fifth of what it had been three years earlier. When national Prohibition went into effect, the California wine industry was thrown into complete disarray; some wine makers switched to growing fruit or vegetables. The legal marketing channels through which wine had been sold were now closed to it; it took a little while for illegal channels to be created. It was only then that California wine sales began to skyrocket. Before Prohibition, the chief competition to California wines had come from European wines. Now the supply of imported wines had been cut off.

From the viewpoint of money making, California grape growers were sitting pretty; from the viewpoint of wine making, the situation was a little different. The demand now was for quantity, not quality. Superior vines of limited yield were grubbed up to make way for grapes which produced more wine per acre, though of a coarser kind. By the time Prohibition ended in 1934, the vineyards were in sad shape. Many of the finest wines, which had been painstakingly selected and imported from Europe, had disappeared. Their place had been taken by grapes suitable only for what was contemptuously called "Dago red" or "red ink."

Prohibition had thus set back by at least the fourteen years it lasted, and probably more, the solving of what had been from the beginning (and still is) the essential problem of the California wine industry—the achievement of quality. In a country whose population was not accustomed to drinking wine the most promising market, for the time being at least, seemed to lie not with the masses, but with the sophisticated minority which had developed a taste for wine by drinking European vintages. If California wines were to make their way into this circle, they would have to be good enough to bear comparison with European wines. Before Prohibition, some of them already were; but during Prohibition quality had gone by the board. Not until 1938 would California begin to regain the ground it had lost.

When Prohibition hit the California wine industry, rather more ingenuity was called into play to defend it against this short-term menace than had ever been put at its service to promote its long-term interests; perhaps it was wine merchants, more resourceful than wine growers, who were responsible for this. They devised "bricks of Bacchus" which consisted of grape concentrate, accompanied with minute directions explaining what the buyer must *not* do to prevent his block of concentrate from turning feloniously into wine.

The technique was law-proof, entirely legal under the Volstead Act which prohibited selling alcoholic liquor, but which did not prohibit selling nonalcoholic grapes. An honest merchant could hardly be obliged to distrust his customers to the extent of imagining that they would be unprincipled enough to make illicit use of licit merchandise. Could a hardware dealer refuse to sell an ax to a man for fear that he might subsequently use it, not on his woodpile, but on his wife? This was a commerce which made everybody happy, except perhaps the Prohibitionist Puritan, who did not enjoy being happy anyway—the merchants who were making sales, the customers who were buying health-giving fruit, and above all the California growers who had found a new outlet for their grapes, which now, wrote John Kobler,

> reached the customers as fresh grapes, bricks of Bacchus or grape juice, the last labeled CAUTION: WILL FERMENT AND TURN INTO WINE. From 1925 to 1939 Americans drank more than 678,000,000 gallons of home-fermented wine, three times as much as all the domestic and imported wine they drank during the five years before prohibition; this figure does not include the wine made from backyard vineyards, from dandelion, currants, cherries and other fruits. . . . Winemaking stimulated the manufacture of numerous related products—grape crushers, wine-presses, fermenting tubes, gelatine to settle the sediment, crocks, kegs and bungs, bottles and corks—on which the home winemakers spent about $220,000,000 a year.

Prohibition was less of a problem for wine growers in the East, who were enabled to weather the drought because they supplied the market for sacramental wine, which escaped the *Diktat* of the Volstead Act. Serving this market had been the specialty of the Hudson Valley and what is called the Chautauqua grape belt, which runs from west of Buffalo along Lake Erie and into the states of Ohio and Pennsylvania. With the coming of Prohibition, other Eastern areas joined in supplying the kosher demand, which may have been sufficient to absorb the entire small production of Eastern wines during the dry period; for by a peculiar coincidence, the size of Jewish congregations suddenly multiplied when the Volstead Act went into effect. There have been persons cynical enough to hint that in many cities of the East, New York especially, large numbers of *Goyim* carried in their pocketbooks cards bearing Hebrew characters which they were unable to decipher, certifying the fact (or, more accurately, fiction) that they were members of one Jewish congregation or another, and thus entitled to buy sacramental kosher wine. This was not a particularly alluring prospect for a connoisseur, for the wines in question were oversweet, syrupy, and thin at the same time, and without finesse; but for Jewish sacramental wine, as for Christian sacramental wine, quality was not the point.

Another large loophole in the Prohibition laws was created by the impossibility of cutting off the supply of alcohol for medical uses. Congress did its best, or worst, by enacting legislation to limit the amount of alcohol a doctor could prescribe and the frequency with which he could allot it to a single patient, matters which should perhaps have been entrusted to the judgment of physicians rather than of legislators.

The American public had long been accustomed to curing almost everything with alcohol. The most temperate of its prescriptions was perhaps the one contained in what seems to have been the very first medical publication in English-speaking North America—a single sheet of paper of which a considerable proportion was used up by its title: *A Brief Rule to Guide the Common-people of New-England How to Order Themselves and Theirs in the Small Pocks, or Measles.* This useful advice appeared when a smallpox epidemic broke out in the Northeast in 1678 and carried all the more weight because its authority was not merely medical, but theological. Its author was Thomas Thacher, pastor of Boston's Old South Church, who began by listing thirty symptoms by which the disease could be recognized, followed by this sage advice:

> As soon as this disease therefore appears by its signs, let the sick abstain from Flesh and Wine, and open Air, let him use small Bear warmed with a Tost for his ordinary drink, and moderately when he desires it.

As a rule it was drink stronger than small Bear which was recommended for maladies, and stronger also than wine, though this was all that was suggested by Governor John Winthrop the Younger at about the same epoch to a friend whose wife was ill: "Good wine is the best cordial for her." Spirits were prescribed oftener, and doctors and folk medicine were more or less in agreement concerning their beneficial qualities. According to the latter, one took for arthritis a mixture of honey, vinegar, and moonshine whiskey, or, alternatively, powdered rhubarb dissolved in white whiskey; for asthma, gin in which pine heartwood had been soaked, or honey, lemon juice, and whiskey; for the blood, yellowroot in whiskey flavored with cherry bark; for colds, cherries soaked in rum, or powdered ginger tea with honey and whiskey, or red pepper in tea and white corn whiskey; for colic (in infants!) asafetida and whiskey mixed in baby's milk; for congestion, white whiskey in which rock candy had been steeped; for coughing, heated white whiskey with sugar, or horehound candy dissolved in whiskey; for dysentery, a mixture of cherry rum, brandy, and essence of peppermint; for gall bladder trouble pure corn whiskey; for measles, whiskey (only a few drops for "tiny children"); for pneumonia, butterfly weed tea in whiskey; for pregnant women and nursing mothers, rum and milk; for rheumatism, a mixture of pokeberry wine and whiskey, or rattleroot, ginseng, red corn root, wild cherry bark, and golden seal in white whiskey, or alcohol in which Castile soap had been soaked for three days, to which camphor and oil of rosemary was added later; for toothache, one part of pokeberry wine to eight parts of white whiskey.

If whiskey predominates in these remedies (contrary to later superstitions, none of the eighteenth- and nineteenth-century books seem to have thought it a remedy for snakebite), it is because a large proportion of them come from the south. Farther north, rum and gin entered oftener into home medicine, and even brandy—sometimes specifically the "finest French brandy" or "old rum"—nothing was too good for a sick man.

But it was in the Middle West that a phenomenon which can hardly be omitted from American folk history developed to the highest degree—the medicine show. This began in artisanal fashion, managed by a single spellbinder with a glib gift of gab, who before each show stirred up a few bucketfuls of branchwater and whatever sufficiently evil-tasting ingredients happened to be at hand, and bottled it under the name of Dr. Somebody's Old Indian Remedy or Magic Snake Oil, which he then foisted off on a gullible public. But industrialism was setting in, so well-organized companies got into the business of putting up standardized remedies in commercial quantity, and though the medicinemen were on hand to serve as sales outlets, they were quickly and ungratefully abandoned to the profit of the pharmacies, while the medicine-show barker's sales pitch was replaced by newspaper advertising, then unregulated, in which the manufacturers of patent medicines could make any claims concerning their miracle-working medicines which they thought the public could be persuaded to swallow, along with their product.

Faith in patent medicines was widespread during the nineteenth century, and though it had cooled somewhat in the more urban areas by the time of Prohibition, there were still enough persons who swore by them to create a problem for the enforcers of the Volstead Act. A large proportion of these panaceas were little more than medically flavored alcohol, but for their users any attempt to crack down on them would have seemed to be an assault on the health of the nation.

There seems to be little data available on the extent to which patent medicines continued to be consumed during Prohibition. It may be that the Puritan-Prohibitionists did not bear down very hard in this area, inhibited by the circumstance that sometimes the very groups which contained the most uncompromising foes of convivial drinking were also those in which, embarrassingly, the consumption of patent medicines was highest. The Puritan who had recourse to a patent medicine when, naturally, he was feeling under the weather, could point to the euphoria which followed swiftly as proof that he had chosen a wise and effective remedy. The end justified the means; and indeed in many cases he may not have been aware of the nature of the means. He was not accustomed to drinking beer, wine, or spirits, and was therefore ill-equipped to identify the sensation of well-being which followed a swig of his favorite medicament as attributable to what was in fact the active principle in most of these concoctions—a liberal dose of alcohol. It was possible to be ignorant of this detail, for although the Pure Food and Drug Act had been passed in 1906, its requirements concerning labeling were neither very strict nor very well enforced; not until 1938 would more effective legislation be adopted. Even those who did know what they were drinking may have reasoned that the bitterness of the herbs assembled more or less at random to give the alcohol a respectably medicinal flavor took the curse off it. It would certainly have been consistent enough with the Puritan mentality to consider that the primary enemy was not the alcohol itself but the sinful joy that the unholy might derive from it.

Patent medicines provided an uncriticizable tipple for those who in their own estimation indulged in none. It was almost symbolic that Andrew Volstead, champion of the Prohibitionists, was a native of Yellow Medicine County, Minnesota. May we permit ourselves also a fleeting smile at another felicitous coincidence in the vocabulary of the Drys?: the Prohibition Party's candidate for President in the elections of 1904 was named Silas C. Swallow.

When Prohibition struck, the American beer industry was much more solidly rooted than the American wine industry; a minute minority of Americans drank wine, the great majority of Americans drank beer, if they drank any alcoholic beverage at all. Beer had been made in the North American colonies from the very beginning, yet the history of its later development was to be closely associated with that of German immigration—it even started with another Teutonic people, the Dutch of New Amsterdam who made the first American beer. Later, the Germans who began entering the United States in large numbers from 1840 on laid solid foundations for the American beer industry and then erected an impressive edifice upon them.

It may seem curious that the colonists from the British Isles, who were there first and came also from a land where beer was the everyday tipple, should have abandoned brewing to the Germans. It may have been because their beer was too weak and too strong—too weak for the serious drinkers, who had a habit in Colonial and post-Colonial times of spiking their beer with other drinkables, especially rum, to make it more potent, and too strong for those who wanted a thirst-quenching beverage rather than alcohol. Early American beer had a higher alcoholic content than that which we drink oftenest today (nevertheless it was considered suitable for children until about 1825, and perhaps it was, since neither the water nor the milk was reliable).

When the Germans produced a beer which offered an alternative to intoxicating drink, the temperate turned gratefully to it; the intemperate did too, for that matter, between drinking bouts, or even during them, when the habit developed of following a shot of whiskey with a chaser of beer. The Germans specialized in lager; their ideal seemed to be something like Pilsner, not a bad model. As the result of their innovation, Americans for the last 125 years have been drinking a milder, lighter and less bitter beer than they had rendered tribute to before. American lager, or, if you prefer, German-American lager, is, indeed, one of our more successful productions—pale in color, only moderately flavored with hops, containing 3 to 3.8 percent of alcohol by weight (the pre-1840 beers contained 5 percent and up).

The first brewery of the second wave of German immigrants was opened in 1841 in Milwaukee, the beer capital of America ever since, though the brewing of beer was pursued also in other cities with important German elements in their populations—New York, Philadelphia, Cincinnati, St. Louis, Chicago.

At the time when Prohibition became the law of the land, beer was a commonplace thoroughly accepted beverage in the United States, often considered harmless even by those who disapproved of hard liquor. Beer alcoholics did exist; it is possible to drink or eat or indulge in anything to excess, including water. But it was stronger drink which seemed the legitimate target of the Drys to most persons, and no doubt there were many who did not anticipate that the term "intoxicating liquors" in the Eighteenth Amendment would be defined as including beer; it was, though. The beermakers were less frightened at their future prospects than the wine makers had been. Beer was big business; the breweries had enough capital on hand to wait out a drought, if it were not a long one. They also had an alternative, temporarily acceptable, to their accustomed activity—it was not too difficult to convert to making soft drinks. Presently Congress gave them something else to do, by deciding that it was permissible to make near-beer. So they made near-beer, though this was something like an act of treason to the noble art of brewing. Near-beer, whose alcoholic content could not exceed one-half of one percent, was such a wishy-washy, thin, ill-tasting, discouraging sort of slop that it might have been dreamed up by a Puritan Machiavelli with the intent of disgusting drinkers with genuine beer forever. However beer drinkers proved not easily disgusted; after fourteen years of near-beer they returned, on Repeal, to their pre-Prohibition habits, drinking the same beers made by the same companies which they had favored before the drought.

During the period when no real beer (theoretically) was being made by professionals, the gap was often filled by amateurs, whose product was apt to be a great deal more dangerous than the brews which had been suppressed.

> The end product of amateur brewing [Mr. Kobler reported] usually fell short of preprohibition standards. If the corks did not pop out or the bottles explode before their contents matured sufficiently to drink, you got a mud-brown liquid, smelling sourly of mash and tasting like laundry soap. As for the effect, one imbiber reported: "After I've had a couple of glasses I'm terribly sleepy. Sometimes my eyes don't seem to focus and my head aches. I'm not intoxicated, understand, merely feel as if I've been drawn through a knothole."

Home beermakers, like home winemakers, could count on the cooperation of an alert mercantile community. New York,

> like most American cities, abounded in shops selling malt, hops, wort, yeast, bottles, crown caps, capping machines, rubber hosing, alcohol gauges and other paraphernalia for home brewing.

> Around these homely activities there grew up a major industry. . . . In New York City alone more than 500 malt and hops shops flourished, with almost 100,000 dispersed through the country, plus 25,000 outlets for assorted home brewing apparatus. The national production of malt syrup in 1926 and 1927 came close to 888,000,000 pounds. Allowing a normal 10 percent for nonbrewing uses, enough remained for 6.5 billion pints of beer. The available hops crop, after export and the manufacture of near beer, was, according to the estimate of Hugh F. Fox, an officer of the United Brewers' Association, about 13,000,000 pounds. For malt, hops, sugar, yeast and machinery, Fox further estimated, the consumer spent $136,000,000. . . . Basing its calculations on the sale of hops, malt, etc., the Prohibition Bureau estimated the quantity of beer brewed at home in 1929 to be almost 700,000,000 gallons.

In the opinion of Samuel Eliot Morison, the enactment of Prohibition put an end to the progress of temperance—genuine temperance, which derives from self-restraint, not compulsion. Before Prohibition, he wrote in *The Oxford History of the American People,*

> the total per capita consumption of alcoholic beverages, reduced to "absolute alcohol," among the people of the United States fifteen years of age up, was 1.96 gallons in 1916-19, the lowest since the 1870's. . . . No sooner had national prohibition become the law than the country seemed to regret it, and a new occupation, bootlegging, sprang up to quench the public thirst. . . . Since beer and wine did not pay bootleggers like strong liquor, the country's drinking habits were changed from the one to the other. . . . College students who before Prohibition would have in a keg of beer and sit around singing the "Dartmouth Stein Song" and "Under the Anheuser Busch," now got drunk quickly on bathtub gin, and could manage no lyric more complicated than "How Dry I Am!" . . . Bravado induced numerous young people to drink who otherwise would not have done so. . . . Woman, emancipated by Amendment XIX, enthusiastically connived at breaking Amendment XVIII and now helped her husband to spend on liquor the savings that formerly went to the saloon. Hip-flask drinking certainly helped the evolution in sexual standards. . . . And it encouraged hypocrisy in politics.

The Dry years, when Prohibition was on the nation's books, are generally conceded to have given birth to a wave of crime and violence attributable to the production, importation, and distribution of illegal liquor. It was then that Chicago gangsters became particularly notorious for their savage competition among themselves, and for their high-handed tactics in extorting tribute from the retailing bootleggers. They had imitators, more or less successful, in every large city, and the loose network created by the interaction of the various gangs still exists in the shape of "organized crime," whose central figures are the inheritors of the rackets of the twenties. Often overlooked, however, are the many crimes of violence and the acts of bribery and corruption which stained the record of Prohibition law enforcers. Convinced of the righteousness of their cause, the Prohibitionists fell back on the Jesuit doctrine that "the end justifies the means," and resorted to every tactic, however underhanded, which might result in arrests and convictions. "Ethics be hanged," said Pussyfoot Johnson, one of the most notorious and unscrupulous of Prohibition raiders. "I have told enough lies to make Ananias ashamed of himself. I spilled liquor wherever found, without bothering about any legal process."

An escalation in the methods for enforcing Prohibition occurred when the government began denaturing alcohol to make it unfit to drink. We must be charitable enough to suppose that the original purpose of denaturing alcohol was not to poison people, but simply to dissuade them from drinking by making alcoholic beverages unpalatable. It was probably assumed that no one would actually swallow the stuff or use it for making beverages. The bootleggers fell upon denatured alcohol all the same, since it was the cheapest and the easiest to obtain, adulterating it heavily either with the intent of making it less than lethal or perhaps simply to make it salable. When people began to die from drinking this deliberately poisoned alcohol (11,700 in 1927), one might have expected the government to abandon poisoning; instead, the reaction of the Prohibition Bureau was to propose doubling the proportion of poison. The deaths were accepted with equanimity by the militant Puritan-Prohibitionists, who seemed to approve of the strength of the deterrent which was provided by immolating a certain number of sacrificial victims on the altar of virtue. The Bible, after all, had enunciated the principle that "the wages of sin is death," and the Puritans felt that this was the proper penalty for violating the Volstead Act. "The government is under no obligation to furnish people with alcohol that is drinkable when the Constitution prohibits it," Wayne Wheeler remarked. "The person who drinks industrial alcohol is a deliberate suicide." Wheeler's vindictiveness against drinkers did not even end with the grave. "We'll make them believe in punishment after death," he said, though he did not explain how he proposed to enforce his edicts in the hereafter. In the meantime the government continued to make denatured alcohol—"America's new national beverage," in the words of Prohibition administrator Major Chester P. Mills. And during the first ten years of Prohibition, the Federal government arrested more than half a million persons for violations of the Volstead Act and convicted 300,000 of them.

The inevitable happened. The criminals, who had received a handsome gift from the government when an important industry had been declared illegal and thus handed over to them, became popular heroes. They were hardly a recommendable lot, but as the opposition to the detested Prohibition agents they gained public sympathy and even glamour. It is probable that more Americans would have been able to identify with Al Capone than with Pussyfoot Johnson or Wayne B. Wheeler. It was also difficult to refute Capone, who, at a time when respectable merchandisers were raking in millions legally by selling equipment for making liquor, declared speciously, though with apparent reasonableness:

> I make my money by supplying a public demand. If I break the law, my customers, who number hundreds of the best people in Chicago, are as guilty as I am. The only difference between us is that I sell and they buy. Everybody calls me a racketeer. I call myself a business man. When I sell liquor, it's bootlegging. When my patrons serve it on a silver tray on Lake Shore Drive, it's hospitality.

As Daniel J. Boorstin pointed out:

> American gangsters, who only recently had arrived as downtrodden peasants, became rich businessmen and mayor-makers. And these quickly took their place in the iridescent American folklore of adventuring Go-Getters. For the earlier tales of Western sheriffs and desperadoes, American moviemakers in the twentieth century found counterparts on the urban frontier in tales of loyal, smart, ambitious gangsters and corrupt, stupid, indolent cops.

Nostalgic graybeards who tend to wrap the era of the speakeasies in a mist of glamour are for the most part simply expressing their wish to relive their youth. True, the fact that by drinking in them one was defying an unpopular law made the act memorable. Also there was the sense of being a member of a privileged group, an insider of sorts, even if the requirements for membership were of the most elastic sort ("Joe sent me"). For one speakeasy with pretensions to any sort of elegance, there were dozens of drab cellar or tenement bars where no money or thought was wasted on *décor.* When a speakeasy of some standing as a restaurant as well as a bar emerged, such as that well-known New York repair, still legitimately flourishing, Jack and Charlie's 21 (sometimes referred to as "The Twenty-One Club," although it never had official club status), it was because discreet official protection had been guaranteed to it which made the investment gilt-edged. After repeal Jack and Charlie were fond of demonstrating various devices that had been set up to foil raiding Prohibition agents—false-bottomed bins which precipitated liquor bottles into a sink where they were instantly smashed and their contents washed away, secret doors behind which priceless wines and liquors were stored, and so on. The truth of the matter was that the place, at one time one of the best restaurants in New York, had so many friends in high places that any raid by Dry agents was purely a ritual formality. Jack Kriendler and Charlie Berns, both long since gone to the hospitality of Heaven, would never say whether they paid for protection in cash bribes or whether admission to the inner circle of Twenty-One was *quid pro quo* enough for their friends in court.

In time the charm, where it had existed, rubbed off the speakeasies. Their liquor was high in price and low in quality. The circumstances in which drinking was done tended to increase alcoholic consumption, not to lessen it. "The lights of hospitality go out," said the *New York World,* "but the bootlegger thrives on the darkness." Those Americans who wanted to drink, certainly many in a country which had been saddled from its beginning with a reputation for hard drinking, tired of having to skulk into a blind pig whenever they wanted a glass of beer. Any satisfaction which may once have lurked in the do-it-yourself aspect of home brewing had worn thin too; there seemed no point in expending so much time and trouble to produce barely drinkable potions.

Sentiment for Repeal began to be expressed in influential circles. Testifying before the Senate Judiciary Committee, Samuel Gompers, President of the American Federation of Labor, said, "Depriving the American workingman of his glass of beer tends to promote industrial unrest and discontent. . . . Such things as this arbitrary legislation breed Bolshevism." (A few years earlier it had been the Anti-Saloon League which brandished this familiar bugaboo: "Bolshevism flourishes in wet soil. Failure to enforce Prohibition in Russia was followed by Bolshevism.")

The Prohibitionists must have felt themselves betrayed when prominent women began calling for Repeal. It had been the women who had been the first effective opponents of excessive drinking, and the Anti-Saloon League thought them its surest allies. When the Women's Suffrage Amendment went into force a year and a half after Prohibition, dry agent Izzy Einstein had exclaimed exultingly, "Prohibition is here to stay." With fury and spite, the Drys heaped abuse on their women opponents. Grace Root, daughter-in-law of Elihu Root (who encouraged her in calling for Repeal), was denounced from the pulpit of her local church as "a scarlet woman." A paper in Kentucky—Kentucky, the home of bourbon!—wrote that "you cannot find two dozen women in the State who openly advocate the Repeal of the Eighteenth Amendment, who is [sic] not either a drunkard, or whose home life is not immoral, or who does not expect to get in the liquor business when and if it is again legalized," and called them "the scum of the earth . . . flirting with other women's husbands at drunken . . . resorts." The chairman of the National Prohibition Committee described the dissenting ladies as "Bacchantian maidens, parching for wine—wet women, who, like the drunkards whom their program will produce, would take the pennies off the eyes of the dead for the sake of legalizing booze"—a technique whose efficacy is not readily apparent.

Despite the disreputability of the proponents of Repeal, President Herbert Hoover appointed the Wickersham Commission, headed by former Attorney

General George W. Wickersham, to look into the merits of Prohibition, which it described in its report as "police regulation over 3,500,000 square miles of territory, requiring total abstinence on the part of 122,000,000 people who have been accustomed to consume 2,000,000 gallons of alcoholic beverages per annum."

> The Wickersham Commission submitted, in January 1931 [wrote Samuel Eliot Morison], a confused report to the effect that federal prohibition was unenforceable but should be enforced, that it was a failure but should be retained!

Finally, it was not retained because public opinion was by now less indecisive than the commissioners. There is no way of knowing, at this late date, what percentage of the American people, or even of the legislators who had voted for it and the aediles who were sworn in to enforce it, ever thought Prohibition would work. Certainly not all of them, for they were quick to show their disbelief; and in 1933, by repeal of the Eighteenth Amendment, the Noble Experiment came to an end.

The long battle of the Dry forces achieved one thing, at least. If they failed to stop Americans from drinking (two out of three drink some kind of alcoholic beverage) they managed to come close to putting the old-time saloon out of business. Restrictions on the hours of doing business, requirements of cleanliness, heavy penalties for selling to minors, fingerprinting of employees, forbidding wholesalers to own retail drinking shops, rigid record-keeping requirements; all have made life difficult for the publican, who remains at the mercy of police, health department inspectors and tax collectors—Federal, state and municipal. Free lunch has in some cases been limited by law, or abolished. In New York, the price of drinks over the bar has zoomed to four times what it was two decades ago. So, more than ever before, people drink at home, though the saloon, call it "cocktail lounge," "bar and grill," "café," or simply "P. J. Clarke's," is no longer a purely masculine resort which no woman of reputation would dream of frequenting. At home or abroad, women are catching up with men as drinkers, and both sexes are drinking more than before. City folk drink more than rural people (Prohibition had its basic constituency in the sticks), and, believe it or not, the prosperous drink more than the poor. Catholics drink more than Jews, and Protestants drink less than either. A study made back in 1952 showed that younger people were drinking more than they had previously; beer was their first choice, the preference of more than half; liquor came next, with wine the choice of only three percent of the respondents.

In the United States, the trend is toward more drinking of all kinds of alcoholic beverages, especially wine, native and imported, but mostly the abundant American growths which have been coming into their own ever since Repeal. In 1964 we produced 189 million gallons of wine from close to two million tons of grapes, almost all of which was consumed nationally. The most recent figures show that in the last decade production has risen at an average rate of seven percent per year, leveling off only slightly in 1974. The United States produces more wine than any other country in the New World except Argentina, which has about 50 percent more acreage planted to vines; California accounts for 80 percent of the total American production. Even so,

> California's production is not enormous at present [Hugh Johnson points out in *The World Atlas of Wine*]: a quarter of that of Spain; a mere splash compared with Italy and France. But new plantings are speeding up, new valleys seeing the vine for the first time.

It is the convention that the history of our wine industry started in 1697, when the Jesuit Father Juan Ugarte planted grapevines imported from Spain in California—but in Lower California, still in Mexico. Not until the next century were wine grapes planted on what is now the territory of the United States, after the Franciscan Father Junípero Serra established a mission at San Diego. This happened in 1769; it is safe to assume that California had wine shortly thereafter.

The history of wine growing in California is discontinuous. Although a few descendants of the old Spanish plants have survived, notably the famous Trinity vine, believed to have been planted before 1780, which draws tourists to the San Gabriel Arcangel Mission near Los Angeles, it is true that in general the first period of Californian wine growing came to an end in the early 1830s, when the missions were secularized by the Mexican government. The vineyards were abandoned and gradually disappeared beneath an overgrowth of weeds and bushes. The wine makers of the second period, whose beginning overlapped slightly the end of the first period, had to start anew from scratch, or perhaps from a little worse than scratch, for they were burdened by the Mission grape which the Spanish padres had imported, more of a liability than an asset; it is a coarse variety incapable of producing fine wine. It is nevertheless still being grown; ordinary California wines might be better today if the second wine-making period had been obliged to start with no heritage at all from its predecessor.

A tenuous link may have been established between the two periods if it is true that Joseph Chapman, the first commercial wine grower in California, picked up some information about wine making from the Franciscan fathers, as it is believed he did. They do not seem to have been particularly expert teachers if one may judge from the unflattering opinions expressed about the local wine by visitors to California at that time. After all, the good fathers made wine only for sacramental purposes, which do not demand high quality; their major interests lay elsewhere. If Chapman did not seek instruction from the Franciscans, he must have gotten along without any. So far as we know he had no experience with wine making in his background, which is foggy. All we know is that he was a jack-of-all-trades who apparently stumbled into wine growing by accident; but so did most of the first post-Mission vintners. Experienced or not, Chapman planted a vineyard in Los Angeles in 1824, and began selling wine three years later.

If Chapman was California's first commercial wine handler, its first professional winemaker was Jean Louis Vignes (whose very name means "vines"). He was a native of the Bordeaux wine country, though not quite a winemaker there; but his experience had been closely tangential to wine making, for he was a cooper and a distiller. He imported wines from France, planted a vineyard on a site now covered by the Los Angeles railroad station, and was well established by 1837.

In general, the early producers of California wine constituted a decidedly mixed bag, whose chief common characteristic was utter lack of experience with wine. The ex-trapper from Kentucky, William Wolfskill, began making wine about 1839, and must have had a natural gift for it; he soon built up a thriving business and seems to have been the first to establish vineyards in northern California, where the best wines of the state are grown today. A gaggle of Europeans turned up from the wrong countries—a certain Janssens, first name unknown, from Belgium, which produces good beer, but no wine; an Irishman from the Aran Islands, which produces no wine either and not much of anything else except Aran Islanders; and a Finnish sea captain who had prepared for wine making by dealing in furs in Alaska. There was, it is true, another Frenchman, but his previous connection with wine had presumably been limited to drinking it, for he was a Parisian tailor. From wine country too, but not from the wine industry, was a Swiss miller named John Sutter, who started to make grape brandy in 1840 and would probably have graduated to wine in the natural course of events if his attention had not been diverted by the discovery of gold on his property. Also from wine country, but not from wine making, was a German violinist named Charles Kohler, who went into wine on a whim, took in as a partner a countryman named John Frohling, also not previously a maker of wine but a maker of music. After four hard years during which Kohler had to keep up his violin playing to support the business, he found himself at the head of a flourishing concern which among other activities was operating the first wine shop in San Francisco.

The California winegrowers were now joined by another recruit, who did not seem to have been predestined to make his mark in wine, though it was a near certainty that he would make it in something. This was a Hungarian nobleman, Count Agostón Haraszthy de Mokesa, who had been, in his native land, a country squire, a lawyer, a civil servant, and a colonel in the personal bodyguard of Emperor Franz I of Austria. Inconsistently with this last role, he was also a Hungarian nationalist, and an active one, which is why he had to get out of Austria in a hurry, to become a political refugee in the United

States in 1839, at the age of twenty-seven. He went into the contracting and construction business in Wisconsin, but in 1849 asthma drove him to the more lenient climate of California. There he started to grow vegetables and fruit, including grapes; we may assume that he knew something about converting the grapes into wine, for wine had been produced on his country estate in Hungary. He threw himself into viticulture with characteristic energy; and though others had imported European vines before him, it can be said that he was the first to undertake genuinely systematic transplanting in the United States of carefully selected European strains capable of producing fine wines, which he began cultivating in 1851 in San Diego.

His experience with the powers that were in Hungary had not taught Haraszthy the dangers of dealing with governments, so he accepted from California governor John G. Downey what he understood was to be a state-financed mission to endow California with the best varieties of European wine grapes. He traveled through Europe for five months, bought 200,000 plants of 1,400 different varieties from six countries, planted them in his Buena Vista vineyards in northern California pending their distribution throughout the state, and turned in his expense account—twelve thousand dollars. Since his collection of vines has been estimated as worth thirty thousand dollars at the nursery prices of the time, the bill would not seem to have been exorbitant, but the California legislature refused to pay; Haraszthy was a Republican and the legislature was predominantly Democratic. He had to break up this remarkable and potentially highly useful assemblage of vines for whatever he could get for them—possibly enough to recoup his outlay, possibly not. What was worse, to his way of thinking, was that instead of being distributed systematically, to those areas for which each variety was best fitted, and to responsible growers who would know how to handle them, the new vines had to be disposed of haphazardly; many of their buyers allowed them to degenerate or die, and in some cases even lost their name tags, so that they had no idea what kind of grape they were growing.

Haraszthy's chagrin at this contretemps was somewhat assuaged when, in 1862, the California Agricultural Society, which had a higher opinion of his worth than had been manifested by the state legislature, elected him its president. It was also in that year that he first put on the market wine from a grape which had been among his earlier importations—Zinfandel. Zinfandel is a mystery. Haraszthy is supposed to have found it in Hungary, but it has not since been identified there, nor in any other part of Europe either. Possibly a foreign vine planted in strange soil in an alien climate had produced a mutant. Whatever its origin, Zinfandel has become the most important grape in California for table wines; and in optimum conditions it has even produced, from time to time, crops of vintage quality.

Fate was as ungrateful to Haraszthy as the California legislature had been. He was plagued by a series of disastrous losses, including the explosion of a distillery and the destruction by fire of one of his wineries. In an attempt to restore his fortunes, he moved to Nicaragua, probably on the theory that he would have a better chance to succeed in an area where the competition was not as well organized as it was, largely through his own efforts, in California. This theory seemed to be working out, until, in 1869, he simply disappeared. Legend has it that he fell into a stream on his plantation and was eaten by an alligator.

Alexis Lichine has called Haraszthy "the father of Californian viticulture," a verdict concerning which no dissenting opinion has been expressed.

California also used to sell 90 percent of all the wine consumed in the United States, a figure which since Prohibition has been whittled down to 75 percent, despite the increase of Californian production. This results from increased imports of foreign wines, which enjoy a snob advantage over domestic wine. The United States imports many top-notch wines from abroad, but along with them come a great many quite ordinary ones, which, however, sell simply because they are foreign (especially when they are French), and thus profit from the high reputation of the best foreign vintages.

Though beer is, by volume, America's most popular alcoholic beverage, it has never been able to surround itself with the glamorous atmosphere attained by wine. Wine as a drink is older in America than beer, but it has managed to shake off its utilitarian image, except among certain ethnic groups such as Italians in general, and the Californians of the wine growing districts. The rest of the country approaches wine not as part of the ordinary, but as an added attraction, a bit of luxury perhaps, and an evidence of status. Among the young generation (pivot year 1968, let us say) wine was adopted as an accompaniment to the smoking of marijuana, which does not marry well with hard liquor, it seems. That the youngsters' taste ran to the generally sweet "fruit wines," in which flavorful additives made the drink not unlike some of the popular soft drinks, is understandable. Most Americans, when first exposed to wine, either at home or abroad, prefer the sweeter types, and only later accept the more sophisticated complexities of the dryer, flintier, or more tannic vintages, which California can provide. The state has the good fortune to be able to grow almost any of the European grape varieties, *Vitis vinifera,* and hence to produce a range of wines not identical with their Old World counterparts, but having rich characteristics of their own from the coarsest of heavy reds to the most delicate of dry, fragrant whites. The generally dependable California climate has meant that year after year (barring major climatic upheavals) the plants receive their quota of water and sunshine at the proper time of year, with a minimum of variation among the vintage years. Modern methods of vinification have made this assurance doubly sure, and though a California wine of medium price may never show the complex nature of a comparable Bordeaux or Burgundy it will vary little from bottle to bottle, and for those who value reliability it may well be a better buy than the European bottling.

There was a time when California shipped to the rest of the country carloads of fortified wines, cheap sherries for cooking, and bulk wines for bottling by Midwest and Eastern wineries. Some of these were holdovers from the Prohibition period, when they produced wine "for sacramental purposes." Many of them extended their religious vocation to those smaller Italian and French city restaurants where with a table d'hôte meal selling in those days for one or two dollars one could receive, for a dollar more, the benediction of a full bottle of solid native wine. This bulk wine is still available in many such establishments, but the price is more likely to be a dollar a glass. The quality of the wine is somewhat improved over its bootleg predecessor, due to modern vinification.

American wines have never been hampered by the imported kind, as far as the total volume of sales goes. In fact, there is a history of one hand washing the other. The importers have reasoned that although their share of the total wine market would always be small, the pie was growing bigger and bigger and their slice was growing with it. The more Americans drank *some* kind of wine, the more a fair number of them would become interested in experimenting with, and perhaps adopting, an imported French, German or Italian wine. (As it worked out, the trademarked foreign wine enjoying the greatest sale in the United States in the early seventies was not one of these, but a Portuguese pink wine presented in the flask-shaped *bocksbeutel* of Austrian origin.) Desirous of emulating the year-by-year uniformity of the Californian production, French shippers have with some success introduced on the United States market blended non-vintage still wines, sold in jugs resembling the familiar American ones, and similarly priced. Meanwhile, back at the California vineyards, great progress has been made in developing varietal wines, superior vintages traveling under the names of their dominant grape variety and their producer, with sometimes the place and year of the actual vintage. Today these wines, along with a few promising bottlings from other wine regions of the United States, are being sought out by the same sort of connoisseurs who have for two centuries bought and consumed the best wines Europe could offer. So far, the American vineyardists have not come up with anything approaching the truly top wines from overseas, but as far as wines in the moderately priced bracket are concerned, wines better than the bulk wines and lesser than the imported *grands crus,* the jury is still out.

> The American taste for wine is clearly improving [John N. Hutchinson wrote in *Wines of the World*], as is indicated by the shifting balance. The consumption of dry wines is steadily rising, while that of dessert wines is only holding steady. . . . The pride of most California wine-growers today is in the dry wines, and it is in these types that quality reaches the heights of excellence. It is also fair to say that the low-priced California wines are

> outright superior to many wines of equal price in the world's markets. Meanwhile, the best standard wines of the state can hold their own with the best standard wines of the world. California wines which can truly compete with the great wines of France and Germany can be found only in small quantities in private cellars or for virtually private sale. The sweeping generalizations, on the one hand, that California can produce no great wines, and, on the other, that its wines "are as good as any in France" are equally unfair and absurd, and the subjective opinions frequently cited as absolutes are ridiculous. The wine industry in California, as elsewhere, suffers interminably from the wine snob at one end of the scale of opinion and the ignoramus at the other, and often the two are combined in the same individual.
>
> It would be hard to find a dry California wine on a grocer's shelf as poor as French *ordinaire.* It would be even harder to find one which could enter the competition with a first-growth Bordeaux of a good year, or its peer from Burgundy or the Rhine. How many California vintners can lavish the hand labor and attention on their vineyards that are devoted to Château Margaux or La Tâche? And if they could, and the result were as great a wine, how could they develop overnight the world prestige and consequent price advantage of vineyards renowned in the world for 200 years?

It will take more than high quality alone for American wines to surround themselves with the glamour and hoopla which are reserved for imported wines, French mostly, by the militant members of the "Bacchic brotherhoods," the numerous fraternities of wine drinkers and gourmets who celebrate in ritual pomp and circumstance the cult of the vine and its fruits. Such esoteric orders as the Confrérie des Chevaliers du Tastevin (Commanderie d'Amerique) and the Commanderie de Bordeaux initiate their new members according to polyglot texts prepared for them in France, inspired by the ancient rites with which degrees were awarded in the medieval universities. Their rosters include organizational eminences such as *Grand Officier, Grand Argentier, Grand Chambellan, Grand Maître,* and *Grand Pilier Général,* each grade carrying with it the right to wear special colorful robes and decorations. Every meeting of the Tastevin is followed by a banquet at which the wines of Burgundy are featured and discussed; at the Bordeaux dinners, called "Parlements," the talk is all of chateau-bottled clarets, Graves, and Sauternes. The American Tastevin order can boast among its membership of 1,500 the Chief Justice of the Supreme Court, generals and admirals, former Cabinet Secretaries, no end of millionaires, including Rockefellers and DuPonts, and a real live reigning monarch (King Hussein of Jordan, made a Grand Officier by the Palm Beach Sous-commanderie). Though the brotherhoods refrain from direct promotion of particular vintages and wine merchants are admitted sparingly, their activity has not gone unobserved by the American wine-drinking public, and may be presumed to have helped to keep up the prestige of French and other imported wines. The existence of at least two dozen organized national and regional societies devoted to wine and gastronomy also points up Abraham Myerson's 1940 observation (*Quarterly Journal of Studies in Alcoholism,* Vol. 1):

> Men drink in celebration as well as for relief. They drink to lend ceremony, color, and fellowship to life, just as surely as to banish anxiety, dread, and frustration. . . .

In addition to the normal setbacks imposed upon the development of the wine industry by the fluctuations of the economy and the inexorability of Nature, obstacles were created by the short-sighted vintners themselves, so eager to grasp at quick profits that they sacrificed to it the long-range interests of their profession. These had been stated with admirable clarity by Arpad Haraszthy, a son of Agostón:

> The great obstacle to our success . . . is, that the average American is a whiskey-drinking, water-drinking, coffee-drinking, tea-drinking, and consequently dyspepsia-inviting subject, who does not know the use or value of pure light wines taken at the right time and in moderate quantities. The task before us lies in teaching our people how to drink wine, when to drink it, and how much of it to drink.

One of the earliest sins of the wine growers was to try to cash in on the already established reputations of foreign wines by putting European labels on their own wine whenever they felt that they could get away with it. The result was that the only Californian wines which were sold under their own colors were the worst ones; this confirmed a prevailing opinion that the United States was incapable of producing good wine. As business ethics improved and laws on honest labeling became stricter and better enforced, California wine growers shifted to another tactic, inspired, however, by the same desire to enjoy a free ride on the reputations of foreign wines; the American public was submerged in a deluge of California Burgundy, California Sauternes, California Tokay, California port and California sherry. These names were not likely to deceive the wine-drinking connoisseurs the California growers needed to woo in the absence of a mass market for wine, and they prevented drinkers from being able to identify and become acquainted with the characteristics of domestic wine, a study which might have ended by developing a clientele for the California product. Admirers of genuine Burgundy were not likely to be captured by an appeal to them to drink imitation Burgundy. What needed to be done was to educate them to drink genuine Californian.

A start in this direction was made not very many years ago by some of the better growers, who have taken to varietal labeling—that is, they tell you on the bottle what sort of grape went into the wine it contains. The ultimate step has even been taken by a few companies who identify not only the grape, but also the place where it was grown—Livermore Valley Pinot Blanc, for instance. It is still rather unusual for California labels to name the year in which the wine was grown, and sometimes critics point out that the California climate is so equable that wines do not vary appreciably from year to year. It is even objected that place-labeling is pointless too, since the only large area whose wines share a recognizable local quality is the Livermore Valley. (This seems unjust to the Napa Valley, the most famous red wine region of California.) One may suspect again that the real resistance to vintage-year or place-labeling comes also from the circumstance that many Californian wines are blended (blended is a more respectable word than "mixed") from the product of several areas to arrive at a more uniform product—the very thing a devoted wine drinker does not want. It would be difficult in any case, even after making allowances for the different varieties of grapes grown in the two sections, to deny that the wines of the North show marked superiority to those of the South.

The grapes of the East—the native American fruit, *Vitis labrusca, Vitis rotundifolia, Vitis riparia*—are generally considered much inferior for wine making to the *Vitis vinifera* which produces the wines of California (and also of Washington, Oregon, and Arizona, all of which grow small quantities of very drinkable wine). *Vitis vinifera* seems unable to accommodate itself to growing conditions east of the Rocky Mountains. The native grapes of the East are classified primarily as dessert grapes; their slightly musky taste is looked upon with distrust, though it accounted for the richness of pre-war unfermented grapejuice (it supports pasteurization better than *Vitis vinifera).* This muskiness, which results from the presence in these grapes of an ester called methyl antranilate, is sometimes cited as the reason for the nickname given them: fox grapes. Probably, however, all this meant for the early settlers who thus baptized them was "wild grapes."

Opinion is not entirely unanimous about the undesirability of the distinctive flavor of Eastern grapes in wine (more marked in reds than in whites). If you are holding in mind the characteristics of, say, a fine Bordeaux (or even a superior wine from the Livermore or Napa Valleys) when you first sip an Eastern wine, you are not likely to appreciate it, any more than you would be likely to appreciate the delicate flavor of wood strawberries if you happened to be thinking about sardines in oil when you put them into your mouth. If you can manage to approach an Eastern wine with a virgin mind you are more likely to find it perhaps even attractive, but at any rate interesting; and interest is what any devotee of wine with a minimum of curiosity is seeking desperately in these days of humdrum uniformity; even in France the raspy crusty black wine of Cahors has been allowed to die out in favor of an attempt to make Cahors taste like Bordeaux.

The experience of drinking Eastern wines is certainly not disagreeable for everybody, since these wines continue to be manufactured and sold. Our opportunities to encounter them, however, seem to be dwindling; nevertheless more Eastern wine exists, even if much of it does not get beyond the regions where it is produced, than most of us realize. Most Americans, no doubt, are aware of the existence of New York wines; not so many know about Ohio wines (which slop minutely over into Pennsylvania). As for the others, almost nobody has heard about them—Michigan wines, New Jersey wines, Virginia wines, and Maryland wines, although the last have been described by Alexis Lichine as "the best wines made east of the Rockies."

For those who found pure Eastern wines hard to take, one early solution was to water down their muskiness by hybridization. The first identifiable grape that we hear about as having produced wine in the East was the Alexander, named for John Alexander, William Penn's gardener, who discovered it. It is believed to have been an accidental hybrid, a cross produced without aforethought between a variety of *Vitis labrusca* and an unknown European vine which must have been imported by some colonist who left no record of it. Most of the other early Eastern wine grapes were hybrids too, but only of different varieties of native grapes. This seems to have been the case for the Catawba, the grape used for the first systematic production of American wine in Ohio, believed to have dated from 1819. It was certainly the case for the Concord, deliberately achieved by Ephraim Bull, who arrived at it in 1852 after a series of experiments in crossing different varieties of native grapes. The Concord in particular, but also Eastern grapes in general, have found a special vocation in supplying kosher sacramental wine.

Beer was quicker than wine in making its comeback after Prohibition, aided, perhaps, by a new invention which some of us consider a boon and others a flail. Home drinking in America has been affected by television, some brewers believe. Beer consumption is greater during the hours spent before the home screen than it ever was at mealtime or during other evening distractions, such as card playing. There may be some occult relationship between long drawn-out sports programs and a drink which is generally consumed slowly and without ceremony (except in the Teutonic *milieux,* where beer, song, and noisy *Bruderschaft* go together). Much beer is consumed out of doors, apparently, since the glistening aluminum beer can is now a feature of American roadside scenery. Beer is intensively advertised on television and radio, while hard liquor is never pushed on the networks. This is more by common accord among the distillers and their advertising agencies than by an actual legal restriction. It saves the liquor people vast sums which might have been wasted in cut-throat advertising competition. Another curious taboo is the one observed in television's beer commercials: steins, glasses, bottles, or cans may be raised to the actors' lips, but the scene is cut before a drop is swallowed. "Beer is best," the ads proclaim, but actual guzzling is deemed unesthetic.

Unesthetic or not, beer has been welcomed back to the group of legal drinkables to the tune of more than a barrel a year for every man, woman, child and babe in arms in the United States. American beer, after Prohibition as before, was of excellent quality, and was broadmindedly praised as compared to English beer by an Englishman, Alec Waugh, who even went so far as to give the United States credit for a brew which actually it has only borrowed:

> In the United States there is . . . a sweet potation called bock beer. It is made by using the sediment collected from fermenting vats when they are cleaned in the spring of each year. Bock beer is available only at this time, for about six weeks; and it was a good moment in New York in April, 1934 after the repeal of Prohibition to see the newly reopened bars placarded with the slogan, "Bock is back."

Placarded also, Mr. Waugh might have added, with the picture of a goat, "bock" being equated with "buck." Its very name, however, gives away the fact that bock beer is not an American invention, though it has been adequately reproduced in this country. Bock beer takes its name from the Hanseatic town of Einbeck, in Lower Saxony, which the *Deutsches Handbuch für Fremdenverkehr* calls "the oldest brewing city of Germany," credited with having created this type of beer. Even before bock beer made its way to America, the meaning of the name had been forgotten even in its native land and the symbol of the goat had become associated with it. Einbeck was corrupted into *ein Bock,* "a billy goat." German immigrants presumably transferred both the beer and its symbol to the United States. (Einbeck is also responsible for the French word *bock,* meaning a beer glass holding about half a pint.)

There is, however, one authentic American beer worth citing for its special peculiarity—a beer of whose existence the East was unaware until President Gerald Ford took a skiing vacation in Colorado early in 1975. A pilot flying reporters and White House personnel back to Washington found that his plane was carrying so much weight that he had to ask his passengers to redistribute themselves to balance the load in the baggage hold. On landing, he found out why the plane was so heavy—the baggage space was completely filled with cases of Coors beer.

Coors beer is made in Golden, Colorado, and is referred to in that state as "Colorado Kool-Aid." It is distributed mostly in eleven Western states; little of it is sold commercially east of Kansas and Oklahoma, but beer connoisseurs smuggle it east of the Mississippi. The company is, indeed, opposed to sending its beer off on long journeys, for it has to be kept refrigerated from brewery to consumer and drunk fresh. Otherwise its famous flavor would deteriorate, they say. What accounts for that flavor? Colorado water? Quality of hops? Quality of grain? Secrets of brewing? Newspaper reporters speculated about this in writing of the discovery of Coors as a result of the presidential trip, but they did not hit upon the solution, although it was tucked away in their stories as an incidental detail whose importance they had failed to register: it is not pasteurized, and contains no additives.

The persistence of moonshining to this very day may seem puzzling to Americans who, if they drink, drink only legal liquor of well-advertised brands, stamped and sealed by the government to certify that it has paid taxes of about 60 percent of the selling price. If they were obliged to do their drinking in some of the less favored parts of town, in workingmen's bars, or in "ghetto" neighborhoods, the stuff in their glass might well be moonshine, poured from a bottle labeled with a popular brand, as much in violation of the law as anything sold in Prohibition days. Similarly, in those rural areas of Appalachia and the South where moonshining in the old style continues, a traveler with an honest face can buy untaxed corn liquor, "white mule," in a jug or a Mason jar, for half the price of the average legal whiskey. Then, too, there are still areas, dry by local legislation, where moonshine is sold alongside more legal spirits bootlegged in from other countries or states.

Legally made spirits have long since recovered from the blight of Prohibition. Whiskey is doing better than ever: bourbon is even invading Europe with some success. California turns out brandy which its makers would perhaps not dare pit against the finest cognacs or armagnacs, but considering the level to which many popular marks of French brandy have now descended, the American version should be able to hold its own with the lesser lines; it could surpass most Spanish brandy and Italian *grappa.*

Rum has less of a vogue nowadays than it once enjoyed in the United States. Its great importance to New England in America's early days stemmed partly from considerations of commerce which no longer obtain and partly from the use of old-fashioned sugarcane handling processes which left a much richer residue for molasses, and consequently for rum, than escapes today's machinery. Nevertheless Massachusetts, the leading distiller in the palmy days of rum, still makes about 200,000 gallons a year of the sort of dark heavy rum it has always produced. The light rum of the Virgin Islands, whose sugar-and-rum economy was wrecked when Prohibition came in three years after the United States had acquired the islands from Denmark, has now almost disappeared; the inefficient peasant-based sugarcane industry has been deliberately phased out. The equally light rum of Puerto Rico, now the world's leading rum producer, is imported largely by the United States, supplying 70 percent of the diminished consumption. Perhaps Americans lost some of their taste for rum when they were cut off from the fine light Cuban Daiquiris and Bacardis which they were used to drinking. Finally we might note that there is still a ready market for New Jersey's applejack.

The United States is the world's third largest consumer of spirits, after the Soviet Union, where 14.8 liters of 100-proof alcohol are drunk per capita every year, and Poland, 6.8 liters. The United States drinks 5.8, followed by West Germany (5.5), Sweden (5.2), Yugoslavia (5.2), East Germany (5), and Spain (5).

Besides the classic drinks of the wine-beer-spirits triad, what do Americans drink today, more than forty years after Repeal? Modern Americans drink anything and everything, as they have done since the country was first discovered and settled. There have been changes in fashions in drinks, and changes in the where and how of drinking. The Colonial gentry fancied Madeira, today a wine used mainly in cooking. Port was an aristocratic drink through the nineteenth century, but is out of favor now. Sherry, after a period of slump, is doing better. The cheap California imitations of sherry and port have long been the standby of skid-row alcoholics who appreciate their low price and high content of added alcohol.

The straight shot of whiskey from a small glass, placed with the bottle on the bar before the customer, refillable by him at his pleasure, was the old American style of drinking, now mostly relegated to scenes in Western movies. Removing the bottle before the client was through with it was considered offensive. In higher-type saloons the bartender was presumed to be fully familiar with all the cocktails, coolers, cups, juleps, rickeys, shrubs, slings, smashes, flips, fizzes, and toddies listed in the *Bartender's Guide,* plus an invention or two of his own, but this art, or craft, became lost some time after World War One. The mixed drink was largely an American creation, reflecting the ostentation of the Gilded Age, the ceremonial element of Nordic drinking challenges, and the national desire to mess around with the old and to produce something new. There were over one thousand mixed drinks listed in various guides; today the average barkeep pours short and long whiskeys and gins, mixes a few martinis or Manhattans, makes Gibsons by adding a pickled pearl onion to either gin or vodka, poured directly from the bottle into a short, fat glass full of ice cubes (if the order is "on the rocks"), and draws beer. He is chosen for his ability to endure the clients' recitals of their personal obsessions, political or other, without committing the establishment by any bias of his own. He should have charisma of a vague sort, but it should not be too pronounced. Nor is he supposed to drink while he is working.

The reduction in the variety of commonly ordered cocktails and other mixed drinks (some of which were so fantastic that they are not likely to be missed) is only part of the general current evolution toward uniformity, which in the case of food and drink results from mass marketing, the growth of national brands, advertising promotion concentrated on a limited list of leading products, and general simplification in the interests of efficiency and economy. These factors are bound eventually to reduce local diversities as well, but in the meantime many cities and regions still preserve traditional specialties which are resisting the process of levelling down to the lowest common denominator. Some local drinks may be expected to survive indefinitely, since they are economically strong as salable packages of nostalgia or folklore. Who, for instance, would want to visit a gastronomic city like New Orleans without tasting some of its characteristic beverages? Indeed, the tourist will find it difficult not to sample them, for New Orleans takes pride in its fancy drinks and presses them insistently upon the visitor. *Café brûlot* is one of them, an elaborate production involving orange and lemon peels, cinnamon sticks broken into a silver bowl with coriander seeds, bay leaf and cloves. Adding sugar lumps and a jigger of brandy per person, the bowl is warmed so that the brandy may be set aflame at the proper moment, after which the coffee is poured into the bowl before the flames expire. It makes a pretty sight at a dinner party and doesn't do much harm to the coffee. (When it is made with only lemon peel in it, it is *café diable.*) The Ramos gin fizz calls for gin, cream, white of egg, lime juice, sugar, and orange-flower water shaken briskly with ice cubes, and is recommended as a morning-after pick-me-up. The Sazerac cocktail features sugar and bitters muddled together as for an Old Fashioned, to which two jiggers of rye whiskey (previously it was brandy) are added. Another identical glass is rinsed with absinthe, two ice cubes are put in it and the contents of the first glass are poured into the second. (Absinthe was produced in New Orleans for some years after it had been banned in France as narcotic and dangerous. Today's American absinthe, like France's modern anise drinks, such as Pernod and Ricard, is a synthetic with no drug in it but the alcohol.) Otherwise, except for planter's punches and various long cooling drinks, New Orleans slakes its thirst as does the rest of the nation.

Florida's local beverages have been less well publicized than those of Louisiana, but they include some rather curious ones. Old Sour is a commercial product of great potency made from the fermented juice of Key Lime, but most of the other specialties of the Peninsula are homemade. It is difficult to decide whether you are in the presence of a drink or an act when a Floridian cuts a coconut from a tree, slashes off its top with a machete, pours a generous portion of rum directly into the coconut juice, and invites you to drink the mixture straight from the nut, a feat best performed in a bathing suit. Homemade sand pear wine gives the impression that it is burning a trough to run through as it proceeds down the throat. Orange wine will be found only in the homes of orange growers, one of whom Eugene Walter encountered, learning from him that "the oranges must be past ripe, even better if they're moldy," as he tells us in *American Cooking: Southern Style:*

> You need about 12 pounds of oranges; I pick up some off the ground, or find moldy ones in the bottom of a basket. . . . I slice 'em up in a big vat and pour 3 gallons of boiling water over 'em and stir 'em all up good, and put a cloth tight over 'em. I leave 'em three weeks without touching 'em. If the oranges were good and moldy you've now got a crust of mold on the vat. You have to get that crust off without breaking it, if you can manage. Then you strain the liquid carefully into another vat, put in 9 pounds of sugar

> and go on stirring until it is dissolved, then cover the bowl real tight with cloth and leave it there for four days. Every morning about 10 o'clock I uncover it and stir it up real good. After four days you're ready to put it into bottles. After a month you taste it. Every batch will come out slightly different; you might have to put a little sugar in each bottle. But if it tastes sweet when you try it after a month, then leave it alone. After about a year and a half you've got as fine a wine as ever was . . . and strong, too. Nothing sissy about it.

In Philadelphia the traditional drink is of course the famous Fish House Punch, which is "built"—it would be a social error to say "made"—by dissolving one and a half cups of ultra-refined sugar in a quart of fresh lime juice or lemon juice. Two quarts of 80-proof light rum (Puerto Rican is excellent for this purpose) are then stirred in, followed, austerely, by two quarts of cold water and, less austerely, by a quart of cognac and a modest four ounces of peach brandy. The mixture is allowed to stand (*not* in the refrigerator) for two hours, during which time it is stirred occasionally. When it is to be served, a large block of ice is placed in the bowl; at this point some persons who do not believe in letting well enough alone add sliced peaches. It is also in Pennsylvania that you may come across what is referred to disdainfully by males as "women's wine," made from wintergreen leaves after they have turned red in the fall; it is weak in alcohol and a girlish pink in color.

New England is the right place to find cranberry cocktails (cranberry juice plus vodka), but cranberry wine, almost as strong as the cocktails, seems a trifle out of place in Alaska; it is not made from genuine cranberries, but from what are called highbush cranberries—the fruit of a species of viburnum, or, if you want a popular name for it, witch hobble. Alaska is ingenious when it comes to drinks: one favorite, called "salty dogs," is a little less than indigenous—it combines vodka with grapefruit juice, neither of them native to Alaska. (The name comes from the fact that it is served in glasses with salted rims.) Less deadly, but not quite innocuous, is home brew made from hop-flavored malt and honey, served cold; despite the honey it has an ale-like character.

Iowa produces a fruit wine called Piestengel, which starts out from a rather unexpected base—rhubarb juice. The humble sap of the pie plant is treated with the same respect as the noble juice of the vine, is aged in oak barrels, and, in the opinion of its makers at least, develops from time to time a quality which justifies it in being described as the product of a vintage year.

It is of course Texas, the repository of virility, which comes up with what may well be the most potent of local drinks (though with Mexican help). This is Border Buttermilk—lime juice and tequila.

Do Americans still drink too much? Some persons not themselves given to total abstention think that they do; even the wine-drinking brotherhoods, dedicated promoters of alcoholic drinks (but alcoholic drinks of quality), include members who deplore the abuse of alcohol and would deplore a return to the American drinking habits of the early nineteenth century even more. They disapprove unrestrained drinking by those they consider to be less wise, less stable psychologically and economically than they consider themselves to be, and would not object to measures restricting the drinking habits of such persons, though without going to the extremes that led to the catastrophe of Prohibition.

Drinking will continue to exist, as it always has, and will create the same anxiety among good citizens as the present abuse of narcotics does, though in lesser degree. The problem of alcoholism is a grave one and does not seem near solution in our time, for there are still militant, politically minded Drys on the one hand, and, on the other, as Howard W. Haggard pointed out in 1945 in the *Quarterly Journal of Studies on Alcohol,* Vol. 6, the paranoid minority among the distillers, who see a return to Prohibition in any acknowledgment of alcoholism as a national problem. Together they prevent a full scientific approach to the concept that "alcoholism is an illness, and that the alcoholic deserves not moral degradation, not jail sentences, but the dignity of medical care which is the right of every man who is ill."

Looking backward two centuries or more, it is fair to say that America's beer, wine, and spirits have become of better quality and variety, thanks to native enterprise and government regulation of manufacture and sale, while our drinking water, on the whole, has become, due in part to increasing pollution and, in part, to corrective chemical additives, much less palatable than it used to be. "The water in most of the great cities (except . . . Boston)," wrote the French gastronomic guidebook authors Henri Gault and Christian Millau, after visiting the United States, "has a terrible taste of chloride, which it cannot help passing on to vegetables and fish" boiled in it.

This puts us back to the *status quo ante,* or, in less learned language, this is where we came in. One explanation given for the heavy drinking of the eighteenth century and the beginning of the nineteenth is that nobody dared drink the water, in towns and cities at least. The United States, after having developed adequate municipal water supply systems, enjoyed a blissful century of dependable water; but today, where we had once solved the problem of the pollution of water by man, we are now confronted by the problem of the pollution of water by man's industries, and we have found no solution other than pumping into the water a dosage of man's chemicals to undo some of the damage. It is enough to drive man to drink—but not water.

Even that one-time haven of health, milk, is now distrusted. The demand for milk in the United States has dropped by 10 percent in ten years, which represents an even greater decrease for milk provided in liquid form for drinking purposes, since during the same period there has been a heightened demand for milk to make cheese, of which consumption has risen substantially. Part of the decline in milk drinking may be attributed to the comparative tastelessness of milk and to its unappetizing thinness since it has been subjected to such manipulations for the market as the plentiful use of preservatives. This, however, does not appear to be the main reason (any number of foods have achieved tastelessness without losing sales). The main reason is fear—fear of pollution by pesticides and fear of pollution by radiation. The public has been abundantly educated to the facts that milk readily picks up strontium-90 from radioactive fallout and that DDT is frequently detected in cows' milk. When such milk is found to contain more than 0.05 parts of DDT per million, the law forbids it to be sold; but there are certain areas into which it is difficult for the most vigilant officers of the law to peer. Breast feeding, once advocated by most doctors as the healthiest way to bring up human infants, has become discredited since the discovery that, in our poison-drenched world, mother's milk frequently contains four times as much DDT as the legal limit permitted to cows. "If it were packaged in any other container," conservationist David Brower remarked to a House of Representatives committee, "we wouldn't allow it across state lines."

So how shall we quench our thirst? By taking a leaf from our ancestors' book and substituting alcohol for water? But alcoholic drinks have been tagged for us as potentially dangerous. We are also being warned against abusing coffee or tea, and, even before it caused concern about its possible pollution, milk, suspected of connivance with cholesterol. Beer, popular in the United States and an excellent disposer of between-meals thirst, accommodates itself at meals only to a limited range of foods. Wine, of which one variety or another can be found to do honor to almost, though not quite every, food is relatively incompatible with the American cuisine and consequently has never quite been clasped to America's bosom. There remains, however, one family of beverages to which Americans have proved susceptible.

While selling mild thirst quenchers to the populace was traditionally the job of the brewer and the cider presser, much of this role has now been taken over by the soft-drink manufacturer. Soft drinks slake thirst for the moment, but the effect is fleeting. Their sugar and other sweetening substances also *cause* thirst, creating a demand for repeat sales, a circumstance which does not disturb their makers, who have no more objection to filling new orders than have automobile manufacturers who assure them by building planned obsolescence into their vehicles. The United States has become submerged in a sea of syrupy soft drinks, which may be dangerous too, but so far no one has managed to have affixed to their bottles and cans warnings like those printed (and ignored) on packs of cigarettes. It might be justifiable to do so.

XXIX

The Great American Sweet Tooth

DO AMERICANS make excessive use of alcohol? A good many observers, especially foreign observers, would say, Yes. Do Americans make excessive use of soft drinks? Let us consult the figures:

In the year 1974, the American public bought 4,460,000,000 cases of soft drinks, 107,040,000,000 bottles, or, figuring the population at 220 million, 485 bottles a year for everyone in the United States, including those still, let us hope, on mother's milk—about a bottle and a half per day. These figures do not include the hundreds of thousands of gallon jugs of concentrated liquid flavorings sold to soda fountains or the tons of flavorings provided to bottlers and consumers in the form of colorless crystals which look like coarse-grained salt, labeled as representing lemon or orange or pineapple, sometimes extracted from fruit and sometimes from chemical retorts. It is probably impossible to do more than guess at the total amount of soft drinks which go down the American gullet annually; but after all it is not basically the American intake of soft drinks which interests us, but the intake of the most important ingredient of soft drinks—sugar.

Soft drinks provide only one of the forms—an important one, it is true—by which more sugar is shoveled into our bodies than the human system can be reasonably expected to absorb. Closely related to soft drinks—and often operating from the same terrain, the soda fountain—is another sugar-charged nutrient, ice cream, of which Americans eat more than twice as much as anyone else in the world, with the exception of Australians, New Zealanders, and Canadians, all of them, it is pertinent to point out, joint heirs with ourselves of the dubious eating habits of the British Isles. It was from England that we inherited our penchant for sugar, and in some departments of sweets, England is the only country which sins more than we do. Americans consume about six ounces per person per week of candy, but the

United Kingdom in 1954 hit a high of nine ounces, while its normal consumption varies between seven and eight. Altogether American sugar consumption is ninety-nine pounds per capita per annum, or a quarter pound per day, a figure again exceeded by the United Kingdom, which eats 111, not the record—Australia, Holland, and Ireland eat more, countries of which two, again, share the gastronomic heritage of Great Britain (the third shares its damp climate). France, a country universally conceded to eat well, consumes only seventy-six pounds per capita.

> Americans have a nearly childish weakness for sweets in general [said the French gastronomic writers Henri Gault and Christian Millau], for all foods which are sweet, soft and colored. One must not, however, sum up their pastry as consisting solely of those wedding or birthday cakes one sees in the moving pictures, whose tastelessness is equal only to their size. You can eat, especially in New England, delicious desserts of American or English origin, like Indian pudding, apple pie, blueberry pie, cheesecake, strawberry shortcake, etc., without forgetting lemon chiffon pie, fruit cakes, or waffles doused in maple syrup.

The authors will not renounce their allegiance to strawberry shortcake (made with real shortbread, not with the over-sweet spongy cake substituted for it in many restaurants), nor to blueberry pie (or even better, blueberry bread), but they are obliged to point out that for that universal American dessert, pie, we compound the load on our stomachs by making it in most cases with two crusts, thus doubling the carbohydrate intake we pile on top of its sugar. Europe prefers open-faced fruit tarts, with only a bottom crust, except in the case of meat pies, into which sugar does not enter. Unfortunately we do not stop with saturating our desserts with sugar; we put it in everything, even salad dressings, to the horror of most foreigners.

Most of us are familiar with the chief disadvantages of over-indulgence in sugar—bad teeth, excess weight, dyspepsia, clogged arteries, with the attendant risk of heart trouble. Attempts are occasionally made to reduce sugar consumption by using substitute sweeteners, but most of them comport dangers to health more serious than those of sugar—or rather of excess sugar, for it is excess which is at fault, not sugar, a natural food not only useful but necessary in one form or another. An educational effort to reduce the excessive use of sugar might well be as important socially as similar efforts to reduce the excessive use of alcohol.

The evil effects of too much sugar in the diet are well known. Less attention has been paid to its evil effect on gastronomy. It is disastrous.

The modern American soft drink is a descendant of the non-alcoholic beverages prepared at home in America's early days—drinks like pennyroyal tea, sassafras tea, cranberry juice and the like. It may be that no very great distinction was made between alcoholic and non-alcoholic drinks, except in the case of really hard liquor—in those days. Either could be employed to wash down a meal, and which the housewife prepared might depend upon the accidents of the moment. If she had elderberry plants at hand, she might make elderberry tea from the leaves, or elderberry wine from the berries, or both, depending on what was most convenient. Some drinks made the choice themselves, especially fruit juices. Prepared to be drunk fresh, they might, if left to their own devices, ferment and become alcoholic. Sweet cider could become hard cider in this fashion even when it had not been the intention in the first place to produce an alcoholic drink.

The use of effervescent water in beverages may be considered as a development from a natural beginning too—gaseous mineral waters, as they are found in nature, were eventually imitated artificially by the manufacture of aerated or carbonated waters, usually more gaseous than those imagined by Nature. A way of doing this was discovered as early as 1767 by Joseph Priestley, an Englishman better known for his exploit in isolating, and thus discovering, oxygen. He apparently regarded the production of carbonated water as no more than an amusing laboratory trick, and did nothing to exploit his invention even when he moved to the United States, where he spent the last ten years of his life and died, in Northumberland, Pennsylvania, in 1809, quite unconscious of the fact that he had started a multi-million dollar industry. The first person to produce and bottle soda water in commercially significant quantities in the United States was also unaware of the possibilities of the beverage. This was Benjamin Silliman, a professor of chemistry at Yale, who put his then unflavored water on the market in 1807. Apparently it did not occur to him that there was anything patentable, or worth patenting, about so simple a process as pumping carbonic gas into water, so the field was left open for a soda water maker more astute or more acquisitive, Joseph Hawkins, who took out the first soda water patent in 1809; that is, he did not patent the idea of making artificially gaseous water, but the machinery he had devised for doing it. The promotion genius of the business turned up in 1832, with the arrival in the United States of a young man named John Matthews, who would probably have made his mark in any activity he chose to enter, but since he happened to know how to make carbonic acid gas, he went into the manufacture of soda water. His soda water may have been no better than that of his competitors (there were several of them by now), but his advertising was. The style of the times was a little dithyrambic and he composed his publicity accordingly. "Youth as it sips its first soda," he told potential customers, "experiences the sensations which, like the sensations of love, cannot be forgotten." Was this the first harnessing of sex to the chariot of advertising? It would not in any case be the last. It is hard to believe that the unforgettable sensations which Mr. Matthews was purveying were produced by soda water still flavorless.

The progression from plain gaseous water to flavored gaseous water might seem in retrospect to be a step which should have been taken almost automatically, but in fact it was something like half a century before anybody thought of it. Nobody really knows who first put flavor into a bottle of gaseous water, but the prevailing theory is that it was one or the other, probably the second, of two Frenchmen who figure in the early history of soda. The first was Elie Magliore Durand, a pharmacist of Philadelphia, who in 1825 added cigars and soda water to his stock, thus starting the drugstore on its way to becoming an emporium which would sell a little of everything except drugs. The second was Eugène Roussel, who set up in Philadelphia too, and the business to which he added a soda counter in 1838 was a perfume shop. The first flavored sodas appealed mightily to an eager public. A mere ten years later, in 1849, there were sixty-four soda plants in the United States, and in 1859 123, which had already made "mineral waters and pop" (the inelegant term "belch water" had not yet come in) a million-dollar business—$1,415,000 to be exact. "Soda water," said *Harper's Weekly* in 1891, "is an American drink." The soda industry had now taken the bit in its teeth and would not let go. In 1900 there were 2,763 bottling plants doing $25 million worth of business. By 1955 they employed about 100,000 people, and 1,200,000 tons of sugar was being consumed by the American public in sodas. By 1960, thirty billion bottles a year were being produced, and Americans were drinking 185 bottles a head. We are doing more than three and a half times better now—or worse, as you happen to feel about it.

The early soda flavors upon which the public fell with avidity included root beer, birch beer, spruce beer, pepsin, ginger, lemon, kola, cherry, sarsaparilla, champagne, and claret. Ice cream and soda were soon being sold in the same places, and it would not seem that a great deal of imagination was necessary to think of putting one into the other. But inspiration was slow; it was something like thirty-five years after flavored soda had appeared before the combination occurred to anybody, and even then it did not *occur* to the official creator of the ice cream soda, it *happened* to him. The man to whom it has been decided to award the laurels for this innovation was Robert M. Green, who held the soda fountain concession at the semi-centennial of the founding of the Franklin Institute in, once again, Philadelphia. He made his sodas with cream, but one day, running out of cream, he surreptitiously slipped in a spoonful of vanilla ice cream instead, hoping that nobody would notice. Everybody noticed—and everybody clamored for more. Before the end of the semi-centennial, his sales had multiplied from six dollars a day to six *hundred* dollars a day. This bonanza did not escape the notice of the concession sellers of Philadelphia, decidedly the capital of this sort of nourishment, and when James M. Tufts applied for the ice cream soda concession at Philadelphia's commemoration of the centennial of the Declaration of Independence, they charged him fifty thousand dollars for it. He made a fortune.

Some of the first flavored sodas, those made from bark, for instance, must have been coarse in character and unlikely to wring enthusiastic praise from gourmets; but they were products uncomplicated by chemistry, except Nature's, and if they did the cause of gastronomy no good, they did the human body no harm—except when they were overloaded with sugar, which seems to have been less often the case then than it is now. More pure fruit juices were consumed in those times too; but Americans today drink nearly twice as much soda pop as fruit and vegetable juices. From the simplicity of such beverages we have since progressed to the complexity or apparent complexity of what are undoubtedly our most popular soft drinks today, those of the cola family. Of the top ten brands of bottled drinks sold in the United States now, half are cola drinks.

The first of all the cola drinks, and the one which still outsells all its competitors, is Coca-Cola, devised in 1886 by a druggist of Atlanta, Georgia, John S. Pemberton, to whom it may not have occurred that it would become a beverage drunk for pleasure, for he saw it as a remedy for headaches and hangovers. The story goes that Pemberton mixed the first batch of his concoction, put together from extracts of coca leaves and cola nuts, in an iron kettle in his backyard, and stirred it with an oar. There were enough hangover or headache sufferers in Atlanta to consume twenty-five gallons of Coca-Cola, as he immediately named it, during the first year it was on sale in his drugstore, its only outlet. It gave him fifty dollars profit—not bad, but no bonanza. He must have peddled it thereafter to some of his fellow merchants, for it was a second Atlanta druggist, an anonymous one, who is credited with having taken the next step, by accident. He spilled some soda water into his Coca-Cola, and found that this gave it more pep. Finally a third Atlanta druggist started Coca-Cola on its meteoric course to fortune when he bought Pemberton's formula for two thousand dollars. (The Coca-Cola recipe is carried on the books now at $42 million, but it is actually impossible to put any realistic value on a mixture—or is it the value of a name?—which brings in a billion dollars a year from sales in 130 countries.)

The man who bought Pemberton out may have been attracted to Coca-Cola originally by its medical aspect; he was a dyspeptic plagued by frequent violent headaches. If so, he was quick to realize that Coca-Cola had more than medicinal possibilities. His name was Asa G. Candler, and it was under his management that Coca-Cola began its rise toward its present position as the leading soft drink of America and probably also of the world. The reasons for the spectacular success of a drink somewhat medicinal in flavor are difficult to discern, so an explanation was sought in sorcery—it was suggested that Coca-Cola contained some habit-forming drug, for instance cocaine, which bewitched consumers and converted them into permanent imbibers willy-nilly. Cocaine is indeed derived from coca leaves, and it is possible that the original drink stirred by Pemberton's oar did contain an infinitesimal residue of it, simply because the mechanical skills of the times were not up to the task of eliminating all the cocaine when an extract was made from coca leaves. However it is more probable that the nation acquired the habit of drinking Coca-Cola because of the aggressive and skillful advertising methods used to promote it. The makers of Coca-Cola were aided powerfully by the possession of a mellifluous name, easy to pronounce, easy to remember, and reducible to a homely familiar abbreviation, Coke. None of the rival companies which sprang up in imitation of Coca-Cola hit upon a succession of syllables which ran so trippingly off the tongue, which may account partly for the fact that none of them ever succeeded in catching up to the leader.

Cola drink manufacturers have reminded customers from time to time that Peruvian and Bolivian Indians derive energy to cope with exertion at high altitudes by chewing coca leaves (true), while West Africans achieve a similar stimulus by masticating cola beans (also true). But true as these statements may be, they are irrelevant. It may be doubted that Coca-Cola today contains either coca or cola. It certainly did not in 1906 when the company was prosecuted for mislabeling in a case filed in judicial annals under the picturesque title of *The United States vs. Forty Barrels and Twenty Kegs of Coca-Cola.* The government maintained that the name Coca-Cola was misleading (one wonders if it mattered, since not one American in a thousand could have identified accurately either coca or cola), and the court was not impressed by the defendants' observation that nobody was bothering to prosecute the company which made Grape-Nuts, though it contained neither grapes nor nuts. Having lost its case, the company presumably returned these two ingredients to their mixture, but in amounts so small that they cannot be detected by chemical analysis. The uplift (if there is any, apart from that implicit in any form of refreshment) of cola drinks is possibly attributable to the caffeine they contain, though a bottle of the soft drink offers less of it than a cup of tea or coffee. A likelier source of energy is the sugar which is the main ingredient of the drink, except for water—about five teaspoons in a small bottle.

A second category of soft drinks is constituted by those based on milk, already a rich drink on its own—too rich indeed for many adults, who, unlike children, do not require a type of food particularly useful for bone-building and other growth processes. (Some Asiatic and African adults cannot digest milk at all.) One thing milk certainly does not require is the added dose of sugar in the thick rich syrups which go into milk shakes, in some of which the overload of sweetness seems particularly superfluous. California, for instance, has a specialty of date milk shakes, to which, it appears, some of the local citizenry become unweanably addicted. The very idea may seem nauseous to non-Californians, even when they imagine it to be, like other milk shakes, simply a combination of milk and a flavoring syrup, in this case one which tastes like dates. The reality is richer. "Put about three quarters of a cup of pitted dates in a blender with half a cup of milk and blend until they are nearly smooth," the recipe goes. "Then add a pint of vanilla ice cream and another half cup of milk and blend some more."

As though the milk shake were not already rich enough, the American repertory of soft drinks moved on to malted milk, adding to the original sugar of the milk itself (about 4.9 percent of its weight) and to the sweetening contained in the flavoring syrup, the maltose sugar of the grain which makes up about half of malted milk powder. The drying of the milk which makes up the other half also concentrates the milk fats, so that instead of the 3.9 percent of fat normally found in liquid milk, you get 8 percent in malted milk. The soda jerk is not yet through with us; sometimes he adds an egg to the malted milk, by which time the next meal has become unnecessary.

Superfluous richness is added to the milk shake in another fashion when it is converted into a float by adding a scoop of ice cream to the drink. Ice cream is also often added to malted milk, in which case the digestive system had better gird its loins for action. The final step is to beat the ice cream into the drink, producing a liquid so thick you can feel it in the mouth as well as taste it.

Ice cream is a symbol of America, so thoroughly associated with it that during the last war eating it was discouraged in Japan as indicating a suspicious sympathy with the enemy. The opposition came originally from high military circles, which may also have looked upon ice cream as a namby-pamby food capable of sapping the will to win. In this, Japanese and American generals seem to have been as one, if we may judge by the attitude of Marine General Lewis B. Puller, who roared that his men were not issued ice cream, adding that the proper nourishment for Marines was beer and whiskey. The rank and file was not in complete agreement with the big brass, as sometimes happens, and indeed during the fighting in the Pacific Islands, Marines had to be dissuaded from collecting "souvenirs," a euphemism for enemy ears and buck-toothed skulls, by a promise of ice cream for those who desisted. During the Korean War General Puller's fulminations against the "ice cream and candy" Marines backfired; the Pentagon reacted by announcing that ice cream would be served at least three times a week to the troops in Korea.The United States Navy did not agree with General Puller either. When the aircraft carrier *Lexington* was sinking, the crew pulled its cans of ice cream up onto the deck and dug into them until each man's turn came to go over the side. General Puller should have looked back to the history of individual fighting men before he formulated his theories on the proper diet for battlers, to the time when Gentleman Jim Corbett, who was fond of ice cream, defeated heavyweight champion John L. Sullivan, who had trained on, precisely, beer and whiskey—and, or so the story goes, switched thereafter to ice cream himself, but too late to regain the championship.

The Founding Fathers indulged in ice cream, led in this, as in everything else, by George Washington. His home at Mount Vernon numbered among its utensils what the inventory called "two pewter ice cream pots." The books of an early ice cream seller in New York which have luckily come down to us list an account for Washington which reveals that he spent two hundred dollars on ice cream during the single summer of 1790, which at current prices must have bought a good deal of ice cream. He was accustomed to serving "iced creams" at the formal dinners he gave every Thursday, and it may have been to make them that he bought in 1784, in Philadelphia, already the capital of ice cream making, something described as a "Cream machine for Making Ice"—cost, one pound, thirteen shillings, fourpence. What was it exactly? Certainly not a machine for making ice, which he did not need, for he had an ice house on his property. Did some kind of ice cream freezer exist long before we have any official record of one? José Wilson suggests that the "iced creams" Washington served may have been

> more like iced or chilled creams than the hard-frozen type of today. The first printed recipe for this treat, in a Philadelphia cookbook of 1792, directs that the mixture of cream, eggs and sugar be stirred at frequent intervals in a pewter bowl set in a larger bowl filled with ice, and that care be taken to prepare it "in a part of the house where as little warm air comes as you can possibly contrive."

It is true that it was not until the middle of the nineteenth century that anything comparable to our modern ice cream freezer is known to have appeared in America, but ice cream of reasonably firm consistency was being made nevertheless. The cream was beaten with a spoon until it became too stiff for further beating, after which the container was twirled around by hand in a bucket of salt and ice. There is also the possibility that George Washington's machine was a foreign contraption. After all, the Italians, who introduced ice cream to Europe, had been making it for a century or two and might conceivably have developed some sort of machine to facilitate the process.

Thomas Jefferson had an ice cream machine too, but we do not know if it was of the same type as Washington's. We do know that Jefferson brought back with him from France, in 1789, an ice cream recipe so elaborate that it required eighteen separate operations. He preferred his ice cream enveloped in a crust of warm pastry: he had invented baked Alaska a century and a half before anyone else thought of it.

Among the hostesses of the times who served ice cream was Mrs. Alexander Hamilton, caught in the act precisely because one of the persons to whom she offered it was George Washington. Dolley Madison presented ice cream too.

> Last night I was bid by our President to the White House [wrote a personality of the time], and it was a most unusual affair. Mrs. Madison always entertains with Grace and Charm, but last night there was a sparkle in her eye that set astir an Air of Expectancy among her Guests. When finally the brilliant Assemblage—America's best—entered the dining room, they beheld a Table set with French china and English silver, laden with good things to eat, and in the Centre high on a silver platter, a large, shining dome of pink Ice Cream.

It was perhaps this account which inspired James Trager to write that "James Madison's wife, Dolley [sic], made ice cream popular." but with all due respect to one of the most brilliant hostesses of the times, Dolley Madison could hardly have been the innovator. She did not marry Madison until 1794 and could not have been hostess at the White House before 1801, when Jefferson entered it, and, having no wife himself, borrowed Dolley to preside over White House meals. We have just seen that ice cream was already well enough established in 1790 so that Washington could run up a bill at an ice cream store, and if we go back to the year before that, we find Mad Anthony Wayne, after the Battle of the Fallen Timbers, sitting down to a victory meal which ended, in the words of historian Harry Emerson Wildes, with "dishes of ice cream, a dainty which the Army had not seen since it left the East"—so ice cream was obtainable in the East from sources less elevated than the White House. Brillat-Savarin, who came to the United States in 1794, wrote about those of his compatriots who, having fled the Terror like himself, were making a living in the United States by exploiting one gastronomic specialty or another. Of one of them he reported:

> Captain Collet made a great deal of money in New York, during the years 1794 and 1795, by selling ice cream and sherbet to the inhabitants of that busy city. The ladies especially never tired of a pleasure so novel to them; nothing was more amusing than to watch them smirk and simper as they tasted it. They could not understand how it could be kept so cold.

The history of ice cream in America in fact goes farther back than Dolley Madison or George Washington. The first known reference to it in America dates from when a guest of Thomas Bladen, governor of Maryland from 1742 to 1747, wrote to a friend that some of the foods served at the governor's dinner had been rather strange and that

> we had dessert no less Curious; among the Rarities of which it was Compos'd was some fine Ice Cream which, with the Strawberries and Milk, eat most deliciously.

If it was Annapolis which saw the first private appearance of ice cream in the United States, it seems to have been New York which was the scene of its first public appearance. The earliest known advertisement for this confection appeared in the New York *Gazette* on May 12, 1777, announcing to buyers that ice cream "may be had almost every day" at the confectionery shop of Philip Lenzi. The name seems to be Italian, and so many other Italian names crop up in the early history of American ice cream that it is not unreasonable to suspect that it was Italians who first introduced ice cream to America, commercially at least, just as it was Italians who introduced it to France and England. However it may have been French influence which captivated our early Presidents. The French representative gave a dinner in 1782 at which he served ice cream. George Washington was present, and it is not impossible that it was there that he made acquaintance with the dish; it was not until two years later that he bought his "Machine for Ice."

In the meantime commercial ice cream was making its way in New York. In 1781 another ice cream seller advertised in the New York press, one Joseph Corre, a name which might be Italian too. The third known advertiser, however, sounds Anglo-Saxon enough. He placed an advertisement in the New York *Post Boy* in 1786 which read: "Ladies and Gentlemen may be supplied with ice cream every day at the City Tavern by their humble servant Joseph Crowe." (Or had Corre Anglicized his name?) In 1800 Italy was back in the lists again, in the person of an Italian confectioner named Bosio, who placed what was perhaps the first advertisement for ice cream in Philadelphia. He announced the opening of an ice cream parlor offering "all kinds of refreshments, as Ice Cream, Syrups, French Cordials, Cakes, Clarets of the best kinds, Jellies etc." Dolley Madison was not yet on the job.

The *Louisiana Courier* of New Orleans carried an advertisement of the Exchange Coffee-House in 1808 which announced that it served ice cream daily between noon and 9 P.M. Dolley Madison was still in the White House then, but this development was unrelated to her sponsorship of ice cream; it stemmed from the fact that New Orleans was just beginning to receive ice from the North.

When Captain Frederick Marryat arrived in America in 1837, ice cream was already familiar. There was, he wrote, "one great luxury in America . . . the quantity of clear, pure ice . . . even in the hottest seasons, and ice creams are universal and even cheap." He also expressed his surprise at seeing "common laborers" take time out in the middle of the day to eat a dish of ice cream.

Eighteen forty-six was a big year in the history of ice cream; it was then that Nancy Johnson invented the ice cream freezer, in a form small enough to be portable and a size suitable for family use, requiring no other energy for its operation than human muscle. Once again an innovator in this category of foods did not think of patenting the idea, so, two years later, naturally, somebody else did—William G. Young, who did not even bother to disguise the fact that he had taken over the invention from somebody else, for he put it on the market as the "Johnson Patent Ice-Cream Freezer." It was virtually the same machine many of us knew in our youth, using a battery of paddles turned through the cream by means of a hand crank affixed to its cover, with ever diminishing speed through ever increasing resistance until finally the ice cream became so stiff as to defeat the strength of the operator.

Godey's Lady's Book, a sort of Bible for the housewives of the times, ruled in 1850 that ice cream had become one of the necessities of life. "A party without it," it opined, "would be like a breakfast without bread or a dinner without a roast." A year later a cookbook appeared in—of course—Philadelphia, which gave thirty-four recipes for different kinds of ice cream and eighteen for sherbets. Ralph Waldo Emerson sounded a sour note: "We dare not trust our wit for making our house pleasant to our friend so we buy ice cream."

Ice cream became big business in 1851. Previously it had been produced locally, on a neighborhood, or at the most a city-wide, scale and sold directly to the consumer by the manufacturer. But in 1851 Jacob Fussel, a Baltimore milk dealer, set up what seems to have been the first wholesale ice cream business in the United States. Once again a new development in pleasure foods seems to have been partly accidental. Plagued with a surplus of cream for which there were no buyers, he decided to turn it into ice cream, and as it was a by-product, he was able to undersell—drastically, twenty-five cents a quart instead of sixty-five—the small-scale ice cream dealers serving restricted markets. He found himself doing better on ice cream than on milk, and decided to concentrate on ice cream alone. From Baltimore he invaded other markets, the first in 1885, when he opened an ice cream plant in Washington, and then Boston, New York, Cincinnati, Chicago, and St. Louis.

In 1890 another innovation exploded in the sweet foods universe—once again a development which now seems obvious enough, but which had taken its time in coming. This was the sundae, ice cream embellished with additions of various kinds—syrups, jellies, fruits, nuts, candy, marshmallows, whipped cream and *tutti quanti,* not to mention combinations of differently flavored ice creams and sherbets, with or without the intrusions of foreign elements—Nabiscos, perhaps, or bananas, leading to the classic banana split, which from classic quickly became baroque. At first these concoctions were presented under names which were reasonable descriptions of what you might expect—chocolate walnut sundae, for instance, was composed of chocolate ice cream, chocolate syrup and chopped walnuts, with or without whipped cream, topped perhaps with a maraschino cherry. But fantasy quickly gained the upper hand, and sundaes were presented under titles which gave less information about what the dish contained than about what its creator's imagination contained—for instance, to give a pair of comparatively simple early examples, Buffalo Tip or Heavenly Twins.

As for the name "sundae" itself, it is generally assumed that it is a purposeful misspelling of "Sunday," possibly in the interests of reverence; one may wonder if it did not result from the same Puritan attitude which gave us baked beans and brown bread on Sunday because they could be prepared on Saturday and thus provide a meal uncontaminated by violation of the prohibition against working on the Sabbath. Ice cream and its decorations were prepared ahead of time too, and it may be supposed that the name "sundae" was intended to indicate that it could be consumed with a minimum of sin on a day when in principle the only permissible enjoyment was reflection upon the ingenuity of the tormenters of Hell. But where the name—and, it may be presumed, the dish also—originated is in dispute. Paul Dickson, in *The Great American Ice Cream Book,* presents two leading candidates for the honor:

> The first claim goes back to the 1890s in Evanston, Illinois . . . where civic piety had reached such a state that it became the first American community to recognize and legislate against the "Sunday Soda Menace." This prompted confectioners to create Sundays so that they could do business on the Sabbath. Ironically the soda was later given a strong boost from this community when the Evanston-based Women's Christian Temperance Union . . . championed it as a pleasant alternative to alcoholic drinks.
>
> The Two Rivers, Wisconsin, claim goes back to the same era and, so the story goes, was created when a youth named George Hallauer went into Ed Berner's soda fountain for a dish of ice cream. As the ice cream was being scooped, the daring Hallauer spied a bottle of chocolate syrup normally used in sodas and asked Berner to pour some of it over his ice cream. Berner sampled the concoction and liked it enough to begin featuring "ice cream with syrup" in his shop for the same price as a dish of ice cream. The name *sundae* was given to the dish when George Giffy, an ice cream parlor proprietor in nearby Manitowoc, was forced by customer demand to serve the popular Berner concoction. Giffy was convinced that the nickel dish would put him out of business and at first served it only as a Sunday loss leader. In Manitowoc it soon became known as "the Sunday." Giffy soon found that he was making money on the dish and began advertising his "Ice Cream Sundaes," with the spelling changed so that it would lose its Sunday-only association.

In 1904, there was another great breakthrough on the ice cream front—the ice cream cone was invented, again apparently by accident. Or, more precisely, it was in 1904 that the event occurred which was long accepted as constituting the original appearance of the ice cream cone in the United States, though at least four other claimants for the credit have appeared since, two of them referring to the same place and date, the other two going farther back. The coeval claimants all place their discoveries at the St. Louis World Fair of 1904, and indeed this ice cream container was once called the World's Fair Cornucopia by some of its makers and simply a cornucopia by others; the term "ice cream cone" does not seem to have entered the language before 1909.

The original (and then generally undisputed) story credited a Syrian named Ernest A. Hamwi with inventing the cone (stumbling upon it would perhaps have been a more exact description). Having arrived in America in 1903, he turned up the following year at the St. Louis Fair with a concession to sell *zalabia,* a type of waffle represented as being Persian. His stand stood cheek by jowl with that of an ice cream dealer who sold the confection by five- and ten-cent dishes. On one particularly hot day he ran out of dishes; Hamwi rolled a *zalabia* into a cone and handed it to him as a substitute for a dish. Other waiting customers immediately demanded their ice cream in a waffle too. The ice cream cone was in.

It appears today that Mr. Hamwi and the other claimants for the honor of having invented the ice cream cone had all been outdistanced by an Italian named Italo Marchiony; there is documentary evidence to prove it. He is said to have started to sell ice cream cones in 1896; it is on record that he applied for a patent on a mold to produce "small round pastry cups with sloping sides," and it was granted in 1904—before the St. Louis Fair. If Marchiony had dropped out of the picture, it was because he never succeeded in exploiting his invention commercially, surprisingly enough, for all the others made money out of it. The ice cream cone was clearly a natural for a public which doted on sweetness added to sweetness, and felt a particular affinity for foods which could be eaten standing up, or held in the hand, or consumed rapidly, all virtues offered by the cone. By 1924 the United States was eating 245 million ice cream cones annually.

The Eskimo Pie burst upon the brain of Christian Nelson, so the story goes, in 1919, when a boy in his candy store had trouble making up his mind whether he wanted an ice cream sandwich or a candy bar, which gave Nelson the idea of offering both in one. The first chocolate-covered ice cream bars, without sticks, appeared on the market under the registered name of Eskimo Pie in 1921; a year later the company was selling a million Eskimo Pies a day. At the time of writing, 750 million Eskimo Pies are being sold annually in half a dozen countries.

The Good Humor bar was started on its way in 1920, already equipped with a stick; its striking success may have been largely the result of its conspicuous selling technique, based on the uniformed Good Humor man. Popsicles were patented in 1924, and have now reached a sales figure of three million pieces a year. It was about this time also that Ralph A. Lee developed the first thermal bag to preserve more orthodox forms of ice cream for distant delivery, a convenience which was followed by the familiar packing of ice cream in "dry ice"—solidified carbon dioxide.

We have little information about the flavors offered in the first American ice cream, perhaps because its eaters were too much impressed by the fact that they had any ice cream at all to think of recording the details. We might expect them to have been fairly primitive, like the early soda flavors, but this was perhaps not the case, since the circumstances were different. Americans were apparently the first to flavor soda water, so, without precedents to guide them, they had to start from scratch with whatever was at hand. Ice cream, on the contrary, was already in vogue in Europe and had presumably developed flavors there which could be passed on to America. It is probable, though, that the two top flavors in the United States today, vanilla (51 percent of all ice cream sales) and chocolate (13.5 percent) were not present among the early flavors. Both vanilla and chocolate are natives of tropical America, and do not seem to have reached North America directly, but were relayed from Europe only after Europe had received them from South America and had become familiar with them, which took a century or more.

The demand for vanilla beans as American consumption of vanilla ice cream increased did give a welcome fillip to the trade of several South and Central American countries, and has never ceased to do so, since the American demand for vanilla for ice cream alone exceeds the amount of all the vanilla produced in the world. Most Americans eat vanilla ice cream flavored with vanillin derived from some other source than genuine vanilla, but Philadelphians, our top ice cream gourmets, sometimes get the real thing because they know what it looks like—dead white (not yellow), containing tiny black specks, minute morsels of the vanilla bean. (Modern science, however, is equal to the task of inserting spurious black specks into ice cream.)

After vanilla and chocolate, the statistics give strawberry as the nation's third choice, but its percentage of sales is so low (six percent) that it hardly belongs in the same class as the first two; but it is true that strawberry still sells more than twice as much as Number Four, which is not always the same flavor. Among sherbets, orange is dominant, followed at respectful distances by pineapple, lime, lemon, and raspberry (the last in the United States is the first in France). Coffee-flavored ice cream accounts for only one percent of national sales, concentrated in the Northeast. "Time was," remarks Paul Dickson, "when it was all but a New England exclusive," and he adds, "New Yorkers generally like their coffee ice cream strong, while Bostonians go for a milder blend."

Local option is an all-important factor in the ice cream market. If you were asked to guess which state consumes ice cream most avidly, would you look for the leader in the South, among the hotter states? If so, you would be wrong. The answer is Alaska. Alaskans put away six gallons of ice cream per person per year, approximately twice the national average. Regional flavor preferences are often explicable by reference to favorite local foods in unchilled forms, but not always. It is normal enough to find Canada demanding maple ice cream, but the demand seems to have fallen off in New

England. No explanation is required for the preference of Texans for pecan ice cream nor for the willingness of other Southerners to accept peanut ice cream (why candy ice creams are also welcomed by the latter is a trifle more difficult to explain). It is normal enough also for Florida to like citrus flavors, in ice cream as well as in sherbet, and for California to buy date or prune ice cream, virtually unsalable elsewhere. New Englanders seem to be the most eccentric in their preferences. They are the top consumers of frozen pudding, of which there are two varieties, for drinkers and for abstainers; frozen pudding should include a dash of rum or sherry, but it is also made without any alcoholic ingredient, in which case strict constructionists insist that it ought to be called tutti-frutti. Ginger ice cream sounds like a stranger choice, but it can be explained as a derivative of the habit of munching candied ginger, which many New Englanders acquired in the days when Yankee Clippers were active in the spice trade. But why grapenut ice cream? Why mint tea ice cream? The latter, it appears, was developed expressly at the request of a Boston ice cream maker by the University of Maryland.

The proliferation of flavors which set in about the second quarter of this century was partly a function of another proliferation, that of chains of ice cream outlets, most of them devoted not to ice cream alone, but featuring it against the background of other merchandise—candy, perhaps, or nuts, or even full meals. This was one segment of what was becoming an increasingly popular form of merchandising, through licenses granted by a parent house which supported by national advertising the individual dealers to which it granted franchises to handle its products. It has been claimed that the Howard Johnson chain of restaurants, whose advertising threw its ice cream into higher relief than its food, was the first example of franchising, or at least of food franchising. This chain was, at least, typical of the franchising technique, which usually included conditions imposed by the central organization as to installations and methods of presenting and handling its products. One of the conditions applied in the Howard Johnson chain was the construction of buildings in a similar, and consequently easily recognizable, style of architecture, and this was probably one of the reasons why the chain impinged sufficiently on the national consciousness so that Howard Johnson became a household word, like Coca-Cola and Good Humor. This may have been partly due also to the fact that here, once again, the name was easily pronounceable and easily memorable, more so than those of some of its competitors, like Baskin-Robbins, the giant enterprise which in 1972 sold $85 million worth of ice cream. Distributing food through franchising was a gadget of the twentieth century, whether it was Coca-Cola and Seven Up, which licensed bottlers, manufacturers, or wholesalers, or the companies which specialized on retail outlets—Mister Donut, Dairy Queen, McDonald's Hamburgers, Dunkin' Donuts, Colonel Sanders' Kentucky Fried Chicken, Fanny Farmer, Chock Full o' Nuts, Yum Yums, or Zum Zums.

The vendors concentrated on flavor, but perhaps they concentrated too hard; or they were led astray by the letter and forgot the spirit, putting out new varieties not on the reasonable basis of increasing our repertory of harmonious and, we might say, understandable taste sensations, but on that of having a name to advertise, even if the reality behind the name consisted only of a senseless hodgepodge of incompatible flavors thrown together with little respect for the subtleties of the palate. Ordinarily gourmets applaud any attempt to expand the choice of savors offered them, but they must be coherent savors, capable of constituting, in one fashion or another, an interesting experience in the realm of taste. Competition, however, created a temptation to devise novel flavors for no other reason than their novelty. The pressure for something different—bad or good, but different—was created by those chains of ice cream outlets which had come up with the merchandising idea, not necessarily vicious in itself, of providing their customers with a wide choice by having always on hand a considerable number of different ice creams—the twenty-eight flavors of the Howard Johnson chain or the "31 flavors" of Baskin-Robbins (in practice, often thirty-four, since the three leaders, vanilla, chocolate, and strawberry, remained fixtures, and more expensive). The worst sellers were periodically replaced by other new and imaginative creations, which disappeared in their turn as soon as they had worn out their welcome; each new flavor enjoyed a curiosity sale for a few weeks until the public discovered that there was nothing particularly ingratiating about it, whereupon it would be escorted without fanfare to the oubliettes.

There must have been a great deal of good sense and sound taste in the population since, after consulting the long list of extravagant ice creams, the majority ordered vanilla; so it seems rather strange that there was not more demand for what might be called other natural but neglected flavors instead of the artificially created nightmares. Varieties like peach or grape, made in season from fresh fruit, can be superb, especially when prepared at home from the flavoring ingredients picked in one's own backyard. Backyards capable of growing fruit are, of course, becoming ever more rare in these days of galloping urbanization, when the alternative often boils down to a farm or nothing. The making of homemade ice cream, which, when conscientiously pursued, is a two-day process, is also discouraged nowadays by the ease with which frozen desserts can be prepared in the refrigerator, including what for many persons is an acceptable substitute for ice cream. If it is not as good as well-made ice cream should be, it does come close enough to justify renouncing the pains required to produce ideal ice cream. We are faced here with the same balancing of quality against effort which has debased our bread.

Among the ice creams which have been commercially manufactured in the

United States, offered to the public, and, we may suppose, bought, if only briefly, are these: apple štrudel, banana daiquiri, banana marshmallow, borscht, boysenberry cheesecake, brassicaceous beer (root beer and horse radish), bubble gum (and *pink* bubble gum), Burgundy cherry, buttermint toffee, caramel coconut, casaba melon, chile con carne (this one, dreamed up by Good Humor, was, to the credit of the American people, one of the quickest failures in ice cream history), chocolate chip candy, coconut pineapple, Danish fruitcake, eggnog, English toffee, espresso, German chocolate cake, ghee (Hindu clarified buffalo milk), gum drop, iced tea, jelly bean, lemon crunch, licorice, locust gum, macadamia (a favorite of President Nixon), mince pie, Mocha chip, mustard, peppermint stick (and green peppermint), persimmon, pickle (dill), pineapple pecan, pistaschio almond fudge, potatoes and bacon, pumpkin (plus pumpkin licorice and pumpkin-pie marble), rhubarb, root beer, rose, sarsaparilla, squash, sunflower seed, tequila, truffle (the Delmonico invention already noted), Vermont maple pecan, violet, and wild blueberry. Curiously missing—but possibly they exist beyond the authors' ken—are fig (which can be imagined as a defensible flavor), mango, and passion fruit, an ice cream of incomparable delicacy and subtlety which is obtainable in Paris.

American sherbets include, in addition to the well known varieties, boysenberry, cranberry, grape, mandarin chocolate, mint and raspberry, nectarine, ollallieberry, pink grapefruit, sauerkraut, tangerine, watercress, and watermelon. There are also Here Comes the Fudge ice cream, Red, White and Blueberry ice cream, and others in a similar literary vein. We have been spared, however, Grape Britain, Sophia Lemon, Nudie Fruitti, Berry Goldwater, Can't Elope Tonight, U. S. Mint Green, and Tarzan and the Grapes, all considered by the Baskin-Robbins chain, but turned down in the interests, one may suppose, of sanity. Baskin-Robbins, probably the world's largest operator of ice cream chain stores, with 1,200 outlets at the end of 1973, had already been credited in the *Guinness Book of Records* with having 401 kinds of ice cream on tap in 1971, the company's twenty-fifth anniversary, which according to Paul Dickson had become 431 by 1972. The company must then have decided to prune its list, for in October 1973, the number of approved flavors was given by one of its executives as 330 (about fifteen new varieties are added each year, but some old ones are allowed to withdraw to deserved retirement). Bresler's Ice Cream Company, a Chicago outfit, had 201 flavors in 1972.

Few foods lend themselves more readily than ice cream to adulteration, not necessarily a case of fraud. As a rule you get in ice cream what you pay for. If you choose to buy cheap ice cream you receive, naturally, the sort which can be provided profitably for the price you are willing to pay. You can hardly expect more: first-rate ingredients command top-notch prices.

> Most ice creams [*The New Yorker* pointed out in its *Talk of the Town* department on August 19, 1974] contain dextrose, lactose, fructose, calcium hydroxide, alginate, polysorbate 65 [or polysorbate 80], propylene glycol, gum acacia, carboxymethylcellulose, and plastic cream (trade name for concentrated milk fat). Federal Food and Drug Administration standards also permit the inclusion of imitation flavors, antioxidants, surfactants, artificial dyes, stabilizers (bring smoothness), emulsifiers (make ice cream less than it looks like).

This list of chemical terms sounds grim, but actually the additives and adulterants used in ice cream are not noxious to the health, though they do short-change the public on taste and nutritive value. The most important ice cream adulterant is one of which nobody need be afraid, except when absorbed in our city streets—air. The volume of ice cream can easily be doubled by pumping enough air into it (one of the functions of emulsifiers is to persuade ice cream to retain the extra air), a process to which the Food and Drug Administration puts a limit by ruling that ice cream may not weigh less than 4.5 pounds per gallon. (Homemade ice cream weighs twice that.) It also stipulates that ice cream must contain at least 10 percent butterfat. (Homemade ice cream runs from 18 percent up.) One of the roles of stabilizers is to prevent ice crystals from forming in the ice cream, useful when it is made in large quantities by mechanical means with a minimum of human attentiveness, but superfluous for carefully made ice creams, since it is possible to avoid "heat shock," which is what causes ice crystals to form. Unfortunately the use of stabilizers in any considerable amount robs the ice cream of taste. Other additives avoid the use of expensive ingredients like fresh cream, cane sugar and eggs, substituting instead dried eggs, powdered milk (depleted of some of its content), dried cheese whey, seaweed derivatives (like carageen or Irish moss, used also in blanc mange), or dried corn syrup.

Most of the leading ice cream manufacturers, who have national reputations to sustain, do a great deal better than the legal minimums; it is the supermarkets, where price is an all-important factor, which cleave most closely to them. "The proverbial purchaser of a pig in a poke had nothing on the buyer of ice cream in our modern age of palatial supermarkets," the *Consumer Bulletin* once remarked.

Good or bad, the United States now eats more than 750 million gallons of ice cream a year, or fifteen quarts per person (twenty-three, if you define as ice cream all commercially produced frozen dairy products). American ice cream is also widely exported, one of its markets being China, a carrying of coals to Newcastle indeed, if it is true, as many food historians believe, that the Italians who gave ice cream to the rest of the West got it themselves from the Arabs, who got it from the Chinese, who are supposed to have invented it, probably first in the form of sherbet. If so, the Japanese seem to have roamed unnecessarily far afield in looking upon Americans as the instigators of ice cream.

While "soda water is an American invention," and ice cream, whatever its origin, has become so Americanized that the Japanese took it for a typical Yankee confection, there is a third food which falls in the same general category of aliments, so indisputably American that no other country has ever tried—or even desired—to usurp credit for it: chewing gum. Chewing gum a food? Certainly. One stick of chewing gum provides nine calories of nourishment, and there is a feeble residue of anti-scorbutic vitamins in the juice which is swallowed when it contains such flavorings as peppermint or spearmint, America's two top favorites. The juice also includes some of the 60 percent of sugar and 19 percent of corn syrup which most chewing gum flavorings contain. Gum chewing, unlovely though it looks, offers other assets too. Chewing gum stimulates the flow of saliva, the first step in digestion, and, as everyone knows, relieves pressure on the ears in rapidly rising or descending aircraft, though this advantage was not perceived by the first gum chewers. The ruminant rhythm of the jaws, resorted to in some other parts of the world as well (by betel chewers in India, for instance) seems to have a soothing effect on the nerves, a precious contribution to survival in the maelstrom of modern life; consumption of chewing gum rises in periods of tension, as it did during and after both World Wars.

The United States chews more gum per capita than any other country in the world; Canada is second. After them come the Latin American countries. Gum chewing is thus concentrated in countries inhabited originally by American Indians; and it was indeed from Indians that the Anglo-Saxon colonists of North America and the Latin colonists of South and Central America inherited the habit of chewing gum. In New England, the Indians masticated the resin of the black spruce and taught the Pilgrims to do the same; in Central America, the Mayans masticated chicle (from the Nahuatl *chichtli),* the coagulated latex of the sapodilla tree, and taught the Spaniards to do the same.

The first chewing gum produced commercially seems to have been that made about 1850 in the state of Maine, which, following the Indian example, was based on spruce resin. Various other flavorings and chewy substances were experimented with subsequently, the nadir of nutrition being reached when chewing gum was made from paraffin wax, described by the *Encyclopedia Britannica* as "devoid of taste and smell and characterized by chemical indifference." About 1890 the United States, which had been importing chicle as a rubber substitute, suddenly noticed that South American Indians chewed it, and decided to try it out in gum. It proved more resilient and a better carrier of flavors than any substance previously used, and its career as rubber was abruptly terminated: it was worth much more for chewing gum. Intensive advertising of gum began about 1900, with such success that by 1924 the United States was using up the entire Latin American output of chicle and needed more. Other gummy materials from tropical America were pressed into service, while jeluton and sorva were brought in from the East Indies. This was still insufficient, and today the base of most American chewing gum is some synthetic compound.

If Americans have become the world's greatest gum chewers, it is for the same reason that the Indians were gum chewers—they suffer from dietary deficiencies. The Indians chewed spruce gum or chicle because their diets were badly balanced. Psychologically, the physical act of chewing may be interpreted as an attempt to deceive the body into believing that it is being nourished (and so it is, but to an insufficient extent). Gum chewing is a more sophisticated development of twig chewing, generally recognized as a sign of dietary deficiency. Twig chewing, before chewing gum came along, and to a lesser extent afterward, has been habitual particularly in those sections of the country which are the most poorly fed, such as parts of the Southeast and the Middle West. (The betel chewers of India live in a country subject to famine.) Twig chewing has been so widespread in the United States that a popular name for one of the plants oftenest chewed, sassafras, is "chewing stick."

The chewing of sassafras and spruce twigs is not solely a trick to fool the stomach; twig chewing supplies vitamins. As recently as 1933, Mandel Sherman and Thomas R. Henry reported in their book, *Hollow Folk,* that in a badly nourished mountain community they had observed children gnawing instinctively on young twigs. Writing of the unbalanced diets of the first half of the nineteenth century, Richard Osborn Cummings remarked:

> Safeguards, now little thought of, served to protect against vitamin deficiencies. A popular drink, spruce beer, made by brewing the tips of young spruce, was an anti-scorbutic. Twig-chewing perhaps supplied vitamins. A combination of these two practices appeared in spruce chewing gum, put up by a Maine firm and widely distributed in the fifties.

The habit of gum chewing in the United States appears thus to reveal Americans as suffering from dietary deficiencies, which were present at the beginning of our history and are still with us. They were not created basically by poverty, but by bad eating habits, for deficiency is betrayed by other types of obsessive near-eating in circles where it is obvious that poverty cannot be the cause. Thus in Townsend Hoopes' *The Devil and John Foster Dulles,* we learn that the late Secretary of State was given to picking the wax drippings from candles at formal dinners and eating them, a classic giveaway of dietary deficiency.

"Now, Mr. Dulles, I scold my children for doing that," said one outspoken woman. "It's bad manners and it messes up the tablecloth." "I know; it's awful. It's a terrible habit," replied the Secretary. "But I just love to chew candle grease. I've been doing it all my life."

Much earlier James Fenimore Cooper, no doubt prejudiced by seven years in Europe, had been more vehement, but perhaps not far off the mark, when he wrote:

> The Americans are the grossest feeders of any civilized nation known. As a nation, their food is heavy, coarse, and indigestible. . . . The predominance of grease in the American kitchen, coupled with the habits of hearty eating, and of constant expectoration, are the causes of the diseases of the stomach which are so common in America.

"Constant expectoration!" The unlovely habit of spitting, which made the cuspidor a once all-too-American article of furniture, was frequently referred to with distaste by European visitors to the United States. It may have been a symptom of dietary deficiency too, especially when it was associated with the chewing of tobacco. That chewing tobacco was most common and lasted longer (but it is not dead yet) in the South may be not entirely the result of the fact that this is tobacco-growing territory. Nicotinic acid is used in the treatment of pellagra; the only region of the United States where pellagra has ever been a problem of any importance is precisely in the badly nourished "hog and hominy" belt. It may be that chewing tobacco was an instinctive defense against pellagra as clay eating had been an instinctive palliative of hookworm.

Another sign that a nation is not being well fed at its meals is a habit of eating between them. It is also a means of assuring that there will be no improvement in this evil situation, for it sends its victims to the table without appetite and therefore without the capacity to absorb a sit-down repast which in the ordinary course of things should be at least better balanced than the random samplings of food with which the average American stuffs himself throughout the day.

> Americans are the world's greatest snack eaters [Dale Brown observes]. . . . It has been estimated that we spend more than a billion dollars a year on potato chips, pretzels, crackers, corn chips, packaged nuts, cracker sandwiches, shoestring potatoes and other tidbits. And this figure, enormous as it is, does not include the money we spend on such other preferred snacks as candies, cakes, doughnuts, cookies, yoghourt, hors d'oeuvre, cheese dips and gourmet-type [sic] nibbling foods. No one really knows why Americans are such great nibblers. The habit goes way back and probably has something to do with our restlessness. . . . Snacking as a full-fledged national folkway probably got its impetus from the free-lunch counters set up on top of bars in the 1800s to encourage drinking—and to provide men in a hurry, as even Americans of the 19th century could be, with a quick snack of raw oysters, salty ham or pretzels. "Gobble, gulp and go" was a motto of the day. [And

still is.] In modern times the supermarket has encouraged the habit as much as anything, putting temptation on the shelves that are easiest to reach. The automobile no doubt has helped. "Let's pull up for a bite to eat" has so long been a national refrain that entrepreneurs have marred the landscape with roadside "eateries" of all shapes and sizes, including two-story tin pineapples and hot dogs as big as trucks. Largely as a result of motoring, many food fads have spread fast. The taco has worked its way up from the Southwest to Oregon and Washington, and even now this crisp-fried tortilla, its pockets filled with chili, cheese and chopped iceberg lettuce, may be heading east. Meanwhile the pizza continues its boom . . . in restaurants and diners across the country motorists are cramming themselves at this minute with hot dogs, fried clams, frozen custards—an almost limitless variety of snacks.

The foods Mr. Brown cites in this passage constitute a very mixed bag: a good many of them certainly deserve to be classed with junk foods. There is indeed a broad overlap between the categories of junk foods and fast foods; one is tempted to wonder if the second term is not simply a euphemism for the first: however blameless the nature of a fast food, it risks becoming junk food from the very fact of being eaten fast. To get full value out of our food, we must pay some attention to it as it goes down. Digestion is not as gross a function as you may think: the stomach is a slave to psychology, responsive to mind as well as matter. Gulping down television dinners with attention to nothing except the mayhem occurring on the screen is viewed by the stomach as an insult. It broods, and refuses to separate from this merchandise whatever small proportion of nourishment it has been allowed to retain by a manufacturer more alert to salability than to dietetics.

Another factor which often prevents the American from deriving full value from his food is timidity. Many Americans do not like to eat and many other Americans are afraid to eat. This may be a transfer of the Puritan distrust of food as a tempter from the moral to the hygienic context.

American food [wrote Gault and Millau, in their guide to the United States] is . . . placed under the double sign of mass production and the sacrosanct fear of microbes. . . . The fear of microbes . . . completes the gastronomic ruin of American food. We French swallow an impressive number of microbes and we even boast of having gotten along well with them for a score of centuries: *Si vis pacem, para bellum!* [If you want peace, prepare for war.] The American, a perfectionist, abandoning resistance tactics, has declared an offensive war on microbes. A total war.

Pasteurization has not only debased butter and cream. It touches nearly everything, from Camembert and Brie to, in the state of New York at least, trout. . . . Haunted by microbes, American industry has not ceased to "enrich" its products. It is impossible to put anything into a can or a bottle without adding to it vitamins and products with complicated names,

> intended no doubt to impress the user, who, without them, would think himself cheated. . . .
>
> It is not for us to judge if the digestive troubles which affect a great number of Americans, along with numerous cases of gastro-duodenal ulcers, come partly from the chronic chemical irritation of their intestines. More modestly, we accuse their chemistry, if not of killing people, at any rate of killing taste.

When the American goes abroad, he often avoids the food on which foreign peoples are obstinately thriving because he is afraid of it. ("Don't drink the water.") Wherever the American Army or Navy maintains foreign bases permanent enough to justify the implantation there of service families, the visitors get their food from the Post Exchange or the ships' stores. In every foreign city which shelters a more or less fixed American population of any size, commissaries are organized to provide the cautious citizens of the United States with breakfast cereals and canned soups from home, to preserve them from the dangers which lurk in *boeuf bourguignon, tagliatelle alla bolognese,* and *arroz con pollo.* In Paris, the world capital of good eating, there is not only an American Embassy commissary, to which some privileged persons in addition to Embassy personnel are admitted, but a privately organized American businessmen's commissary, which imports safe nourishment from the States. Americans may be adventurous in the matter of the places to which they go, but not in what they eat when they get there. On July 4, 1975 (a date chosen, let us hope, without sarcastic intent), the *International Herald Tribune* subjected Americans to a humiliating experience—gastronomic reproof from a citizen of the nation which had bestowed its bad habits on us. James Fenton, an Englishman, wrote in that paper a report on the Americans who had stayed on in South Vietnam after its military collapse:

> There are more than 10 Americans in the provinces and more than 60 in Saigon. One place to meet them is at the Viet-My ("Vietnamese-American") restaurant, a place where unadventurous Americans used to eat food they felt they could trust. The management has now passed into the hands of the Provisional Revolutionary Government, although the name has been kept for the moment. Only the central section of the restaurant is illuminated. The singers and the band, I suppose, are now in Guam. But the menu, although reduced, retains its former lack of character.

There must certainly have been enough American food left behind to feed a mere sixty customers for some time, and there is perhaps no other market for it in Vietnam, a country which has a subtle and imaginative cuisine of its own, seasoned with *nuoc-man,* not catsup.

Another example of an American abroad avoiding foreign cooking was spread before the French public on June 6, 1975, by Philippe Bouvard, columnist for the mass-circulation evening daily, *France-Soir:*

> The cooks of European royal and presidential palaces are not happy; the subtle dishes that they prepared with the greatest of pains for President Gerald Ford are being replaced *in extremis* by stews prepared by a United States chef in an American military base and delivered by helicopter. After which, before the successor of Nixon sits down at the table, an official "taster" makes sure that the dishes destined for him contain no poison. Gastronomy and confidence reign.

The experts seem to be in agreement—in the midst of plenty, the American today is undernourished, not because he does not have the right foods at his disposition, but because he doesn't eat them. His most conspicuous lacks are calcium and iron. Certain other minerals, and some vitamins, are neglected too, and putting them back into foods from which they have previously been removed does not produce quite the same effect. Moreover we are beginning to find out that our recently acquired habit of stuffing ourselves with vitamins has its ominous side. The theory used to be that if you took more vitamins than you needed, the rest would be excreted automatically, and if vitamins did you no good, at least they would do you no harm. This comforting opinion has now been revised. It appears that a glut of vitamins—of some vitamins, at least—can affect health adversely. Pills are no substitute for food.

The American contrives to combine deficiency with excess: he does not absorb enough calcium and iron, yet he does absorb too much salt—ignorant, no doubt, of the fact that a high sodium diet encourages blood pressure to rise and is associated with cardiac vulnerability. It is perhaps because he is accustomed to overseasoning his food—being uneducated to the perception of subtle flavoring—that the introduction of monosodium glutamate (MSG) into the United States was accompanied by outbreaks of the "Chinese restaurant syndrome." In America MSG produced disorders unknown in the Orient, where MSG had long been a commonplace in the diet. Is MSG dangerous in itself, or is it American excess in its use that is dangerous? Are we not, indeed, a people given to excess? We eat excessively, we drink excessively, we season excessively—and when someone convinces us that we are in error, we react excessively by plunging headlong into a food faddism as pernicious as the eating habits from which we want to escape.

As for our excessive use of sugar:

> Convinced health foodists [writes Sidney Margolius] fear the potential damage to health from sugar, and they may be right. Dr. [Roger J.] Williams said in *Nutrition against Disease* that sugar "appears to be statistically more conducive to arteriosclerosis than is starch," and some other researchers agree. (An English researcher, Dr. John Yudkin, reported that a person taking more than 100 grams—3.5 ounces—of sugar a day is

five times as likely to have heart problems as a person taking less than 60 grams.)

(May we add that the food faddists who try to escape the dangers of sugar by switching to honey are fooling themselves? The various claims made for honey, for instance that it is less harmful to the teeth than sugar, are fallacious. In some respects, sugar is a healthier sweetener than honey.)

Following the moderate example of Gault and Millau, we will not accuse sugar of killing people, but only of killing taste. Of all the factors that have brought American food to its present pass, the sweet tooth is probably the most culpable. As we have pointed out earlier, the ubiquitous use of sugar is incompatible with a general use of wine, which as an accompaniment of food has been the great shaper of subtlety and savor in the development of such cuisines as the French and the Italian. However, wine is not essential to the development of a fine cuisine, as Chinese cooking demonstrates. Chinese food is customarily accompanied by tea, and it is significant that on its home grounds, the tea is not sweetened. Elimination of sugar from the drink leaves room for the use of sugar, discreetly, in the food—without overdoing it, as is our habit when we wash down our sweetened food with sweetened coffee and milk, or, even worse, with soft drinks. Many Chinese dishes do in fact include sugar in their sauces, but often the taste-deadening effect of the sugar is corrected by an accompanying tartness, for the sweet-and-sour theme is often sounded in Chinese cooking. For Western cuisines, though beer is a permissible companion to heavy, coarse, unimaginative food (German cooking, say), wine is the great encourager of quality. By virtually ruling out wine as an everyday, every meal, every man beverage, the high sugar content of American food has dealt the first blow, a heavy one, to our ability to produce or to appreciate superior food.

Sugar is probably the least subtle of all seasoners (except salt, of which we make abusive use also). It blankets all other flavors and prevents us from really tasting them. Even when sweetness is the whole point of something we venture to take into our mouths, we manage to overdo it—consider that pair of beach-resort and country-fair favorites, cotton candy and saltwater taffy, of cloying sweetness, both almost pure sugar.

Deadly also is the effect of the onslaught of sugar in achieving the gastronomic corruption of the young. How does today's youngster educate his sense of taste? By submerging it in a sea of sugar from the time he gets up to the time he goes to bed. Sugar on his cereal, soft drinks at intervals during the day, sweet between-meal snacks, and, when he sits down at the table, a sweetened beverage with his excessively sweet food. He learns to taste nothing except sugar.

Two generations of such a regime—or perhaps no more than one at the present rate of the ingurgitation of sugar—and the good tastes of simple foods and of well-cooked foods may well be forgotten. There will be no demand for them, because no one will be aware that they can exist. They will drop into the oubliettes of history. More justified than ever will be the cries of the Cassandras who warn us that we are still cherishing dyspepsia as a national malady, and that more and more we are sinking into the engulfing quagmire of gastronomic illiteracy.

XXX

Where We Are Now

VERY LITTLE in the history of the United States from 1776 to our times presages the confusion and near-collapse which from mid-century on has overtaken American eating. Were it possible to envisage in one great glob the totality of what is now eaten in a single day by our fellow-citizens, whether at home, in institutions, in fast-food joints or in expensive restaurants, and to judge it in the light of what the country has produced in the past, and what it might produce again, the word "garbage" would rise inevitably to mind and gorge. Americans are consuming, along with unheard-of amounts of valuable proteins in their meats and cereals, and along with vast quantities of fruits and vegetables full of good nutrients and vitamins, tens of billions of dollars worth of packaging, additives, and advertising, as part of their total estimated two hundred and fifty billion dollar contribution to the food industry, agribusiness, and the conglomerate corporations that decide what we will be allowed to eat.

This American gorging on good food, bad food, and non-food must be seen against a background of ever-increasing scarcities, particularly in cereals, that face a world population which threatens to double itself in the last quarter of the twentieth century. For a long time now, countries of Asia and Africa have depended on the availability of United States surpluses either as gifts or as purchases, but if North America has a few bad crop years, or if cash clients raid the granary as the Russians recently were able to, there "won't be any core to this apple"—nor any surplus to give away. And besides, the formerly overfed Americans, still without a population-growth problem equal to that of the rest of the world, are going to have to tighten their belts one way or another. The majority will probably manage to fill their stomachs every day, with food of decreasing quality "extended" with various substitutes, rammed down the consumers' throats by intensive advertising, and priced to cover ever-mounting distribution costs.

The inflation of the early 1970s has already played its part in the drama, for rising food prices have added millions of people to the already swollen ranks of the undernourished and filled the usually well-fed with anxiety. To the poor, who live at the arbitrarily determined "poverty level" or below, the Federal government tries to offer some relief. After various types of means tests, the poorest may become eligible for food stamps or surplus foods. Their children may receive free school lunches whose menus are in good part determined by what surpluses agribusiness has on hand to sell to the government (and thus avoid causing any price decline). But the latest victims of inflation include those pensioners and the like who once considered themselves at least relatively secure. These are the new customers for dog and cat food who have no pets, and the new recruits for petty crime who are tempted to try shoplifting in the supermarkets to improve their ordinary diet.

Thus the chronicles of American eating are bound to include non-eating, or at least the failure of a large part of the nation to eat as well as it deserves. This failure has been thoroughly documented by the nutritionists, to whom the authors must perforce refer the reader for voluminous technical substantiation, and has been actively contested by the food industry, which by its advertising seeks to convince us that we never had it so good, thanks to in-house geniuses such as those who found ways to remove the natural properties of wheaten flour and to replace them with synthetic vitamins and minerals. Catchy jingles conceived on behalf of the manufacturers of soda pop remind us that the truly best thing in life is a cola drink, while competing commercials declare the virtue of another soft drink to lie in its absence of cola. All proclaim that their slop is "natural," whatever that much-abused term means today, and since the bottlers are not required to specify all that goes into their products, we may only be sure that the ingredients are as natural as the rapacity of the merchandisers and producers.

The supermarket is today a worldwide institution; it is here to stay, and deserves to be examined more closely, particularly as it affects the housewife. In the United States it has been the barometer of skyrocketing food costs and the constant witness to the displacement of non-branded items (which may be assumed to carry less advertising and promotional costs) by the national brands (which must bear their share). For years supermarket chickens, culled young from the poultry factories as unlikely egg layers, were a cheap if not particularly enticing buy in meat. A skilled buyer would prod breast bones until she found a good bird and would have it weighed. Today she is confronted with either brand-named birds at premium prices, or a debris of chickens and chicken parts, pre-chopped for her alleged convenience, pre-weighed and securely wrapped.

The vegetable and fruit departments are beginning to discourage picking and choosing by pre-packaging citrus fruits, tomatoes, turnips, radishes, lettuce, cabbage, and onions. Potatoes are usually exempt from the wrappings, but green corn, which is wrapped by nature, is sometimes plasticized on trays of three or four ears to prevent the buyer from peeking at the kernels.

Anyone who roamed through the produce markets of our cities in the first half of this century can recall the profusion of stacked vegetables and fruits that was usually invitingly displayed. Butchers would gladly trim a cut of meat before the buyer's eyes. Though he traditionally weighed his thumb with the steak or roast, the butcher had not yet adopted the electric band saw which invariably cuts a steak too thin at one end and too thick at the other. A proper grocer would sell flour in bulk, beans and coffee from the sack, and weigh any of them out as required. A few items were pre-packaged, mostly the new-fangled breakfast cereals, salt, and of course jams and canned goods. The selling system was personal and involved persuasion by the storekeeper or his clerk, recommendations and information about the merchandise on hand that day, and a right of free reply by the consumer. Today massive national advertising replaces most discussion; the customer talks to the supermarket help only (1) to complain about prices; (2) to ask why an item is no longer carried; and (3) to ask where the store has hidden some item which is essential but not known by a brand name. If the client has not been sufficiently conditioned by advertising, another silent salesman is on the job—the studied layout of merchandise in the aisles of the supermarket, and the placement of various items on the shelves. To locate staples the buyer passes *chevaux de frise* of highly advertised branded goods, including costlier versions of the item being sought. At toddlers' eye level are laid out those products a child has seen advertised on television, the cereals, snacks, and other sugared junk he has been taught to dun Mommy for, and to place in her shopping cart if she fails to respond to a hint.

Nobody eats in supermarkets, it is true, but the supermarket, the super-hyper-supermarket, and even the lowly "superette," the Mom and Pop version, all reflect the marasmus of American nutrition.

Of course in present-day eating there are high and low points to be observed, and there will never be an end to discussions about taste, in the sensory definition. If the authors deplore the overloading of breakfast cereals with sugar that has taken place in the past forty years, they might also applaud the apparent drift of American wine drinkers away from the fortified (with sugar) wines to more natural table wines. If they feel that the American household has gained nothing but time in the ever-increasing use of convenience foods, and that the extra time is probably devoted to the absorption of more television advertising for other "convenience" products, from microwave ovens to pancake mixes, they must also note that many young households are attempting to find their way back to the simple if time-consuming satisfactions of baking their own bread, canning tomatoes, beans, and corn, and studying the recipes of other nations and our own past. But if the couple has children, the in-house cook and dietitian will have to battle with the forces of Madison Avenue for the minds and hearts of the young. Mommy's healthful creations may seem pale to kids who have watched animated bears singing to them about crunchy sugared treats or have been given the live example of a couple of their peers joyfully hauling Daddy off to the hamburger joint to give him the finest meal of his life, a double-decker of ground beef drenched with a proprietary sauce, washed down with a cola or a shake, ingredients not necessarily revealed. Not many mothers, or fathers either, are prepared to put on a show equal to what television offers on behalf of its clients, and as a result when the toddlers become pre-teenagers with buying power of their own, the majority are likely to seek out the joys of the group-munch of junk-eats at their favorite fast-food place.

It should be remembered that the process of education by advertising which has destroyed regional eating in most of the United States is no new thing, and that in the last quarter of the twentieth century its force will be at its maximum. If the current inflation is not stopped, the alternatives to the banal diet of industry-selected and industry-backed foods will have become prohibitively expensive or may well have vanished.

The authors, in attempting to evaluate the present state of American eating, have recourse to some simple criteria (it has been the fashion to call these things "guidelines") which they have not concealed:

> They believe that fresh food is preferable to preserved, and that food grown not too far from the place of consumption is the best, even if it is only available in season.
>
> They believe that variety in ingredients and in ways of preparation of dishes makes eating more enjoyable and probably more healthful.
>
> Choice of foods should be, within reason, up to the consumer instead of reflecting the wishes of agribusiness and the food industry giants (e.g. the "hard-ripe" tomato).
>
> Most industry-created foods, such as the sugared breakfast foods, "potato chips" synthesized from powdered dessicated potatoes, synthetic fruit drinks notably shy on fruit, dry soup mixes, and meat and fish "extenders," are in the opinion of the authors properly called junk and should be so regarded.
>
> They believe that mankind is meant to drink milk (for a starter), water, wine, beer, tea, coffee, and some spirits if desired, but never should we sluice down pop, crushes, colas, "un-colas," or milk-shakes which must be called simply "shakes" since they contain no verifiable quantity of milk.
>
> They fancy the idea of eating with a certain decorum, preferably

> while seated in a quiet place with or without company, and taking their time. The idea of talking about food at table does not shock them.
>
> While they admire quality and diversity of food, they deplore its conspicuous waste as evidenced in over-large servings. The steak house which grossly overcharges its clients for more than they can eat does not atone by offering a "doggie bag" for the uneaten portion. Restraint is appropriate in home cooking, too, unless the cook is a genius at using leftovers.

Unfortunately ideally fresh or nutritious food is not readily available, even at a price, in most small American communities. Only banal prepared and semi-prepared food is generally at hand. Yet a substantial, balanced diet for the whole community requires government aid, from whatever level, either by subsidies, by education of consumers, or by supplements in the form of stamps and free lunches. If these are absent the signs of malnutrition are going to increase. At present the forces of the marketplace are narrowing the consumer's choice, depriving him at one end of the scale of high-quality foods and at the other end making the basic nutrients more and more expensive. The need for many households to have both husband and wife at work has cramped the style of many otherwise willing home cooks, and has driven the family out to the fast-food places which have proliferated across America. The estimated take of all these chains for 1974 was over thirty billion dollars; in 1973 they took in twenty-eight billion, or roughly ten percent of the food-industry total of about $250 billion. Of course, their clientele did not consist solely of harassed housewives, but rather of a good cross-section of eating Americans.

Two chains lead the pack: McDonald's with 1973 sales of a billion and a half dollars, and Kentucky Fried Chicken with sales of a billion. Twenty-three other chains followed, the least of them selling sixty-six million dollars' worth of its specialty.

According to John C. Maxwell, Jr., writing in that well-informed weekly *Advertising Age,* it cost folks more to eat at home than to eat out in 1973. In 1965 one meal in four was taken outside the home, in 1973 one in three, and the projection for 1980 is that every second meal will be taken in some sort of eating place, and not from Mom's kitchen. There will be some in the food industry to debate this, and such inroads on sales for home consumption will be fought by every possible type of convenience food old and new, and by massive doses of TV, radio, and print advertising. In mid-1974 General Mills was testing Mrs. Bumby's potato chips made from dried potatoes, packaged in a re-sealable aluminum tube, and in 1975 a similar product, Pringles, successfully invaded the chips market. A subsidiary of H. J. Heinz was testing "frozen self-sizzling deep fries" and brown potatoes in butter sauce. Lipton,

Thomas J., Inc., had launched a flavored soy meat extender as "Make-A-Better Burger," while Ocean Spray was seeing whether frozen cranberries would find consumer approval in Columbus, Ohio, and Minneapolis. Professor Theodore Hedrick at Michigan State University had invented his own way to make children (and some adults) find cheese scraps more palatable by adding cocoa, marshmallows, peanuts, and non-fat dry milk with milk solids. The result is nutritious and chocolatey, but at the same time back in the chocolate candy factories other experts, appalled by the rising cost of cocoa beans, were seeking a synthetic chocolate substitute which would be legally permissible in or around candy bars. Through a subsidiary of Monsanto Corporation a combination of an artificial flavor and a "bulking agent," with a chocolate-like appearance and taste, was found which may fill the bill.

Pet, Inc., was trying out Downyflake "natural" waffles, and Heartland "natural" bread, as part of the industry trend to associate the word "natural" or a synonym with almost any product. The biggest soft drink maker of all was having his airwave minnesingers chant that his cola was the "ree-al thee-ing" in four syllables, having years ago musically convinced his audience that "Coca-Cola is Coke" in a bit of legalistic singing double-talk contrived to drive off imitators. As S. I. Hayakawa the semanticist has said, advertising thrives on rhythm and ambiguity.

While the merchandising power of the food conglomerates bears down heavily on the average consumer, and the lobbyists for the industry put their pressure on the governmental agencies that are supposed to make the rules, the motivational researchers such as Dr. Ernest Dichter have been pursuing their analyses. Over ten years ago, Dr. Dichter put his question "What is the psychology of soup; what is the right marketing approach for spaghetti and for meat?" and seemed to find his answer in the obvious fact that foods were not purchased for nutritional values alone (he said that if they were, most of us would be living on Metrecal, a balanced-ration compound then popular with weight watchers) but really were chosen for their potential to make us happy.

Today's food world is "so full of a number of things, I'm sure we should all be as happy as kings," as Stevenson suggested, so we might take a look at how the "kings" of American eating, those gastronomists who have both the means and the inclination to go all the way in search of food-happiness, are making out. No simple ritual like the old Scottish grace "We ha'e meat, and we can eat, and so the Lord be thankit!" is enough to rally the American *Fresser* of today. Instead, the trend is for organization, membership in one or more of the fine-food societies such as the International Wine and Food Society, Les Amis d'Escoffier, La Chaîne des Rôtisseurs, La Confrérie des Chevaliers du Tastevin, La Commanderie de Bordeaux, et cetera. Locally, countless groups are formed in honor of food and wine, sometimes by professions (M.D.'s and D.D.S.'s are notable joiners), sometimes around a special group of wines (Italian, German, Alsatian, Provençal, California). The nucleus is usually an amateur anxious to share his knowledge with friends and neighbors, or, in the case of the more elaborate cult groups, a man or woman with time and money who has no objection to becoming the center of an exclusive society where membership is supposed to connote affluence, good taste, and, of course, social status and acceptability. Such a person may either form his own small group under its own banner as, say, "The Middletown Society of Gourmets," or seek affiliation with one of the national orders by demonstrating that he has put together a dozen or two presentable members capable of paying their dues to the national organization, and of holding three or four dinners a season in a style which passes for high gastronomy in his city.

The problems presented for all gourmet societies are identical, varying only in degree from one city to another. Once membership exceeds what the richest member can serve in his own home, the group must depend on public or semi-public eating places—hotels, restaurants, or private clubs. And of course, the Middletown Gourmets are not going to be satisfied to sit down to eat whatever the Union Hotel or the City Club provides every day. The meal must be special, or the *raison d'être* is lost, and at this stage there begins a ceremonial courtship ritual between the dinner chairman and the head chef. The maximum of bundling is when the establishment is required to provide an actual rehearsal of the menu to be served, and to subject itself to more or less intelligent criticism by the committee; the minimum is when the gourmet chief brings in a suggested menu, the chef points out his limitations, and *faute de mieux* it is agreed that the meal will be something a bit out of the ordinary, and the best the establishment can provide for the price.

The price! In the inflation current as this is written it can be almost anything. Dinners costing the subscribers seventy-five to a hundred dollars each are usual in New York, and frequently all the wines served have been donated or acquired separately from another budget. Becoming a certified gourmet by this route is by no means inexpensive. In any of the top societies, the Tastevin for example, the initiation fee, an annual membership, and the charge for two or three dinners runs about $500. Should the novice eventually become one of the superior officers of the Order he must order a crimson and gold robe and hat costing about the same, and must pledge himself to make a pilgrimage to France to attend one of the Chapitre dinners held in the Château du Clos de Vougeot, at Nuits-Saint-Georges, in Burgundy. Many of the faithful manage the trip every year, and declare it well worth the detour, as the Michelin Guide might say.

The dinners of American gourmet groups have much in common with each other, though they are far from identical in actual menus. Usually they begin with a "reception," which is in effect a cocktail party, though the drink may be champagne or aperitif wines. Contrary to the French tradition to which most of them pay lip service, the reception includes a lavish spread of hors d'oeuvre, hot and cold, and sometimes freshly opened clams, oysters, or scallops. Frozen crab claws, once the rage, seem to have vanished. Until the late sixties, caviar was available in generous spoonfuls, but lately even the most lavish gourmet societies have been priced out of the caviar market, for one greedy guest could easily eat sixty dollars' worth of the best fresh Malossol before being elbowed away from the buffet. Of course, few guests made such pigs of themselves. If a good champagne was served, ten or twelve cases were no more than enough for a reception crowd of 250–300.

The dinner was still to come, of course, in another room, decorated in the style of the season or the colors of the gourmet clan, with tables set for ten or twelve, and a head table for the dignitaries.

First course, a clear soup or consommé (which is where a classic French dinner would have begun) with no wine, except perhaps a splash of sherry or Madeira. Next, the fish, usually in a mousse or *turban,* but sometimes poached whole, always with a sauce reflecting for better or worse the talents of the kitchen brigade. With the fish a white wine, often the best table wine of the evening, since it could withstand the rough handling of part-time waiters in a way the older red wines coming later never could. America possesses no such craft designation as *sommelier,* and hanging a cup and chain on a waiter's neck does not teach him to handle old wines as if the bottle contained nitroglycerin, or to fill a proper wineglass between one-third and half full, not more. These little techniques are being learned by thousands of American civilians who will practice them in their own homes as part of their attempt to shine up their life-style through gastronomy, but they will remain forever foreign to the great majority of waiters mobilized for the grander gourmet occasions.

After fish, meat. Beef, lamb, veal and pork: beef enveloped in pastry (beef Wellington) somewhat more popular than roast saddles of lamb. Veal usually "Orloff," and not much in demand at that; pork of any kind has proved a sure loser at most banquets. Out comes the best red wine at this point, unless the wine committee has mistakenly saved it for the cheese, two courses later. A cold game or poultry dish, the portions carefully glued to the serving platter in an aspic, get the second-best red wine as its accompaniment, but between the two high-protein items there may have been served a sherbet doused in Calvados, fruit alcohol, or brandy, a *trou Normand* or *coup du milieu* which serves to stun and anesthetize the taste buds.

Sometimes the *chaud-froid* has a bit of fruit or a leaf or two of salad accompanying it, or occasionally the salad turns up with the cheese course, a practice frowned on by the wine lovers, even though lemon juice substitutes for vinegar and the oil used is mild. But the cheese course, however sumptuous in the variety of cheeses displayed, is likely to reveal the American gourmet's failure to protect his own interests. There are some good American cheeses, even of the soft-ripened variety, but protectionist legislation originating in Wisconsin has for some years prevented the importation of the many unpasteurized, naturally ripened cheeses of the Brie and Camembert type which at their best are among the glories of gastronomy. So when the cheese platter is offered to the banqueter it is likely to have on it a tasteless soft-ripened domestic cheese which spent the night in the refrigerator, in company with a desiccated French goat cheese and, perhaps, a segment of Roquefort (the real thing) which luckily has survived the usual mishandling. The final red wine is offered at this point.

The feast reaches a climax with a fancy ice, a *bombe* perhaps or a frozen soufflé which has been prepared in advance, as the whole meal must be. (Even a roast will usually be cooked about half-way, then given a final blast a few minutes before service time.)

Our typical banquet comes to an end with coffee, cigars, brandy and liqueurs. (There may have been a sweet wine or a second champagne with the dessert, but not always.) Then come the speeches, and the chef, with his principal assistants, is invited in for a glass of something, compliments from the chairman, applause from the diners, and at the French-linked gatherings, the so-called *accolade,* where the presiding gourmet gives each chef a ritual peck on each cheek.

It is no secret to anyone that everywhere in the United States, and to some extent wherever Americans travel, dollars they spend on the costlier restaurants are expense-account dollars, at least fifty percent of the total. In certain establishments the percentage is even higher, and as the late and lamented Jack Kriendler, founder and partner of New York's Jack and Charlie's 21, confided to one of the authors some years ago, "If corporate spending for entertainment were to be outlawed, we would have to close." The heirs of Jack and Charlie (Berns) have by now become owners of considerable choice Manhattan real estate and would survive such a closing handily, but the same could not be said of their competitors.

American restaurants above the mechanical production-line category, standing apart from the fast-food chains, yet below the de luxe category, do indeed exist, and some of them are doing exceedingly well. Usually their owners are the managers, and spend long hours on the premises. It is not at all necessary that they be familiar with an international or a complicated cuisine, but rather that they have the sense of quality, and know when something is good and when it is bad, either among the aliments going into their kitchen or the dishes coming out. One could name in every large city of the United States a sincere and successful restaurant which has earned its fame in no other way. But one might be hard put to it to name a second or a third.

Other restaurants have achieved renown simply by staying in the same place a century or so (Fraunces' Tavern, Durgin Park, Antoine's, et cetera), by their location at the seaside or in mountains, by a combination of exclusionary tactics coupled with lavish hospitality to those admitted (New York's Stork Club, now replaced by a mini-park open to all with waterfall and hot dogs), or by such ostentatious mnemonics as the unfailing recognition of every guest who has ever appeared there once, even if it was ten years before (New York's previously mentioned "21"). Not one of these historical, geographical or social attributes is in any way a guarantee of first-quality food. In fact the monomaniacal fervor of a quality-mad restaurateur may well drive him to neglect all the promotional aspects of his trade and, disregarding usual practice, serve a stranger just as well as he would an habitué. Such places acquire a fame which builds from mouth to mouth, no one quite knows how, until perhaps the proprietor finds his clientele has outrun his ability to find or produce profitably the food he believes in, and he disappears. Sometimes, after a period in the wilderness these prophetic geniuses surface in a new environment, but their second dispensation is rarely equal to their first. Cooks finally do get tired or bored (one thinks of Dumaine and Guérard); while inspired non-cooking restaurateurs tend to die on the job (Point and Soulé).

At no point in its culinary history has the United States been able to create an educational structure turning out personnel for hotels and restaurants in the way the French and Swiss do, yet it is not for lack of trying. Perhaps what is lacking is the system of apprenticeship which smacks of peonage to Americans, though it has produced thousands of competent and successful craftsmen throughout Europe. Americans realize that careers in food preparation will always involve long hours, put in at odd times, and this for many young people outweighs the fact that wages are now competitive with other trades. Unionization of the culinary trades is only partial, but where union contracts exist, as for instance in the big hotels, there are twenty different jobs covered, from chef down to cook's helper, the starting grade, and the establishments themselves are graded by the unions and told how many men or women must be employed.

One system of grading is by the number of items on the menu. The "specialty menu" category of restaurant serves fewer than twelve items, including beverages, and here is where one finds the McDonald's, the Burger Kings, and most fried chicken chains. The "limited menu" class may serve up to thirty items in all, and may well stick to meat or fish with potato and salad, skipping vegetables but offering a selection of desserts. The "standard menu" may run to fifty or eighty items, and is the type of fare offered by most restaurants and hotels making some culinary pretense. The top category is that of the "extensive menu" which may carry over one hundred items and requires a large crew, with most specialist jobs filled. According to Robert G.

Haines, an expert writing for the American Technical Society, if one adopts the extensive menu "you can use all the leftovers"—or feed them to the help.

Leftovers, about which was written the French saw: *"Faire la cuisine, c'est l'art d'accommoder les restes"* (Cooking is the art of making leftovers taste good), are conspicuously absent in those American restaurants where the newest technology is to bring in pre-cooked dishes in a frozen state and defrost them as they are ordered. This procedure, which originally was brought into being by the airlines, has proved successful and efficient—except from the point of view of the consumer. In one major city an attempt was made by a consumer group to have a city ordinance passed which would require restaurants to specify on their menus that such and such a dish was frozen and had been made off the premises. The attempt failed, and so did a compromise which would have required the restaurant to indicate that it served pre-cooked frozen food without specifying just what. The quasi-unanimity of the purveyors in fighting the proposal and the compromise is indicative of the extent to which such congelations are already being used, without identification. A restaurant which features brook trout, for instance, runs the risk of a considerable loss if it has a supply of fresh fish on hand and nobody orders any for a few days. If they all come in frozen solid, awaiting only the magic touch of the micro-wave oven, they can stay for weeks without loss to the restaurant. They may not have the quality of a fresh fish, however, but how many diners will complain so long as theirs isn't actually rotten?

A well-known pancake chain which features Brittany *crêpes* with various fillings creates all those stuffings at a central kitchen and delivers them frozen in appropriately sized containers, ready to be decongealed as demand requires. Howard Johnson's has denied that it pre-cooks and freezes its hamburgers, although it admits to having pre-cooked its one-piece steaks in the past. Nobody seems to have been upset by this revelation, made by Pierre Franey, famous French chef who is now a consultant to the chain as well as a collaborator with Craig Claiborne, star gastronomist of *The New York Times.*

The authors do believe there is some light at the end of the tunnel of present-day American eating, but not many of the chinks through which it shines are those of public eating places. Most of the practicing gastronomes find something to admire in our so-called "ethnic" restaurants. Top rating in this field goes to the Chinese, in recent years, for the variety and ingenuity of their cuisine. Where once the dishes were strictly Cantonese and cheap, compared to other American restaurant food, today the range is over several Chinese regional styles, while the prices in the spruced-up Chinese restaurants are comparable to those practiced in equivalent American, French, Italian, or German places. Nor is it rare to find households where the amateur cook has experimented with Chinese stir-frying in a *wok,* that unique and indispensable pan which is perhaps the most widely useful kitchen utensil ever invented.

The larger American cities now make a place for the various foreign cuisines mentioned above, and restaurants serving them are patronized by average citizens not specially conditioned by ancestry or national origin. There are two exceptions, however. Kosher cooking has never attained much popularity among those who were not brought up in Jewish households, despite the fact there are a number of excellent dishes traceable to Germany, Bohemia and the Balkans to be found among this otherwise somewhat bland treatment of food. And "soul food," the good-times cuisine of the American blacks, perhaps the cooking most directly traceable to the early days of America and plantation life, gets little attention from the white population of a city as big and cosmopolitan as New York. Obadiah Green's "Obie's" at the crossroads of Harlem at 135th Street and Seventh Avenue welcomes the white gourmet and sets out the finest traditional black dishes, yet it is little known even to the dozens of restaurant sleuths who write for the metropolitan weeklies and dailies.

As the twentieth century's final quarter arrived, American eating habits were endangered by the inflation of the two preceding decades, which lifted the price of meat, milk, and sugar, the favorite constituents (with wheat flour in its various forms) of our national fare, to what might once have seemed intolerable heights. Family income for most people had risen, too, but there was a new element to be dealt with, the need of other countries for their share in the United States agricultural production and the need of the United States to sell it in order to buy oil, which America needs almost as much as it does food. In this situation, food in general is not going to come down in price, agribusiness is not going to have to change its ways to please the consumer, and the manufacturers of processed foods are most unlikely to improve the quality or increase the quantities in their packages. Instead, they can be counted on to reach new heights in salesmanship and the arts of merchandising, packaging and promotion. Wheat or pork or sugar may be in short supply, but advertising never.

We may conclude that the American gourmet, if we may assume his existence as a group or even an attitude, is not today enjoying any real renaissance, and that the average diner-out is offered less variety and poorer quality in what he gets for his money. The rich and the very rich will always be able to eat relatively well, but the simple diner-out feels the deterioration and blames it on inflation, not realizing or caring that his food has been gradually becoming more banal for several decades. On the composite authority of a number of older professional cooks who have been feeding Americans for at least a score of years, the diner-out's taste has been dulled, while his attention has been drawn off by the interior decoration of eating places, by flowery menu descriptions of dishes, and by technical tricks of presentation—not that the customer is blameless, since he may bring to his restaurant his own prejudices, or his latest diet fad. In most cases these attitudes have to do merely with what he will *not* eat or, if he will, how long he believes it should be cooked, neither much of an inspiration to the restaurateur or his chef. When French gastronomy adopted as a principle the theory that good restaurants are in great measure made by difficult customers it took as basic the idea that for every dish there is a right and a wrong way of preparation, and that a paying guest should be presumed to know which was which. The American tragedy, so far as French-schooled chefs are concerned, is that the public doesn't know and doesn't give a damn, and that a special effort or careful presentation is usually a waste of time. Since few cooks have the abnegation of the Carthusian monks, who would construct a work of art or piety in the solitude of their cells only to destroy it before it could be admired, it is no wonder that when creations are sent out of the kitchen and no appreciation comes back, interest flags, the cook's ability diminishes and his creations become few and far between.

It would be gratifying if one could report that in average American homes eating is a joy, and that home cooking promises the revival of honest gastronomy. No Gallup, Harris, or Roper poll will ever be able to analyze all the conflicting views on how well or badly Americans (those above the starvation level) are faring, for the criteria are non-existent. An author like Calvin Trillin may go into ecstasies over the hamburger served at a Kansas City beanery, and a doubting reader may go there to check him out. If Craig Claiborne hangs laurels on the brow of André Soltner for his *mousse de brochet,* gourmets with the price can scurry to New York's Lutèce to see if it is deserved. But no guest in an American home has ever admitted, except under torture, that the food served him was execrable. No husband ever brags about what a rotten cook his wife is, or if he lives on a more elevated scale, how bad a cook his cook is. That is, unless the cook was just fired, in which case we may assume the ex-employer is telling us rather how high his own gastronomic standards are.

What can be said, however, is that the seeds of a new recovery and the birth of an American cuisine suited to our own times and our present-day restricted sources of supply are sprouting in the kitchens of some of our middle-class homes. Not yet in sufficient strength to stand up against the flood of glop and slop which flows like slime through the supermarkets, the sprouts may yet flourish. For one thing, today's houseperson (we might as well settle for the term, since househusbands are shopping and cooking, too—"houseman" has a different and largely archaic definition) is more literate than in previous centuries, and is exposed, though fleetingly, to more varied ideas on what is edible, particularly in the area of health and nutrition.

Nutrition as a cult has made considerable waves in the twentieth century, both in Europe and America, but are the people actually better fed? In the case of children, the answer is certainly yes. A whole generation of post-war European children grew taller (and presumably, but not certainly, healthier) because their parents became aware of their needs for milk and other proteins during the stressful years of the Second World War.

Despite all handicaps the enlightened middle-class American home cook really tries for excellence. Where there are children there is emphasis on the healthful qualities of the food provided at meals, and some surveillance of the amount of snack junk consumed. Not only is there a cookbook library ranging from the giveaway brochures of the appliance manufacturers, some containing sound recipes, and standard works such as *The Joy of Cooking,* Fannie Farmer, and various James Beard tomes, but also esoterica such as *Mastering the Art of French Cooking.* When it comes to teaching the cook of the house, television is variably helpful. Programs dealing exclusively with Greek and Italian cooking, though their appeal is limited and few viewers actually tackle the recipes presented, have reminded our enlightened houseperson that such cuisines do exist. Since their standard dishes tend on the whole to be easier to make than many in the French repertory, their contribution is not to be ignored. American home cooking is belatedly becoming international, in a small way.

We do much reading of recipes, in cookbooks and in newspapers and magazines. All the women's magazines feature recipes, menus, table settings, and their accessories. Such institutions as the magazine *Gourmet* have prospered mightily by offering, more for contemplation than execution, the dishes of the whole wide world in glorious color and dithyrambic text, plus a sagacious dosage of homely American recipes which an ordinary cook can manage. The formula of two-level discussion of cuisine, pie in the sky on the one hand and nuts-and-bolts advice on the other, is seemingly the most successful. Yet a well-financed magazine, *Epicure,* which attempted to "do food" in a style apparently aimed at fun-loving young couples presumed ignorant of and uninterested in gastronomic history and jargon, foundered after only a few issues. Yet it did not ignore the mythic needs of people who like to read about food as well as eat it. As available food becomes more uniformly banal, whether in stores or restaurants, the mythical element becomes more necessary, and the admen are there to supply it. The big hamburger chain created its own personalization, Ronald McDonald, a pantaloon figure pleasing to kids, and later undertook to teach children to fight inflation ("a big word") by eating a special combination package of hamburger, French fries and cola. In the TV commercial of a different firm, a loving wife earns favor with her lord and master by donning a kimono and mixing into his hamburger some Japanese-style vegetables. It's all in a spirit of fun, good citizenship or love, and demonstrably it works, as does the good-fellowship hoopla which permeates the flourishing American "gourmet" associations. But whether it does anything for American eating as such is doubtful. The substitution of myth for meat has enhanced the American concept of good cooking to a considerable degree, and has encouraged a great deal of experimentation, some of it successful, by home cooks. Beyond this, deponent sayeth not.

If one reads the vast literature on modern American food, American hotels and restaurants with their exoticisms and embellishments, and the gastronomic flights of fancy of the rich, one might conclude that American eating was never better. This is not the case, unfortunately. Richer, more costly, more wasteful, yes. But better, no!

XXXI

Where Do We Go From Here?

OUR SURVEY of more than four centuries of American eating, the last two those of the independent nation which calls itself the United States but which has shown and acted out its divergencies every step of the way, can only be brought to a close by an attempt to project what is coming next. The authors have no illusions of omniscience, and the field of food production and use is so vast that everything one can say about it is provably true and provably false at the same time. Taste, despite Latin proverbs, is and will be continuously in dispute; therefore it is no use trying to guess whether Americans will like what they are going to have to eat for the next twenty years, or whether they will hate it.

The outlines of what they are going to get are fairly discernible. To begin with, more and more of the nation's food will come from industrial sources, and these will be set up for maximum production with high mechanization and minimum human labor. The farmer's machines will be more powerful and more efficient and will be used for a shorter repertory of crops. What this farmer (probably a corporation) plants may have been improved by such hybridization as has already given birth to the "Green Revolution" that has increased yields in rice and other grains, and its growth will have been controlled by even more elaborate fertilization and similar chemotherapy. Already some populations have objected to the new high-yield rice as less palatable than their former staple, but there is not much chance that they will be listened to, nor is it likely that the California and Florida industrial truck farmers will give up their hard-ripe tomatoes, bred for toughness under transport conditions, for something more tender and more tasty.

A threatened shortage of corn and wheat, shortage taking into account America's need to export for cash and for famine relief, means that more beef will be grass-fed, not grain-fed, and leaner meat will replace much of the marbled prime and choice cuts. The public may well be eased painlessly into the change by a switch in grading procedures, and there is little chance that prices will be lowered in consequence. Doctors will applaud the downgrading as better for the nation's health, while beefsteak amateurs will be unhappy but will continue to demand the national treat of broiled steak, baked or fried potatoes, and salad with the "house dressing." In meat as well as poultry and vegetables and fruit, the national supply will have less variety, and the quality will continue to flatten out. The standards of basic cleanliness and nutrition will undoubtedly improve, thanks to consumer pressure groups, but throughout the whole system of food production, preservation, and distribution there has always been room for improvement in sanitation and surveillance. Perhaps the government agencies that watch over our diet will be less deferential to the giants of the industry than they have been in the past.

The contribution of the smaller, independent producer will continue, of course, with its ups and downs for him, and variable results for the consumer. Farmers will generally try to adopt the commercially viable techniques which can assure them a dependable market, but a few will try to specialize in better-grade fruits and vegetables, and even in more succulent poultry or leaner, tastier hogs. These products will not usually find their way into the mainstream of food distribution (except in desperation and at a loss to the grower) but they will nevertheless come to market. The specialists' crops may find their outlet in the top grade of supermarket, and in the luxury retail stores of the more affluent neighborhoods and suburbs, but in diminishing volume as compared to the straight industrial crops.

Whether or not the United States remains in a recession, there will be a continued upswing in home gardening, including an increasing number of those following the organic theory by avoiding chemical fertilizers, and by composting leaves and vegetable wastes. Wherever the labor cost is no problem, and when the investment in equipment is held to a minimum, home gardening can be a profitable and healthful occupation for the family, and provide a desirable variety of foodstuffs which the big stores cannot match. Vine-ripened tomatoes, fresh-picked lettuce of the tender varieties the industrial growers refuse to handle, or corn grown within yards and minutes of the pot can provide the householder not only with gustatory delights but also with an insight into what the big business of agriculture is failing to deliver at any price.

The restrictive nature of agribusiness, by which growers must concentrate on relatively few crops and few varieties of each, is to be noted again among the food processors. Let the consumer beware of the words "new" and "improved," as he should of "natural" and "farm-fresh." "New and improved" is a phrase which has covered a host of frauds, fakes, and adulterations, intended to facilitate marketing. On this, a most pointed comment has come from the pen of a man who knows his way in the field of promotion, the artist and movie maker Andy Warhol, who says, "Progress is very important and exciting in everything but food. When you say you want an orange, you don't want someone asking you 'An orange what?' "

Let us ignore the vague if promising words and concentrate on reading the fine print, wherever such information exists on can or package. In the foreseeable future processors will be obliged to come clean, more and more, as to what goes into their goodies, for although the consumer movement has had some setbacks, as has the campaign to save our environment, there is every reason to believe that though we will never achieve truth in advertising, truth in packaging is an enforceable ideal.

A critic of the British system of government once nastily said that it was "designed to give the Englishman the *sensation* of self-government." It will be many a year before the American consumer is rid of the highly advertised and skillfully merchandised foods and drinks which at best provide principally the *sensation* of nourishment. Not many (but still quite a few) Americans experience actual pangs of hunger. Those who do hardly constitute a rich market for the inventors of "new" food preparations, so the appeal will most often be directed to "flavor-cravers" (another Madison Avenue word and concept devised for a soft-drink account). Basic foodstuffs, clean and bland but otherwise bereft of any distinctive flavor or consistency, will be given new characteristics by the addition of those substances which can most closely duplicate the nostalgic virtues promised by the advertising. Product names will continue to evoke the mythic and emotional associations, as in the past, by liberal use of terms like "log cabin," "chuck wagon," "Grandma's," "home-style," et cetera, which evoke but don't inform. Thus foods which once had their own very special identity will be turned into vehicles for the presentation of new conceptions of their nature which have been determined by market research, computerizations of sales histories, and "creative" product managers. As examples, the transformation of yogurt, once a dairy product with a characteristic slightly acid taste, into a sweetened concoction flavored with fruit jams, chocolate, and other flavorful additives proved so successful that plain yogurt became hard to find in many supermarkets. So the metamorphosis of peanut butter, memorable for sticking to the roof of one's mouth, into a salvy fluffed unguent flavored with whatever the computer has indicated as the current taste, can hardly be far behind. Thanks to the alchemy of the flavor blenders, it may be possible to eliminate the actual peanut and put in its place a less expensive vehicle for the chosen taste effect. It is not likely anyone will die from ingesting these "new" and "improved" foods, and those inventions that succeed will make fortunes for their adapters.

The trend toward convenience is already exemplified in one of the recent products launched by General Foods. For centuries people have been wrestling with the problem of how to make coffee to their taste, from the heady Oriental brews and the pungent *espresso* to the thin tinctures popular in American roadside diners. Recent versions of soluble "instant" coffee, with or without caffeine, have proved popular. Now, evoking the image of the French breakfast drink, with its pair of pitchers, one containing a strong black brew of coffee (and sometimes chicory), the other full of heated foamy milk, General Foods has created "Cafe au Lait," which should give, by the simple addition of hot water, the sensation of enjoying breakfast in Paris or Geneva. However, the *"lait"* in question is not milk at all. Vegetable oil, corn syrup solids, sugar, sodium caseinate solids, monoglycerides and diglycerides, dipotassium phosphate, lecithin, artificial color, and artificial flavor, plus coffee, of course: there you have "Cafe au Lait."

We repeat, we should all learn to read the fine print.

Home canning and freezing of foods, which fell into something of a slump during the years of great affluence prior to 1972, took a turn upward as hard times seemed to threaten. The statistics in support of this are derived from the sales of jars and caps, up 175 percent from the preceding year. The rise in food prices awakened home gardeners, and the home canners who attempt to profit by seasonal abundance of fruits and vegetables in their local markets. It is interesting to note that the jar, cap, and lid industry, including sales from sideline divisions of the big glass producers, totalled well over $70 million, with an advertising budget of less than $400,000, some of it spent explaining to the public that the manufacturers had underestimated the 1973 demand and asking home canners to be patient.

The future of America's bread promises to be an exciting contest between the huge baking firms and the small specialty bakers. Since 1970 the industry has claimed that fifty-two million pounds of white bread are consumed each day in the United States, yet they admit that this figure has not increased since then. The introduction of other breakfast products such as protein-charged drinks and sweet chunks resembling something between fudge brownies and a soldier's iron ration has cut into the sales of their soft, spongy product, they say, but they are not inclined to attribute this to a change in public taste. The industrial bakers plan to maintain their preeminence by heavier advertising or the insertion of child-aimed premiums in the bread package itself. Nevertheless there will be other attempts to improve the image of the white loaf, presumably by a well-heralded addition of proteins or minerals, rather than by improving the bread through any change in the basic proportions of flour or shortening. In 1973 the United States Department of Agriculture found that of the $13,200,000,000 spent by consumers for bakery products, 80 percent went for the various procedures of marketing, while only 20 percent represented "farm value"—what the producers of the raw materials received.

The specialty bakers, smaller local firms for the most part, have less marketing cost, but on the other hand have none of the economies of mass production. Their bread products will continue to be more expensive for the consumer, but some of them will be more interesting and of higher quality, as well as more directly nutritious. This will not help the poor, who will continue to buy the inflated white loaf because it is cheaper and readily available. Some young households will get around the problem by baking their own bread, with a few of them grinding their own wheat and other grains in little kitchen mills. They may not save any money this way, but it should provide interesting loaves.

Though many young people will turn toward home cooking, the statistical curve seems to show that by the time our nation is in its third century of independence, it will have every second meal away from home. Since breakfast, whatever it consists of, is to be counted as one of those meals, it sounds as though the urban habit of skipping that meal at home and having something to eat at a quick-lunch place on the way to work will continue. So, too, the practice of having the coffee, juice, and pastry ("Danish" in New York) sent in from outside, to be eaten at the employee's desk. The 1974 recession made the "brown bag lunch" popular, especially in the Wall Street district, where many a handsome briefcase contained the luncheon sandwich brought from home. Normally, mid-management executives would have been able to lunch at company expense in the course of entertaining a client or a prospective client, and to do it in a restaurant of some standing, but the lean years caused a sharp reduction in many such perquisites, particularly those of industry's lesser ranks. Meals eaten away from home, for statistical purposes, may have been prepared at home as was, and is, the worker's lunch box, but most such meals will be eaten and paid for in establishments ranging from the greasy-spoon lunch counter and its local variants up through the more efficient and pretentious fast-food shops to the sit-down "family" restaurants, the steak houses, the fish restaurants, the "ethnic" galaxy, and finally the truly de luxe restaurants and clubs.

At the peak of the years of affluence, the American public was spending less than twenty percent of its income for food, a lower proportion than in any other country. Should this rise to thirty percent, a figure comparable to that of Great Britain, experts like William G. Phillips, chief executive officer and chairman of International Multifoods, predict that there will be some major changes in what Americans purchase, and in consequence eat. But until then, Phillips feels, the consumer will continue to demand beef unstretched by soy extenders, sugar on his doughnuts, and more new products, emanating from the research and development efforts of the industry. "The average young housewife is better educated and has more knowledge of nutrition," he commented, adding that marketers must do a better job nutritionally, without specifying just how.

Nutritionally speaking the citizen with money in his pocket can pick up the various elements he needs for good health in his supermarket or in the restaurant of his choice, provided of course that he knows how to pick and choose from the shelves and display cases or the menu handed him. We have every reason to believe that this will still be true, short of some nuclear holocaust or planet-wide catastrophe. But the form in which his proteins, starches and complementary elements will be presented may well be less varied, less attractive, and, if recent experience is any guide, the American consumer will have only slight reaction and even less redress. If the food industry accepts the responsibility not to poison him and not to let him starve, and if the government maintains some effective control over the industry, that is about all the consumer can realistically expect. The choices must inevitably be his own, though the items spread out before him differ in their packaging and promises, rather than in their nature.

Restaurants of every category will continue to stress all those attractive qualities having little to do with what turns up on the plate: prestige, location, exclusiveness, hospitality, charm, décor, high prices, low prices, bright lights, low lights, historical associations, elegance, homely simplicity, ample parking space, beer, wine, spirits, discounts, credit cards accepted, friendly waiters or waitresses, arrogant *maîtres d'hôtel,* notables to stare at, crowded tables, spaciousness, glowing recommendations from various critics, plaques awarded by various magazines, insignia of gourmet societies past and present, insignia of local service and luncheon clubs, or autographed photos of sports and show-business personalities, furnished by their press agents. If the establishment's image is personalized by the name of a chef (dangerous unless the chef is securely pinned down by contract), or by a food specialty he is supposed to have originated, it at least will indicate that the management believes that the culinary aspect of the enterprise has some meaning.

The problems of the restaurateur who wants to make and sell the best food, attractive to a sophisticated "gourmet" clientele, will multiply in the years ahead. In addition to the difficulty of obtaining prime meat, poultry, and fish beyond any reproach, he will have a hard time finding the personnel he needs, either for the kitchen or the dining room. Immigration from those countries which traditionally provided the best-trained craftsmen has slowed to a trickle, partly due to United States regulations having been tightened up and partly because conditions in Europe have been more favorable to the worker, who in several countries is as well paid and even better protected by social insurance than in America. Anti-discriminatory measures, laudable in their intent and workable in most cases, come down hard on a restaurateur who is attempting to put together a kitchen brigade along classic European lines. Though many hotel and restaurant schools, some attached to major universities like Cornell, others subsidized by industry, as is the case of the Culinary Institute at Hyde Park, New York, are turning out competent and enthusiastic graduates, few of these young people will consider a further apprenticeship in a de luxe *bistrot,* where advancement will necessarily be slow, when they can find work in the mass-feeding chains or the major hotel circuits with the prospect of early promotion to a supervisory or management job. Moreover, the culinary training they receive will inevitably include the use of many short cuts such as the use of pre-mixes, congelations, and various handy additives which a true *toque blanche* would disdain, but which have become increasingly common, and it would appear nonsensical to many of these graduates to return to the laborious hand work of a bygone era.

What *is* the restaurant of the future going to be like?—a matter of some interest to those of us who expect to survive automobile accidents, asphyxiating smog, and the poisons and pollutions of our environment, since the futurologists tell us that we are going to take ever more of our meals outside of the home. We have already with us an example which may represent the apotheosis of the Machine Age (the present) or the opening of—what? The Nuclear Age? The Space Age? In any case, the future.

At the lower end of Manhattan Island, looming large over the area which once included New York's famous Washington Market, a happy, noisy warren of booths selling meat, poultry, game, vegetables, flowers and cheeses, with shrubs and plants in springtime, stand the twin towers of the new World Trade Center, the city's tallest building complex. Built on a $950 million budget which the Port Authority of New York and New Jersey had no trouble financing, the Center has been subject to extended controversy as to its utility and its esthetic value to the skyline and some doubt as to the likelihood of its filling up with rent-paying tenants. Under the guidance of Joseph Baum, a small, dapper man who is recognized as a prestidigitator in the restaurant world, there is evolving a feeding machine which must eventually satisfy, in various clubs, pubs, cafeterias and shops, the hungers and thirsts of the fifty thousand tenants who will inhabit the Trade Center, the eighty thousand visitors who will swarm in and out of the offices, and the estimated 250,000 New Yorkers and New Jerseyites who twice a day traverse the street-level concourse area of the Center in order to reach the subways and trans-Hudson trains that bring them to the downtown Wall Street area and take them home. When, as, and if the buildings are fully occupied, this task will be assigned to forty individual eating and drinking places, located at strategic spots that market surveys have demonstrated as being where the people will most often have to be, such points as "lobby floors," where one transfers from an express elevator to a local. These "sky lobbies" will give the consumer a chance to have a hair cut, a beauty treatment, to patronize a newsstand or deposit his pay check in a bank branch, as well as to see to his or her needs in food or drink.

On the concourse level, ground and basement floors, where the traffic is heaviest, the accent will be on fast-food eating and stand-up drinking. As the morning crowds arrive, these shops will serve hurrying employees the ritual breakfast package of coffee and pastry, to be eaten at the desk on the boss's time. Most of the eating places on the floors above will concentrate on serving lunch, at a reasonably priced average check. Thanks to the elaborate production systems involved, by which all basic dishes are prepared at least in part in a central service area below decks and sent aloft to the pantry and serving areas to meet the demand, Baum and his fellow consultants hope to achieve impressive economies in a business where labor costs have always been the dominant concern. Given the large population to be fed, the central service kitchens can afford to do all their food preparation from scratch, using fresh materials rather than foods prepared outside. Basic sauces, major roasts, soup stocks, and baked goods will flow upward to all the serving stations, where each one in its own individual décor and following its own theme, which might be Italian, French, Greek, New England, or pure fantasy, will convert these elements into dishes as imaginative and varied as possible by adding the touches of the unit's sandwich man or *garde-manger.* By shifting from one restaurant point to another, always within the Trade Center, the resident consumer may hope to avoid food boredom during his working week.

Joseph Baum, who has spent his entire life in the food industry, starting out in a small summer hotel owned by his relatives, is more concerned with motivation of his culinary staff than almost anything else, for he sees in it the key both to restaurant quality and to public acceptance. For his Trade Center venture he has managed to persuade the culinary unions that it is a good idea to permit workers in one specialty to be shifted to other activities, even within the limits of a single working day, as a way of broadening their knowledge of the field and keeping them interested, to say nothing of providing some manpower balance in a business where everything comes in in a rush and goes out in a lull, with the only peak at noon.

In addition to the mass feeding on the concourse floors, and the more relaxed caterings in the "sky lobbies," on the 107th floor of the first tower there is already a club-restaurant surpassing in size, elegance, and complexity anything yet devised to feed, solace, and stroke the executive personality, which in the Wall Street area of New York alone has a wide choice of "executive" luncheon clubs, in addition to the luxurious private dining rooms maintained by individual banks and corporations. "The Club at the World Trade Center," as it is called, boasts thirty rooms and nine hundred seats for lunching or dining. There is a main restaurant called "Windows on the World," with a spectacular view (when there are no low clouds), a bar and grill, and a stone-floored, vaulted-ceilinged "Wine Cellar in the Sky," lined with members' rare wine reserves on display behind glass, and described as "intimate, moody." For those who over-indulge there will be a health club, with exercise room, massage service, a sauna, and a whirlpool bath.

Baum and his associates have established their *bona fides* as analysts of future trends in American eating by having worked in every aspect of public feeding at one time or another and his collaborators share with him a sense that eating is an element of American culture not to be taken lightly, intimately related to every other factor of the economy and the environment.

"Our business competes for appetite, time, and money," says Baum. "We compete with everything, television, backyard barbecues, movies, swimming."

Today more young people are willing to enter food handling as a craft, and Baum feels they will learn to be creative within the present system, a system which has arisen for various reasons, including the failure of the old-line restaurant business to perform. He regretfully notes that many secretaries or clerks today prefer lunching on a hot dog and cola drink to waiting in line for a place in a restaurant where they could well spend four times as much and be treated cavalierly by the person serving. "Today," he says, "the public rejects the investment of time and money in large amounts if it is only to provide a mediocre dining experience. People prefer to make a smaller investment *knowing* they will have a mediocre experience but will save the difference for some other pleasure value, not involved with food. Therefore the steak and salad places are patronized in preference to a so-called high-level restaurant which can still provide only an equally mediocre experience."

For all his realism, Baum maintains, "There is no reason to be in the restaurant business unless you are in love with your work. I love the rhythm of a restaurant, and trying to make of it something more than is expected."

But are the fast-food chains *restaurants* in the true sense of the word, a place which *restores* one, puts one back in shape? Hardly. They are serving points, kitchenless, as distinguished from kitchen-restaurants where food is cooked. Baum foresees a lowering of our standard of living at all levels and in relation to the rest of the world; he believes we will have to give up the present uneconomic feeding of cattle for the sake of more efficient land use; he sees greater use of synthetic fibers and protein in our food as likely. As for convenience foods—their purpose is not so much convenience as devices to aid selling. He shares with his aide, Michael Whiteman, the idea that a long decade ago many restaurateurs, perceiving that people were reading cookbooks and taking an interest in "gourmet" foods, set up restaurants that failed to come up to the promises of what the food buffs were reading. Many of them tried to put over by the use of pre-cooked convenience foods what they could not accomplish in the kitchen. They put glamour into the menu's phraseology—but neglected what they put on the plate. These hustlers, some of them innocently, ignored the fact that more and more Americans were traveling abroad and had learned there was such a thing as a fresh string bean or a ripe pineapple.

Against the traveled sophisticates must be aligned the millions who consider that lunch at McDonald's and dinner at the Hot Shoppe make up a gastronomically adequate day. (Their breakfast may have been Orange-Plus and a Breakfast Square.) The popularity and success of fast-food places, says Whiteman, is a marketing phenomenon, not a food phenomenon, which bears out the contention of the authors that the secret history of food in America is being written in the columns of such journals as *Advertising Age*. Things will get worse, but the limitations the higher echelon of food industry experts detects are not seen as limitations by the Americans who are its mass market. Few sense that there is any burger but a well-done burger. A test of customers consuming "thick shakes" has revealed no interest whatever in the fact that they contain no milk.

The trend of the highway fast-food emporia is now toward another slightly more expensive shop of the Denny's or Sambo's type. Here, in a sort of familiar medley, one may find the same fried chicken one might have had at an exclusively fried-chicken stop, burgers just as from the Burger King, fish 'n chips à la Arthur Treacher, all pre-cooked items, but served to you at a table instead of in paper bags. These are the establishments which, with the long-established Howard Johnson's and the various pancake houses, mark the present evolution of "prole food" outside the home. In the trade, this is known as "cooking by inventory," where at stated times there is always a pre-estimated amount of products awaiting the customer. In the highest-grade restaurants the world over consistency also is sought, so that the house specialities, however complicated, conform at all times to the standard of the master chef. Genius and creativity must yet fit the system of the establishment, or the result is chaos, as occasionally happens. But the "prole" restaurants of America have system, and mighty little else.

It has taken two centuries of national existence for the United States to find itself faced with a threatening dilemma in the handling of its food supply. With inflation rampant and food prices rising everywhere in the world, can the United States afford to ship out its grain (the chief export) either for hard cash or in support of a foreign policy which can be either philanthropic or aggressive, when the retention of our surpluses might, as in the past, assure reasonable prices for the domestic consumer? Is our obligation to the starving of the Third World greater than our responsibility to keep Americans fed at prices they can pay? Is our grain, our most important cash crop, to be used for bringing in the money needed to pay for the petroleum we must import? These questions, with their corollaries, will not be answered easily or soon.

If Americans accept a lowered standard of consumption, notably of food and petroleum products, it does not inevitably mean a reduced standard of living. We were a long time building up to the present level, and those with long memories sometimes think we might have stopped a bit farther back and still be ahead. Radical, wrenching measures have been proposed which would permit us to relieve the immediate pangs of hunger of millions in Asia and Africa, but there is little likelihood that they will be adopted. For instance, a Secretary of Agriculture whose pronouncements have not always been received as nuggets of purest gold came up with the suggestion that the slaughter of half the nation's pets, mainly cats and dogs, would permit a saving of foodstuffs adequate to alleviate pressing Third World hunger. The outcry was of course thunderingly negative, though the annual bill for commercial pet foods is $2,500,000,000. Measures to ration gasoline have likewise been disapproved by four-fifths of the nation, even in the face of a well-advertised shortage, and presumably the same proportion would resist any rationing of food. The suggestion that Africans and Asians straighten things out by population control and a return to subsistence farming on their own account is more agreeable to American ears.

A way out of the dilemma's embrace, worthy of Dean Swift, is suggested by research and testing conducted recently by the manufacturers of Friskies pet foods. With the help of a pharmaceutical house, they have devised a canned food for dogs and cats, available in beef and chicken flavors, which contains a birth control ingredient to prevent pets from coming into heat (it is "reversible"). Should it be possible to treat our food exports to overpopulated countries with a similar ingredient, we might, within a few decades, be relieved of our responsibility to the starving and thus be able to sell all our surpluses for cash again, restore our trade balance and buy all the oil we need.

Prediction is a perilous profession, but any forecast is more acceptable when it contains, along with prophecies of doom, a number of positive elements. Here are a few such:

> The allowable degree of contamination of fish and shell fish by mercury will be reduced by the United States Food and Drug Administration, as new technologies permit better detection of poisons.
>
> Less contamination of condensed milk by lead will be tolerated than previously.
>
> Peanut products will be more sharply watched for aflatoxins, and the present permissible level of thirty parts per billion of these cancer-causing substances, produced by certain molds, will be further reduced.
>
> According to the *Produktschap voor Gedistilleerde Dranken,* a Dutch industrial research group, the drinking population of the United States will in the next fifteen years raise its annual consumption of spirits to nearly three gallons per head. Beer drinking, in the same period, will increase by about a fifth, while wine consumption will come close to doubling. *A votre santé!*

Soft drinks, meanwhile, will find their rate of growth in sales reduced to about three percent yearly, despite great inventiveness on the part of chemists and advertising copy writers. The adoption of plastic throw-away bottles will be slowed by lack of prime petrochemicals needed for their manufacture. Yet by 1985 each person in the United States is expected to buy 142 gallons of fluid per year. Thirty-three billion gallons, in 156 billion containers of all kinds! More states will adopt anti-littering measures, which will lead to recycling some of these containers.

While predicting changes in our life-style, the featured editorial sage of *Advertising Age,* E. B. Weiss, says the consumer will demand higher-quality, longer-lived products. He already notes this trend in cooking ware, for one thing.

Good news for some food processors is that they will be allowed to use up their current supply of labels which have been found by the Agriculture Department to contain misleading information. After that, the words "all," "pure" and "100%" will be prohibited on packages of meat and poultry that contain more than one ingredient; no more "all beef" hot dogs unless they really are.

Prices of foods handled by the specialized health food stores will come down (in relation to the general price trend) as the operators learn more about management and produce is available on a more regular basis. Many freak foods will be dropped in favor of natural (no additives) and organic (grown without chemical fertilizers and pesticides) cereals, fruits, and vegetables.

Available convenience foods will change from time to time as the processors strive to protect their profit margins by getting rid of products whose ingredients have risen in price too rapidly, or that require too much expensive labor. In this way, some of the better-quality packaged foods will give way to more standard banalities which have a cheaper base and will respond just as well to intensive marketing.

More and more supermarkets will accept credit cards for food purchases. Automated checkouts, tied in to computers, will keep constant inventories for an entire chain of stores.

Fixed-price buffet-type meals will become more popular in middle-bracket restaurants in the larger cities, after having proved themselves in resorts of all kinds here and abroad. Their obvious advantages are that they require fewer waiters or waitresses, and in spite of the fact that they provide a lavish display of food, there is not much waste, since much can be recycled for later use. Thus we can freely predict that anyone with money in his pocket will be able to gorge himself on a colorful array of appetizers, build a salad of

> monumental proportions, douse it with a choice of dressings, pick up slabs of cold meats with various garnishes, and return later for a similar foray involving a profusion of pastries, pies, fruits, gelatinous desserts, ices and sherbets—the modern condensation of the sit-down formal dinner of the Victorian age, giving the diner the satisfactions associated with conspicuous waste and unfettered freedom of choice.

And gastronomy?

For several years now the people of the United States have been big buyers of gastronomic literature—both cookbooks and books about food in general. Americans are seeking, it would seem, education in this field; the authors are willing to admit that it is needed. Dare we say nevertheless that we are not sure whether we should greet the spate of food books with gratification or with misgiving?

Misgiving? Yes, for the motivation of this development is not clear. It may be a healthy sign or it may be an unhealthy one. It could be, and we hope it is, the former. Perhaps the increasing deterioration of taste in the nourishment of the Machine Age and the decreasing interest of our industrially produced mass-distributed foods has spurred a desperate public to seek salvation in the guidance of gastronomists. Perhaps Americans have been stirred to rebellion against banality in their daily fare because modern communications have drawn them out of the isolationism of the past, physically if not mentally, and enabled them to make comparisons between the way they eat and the way other nations eat. For at least two centuries Americans have been hearing foreign criticism of their food, but up to now they have shrugged it off. Foreigners' opinions may be listened to tolerantly and with amusement, like those of a child, but they are not to be taken seriously—and, it may be added, those Americans who did acquire a certain amount of gastronomic knowledge abroad were given only too often, on their return home, to dispensing it with the superior air of priests sharing divine revelation, and with a dose of snobbery so enormous as to discredit completely anything they had to say, whether it were true or false. To foreign criticisms of American food, the unruffled American answered simply with what he thought an axiom: "Americans eat better than anybody else in the world."

Today, however, Americans travel abroad *en masse;* and not all Americans on foreign soil avail themselves of the American commissaries dear to the hearts of the more or less permanent proconsuls of business and government. If the traveling American has not had his taste buds irremediably atrophied, he may awake to the revelation that it's true what they say about French bread. And he comes home, perhaps, demanding that American bread, and with it all American foods, should become better. If it is such a demand for improvement which has inspired the present great interest in food literature, good!—for that is an interest in food itself, in its quality, in the reality of eating, and not simply in the artifices too often employed, alas, by those who write about it.

The alternative explanation for American interest in food literature is horrifying. It may be that Americans are falling upon the food books not because of a desire for richer tastes or even for improved nourishment, but as a fad, a distraction, an amusement, a means of making drab lives glitter. They are perhaps seeking new tricks to play with food, not for the sake of the food, but for the sake of the tricks—"conversation pieces." The American addiction to conversation pieces is already a familiar phenomenon in many fields. Are Americans combing the cookbooks for recipes to enrich their eating experiences or for recipes to astonish the neighbors and add sparkle to their chitchat?

The Roman emphasis on the dramatic aspects of eating, expressed in literature by such absurdly fantastic cookbooks as that of Apicius, is perhaps what we are in danger of reproducing. If we are demanding ever more, and sometimes ever more extravagant, cookbooks, it may be because we also are more interested in the drama that can be expressed by our fashion of eating, or the literature that can be derived from our fashion of eating, than in the food we are eating itself. Why might we fear that Americans are in danger of repeating, with modern modifications, the excesses of the Romans at the table, at the same time that we are paralleling their history in other fields and earning the reputation of being the Romans of the contemporary world?

In the days when Nero served his guests nightingale tongues because birdsong is sweet and songbirds' tongues should therefore be sweet also, and Heliogabalus scattered topazes among the grilled ostrich brains at the risk of breaking diners' teeth (conversation pieces both), the Roman Empire, and its food with it, was going to seed—going to seed brilliantly, if you wish, dying in beauty like the leaves of autumn, but dying all the same. Its agony would be long—four centuries. In the meantime, what was the nature of its food?

An observation which occurs frequently in gastronomic works is that the ancient Romans did not cook for the mouth, they cooked for the eye. For the eye? It is this remark which may justifiably arouse our apprehension in the face of the present interest in food literature, for some of it seems to be concerned primarily with cooking for the eye: we are well down that road already. Witness, for instance, the luscious full-color photographs of recommended dishes which cover the glossy pages of our women's magazines. These beautiful pictures are often of inedible matter: food photographers cook, or have cooked for them, special versions of the dishes they want to picture, designed to be photogenic, not to be good to eat—a dish that might melt in your mouth might also melt unappetizingly under studio lights.

Presentation of food so that it will please the eye as well as the palate is, in proper proportion, part of the work of a good cook (indeed, for psychological reasons food that appeals to the eye has an enhanced chance of appealing to the palate also), but proper proportion means that the application of the make-up should never be given so much importance as to alter the quality of the dish. Charles Ritz once remarked to one of the authors, apropos of the prettying-up of food, "While you're putting on the decoration, the dish gets cold." If the appeal to the eye is permitted to become the *raison d'être* of cooking, relegating the appeal to the palate to second place, degeneration has set in. The danger in the United States is that this can happen here—or is already happening. American preoccupation with the *color* of food in advertising and in actual presentation strikes every gastronomically alert foreign observer who reaches our shores.

Gault and Millau underlined this element in American appreciation of food in their guide to the United States, and also that of the dramatic aspect of eating, in which we are in the ancient Roman tradition. When Americans import French chefs and through them discover the French cuisine, they wrote,

> they are naturally drawn to it rather by its spectacular side than by its taste . . . Since a restaurant owner's customers are sensitive above all to the show, why should he deprive them of it? So . . . everything is dressed up or disguised, and tastes are exaggerated . . . "We accept French cooking" [an American hotel manager told us] "only because it is decorative; the dishes have pretty names, and are pleasant to look at." (An essential comment: in the United States you eat above all with your eyes.) [Exactly the criticism formulated about ancient Roman cooking at the period of its degeneration!].

At the very moment of writing, as it happens, a French comment on this aspect of American eating has drifted opportunely into our ken, provided by Jacques Martin, a star of French television and entertainment, and now also of the press, who, visiting the United States, contributed to the July 15, 1975, issue of the mass circulation daily *France-Soir,* an article on American eating.

> In the United States [he said in its course], one eats. One eats all the time. One eats everywhere. One stuffs oneself with food which disguises its extraordinary uniformity under a skillful camouflage of artificial coloring which makes you think that a rainbow has fallen into your plate. Ah! the bright carmine of that candied cherry balanced on a half-slice of orange which was served me this morning with my bacon and eggs!

Alert Americans are themselves not blinded by habit to the prevalence of color in our nourishment. The late A. J. Liebling, in *Between Meals,* wrote of a dispiriting experience when he visited a Connecticut restaurant operated by a French chef who had given up the battle for gastronomic quality because his American customers, though lavish with their praises and generous with their money, were quite as enthusiastic if he gave them bad food as if he gave them good food, and good food requires more effort to provide:

> The Frenchman, discouraged because for four years no customers had tasted what they were eating, had taken to bourbon-on-the rocks. In a morose way, he had resigned himself to becoming dishonestly rich. The food was no better than Howard Johnson's, and the customers, had they not been paralyzed by the time they got to it, would have liked it as well. The *spécialité de la maison,* the unhappy *patron* said when I interrogated him, was jellied oysters dyed red, white, and blue. "At least they are aware of that," he said. "The colors attract their attention."

Americans like color in wine as well as in food, Mr Liebling pointed out, explaining the proliferation of *rosés* as a function of the fact that Americans will drink them. Mr. Liebling himself despised *rosés,* making an exception, however, for Tavel, and for Arbois also, a little obliquely, since, as he points out, Arbois is not really a *rosé,* but a wine of onion-skin color.

> Most often [he writes] *rosés* are made from red wine grapes, but the process is abbreviated by removing the liquid prematurely from contact with the grape skins. This saves time and trouble. The product is a semi-aborted red wine. Any normally white wine can be converted into a *rosé* simply by adding a dosage of red wine or cochineal. . . . Pink champagne, colored by the same procedure, has existed for a century and was invented for the African and Anglo-Saxon trade. The "discovery" of the demand for pink wine approximately coincided with the repeal of prohibition in the United States. (The American housewife is susceptible to eye and color appeal.)

Americans seem already heavily committed to the extraneous aspects of eating—color, drama, showmanship and the providing of something to talk about. Such factors at the best contribute nothing to the intrinsic quality of food; usually they are at war with it. It is this commitment which causes the authors to hesitate before rejoicing at today's devotion to gastronomic literature. What is being sought in it? The basis for a new start, or more material for culinary theater? There are gastronomic writers (and oh! how many restaurants!) who cater to the taste for drama, and whether they do or not, readers have a way of dispensing with the rest. If we are pessimistic about the use the public is likely to make of its gastronomic reading, it is because the worst use is the easiest. The route we are following now is the road to Rome; to continue along it is to follow the line of least resistance, and this, therefore, is what seems likeliest to happen. It is hard to reverse or even modify long established eating habits—so hard as to be almost unnatural.

Are some of the new book readers, discontented, turning to gastronomic books for guidance in an attempt to modify American eating habits for the better? It is a question of education. But education will not be easy in a society which has so often been described as gastronomically illiterate, nor can it be acquired simply by reading books. The sense of taste is, after all, educated by tasting, not by reading, though books can aid mightily as guides and inspirers—or hinder mightily, if they are the wrong kind of books.

Many of us have already been educated *away* from a willingness to grapple with any really assertive flavors; we have been conditioned to prefer insipidity. A. J. Liebling once remarked that the foods we favor most are those with the least taste, not solely, one may suggest, the result of miseducation; the Puritan distrust of food and the timidity with which we approach the unfamiliar play a role too.

> The reason that people who detest fish often tolerate sole [Liebling wrote] is that sole doesn't taste very much like fish, and even this degree of resemblance disappears when it is submerged in the kind of sauce that patrons of Piedmontese restaurants in London and New York think characteristically French. People with the same apathy toward decided flavor relish "South African lobster" tails—frozen as long as the Siberian mammoth—because they don't taste lobstery. . . . They prefer processed cheese because it isn't cheesy, and synthetic vanilla extract because it isn't vanillary. They have made a triumph of the Delicious apple because it doesn't taste like an apple, and of the Golden Delicious because it doesn't taste like anything. In a related field, "dry" (non-beery) beer and "light" (non-Scotchlike) Scotch are more of the same. The standard of perfection for vodka (no color, no taste, no smell) was expounded to me long ago by the then Esthonian consul-general in New York, and it accounts perfectly for the drink's rising popularity with those who like their alcohol in conjunction with the reassuring tastes of infancy—tomato juice, orange juice, chicken broth. It is the ideal intoxicant for the drinker who wants no reminder of how hurt Mother would be if she knew what he was doing.

We are certainly not going to be led away from the reassuring, the familiar and the tasteless toward adventure, innovation, or even the merely new by one form of education which is pressing heavily upon us now, all the more effectively because we do not perceive it as education, nor, indeed, is it meant as such. This is the conditioning of our taste buds by the sort of food supplied to us by the giant corporations which feed us. More and more we are dependent on big business for what we eat, and big business is not interested in gastronomy, it is interested in business. Its point of view is warped further by the circumstance that the great companies which control our food supplies are often not food companies. One could imagine, for example, a national baking company, even though its first thought was for making money rather than making bread, taking pride nevertheless in its product and striving to give us as much quality as possible, short of pruning profits. Man is a perverse creature, whom it is difficult to dissuade from taking pains about his work and feeling satisfaction when it is good. But why should a company concerned primarily, or originally, with long-distance communications give a hoot for the excellence or lack of it of bread made by a company which it happens to have acquired, perhaps more or less accidentally, in some complicated transaction on the financial market? All it wants to know about bread is what figures it contributes to the balance sheet. It happens that at the time of writing the largest national bread making company in the United States, the Continental Baking Company, is owned by International Telephone and Telegraph. Are we entitled to ask "Why?"

> The consumer of tomorrow [William Robbins wrote in *The American Food Scandal*] . . . may, on Thanksgiving Day, as a witness at a Senate hearing testified, bow his head to the deity, but the immediate source of his fare is more worldly. Describing a Thanksgiving dinner of 1971, the witness said: "The Smithfield ham comes from ITT, the turkey is a product of Greyhound Corporation, the lettuce comes from Dow Chemical Company and Tenneco brought the fresh fruits and vegetables. The applesauce is made available by American Brands, while both Coca-Cola and Royal Crown Cola have provided the fruit juices."

The multinational corporations or holding companies which own so many of our big food processing and supplying companies nowadays take pride, like everyone else, in success in what they do, but what they are doing is not making food, it is making money. They do not object if the food sold under their management is good, especially if the profits are good also; but if there is a conflict between producing food of quality and producing food which makes a profit, it is quality which goes by the board. It is almost an axiom that quality in food can be achieved only on the small scale and it is also almost an axiom that profit in business can be achieved only on the large scale. The large scale is what we have.

The result of this situation is that the eager gastronomic student who wants to educate his taste buds is condemned to education without proper textbooks: his texts are tastes, and the tastes he needs to experience are no longer within his reach. He needs to taste as many different kinds of food as he can, but the gamut available is restricted to those foods which can be retailed profitably by the supermarket—the supermarket is now lord and arbiter of what Americans are allowed to eat. He needs to taste, within the limits of a single product, as many different variations on the main theme as he can: the supermarket will usually offer him only one kind of tomato or two kinds of apples at a time, though there will be slight variations as the seasons change. He needs to taste his foods pure—untampered with, unadulterated, without additives or chemical hocus-pocus: purity no longer exists.

The student of tastes is automatically frustrated in his three main desiderata:

1. He wants to taste as many different kinds of foods as he can.

He should have arranged to live just after the Civil War, a period of expanding opportunity. The development of transportation, particularly by rail, was then bringing foods previously obtainable only locally to all parts of the country, and lengthening the seasons of others. At the same time the development of canning and meat processing was greatly increasing the scope of taste experiences available to all Americans. "Canning," wrote Richard Osborn Cummings, in a somewhat flowery vein (but he was paraphrasing James Collins' *The Story of Canned Foods),* "had provided city dwellers with an Arabian Nights' garden with vegetables and groves of fruits trees always ready for harvest, by the side of a sea where fish and crustaceans of many sorts were plentiful." A trifle later Luther Burbank and his emulators were at work increasing the varieties of fruits and vegetables available to the American public. Then came the Machine Age, and its companion, the Merchandising Age, and Mr. Cummings' Arabs folded their tents and silently stole away. The new foods created so painstakingly by Luther Burbank *et al.,* to public applause, during the last half of the nineteenth century and the beginning of the twentieth, were shoveled into the discard unwanted. The nineteenth century had devoted itself to the increase of variety, the twentieth reversed the current and set out to restrict it. The only foods which remained on the market were those which would produce the most profit for the least handling.

> Persimmons have been forgotten [William Robbins wrote]. Rare, too, are blackberries, loganberries, raspberries and gooseberries. . . . Even many of the finest species of squash have disappeared from most stores, and declining in availability are such old regulars as celery root, parsley, fresh turnip greens, mustard, kale, rape, rhubarb and fresh okra. And even fresh garden peas have faded from most counters.

2. He wants to taste as many different varieties of each separate food as he can. Unfortunately for this desire, the food merchants want to handle as few different varieties of each kind as they can. Once again, the decisive factor is the economic advantage of not fragmenting one's efforts, of concentrating on the smallest possible number of maximally profitable products—to which is added in this case the selection of the single most suitable variety, or at least the fewest number possible of suitable varieties, which fit the seller's specifications. "Suitable" from the merchant's point of view does not mean what it means from the gourmet's point of view, or even from the dietitian's point of view—not the variety which tastes best or nourishes most, but the one which can be transported with the least danger of bruising, which is the most resistant to spoilage, which has the longest "shelf life" (that shibboleth of modern merchandising!), and which looks most tempting to the eye whatever it does in the mouth—you buy before you taste. ("You cannot sell a blemished apple," remember, "but you can sell a tasteless one.")

The Comice, possibly the finest pear in the world, will not be offered you, though it is grown (decreasingly, since there is now so little market for it) in the Pacific Northwest; it is so soft that it can be eaten with a spoon, but this is a characteristic which guarantees a high rate of spoilage in transit and in storage. You will eat the Bartlett instead (79 percent of the total American pear-producing acreage). It is not, as a matter of fact, an unworthy fruit, but if you are to educate your taste, you should be able to sample others. In the case of apples, you will have to go out of your way a good deal of the time to find anything but the Delicious, the nation's biggest seller so far (and the world's, for that matter; the United States exports it). When it first appeared, it was from all accounts a more arresting fruit than it is now; but after a few generations of cosmetic attention and a never-ending succession of sprayings, it has become dependably mediocre.

The classic example of what mass merchandising has done to our fruits and vegetables is the tomato, picked unripe and sold unripe, which we have already mentioned. So has the vigilant Mr. Robbins, who wrote of it:

> Our tomatoes have become hard, grainy and tasteless because government researchers, serving agribusiness rather than the consumer, breed them for toughness rather than quality. . . . You'll find . . . these hard tomatoes, developed primarily to withstand the steel fingers of mechanical harvesters . . . bred for mass production, without regard to flavor, that were picked green, sprayed with an ethylene gas that turns them red but doesn't produce either the vitamins or the flavor of vine-ripened produce. In their cellophane-windowed cartons, they will be lined up on the counter, having been shipped across country, while nearby farmers may have vines heavy with tomatoes that are juicy and ripe in vitamins. . . .

3. He wants to taste his foods in the purest form he can, to become acquainted with their basic natural flavors before they have been distorted by manipulation.

A food must be simple indeed to reach the consumer now without having been subjected to some form of artificial alteration. "Today," wrote Elspeth Huxley, "there are said to be some 1,500 chemical additives that may be put into our food to preserve, dye or bleach it, render it more tender, palatable or nutritious, make it smell more or less, or improve its appearance . . . and the number constantly rises." This figure was published in 1965. In 1970 James Trager raised it to between 2,500 to 3,000, and in 1973, Sidney Margolius wrote: "In all, some 3,000 additives are now in use."

> From 2500 to 3000 food additives are now used in U.S. foods [Mr. Trager's account read], including several leavening agents, nine emulsifiers, thirty-one stabilizers and thickeners, eighty-five surfactants, seven anti-caking agents, twenty-eight anti-oxidants, forty-four sequestrants, perhaps a dozen coloring materials, at least eight acidulants, more than thirty chemical preservatives and over 1100 flavoring ingredients. . . .

> The U.S. food industry in 1969 used more than 90 million pounds of flavor and flavor enhancing additives. In addition it used close to 800 million pounds of additives to improve the culture, texture and keeping qualities of foods. This figure was up from 661 in 1965, 419 in 1955. [It is over a billion now.]

These additives are not necessarily noxious, but whether additives are noxious or not is beside our present point, which is taste; but we might nevertheless take the time to point out that in the case of a great many additives already in use nobody really knows whether they are noxious or not; their very number has prevented adequate testing of all of them. Of some, all we can say is that nobody is known to have been adversely affected by them—yet. But opinions about additives are subject to change, as in the case of vitamins. Not so long ago it was an article of faith that vitamins were good for you. No matter which vitamins, in no matter what quantity, were added to foods, the more, the better. But listen to Sidney Margolius today:

> There *are* dangers in overconsumption of some vitamins. Taking excess amounts of A and D is "unwarranted and potentially dangerous," as the American Medical Association puts it. . . . Chronic vitamin A intoxication occurs more frequently in children than in adults. . . . There is great variation in individual tolerance to large amounts of vitamin D. . . . Some warnings against very high consumption of vitamin C have appeared. . . . An official of the New York State Health Department reported in 1962 that a "wave of vitamin B_{12} addiction" had been . . . stopped by the county medical society, and that "excessive" injections by doctors were dangerous because they could mask certain neurological systems. . . . Dr. Orrea Pye told me: "I don't think it is necessary to take additional Vitamin E, and I have been concerned about people taking too much of it." . . . Vitamin K has been reported to be toxic in large amounts and also riboflavin in very high doses. Nicotinic acid, another of the B vitamins, can be toxic. . . . Dr. Allen Forbes . . . pointed out that a teen-ager might undergo a brain operation for a suspected tumor when it was really "a vitamin A high."

Perhaps we should go back to getting our vitamins from nature instead of from the chemist. "Not enough occurs naturally in foods to be toxic," according to Thelma J. McMillan, professor of Food and Nutrition at Iowa State University.

Toxic or not, what *we* want to know about additives is whether they falsify tastes. The food sellers assure us that they do not—except, of course, when they are added to "improve" the taste. "Improving" taste has now reached a point at which specialized companies exist which promise, by cunning combinations of synthetic chemicals, to impart any desired flavor to any nutritious (or for that matter non-nutritious) base.

The authors are skeptical about the claim that artificial flavors cannot be distinguished from natural ones, and also about the claim that additives do not affect flavor, though there are, no doubt, some which don't. Whether or not you can tell the difference depends, probably, on the acuity of your own sense of taste; but how is anyone today to develop acuity or accuracy in dealing with tastes when no foods with natural taste are ever presented to him? Whether additives serve a good cause (many of them do) or a bad one, they are all enlisted in a conspiracy to deprive us of the arms Nature gave us. When they alter taste, they help reduce the usefulness of a sense which not only provides us with esthetic pleasure, but in extreme circumstances can still play for us the role which we may assume accounted for its existence in the first place—that of warning us against dangerous foods. We still decide not to risk the pâté if it tastes or smells bad, but we are disarmed when the maker of pâtés succeeds in immunizing them in advance against the development of undesirable tastes or smells, whether his pâté is *passé* or not. Meat is another food whose deterioration is easily detected by nose or eye—unless the seller has envisaged the possibility of deterioration before the buyer has.

> In meat [said an Agriculture department expert] we've got a product not only subject to easy contamination but extremely amenable to adulteration and to concealment of adulteration. Partially spoiled meat can be subjected to cooking and curing operations and chemicals that make it look [and smell] fine.

Artificial coloring does not usually affect taste, but it deprives us of another weapon Nature had devised to help us choose superior food. We can learn, if we are permitted the raw material to study, what to expect in goodness from a fruit or vegetable by its appearance; but if the seller has tampered with the appearance, we lose our basis for judgment and possess less defense against trickery. The only sense left us for the assessment of a food's quality before we buy is sight and even sight is hampered. The package may leave visible only as much of its contents as may be expected to arouse the desire to buy; it is a highly sophisticated development of the old-fashioned habit of putting the biggest strawberries in the box on top. There are worthy motives for the use of many additives, but in the case of artificial coloring it is hard to think of anything except deception—to put it harshly, fraud.

And what is the food novice to do when he finds himself faced with foods which are entirely synthetic and offer him no, or few, natural tastes at all as a foundation on which to build his knowledge? For instance, an orange juice substitute whose *total* ingredients are

> sugar, syrup, water, corn syrup, orange pulp and rind, citric acid, gum arabic, vegetable oil, potassium citrate, calcium phosphate, vitamin C, cellulose gum, natural and artificial flavors, artificial color, vitamin A and vitamin B.

This is a mild example. There are other formulas which contain nothing natural at all, not even the orange pulp left over after the fruit has been squeezed for other uses. There are ready-made soups on the market which contain no ingredients whatsoever which have not come out of a chemical factory, except, perhaps, salt.

A member of the younger generation seeking to cultivate his perception of tastes cannot expect much help from the alimentary establishment. Will a diligent student of taste be able to execute a flanking movement around this obstacle by seeking his raw material away from the channels established by the food industry? Unfortunately, no; what he will find in the independent food stores is still supermarket food—food which has been grown for the supermarket but which the supermarket, for one reason or another, has not deigned to accept. For the sake of simplicity, let us confine our explanation of this phenomenon to the field of fruit and vegetables.

Too much money is at stake to permit the big corporations which operate supermarkets, or the even bigger corporations which supply food to them, to take any avoidable risk. They are concerned with assuring the supply of goods which the supermarket is going to sell. On the competitive open market prices can rise uncontrollably, to the ruination of corporation budgets. What the supermarkets need are sure, private, controllable sources, automatically available. What can they do about it?

One thing they can do is to sign contracts with the large-scale farmer. He grows food expressly for them, and they see to it that he does it their way. They tell him what varieties to plant, how and where to plant them, how many plants should be placed in an acre, what fertilizers and pesticides to use (they may even be supplied by the corporation) and how and when to harvest. The once independent farmer has become, in effect, an employee of the corporation, following orders, no matter how experienced he himself may be. The advantage for him is that he has a guaranteed market. His crop is sold before it has been planted. He is protected from almost every risk.

The corporations do not contract for what they expect will be 100 percent of their needs. That would be risky too. A slump of demand, and there they would be with surplus food on their hands which they have to accept because they have contracted to pay for it. So they leave a margin: the difference between their minimum estimated needs and what may turn out to be their maximum actual needs they will pick up on the open market.

This is where the independent small farmer comes in, the one who does not have a contract with one of the big corporations. Theoretically, he can grow what he pleases. What does he please to grow? His neighbor, under contract, grows Hybrid Hard Tomatoes; so he plants Hybrid Hard Tomatoes too, in the hope that they will be picked up by the supermarket buyers. Result: you can't avoid supermarket food. It is all there is.

Or nearly all: there are exceptions to every rule. Defenders of taste have managed to maintain, here and there, a few beachheads. We will still be able to find (but only in the large cities, alas) gourmet food stores which depend heavily on imports for their stock in trade, though some of them make deals with small farmers to provide them with the sort of produce which their enlightened clientele demands. We have always had with us also the fiercely uncompromising idealists, mostly in small country towns, where it may be supposed that the sounder techniques of the nineteenth-century rural home kitchens have been relatively sheltered from the inroads of urbanization and of the Machine Age, who have stubbornly continued to prepare food as Grandmom used to make it, and have built up a market for their homemade products by mail. It is a good sign for American gastronomy that these unreconstructed individualists, whenever their food is of the requisite quality, always succeed in finding the hundred or two hundred or three hundred customers they need to keep their small enterprises going.

Many Vermont farmers process pure maple syrup from their own trees and distribute it among eager customers who are always ready to take more than the farmer can provide. It is virtually the only way to acquire real maple syrup; what you buy in the stores may be up to 95 percent corn or other syrups. Connecticut has a guinea-hen farm, whose birds do not enter into the normal channels of commerce, but go, by individual arrangement, to luxury food shops, to luxury restaurants, or as live chicks to individuals with enough land and patience to bring the guineas to table age themselves. New Jersey has the Wayside Farm, Split Rock Road, Boonton, New Jersey, whose operators are devoted to the apple: they will have one tree, or two, or three, bearing such old favorites as Rhode Island Greenings, Early McIntoshes, Summer Permains, and so forth. On the Pacific Coast there is a food buff who spends his time traveling tirelessly through California, Oregon, and Washington, rooting out small producers or special stores which offer foods of a quality or a kind unfindable in the supermarkets; enough persons are interested in his researches to support a professionally turned out newsletter about them. These are random examples; if the authors know a dozen such enterprises, there must be at least a few hundred in the United States—beachheads of gastronomy.

There is also discernible at present what should be a significant sign of the awakening of a new culinary conscience. Whatever you may think of the level of gastronomy in the last century, you are not likely to disagree with the statement that it began to sink when housewives stopped making bread at home and accepted the professional product. The quality of the professional product has been degenerating ever since, and it may be that it will reach the point where it can no longer be tolerated.

> I believe that today a revival of interest in making bread is in full swing [writes James Beard, in *Beard on Bread*]. People are learning that it is possible to make as little as one loaf at a time with a minimum of effort—or perhaps two loaves, with one for the freezer. They are also learning the extraordinary sense of satisfaction that comes from kneading their own dough, the

> sensual pleasure in smelling a yeasty loaf baking in the oven, the sense of accomplishment in offering real bread at a meal—to say nothing of the knowledge that each loaf is full of goodness instead of being just a starchy filler.

Mr. Beard's instinct is sound. The statistics of flour millers bear him out: the making of homemade bread is indeed on the increase. If the flour makers have registered this fact, they have not yet done much to promote it, for there seems to be a certain incoherence in their industry, as we learn again from Mr. Beard:

> The flour called "all-purpose," which is the most generally available flour . . . is not the best flour to use for making bread. . . . There is no standardization of flours from one brand to another or from one part of the country to another to help the breadmaker produce uniform loaves of bread . . . one can safely say that there are no two flours on the market that really react alike.

It could be that this will turn out to be a favorable circumstance for the home or custom breadmaker of the future. The milling industry has not yet decided that the breadmaker shall use one kind of flour and no other, a standard kind chosen to serve the interests of its purveyors and not the gastronomic interests of its consumers, as the organized general food industry has decided that we shall eat one kind of tomato and no other. Alternatives remain open. If there is a public demand for the right type of flour for home breadmaking, the demand will be filled, for it will be profitable to fill it. It seems that the demand exists: one of the happier signs visible to the gourmet concerned for the future state of American eating.

The authors must admit that though they have hope for the improvement of American eating standards (it is that new interest in breadmaking which impresses them most, plus the increase in home preserving), they are far from optimistic. The United States started their culinary history in full fidelity to the traditions of the British Isles, a poor example in the opinion of most of the other peoples of the world, and they have remained faithful to them ever since. Teutons, Slavs, Latins and members of other ethnic groups have reached our shores, bringing with them varied culinary traditions, and have quickly abandoned them, except, in a few enclaves, as nostalgic local phenomena. The inventions of the Indians and the Negroes have been absorbed, leaving few traces. Even the "native foreign" cooking of Louisiana has never flowed into the main stream to give it color. The United States started out with Anglo-Saxon cooking and it is still paying tribute to Anglo-Saxon cooking. It is unlikely that a tradition so strong and so consistent is going to change.

Bibliography

Books of historical content are like cairns. The authors who sign them have added no more than the latest half-dozen stones to the top of the pile. The major part of the structure is made up of the contributions of those who preceded them. One builds, necessarily, upon the work of others.

Which raises a problem: how can the credit which is their due be given to those who laid the lower courses? To a limited extent one can cite one's predecessors, by name and by work, and this we have done whenever we could without interfering with readability. But any attempt to credit every piece of information to its originator (or, more often, to the last person who recorded it previously) would bog a book down in an incomprehensible jungle of references. One might as well not write a book at all, but simply list the references in order to let the reader consult them himself, one after the other—except that in this case there wouldn't be a reader.

Footnotes are one answer: they are the enemies of style, of which an important element is rhythm. The author's attempt is to maintain a smooth and rhythmic flow, so that his words will pass into the consciousness of the reader without distracting obstructions. A footnote is an obstruction. The little index figure which beckons you to the bottom of the page or the back of the book, whether you obey its peremptory order or not, interrupts the flow.

The alternative is the bibliography, though it is more of a pretense than a solution. Authors thus excuse themselves for not having been able to express their indebtedness by printing at least the names of the works they have consulted. This gives equal credit to all the authors who have been consulted, which means, paradoxically, that it gives unequal credit, in the sense of unfair distribution of it. The book which has helped provide a paragraph gets the same mention as the book which has been basic for building a whole chapter. We have tried to rectify this by adding, here and there in this bibliography, a few words on our special indebtedness to such works as have been more important for us than others, either because of the amount of information they have provided or because they have been the principal sources for certain specific subjects with which we have had to deal.

Bibliography

We suspect that most readers never look at the bibliography. We hope that you will look at this one, and that the recommendations here given will inspire you to buy for yourself works which seem to us to merit your attention. They are books you will be glad to own.

Aresty, Esther, *The Delectable Past.* New York, Simon and Schuster, 1969. An important source of information concerning early American cookbooks—and their contents.

Armstrong, Rev. Lebbeus, *The Temperance Revolution.* New York, Fowler and Well, 1853.

Aykroyd, W. R., and Doughty, Joyce, *Les graines de légumineuses et l'alimentation humaine.* Rome, Organisation des Nations Unies pour l'Alimentation et l'Agriculture, 1964.

Barber, Richard, *Cooking and Recipes from Rome to the Renaissance.* London, Allen Lane, 1973

Bear, James A., Jr., *Jefferson at Monticello.* Charlottesville, University Press of Virginia, 1967. A slim volume, but packed with intriguing details about Jefferson's role as an estate manager.

Beard, James, *Beard on Bread.* New York, Alfred A. Knopf, 1973.

Benét, William Rose, ed., *The Reader's Encyclopedia.* New York, Thomas Y. Crowell, 1925.

Bickerdyke, John, *The Curiosities of Ale and Beer.* London, Spring Books, 1965. Facsimile edition of a book originally published in 1889.

Blond, Georges et Germaine, *Histoire pittoresque de notre alimentation.* Paris, Fayard, 1960.

Bloomfield, Arthur, *Guide to San Francisco Restaurants.* New York, Ballantine Books, 1975.

Boorstin, Daniel J., *The Americans: The Colonial Experience.* New York, Random House, 1958. It would be difficult to exaggerate the interest of Daniel Boorstin's three-volume history of the United States for those who are not content with the routine recital of battles won and lost and the tiltings of professional politicians. Mr. Boorstin tells us how the bulk of the people, who were neither generals nor presidents, live: what they ate, what they wore, how they worked, what they thought; and beyond the details, we see the background of the great movements of our society. From this first volume we have profited particularly from its accounts of the colonization of different parts of the United States, of its exploration and its agriculture.

———*The Americans: The National Experience.* New York, Random House, 1965. Fascinating accounts of the development of American commerce, transportation of food, early American hotels and restaurants, the hardships of railway travel (including the havoc it wreaked on the stomach), and innumerable other subjects.

———*The Americans: The Democratic Experience.* New York, Random House, 1973. Of particular note from our point of view is the brilliant description in this book of the cattle drives which preceded the shipping of steers by rail. But no less valuable are the passages on the development of processed foods and of the

Chicago meat industry, on the dining car, on packaging, and on a score of other subjects.

Borgstrom, George, *The Hungry Planet.* New York, Collier, 1967.

Brillat-Savarin, Jean-Anthèlme, *Physiologie du goût.* Belley, Librairie Gustave Adam, 1948.

Brothwell, Don and Patricia, *Food in Antiquity.* London, Thames & Hudson, 1919.

Brown, Dale, *American Cooking.* New York, Time-Life Books, 1968. Particularly valuable for its information on eating in Colonial times and afterwards, and on early kitchen equipment.

———*American Cooking: The Northwest.* New York, Time-Life Books, 1970. Among the notable passages in this book are those on the pioneers, on domesticated buffalo, on apples, on crabs, on foreign gastronomic enclaves in the United States, and on Alaska.

———*Wild Alaska.* New York, Time-Life Books, 1972.

Carr, Jess, *The Second Oldest Profession, an Informal History of Moonshining in America.* Englewood Cliffs, Prentice-Hall, 1972.

Ceram, C. W., *Le premier américain.* Paris, Fayard, 1972.

Chadwick, Mrs. J. *Home Cookery, a Collection of Tried Receipts, Both Foreign and Domestic.* Facsimile reprint edition, New York, Arno Press, 1973.

Claiborne, Craig, *Dining Out in New York.* New York, Atheneum, 1968.

Collier, John, *Indians of the Americas.* New York, New American Library, 1948.

Cummings, Richard Osborn, *The American and His Food.* Facsimile reprint edition, New York, Arno Press, 1970. This is the standard work on the subject, invaluable especially for controlling the chronology.

Dabney, Virginius, *Dry Messiah: The Life of Bishop Cannon.* New York, Alfred A. Knopf, 1949.

Diaz, Bernal, *The Conquest of New Spain.* Harmondsworth, Middlesex, Penguin Books, 1963.

Dickens, Charles, *American Notes.* London, Thomas Selton and Sons, 1900.

Dickson, Paul, *The Great American Ice Cream Book.* New York, Atheneum, 1973. Tells probably as much as you will ever want to know about ice cream. Our most complete source on this subject.

Dobie, J. Frank, *Up the Trail from Texas.* New York, Random House, 1955.

Dumas, Alexandre, *Le Grand Dictionnaire de Cuisine.* Paris, Tchou, 1965.

Eustis, Célestine, *Cooking in Old Créole Days.* Facsimile reprint edition, New York, Arno Press, 1973.

Farb, Peter, *Man's Rise to Civilization as Shown by the Indians of North America from Primeval Times to the Coming of the Industrialist State.* New York, E. P. Dutton & Co., 1968.

Feibleman, Peter S. *American Cooking: Creole and Acadian.* New York,Time-Life Books, 1971.

Furnas, J. C., *The Life and Times of the Late Demon Rum.* New York, G. P. Putnam's Sons, 1965.

Gault, Henri, and Millau, Christian, *Guide de New York, Boston, Chicago, Los Angeles, New Orleans, San Francisco et Montreal.* Paris, Julliard, 1967.

Gerard, John, *Herball.* Edited by Marcus Woodward. London, Minerva, 1974.

Gibbons, Euell, *Stalking the Blue-Eyed Scallop.* New York, David McKay, 1964. Of the various American writers on wild foods, Euell Gibbons strikes the authors as perhaps the best. He knows the folklore, the history and the taxonomy of the foods about which he writes, and he is always good reading.

———*Stalking the Wild Asparagus.* New York, David McKay, 1962.

Hogan, William Ransom, *The Texas Republic.* Norman, University of Oklahoma Press, 1946.

Hutchinson, E., *The New Family Book, or Ladies' Indispensable Companion and House-keepers' Guide; Addressed to Sister, Mother and Wife.* Facsimile reprint edition, New York, Arno Press, 1973.

Hutchinson, John N. "The Wines of America," in André Simon, ed., *Wines of the World.* New York, McGraw-Hill Book Company, 1962. Brief but excellent treatment of United States wines.

Huxley, Elspeth, *Brave New Victuals.* London, Chatto & Windus, 1965.

Johnson, Hugh. *The World Atlas of Wine.* New York, Simon and Schuster, 1971.

Kephart, Horace, *Our Southern Highlanders.* New York, Macmillan, 1914.

Kimball, Jeffe, and Anderson, Jean, *The Art of American Indian Cooking.* New York, Doubleday, 1965. Fascinating and useful, but one must be careful about accepting its recipes as those of pre-Columbian Indians. It deals also with the cooking of American Indians today.

Kobler, John, *Ardent Spirits. The Rise and Fall of Prohibition.* New York, G. P. Putnam's Sons, 1973. *The* book about the Noble Experiment. As the text indicates, the authors have quoted from it several times. Not only does it present an exhaustively researched account of the Prohibition years, but it goes into considerable detail about the various offensives of the Drys which preceded their victory.

Ladurie, Emmanuel Le Roy, *Histoire du climat depuis l'an mil.* Paris, Flammarion, 1967.

Lark, David, "Early American Kitchens." *Gourmet,* November, 1969. Extremely valuable information about Colonial kitchens.

Liebling, A. J., *Between Meals.* New York, Simon and Schuster, 1962. A delightful book by one of the best gastronomic writers America has ever known.

Leonard, Jonathan Norton, *American Cooking: New England.* New York, Time-Life Books, 1970. One of the most fascinating books in the Time-Life Foods of the World series. Highlights: fishing and seafood, especially lobster; cranberries (Mr. Leonard raises them for the market); maple sugar.

Leslie, Eliza, *Directions for Cookery.* Facsimile reprint edition, New York, Arno Press, 1973. One of the best and most complete of nineteenth-century pre-Civil War cookbooks. This is perhaps the place to thank Louis Szathmary, operator of a famous restaurant in Chicago, for making available old cookbooks from his personal library for reprint by the Arno Press, of which several consulted by the authors are listed here.

Ley, Willy, *Les Poles.* Transl. and adapted by Paul-Emile Victor. Time-Life Books, Amsterdam. 1963.

Lichine, Alexis, *Encyclopedia of Wines and Spirits.* New York, Alfred A. Knopf, 1968. One of the most complete works in its field, and, of the several books of its type consulted by the authors, the one that has been most useful for information on American wines.

Limburg, Peter R., *The Story of Corn.* New York, Julian Messner, 1971. A children's book, but it contains some legends concerning corn interesting also to adults.

Manceron, Claude, *Les Vingt Ans du Roi.* Paris, Laffont, 1972.

———*Le Vent d'Amérique.* Paris, Laffont, 1974. The well-known French historian who wrote these two books was concerned primarily with the history of France, but France's involvement in the American Revolution made early American history part of French history. The view of what was happening in America as seen from the other side of the Atlantic is often thought-provoking; and the book quotes some documents, especially concerning the Marquis de Lafayette, which are perhaps not yet known in the United States. Where letters or journals of French participants in, or observers of, the American scene quoted in this book exist also in the United States, the versions given here may not coincide word for word with texts printed in the United States. That is because the authors have translated directly from the French originals themselves. Americans interested in reading these books are informed that, so far as the authors know, they are not yet being translated, but it seems inevitable that they will be some day.

Margolius, Sidney. *Health Foods: Facts and Fakes.* New York, Walker and Company, 1973.

Matthiessen, Peter, "The Wind Birds," *The New Yorker,* May 27 and June 3, 1967. An essay of genius, which deals with many birds once considered as game, but little eaten now, like the Eskimo curlew, so much appreciated for the table in New England that it was called the "dough-bird," which went the way of the passenger pigeon. Mr. Matthiessen is well known as an expert on birds, but he has a wit which far transcends that of the ordinary specialist.

McPhee, John, *Oranges.* New York, Farrar, Straus & Giroux, 1967. A work which for the whole length of a book never allows interest in a single fruit, which might ordinarily seem a slight subject, to flag for an instant. The passages cited in the present book come mostly from the articles from which the book was born, published originally in *The New Yorker,* a sort of preserve for the protection of gifted writers.

Morison, Samuel Eliot, *The Oxford History of the American People.* New York, Oxford University Press, 1965.

Myers, John, *The Alamo.* New York, E. P. Dutton, 1948.

Perry, George Sessions, *Texas: A World in Itself.* New York, Whittlesey House, 1942.

Pratt, Theodore, *The Story of Boca Raton.* Boca Raton, Patten, 1953.

Les Pyrenées. Paris, Guides Michelin, 1952. This booklet, in the excellent green guide series published by the Michelin automobile tire makers, rather surprisingly provides a considerable amount of information about hunting whales and fishing for cod off the coast of North America before the first settlers arrived.

Rawlings, Marjorie Kinnan, *Cross Creek.* New York, Scribner's, 1942.

Robbins, William, *The American Food Scandal: Why You Can't Eat Well on What You Earn.* New York, William Morrow & Co., 1974.

Shaplen, Robert, "Delmonico." *The New Yorker,* November 10 and November 17, 1956. Everybody knows that Robert Shaplen is a magnificent reporter, and in this pair of articles he has outdone himself. They are studded with picturesque and colorful incidents. The authors had at their disposal seven works dealing with Delmonico, but Mr. Shaplen's stories alone were more useful than all the rest put together. We do not know if these pieces are included in any of the books formed of Mr. Shaplen's various articles, but if they appear in one, they would alone be worth the price of the book.

Skelton, R. A., Marston, Thomas E., and Painter, George D., *The Vinland Map and the Tartar Relation.* New Haven, Yale University Press, 1965.

Smith John, *The Generall Historie of Virginia, New-England and the Summer Isles with the names of the Adventurers, Planters, and Governors from their first Beginning in 1584 to their present 1626.* London, Michael Sparkes, 1626.

Steinberg, Rafael, *Pacific and Southeast Asian Cooking.* New York, Time-Life Books, 1970.

Sunny Florida. London, The South Publishing Co., 1885.

Tannahill, Reay. *Food in History.* New York, Stein and Day, 1975. A thoroughly researched book by a writer gifted with a quiet if deadly sense of humor.

Thompson, Robert, "Les Vins d'Amérique du Nord," in Joseph Jobé, ed., *Le Grand Livre du Vin.* Lausanne, Edita, 1969.

Trager, James, *The Enriched, Fortified, Concentrated, Country-Fresh, Lip-Smacking, Finger-Licking, Unexpurgated Foodbook.* New York, Grossman Publishers, 1970.

Trillin, Calvin, *American Fried: Adventures of a Happy Eater.* New York, Doubleday, 1974. A fecund souce for the history of the American crawfish.

Waldo, Myra, *The Complete Book of Oriental Cookery.* New York, David McKay, 1960.

Wallace, Robert, *Hawaii.* New York, Time-Life Books, 1973.

Walter, Eugene, *American Cooking: Southern Style.* New York, Time-Life Books, 1968. Excellent on Smithfield ham, the aristocratic food of the eighteenth-century South, soul food of course, the mint julep, and the very special foods of Florida—orange wine, palm hearts, stone crabs, conchs, and exotic fruits.

Waugh, Alec. *Wines and Spirits.* New York, Time-Life Books, 1968.

Wigginton, Eliot, ed., *The Foxfire Book.* New York, Anchor Books, 1972. A mine of curious and hard-to-get information on the ways of our Southern mountaineers. A principal source of our section on moonshining.

Wilson, José, *American Cooking: The Eastern Heartland.* New York, Time-Life Books, 1971. An outstanding book of the Time-Life Foods of the World series, which has been a major source of information on Pennsylvania Dutch and Shaker food, on Philadelphian eating clubs, on folk wines, and on nineteenth-century restaurants.

Ziff, Larzer, *Puritanism in America: New Culture in a New World.* New York, Viking, 1974.

Index